BLOOD ROYAL

Throughout medieval Europe, for hundreds of years, monarchy was the way that politics worked in most countries. This meant that power was in the hands of a family – a dynasty; that politics was family politics; and that political life was shaped by the births, marriages and deaths of the ruling family. How did the dynastic system cope with female rule, or pretenders to the throne? How did dynasties use names, the numbering of rulers and the visual display of heraldry to express their identity? And why did some royal families survive and thrive, while others did not?

Drawing on a rich and memorable body of sources, this engaging and original history of dynastic power in Latin Christendom and Byzantium explores the role played by family dynamics and family consciousness in the politics of the royal and imperial dynasties of Europe. From royal marriages and the birth of sons, to female sovereigns, mistresses and wicked uncles, Robert Bartlett makes enthralling sense of the complex web of internal rivalries and loyalties of the ruling dynasties and casts fresh light on an essential feature of the medieval world.

Robert Bartlett is the author of many acclaimed history books, including *The Making of Europe: Conquest, Colonization and Cultural Change 950–1350* (1993), which won the Wolfson Literary Prize for History in 1994, and *Why Can the Dead Do Such Great Things?* (2015). He is Professor Emeritus at the University of St Andrews and is well-known as the writer and presenter of several BBC documentary series, including *Inside the Medieval Mind* (2008), *The Normans* (2010) and *The Plantagenets* (2014).

THE JAMES LYDON LECTURES IN MEDIEVAL HISTORY AND CULTURE

In the millennium between the fall of Rome and the Reformation – commonly known as the 'Middle Ages' – Europe emerged as something more than an idea, and many of the institutions, cultural forces and political ideas we associate with the 'modern' world were born. What is the continuing relevance of this era for contemporary society? And how are we to understand medieval history and culture on its own terms, rather than through the distorting prism of presentist concerns? These are among the most urgent and problematic questions facing medieval scholarship today.

The James Lydon Lectures in Medieval History and Culture, delivered at Trinity College Dublin and named for James Francis Lydon FTCD, Lecky Professor of History at Trinity College Dublin (1928–2013), is a biennial series providing a unique platform to reflect on these issues.

Series Editors:
Peter Crooks, David Ditchburn, Seán Duffy, Ruth Mazo Karras, Immo Warntjes

A full list of titles in the series can be found at:
www.cambridge.org/lydonlectures

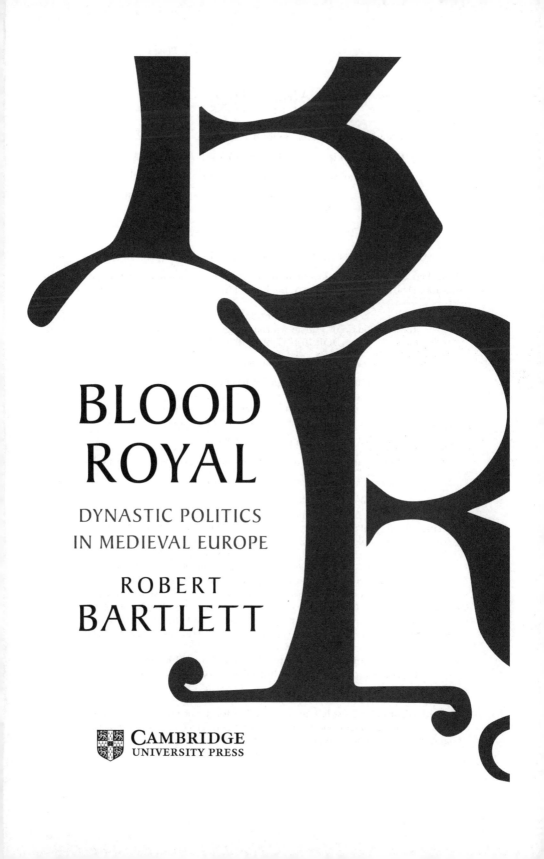

BLOOD
ROYAL

DYNASTIC POLITICS
IN MEDIEVAL EUROPE

ROBERT
BARTLETT

CAMBRIDGE
UNIVERSITY PRESS

CAMBRIDGE
UNIVERSITY PRESS

University Printing House, Cambridge CB2 8BS, United Kingdom

One Liberty Plaza, 20th Floor, New York, NY 10006, USA

477 Williamstown Road, Port Melbourne, VIC 3207, Australia

314–321, 3rd Floor, Plot 3, Splendor Forum, Jasola District Centre, New Delhi – 110025, India

79 Anson Road, #06–04/06, Singapore 079906

Cambridge University Press is part of the University of Cambridge.

It furthers the University's mission by disseminating knowledge in the pursuit of education, learning, and research at the highest international levels of excellence.

www.cambridge.org
Information on this title: www.cambridge.org/9781108490672
DOI: 10.1017/9781108854559

First published 2020

Printed in the United Kingdom by TJ International Ltd, Padstow Cornwall

A catalogue record for this publication is available from the British Library.

Library of Congress Cataloging-in-Publication Data
Names: Bartlett, Robert, 1950– author.
Title: Blood royal : dynastic politics in medieval Europe / Robert Bartlett.
Description: Cambridge ; New York, NY : Cambridge University Press, 2020. | Includes bibliographical references and index.
Identifiers: LCCN 2019039298 (print) | LCCN 2019039299 (ebook) | ISBN 9781108490672 (hardback) | ISBN 9781108854559 (ebook)
Subjects: LCSH: Royal houses – Europe – History – To 1500. | Kings and rulers, Medieval. | Monarchy – Europe – History – To 1500. | Civilization, Medieval. | Kinship – Political aspects – Europe – History. | Europe – Politics and government – 476–1492.
Classification: LCC D131 .B35 2020 (print) | LCC D131 (ebook) | DDC 929.7094/ 0902–dc23
LC record available at https://lccn.loc.gov/2019039298
LC ebook record available at https://lccn.loc.gov/2019039299

ISBN 978-1-108-49067-2 Hardback

For Ros and Len and all their descendants

Contents

CONTENTS

CONTENTS

Figures

LIST OF FIGURES

Preface and Acknowledgements

The subject of this book is the family politics of royal and imperial dynasties in Latin Christendom and Byzantium in the period 500–1500. Family politics means competition and cooperation within the ruling family, shaped at every point by the human life cycle of birth, marriage and death, and also by ideas of what a dynasty was. Hence the two parts of the book, the life cycle and a sense of dynasty. The main dynasties are listed in Appendix A. A full bibliography on this subject would fill a library but references have been given for all direct quotations and for facts other than those easily accessible. A few directly relevant titles have also been cited.

The book grew out of an invitation to deliver the Lydon lectures at Trinity College Dublin, a series of four lectures named in honour of the distinguished Trinity historian James Lydon, who was Lecky Professor of History at the College from 1980 to 1993 and died in 2013. The lectures were delivered in April 2017. Warm thanks are due to my hosts, Peter Crooks, David Ditchburn and Seán Duffy, and to the distinguished invited commentators on that occasion, Stewart Airlie, Sverre Bagge, Ana Rodríguez, Katharine Simms and Nicholas Vincent. Discussions at that time helped shape the further development of the book. Warm thanks for help of various sorts are due to Rory Cox, Michael Foster, Tim Greenwood and the late Ruth Macrides. Chris Given-Wilson, John Hudson and Simon MacLean had the great kindness to read through the whole text. I have incorporated their corrections and (most of) their suggestions and am extremely grateful to them for this act of collegiality and friendship.

Abbreviations

AN	Archives nationales, Paris
BAV	Biblioteca Apostolica Vaticana
BHL	*Bibliotheca Hagiographica Latina* (cited by item number)
BL	British Library, London
BnF	Bibliothèque nationale de France, Paris
CCCC	Corpus Christi College, Cambridge
CCCM	Corpus Christianorum, continuatio medievalis (Turnhout)
CCSL	Corpus Christianorum, series latina (Turnhout)
JL	Jaffé (rev. Löwenfeld), *Regesta pontificum Romanorum* (cited by item number)
MGH	Monumenta Germaniae historica
AA	Auctores antiquissimi
DD	Diplomata
SRG	Scriptores rerum Germanicarum in usum scholarum
SS	Scriptores
ODNB	*Oxford Dictionary of National Biography* (60 vols., 2004)
OMT	Oxford Medieval Texts
PL	Patrologia Latina, ed. J.-P. Migne (221 vols., Paris, 1844–65)
Po.	Potthast, *Regesta pontificum Romanorum* (cited by item number)
Reg. Vat.	Registra Vaticana, Archivum Secretum Vaticanum
RHF	Recueil des historiens des Gaules et de la France (24 vols., Paris)
RS	Rerum Britannicarum Medii Aevi Scriptores ('Rolls Series') (251 vols., London)
SHF	Société de l'histoire de France
TNA	The National Archives, Kew, London

INTRODUCTION

Royal Families

MONARCHIES ARE NOW RARE IN THE WORLD, NUMBERING around twenty in a system of almost two hundred independent states, but for hundreds of years monarchy was the way that politics worked in most countries. And monarchy meant power was in the hands of a family – a dynasty – and hence politics was family politics. It was not elections or referenda that shaped political life, but the births, marriages and deaths of the ruling family. This added further unpredictability to the unpredictable business of ruling. Even in modern Western democracies there have been political dynasties producing recurrent presidents, such as George Bush (1989–93) and George W. Bush (2001–9) in the USA, although this is rare. And the crucial thing about these democracies is that while George W. Bush could legitimately inherit personal property from his father, he could not inherit office. It was this separation of property, which could legitimately be distributed on family lines, from office, which could not, that marked the definitive step away from dynastic politics.

In this earlier, dynastic, world where office, including the highest, was family property, biology was a bigger determinant of political life than it is today. Biology does not determine all of human life but it determines a lot of it. Humans are born weaker and need more nurture than other mammals. They become sexually fertile in their teens. The number of children that a woman can bear is limited, the number that a man can father less so, although paternity is notoriously more difficult to establish than maternity. Old age advances on all humans, sometimes bringing with it a weakening of physical and mental powers. In the Middle Ages the absence of contraception meant that fertile women might have numerous children, and poor sanitary conditions and rudimentary health care meant that many of them died before their first birthday. Average life span was low by modern Western standards. Even those who made it to the age of twenty were unlikely to live far beyond fifty. All these things shaped life for everyone, but their impact at the top of society, among the rulers, could have major political consequences. Sometimes those consequences were disastrous.

The main features of the life cycle of an individual can be sketched out easily: birth, childhood, relationships with parents and, probably, siblings, sexual maturity, sexual activity (usually), sexual partner or partners, the birth of children, relationships with children, aging, death. But, of course, this cycle takes place in a world where everyone else is also going through his or her own life cycle, and at a different pace and with innumerable variations. One can make generalizations about certain overall constraints to the human pattern, but that pattern is only truly discoverable in reality as a multitude of individual themes. The best model when analysing dynastic history may well not be the theorems of social science but a piece of baroque counterpoint.

In addition to these biological determinants, family life in the Middle Ages was shaped by assumptions about proper social roles. Medieval Europe was a patriarchal society, ruled, for the most part, by kings, who wished to hand on power after their deaths to their sons. This patriarchal concept of rulership is doubtless linked to the fact that kings were expected to be war-leaders. And the business of war was 'man's business'. An account of the upbringing of Godfrey de Bouillon, a hero of the First Crusade, puts it very succinctly: 'for training in war, there is his father; for the veneration of God, there is his mother!'[1] When recruitment was taking place for the Third Crusade in the late 1180s, men who failed to answer the call to arms were sent wool and distaffs – a parallel to the white feathers of the First World War handed by women to men who had not enlisted but one with a specifically sexual meaning: if you aren't going off to war, you might as well be a woman![2] A French scholar of the later Middle Ages, explaining the purpose of the exclusion of women from succession to the throne of France, put it simply: 'to the end that the commonwealth might be better and more powerfully defended by men than by women'.[3] Conversely, the long-lived fascination with stories of

Amazons, always located in distant lands or distant times or both, must indicate that imagining a society of female warriors was an enthralling violation of ordinary norms and assumptions.

The power-structures of medieval Europe, however, were not shaped by Amazons but by the urge towards male-line succession. Even in the case of monarchies that were in theory elective, fathers were usually expected to be succeeded by sons. Some dynasties were extremely successful in achieving this. The Capetians, who became kings of France in 987, managed to pass the throne from father to son until 1316, an amazing 329 years later. Even when this direct transmission from father to son was interrupted, the French Crown nevertheless continued to pass exclusively through male lines of the dynasty, down to the deposition of the last king of France in 1848. If other kingdoms attained nothing like this kind of continuity, it was still customarily the goal to secure male-line descent. The Plantagenet kings of England could not match the Capetians in terms of father–son succession, but still managed to keep the throne in the hands of the male line for 331 years, from 1154 to 1485. Likewise, the Arpad kings of Hungary, however often they were at each other's throats, passed their title in the male line for 255 years, from 1046 to 1301. All the kings of Aragon from 1162 to 1410, a period of 248 years, were related in the male line.

So, as measured either by father–son transmission or by the looser yardstick of transmission in the male line, there were dynasties that endured for centuries. But not all medieval ruling families attained such dynastic continuity. A striking example is provided by Byzantium, especially in the long period before the fall of Constantinople to the Fourth Crusade in 1204. There are some complex decisions to make when counting Byzantine emperors and their succession, since co-emperorship was common, but a credible approximation is that, of about sixty-five imperial successions between 476, the date of the abdication of the last western Roman emperor, and 1204, only eighteen or so were simple father–son transfers of power, that is, not much more than one in four. All the others involved transmission by marriage, collateral inheritance or, very frequently, usurpation.[4] Only two dynasties in the whole history of Byzantium in this period, the Heraclians and Macedonians, produced emperors in five successive generations. In this respect succession in the Byzantine empire resembled that in the state from which it had grown, the Roman empire, which also had very few long-term dynasties. Foreigners noticed this distinctive pattern. 'Why', asked an envoy from the Khazars of the Asiatic steppes, 'do you follow the evil custom of replacing one emperor with another of different lineage?'[5] The eleventh-century Armenian writer, Aristakès of Lastivert, also recognized this trait, contrasting Byzantine practice with that of other peoples, among whom the ruler's son succeeds him. Patrilineal succession is like iron, he says, the Byzantine custom of intrusion by outsiders is like mere brick.[6]

At the other end of Europe, it is also evident that in the Celtic and early Scandinavian worlds the nature of a ruling dynasty was different from that of, say, the Capetians or Plantagenets. Irish royal succession is a subject which non-specialists approach at their peril, but it may be possible for an outsider to sketch the general outline.[7] It seems that in Ireland, as in Wales and in early Scandinavia, it was assumed that the new king would be an adult male, that hereditary right would be only one of the grounds he would put forward to justify his claim to succeed, and that this hereditary right could look different from the hereditary rights asserted by royal claimants in other parts of western Europe. In particular, there was a much larger pool of candidates for kingship, because of concubinage or frequent divorce and remarriage, the recognition of the long-term rights of collateral branches of the dynasty, and hence a smaller role for primogeniture.

The distinctive features of the family structures of the ruling classes of Ireland, Wales and early Scandinavia were noted, usually disapprovingly, by their neighbours. Adam of Bremen, a German observer of things Scandinavian, remarked that when King Canute died in 1035, he left three sons, two of whom 'were born of a concubine, and who, as is the custom among barbarians, shared an equal part of the inheritance as Canute's children'.[8] He also described the polygamy practised by the Swedish chieftains: 'in coupling with women they know no measure; each has two or three or more at the same time, according to his means; rich men and rulers have them without number; the sons born from such unions are deemed legitimate'.[9] Anglo-Norman and English ecclesiastics of the eleventh, twelfth and thirteenth centuries reiterated complaints about Irish and Welsh practices: incest, that is, cousin marriage; the dissolubility of marriages; the equal standing of legitimate and illegitimate children.[10] It is clear that if one combines recurrent divorce and remarriage, or the public recognition of women other than the wife, with acceptance of the rights of the children of several, or even all, sexual partners, the chances of a ruler leaving sons will be greater than in a system of indissoluble monogamy and rights only for the legitimate, which was the rule, at least in principle, in many other parts of Christendom. This is why Irish royal dynasties did not face the issues of female succession or succession by minors, since there would always be adult male claimants when a king died.

If we turn to look at the workings of the dynastic system prevalent in most parts of Europe, we find its underlying and basic principle expressed very cogently in the following statement by Margaret of Burgundy, the sister of Edward IV and Richard III of England, writing in 1495: 'In this kingdom, as is well known, a king is constituted not by the wishes of the people or by election or by the right of war but by the propagation of blood.'[11] 'Propagation of blood' means sex and child-birth, and hence the human life cycle. One could begin one's analysis at any phase of that cycle, but the search for a bride is a reasonable starting point.

PART I

THE LIFE CYCLE

CHAPTER 1

Choosing a Bride

FOR A DYNASTY TO SURVIVE, IT HAS TO REPRODUCE. BY THE eleventh century, in most parts of western Europe, for the ruling families, reproduction meant marriage as defined by the Church. A king was expected to have one wife at a time, marriage could be ended only by death or in very precise circumstances laid down by the Church, and only offspring of these sanctified monogamous marriages were legitimate. Earlier, more casual, arrangements had been replaced or marginalized. So, for these ruling families, formal marriages were an essential part of their strategy and hence a never-ending subject of debate, discussion and disagreement. Sometimes this even involved babies being committed to future brides or bridegrooms. The first step, logically, was for a wife to be found for the king or future king. Indeed, from the point of view of the ruling dynasty and its advisers, one of the most important political decisions to be made was which bride to choose for kings or princes. *Car feme prendre est molt grans cose* – 'to take a wife is a very big thing'.[1] Marriage could even be classed, along with warfare, as one of the two things necessary for the state: 'those things and activities without which the earthly commonwealth cannot be sustained, namely, marriage and the use of weapons'.[2]

The bride's status was important. In the early Middle Ages, the Merovingian kings of the Franks sometimes took wives of very low social status, including slaves. Charibert (561–7) married the daughter of a wool worker, who had been a servant of his previous wife, and later took as another of his queens the daughter of a shepherd.[3] Bilichilde, queen of Theudebert II (d. 612), was a slave who had been purchased from some merchants by his grandmother.[4] Nantechildis, queen of

Dagobert I, was chosen by the king from among his servant girls.[5] The great historian of the Merovingian dynasty, J. M. Wallace-Hadrill, saw this practice as a reflection of the eminence of the royal kindred: it was 'a family of such rank that its blood could not be ennobled by any match, however advantageous, nor degraded by the blood of slaves'.[6] But this pattern, akin to the practices of the Ottoman sultans of Early Modern times, was unusual. Sexual unions with slaves or commoners were not characteristic of the ruling dynasties of Christian Europe later in the Middle Ages. A royal bride had to be high-born. One of the objections raised by his enemies against Charles of Lorraine, the last Carolingian claimant to the throne of France, was his marriage to a woman below him in status: 'He has married a wife who was not his equal, from the knightly class.' How, they asked, could a great duke of France allow such a woman 'to be made queen and rule him'?[7]

But, granted that a royal bride should be high-born, this still left a vital decision: was she to be from a local aristocratic family or a high-born foreign bride? It was a subject on which there were strong opinions. Erasmus, for example, thought it would be 'by far the most advantageous to the state if the marriage alliances of rulers were confined within the borders of the kingdom'.[8] But both strategies had their advantages and their drawbacks. Indeed, in a fictional dialogue composed in Russia in 1776, the protagonist of the view that the tsar should marry a foreign princess claimed, 'I can give you forty reasons to show the advantage' of that policy; his opponent, however, was not impressed: 'And I could lay before you 400 reasons to prove the advantage of marriages with their own subjects.'[9]

When discussing the advantages and disadvantages of each policy, the crucial point is that marriage not only created a new married couple but also created in-laws, relatives by marriage. Ruling dynasties relied on powerful noble families for support, and a marriage alliance with one of these powerful kindreds could cement and symbolize internal alliances of this kind. On the other hand, a miscalculation might upset the balance of aristocratic power. The impulsive and imprudent marriage of Edward IV of England to Elizabeth Woodville, one of his 'own subjects', had this effect: the speedy advancement of the new queen's relatives seems to have irritated the established aristocracy and undermined support for Edward's regime.[10] Foreign brides, on the other hand, brought links with other ruling dynasties, which could be useful, and they were free, at least initially, of any alignment with local aristocratic factions. This could be attractive. After he seized the throne in 1078, the Byzantine emperor Nicephorus Botaniates was advised to marry the Georgian princess Maria of Alania, the wife of his predecessor, 'because she was a foreigner and there was no crowd of relatives attached to her to pester the emperor'.[11] Maria of Alania may have been exceptional in this respect, however. Many foreign brides did bring crowds of relatives with them, who provoked distrust and envy.

Marriage with Local Aristocrats

Some ruling families concentrated their marriage strategy upon creating ties within the kingdom rather than beyond it. An example is the Carolingians.[12] They had long been the most powerful aristocratic family in the Frankish realm before they seized the throne in 751 and they then expanded Frankish power throughout western Europe, ruling territory that covered all or part of nine or ten modern European states (some historians assess the Carolingian empire at a million square kilometres or more).[13] Charlemagne was crowned not just king but emperor in 800. Yet, despite the huge territories they ruled and their ascent to the imperial title, the Carolingians tended to marry among the daughters of their own Frankish aristocracy. Charlemagne's son and successor, Louis the Pious, married, first, Ermengard, daughter of the Frankish duke (or count) Ingram, and then Judith, daughter of the Frankish duke (or count) Welf.[14] Louis actually forbade his sons from marrying foreign wives. When he issued his ordinance of 817 regulating the succession, he urged the younger brothers, if they were to marry after his death, to do so with the advice and agreement of their oldest brother, adding, 'however, in order to avoid disagreements and to remove any pretext for anything harmful, we decree that none of them should presume to take a wife from foreign peoples.'[15] Louis' sons, Lothar, Louis the German and Charles the Bald, followed this advice. Louis the German actually followed his father's example quite closely, marrying Hemma, Welf's daughter and hence the sister of his own stepmother. And Louis the

German's three sons, each of whom was granted a sub-kingdom, married women from the Frankish aristocracy of Bavaria, Saxony and Alsace, the areas where their power was initially based.[16]

This pattern was general in the dynasty. Of Charlemagne's descendants in the male line, twenty-six bore the title of king or emperor. The last of these died in 987. It is not always possible to name their wives or say much about their origins, but there are twenty-three cases where this can be done.[17] Of these twenty-three royal wives, twenty came from the Frankish aristocracy in the kingdoms where their husbands ruled. The pattern only begins to change slightly in the tenth century, when there are three generations of West Frankish kings of Carolingian descent who sought royal brides outside their kingdom. Around the year 919 Charles the Simple, king of the West Franks, married Eadgifu, daughter of Edward the Elder, king of Wessex, the first time a royal descendant of Charlemagne had married into a foreign royal family. The son of Charles and Eadgifu, Louis IV, who eventually succeeded to his father's throne, married Gerberga, daughter of Henry I of the East Franks. By the time they wed, the kingdom of the West Franks and the kingdom of the East Franks had been separate for fifty-two years (887–939), so the union between Louis and the non-Carolingian Gerberga can be regarded as a marriage between members of two separate royal families, although, for Louis, what was doubtless of greater political importance was that Gerberga was the widow of the duke of Lotharingia, a vast duchy much disputed between the kings of the West Franks and the kings of the East Franks. Finally, Louis and Gerberga's son, Lothar, who ruled the kingdom of the West Franks from 954 to 986, took as his bride Emma, daughter of Lothar, king of Italy, and Adelheid of Burgundy. By the time of this marriage Lothar of Italy was long dead and Adelheid had remarried Otto, king of the East Franks, so the bond was in reality again with the East Frankish kingdom. But these cases are exceptional when placed in the context of the Carolingian dynasty as a whole.

Kings of the house of Wessex, who became kings of England from the tenth century, tended, like the Carolingians, to marry the daughters of their own great aristocrats (*ealdormen*). There were exceptions, such as Æthelwulf (839–58) who married as his second wife Judith, daughter of Charles the Bald, king of the West Franks, or Æthelred the Unready

(978–1016) who married Emma, daughter of Richard I of Normandy, but the usual pattern was to create a bond with native families. An example that shows both the advantages and disadvantages of such unions is the tie between Edward the Confessor, last of the kings of the Wessex line, and the family of Earl Godwin, whose daughter, Edith, the king married. This powerful noble family provided support for Edward's succession in 1042, and the king in return bestowed earldoms upon Godwin's sons. The marriage between Edward and Edith took place in 1045. But relations were complicated by factional divisions and, in 1051, Godwin and his sons were outlawed and Edith placed in a nunnery. However, the family had sufficient military might and support within England to return in the following year, re-establish their position and make Edward take Edith back as his queen. After the death of Godwin, his son Harold became the most powerful man in England and succeeded the childless Edward in 1066. Whether it is fair to describe Edward as a 'puppet king' of the Godwinsons is arguable,[18] but they are clearly a good example of an aristocratic family whose marriage tie with the king was both consequence of and contribution to their immense political power. For Edward, this alliance was a strength and a hindrance.

The Byzantines, as the embodiment of the Roman empire, were especially conscious of the high prestige that a marriage alliance with them might bring, and even claimed that there were strict rules governing such alliances. Around the middle of the tenth century, the emperor Constantine Porphyrogenitus wrote that there was a law of Constantine the Great, the first Christian emperor, engraved in Hagia Sophia, 'that an emperor of the Romans shall never make a marriage alliance with a people who differ from and are alien in their customs to the Roman order ... except with the Franks alone'.[19] A generation later, when the envoy Liudprand of Cremona came to the Byzantine court seeking a marriage alliance for his lord, Otto (later Otto II), he says he was told, 'It is unheard of that a daughter born in the purple to an emperor born in the purple should be joined to a foreigner.'[20] This was in fact untrue, although it might have been a way of avoiding simple rejection of Otto. Anna porphyrogenita, sister of Basil II, was married to Vladimir, Prince of Kiev, not long after Liudprand's humiliating rebuttal at the Byzantine court.[21] She brought with her to Russia not only the glamour of an older and wealthier civilization, but also Christianity.

One function of internal marriages was to create bonds between great families. If a marriage was arranged between two warring families as part of a settlement, the bride might be described as *obses pacis*, which can be translated as 'pledge of peace', but also as 'hostage for peace'. For example, when the rebellious noble Erchanger came to terms with Conrad I of Germany, 'the king received his sister in matrimony, as a pledge of peace'. And the twelfth-century counts of Cappenberg prided themselves on descent from the lineage of both Charlemagne and his great Saxon opponent Widukind (called 'King Widukind' in their traditions): 'they say that Charles gave a daughter of his sister to Widukind's son as his wife and a pledge of peace'.[22] When the chronicler William of Malmesbury described how the Frankish king Charles the Simple gave his daughter Gisela to the Viking adventurer Rollo along with the land that later was called Normandy (a purely legendary event), he calls Gisela 'a vessel of peace and a pledge of the treaty'.[23]

The marriage of a king's daughter with a powerful local aristocrat might give that noble, or his heirs, the chance to claim the throne themselves, if the king left no surviving sons. When, in 1079, the emperor Henry IV betrothed his young daughter Agnes to Frederick, duke of Swabia, he already had one son and was to have another, but neither of those sons themselves had sons, so that when the second of them died in 1125, the male line of Henry IV's family was extinguished. At this point the son of Agnes and Frederick, duke of Swabia, another Frederick, became a candidate for the throne. Since the empire was elective rather than hereditary, he could not claim hereditary right, but his prospects and his expectations were clearly shaped by the fact that he was the grandson of Henry IV.[24] As it turned out, Frederick was not able to establish himself on the throne, but his younger brother Conrad was ultimately more successful and became the first German ruler of the Hohenstaufen dynasty in 1138. A royal–aristocratic union in 1079 had thus helped to bring a new dynasty to the throne fifty-nine years later.

The ties that marriage created between a royal dynasty and local aristocrats could clearly be both useful and awkward. This may explain why some rulers kept their daughters unmarried, removing the problem of sons-in-law entirely. Charlemagne famously kept his daughters to himself:

> Remarkable to relate, because they were very beautiful and greatly loved by him, he was not willing to give any of them in marriage to anyone, his own men or foreigners, but kept them at home with him until his death, saying that he could not bear to lose their company.[25]

Since access to these beautiful princesses was not, apparently, completely controlled, Charlemagne's policy gave him, as an indirect result, some illegitimate grandchildren, but it led to no other dynastic complications. Two generations later, in 867, when Basil I seized the Byzantine throne, he also avoided sons-in-law, but in a completely different way. He made three of his sons co-emperors, but placed all his four daughters into the family nunnery.[26] But such cases of rulers keeping their daughters unmarried were exceptional. Royal women were usually regarded as a valuable medium of exchange. This is most clear in the case of foreign queens.

Foreign Queens

In several kingdoms, the foreign queen was the rule not the exception. Between 1066 and 1464 no English king married an English woman.[27] Most English queens in this period were French, indicating the central place of France in the world of the Norman and Plantagenet kings, although, since many of the kings were more French than English, perhaps the word 'foreign' for these queens is not quite right. 'Foreign' is a relative term. Of the thirty queens of Denmark between 1000 and 1500, only three were Danish.[28] In the earlier part of that period, Danish kings found their brides among princesses from other Scandinavian kingdoms or from the Slavic world, including Russia, while in the late Middle Ages marital links were primarily with the princely houses of northern Germany, many of which by this time had a status and resources only slightly below royalty.

The circulation of these high-born brides was one way in which the various courts of Christian Europe maintained contact. In fact, one could

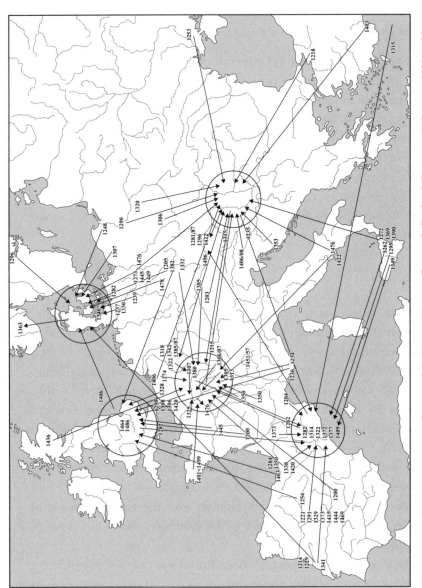

Figure 1 Map depicting marriage alliances of the kings of Aragon, Denmark, England, France and Hungary, 1200–1500. Redrawn from Karl-Heinz Spiess, 'Europa heiratet. Kommunikation und Kulturtransfer im Kontext europäischer Königsheiraten des Spätmittelalters', in *Europa im späten Mittelalter: Politik, Gesellschaft, Kultur*, ed. Rainer C. Schwinges et al. (Historische Zeitschrift, Beihefte, Neue Folge, 40 Munich, 2006), pp. 435–64, map 15.

define the culture-areas of medieval Europe by plotting which realms exchanged brides and which did not.[29] Although Byzantine brides were occasionally sent to western Europe, Byzantine emperors rarely married foreign brides in the early Middle Ages. There was one such marriage in the seventh century, one in the eighth (both with Khazar brides), none in the ninth, and one in the tenth.[30] It is true that more marriages with Westerners were negotiated than were finally concluded,[31] but this pattern still means there was a lack of the permanent links between courts that international marriages produced. The marriage between the emperor Isaac Comnenus (1057–9) and Catherine, daughter of a Bulgarian ruler, is no exception because it took place long before anyone expected him to become emperor, and, by the time he did, Bulgaria had long ceased to be an independent state.[32] After his reign, however, the pattern began to change, with marriages such as that between Michael VII Doukas and the Georgian princess Martha/Maria, while, from the time of the marriage of John Comnenus, heir to the imperial throne, and a Hungarian princess in the first decade of the twelfth century, down to the extinction of the empire in 1453, foreign brides, mainly from Latin Christendom, formed a majority of the Byzantine empresses.[33] The dramatic reorientation of the Byzantine political situation from the late eleventh century is thus reflected in imperial marriage patterns, as the large and autonomous empire of the earlier period was transformed into the much smaller state of the later Middle Ages, with its multiple connections, good and bad, with the West.

Marriages between eastern (Greek, Orthodox) and western (Latin, Catholic) Christians were originally simply marriages between partners of different cultures, but, as the theological temperature became heated and political and military relations more confrontational, culminating in the Latin conquest of Constantinople in 1204, such marriages might indeed be considered 'mixed marriages'. Innocent III, the pope at the time of the capture of the Byzantine capital, certainly expressed himself as if he thought so. He was considering the complicated case of Margaret, daughter of the king of Hungary, who married the Byzantine emperor Isaac II in 1185 when she was about ten. She took the Greek name Maria and was brought up following Byzantine customs. After the death of Isaac and the conquest of Constantinople, she married again, this time one of the Latin conquerors, Boniface of Montferrat. This marriage was carried out according to Latin rites, but, according to the pope, Margaret-Maria 'nevertheless shrank from returning to Latin ways so immediately, as a too impudent champion of Greek custom'. Eventually, under pressure from both her husband and the papal legate, she 'accepted a Latin blessing and received the body of Christ, consecrated according to Latin traditions'. Pope Innocent wrote to congratulate her and took her under his protection.[34] In this case, some very palpable signs were being read as markers of identity and allegiance: the use of leavened or unleavened bread for the Eucharist, the language of ritual. Royal brides had to decide.

Although it was not a very common practice, there were dynastic marriages that crossed the boundary between the Christian and the Muslim world. These were almost entirely between Muslim male rulers and Christian princesses, for, while the Koran explicitly allowed a Muslim man to marry a Christian or Jewish woman, Muslim societies prohibited and penalized sexual relations between Muslim women and Christian or Jewish men.[35] An example is found in Iberia very soon after the Muslim conquest, for both Christian and Muslim sources report that 'Abd al-'Aziz, the Arab governor 714–16, married the widow of the last Christian king of Visigothic Spain. She encouraged his separatist ambitions, which led to his downfall.[36] By the later eighth century, such unions were so common that, when Pope Hadrian I (772–95) wrote a long letter to the Spanish bishops, it was specifically the practice of Christian families giving their daughters in marriage to Muslims that he condemned.[37]

Some of these marriages represented political dealings at a high level. For instance, a Christian chronicler reporting the revolt of a Berber leader in north-east Spain in the early 730s describes a marriage alliance he had made earlier with the duke of Aquitaine: 'A duke of the Franks named Eudo had long ago given his daughter to him in marriage, for the sake of alliance and to put off the attacks of the Arabs.'[38] Occasionally there were marriages between members of powerful Muslim clans and aristocratic or royal women from Christian Spain during the ninth and tenth centuries.[39] An Arabic source which describes the fifty-six raids undertaken by the great Muslim general al-Mansur records, of the six-teenth raid, that he forced the Christian king (probably Sancho II of

Navarre) to make an agreement and give al-Mansur his daughter in marriage.[40] Such marriages were, however, rare, and ceased completely after the eleventh century when the power balance between Christian and Muslim states in the Iberian peninsula began to tilt in favour of the former.

An exception to the pattern 'Muslim male–Christian female' is found in the case of Zaida, wife or mistress of Alfonso VI of Leon and Castile. She later became a legendary figure, but there seems no doubt that she was real, and probably to be identified as the widow of al-Fath al Ma'mun, son of the ruler of Seville. In 1091 Seville was conquered by the Almoravids, invading from Morocco, and al-Fath al-Ma'mun was killed. It was probably at this point that Zaida (the name is simply the Arabic for 'Lady') sought refuge with Alfonso and became his mistress and perhaps his wife. Zaida is reported to have converted to Christianity and borne a son, Sancho (see below, p. 69).[41]

Eastern Orthodox Christians had faced the pressure of the Muslim world since its creation in the seventh century, and that pressure increased as the Mongols and Turks, peoples who both eventually converted to Islam, expanded their territories in the later Middle Ages. Warfare was one reaction, but diplomacy was another, along with its tool, the dynastic marriage. The Byzantine emperor Michael VIII (1258–82) gave illegitimate daughters in marriage to the Mongol ruler of Persia (the Ilkhan) and to the khan of the Golden Horde (in southern Russia), while between 1297 and 1461 at least thirty-four Byzantine and Serbian princesses married Mongol or Turkish rulers.[42] When the Muslim traveller Ibn Battuta visited the court of the Mongol khan Uzbeg, ruler of the Golden Horde from 1313 to 1341, he was entertained by one of the khan's wives, who turned out to be a daughter of the Byzantine emperor. She was pregnant and received permission to return to Constantinople for the birth. Ibn Battuta travelled in her entourage and remarked that, as soon as she was in Greek territory again, she abandoned Islamic religious practice and commenced drinking wine and eating pork.[43] Both of the rival Byzantine emperors of the mid-fourteenth century, John VI Cantacuzenus (1341–54) and John V Palaeologus (1341–91), married their daughters to Ottoman rulers, in the pursuit of Turkish military support. In 1346 Theodora, daughter of

John VI, married the Ottoman ruler Orhan, who sent thirty ships and a troop of cavalry to escort her from Greek to Turkish territory, and in the following year John entertained Theodora and Orhan's four adult sons (by other wives) on a summer visit to Byzantium.[44]

Dynastic marriages between Muslim and Christian states were almost entirely of one kind, with Christian princesses coming from countries adjacent to, and often subordinate to, powerful Islamic realms, such as those of al-Andalus in the earlier Middle Ages, or those of the Mongols and the Turks in the later Middle Ages. The Muslim ruler, not bound to having only one wife and allowed by the Koran to take a Christian wife, could easily add one as an attribute of prestige and without regarding the marriage as an alliance of equals. As an early Islamic authority put it, 'Our men are above their women, but their men are not to be above our women.'[45]

When a royal bride passed from the Christian to the Muslim world she would be surrounded by a different religion and culture. Passage from Latin to Greek Christian society, or vice-versa, was not so drastic a voyage but still involved adopting or adapting to unfamiliar language, religious practice and social habits. Within Latin Christendom itself, some courts exchanged brides more regularly than others, and these patterns might change over time. The political and cultural geography of medieval Europe is, in part, constituted by who gave brides to whom. For example, the position of Bohemia and Moravia between eastern and western Europe is reflected in the marriage choices of the ruling dynasty, the Premyslids: most of the wives of the male members were from German princely houses, sometimes including the highest, as in the case of the wife of Wenceslas I, who was daughter of the German Hohenstaufen king, Philip of Swabia, or the first wife of Wenceslas II, who was the daughter of Rudolf of Habsburg, another German king, but there was also considerable intermarriage with the ruling dynasties of Hungary and Poland, links which in the last days of the dynasty even led to Premyslid rule in those lands. On occasion, too, the Russian princely houses supplied wives, such as Cunigunda, second wife of Premysl Otakar II, who was the daughter of a Russian prince of the house of Chernigov and a Hungarian princess. Premysl Otakar combined the introduction of his new wife to Prague at Christmas 1261 with his regal coronation. The archbishop of Mainz (the metropolitan of the diocese of Prague) offi-ciated, in the presence of the two bishops of the Premyslid lands, plus the bishop of Passau and two bishops from Prussia. Secular dignities present included the margrave of Brandenburg and his family, Polish dukes and the great men of Bohemia.[46] With its Rhineland pontiff, its German, Czech and Polish princes and its half-Russian, half-Hungarian bride, this gathering is a good example of the way Bohemia and Moravia acted as a literal point of contact between west and east, epitomized in the pattern of its royal brides.

This circulation of women could produce unusual links and connections. Adela, daughter of Robert the Frisian, count of Flanders (1071–93), was married first to Canute IV (or II), king of Denmark, but, after his murder in 1086, she fled back to Flanders with her young son Charles; subsequently, in 1092, she married again to Roger Borsa, duke of Apulia and Calabria, and bore him a son, William. William succeeded his father in 1111, while, in Flanders, after the death of his cousin in 1119, Charles inherited the county. This is how it happened that in 1120 two rulers of territories a thousand miles apart, Apulia and Flanders, were half-brothers.[47]

Rulers with several daughters might choose not to keep them at home, like Charlemagne, but to send them out to foreign courts, creating multiple ties and connections. Four daughters of Edward the Elder, king of Wessex (899–924), went overseas as brides in this way, the first of them, Eadgifu, between 916 and 919, to marry Charles the Simple, king of the West Franks. The policy continued after King Edward's death under his son Æthelstan, brother or half-brother of these royal women. During the early part of Æthelstan's reign daughters of King Edward married Hugh the Great, the most powerful noble in the kingdom of the West Franks and ancestor of the dynasty later called Capetian; Otto, later to be the emperor Otto I; and the brother of the king of Burgundy.[48] In the 930s, therefore, Anglo-Saxon royal sisters were prominent at royal or ducal courts in three continental kingdoms. This has been called 'the high point in cross-Channel royal links in the early middle ages as a whole'.[49]

A yet wider internationalism is expressed in the marriages of the three daughters of Henry II (1154–89), first of the Angevin dynasty to rule

England. The oldest, Matilda, married Henry the Lion, duke of Saxony, at the age of eleven, while her younger sisters, Eleanor and Joanna, married the king of Castile and the king of Sicily respectively. Contemporaries were struck by these wide geographical vistas and exalted prospects. The three daughters were 'three bright beams that illuminated three different and opposite parts of Europe'.[50] The chronicler Ralph de Diceto, dean of St Paul's, showed a touching concern with the fate of these tender girls sent out to foreign parts to fulfil their dynastic duties. He considered that they could seek consolation from the example of their grandmother Matilda, Henry II's mother, who had herself been wed to a German emperor at the age of eleven.

> The stony barbarity of the Saxons, the doubtful conflict of the Spaniards with the Hagarenes (i.e. the Muslims) and the wild tyranny of the Sicilians could have induced continual horror in the daughters of the king of England, dwelling among these peoples so far from England in diet, clothing, behaviour and location. But the nobility of their grandmother, the empress Matilda, and the manly heart in her female body had shown beforehand to her granddaughters the paths of endurance ... to be imitated.[51]

This dynastic internationalism of the Angevin world, manifested in the ties binding ruling families in different parts of the Latin West, had some long-term political consequences. As a result of the first of these marriages, between Matilda and Henry the Lion, a long-lasting alliance was established between the English royal house and Henry's family, the Welfs. When Henry the Lion was forced into exile by the emperor Frederick Barbarossa, he sought refuge with Henry II and spent long periods with him in England and France. One of his sons was born in Winchester. After the death of Henry II, his son Richard the Lionheart proved as strong an ally. Bonds with a sister's son were traditionally important in the Germanic world, and Richard favoured his young nephews, Matilda's children, especially Otto, whom he made count of Poitou and for whom he sought the succession to the Scottish Crown. Under Richard's successor, John, the alliance with Otto, now elected Holy Roman Emperor, was a cornerstone of the English king's policy. Only after the crushing defeat of Otto and his English allies at the Battle of Bouvines in 1214 did the connection between the two families weaken.[52]

Eleanor's marriage to Alfonso VIII of Castile also had important results. Alfonso claimed the marriage deal had been sealed with the promise of Gascony, perhaps with the proviso that the grant would only take effect when its duchess, Eleanor's mother and namesake, Eleanor of Aquitaine, died.[53] This happened in 1204, and Alfonso soon occupied most of Gascony. It required considerable effort to eject him.[54] The kings of Castile did not finally relinquish all claims to Gascony until 1254, claims that were described at that time, diplomatically, as arising 'by reason of the grant that the lord Henry, former king of England, made, or is said to have made'.[55] Another political consequence of this marriage arose through one of the children it produced. Blanche, daughter of Eleanor and Alfonso, married Louis, the son of Philip Augustus, king of France, and when Louis was offered the English throne by rebel barons in 1216, he used this connection to support his claim. John, king of England, he said, had forfeited his rights by his treachery against his brother, Richard the Lionheart, so that, on Richard's death,

> the right to the kingdom of England devolved upon the queen of Castile and her heirs, since she was the sole survivor of his brothers and sisters, except for this John. However, she and her heirs freely granted their right in the kingdom to us and to her daughter, whom we have as wife.[56]

Being married to a granddaughter of Henry II was not enough to win Louis the English Crown but it was a card worth playing.

The third of these Angevin marriages, that of Joanna and the king of Sicily, also involved continued far-flung political and military activity. Joanna's husband, King William, died in 1189 and the throne was taken by an illegitimate relative, Tancred. When, in the following year, Richard the Lionheart arrived in Sicily on his way to the crusade, he found his sister in an unhappy position. Tancred had refused to give her the widow's dower that she was owed and kept her in custody. The presence of the famous military hero as his sister's champion soon induced Tancred to release Joanna and enter into negotiations about her dower. This was settled at 20,000 ounces of gold. When Richard sailed on to the Holy Land in the following spring, he took his sister, and the gold, with him.[57]

In these, often unpredictable, ways, the ambitious marriages that Henry II had negotiated for his daughters in the 1160s and 1170s shaped the politics of Europe for generations: the claims of the kings of Castile to Gascony and the claims of the French prince Louis to the English Crown, the alliance of Plantagenet and Welf that marked the politics of England, France and Germany throughout the late twelfth and early thirteenth centuries, and the unexpected funding of Richard the Lionheart's crusade partly from the gold of Sicily, all were consequences of those marriages.

Sometimes the advantages that a foreign marriage brought were immediate and tangible. For instance, in 1428, when the French king, Charles VII, arranged the marriage of his son and heir with Margaret, daughter of James I of Scotland, the young fiancée crossed to France with six thousand Scottish warriors, a useful reinforcement for the French in the Hundred Years War.[58] Dowries could be sizable, either in cash or land. One of the more extensive territorial acquisitions that came as part of a marriage arrangement between two royal families was the incorporation of the islands of Orkney and Shetland into the kingdom of Scotland. The islands had been ruled by the kings of Norway since the tenth century but in 1468 Christian, king of Norway (also at this time king of Denmark), promised a dowry of 60,000 Rhenish florins with his daughter Margaret on her marriage to James III of Scotland. Of this, 10,000 was to be paid in cash, and Orkney was handed over to the king of Scots as a guarantee that the remaining 50,000 would be paid. The following year, since Christian was unable to raise the 10,000 florins, he also handed over Shetland as a guarantee for this. The dowry was never paid; the islands never returned to Norwegian rule and became an integral part of the kingdom of Scots.[59]

The concrete benefits of marriage alliances with distant courts could be valuable over a long term and in sometimes unforeseen ways, as was demonstrated when the German ruler Conrad III came to Constantinople en route to the Second Crusade, and encountered a Byzantine emperor who was his brother-in-law and who treated him with especial consideration:

For there was a bond between them, since their wives were sisters, daughters of Berengar the Older, count of Sulzbach, a great and outstanding ruler, most powerful in the kingdom of the Germans: because of this he was overflowing with greater favour towards him and, especially because of the empress' requests, felt obliged to pour out more plentiful generosity for him and his men.[60]

Later, after Conrad's return to Germany, he maintained the close link with the Byzantine empress, writing directly to her about the political situation and proposing further marriage alliances between the two dynasties. His young son also wrote enthusiastically to his aunt in Constantinople, boasting to her of his first victory over enemy forces.[61]

The advantages that foreign queens brought could include providing a safe haven in times of crisis. In the 920s, for example, Charles the Simple, king of the West Franks, suffered the indignities of dispossession and imprisonment on more than one occasion, and died in captivity in 929. His young son Louis, whose mother was the English princess Eadgifu, 'fearing to become entangled himself in the storms that had been so disastrous for his father, betook himself to the Anglo-Saxons, invited there thanks to the family connections of his mother'.[62] Louis stayed in England until 936, when circumstances allowed him to return to France as king. His years in the safety of his mother's homeland are evoked by his nickname, 'Louis d'Outremer' – 'Louis from across the sea'.[63] His case is a good illustration of something said centuries later by Christine de Pisan, pointing out the advantages of such marriages: 'the marriage alliances of the beautiful ladies of the blood royal, through which are born new relatives in foreign countries and bonds with distant nations'.[64]

But marriages with foreign princesses might have disadvantages too. Political circumstances might change, rendering the link with the foreign court less relevant or even awkward. And if a king wished to get rid of his wife, her powerful royal relatives might well object. As is well known, one of the reasons Henry VIII of England had such difficulty in divorcing his first wife, Catherine of Aragon, stemmed from the fact that she was the aunt of the Holy Roman Emperor Charles V, the most powerful ruler in Europe and one with leverage over the pope. A similar example of a foreign sovereign championing a wronged queen (although not in this case one rejected because she had not borne children) occurred in the late twelfth century, when Philip Augustus of France repudiated his second wife, Ingeborg of Denmark (see also below, pp. 46–8). She had the backing of her royal brother, Canute IV, who could fund missions to the pope to plead her case, and himself wrote to the pope and the cardinals, urging the imposition on France of an interdict (the suspension of all ecclesiastical services). 'It has always seemed right to us to submit our necks to the yoke of obedience to the Roman Church', Canute wrote to Pope Celestine III in 1196, 'and only if the Roman Church first failed us will we have any wish to separate from her', a nicely phrased threat.[65] As soon as Celestine's successor, Innocent III, was elected pope in 1198, Canute's envoys were on their way to the papal court, complaining 'about Philip, king of France, who had unjustly abandoned his wife, his (Canute's) sister, and married another woman in her place'. Innocent sent a legate to threaten the interdict.[66] An interdict was eventually imposed upon France in 1200 and only lifted when Philip Augustus made a partial submission. After the death of Canute IV in 1202, his brother and successor, Valdemar II, continued support for their sister, until, in 1213, the French king agreed to at least a formal reconciliation with his Danish queen. Ingeborg was grateful for the help she had received from her royal brothers. When, many years later, in 1225, King Valdemar was captured and imprisoned by his north German enemies, a considerable portion of his ransom was sent from France by his sister.[67] If Ingeborg had not been a princess, perhaps Philip Augustus would have been able to get rid of her with less trouble.

Homesick Queens

Foreign brides were not only powerful vehicles of dynastic policy, they were also teenage girls sent into strange worlds, and one of the problems they faced was homesickness. In the late sixth century, as the Visigothic princess Galswintha was about to be sent north to be the bride of a Frankish king, the sympathetic poet Venantius Fortunatus pictured her reluctance, as she clung to her mother and lamented her fate:

I am going as a stranger in those lands and I am apprehensive about what I should learn first: the people, their character, their customs, the towns, the countryside, the woodlands? Whom, I beg, shall I find, as a newcomer in foreign lands, where no fellow countryman, no friend, no relative comes to me?[68]

The Flemish monk Goscelin, writing around 1080, also drew a sad picture of these young girls destined for foreign courts:

The daughters of kings and rulers are brought up in luxury from the time they are babies and know nothing except the glory and happiness of their native land, but then they are sent in marriage to other countries and foreign kingdoms and must learn barbarous customs and unfamiliar languages, and serve harsh lords and observe laws that are repugnant to nature.[69]

These 'barbarous customs and unfamiliar languages' had to be learned, and marriage negotiations often provided for that. When a marriage was proposed between the Byzantine emperor Constantine VI and Rotrud (Erythro to the Greeks), daughter of Charlemagne, the eunuch Elissaios, a notary, was sent 'to teach her the letters and language of the Greeks and educate her in the customs of the empire of the Romans'.[70] Likewise, in the following century, when a marriage was envisaged between Hadwig or Hedwig, niece of Otto I, and a member of the Byzantine imperial family, eunuchs were sent to Germany to teach her Greek.[71] Neither of these planned marriages in fact took place, but they illustrate the general principle that some kind of cultural training was considered necessary for high-born brides being sent into foreign courts where the language and customs were alien. Training on the job was also possible, so brides might also be sent out in the expectation that they would acquire the new tongue and new culture in their future homeland. Matilda, daughter of Henry I of England, was sent to Germany as a bride for the emperor Henry V when she was aged eight. She was betrothed at Easter 1110 and crowned queen on 25 July the same year. The archbishop of Cologne, who had presided at her coronation, then 'commanded that the conse-crated queen should be carefully brought up until a suitable time came for her marriage, and, while she was being brought up, she should learn the language and behave according to German ways.'[72] She married the emperor in 1114, just before her twelfth birthday.

Foreign brides might not only have to learn new languages but also become reconciled to a new name. Especially when women moved from areas of one language family to another, the host court might expect them to drop their barbarous names and adopt something more familiar.[73] When the daughter of Hugh of Arles, king of Italy (926–47), married Romanos, son of the Byzantine emperor, she had to abandon the Germanic aristocratic name of Berta, customary among the Frankish ruling class to which she belonged, and assume that of Eudokia, a favourite name of the Byzantine imperial family.[74] Likewise, in the middle of the twelfth century, when Berta of Sulzbach, sister-in-law of King Conrad III of Germany, married Manuel Comnenus, son of the Byzantine emperor, she became Irene, another traditional imperial name.[75] However, Byzantine commentators noticed that this German noblewoman failed to adapt completely to Greek customs, remarking especially on the fact that she did not use eye-liner.[76] Similar condescension about names can be found elsewhere. Gunhilda, daughter of Canute the Great, had to adopt a more acceptable German name form when she married the heir to the German throne, Henry (later Henry III), in 1036: 'the queen, Gunhilda by name, came to King Henry, son of the emperor, and she received the royal crown there on the feast day of the apostles (29 June) and at the blessing changed her name and was called Cunigunda.'[77] Gunhilda was an old royal name in Scandinavia, Cunigunda a prestigious name among the German aristocracy and royalty. To modern ears they might seem not dissimilar, but a contemporary at the time complained of the difficulty he had tracing Gunhilda/ Cunigunda's descent because of 'the barbarity of Danish and Norwegian names'.[78] A similar disdainful tone can be heard at the end of the eleventh century, after the Anglo-Scottish princess Edith (Eadgyth) married the Norman king Henry I. She and the king were mocked by hostile aristocrats as 'Godric' and 'Godgiva', common English names that obviously sounded barbaric or rustic to aristocratic Norman ears. This helps explain why she adopted the common Norman name Matilda instead.[79]

We sometimes get pictures of these foreign queens pining in their new homes. When the twelve-year-old Blanche of Castile arrived in Paris in 1200 to marry the heir to the French throne, she had, the chronicler Joinville says, 'neither relatives nor friends in the whole kingdom of France'; he repeatedly refers to her as 'a (or the) foreign woman (*femme estrange*)'.[80] Soon after her marriage, the saintly bishop of Lincoln paid her a visit, at the request of her new husband, and 'cheered her up' (*exhilarare* is the verb).[81] Perhaps Blanche, coming from the land where the lemons grow, missed the Mediterranean fruit, as her great-niece Eleanor of Castile certainly did later in the century. In 1289, thirty-five years after her marriage to Edward I of England, Eleanor was still having pomegranates, lemons, oranges and olive oil purchased at Portsmouth from the ships coming from her native Spain.[82]

Foreign Ways

The strange and glamorous fruits that Eleanor of Castile took pains to have delivered to her illustrate the way that foreign queens might bring foreign ways with them. Byzantine brides coming to western European courts had a reputation, at least among the more austere observers, of being pretentiously refined. For instance, the reformer Peter Damian, writing in 1059 or 1060, criticised the Byzantine wife of a doge of Venice for being so delicate as to use a fork for eating: 'She did not touch her food with her fingers, but her meals were cut into small pieces by eunuchs, and she took these to her mouth daintily, with little golden two-pronged forks.' But, Peter is pleased to add, God was so angry with her fancy affectations that he inflicted upon her a terrible disease that caused her to rot and stink, before finally dying.[83] At almost the same time that Peter Damian was writing, another monk recorded a vision of the empress Theophanu, a great Byzantine lady who had been the wife of Otto II (973–83) and regent for her son Otto III. After her death Theophanu had appeared to a nun and explained that she was suffering torments in the afterlife,

> Because I was the first to bring to the provinces of Germany and France, where they were hitherto unknown, superfluous and luxurious ornaments for women, such as the Greeks wear, and, conforming to these rather than

to human nature, I went around wearing this harmful attire and led other women to sin by desiring similar things.[84]

This is characteristic of foreign brides. They brought foreign culture with them and this was not always welcomed. Two other cases from the eleventh century illustrate the commotion that young foreign brides, with their foreign ways, could cause in the royal courts to which they came.

When King Robert of France married a lady from Provence in 1004 or 1005 (Provence at that time was not part of France), the Burgundian monk and chronicler Ralph Glaber responded fiercely to the southern influences she brought with her to the royal court. 'Because of her', he wrote, southerners flocked north:

> empty-headed men, given over to levity, with perverted manners and costume, disordered in their weapons and their horse-trappings, with their hair shaved from the middle of their head, beardless like actors, shameful in their boots and leggings, completely lacking any bond of loyalty or peace.[85]

Not all of this is clearly visualizable, but the strangeness of the new-comers' clothes and hair-styles is obviously objectionable and linked to their moral failings. Worst of all, says Ralph, these new vanities were contagious, and soon the people of northern France and Burgundy became just as bad as the immigrants from the south. He was so incensed by this 'wicked behaviour' that he burst into verse: 'This life now creates tyrants with perverted bodies, men with short clothes, improper, lacking the bond of peace. Because of a woman's counsel, the state is neglected and groans.'[86] It is ironic that this southern hair-style, beardless and with the lower part of the head shaven, is precisely that shown on the Normans in the Bayeux Tapestry. They had presumably picked up the style without any corresponding effeminacy.

In 1043, almost forty years after the marriage of Robert of France, a similar monastic uproar surrounded the proposed marriage of Henry III of Germany to a lady from Aquitaine, Agnes. The objection in the first instance was not her southern French roots but the fact that she and Henry were too closely related.[87] Abbot Siegfried of Gorze spelled out the relationship in detail in a long letter, but then, at the close of the letter, turned to a denunciation of 'the shameful custom of French follies'. These included such novelties as shaving the beard and wearing obscenely short clothes, two fashions also denounced by Ralph Glaber. 'The honour of the kingdom', Abbot Siegfried lamented, 'which in the time of earlier emperors flourished most properly in such matters as clothing and deportment, and weapons and riding too, is neglected in our days.'[88] Like Ralph Glaber, he was particularly worried at the way these foreign customs had been adopted by his own people, and even won favour at court. He is not explicit that the disreputable French customs are linked to the French bride, but the juxtaposition suggests a thought association at the least.

In these two cases, the new bride from the south is associated with the importation of novelties, obscenities and follies that are corrupting the author's own people. Both Ralph Glaber and Siegfried of Gorze combine the gloomy moralism of the Benedictine monk with a lament for the good old days and a strong dash of hostility to foreigners. The court was always more cosmopolitan than the society around it, and the foreign marriage, with the presence of foreign queens and their followers, was one of the reasons for that disjuncture.

Ralph Glaber and Siegfried of Gorze just grumbled, but hostility to foreign queens could take a crueller form. One of the most extreme cases concerns Gertrude of Meran, the German wife of Andrew II of Hungary, a king who ascended the throne in 1205. According to one source, when the king had some difficulty in conquering an enemy castle, the queen suggested, perhaps undiplomatically, that he should raise an army from the Germans who had settled in Hungary. They, our German source says, soon captured the place, and were rewarded with gifts and honours, stirring up resentment amongst the native Hungarians, who plotted to kill the king. The queen was informed of this and encouraged her husband to flee, herself staying behind, confident that the attackers would spare her, 'being of the female sex'. But she had miscalculated. The conspirators broke into the royal camp, wounded her, pushed her down, and when she extended her hands in supplication, they cut them off. They finished the job with their lances and pikes.[89]

Inspection of the Bride

Whether the bride came from abroad or not, care and attention had to be devoted to the process of selection. One of the more striking methods of finding a bride is recorded in the Byzantine empire in the late eighth and ninth centuries. This was the bride-show, where beautiful virgins were sought out from every part of the empire and one was then selected to marry the emperor or the emperor's son.[90] A particularly detailed account of one such bride-show is found in the Life of St Philaretos.[91] It occurs there because Philaretos' granddaughter was the victor, if that is the right word, in this beauty contest (Philaretos was that unusual kind of saint, a married lay man). The Life tells how the empress Irene sent out emissaries to find a bride for her son Constantine VI. They carried three things: an imperial measure, to check the height of candidates, something called a *lauraton*, which has been interpreted as either an ideal portrait or a device for measuring girls' waists,[92] and a shoe (presumably a glass slipper was not available). Coming to Philaretos' home town in Paphlagonia, on the Black Sea, they encountered his beautiful grand-daughter Maria. Rather than making a decision immediately, they took her, her two sisters, and ten other girls back to Constantinople for judging, working on the principle that selection should be made from a field of candidates. Maria was then chosen as the bride of Constantine VI.

An oddity about the Byzantine bride-show, apart from the custom itself, is its chronology. Five instances are reported in the sources and all date to the century between 788, when Maria married Constantine VI, and 882, the date of the marriage of Leo VI and Theophano Martinakia. There are none before or after. No obvious explanation for this pattern springs to mind. And, making matters worse, many scholars think these accounts should be regarded more as fairy stories than accurate historical narratives. Historians are of course a dull lot and shy away from the exotic and colourful, but these sceptics may have a case, pointing to the possible influence of literary parallels from other times and places, especially the biblical story of Queen Esther, who was selected by the king in this way, after 'all the fair young virgins' had been gathered together. On the other hand, perhaps the story of Esther inspired the practice and, in any case, bride-shows are attested in reality in some societies, notably in Early

Modern Muscovy, where there are seventeen documented and five probable cases in the period 1505–1689.[93]

But, whether the Byzantine bride-shows correspond to any reality or are simply the fruit of the heightened imagination of Greek monks, it really was necessary to think carefully about the choice of bride for a ruler or heir, and this might in fact involve a viewing. This seems to have been the case with the Frankish emperor Louis the Pious in 818, who married after 'considering the daughters of his chief men, who were brought from far and wide'.[94] The inspection could involve a demanding physical scrutiny. In one of the Byzantine bride-shows a decision was made between three finalists after the empress, the future mother-in-law, had inspected them in the bath.[95] The envoy sent to Aragon in 1322 to examine the king's daughter Violante, who was under consideration as a bride for Charles IV of France, was instructed 'to see her naked breast', since this would indicate whether she were fit to bear children, 'which the king much desires'.[96] Her capacity as breeding stock did not apparently qualify her to be queen of France, since Charles chose instead Mary of Luxemburg, despite the report that she was cross-eyed.[97] When a later king of France, Charles VIII (1483–98), was debating whether to marry Anne, the fourteen-year-old duchess of Brittany, he sent to her a committee of two dukes, a duchess and one of his most trusted Scots Guards, the last being 'someone employed very often in this kind of business', who reported back that 'they have seen her naked and indeed she limps a little'.[98] The prospect of acquiring Brittany through marriage to Anne was enough, however, to outweigh this little impediment.

Because a royal marriage was seen as a bond between families as much as a union between two individuals, it sometimes did not matter much who exactly was the bride. The English king Æthelstan sent two of his sisters to Germany so that Otto, the heir to the throne, 'might choose for himself in marriage whichever of them pleased him'.[99] He chose Edith (Eadgyth). And this English princess was eventually buried in Magdeburg Cathedral, where, remarkably, her tomb was found and opened in 2008, and her bones and teeth were subjected to scientific analysis, showing that she had indeed grown up in the chalk downlands of Wessex.[100] In 1442, the twenty-year-old Henry VI of England was considering marriage with one of the three daughters of the count of Armagnac, and in a letter to his envoys he underlined the condition 'that we may have choice'.[101] In 1481 an agreement was drawn up between Edward IV of England and the duke of Brittany. Edward's son, the Prince of Wales, was to marry the infant daughter of the duke as soon as she was twelve. However, if she died before that age, he would marry her sister. Likewise, if the Prince of Wales died, his place would be taken by his younger brother.[102] These kinds of replaceable siblings clearly demonstrate that marriage in this world was seen as a bond between dynasties, not individuals.

By the late Middle Ages, it was not unusual for portraits of the prospective bride to be part of the negotiations.[103] At this period they might very well be accurate likenesses. But there are much earlier references to such pictures of prospective brides. In the middle of the tenth century a 'eunuch painter' was sent from Constantinople to Germany in order to produce a painting of the high-born Hadwig, who was espoused to a member of the Byzantine imperial family.[104] And the belief that realistic likenesses were possible was certainly expressed long centuries before oil painting and perspective began to shape Western perceptions of pictorial realism (see below, p. 376).

Marriage to the Royal Widow

A very distinct type of dynastic marriage was marriage to the previous ruler's widow. Examples from the sixth century are fairly numerous. In the Visigothic kingdom of Toledo, Goswintha was successively wife of King Athanagild (555–67) and King Leovigild (568–86).[105] After the death of Miro, king of the Suevi, a Germanic people ruling north-west Spain, in 583, his son succeeded but was soon deposed by his brother-in-law, Audica. Audica then married Miro's widow – 'he took the wife of his father-in-law and obtained the kingdom'.[106] During the course of his fifty-year reign, the Frankish king Clothar (Lothar) I twice seized the opportunity to unite with royal widows, who had, in both cases, been wives of his own relatives. On the death of his brother Chlodomer in 524, Clothar married his widow 'without delay', excluded Chlodomer's sons and took a large share of his kingdom.[107] Thirty-one years later, in 555, on the death of Theudebald, great-grandson of Clovis, Clothar, his great-uncle, 'received his kingdom and took his wife Waldrada to his bed', although he gave her up after the clergy complained.[108] Such marriages could be interpreted as declarations of intent to rule, even if they did not succeed. For example, after the assassination of King Sigebert in 575, his widow Brunhild was quickly taken in marriage by the young Frankish prince Merovech, Sigebert's nephew. Merovech's father was supposedly upset at this breach of canon law but seems also to have suspected a plot to dethrone him ('he began to have his suspicions about his son Merovech on account of this marriage with Brunhild'), and pursued Merovech mercilessly.[109]

In the Lombard kingdom of Italy there are two cases of an interesting variation on the theme, in that the royal widows were supposedly allowed to choose their husband and hence the king. After the death of her husband, King Authari, in 590, his widow Theodolinda 'was so pleasing to the Lombards that they allowed her to keep her royal status and advised her to choose from all the Lombards the husband she wished, such a man who could rule the kingdom successfully'. She decided upon Agilulf, duke of Turin, and sent for him. When he respectfully kissed her hand, she told him he should not be kissing her hand but her mouth. They were soon married and in the following spring Agilulf was inaugurated as the new king.[110] A similar situation occurred again under Theodolinda's daughter, Gundeberga, who had married a later Lombard king, Arioald. After his death, in 636, it was a condition of the accession of the newly chosen king, Rothari, that he should abandon his own wife and marry Gundeberga. Then 'all the Lombards raised him to the kingdom, through her (*per ipsam*)'.[111] A story told of Gundeberga recounts that she was falsely accused of plotting with Duke Tasso to kill Arioald, marry Tasso and 'raise him to the kingship'.[112] Even though the accusation was false, it demonstrates that among the Lombards marriage to a widowed queen was a commonly imagined pathway to becoming king.

A notable example of a conqueror marrying the widow of a defeated rival occurred in 1017 when Canute of Denmark, after conquering England, married Emma of Normandy, the widow of the vanquished King Æthelred. The author of the *Encomium Emmae*, which was commissioned by Emma after Canute's death, gives an audaciously inaccurate account of how this came about, turning the widow into a virgin:

> Nothing was now lacking to the king except a noble wife, and he ordered one
> to be sought everywhere, so that, when she was found, he would take her in
> legal marriage and make her partner in his rule. So, they ran about through
> the kingdoms and cities, in search of a royal spouse, but it was with difficulty,
> after seeking far and wide, they at last found one who was worthy ... But she
> said she would never be Canute's wife unless he swore to her on oath that he
> would never have the son of another wife rule after him, if it happened that
> God gave her a son by him ... The virgin's words were acceptable to the king
> and, once the oath had been sworn, the king's will was acceptable to the
> virgin, and in this way, thanks be to God, the lady Emma, most noble of
> women, became the wife of that most powerful king, Canute.[113]

This picture of a supposedly free and unrestricted bride-search sits rather
uneasily with another comment that the author of the *Encomium* makes.
Writing of the violent struggle Canute had to undertake in 1016, he says,
'perhaps the war would scarcely or never have ended if he had not at last
received this most noble queen in the bond of marriage'.[114] Clearly the
significance of the link with Emma is that she was the widow of Canute's
predecessor, although the author never says so. The German chronicler
Adam of Bremen, writing a little later, put it all more succinctly: 'Canute
took Æthelred's kingdom, and his wife'.[115]

There are also examples of this practice from Byzantium. Nicephorus
Phocas (963–9) married Theophano, the widow of his predecessor
Romanos II. Objections were raised to this marriage, not because
Nicephorus was marrying his predecessor's widow, but because he had
supposedly acted as godfather to their children, hence creating a tie of
spiritual kinship that would make the marriage technically incestuous.[116]
In 1183, Andronicus Comnenus, who had forced his young cousin Alexius
II to accept him as co-emperor, had him murdered, and then married his
widow, Agnes-Anna, the twelve-year-old daughter of the king of France.
Andronicus was in his sixties, with a string of sexual partners behind him as
well as a current mistress. Archbishop Eustathios of Thessalonica
expressed, or imagined, the feelings of the poor young bride:

> she shrank from the union. Being high-minded and having experienced
> a different kind of gentle loving, she loathed his roughness. Sometimes,

they say, she would imagine the young man in her dreams and would cry out 'O Alexius!' She alone knew what she suffered.[117]

An exceptional variation of the practice of marrying one's predecessor's widow was marrying one's predecessor's widow when she was also one's own stepmother. This happened in the case of Æthelbald, king of Wessex (858–60), who married Judith, his father's widow, in 858. Judith was no older than fifteen at this time, since there had been an age gap of at least thirty years between her and Æthelwulf, Æthelbald's father. The sense of revulsion in the account of this event given by Bishop Asser, writing in the reign of Æthelbald's youngest brother and eventual successor, King Alfred, may be political as well as moral, since Asser regarded Æthelbald as divisive and unfilial:

> After King Æthelwulf died, his son Æthelbald, against God's prohibition and the dignity of Christians, and also contrary to the custom of all pagans, climbed into his father's bed and married Judith, daughter of Charles, king of the Franks, to the great scandal of all who heard of it.[118]

The situation was indeed 'against God's prohibition', since Deuteronomy 22: 30 declares tersely, 'a man shall not take his father's wife (*non accipiet homo uxorem patris*)'. Asser then underlines the scandal of the marriage by claiming that even pagans do not marry their stepmother, in this following the lead of St Paul, who had described marriage with one's stepmother as 'such fornication as is not even found among the pagans'.[119] But there is contrary evidence that this was a pagan practice. Eadbald, king of Kent, married his father's widow in 616, and although Bede, commenting on this marriage, cited Paul's words, one version of the Anglo-Saxon Chronicle saw it as a consequence of Eadbald's paganism: 'he lived according to pagan custom, so that he had his father's widow as wife'.[120] He certainly abandoned that wife when he converted to Christianity.[121] And one of the missionary questions supposedly put to Pope Gregory the Great was whether it was allowed to marry a stepmother, suggesting that it was a practice found among pagan populations.[122] Moreover, a penitential apparently from the eighth-century Frisian mission field allowed those who married their stepmothers to remain married to them if they had done this while still pagans.[123] And it seemed to be a practice that required general legislation. A law of the Frankish king Childebert II of 596, twenty years before the marriage of Eadbald and his stepmother, specified the death penalty for those who married their father's wife.[124] In her reforming mood, St Margaret, foreign-born queen of Scots in the late eleventh century, demonstrated to her subjects 'that marriage to a stepmother, and likewise marriage of a surviving brother to his dead brother's wife, such as had previously been practiced there, were totally execrable and to be avoided by the faithful like death itself'.[125] The implication is that marriage to a stepmother was customary rather than an occasional scandal.

The sixth-century historian Procopius tells a story about marriage to a stepmother which, although highly unlikely to be true, throws some light on thinking about such a match. It concerns Hermegisclus, king of a Germanic people, the Varni. Hermegisclus has married the sister of Theudebert, ruler of the Franks (a Frankish king of this name ruled 534–48); Radigis, his son by an earlier wife, is engaged to an Anglo-Saxon princess. But Hermegisclus learns that he is dying, and he gives the advice that Radigis should break off his engagement and, after his father's death, marry his widow, that is Radigis' own stepmother. This is his reasoning:

> I think then, for the Varni, it will be more profitable to make a marriage alliance with the Franks than with the islanders. For the people of Britain are only able to have contact with you after a long time and with great difficulty. The Varni and the Franks have between them just the waters of the Rhine, so that as close neighbours to you, who have increased their power a great deal, they are at hand to do good to you and to harm you, at a time when they wish. They certainly will harm you, unless they are checked by this marriage alliance.[126]

In fact, the Anglo-Saxon princess turns out to be a determined and bold champion of her own interests, leads a fleet of 400 ships across the Channel, captures the fiancé who has spurned her and, taking pity on him, accepts him as her husband after Theudebert's sister has been sent home.

None of this is eye-witness reportage. The story does, however, give one view of why marriage alliances with neighbouring peoples were important: such neighbours can help you and harm you, and a marriage alliance might prevent the latter. Moreover, in these circumstances, it is a reasonable ground for marrying your predecessor's widow, even if she is your stepmother.

Marriage with a predecessor's widow was not only a feature of the early Middle Ages. In the summer of 1350, when the young king of Castile, Peter I, fell gravely ill, two parties formed around two possible claimants to the throne if he should die, and it is significant that both of these potential successors were advised to marry the queen mother, Maria, widow of Peter's father and predecessor Alfonso XI. In fact, Peter's recovery meant that such a marriage did not take place, but the common advice given to the rival candidates shows how valuable marriage to a predecessor's widow appeared.[127] After the death of Albert of Habsburg, king of Hungary and Bohemia, in 1439, the Magyar nobles offered the Hungarian Crown to the young king of Poland, Wladyslaw III, and wanted to confirm this offer by a marriage between Wladyslaw and Albert's widow, Elizabeth. As Elizabeth was the daughter of Sigismund, king of Hungary (1387–1437), she embodied legitimacy and hereditary right, and could bring those things to Wladyslaw just as she had brought them to Albert. She pretended to agree, but in fact was committed to ensuring the rights of the child she bore in her body at the time (see below, p. 58). Although this too is a case where the royal widow did *not* marry her husband's successor, the assumption of the Hungarians was that this would have been desirable and appropriate.[128] A few years later, when Christian I was elected to succeed Christopher III as king of Denmark by the Danish State Council in 1448, it was agreed that he should marry Christopher's widow, Dorothea of Brandenburg, which he did the following year. The main motive for this was financial: at her marriage to Christopher, Dorothea was given a huge dower in all three Scandinavian kingdoms; if she left the kingdoms, she was due 45,000 Rhenish guilders in compensation for this dower.[129]

Later in the fifteenth century another case, a fairly complex one, arose in Hungary. The princess Beatrice of Aragon had married Matthias Corvinus, king of Hungary, and, on his death in 1490 without legitimate children, the Hungarian nobles insisted that the new claimant to the throne, Vladislav II, king of Bohemia, marry her. According to the queen herself, the nobles supposedly said, 'that if the devil should happen to tempt him to refuse to take our majesty as a wife' then they would abandon him and adhere just to her.[130] Vladislav was elected king on 14 July 1490. By 8 August the gossip in the north Italian courts was that 'the king of Bohemia has been elected king of Hungary and has taken the queen as his wife'.[131] The gossip may have been premature but Beatrice claimed that she and Vladislav exchanged vows. He was very happy to take her money to pay his troops but showed a worrying reluctance about the marriage. Beatrice noticed that he did not refer to her as his wife in his letters, and he made endless excuses about having a public nuptial celebration. Eventually he told her that he acted this way 'because of a certain secret impediment' that he could not reveal.[132] This impediment seems to have been the fact that he was already married. The resulting legal case dragged on, as such cases do, until the marriage of Beatrice and Vladislav was annulled in 1500. Vladislav had got Hungary, and Beatrice returned to her childhood home, where, in 1507, a year before her death, she was signing herself 'the most unhappy queen of Hungary'.[133] The case shows several things: the demand of the native aristocracy that a new king would be required to marry the royal widow; the widow's own desire to hang on to power; and the ability of the new king to worm his way out of the situation by, in the long run, disregarding both.

Another remarkable case occurred at just this time in France, where marriage with a predecessor's widow was actually agreed years ahead of time. When Anne, duchess of Brittany, married King Charles VIII in 1491, she finally brought the semi-independent duchy to the French Crown, and Charles was determined that it would stay in royal hands. Hence, the marriage contract specified that, if he should die before Anne, and they had no children, Anne 'shall not remarry, except to the future king'.[134] Charles did indeed die before Anne and she did indeed marry his successor, his cousin Louis XII (1498–1515), although Louis had to have his existing marriage annulled first. Brittany became a full part of France. The motives here need no discussion.

The explanations that modern historians give of the practice of marrying a predecessor's widow range from level-headed political calculation to the extremes of cultural symbolism. On the one hand, some see it as

Figure 2 Anne, Duchess of Brittany (1488–1514), who married the king of France on condition that, if he died without children, she could remarry only his successor. This did happen, thus ensuring Brittany remained incorporated into the kingdom of France. Paris, BnF, lat. 9474 (Jean Bourdichon, Grandes Heures d'Anne de Bretagne), fol. 3.

'a vehicle on which claims to the royal succession could be carried to a second husband', or a way for the new king to strengthen his kingship.[135] It 'served as a lever in the attainment of power'.[136] A widowed queen could be 'a vessel of royal power'.[137] The new king would acquire the queen's treasure and followers and, especially in the case of conquerors and usurpers, such a union might serve to legitimize the new ruler. But other historians look for illumination from a quite different source, Celtic or Germanic paganism. In early Irish mythology, sovereignty was imagined as female, and accession to kingship as a marriage between the king and this female power, in origin a goddess: 'Sacred union with the goddess of the land was seen to initiate the fertility and prosperity of a sovereign's reign.'[138] The legendary Irish Mebh, like the Lombard queens Theodolinda and Gundeberga, chose her own husbands, who then became kings. Germanic myth can be interpreted in the same way, as marriage between goddess and mortal king: 'As the northern ruler had once been the husband of [the goddess] Freyja, the new king must possess the old queen who came to represent that deity.'[139]

But, in addition to rational calculations, on the one hand, and echoes of the *Golden Bough*, on the other, there might also be a rougher kind of sexual appropriation involved. After Fáelán mac Murchado defeated and killed his older brother Dúnchad, king of Leinster, in 728, 'he took the kingship of Leinster, and married Dúnchad's wife'.[140] In a similar style, after Vladimir of Novgorod killed Rogvolod of Polotsk and his two sons around 978, he married Rogvolod's daughter, and he also fathered a child on the widow of his half-brother Yaropolk after having arranged his assassination.[141] Following up a killing by sleeping with the daughter or wife of the man you had killed could be a way of finishing the job, taking his women as well as his land. As Adam of Bremen said of Canute (above, p. 36), 'he took Æthelred's kingdom, and his wife'. The association of taking the royal widow and violent seizure of power also comes out very clearly in Hungary in 997, when the Hungarian ruler Duke Géza died, and his son Stephen (later St Stephen) had to face the rival claims of Duke Koppány: 'Koppány wanted to join himself in an incestuous marriage with the mother of St Stephen the king and kill St Stephen and subject his duchy to his power'.[142] The accusation that the marriage was 'incestuous' implies that Koppány was a relative of Géza's but it is not certain how. In any event, Stephen got Koppány first and had his quartered body displayed in four cities of the kingdom.

Apart from such 'incestuous' marriages, there is some evidence that marriage to a predecessor's widow could be seen in itself as violation and pollution. In 683 a council at Toledo, summoned by the Visigothic king Ervig, issued a long and animated ruling, of which the following is a section:

> It is an appalling crime and a deed of very frequent wickedness, to seek the royal bed when kings die leaving behind their wives, and to befoul it with the horrific stains of pollution. For which Christian can bear it with equanimity when the wife of a dead king is enjoyed afterwards in another union, or is subjected to the lust of the following ruler? ... No one therefore will be permitted to marry a surviving queen, nor stain her with filthy touches. This shall not be permitted to the following kings, nor to any man.[143]

The tone here is not exactly rational. The belief is that, once wedded to a king, a woman should not be touched by any other man. Under Ervig's successor, Egica (d. 702), the rule was strengthened by specifying, in addition, that the king's widow must enter a nunnery.[144] Some men, like Fáelán mac Murchado and Vladimir of Novgorod, clearly regarded such a taboo as a challenge to be broken. Yet for others, like the Danish and Hungarian nobles of the later Middle Ages, there seems to have been no taboo to overcome. The variety of responses meant that a king or prince looking for a bride might find a royal widow prescribed or proscribed.

Prohibited Degrees

In the eleventh and twelfth centuries, the Church settled its rules on marriage in ways that might appear paradoxical. On the one hand, it came down decisively in favour of a view of what constituted marriage: consent of the two parties. A church service was not necessary, the presence of a priest was not necessary, and neither did consent of the families or a transfer of property, however desirable or customary, have any constitutive function. What mattered was two people agreeing to marry. This is remarkably informal. But in contrast, over the course of the early Middle Ages, the western Church established the most restrictive rules about *choice* of marriage partner that the world has ever seen. In the fully developed system, as evidenced in sources of the eleventh and twelfth centuries, the prohibition on marrying a cousin was extended far beyond first cousins, to include second, third, fourth, fifth and sixth cousins.[145] In other words, having a common great-great-great-great-great-grandfather debarred a couple from marrying.

Rigorous churchmen would label marriages that broke these rules 'incestuous'. A conscientious layman might consequently have to look far afield for a permissible bride. Constance Bouchard suggested that this explains such unusual marriages as that of Henry I of France with Anna of Kiev in 1051 (a taste of the exoticism that foreign queens could represent is exemplified in a charter issued by Philip I of France in 1063, in which his mother, Anna, signs her name in Cyrillic script),[146] and also the willingness of the great dukes and counts of eleventh-century France to take brides from outside their caste, from among knightly families.[147] Even if such brides were in reality the sixth cousins of the dukes and counts they married, the chances are that such a distant relationship would be unknown. The search for wives of the right status who were not technically within the prohibited degrees could thus be complex and convoluted.

The process of evolution towards this extreme situation had been gradual and long. Marriage between first cousins was not unusual in ancient Rome but had been prohibited by the Christian emperors of the fourth century. Marriage to cousins beyond this degree of relationship was accepted, as is shown by the case of the western emperor Valentinian III, who in 437 married the daughter of his first cousin. However, during the course of the early Middle Ages, in both east and west, the prohibition came to be extended to marriage between second cousins. Important milestones in this process are the council of Epaon in Burgundy in 517, and the *Ecloga* of the emperor Leo III, issued in 741.[148] A relationship with a second cousin was still likely to be within the boundaries of what a family might know about its members. Indeed, defining the prohibited degrees by the limits of known relationships might seem to make sense, and some ninth-century rulings from popes and councils refrained from defining their exact extent but stipulated 'we command that no Christian is permitted to take a wife from his own relatives or kindred, as far as the relationship is recalled, known or remembered.'[149] This definition would usually mean that marriages between very distant cousins would be possible because there would be no memory of the kinship. It is the drastic extension of the prohibitions around the year 1000 that created a dilemma. Given the complex network of marriage alliances among western kings and aristocrats, it might have seemed to them virtually impossible to find anyone to marry, given the newly defined rules. The Church itself finally recognized that the rules about illicit marriages were extreme, and, at the Fourth Lateran Council in 1215, reduced the prohibited degrees from seven to four, thus only debarring marriage with one's third cousins.

Throughout the medieval period, therefore, choice of marriage partner was limited by law, both Roman and canon. Marriage of first cousins, which had been banned in the fourth century, was rare. Karl Ubl, in his comprehensive analysis of this topic, found only three cases in the Merovingian period.[150] Later instances do occur, like the marriage of the Welsh ruler, Owain Gwynedd, ruler of Gwynedd (d. 1170), and his first cousin Cristina, but that was highly controversial. Charles IV of France (1322–8) married his first cousin, Joan of Evreux, but required a papal dispensation to do so. Cousin marriage beyond that limit, however, was a different matter, allowed with third cousins in the Byzantine empire and in the early medieval west, and with fourth cousins in the Latin Church after 1215. The really extreme regime was thus that in the west from 1000 to 1215, and there are plenty of examples to show the difficulties, as well as the opportunities, that such a system generated. The first difficulty, of course, was knowing who your sixth cousins were. Even today, when research into family history is the second most popular use of the internet, it is not simple to establish a genealogy of this extent. The development of genealogical literature in this period and the rise of the pictorial family tree (discussed below, pp. 326–39) show how ruling and aristocratic families grappled with their deep ancestry and the complications it might bring to their choices of marriage partner.

The intrusive and sometimes combative nature of papal policy on dynastic marriages can be exemplified by the activities of Pope

Innocent III (1198–1216), recognized as one of the most energetic and influential of all medieval popes.[151] Innocent fought vigorously against what he saw as a storm of incestuous marriages. 'In the East', he wrote, 'one woman has been joined incestuously with two men, while in the West one man has dared to join himself with two women through incest.'[152] In both these cases he was, of course, referring to consecutive rather than simultaneous unions. The woman was Isabella, daughter of Amalric I, king of Jerusalem, who brought royal power to her successive husbands in the 1190s. The pope's objections were to husbands two and three, Conrad of Montferrat and Henry of Champagne. Conrad was the brother of William of Montferrat, who had been married to Isabella's half-sister, a relationship close enough to qualify as incestuous, although whether the relationship between Isabella and Henry of Champagne was technically within the prohibited degrees is doubtful – later Innocent simply called it 'less than legitimate, as is said'.[153] In any case, Innocent saw the hand of God in the swift and unexpected deaths of the two husbands, one of whom was assassinated in 1192, while the other fell out of a window to his death in 1197. The other case Innocent mentions ('one man has dared to join himself with two women through incest') was Alfonso IX of Leon, who married first Teresa of Portugal, who was his first cousin, and then Berenguela of Castile, who was the daughter of his first cousin. Both marriages were eventually annulled, but not before Alfonso had fathered eight children by these two wives. One of these children, Ferdinand III, was to inherit both Leon and Castile, reuniting those two kingdoms permanently. Although Pope Innocent had deployed all the weapons at his disposal – interdict, excommunication, declaration that Alfonso's children were illegitimate – and although the marriage of Alfonso and Berenguela had been ended, the dynastic bond proved stronger than canonical rules: a marriage between members of two royal families (or two branches of a royal family) had produced a new (or restored) kingdom (see also pp. 183–4).

Innocent's intransigence was also shown in the long and tangled case of Philip Augustus of France and Ingeborg of Denmark, whom the king married in 1193 and then repudiated the very next day (see also p. 26).[154] His grounds for this action have been much debated, and there has been speculation about some kind of pathological reaction on Philip's part, but, be that as it may, he immediately made determined efforts to obtain an annulment of his marriage to Ingeborg. His servants and ministers got to work producing a lengthy genealogy designed to demonstrate that Philip's first wife and Ingeborg were too closely related for Philip and Ingeborg to be married, and a tame council of bishops and nobles was assembled to swear to this.[155] A copy of the genealogy was even entered into the French royal registers.[156] When Pope Innocent took over the handling of this case after his accession to the papacy, he was not impressed: he described the sentence annulling the marriage, passed by Philip's council, as 'a ludicrous fairy tale',[157] and went as far as to impose an interdict on the kingdom of France in order to induce Philip to take Ingeborg back. A complication was that Philip, relying on the decision of the council of French bishops and nobles, had remarried. His new wife (as he saw her), Agnes of Meran, bore him two children, including a son, Philip's second and a welcome insurance against the possible death of the first. Innocent insisted that Philip and Agnes should separate and Ingeborg be received back:

> He commanded that the intruder (Agnes) should be removed from the king's company, both physical and local, so that she should be excluded not only from the king's embraces but also from the boundaries of the kingdom, and that the queen should be solemnly received by the king and treated as befits a queen.[158]

Philip eventually agreed to these terms, leaving open the question of whether his marriage to Ingeborg might later be annulled. Further proceedings were inconclusive, but then Agnes helpfully died. In a conciliatory gesture, Innocent legitimized her children by Philip, acknowledging the king's plea that he had acted in good faith when he married her and recognizing that Philip only had one other child and that legitimizing the two new children would serve 'the utility and needs of the kingdom of France'.[159] Innocent was determined, but also had to balance competing ends. He wanted Philip's political support despite being committed to a strict line on marriage. Even when he had imposed an interdict on the kingdom, suspending all religious services except baptism and absolution, he had made an exception for crusaders, who were allowed to hear mass and receive Christian burial – the crusade remained one of the pope's highest priorities.[160] The case of Ingeborg and Philip dragged on over the years until eventually, in 1213, Philip 'received into his favour and conjugal affection his legitimate wife, queen Ingeborg'.[161] The fact that he now had two adult sons, and his ability to ignore Ingeborg henceforth, had convinced Philip that this was the easier path in the face of Innocent's persistence. Innocent did not always gain complete victories in these matrimonial cases (and he had other important ones to deal with too),[162] but the decrees of canon law and the attitudes of individual popes were things that the rulers of the high and late Middle Ages had to take into account when choosing a bride.

The Case of Joan of Woodstock

A case-study can illustrate many of the procedures and perils of choosing a royal bride. In 1345 envoys from the king of Castile arrived in London, seeking a wife for their master's son. 'After a careful inspection of the two daughters of the king of England, they chose Lady Joan of Woodstock, the king's younger daughter, saying that she suited her future husband better because of her age.'[163] Joan, the third child of Edward III and Queen Philippa, was eleven at this time, her older sister thirteen. The proposed husband, later notorious as Peter the Cruel, was exactly Joan's age. But, young as she was, this was not the first marriage that had been proposed for Joan.[164]

Joan was born late in 1333 and by the summer of 1335, when she was about eighteen months old, plans were being made for her marriage. On 18 July of that year, her father, campaigning on the Scottish border, issued a letter authorizing his envoys 'to deal and make agreement with that noble and powerful man, the duke of Austria ... about contracting a marriage between the duke's eldest son and our dear daughter Joan'.[165] The duke of Austria in question was Otto of Habsburg, youngest son of King Albert I. Otto's eldest son, Frederick, was six years older than Joan, so around eight years of age when these negotiations were taking place. An agreement was reached that the young princess should actually be sent to Germany to be brought up there until of marriageable age. It took several years before this happened, and, in the meantime, the outbreak of war between King Edward and his rival, Philip VI of France, gave the alliance with the Habsburgs greater significance, since Edward was hoping to build up a coalition of Rhineland princes as a threat on France's eastern border. In the summer of 1338 the English royal family crossed to Antwerp and made their way up the Rhine for a summit meeting with the emperor Louis the Bavarian. Louis was married to Margaret of Hainault, sister of Edward's queen, Philippa of Hainault, so she was Joan's aunt. It was decided that she should take care of the young English princess, and when her parents returned north, Joan went south to Munich, the court of Louis and Margaret. Here she spent almost a year.

Her time there seems not always to have been easy, for the English royal accounts record that money had to be spent on food for her and her companions 'when they did not have sufficient food and drink from the emperor'.[166] Duke Otto continued to request that she be sent to Austria, and Edward appears eventually to have agreed to this, but all was put in doubt by Otto's death in February 1339. Joan was recalled in the spring of 1340 and joined her mother in Ghent, where the queen gave birth to a young brother for her, John of Gaunt (that is, 'Ghent'). By the summer, Joan, now aged six, was in her apartments in the Tower of London, along with her older sister Isabella and her loyal French nurse. The Habsburgs continued to consider the marriage as agreed, despite discouraging noises from the English side. In the summer of 1341 Edward III wrote to Albert of Habsburg, Frederick's uncle and head of the family, suggesting the marriage be postponed, especially since the emperor Louis had now gone over to the French side.[167] Over a year later, on 28 October 1343, the young Duke Frederick, now sixteen, wrote to Edward from Vienna, urging speedy marriage to Joan.[168]

But by this time the Castilian marriage had already been mooted as an alternative. King Edward's cousin and friend, the earl of Derby, participated in the siege of the Muslim city of Algeciras in 1342–4, a major military undertaking of Alfonso XI of Castile, and used the contact to broach the question of a marriage alliance between Alfonso's eldest son, Peter, and one of King Edward's daughters. Alfonso responded favourably, and envoys began to cross back and forth between Spain and England (or Edward's duchy of Gascony). Edward's instructions required his ambassadors to drive as hard a bargain as they could. Their opening offer for a dowry would be £10,000; if this was not acceptable, they could go to 20,000 marks (roughly £13,333); if this was not enough, they could offer £15,000, then £20,000. If this still did not secure the agreement, they should then consult the king again.[169] Negotiations were hampered by various problems. One was simply the difficulty of travel and communication. On one occasion, the king sent his envoys by land across France to Bordeaux but he was unwilling to entrust their documents and credentials to this risky journey across the territory of his enemy, so sent them by sea; unfortunately, the ship carrying them sank and duplicates had to be arranged.[170] Another issue was the competing offer from Philip VI of France, who also had a daughter suited for the Castilian prince and could promise a dowry more than twice as large as Edward's maximum. Alfonso XI was happy to accept Philip's offer but did not see any reason to stop negotiations with Edward. Indeed, he revealed Philip's terms to Edward and promised that he would prefer the English alliance, even with a lower dowry.[171] The English king was assiduous in cultivating support at the Castilian court through letters and gifts, making sure that he had the backing of both Alfonso's wife, Queen Maria, and his mistress, Eleanor de Guzmán. Even the lower dowry was a problem for Edward, engaged as he was in constant warfare. One ingenious suggestion was that he could marry his eldest son, later known as the Black Prince, to a daughter of the king of Portugal and thus acquire a dowry from her that he could then use to provide one for Joan. Queen Maria, who was herself a daughter of the king of Portugal, was a supporter of this scheme.

Edward's instructions to his officials show an insistence that any son of Peter and Joan would have the right to succeed to the throne of Castile, coupled with lingering doubts: 'if they arrive at Bordeaux and have certain news that the prince of Spain has married another, the lady will return immediately to England.'[172] Finally, in spring 1348, Joan set out from Plymouth to sail to Bordeaux and then to travel on to Spain. Her entourage contained knights, bishops, officials, ladies and 130 archers, as well as a minstrel of Prince Peter returning to Spain. She took with her a spectacular and enormously expensive array of clothes, textiles, jewels and furnishings. On 31 March she reached Bordeaux, where the four-teen-year-old girl was to await her Castilian prince. But the marriage was never to be consummated, for, later that year, the Black Death swept through Europe, carrying her off on 2 September. Peter settled for a French wife five years later.

The case of Joan of Woodstock illustrates the character of medieval marriage diplomacy: plans made while the princess was just a baby, the arbitrary switch from a proposed marriage that would take her to Vienna to one that would see her in Burgos and Toledo, the seemingly interminable negotiations, the double-dealing and dissimulation, the flattery and hard bargaining, all at any moment to be punctured and dispersed by sudden death. In the words of Mary Anne Everett Green, who in the 1840s delved into the English royal records to learn about the young princess, 'How little did she imagine while contemplating her luxurious array, that it was all vainly lavished on one who was soon to be the bride of death!'[173]

CHAPTER 2

Waiting for Sons to be Born

THE SEARCH FOR A BRIDE, WITH ALL ITS COMPLEXITIES, ITS political implications and its possible cultural consequences, had a simple goal: the birth of a child. This was the biological event on which the fortunes of kingdoms turned. Rulers in the patriarchal and dynastic world of medieval Europe were expected to be brave, violent, aggressive, forceful – qualities that were associated with men. But the thing on which dynastic continuity, and indeed the very existence of dynasties, relied was the female body and what it alone could do: conceive and give birth. So, once the new bride had been chosen, attention focussed on her ability to conceive children, especially sons. The natural fertility and mortality of upper-class and lower-class people were probably quite similar, but age at marriage might be different. In late medieval England, it has been calculated, women of the top level of the aristocracy married, on average, at seventeen, men at twenty-two.[1] It seems, however, that practices at the very apex of the social hierarchy, the rulers, often included much earlier marriage.

According to the canon law of the western Church, girls were permitted to marry at the age of twelve, but ecclesiastical authorities recognized the possibility of marriage before that age 'for the sake of reconciliation and peace between rulers or great men'.[2] Richard II of England married Isabella of France just before her seventh birthday. Henry the Young King (as he is known), son of Henry II of England, was married at the age of five to the even younger daughter of the king of France. Contemporaries noted with some disapproval this marriage of 'little children still wailing in the cradle',[3] but it brought Henry II the important border territory of the Vexin as the baby princess's dowry.

52

There are cases of aristocratic women in Ottonian Germany not only marrying at twelve but also bearing children at that age,[4] although it was not usual that sexual activity would begin so young. One careful study of upper-class marriages in late medieval England, by John Carmi Parsons, suggests that, whatever the age at marriage, sexual relations usually did not begin before the girl was around fifteen, and this is likely to be true of royal marriages too.[5] A good example of this pattern is provided by Margaret, daughter of the king of Denmark and later ruler of all three Scandinavian kingdoms, who was engaged to the king of Norway when she was six and he was eighteen, married him aged ten and bore a child aged seventeen. Matilda, daughter of Henry II of England, married Henry the Lion, duke of Saxony, at the age of eleven; her husband was then thirty-eight. She seems to have borne her first child around the age of sixteen.

But the age imbalance was not always between older men and younger women. When, in 1281, the twenty-year-old Margaret of Scotland was sent to Norway to marry the Norwegian king Erik, who was not yet fourteen years old, the Scots insisted that, when she arrive, she be given separate lodgings until the wedding, 'in such a way that the king of Norway might have no dishonourable or carnal contact with her in the meantime'.[6] The raging hormones of a pubescent boy could not be allowed to upset the course of a carefully negotiated dynastic marriage. Such disparities in age between older brides and younger grooms are to be explained by the politics of dynasty and inheritance. When Matilda, daughter of Henry I of England, married Geoffrey of Anjou on 17 June 1128, she was a widow of twenty-six and he fifteen, and when Constance of Sicily married Henry, son of the emperor Frederick Barbarossa, on 27 January 1186, she was thirty-one and he nineteen or twenty. These ten- or eleven-year differences in age were outweighed by the fact that in each case the bride had a hereditary claim to the kingdom, a claim that was formally acknowledged in the case of Matilda, and may have been in the case of Constance. Both women bore sons, Constance at the age of thirty-nine, and these sons became kings of England and Sicily respectively. In the case of Matilda, relations with her younger husband were initially stormy, though there is no reason to assume that the age difference was the explanation. Less happy was the marriage of Louis V, joint king of the

West Franks, and Adelheid of Aquitaine in 980. He was fourteen, she in her thirties:

> There was almost no wedded love between them. For, since he was still a teenage boy and she was an old woman, they had quite different ways. They did not sleep together ... when they needed to speak, they did so outdoors ... Their ways were so discordant that not long afterwards they separated.[7]

Perhaps, as has been suggested in a later, similar case, Adelheid felt their marriage was 'like being wed to an annoying younger brother'.[8]

In the dynastic world, it made a fundamental difference whether the ruler had a son or not. The worry and concern about this issue are often made explicit. 'Woe to those peoples who have no hope that offspring of their lords will succeed to rule', wrote Thietmar, bishop of Merseburg, in the early eleventh century.[9] Everyone in a kingdom knew whether the ruler could expect a son to succeed him, and knew too that if he could not, there would be consequences for all. Thietmar was here expressing a justified foreboding, for this was exactly the predicament that would face the Germans when the ruling emperor, the childless Henry II, died. Later in that same century, in the reign of a subsequent ruler, the same note of concern is heard in the words of the archbishop of Cologne calling for universal prayers 'that a son should be given to the emperor by the heavenly mercy, so that the peace of the realm might continue'.[10]

Pregnancy brought no unqualified reassurance. The world of dynastic politics was full of uncertainties, but these were of two kinds: there were certain uncertainties and uncertain uncertainties. Among the certain uncertainties was childbirth, which was always happening but, on any given occasion, had a doubtful outcome. Would the child survive? Would the mother survive? What sex would the child be? Careful negotiators would have to think through the possibilities. After the wedding of Isabella, daughter of the king of France, with Edward II of England in 1308, the French diplomats wanted to discuss all the permutations:

> in the case where there are several sons and daughters, what provision will be made for the younger sons and the daughters; in case my lady

dies without sons and there are several daughters, what provision will be made for the younger daughters; and if the eldest will be queen; and if my lady dies without a son but there is a daughter or there are several daughters, and the king of England has a son by a second marriage, what provision will be made for the daughter or daughters of the first marriage?[11]

Death in Childbirth

Among ruling families, childbirth was a political matter. It was also, for the mother, one of the most dangerous moments in her life. Modern maternal mortality rates vary enormously. In the early twenty-first century, the maternal mortality rate in western European countries was 4 to 10 per 100,000 live births, but in Afghanistan it was 1,575. In other words, it was 150 to 400 times more dangerous to give birth in Afghanistan than in western Europe. We do not have such statistics for the Middle Ages, but reasonably reliable figures for seventeenth-century England, when conditions were probably similar, suggest a rate of 1,500–1,600 per 100,000, a rate like Afghanistan.[12]

High rank did not make the chances of death in childbirth any less. There are examples of queens dying in this way throughout the Middle Ages and in every part of Christendom. At least four Capetian queens of France died in or immediately after childbirth. In 1160, Constance of Castile, the second wife of Louis VII, 'died during labour, but the daughter who was the cause of her death survived'.[13] Thirty years later, Elizabeth (Isabella) of Hainault, the first wife of Philip Augustus, died giving birth to twins.[14] In 1324, Mary of Luxemburg, the second wife of Charles IV, gave birth prematurely, both baby and mother dying:

> Around the middle of Lent, as King Charles was returning from the region of Toulouse, and had arrived at the castle of Issoudun with his pregnant wife, she, perhaps worn out by the journey, gave birth to a male child a month or so before its term; he was quickly baptized and, after a little while, breathed his last; and in a few days the mother followed her son and departed this life.[15]

And Joan of Bourbon, wife of Charles V, died on 6 February 1378, soon after the birth of her daughter Catherine, according to one account because she had taken a bath against her doctor's advice.[16] Joan was just forty and Catherine was her ninth child.

One of the sadder cases of death in childbirth is Isabella (or Yolande), queen of Jerusalem. Isabella's mother, who was also queen of Jerusalem, died giving birth to her; she was about twenty at the time. As queen of Jerusalem, Isabella was a very desirable bride and she was engaged to the Holy Roman Emperor, Frederick II, at the age of ten or eleven, marrying him two years later. Frederick was seventeen years her senior. In 1228, aged fifteen or sixteen, Isabella died giving birth to a son. This melancholy story shows how childbirth could sweep women away in each generation. Another of the wives of Frederick II, Isabella of England, also died in childbirth.[17]

Death soon after giving birth, from puerperal fever, was common. The account of the death of Queen Guta or Judith of Bohemia in 1297 describes how she used her last days to set her affairs in order:

> But as the sickness that she had contracted during the recent birth of a baby grew stronger, the lady queen, the pious and renowned Guta, recognized from the terrible pains, like unmistakable messengers of death, that the last days of her life had come, and she began wisely to make arrangements for her property and household and to think what might benefit her soul.[18]

Guta, daughter of Rudolf of Habsburg, had married Wenceslas II of Bohemia shortly before her fourteenth birthday, borne him ten children and now died at the age of twenty-six.[19]

It is thus not surprising that pregnancy and childbirth constituted a time when supernatural help was welcome. In November 1244 Henry III of England ordered a thousand wax candles, each weighing half a pound, to be placed around the shrine of St Thomas Becket in Canterbury Cathedral, and a like number to be placed in St Augustine's, Canterbury, 'for the preservation of the health and for the safe delivery of the queen, who is pregnant'. Later, two nuns brought 'St Edmund's cloak' to Westminster 'in preparation for our queen's delivery'.[20] Probably the intention was to wrap this around the heavily pregnant queen. She gave birth to a son, Edmund, on 16 January 1245. Likewise, when Scottish queens were preparing for labour, the 'sark' or chemise of their saintly predecessor, St Margaret of Scotland, was sent for.[21] Judging from other similar use of saintly relics, it is probable that the pregnant queens would wear this holy garment to ease the pain and ensure a healthy birth.[22] Isabella of Bavaria, the queen of Charles VI of France, visited the relic of the belt of the Virgin Mary at St-Sanctin-de-Chuisnes, near Chartres, during each of her twelve pregnancies.[23]

The Uncertainties of Pregnancy

In one case, we can actually hear the apprehensive voice of a queen pregnant for the first time. One of the most remarkable documents of the whole Middle Ages is that issued by Queen Petronilla of Aragon on 4 April 1152. Its opening words are, 'I, Petronilla, queen of Aragon, lying and labouring in childbirth at Barcelona . . .'[24] The queen is actually issuing this document during her labour. She wishes to make provision for the child, whichever sex it may be – whether it is a boy that 'is to proceed from my womb, by God's will', or 'if a daughter should proceed from my womb'.[25] The conjectural boy is to have the kingdom of Aragon, although Petronilla's husband, Count Raymond, will rule it during his lifetime. If the boy dies, her husband will have the kingdom. He will also have it if Petronilla's child is a girl, being required only to ensure that she marries well. Petronilla's own apprehensions at this time may be signified by the last clauses in the charter, whereby she grants 2,000 gold coins to the churches of Aragon and Barcelona for the sake of her soul. She was only fifteen at this time. As it turned out, Petronilla gave birth to a healthy child, and survived to have four more. It is hard to imagine a more vivid example of the bond between the female body and the body politic, as this teenage girl strains in childbirth, wondering what will 'proceed from her womb'.

An even more uncertain situation could arise when a ruler died leaving a pregnant wife. A famous instance, with far-reaching political consequences, occurred in 1316. When Louis X of France died on 5 June in that year, he left a daughter by his first wife, but she was of dubious status, since her mother the queen had been found guilty of adultery and imprisoned for life. After the death of this imprisoned first wife, King Louis had married again, to Clemencia, a distant cousin, and she was four months pregnant at the time of his death. The succession to the kingdom was now in suspense. If Clemencia gave birth to a boy, there was no question that he would be king, with a long minority ahead of him, but arrangements had to be made for the eventuality that she might give birth to a girl. In the words of one contemporary account, the dead king's brother, Philip, was to control the government, 'with the title of regent (*sub nomine regentis*), until, if a male child was born, he reached the age of understanding, that is, fourteen, but, if a daughter was born, Philip would himself become king of France and rule'.[26] Provisions were made for a landed endowment both for Louis' daughter by his first wife and this possible daughter by his second wife: such hypothetical children were often major actors in the world of dynastic politics. Meanwhile, from 5 June until the 14 November 1316, more than five months, the kingdom and its ruling dynasty waited for Clemencia to come to term.[27]

Similar uncertainty went through the mind of Albert of Habsburg as he lay dying on 23 October 1439 in the Hungarian village of Neszmély (Langendorf) on the banks of the Danube. His thoughts turned first to his own chances of salvation, but then to the future of the child that his pregnant wife, Elizabeth, was carrying. Albert was not only 'king of the Romans' (Holy Roman Emperor elect), a title that was not hereditary, but also duke of Austria, king of Hungary and king of Bohemia. Albert made careful stipulations for the event that his unborn child were a boy. He named Queen Elizabeth and the oldest male of the house of Habsburg as regents (*verweser*), who would exercise power in Austria, Hungary and Bohemia, with the advice of councils from those three domains; he instructed that the boy should be brought up in Bratislava (Pressburg) because it was close to all three of his realms; and he directed that officials in the three dominions should be chosen by the local bishops and nobles with the advice of the two regents, and that these officials should render accounts to his son when he came of age.[28] A whole imagined future was passing through his mind. Albert died a few days later, on 27 October 1439, and Elizabeth gave birth on 22 February 1440, almost four months later. The child was a boy, known as Ladislas 'Postumus', and, after many years of struggle by his partisans, he was able to succeed to all three of his father's titles, although he died young.

Yet more perplexing difficulties arose when a ruler died leaving a wife who might or might not be pregnant. When Alexander III of Scotland died in a riding accident on 19 March 1286, he left no surviving children. Just five months earlier he had, however, married a young French noblewoman, Yolande of Dreux, and there was a possibility that she was pregnant. For much of 1286, it seems, the regency council that had been appointed was waiting to see whether Yolande would produce a child. One sober chronicle source for that year simply reports: 'the event did not take place, or there was a miscarriage'.[29] A much more dramatic tale is told by a contemporary Franciscan, who had good contacts at the Scottish court but whose account is also coloured by an almost hysterical misogyny. He reports that Queen Yolande, 'employing her feminine wiles, said falsely that she was pregnant'. She refused to let 'honest matrons' inspect her state and 'determined to deceive the people forever by substituting someone else's baby'. She had a new font made of white marble and she arranged to acquire a baby boy, the son of an actor, but her trickery was discovered at the last moment by a loyal earl, and 'she left the land covered in shame'. This all shows, concludes our author, how much trust you can place in women.[30] This might all seem like fantasy, but a Scottish historian as hard-headed as Archie Duncan of Glasgow accepted that the queen was pregnant, suggested she might have lost the baby in August 1286, and was at least prepared to consider the possibility that this might have been concealed, and hence, at that stage, became a false pregnancy.[31] We do know, at least, that Yolande was fertile because she went on to have many children by her second husband, the duke of Brittany.

Celebration

The story was told that when Margaret of Provence, the wife of Louis IX of France (St Louis), gave birth to her first child, which turned out to be a girl, 'they did not dare to break the news to the king' and called on the bishop of Paris to convey this unwelcome information, which he did with a jest to soften the blow.[32] Conversely, the worry and concern about whether a son would be born could be explosively dissolved in celebration when one arrived. It was a time for grand public gestures, like the one made by the Frankish king Chilperic in 582. When a son was born to him, after several sons had been born and died, he celebrated by a general amnesty: 'the king commanded all the prisons to be opened, those in chains to be freed and the fines that were owing to the treasury by delinquents not to be demanded'.[33] Despite this act of thanksgiving, however, this little boy also died as an infant, aged two.

Elaborate celebrations for the birth of a son to the Byzantine emperor are described in *The Book of Ceremonies* of Constantine VII Porphyrogenitus (913–59). The patriarch of Constantinople and his clergy, and the senators in ceremonial dress, are to visit the palace to offer prayers and congratulations. On the third day after the birth, receptions are held and chariot races take place in the hippodrome. On the fifth day, 200 representatives of the Byzantine people assemble in the hippodrome and call out the boy's name. On the eighth day, the empress' bedchamber is decked with golden curtains and she receives a procession of high-born women, then high-born men, bringing prayers, congratulations and gifts. For a week, a special 'childbirth-brew (λοχόζεμα)' is to be distributed freely in the streets.[34]

The longer the wait, the greater the relief, and sometimes the wait was protracted. Louis VII of France was in his mid-forties and had been on the throne for twenty-eight years when he finally had his long-desired son. Ralph de Diceto, dean of St Paul's, London, looking across the Channel, describes how 'in his last days a happier fortune smiled on Louis, king of the French'. 'The king had had only four daughters from his first and second marriages; at last, from the third, much more happily, he happily fathered a son, desired by the people and devoutly and keenly besought by the clergy.' Indeed, he says, the very reason for Louis' three marriages (*trigamia*) was 'to bring forth masculine offspring'.[35] Louis' biographer describes how the king 'feared that the kingdom of France would not be governed by an heir who had issued from his seed'.[36] A poem written to celebrate the birth of this son, Philip, in 1165, puts it pithily: 'The boy is peace (*Pax puer est*).'[37] This same poem, which was written by a French student in Paris at the time (Paris was in the process of giving birth to the university as well as a Capetian prince), conveys the suspense and tension of waiting to find out the sex of the new child:

> It was night and the queen was in labour in this famous childbirth;
> the city beseeches you about this, O Christ, with wakeful prayer.
> The eager wishes of the city beg that it be male;
> the tearful court asks God for a male.[38]

Another student in Paris that night was woken from his sleep by the noise of the city rejoicing:

> As the news was heard in the city and received with a joy such and so great that it cannot be expressed with the tongue, immediately such a great sound and ringing of all the bells broke out everywhere throughout the breadth of the city, and so many wax lights were lit through all the streets, that those who did not know the cause of such a great sound or such an unusual tumult or the vast amount of lights at night-time, thought that the city was threatened with fire. Hence, also, the author of this work . . . woken from the bed where he had already laid down to sleep, leapt at once to the window, and, looking out, he saw in the street two old women, very poor, but holding wax torches in their hands, rejoicing in expression and voice and every movement of their bodies, and rushing to and fro with swift steps. When he had asked them the cause for all this noise and rejoicing, one of them looked at him and answered, saying, 'We now have a king given to us by God and a powerful heir to the kingdom by God's gift.'[39]

Even two years later the bishop of Orleans made a grant 'from joy at the birth of the illustrious boy Philip, son of the lord king'.[40] No wonder that Philip, later to be famous as Philip Augustus, also had the soubriquet *Dieudonné*, 'given by God'.[41]

An account of the birth of the son of Charles VI on the night of 6 February 1392, over two hundred years later, depicts the Parisian response in equally enthusiastic terms: all the church bells rang, and as royal messengers cried out the news, everyone came onto the streets with lighted torches, playing music and singing all night, while ladies doled out wine and spices from trestle tables set up in the streets.[42] Just like King Chilperic in 582, more than eight centuries earlier, Charles VI authorized the release of prisoners 'because of the joyous arrival and nativity of Monsieur the Dauphin'.[43] Bells ringing, music and all-night street parties show that the population at large might have shared the dynastic concerns of its rulers. The birth of a royal son, promising dynastic continuity, might also promise peace to the kingdom at large.

But even when the long-awaited son was born, there was no certainty he would live. High child mortality meant that rulers had to get used to a rapid turnover in their presumed heirs. Edward I of England, for example, had a son, John, born in the summer of 1266, before Edward himself became king. For the following five years John was next in the line of royal succession after his father. But the young prince died in the summer of 1271, which meant his young brother Henry, who was four at the time, took his place as heir. But in three years or so, with Edward now king, Henry also died, leaving the role of heir apparent to the baby Alfonso, who was not yet a year old. For almost ten years, from October 1274 to August 1284, it was Alfonso who was treated as the expected inheritor of the throne. But there was to be no Alfonso I of England, as the prince died before his eleventh birthday. Fortunately for King Edward, he had just had another son, born in April 1284 and christened with the king's own name. He grew up to be Edward II. But the constant changes over many years show the uncertainties of succession, as well as highlighting the many 'might have beens' of history. If Prince Alfonso had lived and succeeded his father, perhaps Alfonso would have become as common a name in English history as Edward, and we might admire the *Decline and Fall* of that great historian Alfonso Gibbon, or laugh at the nonsense verse of Alfonso Lear.

Childlessness

The purpose of a royal marriage was to produce children, or, more specifically, a son. A childless king not only created, and had to deal with, uncertainty about the succession but was also more vulnerable in his lifetime. If an opponent got rid of him, there would be no sons to fight back or pursue revenge. When Henry Bolingbroke usurped the throne from Richard II of England in 1399, he faced opposition, criticism and, sometimes, rebellion, but Richard had no son to fan the flames. In contrast, when Bolingbroke's grandson, Henry VI, was removed by Edward of York in 1461, there was a son, and Edward's regime was not truly secure until the killing of that son ten years later.

There were occasions when childless rulers or nobles sought to bequeath everything to ecclesiastical institutions but such radical measures faced opposition from their wider kindred. Alfonso the Battler, king of Aragon and Navarre, who died in 1134, left a will in which he bequeathed his kingdom to the Templars, the Hospitallers and the Order of the Holy Sepulchre, international Orders based in the Holy Land:

> After my death I leave as my heir and successor the Sepulchre of the Lord that is in Jerusalem, and those who keep it and watch over it and serve God there, and the Hospital of the poor that is in Jerusalem, and the Temple of Solomon with the knights who are on guard there for the defence of the name of Christendom. To these three I grant my whole kingdom . . . so that they should have and possess it in three fair and equal portions.[44]

If Alfonso's will had been carried out, his kingdom would have become three states run by the crusading Orders, just like the later *Ordensstaat* ('Order State') of the Teutonic Knights in the eastern Baltic, or the Hospitallers' Rhodes.[45] the leaders of Aragon and Navarre were not prepared to tolerate this. In Navarre the nobles chose as king a descendant of an illegitimate son of a king of Navarre who had ruled eighty years earlier, thus separating the two kingdoms again. In Aragon, Alfonso's only close male relative, his brother Ramiro, was a monk, but this did not stop the leaders of Aragon hauling him out of his monastery, marrying him to a noble French lady and only allowing him to return to it when she had given birth to a child, a daughter who thus became queen of Aragon before her first birthday. 'This', commented a Castilian chronicler, 'was a great sin before the Lord, but the Aragonese, having lost their dear lord, did this so that sons might be raised up from the royal seed.'[46] This infant queen, Petronilla, mentioned above (p. 57), was betrothed to Raymond Berengar IV of Barcelona, twenty-three years her senior, in 1137. He took over the running of Aragon and secured renunciation of their claims by the Hospitallers and the Order of the Holy Sepulchre in 1140, in return for generous grants within the realm.[47] A few years later, in 1143, the Templars accepted compensation in the form of a huge endowment in Aragon.[48] Later, the renunciation by the Orders and Raymond's possession of 'all the land which Alfonso, former king of the Aragonese, dying without an heir, left to the Sepulchre of the Lord, the Hospital and the Temple' was confirmed by the papacy.[49]

The same urge that motivated Alfonso the Battler can occasionally be found among the higher aristocracy as well as amongst sovereign rulers. The childless Welf III (d. 1055) wanted to leave his entire estate to a monastery but his nephew turned up from Italy to claim it.[50] In English law it was even forbidden to make a bequest of land to a religious house on one's deathbed, to avoid this situation.[51] There were to be states run by the international Orders in medieval Europe but they were created by conquest, not by the wishes of childless kings. The swift action of the Aragonese nobles in finding a blood-heir shows very clearly that this was an elite who thought in dynastic terms.

One story that could be told about childless kings was that they preserved their virginity to maintain their moral and spiritual purity, in accordance with the teaching of the medieval Church that virginity was one of the highest goods. Two childless eleventh-century kings, Henry II of Germany and Edward the Confessor of England, were declared saints, the former in 1146, the latter in 1161, and on each occasion the monarch's lifelong virginity, despite being married, was given as one of the signs of their sanctity.[52] But saints are, by definition, rare. Most childless kings wished to take action to remedy the situation. Should a childless queen be dismissed and replaced by another, possibly fertile, one? How many times could this be done? Or was it better to wait out the first wife and hope for her early death, perhaps while giving birth to a girl? And, failing all else, was it desirable to make arrangements for a successor who was not a son or daughter – perhaps a relative, perhaps not?

Repudiation of Failed Mothers

In the High Middle Ages, the Church did not permit divorce, in the sense of the ending of a valid marriage, but did allow annulment, which was the recognition that the marriage in question had never been valid in the first place, and hence the partners could separate and marry others. One of the most common grounds for annulment was too close a family relationship between the partners, and the Church defined 'too close' in remarkably demanding terms (see above, pp. 43–5). But if that was the most common grounds, in the sense of legal justification, then the most common motive for an annulment was the fact that the wife had borne no sons. Commentators sometimes blithely combined the motive and the justification: 'they had parted because they were closely related and she had borne him no children'.[53]

An annulment of this kind with enormous political implications was that of the marriage of Louis VII of France and Eleanor of Aquitaine in 1152. At this time, although the king of France had an undisputed position as sole consecrated monarch in the kingdom, real power in most areas was in the hands of the great dukes and counts. Amongst the greatest were the dukes of Aquitaine, ruling the south-west of the country from the Loire to the Pyrenees. Eleanor's father, Duke William X, died unexpectedly in April 1137, leaving no sons. Within four months Eleanor was married to Louis, son of Louis VI and already crowned in his father's lifetime (the older Louis died just after this marriage). As husband of Eleanor, the king of France now had direct authority over the huge duchy of Aquitaine. It could have been a turning point in the history of the French monarchy. But there were two sources of tension in the marriage. One was a personal incompatibility. Eleanor supposedly complained, 'I have married a monk not a monarch!'[54] The other was the fact that during the fifteen years of the marriage she bore only daughters. The Capetian dynasty had either to face the problem of the failure of that series of father–son successions that had characterized it for well over a century, or give up Eleanor and Aquitaine. The decision was made in favour of the latter, justified, and perhaps even partly motivated, by the discovery that Louis and Eleanor were related within the prohibited degrees (they were fifth cousins). Louis' rivals were willing to gamble on the young Eleanor still being able to have sons in return for the acquisition of Aquitaine, and wasted no time. The marriage of Louis and Eleanor was nullified by a council held during Lent, that is, February to March, 1152, and she married Henry of Anjou at Pentecost (Whitsun), 18 May, the same year.[55] Henry already ruled Anjou and Normandy and with his marriage to Eleanor and then his accession to the English throne in 1154 there came into existence the huge conglomeration of territories, sometimes called the Angevin empire, that dominated the history of north-west Europe for the next half-century. And Eleanor went on to have five sons with Henry. The accident of her having borne only daughters with Louis VII thus shaped European political and military affairs for generations.

Getting rid of a wife who produced no children, or only girls, had political as well as legal consequences. If she were a member of a family that was important within the kingdom, then her relatives might well object and oppose. When the English king Edward the Confessor fell out with the powerful Earl Godwin and his sons in 1051 (see above, p. 13), driving them into exile, he also repudiated his wife Edith, Godwin's daughter, and sent her to a nunnery. Moreover, he stripped her of all her property: 'the king forsook the lady, who had been consecrated as his queen, and had her deprived of all that she possessed, in land, in gold, in silver and in everything'.[56] Edward and Edith had been married for more than six years but had no children. However, the next year the Godwin family returned in force, were reinstated in power, and consequently 'the queen, the earl's daughter, was brought back to the king's bed'.[57] The king's failure to break the Godwin family meant that he could not now seek another, younger and potentially fertile bride, and that he died childless, with the throne being taken by Godwin's son, Edith's brother, Harold, a move that provided the impetus for the Norman Conquest of 1066.

Some royal marriages were ended without much fuss. In 1153 Frederick Barbarossa, who had become 'king of the Romans' (Holy Roman Emperor elect) in the previous year, had his childless marriage to Adela of Vohburg dissolved easily and with no long-term consequences. The grounds were 'the bond of consanguinity', that is, they were too closely related.[58] Both remarried, he to the heir of the county of Burgundy, she to a member of the German lower aristocracy, and both had children from these second marriages.[59] Their marriage had lasted only four years or so, and consequently it is not clear that childlessness was the actual motive for this act rather than political considerations, such as the acquisition of Burgundy. The marriage was dissolved by papal legates, so the pope clearly raised no objections.

A very different situation faced Alfonso III of Portugal in the following century. He had married a great French noblewoman, Matilda of Boulogne, in 1239, many years before he became king – his elder brother Sancho II was ruler of Portugal – but he replaced Sancho as king in 1248 and now had to think seriously about the succession. His marriage with Matilda was childless and she was older than him, well into her forties. He therefore contracted another marriage. It is not clear what form of separation with Matilda took place. His new bride, who was not yet twelve, was Beatrice, the illegitimate daughter of Alfonso X of Castile, a match negotiated as part of a wider settlement of territorial disputes between the two kingdoms. Beatrice appears as 'wife' and 'queen' in Alfonso's charters from 1253.[60] Matilda, however, did not accept this without protest and appealed to the pope, who first delegated the case to the archbishop of Santiago and then, when the king failed to respond to the archbishop's summons, himself cited the king. Alfonso failed to send representatives, but Matilda's lawyer argued that, although Matilda 'was the king's legitimate wife, the king had publicly contracted a de facto marriage, or rather cohabitation, with the daughter of the king of Castile', and hence the pope should grant Matilda's request for a formal separation and the return of her dowry. The pope agreed to this.[61]

Alfonso continued to ignore the pope, even when he imposed an interdict on Portugal, and soon his teenage bride produced three sons. He was concerned that they should be declared legitimate, and his path was eased by two developments: a new pope in 1261 and the death of Matilda in 1262. In June 1263 the new pope, Urban IV, wrote to 'his dearest son in Christ, Alfonso, the illustrious king of Portugal', recording how the king had approached him, explaining

> that in the past, at the time when you received the reins of government of the kingdom of Portugal, on account of the pressing necessities with which your highness was faced and in order to avoid the grave and manifest dangers that were imminently at hand and also on account of the fear which can strike even the steadfast, you contracted a de facto marriage with the noble woman Beatrice, daughter of our dearest son in Christ, Alfonso, the illustrious king of Castile, while Matilda of precious memory, your legitimate wife, was still alive.[62]

Not only had Alfonso married while his first wife was alive, he had also married a girl who was underage and too closely related to him. But the pope notes that he has the power to suspend the rules if public necessity is great, especially in the case of rulers. Urban goes on to explain that he has taken many things into account – the loyalty of past kings of Portugal to the papacy, the fact that Portugal made an annual payment to the pope, the support for Alfonso's request from the king of France and from the Portuguese bishops – and declares that Alfonso and Beatrice may stay together and that their children are legitimate and have the right to inherit the kingdom. The kings of the Iberian peninsula had a tradition of making marriages that broke canon law and then outfacing papal disapproval to get their desired end. This is exactly what Alfonso III had done: he had dismissed his first, unfertile wife and found another, much younger one, with whom he had the sons he desired; then he had them legitimated. His male-line descendants ruled Portugal down to 1580.

A similar awareness of political realities is evident in the dealings of Urban IV with Premysl Otakar II, king of Bohemia. Premysl determined to obtain a separation from his wife, Margaret of Austria, 'since they were not able to have children'.[63] In 1261 'the sterile queen was repudiated' and Premysl married Cunigunda, the teenage granddaughter of the king of Hungary.[64] The pope was willing to accept this on various grounds, even though Premysl and his new wife were too closely related by the rules of canon law. One reason was that it was argued that Margaret of Austria had been a Dominican nun and therefore could not have entered a valid marriage with the king. Another was that 'from the continuation of the marriage contracted between you and Cunigunda peace will be preserved in the kingdoms of Hungary and Bohemia and the adjacent provinces'.[65] Urban therefore confirmed the annulment of the marriage with Margaret and gave a dispensation for the marriage with Cunigunda. Premysl was indeed succeeded by his son by Cunigunda. International peace was a good reason for being flexible in the application of rules about marriage.

Remarriages

The Byzantine emperor Manuel Comnenus, who had only daughters from his first marriage, married again, 'since he longed to be called the father of a male child'.[66] Remarriage was not uncommon after the death or repudiation of a childless queen, or one who had borne only daughters, and kings could then continue to father children with young brides. The English king most notorious for notching up wives is Henry VIII, who had six all told, motivated mainly by the desire to secure his relatively new dynasty through male heirs. In the end, he produced a son and two daughters, but all three died without children and so with them the Tudor dynasty came to an end. Henry's activities even left a mark on popular culture, with a mnemonic about how to remember the fate of his six wives: 'Divorced, beheaded, died; divorced, beheaded, survived.'

One medieval king who came close to rivalling Henry was Alfonso VI of Leon and Castile (d. 1109), although he did not execute any of his wives.[67] His first wife, Ines or Agnes of Poitou, who is recorded as queen in the 1070s, when Alfonso was in his thirties, left no children. After her death or divorce, Alfonso married another great French noblewoman, Constance of Burgundy, who gave birth to a daughter, Urraca, later to be the first queen regnant in medieval west European history. Constance seems to have had no further surviving children, and very quickly after her death in 1093, the king married again, to Berta, of uncertain but probably Italian descent. No children are recorded. The year after Berta's death in 1099 Alfonso married Elizabeth (or Isabella), another queen of uncertain descent but probably French, like two of his earlier wives. By her Alfonso had two more daughters, Sancha and Elvira. By this time the king also had several illegitimate children, two of them daughters, Teresa and another Elvira, by a Spanish noblewoman, and, most significant from his point of view, a son, Sancho, by his Muslim mistress Zaida (on her, see p. 19). A contemporary chronicler reports that Zaida converted to Christianity and took the new name Elizabeth, and this has led to conflicting theories about whether she is to be identified with Alfonso's fourth wife or whether she succeeded her, confusingly with the same name. At the very end of his life, when the king was again free to marry, after the death or divorce of the preceding Elizabeth or Elizabeths, and now around seventy years of age, Alfonso took a wife called Beatrice, who survived him. He thus had five or six wives but fathered only one son. This son, Sancho, died in battle the very year before the death of his father, hence the succession of Urraca. Alfonso's matrimonial history suggests that the pursuit of a male heir was a constant purpose and led to remarriage very quickly after the death of a queen.

One of the most controversial remarriages of a medieval monarch was the fourth marriage of the Byzantine emperor Leo VI.[68] His first wife, Theophano Martinakia, whom he had married in 882, was chosen for him by his parents. They had one child, a daughter, Eudokia, but relations between the spouses were not good, and the emperor began a relationship with another woman, Zoe Zaoutzaina. There were discussions about a separation between Leo and Theophano, especially after the death of their daughter. After Theophano's death in 897, Leo's plans to marry Zoe Zaoutzaina met with some opposition. Partly, this was due to a general Christian hostility towards second marriages, which can be traced back as far as St Paul and was also expressed in penitentials and canon law. St Jerome gave practical advice to those contemplating a second marriage: 'think every day that you are going to die, and you will never think about a second marriage.'[69] A century before Leo faced his own decision, Theodore, influential abbot of the Stoudios monastery in Constantinople, had put it very succinctly: 'a second marriage, even though it is permissible, still requires penance'.[70] But opposition was also inspired by Zoe's moral reputation, which was not good, since she was suspected of poisoning her husband, as well as being acknowledged as the emperor's mistress. Because of this, the patriarch of Constantinople refused to take part in the marriage ceremony, and the priest who did so was degraded from office. Zoe Zaoutzaina gave birth to a daughter, Anna, but died after only twenty months as empress. Leo now took a third wife, Eudokia Baiane, but she died in childbirth on 12 April 901, her baby boy also dying.[71]

If a second and third marriage were deemed 'permissible but requiring penance', a fourth was unprecedented in Byzantium. Yet, after Leo had buried his third wife alongside his first two in the Church of the Holy Apostles, the imperial mausoleum in Constantinople,[72] he not only took as his mistress Zoe Karbonopsina ('black-eyed Zoe'), but, after she had given birth to the long-desired son, Constantine, on 3 September 905, he married her. In a reprise of his second marriage, the priest who conducted the ceremony was later degraded from office. This fourth marriage was, however, an even more serious matter, and Nicholas, the patriarch of Constantinople, who had been willing to baptize the baby Constantine, was not willing to countenance the marriage and debarred Leo from entering church. He could be justified by the strong tradition in the eastern Church that condemned fourth marriages as bestial and iniquitous.[73] Patriarch Nicholas later claimed that he had agreed to baptize Constantine only in return for a promise from Leo to give up Zoe.[74] Matters became embattled. The emperor sought support for his position from Rome, for western canon law put no limit on the number of remarriages. Patriarch Nicholas berated the western Church for allowing not only fourth marriages, but fifth marriages, sixth marriages and so on indefinitely, and this was not a caricature.[75] The greatest legal expert of the thirteenth-century Roman Church argued that second marriages were licit and defined 'second' to mean any marriage after the first, 'even the thousandth'.[76] Nicholas vacillated in his position, but eventually came down for a hard line. Leo then pressured him into resigning, sent him into exile and secured a new patriarch. He obtained his dispensation and Zoe stayed on, later ruling as regent in the reign of her son Constantine.[77]

The emperor's fourth marriage created deep and long-lasting divisions in the Byzantine Church. Some episcopal sees had two bishops for a period, one loyal to the old patriarch, one to the new. Seemingly as part of the process of obtaining a dispensation for his marriage, Leo had to agree to a law forbidding fourth marriages, which thus made him 'the first and last person in the history of Byzantium to have been allowed to marry for a fourth time'.[78] His persistence in the face of opposition, his willingness to endure the disruption this entailed and his disregard of deep moral traditions all indicate a total commitment to the dynastic ideal of having a son to succeed him.

Leo VI finally obtained his son, and his dynasty continued on the Byzantine throne for another 150 years. But having just one son was a precarious position, given the high rate of infant death in the period. Most rulers would prefer more, 'an heir and a spare' as it is sometimes flippantly expressed. Edward I of England, after producing at least fourteen children with his first wife, Eleanor of Castile, had three more when he was in his sixties, with his young bride, Margaret of France. This was not simply from emotional or sexual motives. When Eleanor died, only one of the four sons she had borne survived, so Edward's line hung on a thread. The two further sons that Margaret bore were a guarantee. Extinction of the line was a frightful prospect for patriarchal dynasts like Edward.

The End of the Line

Kings often died without children, or without sons, or without male descendants, or without legitimate children. In all such cases, there would almost certainly be more than one claimant to succeed and the politics of the kingdom would be dominated by the issue until a secure outcome was reached, which might take years or even decades and involve the shedding of large amounts of blood. The long-term fate of kingdoms could be decided by a ruler's childlessness. After the death of the childless Rudolf III in 1032, his kingdom of Burgundy came into the hands of the Holy Roman Emperors and lost its political identity. Thirty-four years later, in 1066, the death of the childless Edward the Confessor, king of England, set off a ferocious conflict among his potential successors and led to the most dramatic transformation ever experienced by the medieval kingdom of England. In Germany, kings died without leaving children in 911, 918 (although in this case with an adult brother), 1002, 1024, and 1125. This was one reason why German kingship remained elective, since on these occasions the great nobles and higher clergy decided the succession, establishing precedents for election rather than hereditary monarchy. Famous dynasties that died out though lack of male heirs included the Arpad kings of Hungary in 1301 and the Premyslids of Bohemia in 1306, in each case after ruling for centuries in their ancestral realms. In both cases, many years of political uncertainty, military conflict and outside intervention followed. Neither Hungary nor Bohemia was ever ruled by a native dynasty again (as distinct from one individual king), and in the long term both became part of the domains of the Habsburgs, who acquired these realms permanently in 1526 and 1527 and lost them only in the turmoil at the end of the First World War.

The cases of Scotland in 1286 and Aragon in 1410 show very well the big political consequences that could result from kings dying without male descendants. The Scottish example is exceptionally enlightening about the thinking of the nobility and higher clergy in such times of dynastic crisis.[79] The unexpected death of Alexander III in 1286, leaving no male descendants, did not result immediately in a contest for the throne, as it would in many dynastic systems, since, by this time, Scottish royal succession had not only been monopolized by one lineage, but also explicitly recognized the right of female heirs. In 1284, two years before Alexander's death, the nobles of Scotland acknowledged Margaret, 'the Maid of Norway', the king's daughter's daughter, as heir to the kingdom.[80] So, after the king's death, there was no question about who should succeed.[81] But Margaret would be the first female ruler in Scottish history. The nobles could accept this, but presumed that Margaret would marry, not only to have children to continue the dynasty, but also to have a man to govern and make war. The question then arose as to whom she would marry. Edward I, king of England, Scotland's large and powerful southern neighbour, had a suggestion: his own son and heir, also called Edward, who was two years old in 1286, a year younger than the Maid of Norway.

The committee of Scottish lords and bishops that acted as a regency council for Margaret, the absent child ruler, entered into negotiations for this marriage and in 1290 a detailed agreement was drawn up, carefully designed to preserve the separate identity of Scotland after the marriage of the heir of England and the heir of Scotland.[82] If Margaret and Edward had married, any son of theirs would have become both king of Scotland and king of England, but the two realms would not then be united into one (this exact situation did occur in 1603). All this care came to nothing, however, with the death of Margaret on her way to Scotland. There now really would be a contest for the succession.

Fourteen claimants made their case to succeed, but it was generally recognized that only two, John Balliol and Robert Bruce, had a strong basis for their claim (see the family tree in Appendix D). Rather than see civil war, the leaders of Scotland agreed to seek a judgment on the matter from Edward I of England. He first required recognition as overlord of Scotland, and then set up a court of 104 men, twenty-four from his own council, forty nominated by Balliol and forty by Bruce. Both Balliol and Bruce were descended from David, earl of Huntingdon, brother of King

William the Lion. The legal argument boiled down to a simple issue: did Balliol, as grandson of Earl David's oldest daughter, have the better case, or Bruce, as son of a younger daughter of Earl David? On grounds of primogeniture, Balliol's case was hard to refute, so Bruce's lawyers had to argue that, as a son of David's daughter, not a grandson, he was 'nearer in degree', that is, closer as counted by generations.[83] This did him no good. On 17 November 1292, at a great assembly of the lords and bishops of Scotland and England in the castle of the border town of Berwick-upon-Tweed, judgment was pronounced in favour of John Balliol.[84]

It might seem that the matter had been resolved, but that was not the case. Edward I had used his opportunity to win recognition as overlord of Scotland and Balliol had to swear fealty and perform homage to him. Although Balliol was now 'King John', he had a superior in England with a powerful sense of his own rights and privileges. Very quickly points of tension arose, notably the hearing of appeals from Scotland in the English royal lawcourts and the demand for Scottish military service in King Edward's war in France. The Scots leaders decided that resistance was better than compliance and entered into an alliance with Edward's enemy, the king of France. As soon as he could, Edward invaded and conquered Scotland, deposed John Balliol and took the country into his own hands. This was a turning point in relations between Scotland and England. In the previous two centuries, there had been only nine years of war between the two kingdoms but after Edward's invasion of 1296 warfare was the usual condition, down to 1560. It was the deaths of Alexander III, last of the old line of Scottish kings, and of his grand-daughter Margaret, that triggered this shift from two centuries of almost continuous peace to two and a half centuries of almost continuous war. An entirely different history of relations between the two countries could be imagined if the Scottish royal dynasty had not faced the crisis of extinction in the male line.

More than a century later, in 1410, Martin I of Aragon died leaving no legitimate male descendants.[85] He did, however, have an illegitimate grandson, son of his predeceased son, and a nephew and a great-nephew who descended from the Aragonese royal family in the female line. Moreover, there were two more distant relatives who descended in an unbroken male line from earlier kings of Aragon (see the family tree in Appendix D). The complexity of the situation, of weighing the claims of legitimate versus illegitimate birth, male-line versus female-line descent and closer or more distant relationship, was compounded by the starker question of the balance of power between the claimants. Unlike the Scots lords in the later thirteenth century, the ruling classes of the lands of the Crown of Aragon (which comprised Aragon, Catalonia and Valencia) decided to settle the question of the succession themselves, not by referring it to any outside power. This involved a long and sometimes difficult process, harmonizing the parliaments of Aragon, Catalonia and Valencia, dealing also with those claimants who were resorting to violence, and maintaining authority in the islands of the Mediterranean subject to the Crown of Aragon, where, in Sicily, there was a move to have Martin's illegitimate grandson crowned.

The five contenders were Alfonso de Gandía, grandson of James II and quite old at the time of this crisis, who died early in 1412, whereupon his claim was taken up by his younger brother, John of Prades; James of Urgell, great-grandson of Alfonso IV and notorious for his violence; Frederick de Luna, the young illegitimate son of Martin I's son; Louis (III) of Anjou, always on the lookout for a crown; and Ferdinand of Antequera, the younger son of John I of Castile, and from 1406 regent for his young nephew John II of Castile, who was the son of Ferdinand's older brother Henry III. Ferdinand was also extremely wealthy and experienced in warfare, both attractive qualities in a candidate for the throne.

In February 1412, almost two years after the death of Martin I, the parliaments of Aragon, Catalonia and Valencia each chose three representatives, thus forming a committee of nine, who were granted the power to decide who should be the next king. Among the nine commissioners were bishops, legal experts, representatives of the towns and also Master Vincent Ferrer, a Dominican friar from a wealthy Valencian family who was one of the most celebrated charismatic preachers of his time (and who was canonized in 1455). A decision of at least six of the nine would be valid, on condition that they included one from each of the three lands of the Crown of Aragon. The nine spent the spring and early summer of 1412 in their deliberations in the town of Caspe, close to where Aragon, Catalonia and Valencia adjoined. They read the documents submitted to them and heard the arguments made on behalf of the claimants. On 28 June 1412 they went to the church of Caspe to publish their decision. An altar had been set up at the doors of the church, facing the square, and benches placed around it. Representatives of Aragon, Valencia and Catalonia, including lawyers, nobles, clergy and others, took their places here. The archbishop of Tarragona celebrated mass at the altar. Master Vincent Ferrer preached a sermon and then proceeded to announce the decision about the succession:

> There, publicly, in a loud and comprehensible voice, before the lord ambassadors and the people assembled in that place, he solemnly published one of the documents concerning our lord and king, reading word for word. And when in this publication there was a passage in which the name was mentioned of the most excellent and magnificent ruler and lord Ferdinand, our true king and lord, Master Vincent and the others and all present, expressing their happiness and joy in a great and loud voice, exclaimed many times, '*Viva, viva nostre rey e senyor don Ferrando!*'[86]

The local garrison then raised a huge banner with the arms of the kings of Aragon, and church bells were rung and trumpets sounded. Everything was being done to make this decision as public and as loud and joyful as possible, and hence irreversible.[87] Not everyone rejoiced. James of Urgell refused to recognize Ferdinand and had to be defeated in battle. He spent twenty years a prisoner and his county of Urgell was incorporated into the lands of the Crown. This is how a junior branch of the royal family of Castile came to rule also in Aragon. Ferdinand's grandson, also called Ferdinand, married his cousin, Isabella of Castile, thus effecting the dynastic union of Aragon and Castile on which modern Spain is based.

In both Scotland and Aragon the ruling classes, lay and ecclesiastical, had contrived to create institutions and procedures to deal with a crisis in the succession without simply lapsing into civil war. The Scots, however, had submitted their case for judgment to a ruler outside the kingdom, and moreover one who would have a very determined and intransigent view of the proper relationship between England and Scotland. That is why, although the judgment in favour of John Balliol was undoubtedly the correct one in terms of the rule of primogeniture, recourse to Edward had left the Scottish kingdom in a vulnerable subordinate position. Perhaps the Scots ruling classes thought they had little choice between accepting Edward as arbiter and seeing a Bruce–Balliol war, although in the long run they got both, since in 1332 John Balliol's son launched a campaign for the kingship against the incumbent Bruce dynasty that lasted for a quarter of a century. In the lands of the Crown of Aragon the decision was put into the hands of a committee representing the three constituent lands and was reached as much on grounds of utility as of legal custom. Indeed, one account of the proceedings at Caspe alleged that one of the nine commissioners, the archbishop of Tarragona, 'believed that the duke of Gandía and the count of Urgell, as legitimate males and descendants in the male line of the stock of the kings of Aragon, had greater right', but had to concede that 'don Ferdinand was more useful for the government of the realm'.[88]

The failure of a dynastic line, especially if it was dramatic, often stimulated chroniclers and others to provide an explanation, usually in terms of providence and punishment rather than in terms of biology. One of the more notable cases was the successive deaths in 1314, 1316, 1322 and 1328, of Philip IV ('the Fair') of France, his three sons and a grandson. A king who was the most powerful in Europe and had, at the time of his death, three adult sons, left no male-line descendants just fourteen years later. It is a perfect example of the uncertainty of the dynastic world and no surprise that these kings have been christened *les rois maudits* – 'the accursed kings'. A chronicler writing in Castile a little later tells the story of the successive deaths, concluding,

> and in this way there came to an end the line of King Philip of France, whom they call 'the Great' and in France 'the Fair'. And some say that this death of King Philip and also the failure of his line came about because this King Philip had the pope captured. And others say ... because this King Philip in his time made great extortions in the kingdom of France ... and some say because this King Philip expelled the Jews from all his realm ... but the reason why this happened, God knows.[89]

Such a superfluity of explanation suggests the inexplicable.

Adoption

There was one institution that might seem to solve the problem of the childless ruler. In his will, which was read out after his assassination in 44 BC, Julius Caesar bequeathed three-quarters of his property to his great-nephew Gaius Octavius, and also 'adopted him into his family and name'.[90] Octavius then became 'Caesar' and was launched on his path to becoming 'Augustus', conventionally regarded as the first Roman emperor.[91] When planning for the future, Augustus himself also employed the institution of adoption. After the death of two of his grandsons, Augustus adopted the remaining grandson and also Tiberius, who was both his stepson and his son-in-law. The grandson proved unsatisfactory and was soon disinherited, but Tiberius entered fully into the role of adopted son. In return Augustus made every effort to increase Tiberius' power and glory, for 'it was now certain that hope of the succession inclined to one person alone'.[92] These examples show how important adoption was in Roman society, often determining the transmission of power at the highest level.

This tradition continued in the Byzantine empire, where succession to the imperial throne was sometimes by means of adoption: thus the emperor Justin (518–27) adopted his nephew, who took the name Justinian, and succeeded him as emperor, and Michael III (842–67) adopted Basil, his chamberlain, with a view to Basil succeeding (although Basil hastened events by murdering Michael), while the eleventh century saw several examples of adoption being practised or proposed to secure imperial succession.[93] It was such a readily conceivable possibility in Byzantium that when Nicholas, patriarch of Constantinople, was justifying his refusal to sanction the fourth marriage of the emperor Leo VI to his mistress Zoe in 906 (discussed above, pp. 70–1), he rejected Leo's argument that the marriage was required to legitimize the son Zoe had borne him, by saying that it would be perfectly easy for Leo to adopt the boy; this would legitimize him and there would then be no need for the marriage.[94]

In contrast to Byzantium, adoption became marginal in the medieval west.[95] It is mentioned in the Frankish and Lombard laws of the early medieval period, and legal formulae for the procedure are found in formularies from the Frankish empire,[96] but cases are few, and even fewer among rulers. There are three instances of adoption among the Merovingian kings, although one of them is doubted by some scholars.[97] The most fully depicted case, because it is described in the history of Gregory of Tours, is the adoption of the child king Childebert II by his uncle King Guntram – this was a period when the Frankish realms were divided amongst several members of the Merovingian dynasty. Gregory describes how, in the spring of 577, Guntram arranged a meeting with the young Childebert, along with the chief men from both their kingdoms, and said, 'It has befallen me, because of my sins, that I am without children, and so I request that this nephew of mine should be as a son to me.'[98] He then placed Childebert on a throne, bestowed on him the entire kingdom[99] and promised that, even if he had a son in the future, Childebert would be that child's equal. Thereafter, Guntram referred to Childebert as his son or adopted son.[100] Some years later, in 585, this bond was strengthened. At a meeting between the two kings, Guntram placed a spear in the hands of Childebert, who was now about fifteen, and said, 'This is a sign that I have handed over my whole kingdom to you . . . For, because of my sins, none of my stock remains except you alone, the son of my brother. For you succeed in all my kingdom, all others excluded from inheritance.'[101]

In whatever way one interprets these early medieval cases and the references in laws and formularies, there is no doubt that they are few in number and dry up soon after the Merovingian period. From the tenth to the twelfth century there is virtually silence on the subject of adoption in west European sources. The story then recommences but at a very abstract level. The learned lawyers of the twelfth, thirteenth and fourteenth centuries often discussed adoption, since it appeared in the texts of the Roman Law that they studied, but it is clear that, in general, these discussions were theoretical and hypothetical.[102] In Spain adoption appears in law codes such as the famous *Siete Partidas*, but 'research undertaken in judicial and notarial sources to study the practical application of adoption has produced nothing'.[103] Only in the late Middle Ages was there a muted revival of the practice of adoption. There is evidence of adoptions, at various social levels, from the fourteenth century in Sicily and from the fifteenth century in Florence, Provence and southern

France, with isolated examples elsewhere.[104] These were all areas where written law, as distinct from unwritten custom, was important, and this distinction was recognized at the time, one legal expert, after defining adoption, pointing out 'this happens more in written law than in custom'.[105] Roman Law, with its prominent place for adoption, provided a model in these regions.

Adoption could be used by peasants to bring a strong young man into the family, who would support them in their old age, but it could also be used by aristocrats for dynastic purposes, especially to preserve the family name if they had no sons of their own. The 'adoption of name and coat-of-arms', as it is called, enabled dynastic continuity to be salvaged even if the biological male-line transmission was broken. Thus, Lourdin de Saligny, chamberlain of the duke of Burgundy in the mid-fifteenth century, lacking a son, named his daughter as his heir but then 'substituted' her son for her. His grandson thus became 'his substitute son'. This substitute son would inherit all Lourdin's property, and so would his sons after him if he had any; if not, the property would pass to his younger brothers in turn. A condition of their receiving the inheritance was that they 'should be held to bear the name, surname, heraldic motto and arms of the testator'.[106] In this way generations of men with the name Lourdin de Saligny, and with Lourdin's coat-of-arms, would march into the future, bridging the gap in male transmission that Lourdin's daughter represented.

In adoption, the dynastic world would seem to have found an ideal safeguard against rupture of the family line. This was indeed how the institution was used in ancient Rome. However, medieval cases of transmission of royal power in this way are few. Apart from the Merovingian examples already discussed, there are isolated later cases, some of which are hard to interpret. For example, annalists describe a meeting in 887 between the emperor Charles the Fat and his young kinsman Louis, 'whom the emperor attached to himself honourably as his man, like an adopted son'.[107] This word 'like (*quasi*)' can be interpreted as having a stronger or weaker meaning, and some scholars have viewed this as a genuine adoption with Charles accepting Louis as his heir, while others view it as a vaguer 'ritual of peacemaking'.[108]

A case of royal succession by adoption occurred in Hungary in 1038. A well-informed Bavarian chronicler describes how Peter Orseolo, whose father was Otto Orseolo, doge of Venice, and whose mother was a sister of King Stephen of Hungary, came to the throne: 'Since his own son had died during his lifetime, and he had no other, Stephen, his uncle, made him his adoptive son (*adoptivum*) and appointed him heir to the kingdom.'[109] To do this, Stephen had to kill or exile other relatives, and Peter's reign was precarious: he was deposed in 1041, restored by the German emperor in 1044, and again deposed and blinded in 1046. This adoption of a sister's son, which is a particularly close relationship in some societies, thus misfired in the face of the claims of other members of the ruling dynasty and also hostility to Stephen's christianizing policies.

A more successful attempt to alter the succession by some kind of adoption marked the end of the civil war in the reign of King Stephen of England (1135–54). Stephen had faced the competing claims of his cousin, the empress Matilda, and her son Henry of Anjou. Eventually, in 1153, after years of war and the death of his eldest son, King Stephen came to terms, agreeing that Henry would succeed him when he died. The document recording this agreement does not use the language of adoption explicitly, Stephen saying 'I have appointed Henry my successor in the kingdom of England after me and my heir by hereditary right . . . I have also given him my assurance on oath that I will support him as my son and heir', but the chroniclers did not hesitate to describe this act as adoption: 'the king accepted him as his adoptive son and made him heir of the kingdom'; 'an agreement of mutual adoption was made between Stephen, king of England, and Henry'; 'Henry, whom King Stephen adopted as his son'.[110] This language of adoption might have inspired the fantastic story, current in the thirteenth century, that Henry was actually Stephen's biological son, whom he had fathered on the empress Matilda in a ship in the English Channel.[111]

The most notable instances of adoption by a ruling sovereign occurred in the late medieval kingdom of Naples: both Queen Joanna I (1343–81) and her great-niece Joanna II (1414–35) adopted heirs. The kingdom of Naples, which covered the whole of mainland southern Italy, was in the region of written law where, as was noticed, adoption was more common than in northern Europe. The background to these adoptions was the long and vicious feuding between different branches of the ruling family. In 1380 Joanna I was facing a serious threat from Charles of Durazzo, representative of one of these rival branches. Joanna was in her fifties at this time and, although she had had three children from her four marriages, none had survived beyond their third year. She was thus able to offer to adopt an heir, who would be chosen for his ability to back her cause against Charles of Durazzo. She therefore negotiated with her cousin, Louis of Anjou, younger brother of the king of France, and, on 29 June 1380, issued a document adopting him:

> we have adopted, received, admitted and ordained lord Louis as our legitimate son, wishing that lord Louis, our legitimate son, should enjoy and possess all the privileges and rights that legitimate adopted sons can and should enjoy and possess. Moreover, we, honouring lord Louis, our legitimate adopted son, with full and maternal affection, have named, pronounced, declared, made, instituted and ordained, him, and his successors after him, as future king, as our legitimate heir and successor after our death.[112]

Joanna could now hope for military backing from the powerful French prince. Louis, however, acted with deliberation rather than haste. Charles of Durazzo was able to conquer the kingdom of Naples, capture Queen Joanna and have her murdered before Louis even arrived in the kingdom. But Louis was not deterred from pursuing his claim, just as his son and his grandsons did after him. The act of adoption of 1380 thus helped to shape the politics of Italy, and beyond, well into the fifteenth century.

During the course of this long struggle, adoption was again used as a tool. Joanna II, daughter of Charles of Durazzo, succeeded to the throne of Naples in 1414 but soon faced a serious threat from Louis (II) of Anjou, the son of the man adopted by Joanna I, and, after his death, from his son Louis (III). Joanna was childless and in her forties and hence, like her earlier namesake, was free to offer her inheritance in return for immediate military support. She turned to the king of Aragon and Sicily, Alfonso V, whom she adopted as her son and heir in 1421. Alfonso could provide powerful fleets and had a nearby base in the island of Sicily. He made a grand entrance to the city of Naples on 8 July 1421 and was greeted warmly by his adoptive mother. But these good relations did not last. Alfonso's military success was limited, and soon serious distrust arose between him and his followers and Joanna and her court. By 1423 relations had broken down completely and Joanna revoked her adoption of Alfonso and Alfonso himself sailed back to Barcelona, while Joanna changed her position entirely and adopted Louis of Anjou in his place.[113]

There seem to be a few other late medieval cases, but the total number of adoptions by rulers in the Middle Ages, outside of the Byzantine empire, cannot exceed ten or twelve.[114] The question naturally arises of why so few childless, or sonless, medieval rulers took this route. The influential anthropologist Jack Goody advanced the thesis that the disappearance of adoption as a general practice in medieval Europe was the result of a concerted effort on the part of the Church, which attacked cousin marriage and concubinage as well as discouraging adoption:

> If the Church introduced and encouraged procedures for acquiring land and other property for itself, did it also discourage, at least in consequence if not in intention, those practices that might provide a family heir for the property of a dead man or woman? If so, this would provide some explanation for the dramatic shift from close to distant marriage, as well as the abandonment of adoption, widow inheritance, concubinage, divorce and remarriage and other strategies of heirship.[115]

Goody sees a pattern here: 'it does not seem accidental that the Church appears to have condemned the very practices that would have deprived it of property'.[116] It is not quite clear how attacks on cousin marriage helped the Church accumulate property, although the other two prongs, hostility to concubinage and adoption, would indeed increase the chances of childlessness, and hence of a bequest to the Church. But there is little evidence of official ecclesiastical hostility to adoption, with one exception, Salvian, a priest from fifth-century Gaul. The uncompromising Salvian is indeed scathing about childless people adopting rather than bequeathing their property for pious purposes, that is, to the Church:

A number of people without sons, paying no attention to their own salvation and the remedy for their sins, even though they lack seed of their blood, nevertheless seek others, to whom they award their property, that is, to whom they ascribe the shadow name of family relationship, whom they, as imaginary parents, might make their adopted sons, as it were, and have these offspring born of perfidy succeed in place of those they do not have.[117]

Salvian was, however, a more or less isolated voice. The decline of adoption as a general practice cannot be explained by overt hostility on the part of the Church, because there is so little of it. There remains an enigma. If some rulers, at some times, could use adoption to deal with the problem of childlessness, why didn't all childless rulers do so?

Unmarried Kings and Kings Who Married Late

There is another enigma, although of different degree. If the dynastic world was obsessed with the search for high-born wives to be the mothers of princes, what can explain those cases where kings married late or not at all? There is no doubt that rulers received a constant barrage of advice that they should marry. Ivo, bishop of Chartres, was delighted to hear that Louis VI was intending to marry and urged him to do so without delay, especially since if he died without an heir the kingdom would be torn apart by ambitious men:

> Do not devise any delay for entering the order of married life . . . Hasten so that from your loins there should proceed one who may destroy the vain hope of so many ambitious men and replace fickleness with the hope of one man.[118]

By marrying, Ivo said, Louis would simultaneously serve his own interest, the stability of the kingdom and the peace of the Church.

James I of Aragon, who succeeded to the kingdom in 1213 at the age of five, recalled in his memoirs how his nobles had urged him to marry:

> And we took as our wife the queen, Doña Eleanor, at the advice of our men, who counselled us that, because our father had no other son besides us, that we should take a wife when young, since they had great concern for

our life and that above all they wished that an heir should issue from us, so that the kingdom would not pass from the natural line.[119]

James married Eleanor, a member of the royal house of Castile, just after his thirteenth birthday.

Such advice crops up also in largely fictional accounts. When a hagiographer wrote the Life of Æthelbert, saintly king of the East Angles (d. 794), he needed an explanation for his hero actually agreeing to marriage, a rare thing for a saint. It is the king's advisers who supposedly urged him to take this step:

> Since he had not yet taken a queen in marriage, the whole gathering of his court feared that, if he were snatched from their midst without children, they would fall under foreign rule. Therefore, they counselled the king that he should receive in matrimony a woman worthy of the royal dignity.[120]

Given all this, one would expect that the early betrothal of kings, or heirs to the throne, would be a universal practice. There are indeed, as we have seen, many examples of the betrothal of very young children or even of babies, and the vast majority of kings did marry. But the exceptions to this pattern raise a question: what motivated kings who did not marry, or married late?

The Byzantine emperor Basil II, who died unmarried and childless in 1025, despite the risk to the continuation of his dynasty, presents a rare case. Contemporaries sought to explain his choice by a vow of celibacy that Basil had taken, renouncing sex and marriage in exchange for divine help in war – Basil was a famously successful war-leader (see below, p. 130). Clearly, they thought there had to be some such good reason for his decision never to marry. Later in the eleventh century the case of another unmarried king has provoked speculation about a reason of a different kind. William II Rufus, king of England, came to the throne in 1087 in his late twenties.[121] He never married and his court was criticized by a contemporary monastic writer as a centre of effeminacy, with its 'courtly youths who almost all let their hair grow long like girls'.[122] Monks of the following generation also characterized William's court in this way, adding specific accusations that it was a 'homosexual brothel'[123] and writing of the king that 'he never had a legitimate wife but he applied himself insatiably to obscene fornication and constant adultery'.[124] These authors also launch general attacks on the sodomy that they see all around them, but without making a specific charge against the king. The most thorough biographer of the king concludes that he was probably bisexual.[125]

A similar view has been advanced about Richard I of England, the 'Lionheart'.[126] Richard married Berengaria of Navarre at the age of thirty-three. The lateness of this marriage may be partly explained by his prior, and very long, engagement to another princess. But contemporary sources do report that, during his marriage to Berengaria, he was criticized for neglecting his conjugal duties. The saintly bishop of Lincoln told him to his face, 'the public gossip is that you are not faithful to your own wife', while, after a hermit warned him, 'Remember the overthrow of Sodom and abstain from illicit deeds', the king eventually repented and 'took back his own wife, whom he had not slept with for a long time, and abandoning illicit sexual intercourse, cleaved to his wife'.[127] Some have interpreted these words as indications that Richard was accused of homosexual activity, but it is clear that the invocation of Sodom can often imply only the punishment of wickedness in general, rather than this specific sin.

The matter of Richard's sexuality might have been clarified by a passage by the chronicler Helinand of Froidmont, but we have this in a tantalizing incomplete form. The relevant part of Helinand's chronicle survives only in a seventeenth-century printed edition, not in manuscript, and the passage about Richard describes how the king, during his captivity in Germany on his way home from crusade, made his confession to a certain bishop and proposed 'to be continent henceforth', but another bishop, coming from England and wishing to ingratiate himself with the king, 'persuaded him, for the sake of his bodily health, that he should . . . *dot dot dot* . . . and thus confirmed the unhappy man in his wickedness'. The learned Cistercian editing Helinand in 1669 obviously thought that what the bishop prescribed was unfit for his readers to know. How bad could it have been? And is this the earliest example of the bowdlerizing ellipsis in print? Helinand vouchsafes this story as being told by King Richard himself on his death bed.[128] There is thus no clear and convincing evidence for Richard engaging in homosexual activity but very strong evidence for his sleeping with people other than his wife, and an illegitimate son is recorded. He obviously did not feel that his duty to produce a legitimate male heir was paramount, and he was indeed succeeded by a brother. In this he resembles his predecessor, William Rufus. Both kings, coincidentally or providentially, died in similar ways, the former from an arrow, the latter from a crossbow bolt, a 'coupling of similar things' that was noticed at the time.[129]

Basil II and William Rufus are certain cases of kings who died as unmarried adults. There is also no evidence that Æthelstan (d. 939), often seen as the first king of England, was married. The chronicler William of Malmesbury, writing two centuries later, but perhaps having access to reliable source material, says that the king raised his young brothers with great affection and that 'when they were adults, he made them partners in the kingdom, and, out of consideration for them, he never made any effort to get married'.[130] The implication here is that Æthelstan expected and approved the succession of a younger brother, which indeed was what happened. Such a motive is one of several considered in Sarah Foot's substantial biography of the king. She also mentions his sexuality, along with a sensible caveat:

> Any attempt to talk about the sexual orientation of a tenth-century man is doomed to be anachronistic ... Hypothetically, we could concede that, given both the vocabulary and the opportunity to express such desires, Æthelstan's interests might have tended towards same-sex relations.

Alongside a succession strategy and a sublimated homosexuality, the possible motives for the king's celibacy, she suggests, might also include 'a religious vocation to chastity' (as was suggested for Basil II) although we are warned against the more psychoanalytical theory that it sprang from 'a revulsion against the suffocatingly feminine atmosphere of his father's household'. Foot also seeks to depict the king's unmarried status as nothing extraordinary: 'While bachelorhood was uncommon among secular European princes of his day, it was not a wholly inexplicable life-choice and need not be treated with particular suspicion.'[131] Whether we treat it with suspicion or not, the variety of explanations for the life-choice of unmarried rulers like Æthelstan, whether such explanations appeal more strongly to medieval assumptions (a vow of celibacy) or modern ones (latent homosexuality), shows that an explanation is demanded. Because the number of unmarried kings is so small, and their motivation so uncertain, it remains a safe generalization that kings took it for granted that one of their main responsibilities was to produce a son and heir.

CHAPTER 3

Fathers and Sons

Securing the Succession

THE THIRTEENTH-CENTURY SPANISH LAWBOOK, THE
Siete Partidas, explains that a king can obtain sovereignty justly in
four ways: by inheritance (by being the eldest son, or other near relative);
by election by the people when there is no such heir; by marriage to the
heir to the kingdom; and by grant of pope or emperor.[1] There are
examples of all four types in medieval Europe: cases of inheritance are
too numerous to mention; cases of election are less common, but there
are many examples, some of them very significant, such as that of the
Holy Roman Empire, where, eventually, elaborate rules about election
were developed and a class of 'Electors' was defined (see below, pp. 401–
2); the third way, marriage to an heir, brought the Hohenstaufen dynasty
the kingdom of Sicily in 1194, and led to the fifty-year reign of Sigismund
of Luxemburg in Hungary (1387–1437); grants by the pope created the
kingdom of Sicily in 1130 and transferred it to a new dynasty in 1265,
while grants by the emperor conferred the royal title on Polish and
Bohemian dukes, either for an individual's lifetime or permanently.[2]

If we turn to the first category in this list, inheritance, it is clear that in
medieval Christian Europe there was a range of inheritance patterns,
both in the sense of varying norms and customs and in the sense of actual
degrees of order or disorder. In Ireland a large group of relatives, more
or less distant, was eligible to succeed, and there were also overlapping
hierarchies of kings, and in Merovingian Gaul division of the inheritance
among members of the ruling dynasty was common, while, in contrast,

the main continental dynasties of Frankish descent had, by the tenth century, adopted unitary and impartible kingship. If we look at actual practice, in eleventh- and twelfth-century England there was only one case where the throne passed uncontestedly from father to eldest son, but in France in the same period this was the situation at every transmission of power. Crucial variables were family structure, especially the number of spouses, the number of sons and the rights of daughters and 'illegitimate' sons, rules and customs of succession, and the ambitions and scruples of family members.

In the early Middle Ages rules about succession were not usually clear, and rarely written down. This left plenty of room for disagreement and dispute. After the death of Henry I of Germany in 936, leaving three sons, Otto, Henry and Bruno (who had been placed in the Church),

> the chief leaders assembled and discussed the state of the kingdom. Many judged that Henry should rule the kingdom, because he had been born in the royal palace; but others wanted Otto to possess the honour of ruling, because he was older and more prudent.[3]

Here we find three different justifications being advanced for preferring one son to another: being born after one's father had become king; seniority in age; and greater prudence. The first of these was not commonly advanced as a ground, although in Byzantium being born 'in the purple', that is, born when one's father was emperor, and in the imperial palace, was recognized as conveying exceptional status, which might help support a claim to rule. Henry I's case was, however, unusual, in that he was the first king in his family, having been chosen to succeed the childless Conrad I. He did not therefore have the expectation of being a king, so the fact that his son Otto was born while he was just a duke, but his next son Henry was born after he came to the throne, created a sharper and more unusual distinction than would have been the case if the elder Henry had himself been the son of a king. Henry's party supposedly thought that, because of this difference between the brothers, the old king had done wrong in preferring Otto to his younger brother. They asked the younger Henry, 'Do you think your father acted rightly in preferring one who was not born into royal dignity to you, who were so born?'[4] Otto's champions put forward two different criteria of suitability, one entirely objective, Otto was older, and one entirely subjective, he was more prudent. Both types of argument were common when succession was being debated.

A king who wanted to ensure that his son would succeed him, or that a particular son of several would succeed, could employ various methods. Crowning a successor during a ruler's lifetime was one. There were other, weaker, methods, such as designation. Or the ruler might have the great men of the kingdom perform homage to the designated successor, with or without official recognition as heir. Eventually, as medieval Europe moved from the world of memory to the world of written record, to borrow the title of Michael Clanchy's famous book,[5] complex rules about succession came to be written down and endorsed by official bodies, such as parliaments.

In 1115 Henry I, king of England and duke of Normandy, 'had all the chief men of Normandy do homage and swear allegiance to his son William'.[6] William was twelve years old. There was nothing unusual about this, since the Norman dukes of the tenth and eleventh centuries had designated their sons as successors, a process which is described as involving the chief men doing homage and swearing fealty to the son, who might be very young.[7] In the following year King Henry summoned the bishops, abbots and chief men of England to a meeting at Salisbury, since 'he wished to appoint William his heir in the kingdom'. As in the previous year in Normandy, the chief men did homage and swore fealty to William. The bishops and abbots swore that, after Henry's death, they would transfer the kingdom and the crown of the kingdom to William.[8] A contemporary chronicler, recording William's death in the wreck of the White Ship in 1120, calls him 'king and duke designate'.[9] Henry had done what he could to ensure his son's succession. The wreck of the White Ship was also the shipwreck of these hopes.

On occasion, designation as successor might involve handing over regalia, objects with a special power and significance that indicated ruler-ship. For instance, after the death of the Carolingian ruler Charles the Bald in 877, his wife Richildis brought the regalia to Louis, Charles' son and her stepson:

> She brought to him the mandate by which his father, before his death, had
> transmitted the kingdom to him, and the sword called St Peter's Sword, by

means of which she was to invest him with the kingdom, and also the royal robes and crown and a staff of gold, decorated with jewels.[10]

Within a few years, Louis himself felt death drawing near: 'sensing that he could not escape death, he sent the crown and the sword and the other royal trappings to his son Louis, commanding those who were with him to have him anointed and crowned king'.[11] A particularly important piece of regalia was the Crown of St Stephen employed in the coronation of Hungarian kings in the later Middle Ages. When two rivals were contesting the kingship in the fifteenth century, this actually had to be stolen by one party to ensure that their candidate's coronation was legitimate.[12]

Transmission of the regalia need not be a deathbed act. When the childless Rudolf III, king of Burgundy, recognized the emperor Henry II as his heir, he handed over to him his crown and sceptre, although he continued to rule for another fourteen years, until his death in 1032, being then succeeded by Henry's successor.[13] Another case, like this one, of transmission of the regalia to someone who was not a close relative, occurred in December 918, when, according to the chronicler Widukind of Corvey, the dying German ruler Conrad I summoned his brother to him and told him that, although they had fighting men, fortifications and weapons, they lacked one thing: the favour of fortune (*fortuna*). This, Conrad said, Henry, duke of the Saxons, did have. So he told his brother to take the royal insignia – the holy lance, the golden arm-rings, the cloak, the sword and diadem of the old kings – to Henry, who 'would truly be a king and ruler of many peoples'.[14] It has been pointed out that Widukind was writing for Henry's descendants and might have invented this vivid legitimizing scene.

The most drastic way for a ruler to ensure the succession was to have his successor crowned in his own lifetime, with the result that there would be two kings in the kingdom, possibly for a long time. Lothar, king of the West Franks, had his thirteen-year-old son Louis V crowned at Pentecost (Whitsun), 8 June 979.[15] This was the first time a king of the West Franks had associated a son as joint king in his own lifetime.[16] Lothar did not die until 2 March 986, so for almost seven years there were two kings of the West Franks, a situation sometimes acknowledged quite explicitly in their documents: two royal charters issued in 981 are dated 'in the twenty-seventh year of the reign of lord Lothar, his most serene majesty, and the third year of the reign of his son, the distinguished youth lord Louis'.[17] The Capetian kings of France followed this practice of crowning their sons consistently from 987 to 1179, with the exception of Philip I, who designated his son, later Louis VI, as his heir but did not have him crowned.[18] And these ceremonies that took place in the lifetime of the father were genuine coronations. Philip Augustus was crowned and anointed at Rheims on 1 November 1179 and received the acclamation 'Long live the king!', while his father Louis VII was still living, although very infirm.[19] Louis died, within the year, on 19 September 1180, and most modern textbooks give 1180 as the date of the commencement of Philip's reign. He himself, however, dated it from 1 November 1179.[20] Coincidentally, just as France had two kings from November 1179 to September 1180, so, at this very same time, and quite exceptionally, did England, since Henry II had arranged for the coronation of his oldest son and namesake in 1170.

There was a long tradition behind such rituals. In the last months of his life, in September 813, the emperor Charlemagne called a great assembly at Aachen, crowned his only surviving son, Louis, and had him proclaimed co-emperor.[21] A few years later, in 817, Louis conducted the same ceremony at the same place for his own eldest son, Lothar, making him co-emperor 'just as his father Charles had made him'.[22] In both cases the purpose was to ensure a smooth succession: when Charlemagne died, there was already an emperor, Louis, and hence no need for a decision to be made about a successor (although the sitation was simplified by the prior death of all Louis' legitimate brothers); Louis planned a similar outcome, but was less successful in achieving it, largely because he had several squabbling sons, so that, although his oldest son Lothar was emperor after him, he ruled over only a fraction of the empire.

Sharing the throne in this way was a practice commonly found in the Byzantine empire.[23] A French bishop writing in the late tenth century even called such joint rule 'the Greek way'.[24] One advantage of the practice was that it often meant that, when one ruler died, there was already another in place. If an emperor had a son, he might have the child crowned at a very young age. These child co-emperors generally appeared on coins. In the 870s, for example, Basil I appeared on coins flanked by his sons and co-emperors Leo and Alexander, represented on a smaller scale.[25]

The exact status of Byzantine co-emperors, especially child co-emperors, could be complex and variable. An extreme case is that of Constantine VII Porphyrogenitus, son of Leo VI, who was born in 905 and became co-emperor in 908 at the age of two, joining his uncle Alexander who had been Leo's co-emperor for many years.[26] After Leo's death in 912, Alexander became chief emperor and Constantine continued as co-emperor. Alexander died in 913 and Constantine succeeded as chief emperor. In the following years he was depicted on coins alongside his mother and co-ruler Zoe. Although Constantine was named first on these coins, there is little doubt that Zoe was governing, not her son, who was not yet in his teens. In 919, when Constantine was fourteen, Zoe's regime was overthrown and Constantine had to accept the strongman Romanos Lecapenus as chief emperor the following year, Constantine now being in the secondary position. Shortly afterwards, Romanos had his wife, Theodora, crowned empress, and his eldest son, Christopher, crowned co-emperor. In 924, Romanos' other two sons, Stephen and Constantine, were also crowned. There were now five emperors: Romanos, Christopher, Stephen, Constantine Lecapenus and Constantine Porphyrogenitus, who was 'last of all ... having only the appearance and name of emperor'.[27] Constantine endured this position for many years, but was eventually able to change it. Romanos' son Christopher died in 931, and Constantine was able to come to some kind of understanding with the remaining sons, who together overthrew Romanos in December 944. Within a month Constantine Porphyrogenitus outmanoeuvred and removed them and, at the age of thirty-nine, finally became chief emperor in both name and fact. He soon appointed as co-emperor his own son, Romanos, who succeeded him as Romanos II on his death in 959. Constantine is remembered particularly for his scholarly interests and the works he wrote, but his life also demonstrated the dizzying paths that the institution of co-emperorship could follow.

Categorizing co-emperors was a delicate matter for medieval historians, as it is for modern ones. A year after the death of Constantine Porphyrogenitus, Romanos II had his young son Basil crowned on

22 April 960, which was Easter day.[28] Since Basil died on 15 December 1025, he had, from one point of view, a reign of more than sixty-five years. Modern historians, however, date his reign from 976 to 1025, starting it from the time that his co-emperor and guardian, and the real ruler, John Tzimiskes, died. Byzantine chroniclers sometimes distinguish the two periods of his rule. Michael Psellos writes that Basil shared imperial power (συνεβασίλευσεν) until his twentieth year, then reigned fifty-two years 'as sole or chief monarch (autokrator, αὐτοκράτορα)'.[29] John Skylitzes, followed by George Cedrenus, says that he lived seventy years, during all of which he ruled as emperor (βασιλεύσας), and for fifty years of which he ruled 'as sole or chief monarch (αὐτοκράτορα)'.[30]

Sometimes, of course, kings who were crowned in their father's lifetime died before them. Philip, son of Louis VI, was born on 29 August 1116, designated heir on 18 April 1120 and crowned on 14 April 1129, aged twelve, but died in a fall from his horse on 13 October 1131; his younger brother Louis (later Louis VII) was crowned almost immediately to replace him, on 25 October 1131. Louis VI, their father, died in 1137. Tancred, king of Sicily (1190–4), had his son Roger crowned in his lifetime but Roger died a few weeks before Tancred, so never ruled alone. The fact that these young kings were real kings is sometimes reflected in their numbering (see below, pp. 301–10 on numbering). Henry the Young King, the son of Henry II who was crowned in 1170 but predeceased his father, was known as 'Henry III (*Henricus tertius*)' by many contemporaries as well as writers of a later generation. Even in 1307 one learned man referred to the king we know as Henry III (who reigned 1216–72) as 'Henry IV', presumably still reckoning the Young King as 'Henry III'.[31] Writing about this same time, Bernard Gui, in his history of the French kings, took into account the young Philip, son of Louis VI, who had died in 1131; since Gui included this Philip in the numbering, all the kings whom we know as 'Philip II', 'Philip III', etc., appear in his history as 'Philip III', 'Philip IV', etc.[32]

Between the mid-tenth and the mid-thirteenth century, all German kings with sons ensured that they were acknowledged as king during their father's lifetime. There are eleven examples.[33] Not all succeeded their fathers, since some predeceased them, but the majority did, indicating that this tactic worked. It was a way of giving the ruler's child a public and formal status rather than a mere presumption of future succession. These sons were not child heirs but child kings (their average age at election was seven), even if real power was in their fathers' hands. Examples of the father–son relationship exploding are rare (Henry IV and Henry V, Frederick II and Henry (VII) are the notable examples, as discussed below, pp. 111–12). The succession in 983, 1039, 1056 and 1190 all saw crowned kings ready to succeed their fathers, as planned (Conrad IV who succeeded his father Frederick II in 1250 had been elected king but not crowned).

The earliest of this sequence took place in 961, when Otto I arranged for the crowning of his son, also called Otto, during his lifetime. The younger Otto was elected king at Worms and crowned at Aachen in 961, and later crowned emperor by the pope in St Peter's in 967. He sometimes appears in charters during his father's lifetime as 'Otto the Younger ... co-emperor'.[34] Likewise, when the emperor Henry III of Germany had a long-awaited son in November 1050, he sought at once to make his succession secure. At Christmas 1050, when the child was not yet two months old, he had the chief men of the kingdom swear fealty to him. In 1053, at a great council in the imperial stronghold of Tribur, he arranged for his son's formal election as king, and the following year had him consecrated king in Aachen, the traditional coronation site. Henceforth the young boy appears formally in his father's charters as 'our dearest son, King Henry IV'.[35]

Conrad IV, who succeeded in 1250, was the last of such cases for many years. After the extinction of the Hohenstaufen, during the period of alternating dynasties in Germany between 1254 and 1439, kings were not able to secure the election of their sons during their lifetimes, with one exception, Wenceslas (Wenzel), son of Charles IV, in 1376, and the practice did not revive until the Habsburgs established their de facto monopoly of the German and imperial throne at the end of the Middle Ages. There is thus a correlation between the period when the empire was usually hereditary in practice and the custom of child election and designation; the latter was indeed an instrument of the former. Powerful German kings of this period could employ the custom of election as a dynastic tool. In the changed political circumstances of the later Middle Ages, this tool was no longer available.

The custom of crowning sons during their father's lifetime was found outside of the Frankish kingdom and its successor states in France and Germany. It was not uncommon, for example, in the south Italian principalities of the tenth century. Gisulf I of Salerno was appointed co-ruler when he was three: 'When the boy was three years old, all the people, and the great men, along with his father, appointed him to the office of Prince, and they swore oaths to him.'[36] There are examples of Irish kings associating their sons in their rule from the eleventh to the fifteenth century; they are sometimes titled 'king by the side of his father'.[37] It was not always sons who were appointed or crowned. Baldwin V of Jerusalem was crowned during the lifetime of his uncle Baldwin IV (the 'Leper King'). It was clear that Baldwin IV would have no children, and this secured the succession, even though Baldwin V was a child of five:

> He was adorned with royal unction and solemnly crowned in the Church
> of the Resurrection of the Lord, and immediately and without delay fealty
> was paid to the boy by all the barons, with their hands and accompanied by
> the customary oaths.[38]

The sons, and others, crowned in this way were not future kings, but kings. When Valdemar I of Denmark elevated his son Canute as joint king in 1170, the chief men of Denmark 'agreed to assign royal honours to Canute, Valdemar's son, who was acknowledged not only as future possessor of his father's majesty but also as present partner in the office'.[39] Canute succeeded his father as sole ruler in 1182, after being joint king for twelve years. He died childless but his brother and successor Valdemar II continued the practice of having royal sons crowned in their father's lifetime, Valdemar in 1218, then, after Valdemar's death in 1231, his younger brother Erik (Erik IV) in 1232.[40]

When fathers arranged to have their sons crowned during their own lifetimes in this way, it was intended as a guarantee of a smooth succession. Hugh Capet supposedly wanted his son crowned in his lifetime because 'if the king were killed and the country deprived of him, then there could follow discord among the nobles, oppression of the good by the wicked and servitude of the whole people'.[41] Having two kings reduced the chances of this anarchy, since there already was 'a reserve king'.[42] Abbot Suger writes that the purpose of crowning Louis VII during the lifetime of his father, Louis VI, was 'to confute the sedition of rivals'.[43] There could be no clearer way for a king to indicate his choice as successor, and the ceremony of anointing and crowning marked out the new and future king in an unmistakable and indelible way that would pre-empt and deter rivals, including other possible claimants within the dynasty.

Interregna

The association of sons with their fathers during their lifetime was intended to remove the danger of any gap between reigns, interregna. In some kingdoms, in some periods, if the heir had not been designated or inaugurated before the old king's death, then the new reign was not deemed to begin until the election or coronation of the new king. The period in between was a kind of no-man's land. It could last some time. Henry II of England died on 6 July 1189 but his son Richard was not crowned king until 3 September, more than eight weeks later. Ten years later Richard himself died, shot by a crossbow bolt during a siege. This was on 6 April 1199. The coronation of his brother John took place on 27 May. In the intervening seven weeks, knights were paid 'to guard the country after the death of King Richard' and 'all who had castles fortified them with men and provisions and weapons'.[44] The interregnum was a nervous time. In the case of kings dying without clear heirs, or of elective monarchies, the interregnum could be even longer than these seven or eight weeks. Conrad I, king of the East Franks (Germany) died on 23 December 918. There was then no king in Germany until 12 May 919, when Henry, duke of the Saxons, was elected, but even then, only by the Franks and Saxons, not by all the peoples of the kingdom. The interregnum had lasted for almost five months. After the death of the childless Christopher III of Denmark on 6 January 1448, it took eight months of negotiations before Christian of Oldenburg was elected as his successor on 1 September.

People were very aware of the dangers of an interregnum. When the emperor Frederick II had his eight-year-old son Conrad elected king of the Romans in 1237, the electors gave as one of their reasons 'because, after the death of a ruler, the interval of time between the death of a predecessor and the full rule of his successor, which the men of old used to call an "interregnum", could bring great danger to the empire'.[45] An interregnum was viewed as so perilous a time that the chronicler Henry of Huntingdon could scarcely believe the peace and stability that characterized the period of eight weeks between the death of Stephen, king of England, in 1154, and the beginning of the reign of his acknowledged heir, Henry II: 'The king was dead, but kingless England did not lack peace. You, Henry, are the first in the world to have performed this wonder.'[46] Election or coronation during a predecessor's lifetime ensured there would be no interregnum and hence no need to wish for wonders.

The later Middle Ages saw two developments in succession practice: first, the elaboration of written rules of succession, sometimes quite complex ones, often backed by the authority of assemblies or representatives of the kingdom; second, in those kingdoms where coronation had been seen as the constitutive act, the attempt to remove the gap between one reign and the next by deeming that the new king's reign began on the day after the old king's death, or at the very moment of his death, instead of at coronation.

Writing Down the Rules

In the case of societies which had no written rules about succession to the kingship, it might still be possible that unwritten rules and customs can be deduced from actual practice. This has been attempted for early medieval Ireland, although sceptical voices have also been raised. Francis John Byrne wrote:

> Most Irish kings were the sons of kings, though few succeeded their father directly. The great majority were grandsons of kings, and few who were not great-grandsons had any chance. Whether this was a 'law' or a fact of political life can be a matter of debate.[47]

Likewise, J. Beverley Smith doubted whether the divisions of the Welsh principalities between kinsmen in the twelfth and thirteenth centuries reflected a rule or law of partible inheritance rather than being simply the outcome of political and military competition.[48] Writing about succession to the throne of Aragon in the first half of the twelfth century, Alan Forey questioned whether there was a 'juridical tradition' on the matter: 'As it has been set out, the juridical tradition is merely a series of rules formulated by historians on the basis of what happened on a few particular occasions.'[49] These scholars are suggesting that it is possible to describe what happened but not to deduce conscious custom or explicit norms from what happened. It is very unlikely, however, that royal or princely opponents would not make arguments for their case, or that their followers would simply dispense with the need for justifications and explanations for their choice of successor. These would be expressed in a language of right or custom, even if there were no body of law to refer to. The debate over the German succession in 936 (see above, pp. 90–1) is a good example of the way that appeals could be made to general principles, even if they cannot be classified as 'law' or 'juridical tradition'.

Some early medieval societies, however, did produce written documents regulating succession. Writing down the rules about succession can mean two slightly different things: (1) specifying named individuals and the circumstances in which they would succeed to the throne or (2) setting out some general rules (e.g. no woman can succeed). In the early Middle Ages, several written ordinances and agreements of the first kind can be found, sometimes with quite simple provisions, such as the agreement between the Merovingian kings Guntram and Childebert II, who were uncle and nephew, that if one died without sons, the other would inherit his whole kingdom,[50] sometimes with much more elaborate stipulations, as found in some of the Carolingian ordinances about future divisions of the kingdom and relations between successors.[51]

In the later centuries of the Middle Ages, as literacy spread and governments became more bureaucratic, it is not surprising that rules and practices of succession were written down in increasingly exact forms. Sometimes the incentive to do so was a projected marriage, especially with a foreign dynasty, whose members would be very interested in the precise prospects opened up by the match. For example, in 1255, when Alfonso X of Castile negotiated a marriage between his two-year-old daughter Berengaria (or Berenguela) and Louis, eldest son of Louis IX of France, who was then aged eleven, the French court obviously wanted assurances about the girl's expectations, for Alfonso convened an assembly at Palencia to clarify the issue. There, the special rules governing succession to the kingdom were spelled out. Unlike private property, succession to the kingdom was 'indivisible and whole', and, 'according to the general and approved custom of Spain', if the king had sons, the firstborn succeeded to the kingdom; likewise, if he had only daughters, the firstborn daughter would succeed; if he had sons and daughters, the eldest son would succeed, even if there were older daughters. Since, at this time, Alfonso's only legitimate child was his daughter Berengaria, she was his presumed heir, and he had the assembled bishops, nobles and representatives of the towns swear to accept her as queen if Alfonso died without a son. All this was written down, sealed with the seals of the king, his wife, and eight of the nobles and bishops, and sent off to Louis, the young fiancé. The document, with its ten seals, is still in the Archives Nationales in Paris.[52]

The document is significant in two ways. First, it demonstrates very well the unpredictability of dynastic politics and the alternative histories that it could have produced. If Alfonso had had no sons and if the young Louis had not died as a teenager, then France and Castile would have been joined in a dynastic union. Such multiple kingdoms were not at all exceptional (see below, pp. 419–20). In fact, however, a son was born to Alfonso in the very year of the document, 1255. Second, the negotiations over this specific marriage had prompted the king and the ruling classes of Castile to make a very general public statement about the rule of succession to the throne and had it put down in an official document.

A very similar situation occurred in the kingdom of Scotland twenty-six years later, in 1281, when a marriage was arranged between Alexander, eldest son of King Alexander III of Scotland, and Margaret, eldest daughter of Guy, count of Flanders and margrave of Namur. Alexander issued an open letter explaining that, to expedite this marriage, he had consulted with his barons and could affirm that

the custom and usage of the kingdom of Scotland has been from time out
of mind and still is today that if the son and male heir of a king of Scotland
has an heir of the body [i.e. a child, grandchild, etc.] and this son dies
before his father the king, the heir who issued from this son remains and
ought to remain heir to the kingdom.

Consequently, the king can reassure Guy of Flanders that any son of
Alexander and Margaret 'would be heir to the kingdom of Scotland
according to this custom and usage'. No brother of the younger
Alexander would have a superior claim. Moreover, if Alexander and
Margaret had only a daughter or daughters, and Margaret then died
and Alexander remarried, the eldest daughter of Alexander and
Margaret would become heir if any male heirs of the second marriage
died without heirs of their body. Count Guy was being told, as clearly as
the biological uncertainties allowed, 'you will be a grandfather to a king
or queen'. The nobles and bishops of Scotland swore to observe these
customs and usages.[53] Just as the document issued by Alfonso X survives
today in the Archives Nationales in Paris, so this statement of the Scottish
laws of succession is housed in the archives of Namur. In both cases, it was
the court of the proposed foreign spouse that had demanded these
written guarantees.

Some of the features of these two occasions – the assembly of the great
men, their oath, the written record of 'customs and usage' – can be found
in other ordinances about royal succession that were drawn up in other
circumstances, unconnected with any projected marriage. Kings without
a son needed to make decisions about the succession, and these might
have to be revised as their situation was changed by deaths and births in
their family. In 1315 Robert Bruce, king of Scots, who had a daughter,
Marjorie, but no son at the time, convened an assembly at Ayr to determine the succession. It was agreed that, if King Robert died without
a male heir of his body, he would be succeeded by his younger brother
Edward Bruce, who is described as 'an energetic man, extremely experienced in warlike deeds in defence of the rights and liberty of the kingdom of Scotland'; if his line died out, then Marjorie would succeed, or, if
she were dead, the next descendant of King Robert in line. Provision was
made for Marjorie to marry and a regent was named in case any of these

hypothetical successors were under age.[54] All this was sworn to by the assembled nobles, clergy and representatives of the community of the realm and recorded in a document with their seals. Unlike the documents issued by Alfonso X and Alexander III, this makes no claim to represent ancient custom or usage. In fact, by displacing the king's daughter by his younger brother, it could be argued that it was 'neither lawful nor logical'.[55]

A whirl of birth and death quickly rendered all this effort redundant. Within a year or two, Marjorie Bruce was married, gave birth to a son, Robert, and died. And, despite his warlike experience, Edward Bruce was killed fighting in Ireland in 1318. Since two of the main figures named in the document of 1315 were now dead, and King Robert had a male heir of the body in his tiny grandson, new arrangements had to be made. At a Parliament in Scone in late 1318, the infant was recognised as the king's heir. On this occasion, however, more was done, since a general principle governing the succession was enacted, sworn to and recorded in writing:

> Moreover, since, sometimes in the past, some people have called into doubt by which legal principle the succession to the kingdom of Scotland should be decided, if it was not clear, it was declared in this parliament that succession should not in future be decided by the custom that applies to lesser fiefs or inheritances in the kingdom, since such a custom has not been introduced hitherto in succession to the kingdom, but that at the time of the king's death the nearest male in the direct line ought to succeed to the kingdom, and, if there is no male, the nearest female of the same line, or, if that line fails completely, the nearest male in the collateral line. This accords with imperial law.[56]

Here there is no mention of named individuals but a statement of general legal principle, specifying the order of succession to the throne, and buttressed by association with the authority and universality of Roman Law, although without any specific citation of any passage from that law. Such ordinances were to become common across Europe and govern the politics of states up to the present day.[57] They were not always observed. In the long term, patterns of succession were determined by three things in interplay, not just by rules and customs of succession, but also by the biological fortunes of the family and by simple power and violence. All written regulations of succession are attempts to dictate the future, so one would expect a high failure rate. But, as has been pointed out, 'no system of dynastic reproduction and succession ever steadily conformed to its own rules'.[58]

The Prince as Heir

In some kingdoms, the expected successor was designated by a specific term, such as the tanist (*tánaiste*) of later medieval Ireland, although in practice tanists rarely did succeed the king.[59] In Anglo-Saxon England the title atheling (*æðeling*) was used of close male relatives of the king, one of whom might well succeed him, but it did not mean 'designated heir'.[60] The Latin equivalent of atheling was *clito*, an unusual word that crops up in sources from England from the tenth to the twelfth centuries and is apparently an ostentatiously learned coinage, based on the Greek κλειτός, 'famous, splendid'. William, son of Robert, duke of Normandy, who died in 1128, is regularly called 'William Clito', perhaps the last to be so styled. 'Tanist' and 'atheling' were generic terms, referring to a class of person. A new practice that developed in several kingdoms in the later Middle Ages was the association of specific titles with designated heirs. Many of these titles included the term 'Prince', which had not previously been generally used to denote the son of a king. The figure of 'Prince John', wicked younger brother of Richard the Lionheart of England, who appears in Robin Hood stories, never bore this title in reality. The earliest occurrence of his title appears to be in the anonymous Robin Hood play *Looke about you* of 1600, but it only became common usage around 1800, and was then popularized by Walter Scott's *Ivanhoe*. An early example of actual usage of such a title is the creation of the style 'Prince of Salerno' for Charles, son of Charles I, king of Sicily, in 1272, although the next generations of the dynasty more commonly used the title duke of Calabria for the designated heir.[61]

In England, the earldom of Chester was conferred on Edward, son of king Henry III, in 1254, and was thereafter regularly granted to the oldest son of the monarch. In 1301 Edward I's son, also called Edward, was not only granted the earldom of Chester but also made Prince of Wales. Edward senior had conquered Wales and incorporated the lands of the last native prince into the domains of the English Crown. When Edward junior succeeded to the throne in 1307 as Edward II, he did not follow suit and make his own son Prince of Wales, but the practice was revived when this son became king as Edward III. Edward III's oldest son, Edward the Black Prince, was created earl of Chester in 1333, duke of Cornwall in 1337, the first time the title of duke had been used in the English aristocracy, and Prince of Wales in 1343. Since that time the three titles, Prince of Wales, duke of Cornwall and earl of Chester, have made up the standard style of the heir to the English and British throne. After the union of the Crowns in 1603, when James VI of Scotland became James I of England, the title duke of Rothesay, which had been created in 1398 for the heir to the Scottish throne, has also been part of this style.

In France, it was the acquisition of the Dauphiné by the French Crown that provided an equivalent to the English title 'Prince of Wales'. The Dauphiné was a lordship east of the Rhone and hence technically part of the Holy Roman Empire, but it was acquired by the king of France by purchase in 1349, and bestowed on his grandson Charles, later Charles V, who took the title 'Dauphin', which the rulers of the Dauphiné had employed, and quartered his own coat-of-arms with their dolphin.[62] The first royal dauphin was thus the son of the son of the king, rather than the son of the king. After Charles V succeeded to the throne of France in 1364, it was several years before he had a son. During that time, he dealt with his subjects in the Dauphiné as 'king-Dauphin'.[63] When his son, later Charles VI, was born in 1368, his father immediately granted him the Dauphiné, 'and because of this he was called Monsieur the Dauphin'.[64] Subsequently the title was always borne by the oldest son of the king of France, if he had one.

The Iberian peninsula saw similar developments in the fourteenth and fifteenth centuries, with the heir to Aragon receiving the title Prince of Girona from 1351, the heir to Castile that of Prince of Asturias from 1388 and the heir to Navarre that of Prince of Viana from 1423. This last was created by King Charles III of Navarre for his new-born grandson, also called Charles. In the foundation document of 1423, after a general preamble – 'As the human race is inclined and desires that men should wish to consider promoting the status and honour of their children and their children's descendants' – the king turns to Charles, 'our very dear and very beloved grandson', granting him Viana and several other places, and continuing, 'and we have raised and do raise, by this present document, those towns and places to the name and title of Principality, and we have given and do give to him the title and honour of Prince'.[65] Charles, who was the son of Blanca, daughter and heir of Charles III, and John of Trastámara, was not yet two years old when created Prince of Viana.

These new titles gave a clear public recognition to the designated heir and a grander style than had existed hitherto. They did not, of course, ensure that those who bore these titles always succeeded smoothly. Of the eight young men who bore the title Prince of Wales in the medieval period, only four actually succeeded to the throne and, of the four who did, three were deposed and murdered. Charles, Prince of Viana, did not succeed his mother, Queen Blanca, on her death in 1441, since his father, John of Trastámara, retained the royal title he had borne as Blanca's husband. Eventually civil war broke out in Navarre between supporters of John and supporters of Charles, and the son was more than once held captive by his father. He died in 1461 without ever being crowned king of Navarre. Nor did the title of dauphin prevent Charles, son of Charles VI, being disinherited by his father in favour of Henry V of England in 1420. He had to fight for decades, even with the help of Joan of Arc, before he could be crowned, enter his capital and expel the English from France. These titles thus represent the late medieval proliferation and elaboration of titles and honours rather than any new certainty in succession practice.

Abolition of Interregnum

Some medieval lawyers advanced a radical view of coronation. 'A ruler's grants have no validity before his coronation', wrote Accursius, whose views formed the basis of the standard Roman Law commentary.[66] This was an oversimplification. In some kingdoms, such as Scotland before 1329, and intermittently in the Iberian kingdoms, kings were not crowned in any case, as an observer pointed out around 1200: 'the rulers of the Scots, who are also called kings, just like the rulers of Spain, despite the fact that they are not customarily crowned or anointed'.[67] In those kingdoms where coronation was the usual practice, it might still have different meanings. One way of assessing this is by looking at the kings' regnal years, that is, dating in the form 'in the first year of king X', 'the second year of king X', etc., for this shows their own, or their counsellors', idea of when their reign actually began. In the ninth century, for example, the rulers of the West Franks dated their regnal years from the death of their predecessor, but they then began using their coronation as the start of their reign, thus regarding it as the moment when they became kings. In the tenth, eleventh and early twelfth centuries, all French kings used this method, although a few, quite inconsistently, also used the death of their predecessor. In the twelfth century, there was a pronounced vacillation. Louis VII (1137–80) always took the death of his predecessor as the start of his reign, even though he had been crowned in his father's lifetime, but his son Philip Augustus always dated his reign from his coronation, which had also taken place during his father's lifetime. From the reign of Philip's son, Louis VIII (1223–6), however, the Capetians all dated their charters from the dates of their father's death.[68] A final decision had been made in favour of absolute dynastic continuity.

By coincidence, the final abandonment of any hint of an interregnal period occurred in both England and France within a few years and for similar reasons. In 1270, on 25 August, Louis IX of France (St Louis) died outside Tunis, while on crusade. His son Philip was with the army there and immediately received the oaths of his chief nobles and assumed the title of king. Making his will in the camp outside Tunis on 2 October 1270, he styles himself 'Philip, by grace of God king of the French'.[69] He was crowned on 15 August 1271, almost a year after his father's death. Edward, son of Henry III of England, arrived in Tunis shortly after St Louis' death and then continued to the Holy Land to crusade there. Two years later, he was in Sicily returning from the crusade when his father Henry III died, on 16 November 1272. The royal government proclaimed the new king's peace on the following day and buried the old king and organized an oath of fidelity to the new one on 20 November 1272. This last date was taken as the start of Edward's reign, even though he was not crowned until 19 August 1274. The coronation of a French king almost a year after his father's death, not before it, as with the early Capetians, and of an English king almost two years after his father's death, show the stability of these important medieval kingdoms at this period. There was no rush to coronation. In England, the king's reign, which in the Norman and Angevin period had been taken to commence at coronation, was henceforth taken to commence on the day after the death of the preceding monarch. Later, from the time of the Tudors in the sixteenth century, the reigns of English, and subsequently British, monarchs have been deemed to begin on the day of their predecessor's death: 'The king is dead, long live the king!'

Several late-medieval thinkers asserted that coronation actually made no difference to the ruler's power or authority, adopting a position completely opposite to that of Accursius. 'As far as the transmission of succession is concerned, coronation does nothing at all', wrote one legal expert in the 1370s.[70] He was defending the rights of a claimant to the throne of the kingdom of Sicily, who had not been crowned, against the incumbent ruler, who had, so it was important for him to stress that coronation had no constitutive effect. This view tied in with another strand of thinking at the time, which sought to free secular authority from any dependence on ecclesiastical authority. Since coronation usually involved clergy and took place in a church, and the anointing associated with it was indubitably a ritual conducted by ecclesiastics, it was natural to assume that the Church was bestowing something on the person being crowned. Opponents of this view wanted to stress that the king was the king, crowned or not. This was a position advanced with particular energy by the learned men who supported Louis the Bavarian, emperor-elect from 1314, in his conflict with the papacy. William of Ockham, for example, one of the greatest thinkers of the Middle Ages, who was in Louis' retinue after himself escaping persecution by the pope, recorded the argument that 'A king who succeeds by hereditary right does not necessarily receive any power over temporal things from the fact that he is crowned by an ecclesiastical person.'[71] Later writers who followed Ockham dropped that little proviso, 'necessarily'. 'A king who succeeds by hereditary right receives no power over temporal things from the fact that he is crowned', wrote a French royalist author in the 1370s.[72]

This did not mean that French coronations were not extravagant and memorable occasions, of course, and nor did it mean that kings in those countries where there was no custom of coronation were not eager to introduce it. Popes granted this right to the kings of Norway and the kings of Scots, with the first actual ceremonies taking place in 1246 and 1329 respectively. But the implication of the view expressed by Ockham was that they were purely ritual, not constitutive. This way of thinking was well summed up by the seventeenth-century English legal expert Edward Coke, who wrote that, because 'the king holdeth the kingdom of England by birth-right inherent, by descent from the blood royal', 'coronation was but a royal ornament'.[73] If kingship was in the blood, it did not need priests to convey it.

Waiting for Fathers to Die

Kings wanted sons who would succeed them and keep power and authority in their blood line. But adult sons with the expectation of succession also presented a problem in the dynastic system.[74] The novelist Thackeray puts it very well in Chapter 47 of *Vanity Fair*:

> You who have little or no patrimony to bequeath or to inherit, may be on good terms with your father or your son, whereas the heir of a great prince ... must naturally be angry at being kept out of his kingdom ... the fathers and elder sons of all great families hate each other. The crown prince is always in opposition to the crown or hankering after it ... and it stands to reason that every great man having experienced this feeling towards his father, must be aware that his son entertains it towards himself.

This is an excellent summary of the internal dynamics of dynasties. Long-lived kings presented problems. Heirs might become impatient and fractious. Otto, son and heir of the emperor Otto I (936–73), supposedly grumbled about his father, 'He holds onto the kingdoms he has acquired most tenaciously, like a lion, and does not give me, even though I am his son, even one portion.'[75]

Dashing off to the court of your father's enemy was a clear gesture of alienation and defiance. This is what the sons of Henry II of England did in the spring of 1173, when they secretly fled to the court of Louis VII of

France, who was delighted to welcome them, and thus initiated eighteen months of war and devastation across France and England. This is also exactly what Louis the Dauphin, son of Charles VII of France, did on 31 August 1456, when he fled to the court of his father's enemy, the duke of Burgundy. Charles and Louis were already estranged; in fact, the two did not meet for the last fourteen years of the king's life (1447–61).[76] It was known that Louis 'had, for a long time, desired to reign and to have the crown on his head' and this feeling was deepened by the harshness of his father's dealings with him.[77] Louis was thirty-eight when he finally succeeded his father and could return from the Burgundian court to the kingdom of France.

If the young prince had actually been crowned king, as happened in cases where fathers associated their sons with them during their lifetime, he might be particularly prone to impatience, especially if not granted resources of his own. Hugh, the eldest son of Robert II of France, was crowned in 1017 while still a boy. In the course of time, however, 'he realized that he could exercise command over no lordship of his own in the kingdom over which he had been crowned, apart from receiving his food and clothes.' He pressed his father for a lordship of his own, and, when this was refused, 'he joined with some young men of his own age and began to attack and plunder his parents' property at will.' Soon afterwards, however, he was reconciled to them, and was granted 'authority and power everywhere in the kingdom', but then 'suddenly envious death snatched him away from this world'.[78] This was in 1025. The next son, Henry, was crowned in 1027 and succeeded his father as sole ruler on the latter's death four years later.

The fortunes of the restless and ill-fated Hugh were reprised exactly a century and a half later by Henry the Young King, son of Henry II of England.[79] Like the French prince Hugh, Henry was crowned during his father's reign, a unique case in the history of the kingdom of England.[80] And, like Hugh, he grew restless. During the absence of Henry II in Ireland in the winter of 1171–2 some powerful nobles and also, rumour said, Queen Eleanor herself stirred up the Young King's mind against his father, 'suggesting that to some people it seemed incongruous that he was a king but did not exercise proper lordship in the kingdom'.[81] This led to the great rebellion of 1173–4, just mentioned, when the Young

King and two of his brothers, but not John, the youngest and his father's favourite, allied with the king of France and came close to defeating their father. The end of this war did not bring harmony, and fighting between father and son, and among the brothers, continued up to and indeed beyond the death of the Young King in 1183. Writing of his death, a contemporary noted 'He became a parricide of such immoderate passion that his greatest wish was for his father's death.'[82]

Another contemporary observer lamented these notorious family dissensions:

O good gods! If such brothers had observed fraternal agreement among themselves and filial affection as sons to their father and had been bound together by the double bond of good will and nature, how great and beyond estimation, how illustrious and unsurpassed in the ages would have been the father's glory and the sons' victory![83]

Both the case of Hugh and that of Henry show that, even if a son's right to inherit had been recognized by something as formal as coronation during his father's lifetime, there remained the potential for resentment, conflict and even violence, especially if there were powerful allies of the young prince interested in using him for their own ends. In both these cases, too, the son died before the father, so never attained sole rule.

Cases of warfare between royal father and son are numerous, and the outcomes varied. The Holy Roman Emperor Henry IV was imprisoned and forced to abdicate by his son, Henry V, in December 1105, and we can read the old emperor's complaints about the way he had been dealt with in several letters from the last months of his life. He has been treated, he says, 'without due deference, inhumanely and unworthily'; his son 'desired to deprive him of his kingdom and his life'; he had been held in the strictest confinement, suffering hunger, thirst and fear of death.[84] Is there just a touch of ambiguity, or perhaps irony, when he calls his son 'my dearest Absalom'?[85]

Another father–son conflict in the Holy Roman Empire 130 years later had a quite different outcome. Frederick II, whose father, Henry VI, had been both Holy Roman Emperor and king of Sicily, was left an orphan at the age of three in 1198 and had to fight to win his father's thrones, but by the age of twenty he had done so. By that time, he had also married and fathered a son, Henry. Frederick's dominions were vast, since the Holy Roman Empire contained the areas of modern Germany and northern Italy, so Frederick II, who was both king of Sicily and emperor, delegated the rule of Germany to his son Henry in 1220 when the boy was nine years old.[86] They did not see each other for twelve years and by the time they met again in 1232 differences between them had arisen, especially about the policy towards the great princes of Germany. In a letter of January 1235 Frederick complained of his disappointment in his son.[87] That summer he deposed Henry and took him back as a captive to Italy. Here the young man spent seven years as a prisoner, presumably eventually despairing, since while out with his jailors one day taking exercise, he galloped his horse off a high ridge into the depths below.[88] His father expressed his grief in a letter beginning 'at the death of a son nature grieves with us and draws out from the paternal feelings tears which cancel the offenses of the son'.[89]

The chronicler Ralph de Diceto, dean of St Paul's, London, listed numerous examples of father–son conflict from all periods of history. The root of these ferocious struggles was 'the immoderate lust for power (*inmoderata dominandi libido*)'. His examples include some in which fathers triumphed, some in which the sons were victorious, and there is always a moral tone to his reflections: the emperor Henry V, for example, died without children as a divine punishment for his rebellion against his father.[90]

There were occasions when kings disinherited their sons. Two important instances of this type, when a king wrote his son out of the picture, in one case successfully, in the other unsuccessfully, occurred in 1153 and in 1420, in the first case when Stephen of England agreed that he should be succeeded not by his son William but by Henry of Anjou (later Henry II), in the second when Charles VI of France acknowledged as his heir Henry V of England, not his own son Charles, although this Charles did in fact succeed in becoming Charles VII. There were some remarkable similarities between the situations that prompted these unusual decisions. In both cases the throne had been disputed between a crowned and an uncrowned contender: Stephen versus Matilda, whose claim was then taken up by her son Henry, and Charles versus Henry V, who was a crowned king of England but not of France. In both cases the uncrowned contender had had military success. Henry of Anjou waged effective campaigns in the years leading up to his agreement with Stephen, and Henry V won the spectacular victory of Agincourt in 1415 and allied with the duke of Burgundy to begin a sustained war of conquest in France. But it was also probably important that both Stephen and Charles VI lost older sons in the years prior to the treaties they made. They thus were not disinheriting their firstborn, who had lived long years expecting to succeed their fathers.

Stephen's oldest son, Eustace, was five or six years old when his father became king, and from that time he was recognized as the heir to the throne. Stephen even tried to have him crowned joint king during his own lifetime, following a custom of the contemporary French kings. Eustace married royalty: his bride was Constance, sister of Louis VII of France. But Eustace was not only heir to his father's throne but also to his endless war against his cousin Matilda. From the late 1140s he had to face up to Matilda's son Henry. Eustace and Henry of Anjou, the former in his early twenties, the latter in his late teens, campaigned in England and France, with Henry slowly gaining the upper hand. In August 1153, unexpectedly and leaving no children, Eustace died. His father obviously decided that a negotiated settlement, leaving him the Crown and securing a proper place for his younger son William, was acceptable. Within three months of Eustace's death, Stephen agreed terms with Henry of Anjou, recognizing him as his heir and arranging a huge lordship for his son William, and, within another year, Henry had become King Henry II on Stephen's death.

The Treaty of Troyes in 1420 between Charles VI of France and Henry V of England likewise recognized the disinheritance of a royal heir, in this case Dauphin Charles. But Dauphin Charles had only been dauphin, the title held by the heir to the French throne, for a few years at this time. Four of his older brothers had, in fact, preceded him as dauphins, but they had all died without sons. At the time of the great French defeat of Agincourt, Charles' brother Louis was dauphin, but Louis died the same year as the battle, 1415, and was succeeded by the next brother John. John, however, died in less than eighteen months. So, in April 1417, at the age of fourteen, Charles became dauphin. He had not been raised as an heir, and it may be this was one thing that made it easier for some of the French to accept his disinheritance three years later. But Dauphin Charles refused to be disinherited, and he had some unexpected help from Joan of Arc. Her energy and faith brought Charles to Rheims, traditional coronation site of the French kings, in July 1429, where he was crowned. He had regarded himself as king of France since the death of his father in 1422, but there is a possibility that Joan had more old-fashioned ideas and thought of him as simply the 'noble Dauphin' prior to coronation. One of the witnesses at her rehabilitation trial in 1455–6 reported that, after she had sought out Charles in the spring of 1429, saying that she had been sent by God to help 'the noble dauphin', she had been asked why she called him dauphin and not king. She supposedly replied that she would only call him king after he had been crowned at Rheims.[91] Joan was betrayed and burned, but Charles went on to expel the English from their possessions in France, except Calais, and could thus take his revenge on 'the damnable Treaty of Troyes' as later French royalists called it.[92]

Minorities

If royal sons might wait impatiently for their fathers to die, the unpredictable biology of dynasties could also sweep fathers away while their children were still very young and vulnerable.[93] In a world where kings were war-leaders facing endless threats from aggressive competitors, it might seem obvious that the succession of a child would be ruled out. In some dynastic systems, this was in fact the case. In Ireland it was expected that the new king would be an adult male, and he certainly need not be the son of the preceding ruler. In Scotland there are no minor kings before the mid twelfth century, when the model of the dynasty and the nature of succession had shifted towards the kind of primogeniture found in other west European kingdoms. Military needs were indeed cited as an argument against the succession of babies. After the death of Albert of Habsburg, king of Hungary, in 1439, the Hungarian aristocracy was divided between supporters of the succession of his posthumous son Ladislas, and supporters of the king of neighbouring Poland as king of Hungary too. When some of the Polish king's supporters were negotiating with Ladislas' mother, Queen Elizabeth, they were blunt: 'Gracious lady, even if you had a son who was ten years old, we would not accept him as our lord, because he could not lead us against the Turks.'[94]

When, in 890, the bishops and nobles of Provence chose as their king the nine-year-old Louis (later nicknamed 'the Blind'), they acknowledged that 'his age was not suitable to repress the savagery of the barbarians', that is, Viking and Muslim raiders, but stressed, first, that he was of high descent, 'coming from imperial stock', since his mother was a Carolingian, mentioning also that he had grown to be 'a boy of good abilities', and concluding with the confident assertion that the barbarian attacks would certainly be repelled 'by the advice and bravery of the nobles of this kingdom, who are not few in number, and God's help'.[95] They recognized the power of the argument for having an adult male king as a defender of the realm, but thought that high descent, innate ability and a supportive aristocracy could be adduced to outweigh that consideration. The very existence of child kings indicates a strong sense of dynasty. A boy king or girl queen might seem a ludicrous idea in a world of constant armed conflict between competing lords, but, in the dynastic system, the claims of blood counted for much.

Cases where the claims of blood-right outweighed the obvious need for a military aristocracy to have an adult male as their war leader are not rare. There are at least ninety instances from the period 500–1500 (see Appendix B).[96] In Byzantium, minorities, excluding child co-emperors, occur roughly once a century.[97] About half of the Merovingian kings who ruled between Clovis (d. 511), conqueror of Gaul, and 751, when the last member of the dynasty was deposed, came to the throne as minors. For instance, when Chilperic I was murdered in the autumn of 584, he left a four-month-old son. The boy's mother, Fredegund, called on his uncle, Guntram, to act as protector to the baby and regent of his kingdom. The nobles assembled, named the child with the royal name Clothar (Lothar) and secured from the cities of Chilperic's kingdom oaths of loyalty to King Guntram and his nephew Clothar.[98] As Clothar grew up, he, like most Merovingian kings, faced threats from his relatives, and he suffered defeats, but he was also able to reunite the Frankish realms under his rule and died a natural death at the age of forty-five. He is a good example of the way that succession of a tiny infant could work in the Merovingian kingdoms.

The Carolingians, who succeeded the Merovingians, had no child kings for over a century (751–855), excluding those crowned in their father's lifetime, but they are found in the second half of the ninth century in several of the component parts into which the Carolingian empire had broken, the kingdoms of the West Franks, the East Franks and Provence. Thereafter, the situation in the east (Germany, the Empire) came to diverge from that in the west (France). Minor kings inherited the throne in France in 954, 1052, 1226, 1316, 1380 and 1483, roughly once a century, like Byzantium, but because the Empire was not in theory hereditary, there are very few cases of minorities there. There are two cases of very young sons succeeding their fathers as rulers in the tenth and eleventh centuries: Otto III in 983 at the age of three, and Henry IV in 1056 at the age of five. But after 1056 there are no further cases. As election became a stronger tradition with clearer rules, the chances of electing a child vanished.

Minorities were often the result of an unexpected death, which could be natural but might be violent. There is thus sometimes a correlation between the frequency of the violent deaths of kings and that of minorities. In fifteenth-century Scotland, for example, there were four minorities, and three of these resulted from the violent death of the child's father: James I was murdered, James II blown up by one of his own cannons and James III killed by rebels, who included his son, either in or after battle (see also below, pp. 248–9). It is significant, however, that when the lives of these kings were cut short, their young sons were accepted in their place. In eleventh-century Scotland, in contrast, which was even more violent, with six of eight kings being killed in battle, there were no boy kings, for the dead rulers were succeeded by adults of either their own or a rival line. By the end of the Middle Ages the violence was taking place in a different kind of dynastic world.

Minorities meant regencies, rivalries, decisions about and by queen mothers, and, of course, endless negotiations about future brides for the child ruler. Figures at court or noble factions might compete for control of the child king, who could then be their tool. Queen mothers commonly served as regents for their child and were often both protagonists and victims of such factional politics. An early example is Amalswintha, widowed daughter of Theodoric, ruler of Ostrogothic Italy, who acted as regent for her son Athalaric after he succeeded his grandfather as king in 526 when aged eight.[99] For the next eight years she was a major figure in the politics of Italy and beyond, praised for her wisdom and justice, but willing to take harsh measures against her enemies among the Ostrogothic nobility. In 534 her son, the young king, died, and Amalswintha arranged for her cousin Theodehad to become king in his place, reportedly with the stipulation that she would continue to exercise real power. If that were so, she was quickly double-crossed, imprisoned by Theodehad and murdered by her enemies, strangled in the bath according to one account.[100] Her killing provoked Justinian, the eastern emperor, with whom she had had mainly friendly relations, to attack Italy, beginning a war that would last twenty years and end with the complete destruction of the Ostrogothic kingdom. Amalswintha provides a clear example of the way high-born queen mothers could exercise great political power, and of the dangers as well as the influence that brought.

On numerous occasions widowed queens of the Merovingians acted as regents for their minor sons.[101] It was also standard practice in the Byzantine empire: of the seven child emperors in the period 500–1500, six began their reigns under the regency of their mother.[102] In the Western Empire, Empress Theophanu, who acted as regent for her young son Otto III for six years (985–91), won praise for her government during that time, even if clerical writers cannot avoid a note of surprise that a woman could do so well: 'although she was of the weaker sex, she guarded her son's kingdom with masculine care'.[103] After the unexpected death of Louis VIII of France in 1226, at the age of thirty-nine, the misogynist rhetoric was stronger amongst the nobles who opposed the regency of Louis' widow, Blanche of Castile, for her young son. Their spokesman put the feeling into verse: 'France is truly made a bastard, hear me lord barons, when a woman has it to rule.'[104] Blanche went on to devote the next eight years to suppressing or bribing dissident aristocrats, facing down the king of England, leading armies on occasion, and ensuring that by 1234, the year that her son turned twenty-one and took a wife, he could embark on his adult reign with a relatively loyal kingdom.[105] Such struggles between queen mothers serving as regents and aristocratic groups were recurrent features of minority politics.

Ingeborg, daughter of King Haakon Magnusson of Norway, served as regent for her son Magnus VII Eriksson, who became king of both Norway and Sweden in 1319, aged three, but she was deposed by a group of Norwegian nobles in 1323, who accused her of squandering royal revenues and of going to war with Denmark to further the interests of her lover, Canute Porse.[106]

A dramatic example of a struggle to control the young ruler occurred during the minority of Henry IV of Germany, who succeeded his father in 1056 just before his sixth birthday.[107] In the early months of his minority events were controlled by Pope Victor II, who was a German bishop as well as pope and happened to be in Germany at the time of the death of Henry's father, but the regency was exercised by Henry's mother, Empress Agnes. The chronicler Lampert of Hersfeld gave her a warm endorsement: 'Supreme government of affairs and of everything that needed to be done remained in the hands of the empress, who safe-guarded the endangered state with such skill that the unexpected turn of events resulted in no disturbance or dispute.'[108] The German nobles swore an oath that, should the young Henry die, they would consult the empress about his successor.[109] But in the sixth year of her regency a group of dissatisfied nobles, headed by the ambitious archbishop Anno of Cologne, plotted a coup. The key was physical possession of the king, now eleven. He was at the royal palace at Kaiserswerth, at that time an island in the river Rhine. After the archbishop and the boy king had enjoyed a banquet, and were talking cheerfully, Anno invited Henry to inspect his new ship, moored in the river nearby. The moment they set foot on it, the plotters cast off and rowed out to the centre of the river. Henry, fearing for his life, threw himself overboard and was only saved by Count Ekbert of Brunswick, one of the conspirators, diving in to rescue him. Anno tried to reassure the panicking boy, and the ship rowed off to his city of Cologne.[110] Having gained control of the king, Anno was now able to exercise governmental authority himself.

Henry IV grew into a controversial adult ruler with a dramatically disruptive reign and a sorry end. It is not clear if the kidnapping played any part in shaping his character or his political assumptions. In the case of Wenceslas II of Bohemia (1278–1305), however, there is an account that details some of the trauma of a boy king. The opening section of the chronicle written at the Cistercian abbey of Zbraslav (Königssaal) in Bohemia, which comprises an account of Wenceslas II, provides one of the most arresting and personal pictures of a medieval king to be found anywhere (see also below, pp. 233–5). It starts with the pathos of the boy king, whose father was killed when he was not yet seven, being brought up by his uncle in Brandenburg with inadequate revenues, while his mother and her lover, the powerful noble Zawisch von Falkenstein, dominated Bohemia. The psychological consequences for the child included a phobia about cats and about thunderstorms. One way he tried to deal with this latter fear was the construction of a hollow altar within which he hid during storms, while one of his clerks lay at the entrance to the altar, reading to him from the Bible.[111] Wenceslas eventually established himself as king of Bohemia, had Zawisch executed, after his mother's death, and succeeded in becoming king of Poland too.

Queen mothers often acted as regents but they were not always either available or suitable. Another choice would be a senior churchman, who would have authority, experience of administration and, at least in principle, no sons of his own to complicate loyalties. Engelbert, archbishop of Cologne, was the first regent of Henry (VII), who was elected German king ('king of the Romans') in 1220 aged nine. The archbishop is described as the boy's 'guardian, and administrator of the whole of the Roman kingdom in Germany'.[112] Sometimes the pope himself was involved, particularly in those kingdoms with a special tie to the papacy, such as Sicily. This was acknowledged by Constance, queen of Sicily, in her will. When she died in November 1198, she left the 'custody of the kingdom' to Pope Innocent III 'as superior lord', although actual physical custody of her three-year-old son was in the hands of members of the royal household.[113]

Adult male relatives were also available as regents, although relations between uncles and nephews could be tense or worse. Charles VI of France was eleven when he became king in 1380; several years earlier, his father, Charles V, had already made arrangements for a possible regency, entrusting his own younger brother, Louis, duke of Anjou, with the government of the kingdom until his son and successor was fourteen, while reserving a large royal estate for the minor king, who was to be under the guardianship of the queen mother and his two younger uncles, the duke of Burgundy and a maternal uncle, the duke of Bourbon.[114] This rather complex system did not work smoothly, but it gave the royal dukes the chance to run the kingdom in their own interests in the 1380s, although, of course, their interests did not always coincide. The king's fourteenth birthday, stipulated by his father as the age of his majority, was ignored. Throughout these years the king's uncles, including the duke of Berry, who had been excluded from the original scheme, dominated royal government, using royal resources to support their own projects, such as the duke of Anjou's attempts to become king of Naples and the duke of Burgundy's efforts to establish himself in his wife's inheritance of Flanders. These were also years of war with England and serious popular revolts. Eventually, in 1388, as he approached the age of twenty, Charles asserted his personal control of government. At a meeting of the great nobles and clergy in Rheims, the cardinal of Laon acted as his mouthpiece. After praising Charles' qualities and describing the experience he had gained in war, he concluded:

> Since nothing is lacking in him that ought to adorn the royal majesty, I, by the oath of fealty by which I am bound, declare that henceforth he does not need guardians, but the business of government in war and at home ought to be directed by him himself.[115]

The majority present, though not the king's uncles, approved the cardinal's proposal. The king himself tactfully thanked them for the care they had taken during the time of their guardianship and promised that he would continue to value the advice. It was a disputed matter whether the cardinal's death a few days later was due to poisoning.

When a minority was going to end was clearly a big question. There were various rules and customs about when a child ruler reached the age of majority, though they are not all a good guide to actual practice. The laws of the crusader kingdom of Jerusalem, for example, specified that a minor king should be crowned at the age of twelve, but no such case is recorded, and Baldwin V was crowned at the age of seven.[116] Fourteen was a common age of majority. As mentioned, Charles V, in a royal ordinance of August 1374, specified the age of majority for his son as fourteen, citing both biblical and Merovingian precedents for kings of a young age.[117] Majority could be marked by rites of passage: Alfonso II of

Aragon was knighted, got married and issued a new coinage in January 1174.[118] He was sixteen at this time and these were all acts that proclaimed his entry to adulthood. Later ages were also possible. In the kingdom of Navarre a document of 1329 stipulated that if Queen Joanna, who was a queen regnant, died leaving a minor heir, her consort could act as regent until that heir was twenty-one.[119]

The case of Henry III of England, like Wenceslas II a boy king who grew up with a fear of thunderstorms, shows that the end of a minority could be a multi-stage process.[120] Henry succeeded his father, King John, in 1216 at the age of nine, and William Marshal, a tried and loyal servant of the dynasty, was appointed regent: 'our ruler and the ruler of our kingdom', in the boy king's words.[121] The Marshal was supported by the papal legate, Guala, an especially important figure since England was a papal fief at this time, while the bishop of Winchester would look after Henry on a day-to-day basis. Henry was crowned quickly but not at Westminster, the traditional coronation site, since this was in the hands of his enemies, rebel barons and their ally Louis of France. The Marshal's first job was to win the war against them, which he did. In the meantime, royal documents were sealed with his seal since the king did not yet have one. In November 1218, when a new Great Seal was made, the young king proclaimed that 'it has been provided by the common council of our kingdom that no charter, no letters patent of confirmation, alienation, sale or gift, or anything else that can be granted in perpetuity, shall be sealed with our Great Seal until we are of full age'.[122] Clearly there was a worry that royal resources might be squandered, as Ingeborg, regent for Magnus VII Eriksson in Norway, had supposedly done. Henry became fourteen on 1 October 1221, and this is probably the date that the personal guardianship of the bishop of Winchester came to an end. Two years later the king took control of his seal, but still without being able to authorize grants in perpetuity. Finally, in January 1227, when he was nineteen, Henry declared that henceforth he would issue royal charters. Even this was not the end of the matter, for some people thought that the king would only come of age when he was twenty-one, the age of majority for English barons and knights.

Child-rulers faced a wave of critical opinion. It was commonplace to cite the text from the Book of Ecclesiastes: 'woe to you, the land whose king is a child'.[123] And 'boy' was an insult. In 1219, when he had been king for three years, some of his subjects were still deriding Henry III of England as 'not a king but a boy'.[124] Critics sometimes associated the evils of child rule with those of female rule, as during the regency of the empress Agnes for Henry IV of Germany: 'For the king was a boy, while his mother, just like a woman, easily gave way to whatever was suggested to her.'[125] It was this supposedly hazy, yielding quality of rule by children and women that hostile clerical observers stressed: 'The land is cursed where a boy rules and a woman holds the government; a kingdom should be ruled by laws and command, not by entreaties or blandishments.'[126] It was said of Philip Augustus of France, who succeeded his father aged fifteen, that he was a plaything in the hands of his noble advisers: 'For the king was a boy and they could bend him like a reed to their will as they wished.'[127]

But counter-arguments were also made, and it is hard to believe that there could be ninety boy kings and girl queens if the hostile views were the only ones. A letter, written in the year 900, sets out the reasons that had led the bishops and nobles of the kingdom of the East Franks (Germany) to accept as their king Louis, son of the emperor Arnulf, even though he was only aged six – he is indeed traditionally known as 'Louis the Child'.[128] Louis' father, the emperor Arnulf of Carinthia, had made determined efforts to ensure his son's succession. In 897, two years before his death, he 'demanded from everyone an oath of fidelity to himself once more and to his little son Louis'.[129] After Arnulf's death and Louis' recognition as king, Hatto, archbishop of Mainz, one of the leading figures in the kingdom, wrote to the pope justifying this action:

> It remained uncertain for a while whom to elect as king, and, because there was great fear that the unified kingdom would break into separate parts, it was decided, by divine impulse (as we believe), that our lord's son, although he was very little, should be raised to the kingship, by the common counsel of the chief men and with the consent of the whole people; and because the kings of the Franks always come from one family, we preferred to keep the old custom rather than settle on some novel arrangement.[130]

This passage is short but covers a lot of ground: fears of a kingdom disintegrating, something of which there was a lot of experience in 900; the justification derived from the common counsel of the top level of the aristocracy and the agreement of 'the people', usually taken to mean the rest of the aristocracy; a nod to divine will; and, overriding even the fact that Louis was 'very little', the old custom that kings come from one family – one dynasty.

CHAPTER 4

Female Sovereigns

The First Female Sovereigns in Medieval Europe

T HERE IS NO QUESTION THAT DURING THE MIDDLE AGES many female members of ruling dynasties exercised considerable power and influence. The king's wife might be influential, the king's mother might be even more so. Cases of powerful female regents, like Blanche, mother of St Louis, who governed vigorously on behalf of her son for over a decade in all, or queens fighting for the rights of their sons, like Margaret of Anjou, wife of the mentally incapacitated Henry VI of England and champion of the young Prince of Wales, are not uncommon. Sometimes women might also rule in their own right, although it is not always easy to identify which of them ruled formally in this way, rather than as regents and consorts. There seem to be no cases in the medieval west as unambiguous as the long reign of an unmarried queen, like the sixteenth-century Elizabeth of England or the seventeenth-century Christina of Sweden. And the example of Elizabeth's sister and predecessor, Mary Tudor, shows that marriage could change a queen from a sole monarch to a joint ruler, since, after her marriage to Philip of Spain, the royal style became 'Philip and Mary, by the grace of God, king and queen of England and France, Naples, Jerusalem and Ireland' (perhaps the only time when Jerusalem and Ireland had the same ruler).

In Byzantium, it is not clear whether the empress Eudokia Makrembolitissa should best be viewed as a regent or a co-empress. She certainly exercised imperial authority after the death of her husband Constantine X Dukas on 22 May 1067, but on behalf of her young sons.

After she remarried, to Romanos Diogenes, he was proclaimed emperor on 1 January 1068. Then, after Romanos' defeat and capture at Manzikert in August 1071, she again exercised power along with her son Michael, but he exiled her in October 1071 and sent her to a nunnery.[1] Berenguela (or Berengaria) of Castile is another uncertain case. She was the daughter of Alfonso VIII, who died in 1214 and was succeeded by his son Henry, the much younger brother of Berenguela. In 1217, after her young brother's death, Berenguela and her sons attended a great assembly of her supporters. There

> one of them spoke for all, with their universal consent, recognizing, on behalf of the people, that the kingdom of Castile rightfully belonged to the lady queen Berengaria and that they all acknowledged her as lady and queen of the kingdom of Castile. But they all unanimously begged her that she should grant the kingdom, which was hers by proprietary right, to her eldest son, that is, lord Ferdinand, since, because she was a woman, she would not be able to bear the exertion of ruling the kingdom.

She agreed and 'granted the kingdom to her son'.[2] Taking this literally, Berenguela was thus a sovereign for a short time in 1217, but this may not be a useful categorization. Moreover, it has been argued that Berenguela was not merely 'queen for a day' in 1217, but actually co-ruler with her son Ferdinand.[3]

The problem of categorizing Berenguela is compounded by the fact that, in the twelfth and early thirteenth century sometimes the daughters of the kings of Castile, as also the daughters of the kings of Portugal, were called queens.[4] This caused annoyance when they married into the great families outside the Iberian peninsula. The chronicler Gilbert of Mons scarcely ever mentions Matilda, daughter of the king of Portugal and wife of Philip, count of Flanders (d. 1191), without adding 'who had herself called queen', 'who had herself named queen', 'who named herself queen', or 'called queen'.[5] It was clearly a practice that irritated him. Another contemporary explains her title more neutrally: 'She was called queen because she was the daughter of a king and had exercised rule over the kingdom of her father on behalf of her brother, who was not strong.'[6] Here the explanation involves not just the position of being the daughter of a king but also the actual exercise of power. It was clearly a practice that non-Iberian observers thought needed explanation.

However, while one must recognize some ambiguities, it is possible to draw up a provisional list of at least twenty-seven women who ruled medieval European kingdoms and empires as sovereigns rather than as regents or consorts. They are listed in Appendix C, which also indicates those who were named or depicted on the coinage, since this can be a prima facie indication that they were sovereigns not consorts (although absence of such evidence does not indicate they were not sovereigns and their presence on coins is not always definitive evidence that they were).

Byzantium

The earliest were in the Byzantine empire, where there are three cases of empresses ruling in their own right. The first is Irene, who, after blinding and deposing her own son, ruled alone from 797 to 802, issuing coins with her image on both obverse and reverse, and promulgating laws as 'emperor (βασιλεύς)'.[7] All this was quite exceptional. Indeed, according to one western account, the reason that the Frankish ruler Charlemagne was crowned emperor in the year 800, in the middle of Irene's sole reign, was 'because at that time the name of emperor ceased among the Greeks and they had female rule (*femineum imperium*)'.[8] While Irene saw herself as 'emperor', the hostile Franks chose to regard the empire as vacant.

After Irene, there are no examples of sole female rule in Byzantium for the next two hundred years, but in the eleventh century there was the remarkable Zoe, daughter of Constantine VIII.[9] In his last days, in the autumn of 1028, Constantine, having no sons, decided that his successor would be the aristocrat Romanos Argyros. He forced him to put away his wife and marry Zoe instead. Since Zoe was fifty, this could not have been in the hope of grandchildren but must rather have been intended to maintain a family link of some kind into the new reign. But the marriage of Zoe and Romanos was not a success. They soon stopped sleeping together, and Zoe then fell for a young man named Michael, who became her lover. Reports circulated that, when Romanos drowned in his bath, this was no accident. Without delay Zoe married Michael and had him proclaimed emperor, as Michael IV. Their marriage had problems too. Michael's family then arranged for Zoe to adopt Michael's nephew, also called Michael, to ensure that power did not slip from their hands on the death of the older Michael. When this came about, in 1041, Michael the nephew ascended the throne as Michael V. As her adopted son, he did not, of course, have the option of marrying Zoe, but instead he tried to freeze her out of power, and eventually expelled her from the imperial palace and sent her away from Constantinople and into exile. The historian Michael Psellos, our main source for all these events, gives a vivid picture of her, standing on the deck of the ship that was carrying her away, looking back at the palace and recalling her imperial ancestors.[10] But Michael V had miscalculated. A wave of sympathy for Zoe spread through the city. The emperor sought to defuse the opposition by recalling her, but the rebels then found another focus in Zoe's long-forgotten younger sister Theodora. In April 1042 Michael V was blinded and exiled, Zoe and Theodora met, embraced, and, says Psellos, 'the empire now devolved upon the two sisters'.[11] Until now, Zoe had been empress as wife and adoptive mother. In 1042, briefly, she ruled in her own right alongside her sister. Zoe and Theodora are depicted side-by-side on their coins.

Psellos is quite clear that in this short period 'the sisters chose to rule alone'.[12] But, he says, after less than two months, Zoe 'sought strength in marriage' and took Constantine Monomachos, a member of an important Byzantine family, as her husband.[13] He was crowned emperor as Constantine IX. This, writes Psellos, 'marked, for the empresses, the end of their power to act and rule as sovereigns, but, for Constantine Monomachos, the beginning of the establishment of his imperial authority'.[14] Whatever traces of joint rule between Constantine and the two sisters may be found in symbolic language and iconography, notably the so-called Monomachos Crown showing the three of them,[15] the reality was clear. Zoe retired from public life to experiment with the manufacture of different kinds of perfume. She even had to tolerate Constantine's mistress moving into the palace. Zoe died in 1050. She had transmitted her imperial magic to three husbands but had only ruled herself for a few months and then jointly with her sister.

Surprisingly, it was the sister, Theodora, who was to rule alone, outliving and succeeding her brother-in-law Constantine Monomachos, and having a sole reign for more than a year and a half in 1055–6.[16] Psellos

Figure 3 The Byzantine empresses regnant, the sisters Zoe and Theodora, on a gold coin (*histamenon*) in 1042, the year of their joint rule.
© Dumbarton Oaks, Byzantine Collection, Washington, DC.

expressed the general surprise that she did not delegate authority to some noble man but 'took on the supreme authority of the Romans herself with no bad consequences (ἀνατί)'.[17] He describes her as 'acting like a man' or 'taking on the duties of a man',[18] appointing officials, hearing court cases and making decisions. He notes, somewhat bemusedly, that all seemed to go well: the empire was peaceful and prosperous, and equity (ἰσότης) was maintained. Theodora's reputation was high too among neighbouring peoples, the Armenian chronicler Aristakès of Lastivert calling her a 'lioness'.[19]

Irene from 797–802, Zoe and Theodora for two months in 1042, and Theodora alone in 1055–6: these are the only examples of Byzantine empresses ruling alone. All other cases of female rule involve joint rule with husbands or sons, or regencies. Irene's story is extraordinary, as the wife of an emperor who came to exercise sole rule through the violent removal of her own son. The story of Zoe and Theodora, although still unusual, is less strange, and, especially since the sources for it are quite rich, can be used to explore the issue of female rule. Two contradictory points stand out in these sources: the general assumption among men that sole female rule was unnatural and undesirable; and the strong contrary widespread feeling that the imperial sisters had unassailable hereditary rights.

The fact that Zoe and Theodora were female rulers did raise comment. Psellos, although balanced in his judgment of them, expressed the thought that the joint rule of Zoe and Theodora represented a muddling or jumbling of spheres that should be distinct. 'For the first time', he wrote, 'our age witnessed the transformation of the women's quarters into an imperial council chamber.'[20] He accused the empresses of 'mixing the trifles of the women's quarters with the serious matters of the empire'.[21] Incidentally, the Penguin translation of Psellos' history, a translation first published in 1953, renders 'the trifles of the women's quarters' as 'the trifles of the harem', thus orientalizing as well as trivializing the issue. Psellos thought that the empire needed 'a man's care',[22] especially to deal with outside attacks. When describing the sole rule of Theodora in 1055–6, he reports the views of those who claimed that 'it was not fitting for the empire of the Romans to become feminine (ἐκθηλυνθῆναι) after having had a man's wisdom'.[23] He says that this was notably the view of Michael Cerularius, the patriarch of Constantinople at the time, who supposedly gave his opinion that 'sovereign power stands in need of a masculine mind and soul'.[24]

Yet despite this current of definite, but not ferocious, misogyny, contemporaries also stressed the hereditary claims of the two sisters. Psellos recognized that the empire belonged to Zoe 'through inheritance (κλῆρος)'; she was popular, he says, 'as a woman and as an inheritor of power'.[25] He describes her supporters at the time that Michael V sent her into exile asking 'where can she be ... she who has the inheritance of the empire according to law?', and they recall her descent from a line of emperors.[26] The other main source for Zoe's and Theodora's activities, John Skylitzes, writes that, on the death of Michael IV, 'supreme power passed to the empress Zoe, as heir', while in 1055, he says, Theodora acquired 'her hereditary empire'.[27] The Armenian chronicler Aristakès of Lastivert writes that Theodora possessed the empire as 'her own patrimonial inheritance'.[28]

Psellos even writes of Theodora's 'natural (συμφυής)' right or property.[29] Her right was 'natural' because it was a matter of blood and birth. Theodora's blood was imperial.[30] Both Zoe and Theodora were porphyrogenitae, born when their father was emperor, and in the imperial palace. This made them unique at this time, for there were no living male equivalents after their father's death. And it gave them a status that was generally recognized by contemporaries. Aristakès of Lastivert describes the Constantinopolitan crowd asking for Zoe, 'our empress porphyrogenita, who has received the empire as an inheritance from her fathers and grandfathers'.[31] In the reign of Constantine Monomachos, according to Skylitzes, another restive crowd in the imperial city expressed their reverence for Zoe and Theodora, 'our mothers and porphyrogenitae'.[32] During the period of her sole rule, Theodora's coins and seals bear the legend 'Theodora, lady (δέσποινα) and porphyrogenita' and 'Theodora, Augusta and porphyrogenita'.[33]

One could thus say that the two empresses had a strong sense of dynasty. Yet it was very different from the dynastic sense to be found in the west. Future transmission of the line appears to have been treated with astonishing casualness. According to Psellos, neither Constantine VIII, the father of the princesses, nor their uncle Basil II had made any plans for them, even though Basil and Constantine were the last male members of the so-called Macedonian dynasty, the descendants of Basil I who had reigned since the late ninth century.[34] Basil II never married, and a contemporary western chronicler accounts for this by a vow that Basil had taken, promising to live like a monk if God gave him victory in war; from a western viewpoint, a ruler's celibacy needed explanation.[35] Basil's brother Constantine VIII had three daughters: the eldest went into a nunnery; Zoe, the second, was married, as mentioned, only when fifty; the third, Theodora, never married. Psellos describes the ointments and magic charms that Zoe and her first husband Romanos used to try to secure offspring,[36] but it is difficult to believe that continuance of the line could have been a pressing concern if only one of the three imperial daughters was given in marriage, and then at an age when people must have known that a pregnancy was very unlikely. It is hard to imagine western rulers in similar circumstances who would not have started marriage negotiations when the daughters were still in the cradle. The transmission of power in Byzantium was not only different in fact from the transmission of power in the west, but contemporaries conceived of it differently. Psellos, in a panegyric to the empress Theodora, praised her for her virginity and her 'unmarried life'.[37] But, while a virgin queen could have enjoyed such compliments, those who were concerned about the succession knew that she brought only uncertainty.

Latin Christendom

The contrast between the sole rule of women in the Byzantine and western worlds can be explored through the prism of the first western queens regnant. The very first queen to rule in her own right in western Europe was Urraca, queen of Leon and Castile, who reigned from 1109 to 1126.[38] It is worth dwelling on her for a moment, since her story highlights both the possibilities and the limitations of female rule. Her father, Alfonso VI, had fought his way to sole rule in the kingdom and had expanded its territories, most memorably by capturing the great city of Toledo from the Muslims. Unlike the last of the Macedonian emperors in Byzantium, Alfonso had made determined efforts to secure a male heir, marrying five (or possibly six) times but without producing a legitimate son (see above, p. 69). Urraca was his oldest daughter and he arranged a marriage for her with the immigrant French noble Raymond of Burgundy, with whom she had a son, another Alfonso. Lacking a legitimate son, Alfonso VI had supposedly promised the succession to the kingdom to this son-in-law, Raymond of Burgundy, but Raymond died before him.[39] Alfonso then seems to have viewed his own illegitimate son Sancho as his heir, but he too predeceased the king, being killed in battle in 1108, the year before Alfonso died.[40]

Our main chronicle source for Urraca's reign, the *Historia Compostellana*, is written to glorify Diego Gelmírez, the first archbishop of Santiago, who was sometimes Urraca's ally but often her opponent, so what it says has to be viewed in that light, but, nevertheless, it can probably be trusted when it reports King Alfonso's plans after the deaths of his son-in-law, Count Raymond, and his illegitimate son, Sancho. This

Figure 4 Urraca, queen of Leon-Castile (1109–26), the first queen regnant in western Europe.
The Picture Art Collection/Alamy.

is what Urraca herself says, in a speech put into her mouth in the *Historia Compostellana*:

> it is well known to all the inhabitants of the kingdom of Spain that as my father, the emperor Alfonso, was approaching death, he transmitted to me the whole kingdom, and Galicia to my son Alfonso, his grandson, if I should take a husband.[41]

So Urraca was to inherit the kingdom, but part of it, Galicia in the northwest, would be reserved for her son Alfonso if Urraca remarried. Galicia had been Count Raymond's great fief and it would thus be secured to his son in the event of Urraca marrying again.[42] This did happen, in 1109, when, in the immediate aftermath of her father's death and her own succession, Urraca succumbed to pressure to take a new husband.[43] One chronicler, who says he was actually present at the deathbed of Alfonso VI, reports that, as soon as the king had been buried, 'the nobles and the counts of the land gathered together and went to the lady Urraca his daughter, saying, "You will not be able to rule or retain your father's kingdom or reign over us unless you take a husband."'[44] In the speech attributed to her in the *Historia Compostellana* she says that the dying king had ordered her to do nothing important without the advice of the great nobles of Spain, and hence it was at their recommendation that she married, although 'unwillingly'.

The husband chosen for her brought immediate complications, both political and personal. He was Alfonso the Battler, king of Aragon. The marriage of Urraca and Alfonso could have brought about a union of the kingdoms, as happened much later in the Middle Ages with the marriage of Ferdinand and Isabella, if Urraca's son by Count Raymond, Alfonso, had been excluded, but, in any case, arrangements had to be made to deal with the presence of the powerful and warlike Aragonese king as joint ruler of Leon, and negotiations were undertaken about the rights of any children of Urraca's new marriage.[45] The major change that all this involved is reflected in the language of the charters. In a document she issued on 22 July 1109, soon after her father's death, Urraca styles herself 'Urraca, by God's command queen of the whole of Spain', but the following December, after her marriage, a private document is dated 'when Alfonso, king of Aragon, was ruling in Leon'.[46] Her sole reign had lasted about three months. Like the empress Zoe, she had been forced 'to seek strength in marriage'.

Alfonso the Battler deserved his nickname. Soon after the marriage with Urraca he was deeply involved in suppressing a rebellion in Galicia, where the local nobles who were guardians of Urraca's son Alfonso formed a nucleus of opposition. Alfonso the Battler conducted his campaign with all the usual brutalities of medieval warfare and was impervious to reproaches and pleas for mercy. When complaints were made that his Muslim troops had raped nuns in their churches, he supposedly replied, 'I do not care what my army and my fighters do.'[47] More dramatically yet, when a rebel knight, well known to Queen Urraca, fled to her seeking grace, and she wrapped her mantle and her arms around him as a sign of protection, Alfonso, 'like a savage barbarian', grabbed a spear and thrust it through him. Urraca decided to separate from her pitiless husband and made her way back to Leon.[48]

Alfonso the Battler was a man's man. A Muslim historian reports:

> No Christian ruler had more courage than him, more ardour to fight the Muslims without break, more power of resistance. He slept with his mail-coat and without a mattress; and when one day he was asked why he did not sleep with the daughters of the Muslim chiefs he captured, he said, 'A real soldier must live with men, not with women!'[49]

Whether he had slept with Urraca, we do not know. She supposedly complained that he regularly insulted her, struck her in the face and kicked her.[50] The marriage was now effectively ended, and the fact that Urraca and the Battler were closely related allowed the pope to declare an annulment on grounds of consanguinity. Alfonso, however, was not going to surrender his claims to Leonese and Castilian territory. By early 1113 Urraca was appealing for help against 'the Aragonese tyrant'.[51]

Urraca was now at war with both her husband and the supporters of her son. Adding to the family fun was the claim advanced by Urraca's illegitimate half-sister, Teresa. Like Urraca, Teresa had been married to an immigrant French noble, Henry of Burgundy, who had been endowed with a county in the west of the kingdom, a territory that included such important centres as Coimbra and Porto. Teresa had definite ambitions. A sceptical chronicler noted that, soon after the beginning of Urraca's reign, Teresa suggested to her husband that a division of the kingdom would be justified and, 'as is the custom of flattering tongues, this wife of the count was now called "queen" by her household and her knights'.[52] But the essence of being a queen is being called a queen, and the practice has to start somewhere, even if only in one's own home. By 1116, several years after the death of her husband Count Henry, it was not only her servants and retainers who were giving Teresa this pleasant distinction, for a papal letter of that year about a dispute between the bishops of Coimbra and Porto is addressed not only to the archbishop of Toledo but also to 'queen Teresa and her barons'.[53] From 1117 at the latest Teresa was calling herself queen in official documents. And of what was she queen? She was 'queen of Portugal', the name of her husband's county.[54] In this way, from the rivalry of squabbling sisters, a new country emerged on the European scene.[55] In the dynastic world, power-struggles within the family could leave a permanent imprint on political geography.

The problems of Urraca's reign do not appear to have discouraged other western European rulers from attempts at ensuring female succession. Indeed, less than ten months after Urraca's death, Henry I of England, a king just as domineering as Alfonso VI, demanded that his nobles accept his only surviving legitimate child, his daughter Matilda, as his heir.[56] She had been born after his accession, so was a western equivalent of a porphyrogenita. The oath the nobles swore on that occasion (Christmastide 1126), and which was subsequently renewed, did not prevent them ignoring their promise and accepting Henry's nephew Stephen as king after him, but it is unlikely that Urraca's example had much part to play in that choice. Like Alfonso VI, Henry I was willing to envisage a woman on his throne, and her supporters in the civil war that eventually flared up between her and Stephen obviously took the same position. But when Henry made his plans for his daughter, and had her recognized as his heir, he still expected her to marry at his command, both for political advantage and to produce a son to continue the dynasty. Her marriage, to Geoffrey of Anjou in 1128, at first looked as if it would be as rocky as that between Urraca and the Battler, with an early separation, but Matilda and Geoffrey were reconciled and produced three sons, one of whom became Henry II of England. She herself never attained the title 'queen', being only 'Lady of England', that is, uncrowned queen, although she preferred to call herself 'empress', referring to the status she had from her first husband, the Holy Roman Emperor. This is her title on the coins she issued during the civil war.[57] But, while she was never crowned queen, she maintained her cause through war, effectively ruling parts of England for most of Stephen's reign, and passed on her claim to her son Henry, who did eventually succeed to the throne.

And in the very years when Henry I of England was attempting to secure the succession of his daughter and arranging her marriage, exactly the same was happening at the other end of Latin Christendom, in the crusader kingdom of Jerusalem. Baldwin II, king of Jerusalem, had four daughters but no sons, and he determined that his eldest, Melisende, should succeed him.[58] She was in her early twenties and unmarried, so Baldwin saw his first duty as choosing a husband for her. He looked west, to the great princes of France, and in 1127, the year after Urraca's death and only months after the recognition of Matilda as heir to Henry I of England, he negotiated a marriage alliance with Fulk, count of Anjou. Fulk was the father of Geoffrey of Anjou, just mentioned. Fulk surrendered the county of Anjou to his son and went off to the east to marry Melisende, which he did in 1129.

Just as the *Historia Compostellana* is the main narrative source for Queen Urraca, so William of Tyre's *Chronicle* offers the most substantial contemporary comment on Queen Melisende. In his text, the exact status of Melisende's sovereignty is not always quite clear. In William's words, Fulk of Anjou had been promised that after his arrival in the East, 'the king's eldest daughter would be handed over to him with the prospect of the kingdom (*spes regni*) after the king's death.'[59] What exactly this 'prospect' was might of course be debated. Did it mean sole rule with his wife as consort, or would she be queen regnant and Fulk a king 'in right of his wife'? On his deathbed in 1131, King Baldwin summoned Melisende, his son-in-law Fulk, and their child, his baby grandson Baldwin, and 'handed over to them the care of the kingdom and full power'.[60] Three weeks later Fulk 'was solemnly and according to custom crowned and consecrated in the Church of the Holy Sepulchre along with his wife'.[61] The anodyne phrase 'along with his wife' is paralleled in William's description of what happened after the death of Fulk in 1143,

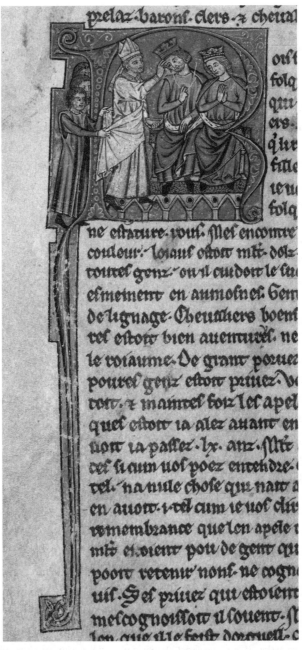

Figure 5 Melisende, queen of Jerusalem (1131–52/61), and her husband Fulk of Anjou. BL, MS Yates Thompson 12, fol. 82v, © The British Library.

when his son by Melisende, Baldwin III, was 'solemnly anointed, conse-crated and, along with his mother, crowned'.[62] Both phrases imply a joint ceremony of some kind, but leave many open questions. The joint rule of Melisende and her young son, if that is what it was, broke down as he entered his early twenties, when frivolous advisers, according to William of Tyre, told the young man that it was unworthy of a king 'that he should always dangle from his mother's breasts'.[63] It was 'shameful', they said, 'that he should be ruled by the will of a woman'.[64] The kingdom was first divided between them; but soon Baldwin besieged his mother in Jerusalem and forced her to retire to the city of Nablus, where she ended her days.

In the cases of Urraca, Matilda and Melisende, the pattern is clear: successful warrior kings of the early twelfth century were willing to champion their daughters as their heirs in the absence of sons, or legitimate sons, but expected them to have powerful husbands. Given that the right of female succession could be asserted as a general princi-ple, it was also clear that female rulers were expected to have a man. With her customary cogency, the late Marjorie Chibnall pointed out that in these cases, 'it was essential to bring in either a husband or a son as a nominal co-ruler'.[65] Alfonso VI told Urraca to follow the advice of his nobles, and their advice was to marry the king of neighbouring Aragon; Henry I married his daughter and heir to Geoffrey of Anjou, who indeed did later provide important military support for Matilda, while Baldwin of Jerusalem married his daughter and heir to Geoffrey's father Fulk, expecting him to bring military and monetary resources to the crusader kingdom. And both Geoffrey and Fulk also fathered sons through their royal brides.

There is not much evidence for how these ruling women viewed themselves. Charter terminology may give some hints, as in the way Matilda seems to have insisted on being styled 'empress', or Melisende's use of the 'by grace of God (*Dei gratia*)' formula, but more explicit and developed images of these queens or would-be queens can only be found in contemporary chronicles, all written by men, either clergy or monks. What we find there cannot be expected to yield a self-image but rather a view of the female ruler from outside, not without its interest despite that.

During her seventeen-year reign Urraca had to fight and negotiate without respite, sometimes in alliance with her son, sometimes in opposition to him, almost always struggling with her half-sister, although gradually less troubled by her battling ex-husband, who, however, retained some important territories in Castile, notably the major centre of Burgos. But heads that wear the crown are often uneasy. Is there any evidence that there was anything different about her reign *because* she was female? Urraca had determined opponents, some of whom made a point of the fact that she was a woman. A Spanish chronicle written soon after her death reports that 'she reigned for seventeen years *tirannice et muliebriter* — tyrannously and like a woman', adding the detail that she died giving birth to a child born of adultery.[66] This is actually not impossible, for the *Historia Compostellana* reports that Urraca had both sons and daughters with her lover, the count of Lara,[67] and the chronicler Orderic Vitalis, writing in Normandy little more than a decade after Urraca's death, also claims that she died in childbirth. His comments on the queen are disapproving. He calls her war against her husband a rebellion, and says she was the cause of destruction to many, and that her death was 'at God's command'.[68]

The author of the *Historia Compostellana*, the fullest contemporary source, describes how Urraca, after being on good terms with bishop Diego Gelmírez, was persuaded by evil counsellors to plan his arrest. 'A woman's mind', the chronicler reflects, 'is weak and unstable and quickly wanders, as is written: Better is the wickedness of a man than a woman who does good.'[69] The last line is a quotation from the book of *Ecclesiasticus*, which has a claim to be the most misogynistic book in the Bible. Later he returns to the attack.

> What does woman's fury not dare to do? What does the cunning of the serpent not presume? What does the most wicked viper not attack? The example of Eve, our first parent, informs us well enough what female creatures dare, presume and attack. Woman's most audacious mind rushes to the forbidden; it violates the holy and confounds right and wrong.[70]

Monastic and clerical opponents of the queen thus wheeled out standard misogyny. There is nothing surprising about that.

Positive evaluation of these queens avoided simple misogyny – women are wicked and fickle – by embracing its more complex twin – women can rise above their natural wickedness and fickleness. William of Tyre's praise of Melisende, which is frequent and warm, stresses the way that she transcended her sex: 'The mother was a most wise woman, with great experience of almost all secular business, overcoming the condition of the female sex so completely that she could set her hand to great deeds.'[71] He describes how she undertook the care of the kingdom 'energetically and fortunately, transcending female power and spirit', although also 'with the advice of the chief men of the region'.[72] When talking of her government, he uses the straightforward vocabulary of rule: 'she ruled the kingdom, she had ruled the kingdom (*regnum . . . rexit, regnum . . . rexerat*)'.[73] Writing of her last illness, William says she had ruled the kingdom for more than thirty years, thus clearly referring to the time between the death of her father in 1131 and her own in 1161 or 1162, including the years after 1152, when her rule had in fact been confined to the city of Nablus. She was 'a resourceful woman, wise beyond the female sex', and 'transcending female power'.[74]

William of Tyre's comments can be compared with those of St Bernard, who wrote to Melisende on the occasion of the death of her husband Fulk and encouraged her in her difficult situation, a widowed mother of a young son. 'The eyes of all are on you', he wrote.

> It is necessary that you set your hand to hard things[75] and show the man in the woman. You must administer everything with such prudence and moderation that all who see you will judge from your deeds that you are a king rather than a queen. But, you will say, I am inadequate for this task. These tasks are the tasks of a man, but I am a woman, weak in body, unstable of heart, neither wise in counsel nor accustomed to business.[76]

Whether Melisende would say anything of the kind is doubtful. But, like William of Tyre, or like Psellos on the empress Theodora, Bernard envisaged Melisende's responsibilities as requiring male rather than female qualities. Matilda, too, was commended in this way. An epitaph written after her death in 1167 praises the empress for 'having nothing of the woman (*nil mulieris habens*)'.[77] Praise indeed!

What may also be significant is that there seems to have been no, or virtually no, opposition to the succession of Urraca, Matilda and Melisende explicitly on the grounds that they were female. Alfonso VI, Urraca's father, was willing to designate her as his successor, although it may be relevant that Urraca came to the throne already the mother of a male child, and accepting the rule of a woman with a living male heir may have been easier for a male aristocracy, because they could picture a future king. What seems to have brought the kingdom into crisis was not the succession of a woman but the imposition on her of an ill-chosen husband, the Battler. This opened up the rivalry of factions, each with a regional base: the Galicia of her son's supporters, the Portugal of her half-sister. Urraca's reign was not a model, but it can hardly be interpreted as a warning against female rule.

Modern historians, including the present writer, have often said that one objection to Matilda's succession was that she was a woman.[78] In fact there is little contemporary evidence for anyone taking this position. There were plenty of other objections to Matilda, or, at least, justifications for opposing her. Some of Stephen's supporters argued that the oath they had sworn to her had been extorted by force; some that Henry I had changed his mind on his death-bed; some that Henry's marriage was 'incestuous', in the medieval sense, since the king's wife had earlier been a nun, and so Matilda had no right of succession; some that Matilda's marriage to Geoffrey of Anjou, made without their consent, cancelled their earlier oath to her.[79] None of this concerns simply her sex. The only time there is mention of this is in a letter of Gilbert Foliot, abbot of Gloucester at the time, and one of Matilda's supporters, who is undertaking to refute the arguments of Stephen's party. He writes that some might object that 'royal sceptres, which suit a son, ought not to be given to a daughter'.[80] He dismisses this idea by citing an Old Testament passage in which God himself upheld inheritance by daughters in the absence of sons.[81] He also emphasizes the natural affection that parents have for their children, both male and female, and defends King Henry's designation of Matilda as his heir on the grounds of divine, natural and human law. But this discussion forms only one part of Abbot Gilbert's argument and is an isolated case. The barons of Norman England were perfectly familiar with female inheritance and did not really require much analysis of it. Between the Norman Conquest of 1066 and 1150 thirty baronies had descended through the female line, and the respondent in one of the most famous cases from twelfth-century England argued simply that 'a daughter is to be preferred to a nephew in cases of a parental inheritance'.[82] In the case of Matilda, her illegitimate half-brother Robert of Gloucester not only recognized her right but became the chief and most loyal supporter of her cause, although her cousin Stephen, nephew of Henry I through the maternal line, obviously did not!

These three active and powerful women, Urraca, Matilda and Melisende, were recognized as heirs to their fathers' kingdoms (the word heiress is a seventeenth-century novelty). An eye-witness account tells how Alfonso VI 'left the lordship of his kingdom to the lady Urraca, his daughter'.[83] Urraca herself constantly stressed her descent, styling herself in her charters most often 'Urraca, by grace of God, queen of Spain, daughter of king Alfonso', and sometimes dating them 'when the lady queen Urraca was ruling in the kingdom of her father'.[84] She never ceased to emphasize her parentage, appearing in a charter the year before her death as 'the lady queen Urraca ... daughter of the lord king Alfonso of worthy memory'.[85] Likewise, when, at Christmastide 1126 Henry I of England insisted that, if he had no sons in the future, his bishops and barons should recognize his daughter Matilda as his successor, 'they solemnly promised the king's daughter, pledging their faith and swearing an oath, that, if she survived her father, they would defend the whole kingdom of the English for her against everyone'.[86] After Henry's death Matilda described herself as 'rightful heir to the kingdom of England'.[87] In a document of 1129 Melisende is referred to as 'the daughter of the king and the heir to the kingdom of Jerusalem'.[88] In these cases, therefore, the female sovereign's right to rule was being asserted as a right of inheritance as a daughter, a right that was seen, in the case of Matilda, as greater than the right of either illegitimate sons or male collaterals such as nephews. As with Zoe and Theodora, the claims of Urraca, Matilda and Melisende were conceived of as the claims of heirs. But, unlike Zoe and Theodora, these western female rulers were expected to marry early enough to produce heirs of their own and transmit their claims to them.

The Later Middle Ages

As mentioned, a provisional list of medieval female sovereigns contains twenty-seven names.[89] The three Byzantine examples occur in the late eighth/early ninth century and in the eleventh century. In Latin Christendom there were seven ruling queens in the course of the twelfth century, beginning with Urraca, but only three in the thirteenth. Then the later Middle Ages sees seven in the fourteenth century, seven again in the fifteenth. A high point of a sort occurs in the 1380s, a decade during which Naples, Sicily, Hungary, Poland and Portugal all had sovereign queens, while at this same time the three Scandinavian kingdoms were ruled by Margaret, who seems never to have borne the title 'queen' except as queen consort but who had all the other trappings of sovereignty – the queen of Denmark who acceded in 1972 clearly thought her medieval predecessor was a genuine sovereign since she chose to style herself 'Margaret II'.

There is a geographical pattern. Of these twenty-seven queens and empresses regnant, twenty-four were from Mediterranean and Iberian realms. The other three comprised one from Scandinavia, if we include Margaret, and two from eastern Europe, all three of these in the late fourteenth century. In recent times, for some reason, European monarchy has had its most solid base in the mainly Protestant social democracies of northern Europe: Scandinavia, the Low Countries and Britain. Several monarchs of these countries have been female. Indeed, the Netherlands was ruled by queens from 1890 to 2013. Meanwhile, Mediterranean monarchy disappeared in the twentieth century, with the unusual exception of Spain, where it was restored by Franco in 1975. The pattern in the Middle Ages, with its strong tradition of female sovereigns in the Mediterranean region, was clearly different. It does not seem to be the case that the contrast reflects a difference in the rules of inheritance of landed property, and it remains a clear geographical pattern without an obvious explanation.

Although it appears there were only three female sovereigns in the thirteenth century, this does not mean that there was a tide of opinion against female rule at that time. In the later centuries of the Middle Ages, as it became more common for rules about royal succession to be set out formally in documents, these rules often explicitly envisage women succeeding as sovereigns. In the negotiations of 1255 about the marriage of the daughter of Alfonso X of Castile, her right to succeed, if the king were to have no sons, was explicitly recognized (see above, p. 101), and the king's law-code, the *Siete Partidas,* was also clear on the subject: 'wise and learned men ordained that if there was no son, the eldest daughter should inherit the kingdom'.[90] In 1265, when Pope Clement IV bestowed the kingdom of Sicily upon Charles of Anjou with the intention of rooting out the last of the Hohenstaufen dynasty, which ruled Sicily at this time, the terms and conditions were spelled out carefully, including the rules of succession. Charles' throne could be inherited by males or females, although preference would be given to sons over daughters. If there were no sons and several daughters, the eldest daughter would succeed, for the kingdom could not be divided. In the case of a ruler of Sicily dying without children, a brother or sister, or an uncle or aunt, could inherit. Female inheritance was thus written into the dynastic structure of the kingdom.[91] Likewise, when Pope Martin IV bestowed the kingdom of Aragon upon a son of the king of France in 1283, he specified that 'if he happens to be survived only by children of the female sex, the oldest of them shall succeed'.[92] As it turned out, this attempt to impose a French prince on Aragon was a disastrous failure, but the recognition of the principle of female succession is just as clear and as explicit as in the case of Sicily. In the following year, 1284, Margaret, 'the Maid of Norway', was recognized as 'the right heir' of her grandfather Alexander III of Scotland,[93] and was expected to become queen of Scotland after his death two years later, although she died at sea on her way from Norway to Scotland in 1290, aged only seven. She was almost never styled 'queen' by the Scots, simply 'Lady of Scotland', just as the empress Matilda was 'Lady of England', that is, uncrowned queen (see above, p. 135).[94] In that very same year, 1290, Edward I of England ordained that his eldest daughter Eleanor should succeed to the kingdom if his son, or any future sons, died without heirs; if Eleanor died without heirs, her younger sister would succeed.[95] These five cases, from Castile, Sicily, Aragon, Scotland and England, did not immediately result in female sovereigns, although the kingdom of Sicily was eventually to have memorable queens regnant, but they do underline the fact that female inheritance of the throne was perfectly conceivable in the minds of thirteenth-century popes, kings and nobles.

It is also certain, however, that these ruling women were expected to have suitable husbands, who might well bear the royal title. In the kingdom of Sicily, the pope ruled, that 'if, in the absence of males, an unmarried female should succeed to the kingdom, she should be married to a person who is suitable for the rule and defence of the realm, after the advice of the Roman pontiff has been obtained'.[96] In the crusader kingdom of Jerusalem men often obtained royal power through marriage to a sovereign queen. Sybilla, daughter of Amalric I, married William of Montferrat, but he died after only a year of marriage, leaving her pregnant with the future, and short-lived, Baldwin V. She married again, to Guy of Lusignan, and, when she inherited the throne in 1186, she crowned him too. Guy used the royal title as 'eighth king' of Jerusalem and kept it for a while even after Sybilla's death in 1190. But the right to the throne now passed to Isabella, Sybilla's younger sister. Isabella married four times, to Humphrey of Toron in 1183, then to Conrad of Montferrat in 1190, after a semi-coerced divorce from Humphrey. Conrad did not take the title king but called himself 'king elect' in a charter of May 1191. The daughter of Isabella and Conrad, Maria, was born that year. After Conrad's murder in 1192, just before his planned coronation, Isabella took a third husband, Henry of Champagne. He was not styled 'king' but is called 'lord of the land of Jerusalem' in some documents. After he died in 1197, Isabella married Amalric (Aimery) of Lusignan, king of Cyprus, brother of Guy of Lusignan, her former brother-in-law. Isabella and Amalric were crowned in 1198, and she is then called queen, and he styled himself 'ninth king' of Jerusalem, therefore ignoring both Conrad of Montferrat and Henry of Champagne. He died in 1205, she soon afterwards, leaving as her heir her daughter Maria. Maria brought the throne to her husband John of Brienne, and it passed after her early death to her daughter Isabella, who brought it to her husband, Emperor Frederick II. Four successive ruling queens of Jerusalem had thus brought the royal title to their husbands.

In the 1380s eastern Europe had its first female rulers. Louis the Great, king of Hungary and Poland, died in 1382, leaving daughters but no sons. His elder daughter Mary inherited the kingdom of

Hungary, while the younger, Hedwig or Jadwiga, was accepted by the Polish nobility as their ruler on condition that she married Jagiello, prince of Lithuania, who had to convert to Christianity to marry her. In this way the last pagan state in Europe was brought into Christendom and the Polish–Lithuanian union came into being. In Hungary, some of the novelty of the situation, and perhaps also the difficulty her Hungarian subjects had in conceptualizing the unfamiliar role of female sovereign, is revealed in Mary's title. The Venetian chancellor, always keeping an eye on Venice's giant neighbour Hungary, reported the young queen's accession, under the regency of her mother Elizabeth: 'Queen Elizabeth, wife of king Louis, along with Mary her daughter, took up the reins of government in Hungary. This Mary was called "king of Hungary".' He goes on to discuss the events in the early years of 'King Mary'.[97] This style is confirmed by the reports of the Hungarian chronicler John of Thurocz: 'all the common people agreed to call this maiden "king"'. After the challenge to her rule by her kinsman Charles of Durazzo had been repressed, Mary's supporters 'gathered in the streets shouting, "King Mary rules!"'. John of Thurocz himself terms Mary 'the female king'.[98]

The Exclusion of Women from Rule

But although female rule was certainly conceivable, it was not always embraced. The most famous case of the exclusion of women from inheritance to the throne occurred in late medieval France. After a remarkable eleven generations of father–son succession, the death of Louis X in 1316, leaving a daughter by his first wife and a pregnant second wife, placed the French monarchy in an unprecedented situation. Louis' wife did indeed give birth to a male child but he lived only five days. This raised the question of female succession for the first time. If female succession were permissible, then Louis' daughter Joanna was clearly the heir. But she was young, about four years old, and, since her mother, the king's first wife, had been convicted of adultery, there were doubts about her paternity.[99] Worse than all this, Joanna had uncles. One of these, her maternal uncle the duke of Burgundy, did seek to protect her rights, which coincided with his own interests, but her paternal uncles,

Philip and Charles, the younger brothers of Louis X, saw her simply as an obstacle. Writing of these uncles, the great French medievalist Robert Fawtier judged that they 'may have been good fathers, good sons, good husbands, and perhaps even good brothers, but they certainly qualified for the title of wicked uncles'.[100] Joanna's uncle Philip, who had already been appointed regent, moved quickly and ruthlessly to exclude his little niece. The posthumous baby son of Louis X, known as John I, had been born and died in November 1316. On the following 9 January Philip was crowned, as Philip V, in Rheims, the traditional coronation site of the French monarchy. One chronicler describes this, tellingly, as happening 'in the presence of the great men and peers of the kingdom (although not all of them)'.[101] Within four weeks a large assembly was held to ratify this act, the masters of the University of Paris adding their approval. 'Then also', says a contemporary chronicler, 'it was declared that a woman could not succeed to the crown of the kingdom of France.'[102]

This general statement was clearly fashioned to justify the wicked uncle's coup. The issue of female succession had not in fact arisen in the previous history of the kingdom, because of reproductive chance. Now the exclusion of women became a general principle, and was applied again in 1322, when Philip's own daughters were excluded, and in 1328, when a male cousin was preferred to the daughters of kings. On this last occasion, one issue at law was whether a woman could transmit a claim even if she could not herself rule. If she could, Edward III of England would become king of France, if not, then Philip of Valois would succeed. Learned lawyers were consulted, but, as a contemporary chronicler makes clear, it was not only law that mattered: the French lawyers, 'not bearing it with equanimity to be subject to the rule of the English', denied the right of a woman to transmit a claim.[103] Later, the French royal ordinance of August 1374 about royal minorities simply assumes male succession.[104]

At first there was no mention of the roots or basis of this rule, but during the century after the compliant assembly summoned by Philip V there appeared the claim that the exclusion of women was actually based on the ancient Salian or Salic Law of the Franks. Some cooking of texts was necessary for this to have any plausibility, but texts can be cooked. Although there are isolated references to the Salic Law in royalist discussions of the second half of the fourteeth century, it was the work of Jean de Montreuil in 1413 that was really significant. This was because he took a clause of the Salic Law, which deals with the exclusion of females from the right to inherit a particular kind of private property and augments it with two words which are not in the text: 'A woman shall have no share *in regno* – in the kingdom.'[105] Thereafter Salic Law became a kind of shorthand term for the exclusion of females from succession, or, yet more restrictive, even the transmission of a claim to succession through the female line. In the age of the Hundred Years War, when the English kings claimed the French throne on exactly this basis, the political point was clear.[106] This is one of the most obvious cases of an ancient law or custom being invented to meet pressing contemporary political needs. Women were not excluded from the throne of France because of the Salic Law, rather the Salic Law was dug up and doctored because women were excluded from the throne of France.

After this political choice had been made at the beginning of the fourteenth century, arguments for the exclusion of women from French royal succession could be elaborated. There was indeed virtually a literary genre on the topic in the late Middle Ages.[107] Of these many tracts, one of the most influential is known by its opening words as *Pour ce que plusieurs*.[108] This was written in 1464 and is bold in its assertion that the Salic Law, which was the first law of the Franks, going back to 'the time when the French still lived on the banks of the Rhine',[109] unequivocally prohibited women from inheriting royal power. But the author is not content simply to appeal to ancient law. The exclusion of women from sovereign power can be supported by other arguments. God had commanded women to be subject to men. As God said to Eve in Genesis 3: 16, 'you will be under the power of the man and he will be your lord'.[110] And women should not have the power to hear criminal cases and condemn people to death 'because their thoughts and their judgments could be a little too sudden (*un pou trop soudains*)'.[111] Or a queen might marry a low-born man, or an enemy of the kingdom, and, in such cases, there was almost certain to be civil war. Moreover, the custom of the Ile-de-France is that, if there are only daughters, the estate should be divided among them, so, if women were allowed to inherit, and the king of France had fifteen daughters, France would be divided into fifteen.[112] The author concedes that 'great and notable things' had been done by past queens of France, but these queens were widows and mothers of kings, not queens by hereditary right.[113] And these are not all of his arguments. It is, of course, an old and wise piece of advice, that if someone gives you more than one reason for something, you should never believe them. The author of *Pour ce que plusieurs* does not enhance his case by multiplying his points. But what is perhaps worth pointing out is that his misogyny is mild, conventional and can hardly be regarded as the animating principle of his text. He has to justify the exclusion of women from succession, or transmitting the right to succeed, because by his time the French royal dynasty was founded on that rule, and this rule (so-called) in its turn sprang from the political circumstances of 1316 and 1328.

In other situations, in other kingdoms, where general objections to female rule were made, often a closer analysis suggests that the real argument on these occasions was not 'we do not want a woman to rule us' but 'we do not want *this* woman to rule us', or, perhaps, 'we do not want this woman, with this husband, to rule us'. This certainly seems to have been important in the opposition to Matilda, who was not only daughter of Henry I of England but also the wife of Count Geoffrey of Anjou, a figure who was at best distant and at worst hostile in the eyes of the Anglo-Norman barons. Some contemporary chronicles did indeed speak as if Henry I viewed Geoffrey of Anjou as a future king of England, one writing that Henry I agreed that, after his death, if he had no legitimate son, 'his son-in-law would succeed him in the kingdom'.[114] Another, writing of the time after Henry's death, when Geoffrey and Matilda were fighting Stephen, notes '*husband and wife* were claiming England'.[115] Another tells how, after Henry's death, Geoffrey 'aspired to the sceptre of the kingdom across the sea'.[116]

Again, after the death of William II of Sicily in 1189, his nearest legitimate relative, his aunt Constance, was passed over in favour of his illegitimate cousin Tancred (see the discussion below, pp. 170–1). According to one contemporary, the issue here was not Constance's sex but her husband:

> The illegitimate Tancred succeeded, by the judgment and election of the
> chief men, who all rejected German authority, for Constance, the dead

king's aunt, who appeared to have the right to succeed him, had married Henry, the son of the German emperor Frederick.[117]

Likewise, a few years later, in 1195, when William the Lion, king of Scots, lay ill and wanted to arrange for the succession by having his eldest daughter Margaret recognized as queen, and a marriage arranged between her and the German prince Otto of Brunswick, a group of Scottish nobles declared

> they would not accept his daughter as queen, because it was not the custom of the kingdom that a woman should have the kingdom while there was a brother or nephew in his lineage who was able to have the kingdom by right.[118]

The general statement of custom here, however, may well conceal a more specific and personal objection to having Otto, a nephew of Richard the Lionheart of England, as king of Scots. Just like the chief men of Sicily, they resisted the prospect of having a powerful German ruler foisted on them. In this they were successful, unlike the nobles of Sicily who found out just how powerful and ruthless Henry, Constance's husband, was, when he conquered the kingdom of Sicily and established his Hohenstaufen dynasty on the throne for the next seventy years.

In 1406 the English Parliament turned an amazing somersault on the issue, excluding female heirs in June and reinstating them in December. The 'Act for the Inheritance of the Crown' of 7 June declared that Henry IV's eldest son, Henry (later Henry V), was heir apparent; if Henry died without a son, the throne would then pass to his next brother; if that brother died without a son, it would go to the third brother, and so on. Any daughters were to be ignored, although they could inherit the Duchy of Lancaster, which Henry IV had held before his usurpation of the throne and was now in the hands of his son. Six months later, on 22 December, this was reversed, because, as the king put it, 'a statute and ordinance of this kind, by excluding the female sex, restricted too much the right of succession of our sons and their children'.[119]

Apart from these very specific political situations, the issue of female succession was sometimes discussed in abstract and general terms. In the scriptural and scholastic world of medieval debate, this involved the citation of proof texts, passages from authoritative works, especially the Bible, that could be considered to support one side or the other of an argument. As mentioned above (p. 141), when he was writing in support of Matilda's claim to the English throne, Gilbert Foliot, abbot of Gloucester, cited from the Old Testament. The biblical passage he invoked is from the Book of Numbers and concerns the daughters of Zelophehad (Salphaad in the Vulgate), whose father had died without sons. The daughters consult Moses who in turn consults God, who declares, 'When a man dies without a son, his inheritance shall pass to his daughter' (Numbers 27: 8). This obviously vindicated the *principle* of female inheritance and could be brought up when expedient.

The passage was invoked, for example, in an illuminated parchment roll glorifying Edward IV of England, who had deposed his distant cousin Henry VI in 1461. Henry was descended from the third son of Edward III (1327–77), Edward from the second, but through females, and hence his claim to the throne rested on acceptance that the right of inheritance could pass through daughters in the absence of sons. The roll includes a family tree of the English royal dynasty showing all this, and identifying Henry VI's grandfather, Henry IV, as the usurper who had robbed Edward's line of the throne. The figure of Moses is portrayed, pointing accusingly at Henry IV and saying, 'By the law divinely given to the daughters of Zelophehad, you are proved to be the usurper of the rights of the lawful heir.'[120]

A rather curious example of the use of this biblical passage is the appeal in verse by the men of Cork to the men of Dublin in 1487, after the latter had recognized the pretender Lambert Simnel, a challenger to Henry VII. This brings in these daughters of Zelophehad to defend Henry VII's right to the throne, for Henry's claim was unambiguously through the female line:

> Moses had of God, by commaundement,
> If a man died without issue male
> His lands should, by lyniall discent,
> Descend to daughters, his heires generall.

The men of Cork appeal to the men of Dublin:

O Dublin! Dublin! Where be the jurours,
Thy noble men of aureat glorie?

And they provide their authority:

... Ye may read this story
Of Sulphact (Zelophehad) his daughters in the booke of Numery.[121]

('Numery' is an old form of Numbers, and here is rhymed with 'story'). It is a striking example of how biblically based argument of this type could reach far beyond the world of Latin learning.

One significant development occurred in the thinking of theorists on the topic of female inheritance. Those who wished to assert that women could not succeed to kingdoms had no desire to extend this exclusion to fiefs and estates within kingdoms, and would find customary law against them if they tried to do so. Hence, they distinguished the rules governing succession to the throne and those governing inheritance of fiefs and estates. This is what we find, for example, in the views of François de Meyronnes, a Franciscan from Provence, a disciple of Duns Scotus. Among many other, more demanding, theological works, he produced an anthology of extracts from Augustine's *City of God*, and this is where the issue of female inheritance crops up. Augustine mentions the old Roman Lex Voconia, a law of 169 BC that prohibited wealthy Romans from making women their heirs. Augustine condemns it in strong terms: 'I do not know what could be thought or said more iniquitous than such a law.'[122] François de Meyronnes cites Augustine's condemnation of the Lex Voconia, and then adds his own comments. A supporting argument for Augustine's hostile attitude to the law, he says, is the passage in Numbers in which the daughters of Zelophehad claim the right to inherit from their father, in the absence of sons, and are given permission to do so by the explicit authority of God. Moreover, he continues, 'by natural law a father is obligated to any one of his children more than to a stranger'.[123] Hence he has patristic, scriptural and natural arguments for female inheritance.

Then, having established this point, François de Meyronnes, in good scholastic style, moves to the arguments for the opposite case. The chief of these is empirical, based simply on what is the case: 'But doubt arises

152

why in kingdoms where the rulership is hereditary women usually do not succeed?'[124] He explains this by a distinction: 'a kingdom is not only an inheritance but also an office that concerns the whole state' and women 'are not entitled to office as they are to an inheritance'.[125] This is an important distinction, and one that would eventually undermine the dynastic system itself. Rule of the state is one thing; the transmission of private property another. François de Meyronnes does not use the words 'private' and 'public' here, but those are terms that would spring to modern minds when considering his distinction between an 'inheritance' and an 'office', although one should note that he says 'a kingdom is *not only* an inheritance', implying that it is an inheritance. A slightly later author who does couch the discussion in terms of 'private' and 'public' is the Dominican Thomas Waleys, in his commentary on Augustine's *City of God*, a work which survives in more than seventy manuscripts. He notes Augustine's view that the Lex Voconia was unjust, but adds, 'it seems truly iniquitous as far as private persons are concerned although it could be reasonable as far as public persons, such as kings and rulers, are concerned'.[126] He then moves on to the daughters of Zelophehad, but has made an important distinction: exclusion of women may be unjust when it is a matter of private inheritance but just when public persons and rule of the state are concerned. By the time the French apologists for the exclusion of females from the throne of France were elaborating their case, they could cite François de Meyronnes and Thomas Waleys, as well as pointing out the parallel between the Lex Voconia and the Salic Law.[127] A basic difference between private property and public office had been clearly formulated.

Despite this development in France, most kingdoms in medieval Latin Christendom experienced the rule of a female sovereign, once or more than once. In some cases, it might be purely accidental that it did not. England, for example, could well have had a Queen Matilda in the twelfth century. The fact that John of Gaunt, son of Edward III, was unsuccessful when he supposedly tried to induce the English Parliament, 'following the example of the French, to pass a law debarring a woman from being heir to the kingdom', shows that there can have been no assumption that women were debarred.[128] In France, as has been discussed, the exclusion of women was late, and explained entirely by the circumstances of one particular political crisis. Only in the Holy Roman Empire, where monarchy was elective, and continued to be elective despite all attempts to establish hereditary dynasties, was the exclusion of women structural, one might even say constitutional: if the nobles had the right to choose a ruler, they would not choose a woman. No one can deny the patriarchal nature of medieval Europe, but, from Byzantium to Scotland, from Leon to Poland, it was not without its windows and opportunities for female sovereigns.

CHAPTER 5

Mistresses and Bastards

Concubines

I N HIS STUDY OF DYNASTIC SYSTEMS ACROSS THE WORLD DURING the late Middle Ages and Early Modern period, Jeroen Duindam contrasted the harem system, in which the sovereign kept numbers of women for himself (often in seclusion and served by eunuchs), and their numerous children might all be potential claimants to succeed to the throne, with the system established in medieval Europe, where the Church upheld monogamy as a principle and when married rulers slept with women other than their wife it was deemed adultery. He goes on: 'Royal adultery, not uncommon in most dynasties and an acclaimed practice in some, created two characters absent in harem-based reproduction: the mistress and the bastard.'[1]

This is an acute and memorable formulation, and a good description of the contrast between the dynastic world of late medieval Christian Europe and that of, say, the Ottoman or imperial Chinese courts, but it is important to remember that the sharp contrast between harems and (official) monogamy was not so sharp earlier in the Middle Ages, or in some parts of Christian Europe. This is because at that time, or in those places, rulers often had acknowledged female sexual partners who had a status somewhere between a casual lover and a fully legitimate wife. Among writers in Latin, the usual term for such a partner was 'concubine' (*concubina*).

An example from the Carolingian period illustrates some features of the institution of concubinage. In October 869 the Frankish ruler Charles the Bald, having been informed of the death of his wife, took the noblewoman

Richildis 'as his concubine'. In January 870, just a few months later, 'he espoused her, gave her a dowry and took her as his wife'.[2] One can conclude a few things from this: a concubine and a wife had recognized, and different, statuses; a marriage ceremony (*desponsatio*) and a dowry were crucial elements in distinguishing the two;[3] and a concubine could be noble. It is also worth pointing out that this account, written by an archbishop, shows no overt signs of moral disapproval of Charles' actions.[4]

Concubines had been a common and recognized part of both ancient Greek and ancient Roman society. Justinian's *Digest*, the sixth-century compendium of Roman Law, mentions the term 'concubine' some forty times and even has a separate section 'On Concubines'. From these references, it is clear that concubines were systematically distinguished from wives (*uxores*) and concubinage distinguished from marriage (*nuptiae, matrimonium*). They also demonstrate that many concubines were former slaves, but that it was possible for a concubine to become a wife. The legal rulings sometimes throw a little light on social realities: we hear of concubines accused of theft, concubines becoming the concubine of their former lover's son, rules that concubines had to be at least twelve, prohibitions on taking a niece as a concubine, acceptance that officials sent to the provinces could take a local woman as a concubine, rules about bequests to concubines, concubines who were given the clothes of former concubines. A concubine may have been 'she who is in the house in the place of a wife but without marriage', but these references show that she would definitely know she was not a wife.[5]

In the early Middle Ages, Christian writers and ecclesiastical authorities expressed disquiet about concubines, and ruled that men who kept them could not be promoted to the higher ranks of holy orders, but the campaign against concubinage was hardly sustained or zealous. The great canon law collection of the twelfth century, Gratian's *Decretum*, contains the rulings: 'He who does not have a wife and has a concubine instead should not be barred from communion, but he should be content to be joined to just one woman, either a wife or a concubine' and 'I would not say that it is licit for a Christian to have several women or even two women at the same time, but one only, either a wife, or, if there is no wife, a concubine instead.'[6] There is nothing here to suggest outrage at the prospect of a laity happily cohabiting with women not their wives. The tone is quite different from the, sometimes

156

hysterical, note to be found in the utterances of clerical and monastic authorities about 'incest', that is, marriage between cousins.

Perhaps the low temperature of the churchmen on this subject may be linked to the fact that early medieval rulers, and, in some parts of Europe, rulers well into the later centuries of the Middle Ages, took concubinage for granted. These concubines were not necessarily the counterparts of the low-born concubine envisaged by Roman Law, who might have been a slave, who could conceivably be inherited by the master's son and who was expected to tolerate being decked out in a previous concubine's dresses. Merovingian kings had both wives and concubines, sometimes numbers of them. Of Dagobert I it was said:

> He was given to lust beyond measure and had three women as queens and many concubines. These were the queens: Nantechildis, Wulfegundis and Berchildis. It would increase the length of this chronicle too much to insert the names of the concubines, because there were so many.[7]

The four sons of Theuderic II were all born from concubines. One of them was the boy king Sigebert II.

The Merovingians recognized all sons of kings, not just those born of wives: 'those who are born of kings are called the children of kings, regardless of who their mother is'.[8] Their successors, the Carolingians, changed this. They continued to have concubines but their children were generally excluded from succession. This narrowed the field. Thus Charlemagne, who had twenty children by nine or ten different women, did not leave a succession crisis on his death but was succeeded by his only surviving legitimate son, Louis the Pious. And, when the emperor Louis the Pious made arrangements for his own successors in 817, he explicitly excluded 'children born from concubines'.[9] In other societies, like early Ireland, the sons of kings by women other than their wives ('concubines') would not have accepted their exclusion so peacefully. And in some parts of Europe the Merovingian approach continued. A commentator of the late twelfth century noted that 'the custom of the kingdom of Norway until today is that anyone who is known to be the son of a king of Norway, even if he is illegitimate and born of a servant girl, can claim as much right to the kingdom of Norway as a son of the king's wife born of a free woman'.[10] Jan Rüdiger pointed to the parallel: 'In fact the Norway of the sagas followed the view of the Merovingians, that the father's blood was enough to transmit eligibility to the throne.'[11]

While the Merovingians sometimes took slaves as their wives, the Carolingians usually sought high-born women as their concubines, such as Liutswind, concubine of Carloman, son of Louis the German, whose child was Arnulf, 'born of a most noble woman but one not legally married to him', or the unnamed concubine of Carloman's brother Louis, described as 'a concubine of extremely high birth'.[12] Not all Carolingian concubines were of this status, however. The wife of the emperor Lothar died on 20 March 851; less than a month later, on 19 April, Lothar granted her freedom to his slave mistress Doda, by whom he had a son with the royal name of Carloman.[13] The average age at marriage of the Carolingian kings of the ninth century was twenty-five, well after sexual maturity, and they commonly had concubines before marriage.[14]

The chroniclers of the early dukes of Normandy distinguished the sexual partnerships of these rulers as being either 'in the Danish way (*Danico more*)' or 'in the Christian way (*Christiano more*)'.[15] One of these chroniclers, Robert of Torigny, writing in the abbey of Bec in the 1130s, tells how Duke Richard I had several children by his countess, Gunnor, but that when he wanted to appoint one of them as archbishop of Rouen, he was told 'this could in no way be, according to the decrees of the canons, because his mother had not been married'. The duke responded by uniting with Gunnor 'in the Christian way'. During the ceremony, they and their children were draped symbolically in a cloak, and, with everything righted, their son could become archbishop.[16] What is being applied here is the canon law principle that subsequent marriage legitimized the children. Whether it was actually applied in 989, when the event supposedly occurred, or is a retrospective piece of imagination by Robert of Torigni, it is not possible to say for certain.[17] But the distinction between unions in the Danish way and in the Christian way seems to parallel the distinction between concubine and wife. The Burgundian chronicler Ralph Glaber, who died in the 1040s, noted that Norman dukes were born of concubines, but pointed out the good precedents for this: several of the children of the patriarch Jacob, as well as the first Christian emperor, Constantine, were born of concubines.[18]

It is not always easy to ascertain whether a woman was regarded as a wife or a concubine. Charles Martel's mother was called both 'wife' and 'concubine' in the medieval sources, and modern historians continue to disagree about her status.[19] Cases of Carolingian concubines becoming wives may include Pippin III's Bertrada, Louis the Pious' Ermengard and Louis II's Angilberga.[20] Indeed, when chroniclers classify women as either ruler's wives or their concubines, they may be making choices that have nothing to do with the status of these women in fact. As Sylvia Konecny observed, 'the success or failure of a woman's sons or the partisan position of a chronicler often determined whether a woman would be described as a concubine or a wife'.[21] Nevertheless, the distinction existed, and could have political consequences, especially for inheritance (see below, pp. 166–8).

To classify a woman as a concubine could be a hostile act or it could be a simple statement of fact in a world where concubinage was a recognized status. The Latin word *pelex* was used less often than *concubina* and usually with a negative implication. In the interminable dispute involving Lothar II of Lotharingia and his two women, Teutberga and Waldrada, those who championed Teutberga as Lothar's lawful wife and queen frequently labelled Waldrada a *pelex* (or *pellex*).[22] Some Bible commentators, dealing with the rare word *pellicientes* in the Latin text of the Second Epistle of Peter, which means 'alluring' or 'enticing', linked it to *pellices*, the plural form of *pellex*, adding 'that is, prostitutes, who take their name either from pollution or from the beauty of their skin (*pellis*) by which they entice the unwary'.[23] *Pellex* is not a term in Roman Law, like concubine, and it becomes very rare in the later Middle Ages.

Noble Mistresses of the High Middle Ages

When we turn to the twelfth century and later, especially in the central regions of western Europe, the picture is different. Semi-official concubines disappear, while, as Duindam observed, we enter a world of mistresses and bastards. Although these mistresses could be noble and powerful, and produce offspring whose interests they might protect and further, their status was never officially defined, as that of concubine had been by Roman Law or customary law.

Most of these mistresses came from the landed aristocracy. Rosamund Clifford, the most well-known mistress of Henry II of England, belonged to an Anglo-Norman baronial family with landholdings in the Welsh Marches.[24] Her relatives benefited from the connection, since her father's estate was increased by a valuable manor that the king gave him 'for love of Rosamund his daughter'.[25] Henry's affection for her was shown by the care he took over her burial place in Godstow nunnery outside Oxford, endowing the nunnery with lands and having an elaborate tomb constructed for her inside the church, 'in the middle of the choir before the altar, covered with silk cloths and surrounded by lamps and candles'.[26] She entered legend as 'Fair Rosamund'.

Spain saw several royal mistresses who were of great importance and had dramatic lives (and deaths). One was Eleanor de Guzmán, mistress of Alfonso XI of Castile (1312–50). Alfonso had married Maria, the teenage daughter of the king of Portugal, but, after two years, she had borne no children. 'And because the king was a very accomplished man in all his actions', says the chronicler of his reign, 'he felt himself diminished by the fact that he had no sons by the queen; and, for this reason, he sought a way to have sons otherwise.'[27] In 1330 Alfonso met the noble young widow, Eleanor de Guzmán, in Seville, and they formed a liaison that was to last the whole of the king's life and produce numerous offspring. Queen Maria did eventually also have children, two sons, one of whom died in infancy. The other, Peter, was born in 1334, the same year as Eleanor de Guzmán gave birth to her fifth son by the king. The rivalry between the legitimate son and the illegitimate ones was to shape Castilian politics in a fundamental way. Alfonso's concerns are illustrated by a remarkable clause he insisted on including in the treaty he made with the king of France in 1345: that if any future king of Castile should not respect the grants and favours he had bestowed on Eleanor de Guzmán and her children, the whole treaty would be void.[28] It is an attempt to secure the support of the powerful French king for the position of Alfonso's mistress and their many children. Alfonso's apprehensions on this point were realistic. After his death and the succession of his legitimate son, Peter, the new young king sent his father's mistress under guard to Queen Maria's castle of Talavera, where, on Maria's instructions, Eleanor was soon killed.[29]

Alfonso's son and successor, Peter, nicknamed 'the Cruel', also had a complex series of relationships with women.[30] A marriage agreement was drawn up between the young king and a French princess, Blanche of Bourbon, in July 1352, but, when Blanche arrived in Valladolid for the wedding the following February, Peter was not there, since he was 250 miles away in Cordoba awaiting the birth of his first child by his mistress Maria de Padilla. Once that child, a girl named Beatrice, had been born, and endowed with an estate, Peter finally came to Valladolid for his wedding, which was celebrated with pomp and festivity. But then, two days later, he abandoned Blanche and returned to Maria.[31] Subsequently, under pressure from his mother and his senior ministers, he revisited Blanche but only for two days. After that, says a contemporary chronicler, 'he never again saw the queen, Doña Blanche his wife'.[32]

Maria de Padilla lived with Peter for a decade (1351 until 1361, when she died) and had four children by him. The only serious disruption to their relationship occurred in 1354, when Peter married another woman, Joanna de Castro, after having had two tame bishops confirm that his marriage to Blanche was null. It remains a complete enigma why he did this and also why, immediately after the marriage, Peter left her and, in the words of the same chronicler, 'never again saw Doña Joanna de Castro', although she was given an estate and always called herself 'queen'.[33] Blanche remained in Spain and was able to obtain the support of the citizens of Toledo for her cause but was eventually unsuccessful in her efforts and became a permanent prisoner of her husband. She died, still under guard, in 1361, the same year as Maria de Padilla. The circumstances of her death are unclear, but could have been simply natural.[34] She entered the literature of romance, in more than one language, including a full-length English poem of 1855, where she appears 'pale, pensive and alone', as she might.[35]

Throughout her travails, Blanche had a determined champion, the pope, Innocent VI (1352–62). He wrote a series of letters: to Blanche, first telling her to be obedient to her husband and mother-in-law, later writing to console her in the face of Peter's terrible treatment; to Peter, telling him to treat Blanche with marital affection, later congratulating him on the, mistaken, news that the king had separated from Maria de Padilla, eventually exploding at the news of Peter's marriage to Joanna de

Castro – 'you, doing recent things that are worse than what you did before, not dismissing your adulteress nor taking back the queen, have brazenly taken up with another adulteress'; to the queen mother, Maria, encouraging her support for her daughter-in-law; to his legates, Bertrand, bishop of Senez, and William, cardinal-deacon of St Mary in Cosmedin, urging them to vigorous action; to Blanche's supporters in Toledo and to the Spanish bishops; to the king of France and the duke of Bourbon, Blanche's father; to the nobles of Spain.[36] All this epistolary and rhetorical activity had no effect. Peter remained with Maria de Padilla until her death, which was followed the next year by that of Pope Innocent.

After the deaths of Blanche and Maria de Padilla in 1361, Peter announced publicly that he had in fact married Maria before Blanche, so that Maria was truly queen of Castile and his marriage with Blanche null. He had his son by Maria declared his heir and exhumed her body to be re-interred in Seville.[37] It is not possible to say how much truth there is in this claim. The witnesses the king produced to testify to the earlier marriage included relatives of Maria, with a clear interest at stake, but Peter's matrimonial history is impulsive enough to make it possible. In his will Peter expresses the wish to be buried alongside her.[38] Peter was deposed and murdered by his half-brother, Henry of Trastámara (see below, p. 174) but his daughters by Maria de Padilla carried claims to the Castilian throne to their husbands, both of them sons of Edward III of England.

Mistresses Drawn from the Queen's Ladies-in-Waiting

One pool from which royal mistresses were recruited was the body of ladies-in-waiting around the queen, who were mostly young, unmarried and of relatively high social class. These ladies could be seductive. Robert de Vere, earl of Oxford, scandalously separated from his wife and married one of the foreign ladies-in-waiting who had come with Anne of Bohemia, queen of Richard II of England. The inventory of his property after his death included two new saddles 'for the ladies from Bohemia (*pour damoiselles de Boeme*)', and one old saddle 'in Bohemian style'.[39] Queens who were concerned about the reputation of their entourage would keep their ladies busy. The austere St Margaret of Scotland surrounded herself with 'ladies of noble birth and proven sobriety of morals' who spent their time sewing liturgical vestments and whose contact with men was limited to those whom the queen allowed and had no 'disreputable familiarity' or 'wanton levity', while the revered Guta, wife of Wenceslas II of Bohemia, 'did not allow her ladies-in-waiting to be idle but allocated each of them their work, instructing this one in weaving, this one in spinning, this one in sewing'.[40]

But all this needlework did not always keep ladies from the attention of the king. When the illegitimate daughter of the emperor Frederick II, Constanza-Anna, arrived in Nicaea in 1241 as the bride of the Byzantine emperor, John III Vatatzes, she was accompanied by an Italian lady-in-waiting named Marchesina, who soon became the emperor's favourite mistress. He gave her red shoes, customarily reserved for the empress alone, along with a red saddle and bridle, and provided her with a larger retinue than the empress had herself. She was very publicly the empress' 'rival (ἀντίζηλος)'.[41]

Ines de Castro also met her royal lover when serving in the household of his wife. Ines was a high-born but illegitimate Castilian noblewoman, and half-sister of Joanna de Castro mentioned above, who came to Portugal in 1340 in the entourage of Constance, bride of Peter, son and heir of the king of Portugal. Ines and Peter became lovers and, after Constance's death, had four children. Peter's father, King Alfonso IV, was unhappy with the situation, perhaps because of the dominant position being assumed in Portugal by Ines' family, the de Castros, perhaps because of fears about the legitimate successor, Constance's son, and he eventually came to countenance Ines' murder, which took place with his permission in 1355. After Peter became king in 1357, he took a terrible revenge on those who had perpetrated her murder, supposedly having their hearts torn out and then watching from a window, eating his dinner, while their bodies were burned. Peter said that he and Ines had been married and referred to her as 'the queen Doña Ines' and tended her memory. The parallel with the case of Peter I of Castile and Maria de Padilla is striking. Peter of Portugal had an ornate stone tomb made for Ines in the royal mausoleum, the monastery of Alcobaça, which was carved with scenes of the life of Christ and the Last

Judgment and had her effigy above, wearing a crown – if she had not worn one in life, she wore one in death. Ines' body was transferred from its initial resting place in Coimbra to the new tomb, with an escort of knights and a crowd bearing lighted candles. The king prepared an equally elaborate tomb for himself in Alcobaça, where he was eventually placed by Ines' side.[42]

Another lady-in-waiting to the queen who made her way to the king's bed was Alice Perrers, mistress of Edward III of England, who served in the household of Edward's queen, Philippa of Hainault, and was a young widow at the time their sexual relations began. She had a son and two daughters by the king, was publicly acknowledged after Philippa's death in 1369 and was notorious for accumulating lands and wealth. This made her vulnerable when the king was no longer there to protect her, and soon after his death in 1377 Alice was tried, condemned and deprived of all her lands. She spent the rest of her life – more than twenty years – trying to recover what she could. Unlike most royal mistresses of the period, she was not from a noble or knightly background but from a family of London goldsmiths and jewellers, who provided her first link with the royal court.[43] Also recruited from the queen's household was Agnes Sorel, mistress of Charles VII of France. Their liaison began in 1443, when she was twenty-two and he forty-one, and she bore him four daughters, dying in the fourth childbirth in 1450, aged twenty-eight. She came from the lesser nobility of Picardy and was endowed with several manors by the king. Charles erected two grand tombs for her, one in the abbey of Jumièges, where her heart was buried, and which included a statue of Agnes offering her heart to the Virgin Mary, the other at Loches, where her body was buried.[44]

Wives and mistresses were not always rivals. Odette de Champdivers, of a knightly Burgundian family, was provided as a mistress for the mad Charles VI with the agreement of his wife, Queen Isabella, who was not willing to suffer the violence the king sometimes inflicted on her. Odette was 'a very beautiful, delightful and pleasing young woman', bore the king a daughter, and was rewarded with two fine manors. She was nick-named 'the little queen'.[45] Mistresses, and their relatives, including sometimes their husbands, could gain a lot from the relationship with the ruler. Apart from the intangibles of the emotional bond, they were usually endowed with lands, and their family might gain titles and positions. They could be highly prized: ornate tombs such as those of Rosamund Clifford in Godstow, Ines de Castro in Alcobaça and Agnes Sorel in Jumièges and Loches were permanent, visible witnesses to the affection and sense of loss felt by powerful royal lovers. But the life of a royal mistress could be dangerous. Three were murdered in the space of nine years in the middle of the fourteenth century: Eleanor de Guzmán in Castile in 1351, Ines de Castro in Portugal in 1355 and Katherine de Mortimer in Scotland in 1360, the first by a vengeful wife, the second by a repressive father, the last by Scots lords unhappy to see their king return from imprisonment in England with an English mistress.[46]

Bastards

Most kings were powerful, wealthy and aggressive males, and might be expected to produce offspring from women other than their wives. Henry I of England has the record for the number of bastard children, over twenty, ten times as many as all the Capetian kings of France together achieved.[47] The emperor Frederick II had twelve. The kings of the Iberian peninsula also tended to have large extra-marital families. Alfonso IX of Leon (1188–1230) had eleven illegitimate children by five different noblewomen, as well as eight by his two wives.[48] Alfonso X of Castile (1252–84) had four illegitimate children, the eldest of them, Beatrice, by a noblewoman of the house of Guzmán, Mayor Guillén de Guzmán; Beatrice married the king of Portugal. Alfonso XI (1312–50) had two children by his second wife, but a total of ten with his long-term mistress, the noble widow Eleanor de Guzmán, who was the great-great-niece of Mayor Guillén.

Sometimes these children were thus the offspring of a long-term and publicly acknowledged relationship. Their mother might be classified as a 'concubine', with or without derogatory intention, and the sons of such women could then be identified by the status of their mother. For example, one chronicle introduces Tancred, king of Sicily (1190–4), the illegitimate son of Roger, duke of Apulia, and grandson of Roger II, as Roger's son by a concubine: 'He had had a son by a concubine, who was called Tancred, and that concubine had been the daughter of the count of Lecce.'[49] Likewise, Manfred, illegitimate son of the emperor Frederick II, is described as 'born of a concubine'.[50] This way of referring to such children does not label them with a specific term, identifying them instead by the status of their mother. Such terms were, however, also available. Isidore of Seville, whose work was the first recourse of medieval authors in search of a definition, wrote that 'he is called *nothus*, who is born of a noble father and an ignoble mother, such as from a concubine ... the contrary is a *spurius*, who is born of a noble mother and an ignoble father'.[51] Isidore's emphasis on the unequal status of the parents, rather than the simple fact that they were not married, can be traced in later writers who repeated his words.[52] Canon lawyers, however, could use the term *spurius* differently, for a child of prohibited unions, such as incest or adultery, or of a casual encounter, as distinct from a long-term concubinage.[53]

These Latin terms stand alongside the more robust label of 'bastard'. A curious etymology has been proposed for this word. The *Oxford English Dictionary* says it derives from the Old French *bast*, meaning pack-saddle. The pack-saddle, the *Dictionary* helpfully explicates, was 'used as a bed by muleteers in the inns'.[54] This conjures up a picture of casual sex in the straw rather than noble mistresses, but the term was certainly not limited in this way. The earliest occurrence of the word in England is in the Domesday Book of 1086, where a Norman landholder in Devon bears the name 'Robert Bastard', or 'Robert the Bastard'.[55] Another early use is in the chronicle of John of Worcester, who, describing the arrival of Robert, earl of Gloucester, in England in 1139, calls him 'the son of Henry, former king of the English, but a bastard'.[56] This is a strictly contemporary record. The word is found in several European languages and was even borrowed into medieval Greek.[57] The Church courts could 'bastardize' someone by declaring that they were illegitimate, like Hamo de Masci 'who was declared a bastard (*abastardatus*) in the church court'.[58]

In the dynastic world, the crucial question about illegitimacy was whether or not it was a bar to inheritance. When Henry I of England died in 1135 he left numerous illegitimate children including one, just mentioned, Robert, earl of Gloucester, whose wealth and talents could have made him an excellent contender to succeed. A report did indeed circulate that Earl Robert had been advised to seek the throne on the death of his father but that he had followed 'sounder advice' and committed himself instead to the cause of his nephew Henry (later Henry II), son of the Empress Matilda.[59] It seems that on this occasion his illegitimate birth weighed heavily not only with the Anglo-Norman barons but also with Robert himself.[60]

The complex way that the rights of bastards might sometimes be denied and sometimes asserted is revealed in the events of the 880s and 890s, a period when the Carolingian empire finally disintegrated.[61] In 885, the emperor Charles the Fat, lacking a legitimate child, was rumoured to be planning to have Bernard, 'his son by a concubine', made his heir, but was frustrated in the attempt. His intention was to summon the pope to an assembly in Germany, where Bernard's status would be recognized by papal authority, since Charles 'doubted whether this could be done by him himself', but the pope's death en route upset his plans.[62] Charles' doubt and his appeal to the pope suggest that he was considering not simply designating Bernard as his heir but also having him declared legitimate and, if so, this would be the earliest, and for this period an isolated, mention of the possibility of legitimation by the pope.[63]

In 885, therefore, Charles the Fat thought it essential to secure papal backing for the legitimation of his illegitimate son so that he could succeed to the throne. Just over two years later, however, Charles' illegitimate nephew, Arnulf, showing no doubts on the grounds of his birth, deposed Charles and himself became ruler of the East Frankish kingdom and eventually emperor. Partly this is to be explained by Arnulf's ambition and political and military skill and strength, but it also reflects the very narrow range of choice available in the Carolingian dynasty. Apart from Charles the Fat, there were only five Carolingian males in 887: Charles' illegitimate son Bernard, the illegitimate Arnulf and his two illegitimate sons, and Charles the Simple, the eight-year-old representative of the West Frankish branch of the family, whose own legitimacy could also be questioned. As the chronicler Regino of Prüm put it,

> After the death [of Charlemagne] fortune changed and the glory of things, which had overflowed beyond expectation, now, in the same way, began gradually to drain away, until, after kingdoms had fallen away and

the royal stock had partly been extinguished by early deaths and partly withered by the sterility of wives, he alone [Arnulf] of all the numerous descendants of kings could be found suitable to take up the sceptre of the empire of the Franks.[64]

Arnulf was able to have the rights of his two illegitimate sons recognized by the East Frankish aristocracy, but only 'if an heir was not born to him by his legal wife'. In fact, he did have a son by her, and this son, although a child, succeeded him in 900 as 'the only one born of his legal wife' (see above on Louis the Child, pp. 122–3).[65]

Bastard Kings

It is not known exactly why there was opposition to the declaration of Bernard as heir to Charles the Fat, and the case of Arnulf shows that bastards sometimes could inherit, but there is no doubt that there was frequently opposition to bastards succeeding to power, both in general principle and practical politics. A possible early example is Aldfrith, king of Northumbria (685–704/5), an illegitimate son of King Oswiu, fathered during Oswiu's time in Ireland on a princess of the O'Neil dynasty.[66] His contemporary, Bede, calls Aldfrith a bastard (*nothus*).[67] Writing very much later, the historian William of Malmesbury says that Aldfrith was the older son of Oswiu but did not succeed him 'because he was a bastard' and only came to the throne after the death of his younger but legitimate half-brother Ecgfrith.[68] Despite the lateness of this testimony, it is clear that William of Malmesbury had access to materials for Anglo-Saxon England that no longer survive, so what he says may be credible.

Be that as it may, a council held by papal legates in England in 786 was explicit about the issue of legitimacy and royal succession:

in the ordination of kings no one shall permit the assent of wicked people to prevail, but kings are to be chosen lawfully by the priests and elders, and not from among those born from adultery or incest, for, just as in our own times according to the canons a bastard cannot be promoted to the priesthood, so neither can he who was not born of a legitimate marriage be the Lord's anointed and king of the whole kingdom and heir of the land.[69]

The most famous bastard of the eleventh century was William the Bastard, duke of Normandy and king of England, whose conquests not only enormously enlarged his wealth and power but also enabled him to go down in history with the more refined nickname William the Conqueror. He succeeded his father as duke in 1035 while still a boy. His soubriquet dates to his own lifetime, for a German chronicler, writing in 1074, refers to 'this William, whom the French call "the Bastard"'.[70] Orderic Vitalis, writing much later but with good knowledge of the traditions of the Norman aristocracy, says William 'was despised as a bastard by the native nobles and especially by those descended from the earlier dukes Richard' (that is, Richard I and Richard II who reigned 942–1026).[71] Two of these descendants of earlier dukes, Guy of Burgundy and William, count of Arques, were to prove William's most dangerous enemies. Orderic gives William the Conqueror a death-bed speech in which he recalls how Guy 'called me a bastard and ignoble and unworthy to rule', while William of Arques and his brother 'despised me as a bastard'.[72] In the following century, those who resisted the attempt of William of Ypres to become count of Flanders in 1127 declared that they opposed him 'because he is a bastard, born from a noble father and an ignoble mother, who carded wool all her life'.[73] Here the word for 'bastard' is *spurius*, and hence an inversion of the definition in Isidore of Seville (above, p. 166).

Despite such objections, some bastards established dynasties, or even kingdoms. The first kings of Aragon were descended from an illegitimate son, Ramiro I, who was supposedly endowed with Aragon in 1035 by his father, since it was 'a little portion of his kingdom set apart' and would not suggest he was being put on the same level as his brothers, 'because he was not their equal on the maternal side'.[74] There are two notable cases in which illegitimate members of the royal dynasty succeeded to the throne in preference to a legitimate female heir: in the kingdom of Sicily after the death of William II in 1189, and in Portugal after the death of Ferdinand I in 1383. The situations are remarkably similar. In both we see the death of a king leaving a legitimate female heir, but one who was married to a foreign ruler; preference in the kingdom for an illegitimate male member of the dynasty, Tancred of Lecce in the Sicilian case, John of Avis in the Portuguese; and invasion by the foreign king married to the female heir. The only difference was the outcome. Tancred's family was wiped out; John's ruled Portugal for the next two centuries.

The childless William II of Sicily designated his only surviving legitimate relative, his aunt Constance, as his heir, and had the great men of the kingdom swear an oath to 'accept her as mistress and queen if he died without children'.[75] This oath of the Sicilian nobles to Constance, which took place at Troia, probably in 1184 or 1185,[76] is strongly reminiscent of the oath, taken a half century earlier, that Henry I of England made his barons swear, to acknowledge his daughter Matilda as his heir (above, p. 135). As in the case of Matilda, an unpopular marriage complicated the situation. Just as the Anglo-Norman barons objected to Matilda's marriage with Geoffrey of Anjou, so it seems the chief men of Sicily were not pleased at the prospect of having as their ruler Constance's husband, Henry, son of the Holy Roman Emperor and already designated as his successor. In November 1189, when William II died, it was not Constance and Henry who were recognized as successors, but Tancred, count of Lecce, an illegitimate member of the royal dynasty. He was the son of Constance's older brother, who had died in 1149.

A letter written by a prominent Sicilian, probably early in 1190, expresses the fears that the inhabitants of the kingdom had at the prospect of Constance's German husband and his German army. The author of the letter had just heard of the death of the childless William II, and he reflects on 'how great a calamity this change will bring'. The only two possible futures seem to him either 'the storm of hostile invasion' or 'the fierce whirlwind of civil war'. His imagination is heated:

> I seem already to see the turbulent battle lines of the barbarians carried forward in a rush, bringing terror to rich cities and places that have long flourished in peace, slaughtering the inhabitants, devastating them with their plundering, befouling them with their lust.[77]

He pictures men cut down by the sword, virgins raped before the eyes of their parents. 'German frenzy (*teutonica insania*)' knows no bounds. He talks of the Germans as 'a most foul people' and 'a hard and stony race', paints a scene of the native children 'terrified by the gruffness of the barbarian language' and expresses his fears that Palermo, the capital and the focus of his affections, might be 'polluted by the entry of the barbarians'.[78] The only hope for this writer was that the Sicilians would elect a king of their own and then, especially if the Christian and Muslim inhabitants of Sicily could collaborate, 'summon up their forces and fight the barbarians'. But would they be willing to take this course, 'or would they prefer to submit to the yoke of servitude, however harsh, rather than be mindful of their reputation and dignity and the liberty of their country?'[79] Probably already by the time this letter was written, some at least of the Sicilians had decided to elect a king of their own, even if he was illegitimate. Another source represents the arguments that Tancred's supporters advanced against the claims of the legitimist adherents of Constance: 'First learn the emperor's ways, learn his fury! Who can bear German frenzy? … will it be possible for you, like a child, to learn to make barbaric sounds like a barbarian?'[80] Just as in the case of the letter, the German reputation for ferocity and their 'barbaric' language could stir up hostility to the rule of a foreign king. Tancred reigned for four years and was succeeded by his young son, but the dynasty was then annihilated by the irresistible force of Henry and his Germans.

Similarly, two centuries later, when Ferdinand I of Portugal was making arrangements for the succession, there was a legitimate female candidate, his daughter Beatrice, but no son. Ferdinand anticipated that Beatrice and her husband, the king of Castile, would produce a son who would inherit Portugal when of age. Ferdinand died in 1383, when Beatrice was ten, and very quickly Castilian troops crossed the border. Just as in the Sicilian case, the nobles and populace of Portugal were presented with a clear successor, who was legitimate, but one who had the potential disadvantage, in some contemporary views, of being female, and the definite disadvantage of bringing with her as consort the king of a large neighbouring country which had fought wars with Portugal only a few years earlier.

Ferdinand had declared that his wife, Eleanor, should be regent after his death, but there was considerable opposition to her and to the Castilian king's claim to be king of Portugal in right of his wife. The eventual head of the resistance was John, the illegitimate son of Peter I of Portugal (Ferdinand I's father) and his mistress Teresa Lourenzo, and hence Ferdinand's half-brother. John had been publicly acknowledged as King Peter's son – we even know exactly when he was born, 3:00 in the afternoon on 11 April 1357 – and he was raised by a rich citizen of Lisbon, later educated by the Master of the Knights of the Order of Christ, a Portuguese crusading order, and he himself became Grand Master of the Order of Avis at the age of seven, which is why he is usually known as John of Avis.[81] In 1383, in the face of Castilian aggression, an opposition party chose him as regent instead of the queen mother Eleanor, and for two years war was waged between John of Avis, on the one hand, and Eleanor's supporters and the Castilians. John had the backing of the city of Lisbon, which withstood a Castilian siege in the summer of 1384, and on 6 April 1385 he was accepted by the Cortes (Parliament) as king. A crushing victory over the Castilians at Aljubarrota on 14 August 1385 confirmed his position.[82] John of Avis was not only illegitimate but had also taken vows as a member of the Order of Avis. In order to marry, he needed a dispensation from the pope, and he was as assiduous in pursuing this as he was in resisting Castile's armies. In 1391, six years after he had been accepted as king, he received letters from Pope Boniface IX declaring that, although John was of illegitimate birth and had taken vows of poverty, chastity and obedience, he was now legitimized, could marry (which he had already done) and rule as king.[83] Despite continued conflict with Castile, he ruled for forty-eight years. John I entered history and legend as a champion of Portuguese independence and, as such, has a grand equestrian statue in Figueira Square in Lisbon, as well as a medieval effigy, holding hands with his queen, over his tomb.[84]

Sometimes the application of fairly strict rules about illegitimacy increased the chance of there being a female ruler. Blanca of Navarre (1425–41) succeeded her father Charles III in preference to any of his illegitimate sons, as he explicitly recognized: 'Due to a lack of legitimate male sons . . . the daughters of ours will be held to be the first by law to the land of Navarre.'[85] In contrast, in dynastic systems like the Irish, with numerous sons from different unions and recognition of the rights of collateral branches, such a development would be impossible as there was simply no space for sovereign queens. In the case of Sicily in 1189 and Portugal in 1383 the illegitimate male was preferred to the legitimate female largely, it seems, because of the desire to have a native ruler. This preference for a local but illegitimate son over an alien married to a legitimate woman is expressed very well in a parallel case from twelfth-

Figure 6 The Battle of Aljubarrota, 1385, in which John of Avis, bastard son of the king of Portugal, defeated his Castilian rivals and established his dynasty on the throne.

IRHT-CNRS, Bibliothèque municipale de Besançon, Ms 864–865. Besançon, Bibliothèque municipale, MS 865, fol. 239v, digital photography by Colin Dunn, in 'The Online Froissart', ed. by Peter Ainsworth and Godfried Croenen, version 1.5 (Sheffield: HRIOnline, 2013), www.hrionline.ac.uk/onlinefroissart/apparatus.jsp?type=vv&xmlid=Bes-1_27r [accessed 15 August 2019].

century Normandy: 'they preferred to have over them a bastard who was a compatriot'.[86]

One of the most successful dynasties to originate in an illegitimate son of a king was the house of Trastámara, which ruled Castile from 1369, after a short abortive earlier attempt, and later acquired the thrones of Aragon, Sicily, Naples and Navarre. The founder of the dynasty was Henry, one of the ten children of Alfonso XI of Castile and his long-term mistress, Eleanor de Guzmán. Understandably, Alfonso's wife, Maria, and their legitimate son, Peter, regarded them with hostility. On Alfonso's death in 1350, the competition became bloody. Henry and his brothers rebelled, with varying degrees of success, while Eleanor de Guzmán, as mentioned above, was taken into custody and executed. After many years of fighting, Henry was able to defeat Peter and kill him with his own hand. This was in 1369.

Henry's opponents naturally stressed his illegitimacy. The Chandos Herald, who wrote a life of Peter's ally, Edward, Prince of Wales ('the Black Prince'), always calls him 'the bastard', and has Peter's loyal supporter, Ferdinand de Castro, say 'he could not consent that a bastard should hold the kingdom'. In a letter that Chandos Herald claims the Black Prince wrote to Henry before confronting him in the Battle of Nájera, the Prince says, 'you must feel in your heart that it is not right for a bastard to be king'.[87] It is not clear whether Henry felt this. The chronicler Froissart writes that Urban V excommunicated Peter and legitimized Henry in 1362: 'And the Holy Father placed the whole kingdom of Spain in the hands of Henry, bastard brother of King Peter, and he legitimized him to hold the kingdom and the inheritance.'[88] There does not seem to be any corroboration of Froissart's statement but, if it is true, then, at the very least, some of Henry's supporters thought that legitimation would be an asset.

It is customary to label the descendants of Henry of Trastámara 'the house of Trastámara' and the descendants of John of Avis 'the house of Avis', although in both cases there was no break in male-line descent. When the royal secretary and archivist of Portugal, Fernão Lopes, was commissioned by John of Avis' son and successor, King Duarte, to write a chronicle, his task was described as 'setting down in a chronicle the histories of the kings that had previously reigned in Portugal, right up to, and including, the great and most noble deeds of my most able and virtuous father'.[89] This was to be a continuous history of all Portuguese kings, with no hint of a dynastic rupture. Likewise, Pero López de Ayala, commissioned by Henry of Trastámara to write a history of the reign of his enemy Peter I and his own reign, justified Henry's succession to the throne and made his illegitimacy invisible.[90]

In the fifteenth century the kingdoms of Naples and Cyprus were entangled in a web of dynastic and political manoeuvres in which rulers of illegitimate birth figured prominently. Ferdinand (or Ferrante), illegitimate son of Alfonso of Aragon, king of Naples, was legitimized by his father in 1440.[91] After succeeding to the throne of Naples in 1458, he attempted to make his own illegitimate son, Alfonso, king of Cyprus through marriage to the illegitimate daughter of the illegitimate James II of Cyprus.[92] In James' will of 1473 he left the kingdom of Cyprus to his pregnant wife and to the child that she would bear; if that child died, the succession would pass to James' oldest illegitimate son, and, if he died childless, to his next illegitimate son, and so on; if these sons produced no heir, the kingdom would go to his illegitimate daughter, Charla, the girl who was betrothed to Alfonso of Naples.[93] Nothing eventually came of all these plans but the fact that the illegitimate son of an illegitimate but legitimized ruler could seek a kingdom through marriage to the illegitimate daughter of an illegitimate king shows that legitimate birth was not considered indispensable in this world. The succession of James II himself had been a matter of ruthless power by a talented man:

> At this time James, the son of John, king of Cyprus, from a concubine (*e pellice*), took possession of the kingdom after his father's death; his father had understood that he was very eager to rule, it being natural that as he was extremely well formed, of great physical size, very eloquent and gifted with exceptional intelligence, he thought himself worthy of the royal dignity.[94]

Bastard Culture

During the great revolt of 1173–4, when the adult sons of Henry II of England rebelled against him, his bastard son Geoffrey, at that time bishop-elect of Lincoln, fought bravely and successfully on his father's behalf. When Henry and Geoffrey met, the king is reported as saying, 'My other sons have proved themselves to be the real bastards, this one alone has proved to be legitimate and true.'[95] There is plenty of evidence for affection between rulers and their illegitimate children. They were, after all, the offspring of a relationship based on warm personal feelings of love and/or desire, rather than of a marriage that might well have been initially between two complete strangers and was certainly politically motivated. In addition, if it was recognized that they had no right to succeed, a source of major intergenerational tension would not exist. There is no mistaking the note of paternal pride when Richard III of England, appointing his 'beloved bastard son, John of Gloucester', as captain of Calais (then an English possession) in 1485, praised 'the great vivacity of his mind, agility of his limbs and inclination to all good morals'.[96]

The favourite son of the emperor Frederick II, it seems, was Enzio, 'whom', Frederick himself says, 'some time ago we fathered on the German noblewoman Adelheid, when she was single and we were not'.[97] Frederick legitimized Enzio on his own authority in 1239, a power accorded to the emperor by both Roman and canon law, at the same time appointing him his lieutenant in Italy. Enzio was later captured by Italian enemies and spent twenty-two years as a prisoner in Bologna, writing poems lamenting his fate. The fact that those hostile to the emperor and his family said that Enzio's mother was 'disreputable and ignoble' shows the type of invective that was often employed to discredit illegitimate enemies.[98] If we believe the emperor, however, his mother was an example of a well-born mistress providing valued and cherished sons outside of marriage.

Sometimes bastards were marked out by their very names. The Carolingians tended to give different names to their legitimate and illegitimate sons, reserving the 'royal names' like Charles, Louis and Lothar exclusively for the former, while christening their bastards with a variety of names, some of them shared with legitimate Carolingians (Carloman, Pippin) but most not.[99] When a Carolingian king like Lothar II named his illegitimate son Hugh, this was virtually a statement that the boy was not to be considered as an heir or successor to the kingdom.[100] It has also been pointed out that in the ninth century no legitimate

Carolingian fell in armed conflict but five illegitimate ones did, suggesting the former were protected more carefully on the battlefield, so those 'bastard names' implied dispensability.[101] In the late Middle Ages, the rulers of Savoy and Piedmont often gave their bastard sons exotic names, some drawn from ancient names of their dynasties that had fallen out of use, so with an archaic ring, some taken from the heroes of fashionable chivalric literature, such as Lancelot. Later, with the impact of humanism in these courts, illegitimate sons might bear names such as Hector, Achilles and Hannibal.[102] There are examples elsewhere in late medieval Europe, such as Lancelot (d. 1422), son of Charles III of Navarre, or Hector, bastard of Bourbon and archbishop of Toulouse (1491–1502).[103] Humphrey, duke of Gloucester, brother of Henry V of England, followed this custom by naming his two illegitimate children Arthur and, amazingly, Antigone.[104]

One very visible way in which bastards might be distinguished was in their coats-of-arms. By the later Middle Ages the custom had developed of distinguishing the arms of illegitimate branches of the family by a small change or an additional symbol, a 'difference', as it was known. 'In some countries', wrote a French author in the 1370s, 'the bastards bear the arms of the lineage from which they descend with some difference, a custom that seems reasonable'.[105] About twenty years later, a writer in England wrote 'there are those who bear the mark of bastardy, and such people bear the entire arms of their parents with a diagonal bend'.[106] The 'bend sinister', that is, a diagonal band running from (viewer's) upper right to lower left on the shield, became a common difference indicating illegitimacy. It was even made compulsory for bastards by the first king-of-arms of the Burgundian Order of the Golden Fleece in his instructions of 1463 and by Manuel I of Portugal (1495–1521).[107] It was also possible for bastards to bear a blank shield with their father's arms in one quarter, or to place their father's arms on the bend.[108]

In the aristocratic world of those bearing coats-of-arms, the illegitimate were thus being publicly marked out, but it does not seem that this was intended to shame, rather to make an open acknowledgement of their family connections. The bend sinister was borne, for example, by the great French noble, the count of Dunois, illegitimate son of

Louis of Orleans (younger brother of Charles VI) and a companion-in-arms of Joan of Arc, whose arms were 'France, a label argent, a bend sinister of the same over all', that is, the royal arms of France (three golden fleurs-de-lys on a blue ground), differentiated by a silver label (a narrow horizontal band at the top of the shield with three pendants) and a silver bend sinister over all.[109] The label was a difference of Louis of Orleans, so Dunois bore his father's arms with the addition of the silver bend sinister. It proclaimed his illegitimacy at the same time as his royal descent. The sumptuous Dunois Hours, now in the British Library, which he commissioned in the 1430s or 1440s, shows him feasting in a room with a huge wall-hanging decorated with these arms.[110] He was not sheepish about his bastardy.

The dukes of Burgundy, who came close to creating an independent state in the borderlands between France and Germany during the fifteenth century, were well known as fathers of bastards. As in the case of Dunois, there was no attempt to hide or conceal their status; an illegitimate son of John the Fearless, duke of Burgundy, is recorded in the matriculation list of the University of Louvain in 1436 as 'John, bastard of Burgundy'. This John went on to become bishop of Cambrai and himself had at least fourteen illegitimate children by eight different women.[111] A delegation from Bohemia visiting the Burgundian court in 1466 was surprised to be joined at dinner by three of the duke's bastards:

> In those regions, they are not considered shameful, as they are among us ... Some kings and rulers have the custom of maintaining mistresses in their palaces, and they endow the sons they have from them, however many, with lordships for their lifetimes. When the father dies the legitimate sons do not take these away.[112]

The duke of Burgundy at this time was Philip the Good, whose oldest illegitimate son bore the unusual name of Cornelius (Corneille) and signed himself 'Bastard of Burgundy', a phrase also appearing on his seal. After his death, his younger bastard brother, Anthony, bore the title 'Grand Bastard of Burgundy (*Grand Bâtard de Bourgogne*)'.[113]

Illegitimate sons could attain prestigious positions, in the secular or the ecclesiastical world. Two of the many illegitimate sons of Henry I of England became earl of Gloucester and earl of Cornwall, and both of

Figure 7 The Dunois Hours showing the count of Dunois (d. 1468), illegitimate son of Louis of Orleans and companion of Joan of Arc, in a room decorated with his coat-of-arms, which publicly proclaimed his illegitimacy through the bend sinister (the silver diagonal). BL, MS Yates Thompson 3, fol. 1, © The British Library.

them proved loyal champions of their legitimate half-sister, the empress Matilda, and her son, Henry of Anjou, in the political turmoil after Henry I's death in 1135. An illegitimate son of Henry of Anjou, who succeeded as Henry II, became earl of Salisbury, through the patronage of his legitimate half-brother, Richard I. Another rose to be archbishop of York. Illegitimate daughters of rulers might make prestigious marriages. Constance, illegitimate daughter of Peter II of Aragon (1196–1213), was married to a member of the aristocratic house of Montcada, endowed by her father with valuable lordships and proudly bore on her seal the title, 'the lady Constance, infanta of Aragon'.[114] Sybilla, daughter of Henry I of England, married Alexander I, king of Scots. As mentioned above, the illegitimate daughter of Alfonso X of Castile became Queen Beatrice of Portugal. The illegitimate daughter of Frederick II married a Byzantine emperor. There is even a case of marriage to an illegitimate daughter of a ruler being a step to the succession. Filippo Maria Visconti, duke of Milan (1412–47), had no legitimate children but an illegitimate daughter, Bianca Maria, whose mother was a lady-in-waiting to the duke's wife. Bianca Maria's engagement to the mercenary leader Francesco Sforza, despite an age difference of twenty-four years, and their subsequent marriage in 1441, was one part of Sforza's ascent to the duchy of Milan, which he ruled from 1450 to 1466.

Legitimization

Some inheritance systems did not care whether a child was legitimate or illegitimate – the Merovingian dynasty and the dynasties of Ireland or early Scandinavia have already been cited as examples. Others stressed legitimacy. In the kingdom of Sicily it was ruled in 1265, 'No one shall succeed to the kingdom and land who is not born of a legitimate marriage.'[115] But even in systems where it mattered very much, it might be possible for a child to cease to be illegitimate and become legitimate.[116]

The illegitimacy and legitimacy of children was something that the Church devoted a great deal of effort to defining. The Church's definition of illegitimacy was closely linked to its definition of marriage. Sons and daughters of people who were not married to each other were illegitimate; sons and daughters of those who had married in full compliance with the rules of the Church were legitimate. But, in between these clear-cut situations there were dubious cases. As a very restricted set of rules about choice of marriage partner developed, excluding even distant cousins (see above, pp. 43–5), decisions had to be made about the consequences for the offspring of 'incestuous marriage', i.e. that between cousins. A hard line could sometimes be found. In 1065 Pope Alexander II wrote to a Sardinian grandee who had married a relative in the third degree, thundering that this was 'detestable according to divine and human laws' and that if a son were born from such a union he ought not to be regarded as a legitimate heir.[117] This letter, however, was not incorporated into any influential canon law compilation.

Important decisions about the canon law of marriage and legitimacy were taken early in the thirteenth century. At the Fourth Lateran Council of 1215, along with a reduction in the number of the prohibited degrees (above, p. 45), the Church adopted a new definition of 'clandestine marriages', as those that were celebrated without the banns having been previously read, and ruled that the children of such marriages were 'to be deemed completely illegitimate (*prorsus illegitima censeatur*)'. Although the marriage itself was valid, the children could not be deemed legitimate. The same applied to the children of those married even after proper publication of banns if the spouses were related within the prohibited degrees and, crucially, knew of the relationship.[118] For children to be legitimate according to these newly clarified standards, their parents' marriage would have to be a properly publicized union between partners who were either not related within the prohibited degrees or did not know they were. The Decretals of 1234, an official codification, have a specific section, 'which children are legitimate'.[119] It contains rulings that, if a marriage was public and had not faced ecclesiastical prohibition, the children are legitimate and can succeed to paternal property even if the couple are subsequently separated; that a child born of adultery is illegitimate and cannot inherit; and that if two single people had children, their subsequent marriage made their children legitimate: 'The power of marriage is so great that those who were born before marriage are deemed to be legitimate after it.'[120]

Since annulment of a marriage was, technically, not a divorce but a declaration that the marriage had been no marriage at all, the question naturally arose whether the children of such a union were legitimate or not. In English Common Law, the rule was that, if a marriage was dissolved because of consanguinity (being too closely related), the wife could have no dower but the children could inherit.[121] Important questions of royal succession might depend on the issue. When the marriage of King Amalric of Jerusalem and Agnes of Edessa was annulled in 1163 on the grounds of consanguinity, it was specifically stated that 'those who had been born to the two of them should be regarded as legitimate and should obtain the full right of succession to their father's possessions'.[122] The throne of Jerusalem did indeed descend through their children. Similarly, after the marriage of James I of Aragon and Eleanor of Castile was nullified on the grounds of consanguinity, a special effort was made to ensure the succession of their son Alfonso. In 1235, Pope Gregory IX wrote to Alfonso, legitimizing him, 'so that no one can raise an objection to you on the grounds of your birth'.[123]

A separate issue from the legitimacy of children born from consanguineous marriages was the legitimization of children who were admitted to be bastards. From the late 1330s, Robert Stewart, recognized as heir to the Scottish throne, had many children by Elizabeth Mure, daughter of a Scottish knight, but was not married to her. This situation was regularized by a papal letter of 22 November 1347 responding to Robert and Elizabeth's petition, which had the powerful backing of both the king of Scots and the king of France. In it, Pope Clement VI authorized the bishop of Glasgow to grant a dispensation to allow them to marry, which was necessary both because Robert had also slept with one of Elizabeth's relatives, creating an impediment to their marriage, and because they themselves were related. 'They had lived together for a long time, producing a multitude of offspring of each sex', but they had at first been ignorant of the relationships that constituted the impediments. Now, because these offspring 'are hoped to be a great future support' to the king and kingdom of the Scots, the bishop should allow the public marriage of Robert and Elizabeth and declare their children, past and future, legitimate. They did marry in 1349. Robert succeeded as king of Scots in 1371, the first Stewart king, and his oldest son by Elizabeth, who was born illegitimate but legitimized by the papal action of 1347, followed him on the throne.[124] This long-lasting royal dynasty thus needed an act of legitimization at its outset.

Canon law and secular law sometimes disagreed on their definitions of illegitimacy. For example, the twelfth-century treatise on English law that goes under the name of Glanvill noted explicitly that a child born before his parents' marriage was a bastard according to the law and custom of the kingdom of England but not by canon or Roman Law and that, according to English law, a bastard cannot be an heir.[125] A famous clash between the two views took place at a royal council in Merton in 1236:

> All the bishops asked the magnates to agree that those born before marriage should be legitimate, just like those born after marriage, as far as the right of hereditary succession is concerned, for the Church regards such children as legitimate; and all the earls and barons answered with one voice that they did not want to change the laws of England.[126]

Popes might be willing to be flexible in applying the strict letter of the law in matters of legitimacy if political circumstances warranted it. During his long tussle with Philip Augustus of France over the king's repudiation of Ingeborg of Denmark (see above, pp. 46–8), Innocent III was prepared to take into account the fact that Philip had only one legitimate son and that this made the dynasty vulnerable. In 1201 he therefore responded favourably to Philip's request that he legitimize his children by Agnes of Meran:

> Since Philip, king of the French, has no children other than his first-born son, born of his first wife, except for the boy and girl that the noblewoman, daughter of the duke of Meran, recently deceased, bore him, he, carefully considering posterity, has humbly asked us that we should legitimize them as a favour of the apostolic see.

Innocent, weighing up, among other things, 'what is useful and necessary for the kingdom of France', granted his request.[127]

But Innocent was not always accommodating, as his dealings with Alfonso IX of Leon show (see also above, p. 46). Alfonso had married his first cousin, a Portuguese princess, in a remarkable breach of the canon law of marriage, and, after having had children with her, had finally repudiated her, and then, in the year before Innocent became pope, had undertaken an almost equally 'incestuous' marriage with Berenguela of Castile, the daughter of a first cousin. Innocent III's letters on the subject are inflamed. He demanded that the couple separate and decreed that 'if any offspring has been or should be produced from such an incestuous and damnable union, they should be regarded as completely bastard and illegitimate, with no claim to succeed to paternal property according to the statutes of the law'.[128] Some years after this letter, the pope's anger is evident in a letter he sent to Berenguela's father, the king of Castile, who had arranged for his grandson, the child of the union of Berenguela and Alfonso IX, to be recognized as heir to the throne of Leon:

> although we have declared that offspring produced from an incestuous union of this kind are bastards and at no time whatsoever should succeed to paternal property according to the rulings of the law, you, to our great amazement, cunningly arranged that almost the whole kingdom of Leon should swear an oath to him.[129]

Although Berenguela and Alfonso did separate, Innocent's indignation about the prospect that their offspring might succeed to their inheritance had no effect. Their son Ferdinand became king of both Leon and Castile, reuniting the two kingdoms permanently and becoming one of the most successful Christian rulers in the attempt to conquer territory in Muslim Spain, adding Cordoba and Seville to his kingdom.

Sometimes illegitimate royal children were legitimized with the explicit reservation that this did not give them any claim to succeed to the throne. When the pope legitimized the illegitimate children of Premysl Otakar II of Bohemia in 1260, he explicitly stated this.[130] A similar step was attempted in the case of the Beauforts, the illegitimate, but legitimized, children of John of Gaunt, son of Edward III of England, and his mistress Katherine Swynford, who won the backing of both pope and king to be declared legitimate. Katherine was the daughter of one of the knights of Hainault who had come to England with Philippa of Hainault, queen of Edward III. Katherine had married an English knight, which is how she acquired her surname, but had also been recognised as Gaunt's mistress. In the 1370s she bore him four children. In February 1396, after the death of Gaunt's second wife, he married Katherine. The high-born ladies of the royal dynasty were not amused at this. 'We will not go anywhere she is', they said. 'It would be a disgrace if this duchess, who is low born and was his mistress for a long time when he was married, should have precedence over us. Our hearts would break with grief, and with good reason.'[131] But the ladies were ignored.

It is probable that Gaunt married Katherine in preparation for the next step, because in September 1396 he obtained papal dispensation for the marriage, with explicit legitimation of their children, and in the Parliament of January to February 1397 the chancellor reported that the pope had legitimized Gaunt's children by her and that the king had done the same. The royal charter was read out and at the same time the oldest of the children, called John like his father, was created earl of Somerset.[132] The children of Gaunt and Katherine were given the aristo-cratic-sounding surname Beaufort, and they and their descendants were to be one of the most important political families in England for the next century. In 1407, ten years after their legitimation, John, earl of Somerset, sought a confirmation of the act, and this was issued but with an extra clause excluding the Beauforts from any claim to the throne, which was perhaps inserted by a political rival.[133] The Beauforts were supporters of the Lancastrian kings and suffered heavily in the Wars of the Roses between Lancaster and York, but their line did eventually sit on the throne, since Margaret Beaufort, great-granddaughter of Katherine Swynford, was the mother of the first of the Tudors, Henry VII.

The purpose of legitimation was to clear the way for succession. Conversely, an attempt to demonstrate illegitimacy was intended to bar the way. This could be an important political weapon. When Richard III of England decided to take the throne from his nephews, he thought it necessary to undertake an elaborate process to declare them illegitimate. In English Common Law, although the children of a marriage annulled on the grounds of consanguinity were deemed legitimate, those of a marriage annulled on the grounds of pre-contract, that is, a previous engagement to marry, were not. This is why Richard III was so keen to demonstrate pre-contract by his brother Edward IV, this delegitimizing Edward's sons, the unfortunate Princes in the Tower. Even if no one believed his arguments, he felt it was a case he had to make: if the princes were not of legitimate birth, they could not be kings.[134]

Thirteenth-century Norway provides a good example of a society making a transition from one way of thinking about illegitimacy to another. In 1218, the mother of King Haakon Haakonsson, who had just begun his reign, had to prove his paternity through the ordeal of the red-hot iron.[135] She asserted that his father was King Haakon Sverresson, who had died fourteen years earlier. She carried the red-hot iron and, when her hand was inspected three days later, it was declared to be healing cleanly, thus proving her claim. In 1246 Haakon thought it worth obtaining a papal dispensation for his illegitimate birth, even though by then he had been on the throne for almost thirty years. Innocent IV acknowledged that Haakon's father and mother had both been single when he was born, which was the simplest case in canon law, and granted the dispensation, so that 'notwithstanding this defect, you may be admitted to the honour of the royal throne . . . and also your legitimate heirs may succeed you in lordship and title'.[136] This dispensation was granted a few days after Innocent had allowed Haakon to be crowned, as the first Norwegian king to enjoy a coronation, and must be linked to that.[137] As a crowned Christian king, both he and the pope, it seems, thought it right that he should be legitimate, while the mention of his heirs was intended to secure the succession. Haakon's son, Magnus (1263–80), specified in his law code that the right of succession belonged to 'the oldest legitimate son of the Norwegian king'.[138] Prior to this time, that had been an exceptionally rare qualification for a Norwegian king.[139] When Haakon's mother bore the red-hot iron, she was undergoing this ancient and direful form of proof in order to verify her claim that Haakon was a king's son, for, as in Merovingian Gaul, being the son of a king was grounds enough to raise a claim to kingship. Legitimacy was not an issue. When, a generation later, Haakon decided it was useful to do so, his legitimacy could be obtained through a more bureaucratic and less painful process. A papal ruling could legitimize him, in this new world where educated and legally trained clergy had outlawed trial by ordeal.

CHAPTER 6

Family Dynamics

The Shape of the Dynasty

F AMILIES ARE ALWAYS CHANGING. AS THEY DO SO, THE INDI-
vidual members assume new roles and identities, sometimes happily, sometimes less so. Children become parents, parents become
grandparents, wives become widows. And these identities and roles are
never singular and simple. Younger sons are also younger brothers and
may well become uncles. Your sister is your child's aunt. And a sudden
death might mean new roles had to be assigned. The future Louis VII was
ten or eleven when his older brother Philip died in an accident. Until
then, for fifteen years, Philip had been the presumed heir, and Louis,
who had not been brought up expecting to inherit, now had to take his
place. As a result of these instabilities, family dynamics are complicated
and ever-changing. This is as true for ruling dynasties as for other
families, and hence shaped the high politics of the dynastic world.

Dynasties were never biologically stable. The dynasty that ruled the
Mark of Brandenburg from the time of Albert the Bear in the twelfth
century provides a good example of the way a family could change shape
dramatically in a short time. Albert's great-grandsons founded two distinct lines, each with numerous sons and grandsons. In the year 1295
there were at least fifteen male members of this family alive. Yet in 1320,
a bare generation later, the house became extinct in the male line. This
dynasty had blossomed and then suddenly withered. Childless marriages
and early deaths removed it from history. Processes like these were visible
to contemporaries and are sometimes mentioned explicitly.[1]

For example, a speech attributed to Bretislav I of Bohemia, who died in 1055, has him contemplating the changing biological fortunes of his dynasty, the Premyslids:

> Since my destiny is calling me and black death is now flying before my eyes, I wish to declare to you and commend to your good faith the one who should govern the state after me. You know that our ruling line, partly through sterility, partly through early deaths, was reduced to me alone. But now, as you see, five sons have been granted to me by God. It does not seem to me expedient to divide the realm of Bohemia among them, because every realm divided against itself will be ruined. Proven examples testify to us that from the origin of the world and from the beginning of the Roman empire and up to these present times, friendship between brothers has been rare. For if you observe what two brothers did – Cain and Abel, Romulus and Remus, and my forebears, Boleslav and St Wenceslas – what will five do?[2]

Bretislav was mulling over two kinds of extremes, each of which presented problems for dynasties: too few children or too many.

His solution to the problem of having too many sons was to recommend the principle of seniority. 'Seniority' describes a rule of succession whereby the position of ruler is transmitted not from father to son but to the next oldest member of the dynasty. Bretislav I on his death bed in 1055 urged his family to follow the principle, 'that among my sons and grandsons the oldest by birth should always possess the highest authority and the ruling throne'.[3] The subsequent transmission of ducal authority in Bohemia does indeed show the influence of this principle, even if it was not respected invariably, down to the time of the establishment of the hereditary kingship under Premysl Otakar I. It could even be explicitly invoked during succession disputes, as in 1101, when the Premyslid Udalric objected to the accession of his younger cousin Borivoj, as this was not 'according to the proper custom of the fatherland'.[4] Udalric based his own power in Moravia, a dependency of Bohemia, and this also illustrates the way that subordinate lordships there (for Moravia usually contained two or three duchies) continued to provide a basis for the claims of the junior branches of the dynasty to the title of duke of Bohemia. These claims could be nurtured over many years. An extreme case is Conrad-Otto of Znojmo, who ruled as duke of Bohemia from 1189 to 1191. Neither his father nor his grandfather had held that title, which had last been held in this line by Conrad-Otto's great-grandfather, who had died a century earlier in 1092.

Neither succession by seniority nor the existence of subordinate lordships was unique to the Premyslid lands. Both in Russia and in Poland the principle of seniority governed princely succession for considerable periods of the Middle Ages. The Russian Primary Chronicle includes, under the year 1054, a deathbed speech by Prince Yaroslav very similar in its nature to that attributed to Bretislav I, while in Poland it was Boleslaw III (d. 1138) who was credited with instituting the system.[5] Succession to Irish kingships was also marked by a preference for the oldest member of the ruling dynasty to succeed and a pattern of alternation between different branches.

The political history of the Premyslid dynasty between 1050 and 1200 was in fact determined less by the seniority system or the co-existence of superior and inferior dukes than by the biological accident of a superabundance of male members. As mentioned, Bretislav I left five active adult sons, and four of these ruled as dukes of Bohemia or Moravia, the other becoming bishop of Prague, and three of these brothers produced lines of descendants who continued to the end of the twelfth century or beyond. Cosmas of Prague, the most important Bohemian chronicler of the time, applauded this 'noble set of brothers',[6] but such a multiplication of males was a source of political instability. This was noted at the time. One of the Premyslid castellans remarked on the number of claimants to ducal power in 1109: 'Woe to you, Bohemia, you are not large enough to be subject to many lords in common. Unless I am mistaken, there are now twenty lordlings (*dominelli*) born of the ruling line and of the male sex.'[7] He was right. The third, fourth and fifth generation of Premyslids from Bretislav I each counted ten or more male members, and hence an estimate of twenty or so alive at any time is quite accurate.

The establishment of the hereditary kingship in Bohemia at the turn of the twelfth and thirteenth centuries coincided with a change in the biological fortunes of the dynasty. At the time of the death of Premysl Otakar I in 1230, the only male Premyslids surviving were his son Wenceslas and a few of the 'Dipoltici', exiled descendants of Premysl Otakar's uncle Dipolt. Although long reigns by powerful monarchs characterized the thirteenth century (Premysl Otakar I, Wenceslas I, Premysl Otakar II), a single murder in 1306 brought this ancient native dynasty to an abrupt end when Wenceslas III, the last male Premyslid, was stabbed by an unknown assailant while he relaxed in the summer heat. The continuous succession crisis of too many sons that had troubled the thoughts of Bretislav I was now overshadowed by the stark and evident succession crisis of there being no sons: 'Thus the powerful dynasty of kings was conquered by the bite of death, leaving no male stock.'[8]

Precisely the same thinning process had taken place in Scotland, where the rivalry between different segments of the old ruling dynasty characteristic of the tenth and eleventh centuries was replaced by undisputed male primogeniture in one line by the thirteenth century. The process came to a bloody conclusion in 1230, when a final rising of the MacWilliam family, descendants of King Duncan II (d. 1094), was suppressed, one of the girls of the family having her brains dashed out on the market cross at Forfar.[9] This pruning of the dynasty eventually produced a reasonably clear line of succession, with long reigns by powerful monarchs – William the Lion, his son, Alexander II, and Alexander's son, Alexander III, ruled for a total of 121 years. Yet this narrowing of the dynasty carried with it risks, and a single accident in 1286 ended the male line. The Scottish ancestral dynasty had resolved the problems of intrafamilial conflict only at the price of extreme genetic vulnerability, just as the Premyslids of Bohemia had done. An accident in 1286 and a murder in 1306 snapped the thin thread on which the continuity of the dynasty hung.

In the last centuries of the Middle Ages, father–son succession was taken as the norm in most European kingdoms, and people might recall earlier succession practices with curiosity. In the later twelfth century, Sven Aggesen, writing his *Brief History of the Kings of Denmark* and looking back on the early history of Denmark, tells of the legendary kings descended from Skiold ('Shield'), the first man to rule the Danes. The kingship passed from father to son among his descendants until the time of Ingeld. 'After his time', writes Sven, 'for a period of many centuries no son succeeded his father in the kingdom.' During that time, he says, the kingship passed to the previous king's *nepotes*, which can mean either nephews or grandsons. But these heirs, whether nephews or grandsons, were all, Sven stresses 'descended from the royal stock on one side'.[10] So he is picturing a loose royal lineage of a kind familiar from other parts of the medieval world, such as Ireland. Kingships like those in Scandinavia or Scotland moved from the broader to a narrower concept of the royal kindred.

Brothers

Legend tells of many pairs of brothers, some of them mythic founders or ancestors: Romulus and Remus, Hengest and Horsa. As is clear even from these two examples, brothers might compete or they might collaborate. Not all alliterated. In historical time, the same is true.[11] And there were often many more than two brothers. Medieval families could be large. A healthy, sexually active woman can become pregnant every couple of years, and upper-class women of the Middle Ages married young and did not have their fertility reduced, as the lower classes did, by malnutrition or by breast-feeding, since aristocrats had wet-nurses to suckle their babies. Long marriages and fertile wives could produce large numbers of children. The Holy Roman Emperor Frederick Barbarossa and his second wife Beatrice of Burgundy had ten or eleven children in the 1160s and 1170s; the marriage of St Louis and Margaret of Provence also produced eleven children in the 1240s and 1250s; Eleanor of Castile, queen of Edward I of England, had at least fourteen children between 1264 and her death in 1290; Albert I of Habsburg and Elizabeth of the Tyrol had twelve children over a quarter-century (c. 1280–1305); Isabella of Bavaria, queen of France, wife of Charles VI, bore twelve children in twenty-two years (1386–1407); one of them, Charles VII, went on to have fourteen children with Mary of Anjou over a similar period (1423–46).

These numerous children were, of course, not immune from the high child mortality of the time, so the number reaching adulthood or surviving their parents was much smaller. Only five of the fourteen children of Charles VII survived him. But if custom allowed serial monogamy or polygamy and gave concubines a recognized status, as in native Ireland, then the number of acknowledged sons could be even higher. Toirdelbach Ua Conchobair (Turlough O'Connor), king of Connacht (1106–56), had twenty-two sons by at least six partners.[12] In the harem systems of such societies as imperial China or Ottoman Turkey the numbers were comparable or higher. The emperors of the Tang dynasty

(618–907) had an average of 24.4 children, while the Ottoman sultan Murad III had, at his death in 1595, forty-nine living children.[13]

Fratricidal Impulses

Chapter 47 of Thackeray's *Vanity Fair* not only provides a telling quotation about the relationship of fathers and oldest sons (see above, p. 109) but also has something to say about relations between older and younger brothers:

> Then again . . . you ought to know that every elder brother looks upon the cadets of the house as his natural enemies, who deprive him of so much ready money which ought to be his by right. I have often heard George MacTurk . . . say that if he had his will when he came to the title, he would do what the sultans do, and clear the estate by chopping off all his younger brothers' heads at once . . . they are all Turks in their hearts.

If kings were usually distressed at the lack of a son, they might also have reasonable apprehensions about having too many sons, with the danger of fraternal discord that this brought.

Relations between royal brothers could range from the collaborative to the lethal. It was often the death of the father that was the starting gun opening the contest. As one Spanish chronicler put it, 'royal funerals have been moistened with the blood of brothers'.[14] Another remarked upon the fratricidal strife of their rulers:

> Such was the discord of the brothers in their desire to rule . . . If you read carefully through the deeds of kings, you will find that there is scarcely ever a lasting peace when royal power is shared. Moreover, the Spanish kings are said to have been of such ferocity that when some prince of their line came of age and took up arms for the first time, he was ready to strive for his rights against his brothers, or his parents if they were alive, in order to obtain royal power for himself alone.[15]

Sometimes conflict between brothers was to the death. The Merovingian dynasty was in almost constant family conflict and this often pitted brother against brother. In 612 Theuderic II defeated his half-brother Theudebert II in a series of bloody battles and ordered that his little son should have his brains dashed out on a rock. Theuderic either believed or pretended to believe that Theudebert's paternity was in doubt, and hence he was no brother to him, and not a grandson of his grandmother, the fearsome Brunhild, either. Brunhild was certainly not an ideal grandmother, if that was what she was, since, after the defeated and humiliated Theudebert was placed in her custody, she first had him forcibly ordained a cleric and soon thereafter killed.[16] Forcible tonsuring, making defeated dynastic rivals a cleric or monk, was a not infrequent way of dealing with them, even if they were left to fight another day, but Theudebert was not given that chance.

A dramatic instance of fratricide occurred in Sweden in the early fourteenth century. The king, Birger Magnusson, had two ambitious younger brothers, Erik and Valdemar, who attempted to create their own independent or semi-independent principalities. In 1306 the king was at his manor house at Håtuna, south of Uppsala, when the brothers took him by surprise and imprisoned him. He was eventually released but had to concede to his brothers the whole western half of Sweden and Finland, which was part of the Swedish realm in this period. Birger bided his time. In December 1317 he invited Erik and Valdemar to a feast at the royal castle of Nyköping. Erik was doubtful but Valdemar had already visited the king and thought 'he has utterly changed his mind and only wishes us well'. The two royal brothers went to Nyköping. Accommodation in the castle was limited, so the king suggested their followers lodge in the town. The royal brothers sat down to a feast with plenty of mead and wine. Conversation flowed. 'It is said that one never saw the queen so happy as then.' In the small hours, Erik and Valdemar went to their sleeping quarters, but, as they slept, the door burst open and twenty armed men entered and seized them. King Birger soon followed. Referring to the time when they had captured him eleven years earlier, he asked, 'Do you recall anything of the Håtuna game? I remember it very well.'

The brothers were bound and led off, to be shackled in the dungeon. At dawn a large royal force went into the town and seized all their followers. One knight, attempting resistance, was shot through the heart with a crossbow bolt. Erik and Valdemar were kept in stocks and neck irons. However, as the news spread, opposition to King Birger was aroused, and he was unable even to enter Stockholm because of the townsmen's resistance. At this point he went back to Nykoping, locked up the tower in which his brothers were imprisoned, threw the key into a nearby river and left. Erik survived for nine days without food and drink before dying of starvation, Valdemar for eleven days.[17] The opposition to Birger was so strong that eventually he and his queen had to leave Sweden and take refuge in Denmark, the queen's home country, while the supporters of his murdered brothers executed his son and, in 1319, elected Erik's son, Magnus, king. The fratricide has thus led to the extinction of the perpetrator's line and the victory of the victim's.

Killing your brothers was only one tactic. It was possible to leave them alive but to make them ineligible for rule by blinding them. This was a common way of dealing with deposed emperors in Byzantium, although the emperor Isaac II Angelus, who was deposed and blinded by his brother Alexius III in 1195, remarkably made a brief comeback, ruling again, jointly with his son, in 1203–4 (see pp. 250–1 for blinding). Another, perhaps more humane, method was to lock defeated brothers up for life. After Alfonso VI of Leon-Castile had, in all probability, arranged the murder of one of his brothers, Sancho, he was more restrained with the other, García, simply dispossessing him in 1073 and keeping him in captivity for the remaining seventeen years of his life. Although García was held in chains, he was otherwise treated well and even regarded by Alfonso as a possible successor, should the king have no other heir.[18] Another trio of brothers who sparred in the late eleventh century were the sons of William the Conqueror, and the least successful of them, Robert, endured an even longer captivity than poor García. After being captured in battle in 1106 by the troops of his younger brother, Henry I of England, Robert was a prisoner for the next twenty-eight years, until his death. He was held in various castles in England and Wales, dying in Cardiff castle in 1134 aged over eighty and being given an honourable burial before the main altar in Gloucester Abbey.[19] His captor, King Henry, even handed over a royal manor to the abbey 'to provide a light to burn before the main altar perpetually for the soul of Robert his brother'.[20] In a similar way, Alfonso's brother García had been buried in the royal mausoleum at Leon in the presence of his two sisters, the funeral being conducted by a large number of clergy, including the archbishop of Toledo and a future pope.[21] So, as long as they were kept tightly under lock and key for the whole of their lives, defeated brothers need not be killed, mutilated or treated dishonourably. Robert indeed was said 'to have suffered no evil except solitude, if you can call it solitude when there were endless games and banquets'.[22]

A particular problem in relations between brothers was presented by the 'late lamb', a child born many years after its siblings. Because men have the potential to father children throughout their lives, their oldest sons could never feel quite secure that rivals might not arise in the form of unwelcome baby half-brothers. The unexpected newcomer might well upset property arrangements that had already been made and intrude into a pattern of relationships forged long before. A conspicuous example is Charles the Bald, son of the Carolingian emperor Louis the Pious, born in 823, when the youngest of Louis' other sons, Charles' half-brothers, was already in his late teens. Six years before the young Charles arrived, his father had made an elaborate plan for the three sons he had at that time: Lothar the oldest was crowned co-emperor, while his younger brothers were given sub-kingdoms under him.[23] The question now arose of how to fit Charles into the plans for the succession. The emperor himself supposedly 'did not know what to do for him'.[24] Lothar's two younger brothers had been 'indignant' at the earlier settlement,[25] but all three of them had the chance to be 'indignant' again when their father gave the six-year-old Charles a huge landed endowment in the heart of the empire.[26] This was the beginning of a crisis that would end with the permanent destruction of the Carolingian empire.

The motives for Louis' second marriage are unclear, since he already had three sons by his first wife. This first wife died in October 818, and within a few months a second bride for Louis was being sought. The contemporary annals report that, 'after considering many daughters of his nobles, the emperor took as wife the daughter of count Welf, Judith by name'.[27] A later source, written shortly after Louis' death, expands on this:

> At this time, at the pressing advice of his men, he was contemplating entering the bond of marriage, for it was feared by many that he might

wish to put down the reins of government. But he was compelled and, finally satisfying their wishes and, after considering the daughters of his chief men, who were brought from far and wide, he was joined in matrimony to Judith, daughter of the most noble count Welf.[28]

One wonders why his nobles wanted him to remarry, and whether it was a good idea to have an extra son, half-brother to the other three. The avowed purpose, to keep him from abdicating, seems hard to understand.[29] The consequences, decades of struggle between the brothers, are, however, clear.

In the following century, it was rumoured that Liudolf, son of the German King Otto I by his first wife, was to be disinherited when Otto had a son by his second wife:

After a son was born to the king from his more recent wife, it was said that the king promised to that child his kingdom, which he had earlier assigned to Liudolf, and had had his chief men swear fealty to him.[30]

Liudolf was twenty-three when this younger brother arrived. Whether the rumour of disinheritance was true or not, Liudolf was sufficiently disturbed to rebel against his father, and throughout 953 and 954 led a widely based and serious revolt. Rebellious sons could often rally support from restless aristocrats of their own age, and Liudolf's followers included Duke Conrad of Lotharingia, 'a spirited and bold young man'.[31] The rebels were eventually forced to submit and Liudolf died three years later, in 957. The nineteenth-century authors of the standard factual survey of Otto's reign comment loftily, 'perhaps for him and for the Empire it was fortunate that he was not allotted a longer time of action'.[32] It was good for the Empire, presumably, because the unity of the imperial family was now unimpaired, and good for Liudolf because he did not have to recognize the authority of his younger half-brother! Otto I was indeed succeeded by a son born of his second marriage.

The case of John 'Lackland' did not involve a child of a second marriage but still upset existing territorial arrangements and had big political consequences. John, the youngest son of Henry II of England, was born in 1167, nine years after the youngest of his older brothers, so they were all knights and leaders of men before he had even entered his teens. Moreover, they had all been promised lands and lordships when John was still a baby: Henry the eldest was to have England, Normandy and Anjou, Richard, the next son, Aquitaine, and Geoffrey Brittany.[33] This left nothing for John. Hence his nickname, 'Lackland' (*Sine Terra, Sanz Terre*), which is attested as early as 1185, the year when John sailed to Ireland to visit the new lordship he had been granted there. By that time the nickname was already recognized as out of date: 'John, youngest son of the king of the English, whom they call "Lackland", although he has many and wide possessions and many counties, travelled to Ireland.'[34] The chronicler William of Newburgh, writing in the 1190s, even says that King Henry himself 'gave his fourth and youngest son John, the nickname "Lackland"'.[35] This notion, improbable though it may sound, was also credited by the French writer William the Breton, who wrote a poem in praise of John's enemy Philip Augustus. Addressing John in the poem, William writes, 'Before a trick of fate made you a monarch, you had received the name "Lackland" from your father's mouth.'[36]

It was King Henry's attempt to find a grand landed endowment for this youngest, and favourite, son that triggered one of the great crises of his reign, the rebellion of 1173–4. Marriage to a female heir was a familiar and relatively cheap way of providing for a younger son, and Henry thought he had found one in the person of the daughter of Humbert, count of Maurienne, who possessed numerous lordships on both sides of the Alps, which was the core of the later County of Savoy. Early in 1173 an agreement was drawn up between the king and the count, arranging the marriage of John and the count's daughter Alice, and specifying that John would inherit all the count's lands in the event of his not having a son. Even if Count Humbert did have a son, however, John would still inherit a very large portion of his lands. At some point in the discussions, Humbert asked King Henry what *he* was going to give John, and Henry specified three castles in Anjou, disregarding the fact that Anjou had already been promised to his oldest son, Henry the Young King. Henry the father and Henry the son quarrelled and soon Henry the son sought out the king of France and began the great rebellion against his father.[37] This was the first episode in the long story of violent conflict within the family of Henry II, which only ended thirty years later with John's murder of his nephew and his own humiliating defeat and dispossession of his French lands. In such cases as these, Charles the Bald, Liudolf's new brother and John Lackland, the birth of a brother or half-brother some years after his older brothers (seventeen, twenty-three and nine years respectively) caused family strife, and family strife in ruling dynasties means political conflict and war.

Provision for Younger Brothers

In order to avoid fraternal strife, some kind of provision had to be made for the sons who did not succeed to the throne. One way of attempting to deal with their demands and needs, if the circumstances were right, was to assign to them any lands acquired by conquest or marriage, reserving the ancestral, inherited lands for the firstborn. This is what happened on the death of William the Conqueror in 1087, when his eldest son Robert inherited the duchy of Normandy and his second son became ruler of William's most spectacular acquisition, the kingdom of England. Likewise, after the death of James I of Aragon in 1276, the Balearic Islands, which James had conquered, were formed into a new realm, the kingdom of Majorca, for his younger son James, while Aragon and the other mainland territories, which also included some conquests, went to his eldest surviving son, Peter. In neither case were the sons happy with these arrangements, but they demonstrate one way the claims of older and younger brothers might be addressed.

The younger sons of the English royal family were involved in several schemes intended to set them up in kingdoms of their own. After the failure of the attempt to give John 'Lackland' the lordship of Maurienne, a higher ambition arose. He was meant to be king of Ireland and was sent a peacock crown, although he had to settle for 'lord of Ireland' instead, a title the kings of England bore down to the time of the Tudors, when it was upgraded to 'king of Ireland'. But if the original plan had worked, and if John's older brother, Richard the Lionheart, had not been killed, childless, at the age of forty-one, the result would have been a Plantagenet kingdom of Ireland as a neighbour to a Plantagenet king-dom of England. Edmund, younger son of Henry III, was proposed as king of Sicily, although the only result of this scheme was an explosion of resentment among the English baronage which would contribute to the civil war of 1264–5. John of Gaunt, son of Edward III, claimed and fought for the Crown of Castile. The only English prince actually to establish himself on a distant throne, however, was Richard of Cornwall, the younger brother of Henry III, who became 'king of the Romans', which meant Holy Roman Emperor elect, and was crowned in Charlemagne's old capital of Aachen.

A different approach to balancing the claims of the oldest and the younger brothers is found in the arrangements of 817, mentioned earlier (p. 195), in which the emperor Louis the Pious envisaged that he would be succeeded as emperor by his oldest son, Lothar, but that the two younger sons, Pippin and Louis junior, would be kings under their brother, based in sub-kingdoms in Aquitaine and Bavaria respectively. The brothers would meet together once a year to discuss 'matters relating to common utility and perpetual peace'. The older brother would give the younger brothers aid in war against foreign peoples, but they would make war and peace only with his advice and would keep him informed at all times of the arrival of foreign envoys and their dealings. They would choose a wife only with his consent.[38]

This concept of a 'family firm', of royal brothers guided by the oldest member, failed spectacularly in the Carolingian case, but something like it can be found in Capetian France under Louis IX (St Louis). Louis was the oldest of a number of brothers, all of whom fought for him, supported him and never posed a threat to his rule or his line. There are structural features that might have shaped such sibling relations. Clearly the custom of apanages, large territorial endowments for younger brothers, as was the case with Louis' brothers, gave them power, status and a field for action that might satisfy them. When Louis' father, Louis VIII, made his will, establishing these huge lordships for his younger sons, he explained that he did this 'so that no discord could arise among them'.[39] Apanages were a natural device for a dynasty seeking to balance the claims of younger sons of royal or princely blood with the desirability of unified and enduring political units.

But, in the long run, apanages could lead to decentralization or even disintegration of the realm unless they were reincorporated, and this would only happen if the junior branch died out. The royal house of Bourbon, for example, had its origin in the endowment of Robert, a younger son of

St Louis, with the county of Clermont-en-Beauvaisis. Robert married the heir to the lordship of Bourbon, and their son, Louis, was created first duke of Bourbon in 1327, and from him descended two branches in the male line down to the sixteenth century, when the head of the younger branch, Henry, became Henry IV of France. It thus took four centuries for the cadet line's lordships to be reintegrated with the royal domain.

It might also require vigorous action to reincorporate apanages. When Alphonse of Poitiers, younger brother of St Louis, died in 1271, the year after the king, leaving no children, the new king, Philip III, presumed that Alphonse's great apanage would revert to the Crown. He faced a challenge, however, from Alphonse's brother, Charles of Anjou, who claimed that as a brother of Alphonse, he was a nearer heir than the king, who was only Alphonse's nephew. The case took thirteen years to resolve. King Philip's lawyers claimed that it was 'the custom of France' that, 'if the king gives to anyone a county, barony, castle or fief, and that person dies leaving no legitimate children, the gift reverts to the king who gave it, or to his heir'. Charles' lawyers fought back with a motley assortment of arguments, backed by a fusillade of Roman Law citations: this so-called 'custom' could not be demonstrated; if it did exist it did not apply to this case; the transfer of land from a father to a son, as in the endowment of Alphonse, was not technically a 'gift' but a 'provision'; there was no tacit condition involved in the endowment; it would be 'hard and absurd' to deny to kings' sons the right to collateral inheritance enjoyed by all the barons of the kingdom. In 1284 the final ruling, by the Parlement of Paris, the supreme royal court, dismissed Charles' plea, a judgment that has been called 'a milestone in the development of the reversion clause', since henceforth it was presumed that apanages would revert to the Crown on the failure of direct heirs.[40]

Dividing the Kingdom

Claims of younger brothers could also be settled by a division of their father's realm. In the early Middle Ages, it was not uncommon for a kingdom to be divided on the death of a king. Each of his sons would take a share. This was standard practice in the early generations of the Merovingian dynasty, which ruled the kingdom of the Franks until 751, and could be found at times in Anglo-Saxon England and elsewhere. In 511 the four sons of the Frankish king Clovis split up his realm between them and fifty years later in 561 Clovis' grandsons again divided the kingdom into four.[41] But there was no fixed system: for much of the sixth and seventh centuries the Frankish kingdom was divided not into four but into two or three component parts. Only after 679 was there virtually always just one Merovingian king at a time. It is not clear whether the divisions of the earlier generations represented some kind of accepted norm or custom, or whether they were simply the outcome of a power struggle. The Carolingians, who displaced the Merovingians in 751, reverted to the custom their predecessors had practised in earlier times, with significant divisions or subdivisions of the kingdom in 768, 843, 855, 870, 876, 879 and 888, not to mention numerous other territorial readjustments or planned divisions that did not in fact come to pass. Some of these partitions only lasted a short while, but others shaped European history to the present: it was from these ninth-century territorial arrangements that France and Germany emerged as separate countries.

But there was nothing predestined about this. Other possibilities were numerous. For instance, in 865 Louis the German, who ruled the kingdom of the East Franks, arranged a division of his kingdom between his three sons, to take full effect after his death. Roughly speaking, the oldest son received Bavaria, the second son Franconia and Saxony, the third son Swabia, each with adjoining lands.[42] Accordingly, after their father's death 'the sons of King Louis came together and divided their father's kingdom among themselves and confirmed with an oath that they would keep faith with each other. The text of this oath, written in German, can be found in many places'.[43] If this division had taken effect, there is no reason why these kingdoms might not have become permanent features of Europe's political geography.

The formation of the kingdom of England is often dated to the reign of Æthelstan, who died in 939, but there was also nothing inevitable about England either, and there are later occasions when the kingdom was divided, and these partitions could have endured and become permanent, like that between France and Germany. Sometimes these divisions were based upon the earlier independent kingdoms, as in 957, when the men of Mercia chose Edgar as king in place of his brother Eadwig, who continued to rule in Wessex.[44] This arrangement lasted until 959, when Eadwig died, and England was reunited under Edgar. But it was divided again, albeit for a short time, in the same way in 1016, when the beleaguered English king Edmund Ironside received Wessex and the Danish invader Canute took the rest.[45] After Canute's death in 1035, because of the rival claims of his two sons, 'the kingdom of England was divided by lot'.[46] The nobles north of the Thames chose his son Harold as regent of all England but the leaders of Wessex opposed this and arranged for an alternative kind of regency in Wessex on behalf of Harthacnut, Canute's son by a different mother. This temporary de facto division of the kingdom did not last long, however, and in 1037 Harold was chosen unanimously as king.[47]

Such divisions of the kingdom, however, became unusual later in the Middle Ages. The kingdom of the West Franks (France) and the kingdom of the East Franks (Germany) were not partitioned again after they finally emerged from the last breakup of the Carolingian empire in 888, although they fought over their borders, while the last division of the kingdom of England, as just mentioned, ended in 1037.[48] There were some unsuccessful later medieval attempts to divide kingdoms. During the disputed succession to the Scottish throne in the late thirteenth century, the less plausible candidates argued that the kingdom should be divided, just as great fiefs would be between female heirs, so that they could have something at least. The king of England, who had been called in as arbiter, was not sympathetic: 'the kingdom of Scotland is not partible'.[49] This statement, laconic as it is, unequivocally asserts the unity of the kingdom.

The fate of Galloway in the thirteenth century shows another path, in which loss of regality had as a consequence loss of impartibility. This region, the south-western part of modern Scotland, had its own rulers in the twelfth century, one of whom, Fergus (d. 1161), was actually styled 'king of the men of Galloway', at least on one occasion, and given exactly the same status as the king of Scots.[50] Fergus' descendants did not bear this title but continued to rule their semi-independent lordship until the death of Alan, lord of Galloway, without legitimate male heirs in 1234. His lands were then divided among his three daughters according to feudal custom, although not without resistance. The kingdom of Galloway thus did not become a permanent feature of the political map of Europe but was treated as a fief, divisible among female heirs and subject to the lordship of the kings of Scots, who must have been pleased to see this great lordship subdivided.

In 1316, soon after the judgment that the kingdom of the Scots was not partible, there was another attempt to use the law of fiefs to dismember a kingdom. Upon the death of Louis X of France and of his posthumous son in that year, Louis' younger brother Philip proclaimed himself king, but was faced with the objections of the third brother, Charles, who wanted his legal portion of the kingdom. He does not appear to have suggested sharing the Crown, but wanted a division of the territories that had been acquired by the Crown in the last hundred years, applying a principle familiar from the private law of the Ile-de-France, that is, equal division in the case of collateral succession. Some opportunists also contacted Edward II of England, whose wife Isabella was a sister of Louis and Charles, suggesting that he put in a claim for her share (*purpartie*) of France too.[51] Nothing came of all this, but it shows, like the Scottish case, that the rules about succession to estates could be brought up by interested parties when what was actually at issue was succession to a throne.

There were places where partible inheritance of political units could be found after 1100. The kingship of Norway was shared between two sons of Harald Gille on his death in 1136, and they acknowledged the claims of a third son in 1142. The Welsh principalities of the twelfth and thirteenth centuries, down to the English conquest of 1282, were frequently shared out between members of the ruling dynasty, although, as in the case of the Merovingians, it can be debated whether this was because of a custom or simply the result of power struggles.[52] In that same period, the composite kingdom of Castile-Leon periodically broke into constituent parts, or new ones, ruled by siblings or cousins. Before his death in 1065 Ferdinand the Great divided his realm between his three sons: the eldest, Sancho, received Castile; the second son, Alfonso, Leon; and the third, García, Galicia. He supposedly did this 'so that they might live a quiet life together after his death, if this were possible', but since Leon was the traditional heartland of the kingdom, Sancho might well have felt ill-used, and indeed Ferdinand is said to have loved Alfonso more than the others.[53] Alfonso reunited Castile and Leon in 1072, but they split into the two constituent kingdoms again between 1157 and 1230, each ruled by a branch of the royal dynasty. Before that, Portugal had emerged as an independent kingdom, with an illegitimate daughter of Alfonso VI as its first ruler. But after 1230 the number of Christian kingdoms in the Iberian peninsula was stable and none was to be formally divided again, with the exception of the creation of the kingdom of Majorca (which lasted from 1276 to 1285 and 1298 to 1343) from Aragonese territory.

The country in high medieval Latin Christendom most shaped by partible inheritance was Poland, where after 1138 the ruling dynasty, the Piasts, split into numerous lines, each at the head of a duchy. There were as many as ten or twelve of these at any one time and they were subject to repeated subdivision. Silesia, for example, split into Upper and Lower Silesia, both of which then spilt into three further subdivisions in the thirteenth century, and this was not the end of the process. Repeated division between brothers thus created numerous small states, although the more successful dukes might obtain more than one duchy. During this period, although individual Piast rulers of the eleventh century had borne the title 'king', that title lapsed and there were no Polish kings, only dukes. The revival of the royal title in 1295–6 and 1300–6 and then, permanently, in 1320 marked the end of the extreme fragmentation of the twelfth and thirteenth centuries. The situation in Poland in the years 1138–1320 resembled that in its large neighbour, Russia, where the Rurikid dynasty followed a similar pattern of inheritance and division.

Partibility also came to be a common practice among the great territorial princes of late medieval Germany, such as the rulers of Saxony or Bavaria, producing those hyphenated entities that give a Ruritanian flavour to the map of the Holy Roman Empire: Bavaria-Munich, Bavaria-Straubing, Bavaria-Landshut, Bavaria-Ingolstadt; Braunschweig-Lüneburg, Braunschweig-Wolfenbüttel, Braunschweig-Grubenhagen, and so forth, the example best known outside Germany being Saxe-Coburg-Gotha, a great exporter of monarchs and consorts, including Prince Albert, husband of Queen Victoria of Great Britain.[54] Division had not been practised at the level of the great duchies and counties, as distinct from ordinary aristocratic holdings, before 1250 but it was to mark Germany down to the nineteenth century. The small German mini-states, like the Polish duchies, demonstrate the point that partible inheritance solved the problem of disputes between brothers, but only at the risk of diminishing the family's overall power. The impartible inheritance of Flanders was indeed explained in just these terms by a chronicler writing in the 1070s: 'this was done to avoid the glory of the family being brought low by lack of family property if the province had been divided into many parts'.[55]

Efforts might be made to stop endless subdivision. When Louis the Pious stipulated the territorial division of his empire between the three sons he had at the time, he also specified 'if any of them dies, leaving legitimate children, power should not be divided among them, but instead the people should assemble and choose one of them, according as the Lord wishes'.[56] Louis envisaged three rulers in his place, but not more than three. It has been wisely observed that 'Every dynasty sooner or later faces the choice of either dividing the realm or shedding some of those eligible for the succession, or both.'[57] Louis planned to divide the realm between his three sons, and thereafter to shed any younger sons in each generation.

When Charlemagne dictated the terms of the division of his empire between his three sons after his death, he explained his purposes very clearly: 'We do not wish to bequeath to them, in confusion and disorder, the contention of quarrel and dispute by referring to the whole kingdom but, dividing the whole body of the kingdom into three portions, we are specifying and describing which portion each of them will protect and rule.'[58] This division, which he proposed in 806, included provisions for future relationships between the three parts: the king of one kingdom should not receive political exiles from another kingdom; a king's followers should only be granted fiefs (*beneficia*) within that king's kingdom, although this did not apply to inherited property; a woman from one kingdom could marry a husband from another kingdom, and keep control of her property in her original kingdom, even though living in another; disputes over the boundaries of the kingdoms should always be settled peacefully.[59] These are imaginative precautions addressing practical problems. The issue of men in one kingdom holding lands in another was indeed to be a recurrent issue in medieval politics, as, for example, in the case of England and France and England and Scotland. The harbouring of political exiles from another kingdom was another such issue, with one case, that of Robert of Artois, cited as a justification for the hostilities that were eventually to be known as the Hundred Years War.[60] Division solved one problem, the competing claims of ambitious sons, but created others.

Verdun

The political map of modern Europe is partly a result of family squabbles among the ruling dynasties of centuries past. The clearest, and one of the most important, examples is the division between France and Germany. Neither of these countries existed in the early Middle Ages, since the territories comprising those modern states were included in one vast Frankish kingdom, which, at its greatest extent under Charlemagne, stretched from Barcelona to Hamburg and from the frontier of Brittany to central Italy. But after Charlemagne's death, his descendants fought over the inheritance, and, following a particularly bloody civil war in the early 840s, three of his grandsons agreed on partition. The Treaty of Verdun of 843 specified who got what. It was quite a complex business, involving 120 delegates, forty from each brother, and an empire-wide survey of imperial resources.[61] The partition allotted most of the eastern part of the empire to Louis, the middle brother, and most of the western part to Charles, the youngest, but the oldest brother, Lothar, who already bore the imperial title, was allotted a strange elongated territory, composed of northern Italy, Provence and a swathe of land extending northwards from Provence to the North Sea. Although his realm looks odd on a map, it did give Lothar both Aachen and overlordship of Rome, the two imperial cities; in the negotiations leading to the Treaty of Verdun he had indeed put forward claims for a larger share than his brothers 'on account of the title of emperor and the dignity of the empire'.[62]

After Lothar's death in 855, his unusual amalgam of territories was divided among his three sons, with the northern section, from the North Sea to Burgundy, going to his namesake, Lothar II, who gave his name to the region (*regnum Lotharii*, i.e. 'Lothar's kingdom', whence Lotharingia, Lothringen, Lorraine). After the death of Lothar II in 869, Lotharingia went through an unsettled period, sometimes part of the kingdom of the East Franks, sometimes part of the kingdom of the West Franks, sometimes divided between them, but from 925 it was permanently part of the kingdom of the East Franks.[63] In this manner the lines drawn by the squabbling grandsons of Charlemagne came to be impressed right through the heart of western Europe.

In particular, the line between the kingdom of the West Franks and the kingdom of the East Franks (and its later development, the Holy Roman Empire) was to be the site of future struggle.[64] There were two important features of this political boundary: it did not correspond to a linguistic border, and it carved its path through densely populated landscapes which had centuries of common history. While most of the kingdom of the East Franks, or Germany, was German-speaking, Lotharingia was divided between Romance and Germanic speakers. Likewise, within the kingdom of the West Franks, or France, most of the county of Flanders was Germanic-speaking. Linguistic nationalism was not unknown in the Middle Ages, but this lack of fit between political and linguistic frontiers was rarely an issue in the medieval period and was only to have its full impact in the hyper-nationalism of the nineteenth and twentieth centuries.

This border cut right through the middle of the settled lands of the Carolingian empire. There were wild frontiers in medieval Europe, highly militarized borders that divided peoples of different religions or cultures. The word 'frontier' itself arose in such a borderland, the shifting and dangerous boundary between Christian and Muslim in the Iberian peninsula.[65] The frontiers that were carved through the former Carolingian empire, however, were nothing like that. They were imaginary lines between farms, estates, villages, towns and churches that were otherwise indistinguishable. Later in the Middle Ages, the boatmen on the Rhone and Saône, rivers that divided France from the Holy Roman Empire, simply called the western bank 'kingdom', the eastern bank 'empire'.[66] Their day's work might well take them from kingdom to empire and back many times. The very fact that these boundaries were defined by rivers is significant, since boundaries that follow rivers cut up natural unities, simply for the convenience of a clear demarcation. A contemporary of these ninth-century divisions lamented the fragmentation they entailed: 'instead of a kingdom, we have fragments of a kingdom'.[67]

Later historians recognized that France and Germany had a common origin. A monk of St-Denis near Paris, writing in the 1190s, explained that the phrase *regnum Francorum* had both a larger and a more restricted meaning. In the wide sense, it was a historical term and meant 'kingdom of the Franks' and included Germany, northern France and southern France, but in its narrower sense it meant simply the land between Rhine, Meuse and Loire, 'which is properly called Gaul but modern people call France'. He invoked a helpful parallel from biblical history: both the large kingdom of David and Solomon, and the later truncated version with just ten tribes were called the kingdom of Israel.[68] He clearly sees the kingdom of France of his own time as arising from fission.

These divisions, entirely dynastic in origin, thus determined there would be an eastern kingdom, mainly German-speaking, and a western kingdom, mainly Romance-speaking, and that the fate of the lands between them, which were partly Romance-speaking but fell eventually to the eastern kingdom, would be a tense political issue for a thousand years. As the French monarchy asserted its power within the kingdom of France in the late twelfth and thirteenth centuries, it also began to cast its eyes beyond the boundaries of the kingdom. The eastern boundary of France was long and bordered the highly fragmented lands of the Holy Roman Empire. This was the area where French expansion was to be most decisive in shaping the political and military history of western Europe. The first inroads across the border made by the French royal house were not through direct annexation but by the acquisition of fiefs and lordships. Provence came into the hands of Charles of Anjou, brother of Louis IX of France, in 1246, when he married the heir to the county, and thereafter it passed through the hands of his descendants and later into the possession of yet another cadet branch of the French royal house before being finally incorporated into the kingdom of France in the 1480s. Another important lordship in the Empire was acquired by purchase in 1349. This was the county of Vienne, which had become known as the Dauphiné from the name borne by many of its rulers, Dolphinus, a name that had then turned into a title. After its acquisition by France, the Dauphiné became the usual apanage of the heir to the throne, who consequently was known as the Dauphin (see above, p. 105). This French nibbling gathered pace in the Early Modern period. The bishoprics of Metz, Toul and Verdun were seized in 1552 and officially ceded in 1648, while Louis XIV pushed the French frontier to the Rhine, annexing Strassburg in 1681. How far east France would extend was an open question, and one that constantly provoked war.[69] It is only since 1945 that the frontiers of the French state have had a long period of stability in modern times.

The politicization of Carolingian history visible in French and German textbooks of the nineteenth century has, as its background, this division between the two countries and the struggle over the delimitation of their borders. The millennium of the Treaty of Verdun in 1843 was celebrated in Germany as 'the founding of the German Reich'. The famous German medievalist Georg Waitz gave a lecture with that title and the following year the king of Prussia founded a valuable Verdun Prize, to be awarded every five years for the best work on German history.[70] The Treaty of Verdun was still a standard set-piece of those twentieth-century historians who wrote books with titles such as *La naissance de la France* ('The Birth of France')[71] or *Wie das erste Reich der Deutschen entstand* ('How the First German Reich was Born').[72]

Historians were aware that no one in the ninth century planned or envisaged this long-term effect but they nevertheless stressed the formative nature of those Carolingian divisions:

> Just as no one at Verdun intended to destroy the unity of the Christian world forever, so no one believed that the borders that were defined there would last for long. In fact, the treaty determined the political geography of France for the whole of the Middle Ages and beyond, and, to a lesser extent, that of the future Germany. No one expected these results.[73]

It can still be reasonably argued that 'the treaty of Verdun is like a prefiguration of the political map of western Europe'.[74]

When young Germans and Frenchmen died in the hundreds of thousands fighting each other in the nineteenth and twentieth centuries, the frontier they were fighting on was an inheritance from that distant time. In 1916 Verdun indeed cropped up again as a name of significance. Who would believe that some makeshift dynastic arrangement of the ninth century would be etched permanently on the map of Europe, and that young men might die for that line in 1870 or 1914, a thousand years after it was devised?

Wicked Uncles

Relations between uncles and nephews were different in partible dynastic systems, where the kingdom was customarily divided, and impartible systems. In the former, younger brothers could expect their share, although they could only expand it at the expense either of their brothers or their nephews. The kingdom of the Franks in the early Middle Ages provides a perfect example. As mentioned above, the custom among the Merovingian kings of the Franks was to divide the kingdom among all the old king's sons. This led not only to rivalry between the brothers but also, as their children grew up, conflict between uncles and nephews, which could be brutal. After the death of Clovis, the first Christian king of the Franks, in 511, his kingdom was divided between his four sons. One of these, Chlodomer, was killed in battle, leaving young male children. Their uncles, Chlodomer's brothers, were envious of these boys, especially since they seemed to be favourites with their grandmother. Two of the uncles, Childebert and Clothar (Lothar), asked the grand-mother (that is, their own mother) to send the boys to them, 'so that they may be raised to the kingdom'. Unsuspecting, she did as they asked. Events at this point became complicated, but the eventual outcome was that the two brothers were alone with the two nephews: 'Without delay, Clothar seized the older boy by the arm, threw him to the ground and, driving a knife into his armpit, cruelly killed him.' The boy's younger brother knelt at Childebert's feet, wrapped his arms around his legs and begged for his life. Childebert, clearly the softer of the two uncles, then asked Clothar not to kill the boy. Clothar was unmoved: 'Either you push him off or you will die in his place!', he cried. Childebert pushed the boy towards Clothar, who stabbed and killed him. The uncles then killed the boys' servants and nurses. 'After they had been killed, Clothar mounted his horse and departed, little bothered by the killing of his nephews.' Nor does he seem to have been bothered by the fact that, since he had married his brother Chlodomer's widow, they were also his stepchildren.[75]

The Merovingians have a particularly strong reputation for violence within the family. This is only in part to be explained by their
individual emotions; it is also linked to the dynastic pattern of recurrent territorial divisions. However, impartible systems, such as those
based on primogeniture, also had an intrinsic tendency to produce
wicked uncles. If your father was a king, you might well dream of
being a king yourself, and, although you might have to tolerate your
older brother inheriting the throne, why should his snivelling children have precedence over you? In the early Middle Ages, and in
some regions much later than that, the logic of kingship demanded
that a dead king's younger brother was preferable as a successor to
that king's young children. A king had to be a war-leader, and the
advantages of an adult war-leader are self-evident. But with the crystal-
lization of rules of succession that favoured the sons of kings, even
infant children were regarded as rightful heirs. Their uncles might
not all take a legalistic view, however, and this is when ambitious and
ruthless uncles crop up: the wickedness of wicked uncles is determined by these rights of child inheritance.

One of the wickedest of the wicked uncles was King John of England.
When Richard I 'the Lionheart' was struck by a mortal crossbow bolt
while campaigning in the south of France in 1199, the two main claimants to succeed him were Arthur, the son of his deceased brother
Geoffrey, and John, younger brother of Richard and Geoffrey. Arthur
was not yet a teenager – he turned twelve just before Richard's death – but
he had the support of the lords of Brittany, where he had grown up. His
mother Constance was a member of the old ruling family of Brittany and
the Bretons recognized Arthur as their duke. At first he was also able to
win the support of other parts of Richard's French empire, Anjou and the
surrounding regions, and had the backing of the French king Philip
Augustus. But the war of 1199–1200 saw some serious reverses for
Arthur, and eventually he had to settle for Brittany alone, held as a fief
from his uncle John. War broke out again in 1202. On one side were
Philip Augustus and Arthur, on the other John. In the summer of 1202,
John, showing rare military flair at this point, managed to defeat and
capture his nephew and many of his supporters. Arthur was imprisoned
in Normandy and was never seen again.

What exactly happened will always be uncertain, but there is no doubt that John had both the means and the motive for getting rid of Arthur. Shakespeare, who knew that stories of wicked uncles make great theatre, puts these words into the mouth of an acute observer in his play *King John*:

> John hath seiz'd Arthur, and it cannot be,
>
> That whiles warme life playes in that infants veines,
>
> The mis-plac'd John should entertaine an houre,
>
> One minute, nay one quiet breath of rest.

There is indeed one contemporary chronicle that probably had a good source for the story it tells of Arthur's fate:

> When King John had captured Arthur and held him alive in prison for some time, he finally killed him with his own hand, in the keep of Rouen castle, on the Thursday before Easter [3 April 1203], after dinner, when he was drunk and filled with the devil. Tying a great stone to his body, he threw it into the river Seine. It was found in a fisherman's net and dragged to the shore, where it was recognized, and then buried in the priory of Bec, secretly for fear of the tyrant.[76]

As rumours of Arthur's murder spread, a sense of outrage stirred up his supporters and gave a propaganda advantage to John's great enemy, Philip Augustus of France. William the Breton, a trusted servant of the French king and a propagandist for his cause, painted a pathetic picture of the murder in his verse epic, the *Philippis*, as Arthur pleaded for his life: 'Uncle', he cried, 'have pity on your little nephew; uncle, good uncle, spare, o spare, your nephew; spare your own kindred; spare your brother's offspring.'[77] William the Breton goes on to compare John with Nero, Judas and Herod, the king who ordered the massacre of the Innocents, although Arthur, sixteen at the time of his death, would certainly have been viewed by contemporary standards as a leader of men rather than a 'little nephew'. The murder and the reaction to it thus played some part in John's defeat and his loss of his northern French territories. Perhaps he should have let his nephew live.

John's succession to the English throne in preference to Arthur threw up a delicate legal question.[78] Geoffrey, Arthur's father, had been John's older brother, so, according to one reading, his right to succeed would be superior to John's. Arthur, it could be argued, had inherited his father's right; the legal term for this is 'representation'. Alternatively, it could be said that John had the superior right, as closer in blood to Richard, being a brother, not merely a nephew. These differences could not be resolved by looking up a list or a table, for none such existed, and eventually the issue was determined by war and murder, but it had repercussions in the courtrooms.

Uncertainty about such a case is recognized in the contemporary English lawbook known as Glanvill, which says that 'when someone dies having a younger son and a grandson born to his predeceased oldest son, there is great doubt in law which of them is to be preferred in the succession, the son or the grandson'.[79] The custom of Normandy, which was also ruled by the king of England at this time, was more definite: 'a son, although younger, is the nearer heir of his father than the grandchildren, sons of the older son'.[80] The chief men of both England and Normandy, although not of Anjou, the other main part of the inheritance, accepted John as their lord in 1199. The impact of this decision, that John the younger brother should succeed, not the son of a deceased older brother, has been traced in the ordinary land law of England. In a case heard in the first year of John's reign, for example, in which the descendants of a deceased older brother obtained an inquest into the rights of a younger brother who actually held the land in question, the record concludes, 'it should be noted that this inquest was made through command of the lord king and not through the decision of the court or according to the custom of the realm'.[81] John might well be interested in such an issue. In 1201, two years after John came to the throne, a case was heard in Cornwall, in which a younger brother claimed that he should succeed to his older brother's acre of land, not the son of a deceased middle brother, which was exactly the issue between John and Arthur. The judges record the detail of the case and then conclude 'sine die' – adjourned with no set date for resumption – 'because the judgment depends on the king's will'.[82] It sounds as if they were well aware of just how delicate such cases were. The learned judges of the 1220s and 1230s recognized that the precedent of 'the king's case' (*casus regis*) would prevent a son of a deceased older brother getting a court judgment against his uncle, although this rule silently disappeared in the course of the later thirteenth century.[83]

A similar dispute between uncle and nephew occurred in the kingdom of Sicily a hundred years later. Charles II of Sicily (1285–1309) had several sons. The second one, Louis, became a friar (and later a saint) so was not a contender to inherit. The oldest son, Charles Martel, was recognized as heir in 1289 but died before his father, in 1295, leaving a seven-year-old son, Charles Robert or Canrobert. Charles II decided that he would prefer his third son, Robert, to succeed him, rather than this grandchild, and arranged the support of the pope for his position. On his death, Robert became king of Sicily (that is, the mainland territory also known as the kingdom of Naples). But the older line had not given up its claims, and the situation was complicated by the fact that Canrobert had, through his mother, a claim to the kingdom of Hungary, and this he had eventually been able to assert. The kings of Hungary thus nurtured a grievance and believed that they, not Robert and his family, should be kings of Sicily. The issue was the same as that with John and Arthur, the rights of a younger brother versus those of a son of a deceased older brother.

Both the political implications of the Sicilian case, and its intellectual and legal ramifications, far outstripped those of the earlier one. The king of Hungary invaded the kingdom of Sicily more than once. As early as 1312, just three years into his reign, King Robert was reportedly worried about such an invasion.[84] Hungary and Sicily were not then so far apart as their present geographical associations would lead one to imagine, since in the middle and eastern parts of Italy the kingdom of Sicily extended to latitudes further north than Rome, and the kingdom of Hungary included Croatia, with its coast only 100 miles away, not to mention the land routes around the head of the Adriatic. When he attacked the kingdom of Sicily in 1347, King Louis of Hungary took just six weeks to get from his base at Visegrád on the Danube to the northern frontier of the kingdom of Sicily in central Italy.[85]

Italy was also the home of the lawyers, whom both sides enlisted to back their case.[86] Lawyers can, of course, always produce plenty of arguments. Baldus de Ubaldis, one of the most famous academic lawyers of the Middle Ages, gave ten reasons for and ten reasons against the right of

Robert of Naples to succeed to the throne instead of his older brother's son. He noted that Canrobert's claim was 'in the person of his father', that is, through representation, he thought that the usual law of fiefs would give the succession to the grandson, but he acknowledged that Pope Boniface VIII, the Vicar of Christ, had backed Robert's succession instead and that Boniface had probably taken into account some practical considerations, 'since it is better to be ruled by an older person'. One of the technical issues in Baldus' discussion was the meaning of *primogenitus*, 'firstborn'. Even if it were acknowledged that the firstborn had a greater right to succeed, wrote Baldus, 'a grandson cannot be called firstborn, except by fiction and incorrectly, since that would be against the natural bounds of the truth, and we ought to pay no attention to fictions'.[87]

The main participants in the initial decision to exclude Canrobert in favour of his uncle had also fastened upon this word *primogenitus*. Writing to Charles II in 1297, after the death of the king's first son Charles Martel and the entry into the religious life of his second son Louis, Boniface VIII declared, 'Among your children, he is to be understood as *primogenitus* and to be your successor and heir in the kingdom who, at the time of your death, is found to be prior in degree and older in birth.'[88] The pope was thus authorizing the succession of Charles' oldest surviving son, as indeed occurred. The rather special meaning that *primogenitus* thus acquired comes out vividly in Charles' will of 1308, the year before his death: 'We institute as our heir and universal successor in our kingdoms Robert, our firstborn; we bequeath to Charles, our grandson, the firstborn of our former firstborn, the king of Hungary, 2000 ounces of gold.'[89] Robert was now *primogenitus*, oldest surviving son, while Charles' grandson was the *primogenitus* of a former *primogenitus*.

Lawyers were naturally found to make the case for the king of Hungary. They asserted that, in fiefs, the grandson should succeed the grandfather in the place of his deceased father, and this rule covered the kingdom of Sicily.[90] A memorandum drawn up by a learned Italian lawyer for the king of Hungary in 1376 gave it as 'common opinion that a son of a firstborn son is to be understood as a firstborn (*primogenitus*) in succession and is to be preferred to an uncle', echoing and refuting the phrase of Boniface VIII. He also denied that a mere declaration by Boniface and the agreement of Charles II could change this.[91] The case shaped European politics for almost a century. There was even a brief period in 1385–6 when a great-grandson of Charles II ruled both Sicily and Hungary. And it aroused strong feelings. Dante placed Charles Martel in Paradise and referred to 'the treacheries his seed would suffer'.[92] This uncle–nephew conflict thus won a mention in the greatest poem of the Middle Ages.

The late fourteenth century saw boy kings in both England and France, each with powerful uncles. Richard II succeeded to the English throne in 1377 aged ten, Charles VI to the French throne three years later aged eleven. Three of Richard's paternal uncles were alive: John of Gaunt, Edmund of Langley and, by far the youngest, Thomas of Woodstock, who was twenty-two when Richard came to the throne. Charles VI also had powerful uncles: Louis, duke of Anjou, Philip the Bold, duke of Burgundy, John, duke of Berry, and, on his mother's side, Louis, duke of Bourbon.

Since the difference in age between Richard II and Thomas of Woodstock (who became duke of Gloucester in 1385) was only twelve years, this was a possible difference in age between brothers, rather than uncle and nephew, and it may be one reason that Thomas felt competitive with, rather than protective of, his young nephew. He spoke derisively of Richard's lack of warlike spirit in the conflict with France: 'If there were a good king in charge in England', he reportedly said, 'who desired war and the recovery of his inheritance, he would find 100,000 archers and 6,000 men-at-arms to serve him. I am the youngest of all the princes of England, but I would be the first to renew the war.'[93] In 1387, when Richard was twenty, five great nobles, including Thomas of Woodstock, staged a coup against him. The king remained in power but his favourites were tried for treason and executed or exiled. Among those executed was Simon Burley, former tutor of the young king Richard. Duke Thomas was particularly insistent on the death sentence for him, despite strong opposition to it on the part of his older brother Edmund of Langley. After this, it has been memorably said, 'if Richard had been prepared to bury the hatchet, he had not forgotten where he had buried it',[94] and in 1397 he had three of the five nobles responsible for the coup of 1387 arrested, including Thomas of Woodstock. When the king came with a powerful body of men to arrest his uncle, Thomas pleaded, 'May you act towards me mercifully and spare my life.' The king's chilling reply was, 'You will have the same mercy that you showed to Simon Burley.'[95] Thomas was sent off under guard to Calais, then an English possession, and murdered soon afterwards. He was declared a traitor posthumously, and the king took all his possessions, but he did allow his uncle's body to be buried honourably in Westminster Abbey.

In the case of Charles VI of France, Richard's contemporary, the balance between nephew and uncles was different. Although Richard became king at the age of ten, there was no formal regency, but the arrangements for Charles' minority had been set out by his father, Charles V, some years before, and they gave official positions and authority to his uncles (see above, pp. 119–20). Charles V declared that his oldest brother, Louis of Anjou, 'on account of the very singular, perfect, loyal and true love that he has always had towards us and our children, should have the government of our kingdom', but that another brother, Philip of Burgundy, and his brother-in-law, Louis of Bourbon, 'should be tutors and governors of our children'.[96] What this arrangement guaranteed was a period of fierce rivalry during Charles' minority, as each uncle sought to establish his own position and use the royal resources for his own ambitions. Nevertheless, France was steered through a very difficult time in Charles VI's early years, which included popular revolt, English invasion and the virtual secession of Flanders. Charles came of age in 1388.

What transformed Charles' reign and gave his uncles a quite new significance, was the sudden onset of mental illness that rendered the king incapable of ruling. The political results were disastrous. In the summer of 1392 Charles, then aged twenty-three, was leading a military expedition against the duke of Brittany. According to an eye-witness, his household had already noticed unsettling signs of what was to come: 'foolish words' and 'gestures unbecoming the royal majesty'. But the final outbreak was far more serious. While the army was on the march, 'a most lowly man' terrified the king by calling out, 'Don't go any further, noble king, for you are soon to be betrayed!' Then one of the king's soldiers accidentally dropped his sword. 'The king was moved to a sudden fury by this crash and, as if out of his senses, he brandished his sword and killed the soldier.' He then went on a rampage, charging his own followers and killing four more of them, while shouting, 'I am to be handed over to my enemies!' Only after an hour, when his sword broke, could he be restrained and brought back to the nearest town, tied to a cart.[97] The king regained his senses after a few days, but this was only the first of a series of episodes.

Explanations of his illness varied. After the first dramatic attack, medical opinion was that the cause was black choler, the bodily humour that was the root of melancholy, combined with the king's anger at the slow progress of his army. Many others said it was a visitation from God, 'who chastises those he loves'. But the majority opinion, both among the upper and lower classes, was that it had been inflicted by witches and sorcerers, who abounded in the kingdom of France.[98] The chronicler Jean Froissart gives a characteristically vivid account of the incident, stressing, for his part, the fact that the king had overheated, partly because of the velour jacket he was wearing, and describing how afterwards the king's uncles had inquired carefully about what he had last had to drink.[99]

Charles reigned for thirty years after this first onset, and his spells of madness, termed 'absences' by the court, alternated with brief lucid periods. Often, he had the illusion that he was made of glass, and allowed no one to touch him, and had iron rods sewn into his clothes to protect him.[100] It was clearly necessary to have some sort of regency, even if not an official one. Louis of Anjou was dead by this time, but Philip of Burgundy took effective control of the royal government, in alliance with his brother, John of Berry, and for most of the next decade the king's uncles built up their power and their territorial possessions, siphoned off a high proportion of royal income and made the important political decisions. But a challenger arose in the person of the king's younger brother, Louis of Orleans, who maintained good relations with his brother, even during his periods of insanity. Relations between Louis and the duke of Burgundy were especially bitter and competitive, and the quarrels between their followers continued after Philip's death and the succession of his son John as duke of Burgundy, culminating in murder and civil war (see below, pp. 222–5).

Another king who suffered mental illness was Charles' grandson, Henry VI of England. It is sometimes thought that Henry's madness can be traced genetically to Charles, but they had very different forms of illness. Charles' manic outbursts and his remarkable fantasies, such as the belief that he was made of glass, were nothing like the illness that afflicted Henry, who simply slumped into a stupor, failing to register even the birth of his only son. Henry, like Charles VI, had powerful and ambitious uncles who acted as regents during his minority. Until the birth of the king's son, the oldest of his uncles was next in line to the throne. This led to dangerous territory, such as consultation of experts on the question of when Henry VI would die (see below, pp. 358–9). The uncles of Charles VI had no such temptation since Charles had many children, born both before and after his first bout of insanity, although they still knew how to take advantage of the situation.

The case of Richard II of England and Thomas of Woodstock shows that the age gap between uncles and nephews need not be great. Sometimes, indeed, nephews were older than their uncles. When Henry of Castile, later to be the short-lived Henry I, was born in 1204, his older sister Berenguela had already given birth to four or five children. One of them, Ferdinand, who was born in 1201 or a year or two before, succeeded Henry on the throne of Castile. So, although there was a seemingly natural generational transition, with a nephew succeeding an uncle, the nephew in this case was actually older than his uncle. And the story of Ferdinand's grandson, Sancho IV of Castile, also shows that ambitious uncles did not have to be very old. Sancho was a younger son of Alfonso X (1252–84). When his older brother Ferdinand de la Cerda died in 1275, leaving two young sons, the elder only five, the seventeen-year-old Sancho and his aristocratic supporters asserted his rights as heir to the kingdom over those of his young nephews and won official recognition when the chief men of the kingdom all did homage to him in 1276.[101] Soon thereafter Sancho began issuing documents as 'oldest son and heir of the lord king Alfonso'.[102]

But the rights of the two sons of Ferdinand de la Cerda, Alfonso and Ferdinand, known as the Infantes de la Cerda, still had their champions. Alfonso X's own law code, the *Siete Partidas*, when discussing succession to the kingdom, stated that 'wise and learned men decreed that if the eldest son should die before he inherited, if he should leave a son or daughter that he has had of his lawful wife, he or she should have it, and no other'.[103]

By this law, which recognized the principle of representation, the older of the Infantes de la Cerda was clearly heir to the Castilian throne. And the rights of the young princes were also backed by the noble house of Lara. Moreover, their mother, Blanche, the widow of Ferdinand de la Cerda, was the sister of the king of France. The political situation became yet more complex when Alfonso X and his wife, Yolande or Violante, became estranged. In 1278, Yolande, who was the sister of the king of Aragon, fled to her brother's kingdom, taking with her the Infantes de la Cerda, her grandsons. Alfonso responded by reiterating Sancho's status as heir.[104]

The difficult political relations between the three generations, that of Alfonso X, his son Sancho and Alfonso's grandchildren, the Infantes de la Cerda, were to be a major feature of the history of Castile for the next fifty years, continuing long after the deaths of Alfonso and Sancho. 'Because of this,' lamented one chronicler, 'the kingdom suffered much evil and much damage.'[105] Castile was riven with civil war. Alfonso X was deposed by Sancho and recognized the Infantes de la Cerda as his heirs, but Sancho nevertheless obtained the throne. Alfonso de la Cerda, growing up in exile, sought and sometimes obtained help from his relations in Aragon and in France, and managed on one occasion, after the death of Sancho IV, to establish himself temporarily in Castile. It was not until 1331 that the aging claimant finally came to a compromise with Alfonso XI, Sancho's grandson. He abandoned his claims to the throne in return for the grant of a huge lordship within the kingdom, and his noble descendants were prominent in the later history of Castile. Nevertheless, he remains a classic example of a nephew dispossessed by an ambitious uncle. It was the descendants of that uncle, Sancho IV, who were to rule Castile for the rest of the Middle Ages.[106]

Killing Cousins

Some dynastic systems, such as that of native Ireland, simply assumed there would be competition between cousins. In his great book *Conquest, Coexistence and Change: Wales 1063–1415*, Rees Davies included several family trees of the Welsh princely dynasties of the eleventh, twelfth and thirteenth centuries, which not only showed family relationships but also, through a system of underlining, indicated which family members had been 'killed or maimed by other members of the dynasty'.[107] Of the twenty-three sons, grandsons and great-grandsons of Bleddyn ap Cynfyn of Powys, seven had this unenviable distinction; of the twenty-seven male descendants of Owain ap Hywel Dda of Deheubarth in the following five generations, by a strange coincidence, again seven were killed by other descendants of Owain; in Gwynedd, from 1137, the death of Gruffudd ap Cynan, down to the catastrophe of 1282, family rivalry was as vigorous, but significantly less bloody: only two family members out of twenty-nine males were killed or maimed, although another nine were imprisoned or dispossessed by their kinsmen. As Rees Davies pointed out in his book, his diagrams do not include all male members of the dynasty, so it would be wrong to use them for rigorously statistical purposes, but they do convey an impression, and that impression is that members of Welsh princely dynasties had a one in three or one in four chance of being killed, maimed or dispossessed by kinsmen.

One of the diagrams is labelled 'Segmentary Conflict in a Native Welsh Dynasty', but to use the anthropological term 'segmentary' when talking of early Wales, or Ireland for that matter, may be misleading. The expression was devised in the twentieth century to describe the kinship structures and political workings of some African societies, usually very small-scale ones. Its borrowing by historians of early Wales and Ireland, even if worthily motivated by the desire to integrate history and anthropology, risks by implication placing these societies into the common category of 'primitive'. But if a defining feature of 'segmentary conflict' is the rivalry of cousins for power, then it applies not just to the rural and economically undeveloped worlds of early Wales and Ireland but also to the most sophisticated and urban parts of medieval Europe. The kingdom of Naples, with its networks of towns, high literacy and international connections, was riven by segmentary conflict of this type in the fourteenth and fifteenth centuries, as the lineages descending from four of the sons of Charles II (1285–1309) struggled with each other. They intermarried, but they also murdered one another, and they did so for four generations. Likewise, the so-called Wars of the Roses in England are a perfect example of segmentary conflict: Henry VI was deposed and killed by his third cousins.

In English history, violent conflicts between first cousins repeatedly caused civil war, deposition and murder. The long war in the twelfth century between King Stephen and his cousin Matilda was so destructive that it has been called simply 'The Anarchy'. In the early fourteenth century the struggle between Edward II and his cousin Thomas of Lancaster ended in the latter's judicial murder; interestingly, both parties were later claimed as saints. In 1399 Richard II was deposed, and later murdered, by his cousin Henry Bolingbroke (Henry IV). They had played together as children and were knighted by their grandfather, Edward III, on the same day, but nothing idyllic marked their final encounter.

France and Burgundy

A particularly long and violent struggle between royal cousins marked the history of France and Burgundy in the fifteenth century. The greatest threat to the French monarchy from a junior branch of the royal dynasty arose when the dukes of Burgundy amassed so much land and power that they came very close to establishing a new kingdom of their own in the borderlands between France and Germany. Burgundy has indeed been called 'The Unfinished Kingdom'.[108] The founder of this line was Philip, fourth son of John II of France, who was endowed with the duchy as an apanage in 1363. He married the heir to Flanders and Artois, which he acquired on the death of his father-in-law, Louis de Male, count of Flanders, in 1384, along with the county, as distinct from the duchy, of Burgundy. Because the county of Burgundy was part of the Holy Roman Empire, not the kingdom of France, Philip now ruled an assemblage of lands straddling the frontier between the Empire and the kingdom. This was to be a determining characteristic of the Burgundian state.

Philip and his three successors were major figures in European politics for over a century. Each successive duke of Burgundy added to the family lands, by purchase, conquest or inheritance, gradually building up an almost continuous bloc of territory extending 450 miles (750 kilometres) from the Jura Mountains to the North Sea. As members of the French royal house and as peers of France, they were deeply involved in the violent and sometimes chaotic politics of the Hundred Years War. Their rivalry with other branches of the dynasty, notably with Louis, Duke of Orleans, younger brother of King Charles VI, eventually accelerated into civil war and two dramatic public murders, of Louis of Orleans in the streets of Paris in 1407 and John the Fearless, second Duke of Burgundy, in 1419.

The latter was especially spectacular. By the year 1419 John's opponents were headed by the Dauphin Charles, and, after negotiations between the duke and the Dauphin conducted by Tanneguy du Châtel, one of the Dauphin's trusted followers, an agreement was made that the two great Capetian princes should meet on the bridge at Montereau, where the river Yonne joins the Seine, upstream from Paris. As Duke John neared the town it was reported to him that the party of the Dauphin had

Figure 8 The murder of John the Fearless, duke of Burgundy, by followers of the Dauphin on the bridge at Montereau in 1419, a particularly bloody moment in the long struggle between the two branches of the French royal house.
ART Collection/Alamy.

erected several strong barriers on the bridge, and some of his men advised him against proceeding further. Opinions were divided, but eventually the duke announced in a high clear voice that he would go on and 'await the adventure that it pleased God to send him'. Tanneguy du Châtel informed him the Dauphin was ready, and, with a small group of his nobles, John advanced onto the bridge. Some of the Dauphin's men met him at the first barrier on the bridge, renewed the oaths and promises as to his security and told him the Dauphin awaited him. He passed the first barrier, then the second, which was immediately locked behind him. There waiting was Tanneguy du Châtel, and Duke John slapped him on the shoulder, saying to his men, 'here is the one I trust!' The Dauphin was present, fully armed, leaning on one of the barriers. The duke knelt before him but received a cold response. One of the Dauphin's followers took the kneeling duke by the arm, supposedly to help his rise, but at this moment Tanneguy du Châtel approached, said, 'It is time!', and struck the duke in the face with a small axe, slicing off his chin. John grasped for his sword, but Tanneguy and others gave him repeated blows and he fell dead. A sword was stuck into his belly to make sure. One of the Burgundian nobles who tried to resist was killed, the rest made captive. After the killing of his cousin, the Dauphin, who had been looking on, retired behind the barrier on which he had been leaning, and was escorted back to his lodgings.[109]

The immediate result of the murder of John the Fearless was an alliance between the Burgundians and the English invaders of France. This was agreed in principle within two months of the assassination and embodied in a formal treaty in December 1419. For the next sixteen years Philip the Good, son and heir of the murdered Duke John, cooperated with the English, although not without tension. The most remarkable fruit of this Anglo-Burgundian cooperation was the capture of Joan of Arc in a skirmish before Compiègne in 1430. She was a prisoner of the Burgundians before being sold to the English, tried and burned. But eventually Duke Philip came to terms with Charles VII, that is, the Dauphin who had stood by and watched while his father had been butchered. In the Treaty of Arras of 1435, Charles VII offered 'our cousin, Philip, duke of Burgundy' his excuses for the murder on the bridge at Montereau: he had been young and inexperienced at the time of the murder, it was a wicked deed, and he begged Duke Philip to remove from his heart any hatred towards him that he might have on its account; he would do all he could to arrest the perpetrators, relying on a list of their names provided by the duke; he would establish religious foundations for the soul of Duke John, including a Charterhouse at Montereau itself; as recompense for Duke John's jewels, plundered at the time of the murder, he would pay 50,000 *écus d'or*, representing about 419 pounds or 190 kilogrammes of gold. It was only after all these provisions that the Treaty went on to talk about the territorial concessions Charles would make to Philip and the common front they would offer to the English. The Treaty of Arras, an important turning point in the Hundred Years War, thus opened with detailed provisions regarding a family murder.[110]

But the dukes of Burgundy had ambitions wider than that of being the dominant noble in France. One possibility was for the duke to become Holy Roman Emperor, with its essential preliminary of election as 'king of the Romans' by the leading figures of Germany. Another was the creation of a new kingdom. This hovered on the brink of realization in the middle decades of the fifteenth century. One of the subjects discussed between representatives of the Holy Roman Empire and Duke Philip in 1447 was 'if it pleased him to be a king and take a crown with the title of one of his lands, such as Frisia, which was a kingdom in ancient times, or Brabant, which is the most ancient and excellent duchy of all Christendom'.[111] Nothing came of this, but the idea was opened up again under Philip's son and successor, the fiery but erratic Charles the Bold. Charles was well aware that there had once been a kingdom of Burgundy, which, he thought, France had 'usurped'.[112] It was even reported in 1473, after a ceremonious and well-publicized meeting at Trier, that a definite agreement had been made between Charles and the Emperor Frederick III that all Charles' lands in the Holy Roman Empire would be incorporated into a new 'kingdom of Burgundy', for which he would do homage and render military service to the emperor.[113] For whatever reason, the emperor got cold feet and departed secretly from Trier, leaving behind not only Duke Charles but also an unused crown and sceptre.[114]

From the time of her birth in February 1457, Mary of Burgundy, daughter of Charles the Bold, was heir to the Burgundian domains. As the years passed and it became clear that Charles would not have a son,

Mary, as the most eligible bride in Christendom, was the subject of many marriage proposals. Eventually, despite the complications of their earlier dealings, Duke Charles and the emperor Frederick III agreed that Mary should marry Frederick's son Maximilian of Habsburg. The marriage had not actually taken place when Duke Charles was killed in battle at Nancy in 1477, but it was celebrated soon thereafter, and so the Habsburgs staked their claim to the Burgundian inheritance. Although the French king was able to recover the duchy of Burgundy, most of the rest of the lands of Charles the Bold eventually came into Habsburg hands. The endowment of a junior line of the French royal family in 1363 thus led, two hundred years later, to the establishment along the French frontier of the greatest rivals to the kings of France. But if Charles the Bold had had a son to succeed him, his lands would probably have remained under the rule of his family, and perhaps the dukes of Burgundy might even have obtained the royal title they were so close to procuring. The Low Countries, rather than being under Habsburg rule, could have formed part of a new kingdom between France and Germany. So, the genetic lottery, and luck, again played a central part in European political history.

Queens, Sons and Lovers

Adulterous Queens

Although ruling female sovereigns were uncommon, queens consort, that is, wives of kings, were present in almost all kingdoms most of the time. Such queens not only had the task of giving birth to a son but were also centres of power: they had their own landed estate and treasure, they had a household, followers and servants, they were patrons of the Church and perhaps of writers and craftsmen. But they also had enemies, and because the queen's chief role was sexual, to conceive and bear a son, her enemies might well choose to undermine her by a sexual charge, an accusation of adultery.[115] An adulterous queen threatened both the king's honour and the legitimacy of his descent. Such accusations were very serious and, although not common, there were a sufficient number of cases, and they attracted sufficient attention as public sexual scandals, that they also became a subject in fictional literature.[116] The love triangles of Arthur/Guinevere/Lancelot and Mark/Isolde/Tristan, which centre on adulterous queens, are among the most familiar stories to have come down from the Middle Ages. Perhaps significantly, however, these famous literary cases involve queens who had not borne children, and they thus highlight fidelity, honour and trust between men rather than the legitimacy of the bloodline.

A notorious historical case involved the empress Judith, second wife of the emperor Louis the Pious. When Louis married her, in 819, he was over forty and already had three sons by his first wife. It is not known how old Judith was, but she must have been younger, perhaps much younger, and was renowned as being 'really pretty (*pulchra valde*)'.[117] In 823 she gave birth to a son, Charles, and then dedicated herself to ensuring that he would get his share of Louis' empire, in the face of understandable resentment from Louis' older children, her stepsons (see above, pp. 195–6). A further source of tension at Louis' court was the dominant role of the chamberlain, Bernard, count of Septimania (Septimania is southern France between the Rhone and the Pyrenees). Resentment against him, and hostility to Judith's ambitions for her son, could be neatly combined in an accusation that Bernard and Judith were engaged in an adulterous affair. Their enemies went to one of Louis' sons, complaining about Bernard's arrogance, 'and also asserting, what is horrible to say, that he had defiled the father's marriage bed'. The word used of Bernard here is *incestator*, which can simply mean 'defiler' but also more specifically 'one who engages in incest', a charge based on the fact that Bernard was Louis' cousin and godson. The emperor's lack of response to this shameful behaviour was attributed to witchcraft: 'moreover, the father was so deceived by certain enchantments that not only could he not avenge this but was not even able to notice it'.[118] A shifting alliance of Bernard and Judith's enemies, including Louis' older sons, was powerful enough to have Judith placed in a nunnery and make Bernard flee to Spain. But the situation was volatile, and both of them were eventually allowed to clear themselves by swearing an oath to their innocence. In the end, Judith was successful in her backing of her son Charles, who is known as Charles the Bald and sometimes regarded as the 'first king of France'. One of the things that he did early in his reign was to have Bernard of Septimania executed, although not on a charge of adultery or incest.

Accusations of adulterous relations between queens and bishops were not uncommon, possibly because bishops would have less restricted access to royal women, as advisers or confessors, and this would give plausibility to accusations. In 887 Richardis, wife of the Frankish ruler Charles the Fat, was accused of adultery with Liutward, bishop of Vercelli, 'who was active in the palace, living intimately with her and the emperor', but she was able to refute the charge decisively.[119] A century later, Emma, wife of Lothar, king of the West Franks, was accused by her brother-in-law, Lothar's brother Charles, of adultery with Bishop Adalbero of Laon. Since the issue was public knowledge, a council of bishops was convened to discuss it. Intriguingly, the chronicle describing these events has the section containing their judgment cut away.[120] We have a sad letter of Emma to her mother, complaining of the way her friends have turned against her and how 'they have made up very wicked things against the bishop of Laon, to my shame and the shame of my whole lineage'.[121] The 'queen and the bishop' story became a topos that generated legends, such as that concerning Queen Emma, mother of the English king, Edward the Confessor, who was supposedly accused of sexual relations with the bishop of Winchester but cleared herself through trial by ordeal, walking barefoot on red-hot ploughshares.[122]

The case of the empress Euphrosyne, wife of the Byzantine emperor Alexius III (1195–1203), is strange and complicated.[123] She was a powerful woman, deeply involved in the patronage system, which she manipulated through her minister, Constantine Mesopotamites. Others, including her own son-in-law and brother, felt excluded and plotted revenge. They went to the emperor Alexius and, proclaiming that their loyalty to him outweighed even the bonds of kinship, accused Euphrosyne of adultery. They pointedly combined their picture of her foul deeds in the marriage bed with the suggestion that she was probably preparing her lover to be the next emperor. Alexius was convinced and sent one of his guards off to kill the supposed lover, an otherwise unidentified Vatatzes. Vatatzes' head was sent to the emperor who vented his feelings by kicking it and reviling it. Euphrosyne appealed to have a proper trial, so that she could answer these charges, but Alexius refused, tortured her female servants and interrogated the eunuchs in order to get the information he wanted, and then banished the empress from the palace, sending her to a convent dressed in humble clothes and with two foreign maids who spoke poor Greek.

The picture to this point is fairly clear, with political factions of a purely self-interested kind struggling for advantage and using the particular vulnerability of powerful female figures, their sexual reputation, as a tool. It is perhaps unusual that it was Euphrosyne's own relatives who brought the charge of adultery. The chronicler who tells this story, Niketas Choniates, explains that the accusers had not expected such a dramatic reaction from the emperor and had only wanted to diminish the empress' influence, not have her expelled. They were also conscious of the shame they had brought on their own family and of the hostility of the populace at what they had done. Hence they encouraged Alexius to reinstate Euphrosyne and, six months after she had been sent out of the palace, she was back, regained the emperor's affections and was as powerful as ever. It seems that the twists and turns of events in this case may be best explained by the character of the personalities involved: Alexius' impulsiveness and Euphrosyne's survival skills. Both were to be swept from power when the Fourth Crusade burst upon Constantinople in 1203–4.

One of the most dramatic cases involving the charge of adultery against royal women marked the final days of Philip IV of France. In 1314, which was to be the last year of his life, his dynasty faced a major scandal involving charges of sexual misconduct against not one, but three, royal brides.[124] Margaret, wife of the king's oldest son, Louis, and Blanche, wife of his youngest son, Charles, were accused of adultery with two of their household knights. Moreover, Joan, Blanche's sister, who was the wife of the king's middle son, Philip, was also under suspicion of connivance in these affairs. The three young brides found themselves part of an ominous drama: 'all three were apprehended and conducted in carriages covered in black to be held in custody in strongholds'.[125] Joan insisted on her innocence and was eventually cleared in the Parlement of Paris, the chief law-court, and reconciled to her husband, but the other two were imprisoned for life and the two household knights suffered a gruesome execution. It is possible that doubts about the paternity of Joanna, daughter of Louis and Margaret, played some part in excluding her from the succession after Louis' death (see above, p. 146). Margaret died in prison and Louis remarried, while the marriage of Blanche and Charles was nullified by the pope in 1322, enabling Charles to make two more marriages in the, unfulfilled, hope of producing a surviving son. Between them, the three sons of Philip IV had six marriages but none produced sons who survived childhood. Philip was also the king responsible for the destruction of the Templars and that process shows how ready the king was to believe the most ornate and improbable charges, including those concerned with sexual misbehaviour. The persecution of the Templars culminated in the burning alive of the Grand Master of the Order, Jacques de Molay, on 18 March 1314, at the king's orders. On 19 April 1314 the two knights accused of sleeping with the king's daughters-in-law were tortured and executed. In the last springtime of his life Philip was determined to destroy the perverse wickedness he saw all around him.

Although no public trial was involved, accusations of adultery circulated against Margaret of Anjou, the queen of Henry VI of England.[126] Their purpose was clearly to suggest that her son Edward, Prince of Wales, was not actually Henry's and hence had no true claim to the succession. The beneficiary in that case would be Richard of York and these stories of adultery came from the Yorkist camp. They were given more plausibility by the fact that Margaret and Henry had been married for eight years before Edward was born and Henry, who was mentally ill, had not at first responded to him at all. In 1460 the earl of Warwick reportedly said, 'our king is senseless and, disturbed in his mind, he does not rule but is ruled, power being in the hands of his wife and those who defile the king's bed'.[127] Here the charge is clearly that the queen is sleeping with other men. After the Yorkist victory at the Battle of Northampton in July that year, when the young Prince of Wales was seven, news spread as far as Italy that the Yorkist lords were planning to make a son of the duke of York king and 'pass over the king's son, as they are beginning already to say that he is not the king's son'.[128] But the earliest mention of doubt about the prince's parentage, from 1456, is of a different charge. In that year an apprentice was hanged, drawn and quartered because 'he made writings saying that Prince Edward was not the queen's son'.[129] Around that same time, a chronicler reports, 'the queen was defamed and slandered that he that was called Prince was not her son but a bastard gotten in adultery'.[130] Taken literally, both these cases imply that the rumour was that Edward was not Margaret's son, rather than not being Henry's. Perhaps they should be read as meaning that he was not Margaret and Henry's son. Margaret fought ferociously for her son's rights but could not prevent his killing at the hands of the Yorkists when aged seventeen.

Of course, it is entirely possible that some charges of adultery were true, but it is also clear that the issue involved an explosive combination of male honour and the legitimacy of the blood-line, both of them threatened by such accusations.

Sons and Lovers

The fate of royal widows varied considerably. Some married their dead husband's successor (see above, pp. 34–43). Sometimes foreign queens went back to their homeland, as happened in the case of Matilda, daughter of Henry I of England and wife of Henry V of Germany, who returned to her father's lands after the death of her husband in 1125. Their marriage was childless, but there are cases of foreign royal widows abandoning both their adopted countries and their natural children. A striking example is Isabella of Angoulême, wife of King John of England, who left England in 1217, the year after John's death, to return to Angoulême, where she remarried. Her new husband was the son of the man she had been engaged to before John swept her away. Her children by John, including the nine-year-old Henry III, were left behind. She and Henry did not meet again until 1230. Despite this desertion, Henry proved to be generous to Isabella's children by her second marriage, and his patronage of them in the 1240s and 1250s was one of the causes of the baronial rebellion against him. Aymer de Valence, a son of one of these half-brothers of the king, played an important part in the reigns of Edward I and Edward II. This royal widow thus left a mark on English politics for a hundred years, something that cannot be said of her predecessor as queen, Berengaria of Navarre, who never visited England at all. More significant than such cases were the widowed queens who remained in the kingdom, and here one crucial issue was whether they were the mother of the new king or not. Queen mothers were to be found in every kingdom and every century and often exercised considerable power, especially if their son, the new king, was young, for a respected queen mother could well be seen as a possible regent for a child king. Blanche of Castile, regent for the young Louis IX, is a notable example (see above, p. 117).

Kings were often resentful if their widowed mothers remarried. When Eadgifu, mother of Louis IV of France, remarried after twenty-two years of widowhood, Louis was so angry that he deprived her of her property, giving some of it to his own wife. Perhaps his anger is partly explained by her choice of a new husband, Count Heribert, son of the man who had driven Louis from the kingdom as a child.[131] A later king of France, Philip I, reacted in a similar way to his mother's remarriage. The marriage of Anna of Kiev, widow of Henry I, to Raoul, count of Crépy and Valois, took place in 1062, and was reported in a letter from the archbishop of Rheims to the pope: 'Our queen married count Raoul, which grieved our king exceedingly.'[132] A widowed queen's remarriage was a major event and could have political consequences. Catherine, widow of Henry V of England, was forbidden by an Act of Parliament of 1427/8 to remarry without royal consent on pain of forfeiture of all her lands.[133]

In ruling dynasties, as in other families, a son's relations with his father might be difficult. Relations with a stepfather had yet more potential for conflict. But what of relations with a mother's lover? On more than one occasion young dynasts did encounter the situation where their powerful mothers, ruling as queens or regents, took one of their own nobles as a lover. Urraca, queen regnant of Castile, is an example (on her, see pp. 131–5 above). She had a son, Alfonso, by her first husband and, after the death of that husband and Urraca's succession to the throne, she got married again, to Alfonso of Aragon. An opposition had formed around the figure of her son, which led to warfare between Urraca and Alfonso of Aragon, on one side, and the young Alfonso's supporters, on the other: a mother and a stepfather at war with the mother's son. After separation from her Aragonese husband, Urraca took a noble lover, Peter González of Lara, and had two children by him. Peter appears in sixty-six of her charters (44 per cent of the total 149 for her reign). In the first year of her reign he is called simply 'the queen's squire', but by the last years he has become 'the honourable count, lord Peter de Lara'.[134] After her death and the accession of Urraca's son, Alfonso, Peter rebelled and was exiled, seeking the protection of Urraca's previous husband, Alfonso of Aragon, and was soon thereafter killed in a duel.[135]

This tale is curiously duplicated by that of Urraca's illegitimate half-sister, Teresa of Portugal. She too had a son, Alfonso, by a first marriage but found herself at war with him after her husband's death. She, too, had a noble lover, Ferdinand Perez of Traba, by whom she had two daughters. Between 1121 and 1128 Ferdinand Perez was virtual ruler of Portugal. Even twenty years later a flattering poet could write of him, 'if one were to see him, one would judge him already a king'.[136] This did not stop the austere saint Theotonius, prior of the Holy Cross, Coimbra, from publicly rebuking the couple: 'one day, while he was preaching in the church of Viseu, the queen and count Ferdinand, who was living with her but not her lawful husband, quickly left the church blushing with shame'.[137] They faced opposition of a different kind from Teresa's son, Alfonso, who defeated his mother and Count Ferdinand in the Battle of Guimarães or São Mamede in 1128. Like Peter González of Lara, Ferdinand went into exile, but was ultimately reconciled to his lover's son.[138]

Another young ruler who had to deal with his mother's lover was Wenceslas II of Bohemia (see p. 119). He was not yet seven years of age when his father Premysl Otakar II was killed fighting the Austrians in 1278. Rudolf, king of the Romans (Holy Roman Emperor elect), entered Bohemia and appointed the margrave of Brandenburg to govern it, and the young Wenceslas was taken off to Brandenburg, where, a sympathetic chronicler records, he faced poverty and want: 'He often lacked food . . . he spent several years there in worn-out clothes, . . . and, denied linen clothing, he had to be content with just woollen garments. He frequently appeared with shoes that were falling to pieces, because he had not a penny to give to have them mended.'[139] Finally, in 1282, Wenceslas returned to Bohemia. In the intervening four years the situation in his kingdom had become anarchic, and the country also suffered famine. 'With how great a sting of agitation', asks the chronicler, 'do you think the king's heart was pierced, who found his kingdom completely desolate?'[140]

He also found that his mother, Cunigunda, widow of Premysl Otakar, had taken a lover, Zawisch von Falkenstein, member of a powerful Bohemian noble family who had opposed Premysl Otakar.[141] The chronicler can only explain this distasteful fact by magic:

> Because a woman's mind changes easily, the queen, as they say, deluded by certain tricks of his magic art, loved him warmly and made efforts to please him ... Zawisch, seeing that he had found favour in the eyes of the queen, desired more, and stirred up the queen's heart to love him, deceiving her with certain stratagems of black magic. So the devil, as a deceitful best man, took care that illicit intercourse should be consummated between the queen and Zawisch.[142]

The queen gave birth to a son by Zawisch: 'Thus Zawisch prostituted the pure Cunigunda and stained the bed of the dead king of the Bohemians.'[143]

Cunigunda was, perhaps understandably, apprehensive that her son might be angry, but Wenceslas was more pleased to see her than cross with what she had been doing: 'The king ordered his mother Cunigunda to be cheerful, and thus the boy rejoiced in his mother, he who had previously lived suffering, without a father, in foreign lands.'[144] He was only eleven. Zawisch was also reconciled with the king. He wasted no time in securing control of the royal court, dismissing the current officials and replacing them with his own men, restricting access to Wenceslas and encouraging the young king to indulge in 'childish games', so that 'while he played' he would have a free hand in running the state.[145] Zawisch now married Cunigunda, in May 1285, but she did not long survive this second wedding, dying the following September.

Zawisch's ambitions were still high and he now sought and won the hand of the king of Hungary's sister. When she bore a child, he diplomatically asked both the king of Hungary, his brother-in law, and King Wenceslas, his stepson, to be godparents, and to meet him on the borders of the two kingdoms. Wenceslas' friends feared a trap, designed to get the king away from the crowds of Prague to a remote spot where Zawisch could kill him. Wenceslas devised a counter-plan, asking Zawisch to come to Prague to escort him to the baptism and then seizing him, recovering from him the royal treasure and regalia that he had in his possession and finally, in 1290, executing him before the walls of the castle of Hluboká (Frauenberg), which Zawisch's brother was refusing to surrender. For twelve years, from the age of seven to the age of nineteen, Wenceslas had lived precariously and in the shadows of others. His mother's lover had ruled in his place and had acquired royal estates and royal treasure. Now, at last, his loyal chronicler proclaimed, 'You can live peacefully, young king.'[146]

A similar situation occurred in England a generation or two later, but with a more chilling ingredient. The young Edward III, like Wenceslas II, faced a regime ruled by his widowed mother and her lover, but in this case they had been responsible for his father's deposition and death.[147] The father, Edward II, had a fondness for bright young men and indulged them by granting them lands and titles, freezing out the old aristocracy.[148] His French queen, Isabella, finally left him and resided in France, where she encountered Roger Mortimer, a rebel baron, now living in exile after escaping from the Tower of London. They became lovers by March 1326 and plotted their return to England and the overthrow of Edward II. In September 1326 they landed in England with forces made up of Edward's enemies and mercenaries and very quickly brought down his regime and captured the king himself.

Edward II was deposed in January 1327 and his fourteen-year-old son crowned as Edward III. His mother Isabella and her lover Roger Mortimer governed England for the next four years, despite having no official position. Mortimer used his power to destroy his enemies, build up enormous wealth and even have an entirely new title, earl of March, invented for him. At some point, most people believe, he ordered the murder of the deposed king. Naturally, Mortimer created many enemies, some of whom were willing to support the young Edward III in a bid to free himself from the domination of his mother's lover. In October 1330, the seventeen-year-old king and a band of supporters entered Nottingham castle, where Isabella and Mortimer were sleeping, through a secret underground tunnel. Hearing them approaching the bedchamber, Isabella called out, 'Good son, good son, have mercy on noble Mortimer!'[149] But Edward showed no mercy. Mortimer was taken to the

Tower of London, the same place where he had earlier been imprisoned by Edward II, and, within a few weeks, was hanged like a common criminal. Isabella was retired to a distant castle where she lived on for almost twenty-eight years.

Wenceslas II and Edward III had experienced similar unsettling situations, having the title of king but seeing their mother's lover actually rule. In Edward's case, in addition, the relationship between his mother and Mortimer was adulterous and had led to his father's murder. Wenceslas, on the other hand, had endured deprivation and hardship and was much younger than Edward, only seven, when his trouble began. In their late teens both kings had asserted themselves, capturing and killing their mother's lover, in Edward's case seizing him in his mother's bed. There is no question that Zawisch and Mortimer were powerful nobles who represented a political threat to the young kings, but it is hard not to imagine that there were complex sexual feelings at work when these teenage boys killed their mother's lovers in 1290 and 1330.

Stepmothers

In the pre-industrial world, stepmothers were common, because people died young, and women were especially likely to die in childbirth, leaving youngish husbands who would remarry. In the modern industrial world, stepmothers are common because of the prevalence of divorce. Both situations create a family with particular dynamics. One strong and recurrent conception of the stepmother that emerges from many medieval sources is of a hostile and jealous figure, who hates her stepchildren and tries to influence her husband against them. For instance, Gregory of Tours tells the story of King Sigismund of Burgundy (516–24), who married a daughter of the Ostrogothic king Theodoric and had a son by her, Sigeric. After her death, Sigismund married again:

> he took another wife, who began fiercely to malign and slander his son, *as is the way with stepmothers.* Whence it happened that, one feast day, when the boy recognized his mother's clothes on her, disturbed by bitterness, he said to her, 'For you were not worthy to have these clothes cover your back, which are known to have belonged to your mistress, my mother.'[150]

This stepmother contrived to stir up Sigismund against Sigeric and he had his son killed. The account simply assumes that stepmothers will resent their stepsons. It also provides a credible motive for the son's outburst, seeing this woman dressed in his dead mother's clothes, an unforgivable appropriation of her intimate femininity. A son who had lost his mother would, perhaps understandably, have complicated feelings about his father's new young wife. The sympathetic canoness, Hroswitha of Gandersheim, explained the dissatisfaction of Liudolf, oldest son of Otto I, on seeing his father remarry and the new wife assuming a central place at court: 'from the buried depths of the troubled young man, it brings sighs of the heart for the lost loving of his own dear mother'.[151] Liudolf went on to rebel against his father, and died young.

Philip I of France was notorious for setting aside his wife, mother of his son Louis, and taking up with Bertrada of Montfort, wife of the count of Anjou. By her he had two sons, Philip and Florus, and rumours circulated that Bertrada was determined that Philip, rather than her stepson Louis, should succeed to the throne.[152] Bishop Ivo of Chartres justified the very hasty coronation of Louis in 1108, after his father's death, by the fact that 'there were certain disturbers of the kingdom' plotting 'to transfer the kingdom to another person'.[153] The Norman chronicler Orderic Vitalis gives a colourful, perhaps partly imaginary, picture of Bertrada of Montfort as a wicked stepmother. Orderic disapproved of the relationship between King Philip and Bertrada, which he regarded, not unreasonably, as adulterous, calling Bertrada a *pelex*, the less polite word for 'mistress', and stressing her ambitions for her own sons: 'She greatly desired his [Louis'] destruction and made many attempts, with the help of her companions in evil, to ensure that she would glory in the ruling power and her sons, Philip and Florus, would be securely enthroned in the royal seat if he should die.' Orderic tells the story of how, when Louis visited the court of Henry I of England, Bertrada sent a secret envoy to Henry with a letter supposedly from King Philip, asking him to seize Louis and lock him up for life. The plot failed, however, and, when Louis heard of it, he wished to kill his stepmother. She decided to strike before him and employed three sorcerers to kill him through magic. When the plot was discovered and disrupted, Bertrada turned to poisoners, who were able to bring Louis to the point of death. He was saved at the last minute, not by French doctors, but by 'a hairy man from Barbary', who 'had lived a long time among the heathen and had learned the deep and subtle secrets of nature from his teachers'. Louis recovered but was always paler than before. Soon after his succession his stepmother retired to a monastery.[154]

Stepdaughters could have feelings just as complex as stepsons. Maria porphyrogenita, daughter of the Byzantine emperor Manuel Comnenus by his first wife, was regarded as rightful heir to the empire until the birth of a son to Manuel by his second wife, Maria of Antioch. This might have been grounds enough for resentment on the part of Maria porphyrogenita. The situation became more complicated, however, after Manuel's death in 1180 and the succession of his young son, Alexius II, with Maria of Antioch, his mother, as regent. Although the widowed empress took the veil and adopted the name in religion of Xene ('the foreign woman'), she nevertheless took as her lover Manuel's nephew, the *protosebastos* Alexius Comnenus. The emotions of Maria porphyrogenita are described by the historian Niketas Choniates: 'She almost choked at the thought of the *protosebastos* unholily exploring her father's bed; besides, she welcomed rash deeds, was like a man in spirit and exceedingly jealous of her stepmother by nature.'[155] Here there is a remarkable conjunction of two apparently contradictory emotions: outrage at another man being in her father's bed, but also hatred of the woman her father had been in that bed with. Young kings like Wenceslas II and Edward III had to deal with their mother's lover, princes like Sigeric of Burgundy and the future Louis VI faced antagonism from stepmothers, but Maria porphyrogenita confronted a stepmother who had introduced a lover into her father's bed.

Maria porphyrogenita now gave her support to a cousin, Andronicus Comnenus, in opposition to Maria of Antioch, and plotted to overthrow her, but, after the failure of her coup in 1181, she had to take refuge in Hagia Sophia, saying that she was in flight from her angry stepmother and violent lover, who, she said, 'had sullied the family'.[156] Street fighting between her faction and that of the empress followed, eventually settled by a truce and amnesty. Meanwhile Andronicus Comnenus was closing in and eventually all other participants fell victim to him. The *protosebastos* Alexius Comnenus was blinded, Maria porphyrogenita and her husband supposedly poisoned, the empress Maria of Antioch strangled after Andronicus had secured her condemnation by her own son, the young emperor Alexius, who signed the decree 'as though with a drop of his mother's blood'.[157] Finally Alexius himself was strangled, decapitated and his body thrown into the sea. Andronicus had ruthlessly cleared the field for himself but his first steps were made easier by the clash of stepmother and stepdaughter in Constantinople.

These events, like the alleged adultery of the daughters-in-law of Philip IV of France or the tense relations between Wenceslas II and his mother's lover, Zawisch von Falkenstein, underline how impossible it is to separate the political and the sexual in the lives of members of ruling dynasties. For great men and great women, taking a lover was far from being a private matter. It not only involved them with the family of their lover, with possible consequences for the patterns of power, but also threw a stone into the dark waters of the emotions of their own relatives. Sons and daughters had strong feelings about the sexual behaviour of their widowed mothers or stepmothers and all around were powerful and competitive courtiers and lords eager to use those feelings to gain an advantage for their own position, while an adulterous queen or simply the charge of adultery would unsettle court life and perhaps provide her enemies with the chance to advance their own faction or undermine that of their opponents. What happened in bed had political consequences.

CHAPTER 7

Royal Mortality

Death

VERY MANY MEMBERS OF RULING DYNASTIES, LIKE OTHER people in the Middle Ages, died before puberty. A study of the top ranks of the nobility in late medieval England, whose mortality would be the same as or similar to that of royal families, shows that around a third of children died before they were five. Those who survived, who are the ones we know something about, might live a fair bit longer. Male members of this group who survived to twenty might expect to live another twenty years, while females could anticipate another thirty, the difference being largely explained by the violent deaths of males through execution or in battle.[1] The average age at death of the Plantagenet kings was forty-five. The longest survivor, Edward I, died at the age of sixty-eight. Statistics for German rulers are astonishingly similar. The average age at death of the kings of Germany in the period 911–1273 was about forty-six. Frederick Barbarossa was the oldest, probably sixty-eight, like Edward I of England. The rulers of Castile from 1157–1504 were slightly less long-lived, dying, on average, at forty, with Alfonso X, 'the Wise', being the veteran, at age sixty-three.[2] So these monarchies present a generally similar pattern, with average age at death in the forties and the longest-lived monarchs dying in their sixties.

A normal life, terminated by a 'natural' death, through illness, need thus not be very long. Many lives, however, came to a violent and sudden end. Sometimes this was through accidents. Most members of ruling dynasties lived active, outdoor lives and faced the risks that are unavoidable to those on horseback. Horses are big, powerful animals and riding has its hazards. Philip, the crowned son of Louis VI of France, died when his horse fell on him after stumbling on a pig in the streets of Paris.[3] In 882 Louis III, king of the West Franks, met his death after an accident he suffered while chasing a girl. She fled to her father's house and Louis 'jokingly' pursued her on horseback. He hit the door-frame, however, and injured himself so seriously that he died soon afterwards.[4] When John I of Castile visited Alcalá de Henares in 1390 he was tempted to give his horse its head on a clear open field:

> the king rode on a Castilian roan horse. He went out of the town through the Burgos Gate and, in a fallow field, the king gave the spurs to the horse he was riding and, in the middle of the gallop, it stumbled and fell with the king, in such a way that he broke every bone in his body.[5]

Mary of Burgundy, who ruled the great Burgundian domains in her own right from 1477 to 1482, and was the wife of Maximilian of Habsburg, son of the Holy Roman Emperor (later to be Emperor himself), 'rode a fiery little horse', but while she was out riding in the early spring of 1482 this creature threw her and she hit her head upon a large piece of wood, dying a few days later. News was brought to Louis XI of France, enemy of the house of Burgundy, 'who had great joy of them'. He immediately began planning to undermine Burgundian power.[6] Such was the link between a fall in the woods and the high politics of medieval Europe.

The dangers of riding were heightened during the hunt. In November 1143, Fulk, king of Jerusalem, was accompanying his wife on an excursion outside the city of Acre when their entourage startled a hare in their path.

> The king, unfortunately, snatched up his lance and urged his horse forward to that spot and drove it into a swift gallop in order to pursue the hare. Speeding heedlessly forward, the horse fell headlong to the ground, threw the king and, as he lay there, stunned by the pain of the fall, the saddle crushed his head, so that his brains came out both through his ears and his nose.[7]

He lived on for three days but did not regain consciousness. His body was taken for burial to the Church of the Holy Sepulchre in Jerusalem and his widow and teenage son took up the reins of government.

In this case, Fulk had simply seized an unexpected opportunity for hare-coursing, but planned hunts were also very hazardous and could result in fatal accidents. Since the hunt was a major activity of the European ruling class throughout the Middle Ages (and beyond), there are examples from all times and places, some of them with important political consequences. Aistulf, king of the Lombards, was killed in 756 while hunting in the woods when his horse threw him against a tree.[8] In 884 the West Frankish king Carloman also died from a hunting accident: 'he is said to have been killed by being gored by a boar during a hunt, but in fact he died after being accidentally wounded by one of his followers in that hunt'.[9] In the haste and excitement of the hunt, with the limited visibility of forest terrain, such accidents were not surprising. William Rufus, second of the Norman kings of England, son of William the Conqueror, also died when one of his companions shot him accidentally while on a hunt in the New Forest. One of Rufus' nephews also died in the New Forest, either colliding with a tree while galloping after an animal or, like Rufus, shot accidentally by a companion, and one of Rufus' brothers also died hunting there. The New Forest had been created by William the Conqueror as a royal hunting reserve and required the eviction of most of its inhabitants and the closure of many churches, so it is not surprising that monastic chroniclers saw the deaths of these members of the Conqueror's family as divine judgment.[10] Whether this was the case or not, William Rufus' unexpected death provided his younger brother with the opportunity to seize the Crown and become Henry I of England. Another royal casualty of an accident on the hunt was Valdemar, son and heir of Valdemar II of Denmark, and co-king, who was shot in the foot while hunting at Røsnæs, near Kalundborg, in 1231 and died from the wound, presumably from infection.[11]

The combination of fast riding and wild beasts that the hunt might involve often proved fatal. Three Byzantine emperors died in hunting accidents, either falling from their horse or from the attack of the animals they were hunting.[12] Two of the last three Carolingian rulers of France, Louis IV in 954 and Louis V in 987, died after hunting accidents, the former falling from his horse while pursuing a wolf.[13] This latter incident marked the end of the last Carolingian king. A rather more unusual beast turned up in 1220 when the disaffected Leonese prince Sancho, a potential claimant to the throne, who was on his way to join the Spanish Muslims but had set up a base in an abandoned castle in order to plunder the neighbouring lands, was killed by a bear while hunting in the wilderness.[14]

Riding accidents and hunting accidents thus harvested a crop of rulers. Another permanent threat was human physical violence in this complex, brutal world. It is easy enough when reading medieval chronicles or modern summaries of the political histories of medieval kingdoms to be struck by the high level of violence in political life. Obviously, modern times also provide plenty of examples of political violence, but it is remarkable how often medieval rulers died violent deaths and how common usurpation was. But this violence was not uniform, of a similar intensity in all times and places, and it is worthwhile trying to map out the more and the less violent regimes and societies.

A statistical study of 1,500 European rulers between 600 and 1800 calculated that about 6 per cent died in battle and more than 14 per cent were murdered. It also concluded that the rates of both battle deaths and murders declined markedly over the course of the Middle Ages: battle deaths were common in the period 600–1100, less frequent in the twelfth and thirteenth centuries and insignificant after 1300, while murders of kings and queens were less frequent after 1400 than before.[15] Since these statistics are drawn from a large number of monarchies, including the Ottoman empire and Muslim Spain, and extend to the end of the eighteenth century, the resulting thesis, of a long-term decline in political violence, cannot simply be reapplied to Latin Christendom and Byzantium in the period 500–1500, the world of this book. It is probably more fruitful to look at geographical and chronological variation within that world.

The average length of the reign of medieval monarchs varied from country to country and period to period. This is unlikely to reflect different demographic regimes, such as major changes in overall life expectancy or the impact of new diseases, but rather the level of instability and violence in the political system. For instance, if we compare the average length of reign of the Byzantine emperors with that of the kings of France after 987, the date of the accession of the first Capetian, it is striking that the former, at twelve years, is exactly half that of the kings of France.[16] This is obviously connected with the fact that more than a third of Byzantine emperors came to power through usurpation, while the

French throne descended in an unbroken line of family succession. A calculation has been made that of the eighty-eight Byzantine emperors from Constantine the Great, who founded Constantinople in 324, to Constantine XII, who died defending it in 1453, only thirty-seven died natural deaths in office. That is 42 per cent. Of the rest, three died in hunting accidents and five in battle, but forty-five were either killed, mutilated or sent to monasteries by their supplanters. Blinding was the most commonly inflicted form of mutilation, sometimes done with such gusto that it led to death, as in the case of Constantine VI, blinded on his mother's command in 797, and Romanos IV Diogenes in 1072.[17]

When we compare Byzantium and France, we are in fact comparing, on the one hand, an empire which continued the violent succession practices of imperial Rome, with, on the other hand, the most smoothly functioning dynastic system in western Europe. One of the things that struck contemporary observers of the Capetian dynasty was this peaceful transmission of power from generation to generation. 'They have persisted faithfully in the faith of Christ', wrote Ralph de Diceto, dean of St Paul's, London, in a riot of alliteration, 'and have experienced the most faithful faith of their subjects, so that, raised to the royal crown through the due favour of the Gauls, they have completed the course of life, not with the sword, not by poison, but by the common fate of all.'[18] Gerald of Wales echoed this praise of the Capetians:

> these, always following their father's reign in hereditary sequence and by natural right . . . when they have at last run through the course of temporal life, dying a good death and receiving eternal reward in heaven for such pious and just rule, hand on their realms happily to their sons and heirs.[19]

The calm waters of Capetian rule were occasionally troubled by disputes involving members of the family. The first three generations, in particular, saw kings in conflict with sons and brothers, but after the middle of the eleventh century such dissension was rare. It was reported that Bertrada of Montfort, stepmother of Louis VI, hoped to replace Louis with her son by Philip I, also called Philip;[20] there was apparently an attempted coup by Robert of Dreux, brother of Louis VII, in 1149, while the king was still in the East during the Second Crusade;[21] and, in the early years of the young Louis IX, aristocratic rebels included Philip

Hurepel, son of Philip Augustus, and Peter Mauclerc, a great-grandson of Louis VI. But these challenges are separated by fifty or eighty years and seem to have been brushed off without much trouble. Significantly, in none of these cases does physical violence seem to have been envisaged against the king. In fact, no French king suffered a violent death at the hands of assailants between the death of Robert I in battle in 923 and the assassination of Henry III in 1589, a record that has no parallel in medieval Europe.

Kings were expected to be war-leaders and so death in battle against foreign foes was sometimes their fate. These foreign foes might not be so far away. The competing Anglo-Saxon kingdoms of the seventh century were often engaged in warfare with each other and Bede, the main source for the period, reports the deaths of twelve kings fighting against their English neighbours, as well as the defeat and death of Ecgfrith of Northumbria during his invasion of the land of the Picts. Warfare between the Irish kingdoms was likewise constant and death in battle a common fate of Irish kings. Elsewhere, there might be a clearer cultural division between enemies. The Byzantines conceived of their world as surrounded by barbarians who needed to be resisted and this warfare was endless and sometimes disastrous: the emperor Nicephorus I was killed fighting the Bulgars in 811 and his skull made into a drinking cup by the victors,[22] while in 1453 Constantine XII, the last emperor, died fighting the Turks in the imperial city of Constantinople itself.

It was not only foreign enemies who were to be feared. Probably as much effort was expended in fighting internal rivals as external foes and some civil wars were long and bloody. Several rulers of the western empire ('Holy Roman Emperors') or claimants to that title died in battle against German rivals or rebels. Rudolf of Rheinfelden, elected king in opposition to Henry IV, met him in battle in 1080 and, although Rudolf's side won the battle, he died after having his right hand cut off, a 'most worthy punishment for his perjury', according to Henry's supporters.[23] William of Holland, another 'anti-king', died fighting against the lightly armed and always independent Frisians in the winter of 1256, when his heavy armoured war-horse fell through the ice of a frozen marsh, and the Frisians stuck him full of javelins.[24] In 1298 Adolf of Nassau was killed fighting against Albert of Habsburg, whom the electors had chosen in his place after deposing him.

Some battle deaths marked a dynastic revolution: the replacement of native Anglo-Saxon kings by the Norman dynasty after Hastings in 1066; the overthrow of the Hohenstaufen by the Angevin dynasty in Sicily after Benevento in 1266; the end of the Plantagenets and arrival of the Tudors after Bosworth in 1485. Others did not end dynasties but nevertheless marked permanent political reorientations. After Peter II of Aragon was killed at Muret in 1213, his assemblage of southern French territories and overlordships largely disintegrated and southern France orientated itself towards northern France, not towards Catalonia. The death of Premysl Otakar II of Bohemia at the Marchfeld (also known as the Battle of Dürnkrüt) in 1278 led to the disintegration of his central European empire and opened opportunities for the family of his victorious opponent, Rudolf of Habsburg, father of the Albert just mentioned.

Battles were rare; murder and assassination less so. In some regimes they were constant features. Between 531 and 555 four Visigothic kings of Spain were killed by their own subjects. Bishop Gregory of Tours expressed his distaste for this way of dispensing with rulers: 'The Goths have this detestable custom, that, if one of their kings does not please them, they fall upon him with the sword, and make someone king who is agreeable to them.'[25] It needed the harsh rule of Leovigild (568–86) to end this situation, and Gregory describes him 'killing all those who had been accustomed to kill kings, not leaving alive anyone who pisses against a wall' (that is, any male).[26] But, after the reigns of Leovigild and his son Reccared, dynastic stability was again disrupted and most subsequent Visigothic kings were killed or deposed.

Scandinavia also had a reputation for the killing of kings. The English chronicler William of Newburgh, writing in the 1190s, thought that it was pretty much a law that Norwegian kings came to a violent end:

> for the last hundred years, or more, although many kings have succeeded there, not one of them has ended his life either from old age or disease, but all have died from cold iron, leaving the title of the kingdom to their killers, as if to legitimate successors.[27]

But this was changing even as William wrote. The last violent death of a recognized Norwegian king was that of Magnus Erlingsson in 1184, who drowned during a battle in the Sognefjord. Only six kings before that time had died a peaceful death, so 1184 marks a turning point.[28] It was a change in levels of violence that came to the other Scandinavian kingdoms, for the murder of Erik Klipping of Denmark in 1286 was the very last case of the murder of a Scandinavian king, with the one exception of Gustaf III of Sweden, who was shot at a masked ball in 1792.[29] The example of Denmark also shows that periods of violence could be short and intermittent. Of the thirty-two kings who ruled Denmark in the period 1000–1500, eight died violent deaths, but half of these (i.e. the deaths which occurred in 1134 and 1137, and the two in 1157) were in a period of civil war in the middle of the twelfth century; otherwise, there was one case in the eleventh century and three in the thirteenth, including Erik Klipping's murder. While it is true that a quarter of Denmark's kings in this period died violent deaths, the violence was not a uniform feature of Danish dynastic life.

But the pattern of declining violence is certainly not universal. Dynasties which proliferated into various separate lines had a particular tendency to bloody rivalry. When Charlemagne drew up plans for the future of his empire in 806, he included a provision protecting his present and future grandsons. None of his sons, he ordered, should kill, mutilate, blind or forcibly tonsure any of the grandsons, without a just trial.[30] This provision reveals what he thought were likely events, which needed to be guarded against, namely, violence within the dynasty. This was a striking feature of Irish royal dynasties. For instance, 'between 1274 and 1315 there were no less than thirteen kings of Connacht, of whom nine were killed by their own brothers or cousins and two were deposed'.[31]

The history of the Angevin dynasty of the later Middle Ages, which ruled both Naples and Hungary, is also marked by recurrent murders as the different branches of the family struggled with each other. Notably, the victims included royal women as well as royal men. Andrew of Hungary, the teenage husband, and cousin, of Joanna I of Naples, was murdered in mysterious circumstances in 1345, and Andrew's older brother, Louis, king of Hungary, suspected Joanna's involvement and undertook repeated military expeditions to Naples. In 1348, Joanna fled the kingdom, while Louis captured and beheaded Charles of Durazzo, Joanna's brother-in-law and cousin. Eventually Louis withdrew and Joanna was restored. Louis of Hungary now encouraged the ambitions of Charles of Durazzo's nephew, also Charles of Durazzo, who, in 1381, deposed Joanna I, took the throne of Naples, and, the following year, had Joanna murdered. After the death of Louis of Hungary in 1382, his daughter Mary was proclaimed his successor, under the regency of Elizabeth, her mother, but Charles of Durazzo was determined to assert his claim and invaded Hungary. He deposed Mary and became king of Hungary as well as Naples in December 1385, but was murdered after a few months, at the instigation of Elizabeth. It was not long before Elizabeth herself fell into the hands of her opponents, who had her strangled in 1387. This complex and brutal sequence of events shows competition between different branches of the family reaching a very high level of violence and enduring over generations. There is nothing primitive or backward about the societies in which this savage family drama was played out and it is clearly not part of a story of declining violence.

It is possible to establish the chronological patterns of dynastic violence in individual kingdoms. If we take as an example the twenty-five kings of Scots who died between 1000 and 1500, we find that eight suffered a violent death at the hands of enemies, to which we can add the case of Donald III (Domnall Bán), who was either deposed and blinded or actually killed in 1097. Of those nine cases, seven are found in the eleventh century and two in the fifteenth. Between 1097, the deposition of Donald III, and the murder of James I in 1437, a period of 340 years, no Scottish king was killed by enemies, although one died in an accident and another, John Balliol, was deposed. It is certainly not the case that Scottish history in the twelfth, thirteenth and fourteenth centuries was tranquil and untroubled, but the killing of kings was not part of ordinary political life. In the eleventh century, in contrast, it was the rule: only one of the eight kings who died in that period died a natural death. This was Malcolm II, whose reign was an unusually long one of twenty-nine years. His reign began with Malcolm defeating and killing a cousin, and he was still finding it necessary to kill kinsmen in his last years, so this was not an oasis of peace in a bloody century. At the other end of the period we are discussing, the fifteenth century, two of the four regal deaths were murders by native opponents. In addition, James II was blown up by one of his own cannons while besieging Roxburgh. There thus seems to be a move away from the most extreme form of dynastic violence after 1100 but a return to it in the fifteenth century. If we consider the Plantagenet dynasty of England, a clear chronological pattern emerges, which we can set by the side of the Scottish figure. In the medieval period, excluding those who died as babies, there were fifty-eight male descendants of Count Geoffrey of Anjou, from whom the Plantagenets descended. Of these, twenty-three died through violence, sixteen of them (almost three-quarters) in the fifteenth century, the last century of Plantagenet rule. This century clearly belongs to what the great medievalist Maitland called 'the ages of blood', after an earlier period when the upper classes had been relatively less bloodthirsty in their feuds.[32] A return to high levels of violence in the fifteenth century is thus discernible in both Scotland and England.

An ancient Greek saying was, 'He is a fool who kills the father and spares the sons',[33] and the unfortunate children of deposed rulers might well be finished off along with them, a natural precaution to prevent future trouble. This is what happened to the young sons of the emperor Maurice when he was deposed and beheaded in 602.[34] When Justinian II was murdered in 711, his six-year-old son Tiberius was also hunted down and killed.[35] The same savage efficiency was exhibited by the Merovingians. After the Frankish king Theuderic II defeated his half-brother Theudebert II in 612, 'his little son, called Meroveus, was, at Theuderic's command, seized by the foot and dashed against a rock; his brains burst forth from his head and he gave up the spirit'.[36]

There were ways of neutralizing one's enemies short of murder. Byzantine usurpers sometimes sought to insure their future by castrating the sons of those they displaced. If dynastic continuity depended on 'propagation of blood', then castration was one effective way of ensuring that no propagation took place. To castrate one's enemies meant that their line was at an end and that no sons would grow up as their avengers. The oldest son of Michael I Rangabe (811–13) was castrated at the age of twenty after his father's deposition, while, after the murder of Leo V in

820, his four sons were exiled and castrated.[37] Michael V (1041–2) had the evil reputation of having castrated all his own relatives, presumably to safeguard his position.[38] Blinding of rivals was also a very common practice in Byzantium. In 792 Constantine VI blinded his uncle Nicephorus, who was a contender for the throne, as well as cutting out the tongues of his other four uncles.[39] The Carolingians, too, frequently used blinding as a way of removing opponents without actually killing them. Louis the Pious had his nephew, Bernard, king of Italy, blinded in 818 after he had conspired against him. Louis' son Charles the Bald had his own son, Carloman, blinded after rebellion. Charles the Fat blinded his cousin Hugh, the illegitimate son of Lothar II, in 885 after a conspiracy against him.[40] The practice continued after the collapse of the Carolingian empire. Louis, king of Provence and later emperor, whose mother was a Carolingian, was blinded by Berengar, his rival for the kingdom of Italy, in 905. Berengar justified his action by saying that Louis had earlier sworn an oath not to come to Italy again.[41] A contemporary poet gives a vivid picture of Berengar's men approaching the walls of Verona, where Louis had taken refuge in a church:

> They were admitted straightaway and entered the church where the wretched Louis was, and swiftly seized him, bound him and deprived him of his fair eyes. For he was sitting in the nave, perhaps thinking himself safe, and that is why he lost the kindly gifts of light, and was to be besieged by shadow even at daybreak.[42]

Blinding of rivals, within or outside the dynasty, was also a common feature of dynastic life in Ireland. The *Annals of Ulster* report fifteen cases in the eleventh century alone.[43] The practice continued into the late Middle Ages. In 1444, the *Annals* record, 'Mathgamain Ua Brian was blinded and deposed this year by his own brother, namely, Toirdelbach Ua Brian, and Toirdelbach himself was made king over Thomond.'[44] In the Welsh princely houses the practice of castrating enemies and rivals was common. In one case, the motives, although perhaps obvious anyway, are spelled out: 'Hywel ap Iorweth of Caerleon seized Owain Pen-carn, his uncle. And, after gouging his eyes out of his head, he had him castrated lest he should beget issue who might rule thereafter over Caerleon.'[45] Castrating your uncle meant you did not have to deal with cousins. It has, however, been plausibly argued that Welsh dynastic politics underwent a change in the last century of Welsh independence and that after 1200 'political bloodshed was rare'.[46] Indeed, the last case of castration recorded in the main Welsh chronicle, the *Brut y Tywysogyon*, is in 1175, the last case of blinding in 1193.[47]

After the Holy Roman Emperor Henry VI conquered the kingdom of Sicily in 1194, he ensured that the previous ruler would never pose a threat by blinding and castrating the child-king William III, son of Tancred.[48] Duke Almos of Hungary and his son Bela were blinded by Almos' brother, King Koloman of Hungary, c. 1113, on account of Almos' rebellion. Koloman also ordered Bela to be castrated, but the man instructed to do this, 'fearing God and the sterility of the kingdom', castrated a puppy instead and brought its testicles to the king. Koloman's son, King Stephen II (1116–31), kept Bela in custody but designated him as his successor and arranged his marriage with the Serbian princess Ilona. Bela 'the Blind' ruled 1131–41 and was the ancestor of the later kings of Hungary. Queen Ilona reportedly had sixty-eight nobles executed for their involvement in her husband's blinding.[49]

Burial

Mausolea

It is in the nature of the evidence that we know more about the deaths than the births of members of ruling dynasties. Memorialization of the dead was one of the main activities of the medieval Church, and was one of the reasons that lay people, including rulers, were willing to invest in it, donating vast amounts of property in return for burial sites, commemoration and intercessory prayer. Kings gave a lot of thought to where they wanted to be buried and might have their tombs constructed during their lifetime. The place of burial would often be specified in their wills and sometimes long journeys were undertaken with the corpse to fulfil the king's wish about his last resting place. Medieval genealogies and family trees (discussed below, pp. 326–39) sometimes identified rulers by their places of death or burial. A genealogy of the Dauphins of Vienne from the twelfth to the fourteenth century gives very little biographical information but invariably names their wives and the churches in which the Dauphins were buried.[50] In some texts of this type the circumstances of death might be mentioned if they were unusual. One family tree noted that the West Frankish king Carloman (879–84) was 'killed while hunting' and another labels the unfortunate Philip, the son of Louis VI, crowned in his father's lifetime, whose horse fell on him after stumbling on a pig in the streets of Paris, 'killed by a pig'.[51]

Some rulers wished to be buried in churches that they themselves had founded. This was true of the Norman kings of England: William I was buried in Caen, Henry I in Reading, and Stephen in Faversham, in each case in abbeys of their own foundation. The Angevin kings, Henry II and Richard I, were buried in Fontevrault, not a church of their founding but one they had patronised, and John was buried in Worcester Cathedral at his own request. Of the kings of England 1066–1216, only one, William Rufus, who died in a hunting accident in the New Forest and was buried in Winchester Cathedral, the nearest great church, had no say in his choice of burial site. Similarly, the Byzantine emperors of this period also were often buried in monasteries they had founded in Constantinople: Romanos III Argyros (d. 1034) in St Mary Peribleptos; Constantine IX Monomachos (d. 1055) in St George Mangana; Alexius I Comnenus (d. 1118) in Christos Philanthropos; John II Comnenus (d. 1143) in the Pantokrator monastery.

In contemporary France, Louis VII was buried in the Cistercian abbey of Barbeau in 1180. The French chronicler Rigord, reporting this fact, stresses that Louis was the founder of this monastery and also envisages the main purpose of such patronage:

> His body was buried with glory in the church of Notre-Dame-de-Barbeau, which he himself founded, where, to the honour of Our Lord Jesus Christ and of the blessed Virgin Mary, mother of God, and of all the saints, divine services are celebrated day and night by holy and religious men for his soul and the souls of all his predecessors and for the state of the kingdom of the French.[52]

What was desired was a stream of intercessory prayer, for the dead king, his predecessors and the kingdom, going on for ever until the end of this world. By being the founder, a king might hope that the monks would remember him all the more. Whether or not they founded a burial church, kings frequently specified where they wished to be buried. In 1180, when Ferdinand II of Leon confirmed the property and privileges of the cathedral church of Santiago, he also promised them 'my burial and that of my successors'.[53] He was indeed buried there, as was his son, Alfonso IX. These specifications could be complex. When Charles II, king of Sicily, made his will in 1308, he asked to be buried in the church of Notre-Dame-de-Nazareth in Aix-en-Provence, the kings of Sicily being also counts of Provence at this time. However, he added, if he died in his Italian kingdom he should be buried in the Dominican church at Naples but, within two years, should be transported to Aix (as he was).[54]

Some dynasties developed mausolea, customary burial sites for the family. Churches were used for this as soon as rulers converted to Christianity. The Church of the Holy Apostles in Constantinople, originally founded by the emperor Constantine I or his son Constantius II, served as a mausoleum for Byzantine emperors from the fourth to the eleventh century. Eventually it housed forty-eight tombs containing the remains of emperors or members of the imperial family.[55] It is possible that this imperial mausoleum was a model for Clovis (d. 511), first Christian king of the Franks, when he built a church of the Holy Apostles in Paris as his own burial church.[56] Æthelbert, king of Kent (d. 616), the first Anglo-Saxon king to accept Christianity, founded a burial church for himself in his chief city of Canterbury, in a chapel attached to the monastery of St Peter and St Paul (later called St Augustine's). Subsequent kings of his dynasty were buried in Canterbury for generations, in the church of St Mary within the precincts of the monastery.[57]

In later centuries, the royal abbey of St-Denis came to fulfil the function of a mausoleum for the French kings. Of the twenty-three Capetian kings who ruled between the reign of Hugh Capet (987–96) and the end of the Middle Ages, twenty were buried there.[58] Exceptions were so rare that they provoked comment. Abbot Suger of St-Denis, for example, described how Philip I, who died in 1108 and was buried at the abbey of Fleury, 'had resolved to absent himself from the burial place of his royal forefathers, which is regarded as being the church of St-Denis as if by natural right'.[59] The Norman chronicler Orderic Vitalis gives Philip a deathbed speech in which he says 'I know the burial place of the kings of the French is at St-Denis but because I feel that I am a great sinner, I do not dare to be buried alongside such a great martyr' (Denis was reputed to be an early bishop of Paris who had been martyred at Montmartre, 'martyrs' hill').[60] The Capetians, especially the early ones, are famous for their narrow horizons, spending most of their lives in the royal demesne lands around Laon, Paris and Orleans, and their burial choices reflect this local rootedness.

The pattern of burials of the German rulers was very different. The burial places of the Hohenstaufen kings of Germany, who ruled from 1138 to 1254, show their wide vistas, but also their lack of an enduring territorial base, even one of the modest size of the Ile-de-France. Only two were actually buried in Germany, at Bamberg and Speyer, while the dynasty's acquisition of the throne of Sicily in 1194 led to four of the Hohenstaufen kings having their tombs in Italy, two at Palermo, one at Messina and one at Cosenza in Calabria, while the death on crusade of Frederick Barbarossa explains why his bones came to rest in Tyre.[61] The closest Germany came to a royal mausoleum was Speyer. Eight of the twenty-four kings who ruled in the period 911–1308 were entombed there.[62] But even if this figure represents a third of the monarchs of this period, there were substantial breaks in the continuity of the tradition. Only the Salian dynasty, which ruled for a century from 1024–1125, buried all its members there, often undertaking long journeys with the body of the dead king to ensure it rested in Speyer Cathedral, which the family had built in the midst of their ancestral estates just for that purpose. But after the death of the last Salian ruler in 1125, there was only one royal interment there in the next 166 years.[63] It was no St.-Denis. This contrast in the patterns of the burial sites of the Capetians and the German kings, the concentration of the former, the wide dispersal of the latter, is a contrast between a narrow range with deep roots versus wide imperial horizons.

The royal tombs in St.-Denis became a tourist attraction and, like all such sites, generated guidebooks. Writing in the 1190s, the monk and chronicler Rigord produced a 'handbook (*opus manuale*)' which listed all the kings, gave brief details about them and informed the reader 'where each of them has his tomb'.[64] The same purpose informed William de

Nangis, archivist of St.-Denis, a century later. He explained his object in translating his own brief account of the kings of France into the vernacular:

> Because many people, and high and noble men too, who often come to the church of my lord St Denis of France, where some of the valiant kings of France lie buried, wish to understand and know the birth and descent of their most high lineage, and the wonderful deeds of these kings of France, which are recounted and spread abroad through many lands, I, brother William de Nangis, monk of this church of St.-Denis, at the request of good people, have made a translation from Latin into French so that those who do not understand Latin can know and understand whence such noble and blessed people descended and first came from.[65]

Noble visitors to St-Denis could thus have a handbook in French to help make sense of their tour of the abbey.

Across the Channel, it eventually became a common, though by no means universal, custom for English kings to be buried in Westminster Abbey. Edward the Confessor, last of the Wessex line, who was responsible for rebuilding the abbey church, was buried there in 1066, but it was more than two centuries before the next royal interment, that of Henry III, who died in 1272. Henry revered Edward the Confessor and had himself rebuilt the church. After Henry's death, four more medieval English kings were buried there: Edward I, Edward III, Richard II (after initial burial elsewhere) and Henry V. Westminster's role as a burial church was therefore far more intermittent than its acknowledged status as the place for coronation. There continued to be a variety of burial sites in the later Middle Ages: Edward II at Gloucester, Henry IV at Canterbury, Henry VI and Edward IV at Windsor (the former case a reinterment), Richard III at Leicester, close to the site of his death in battle.

Westminster and St.-Denis have some obvious similarities: both were great abbeys which played a central role in royal rituals, coronation and burial in the first case, guardianship of the royal insignia, though not coronation, and burial in the second, both were situated not in, but close to, the chief city of the kingdom, both produced generations of monastic chroniclers. Yet there were also important differences, notably the fact that royal government in England came to be centred in Westminster, adjacent to the abbey, while in France the royal palace and the central offices of the royal government were located in the capital city itself, in Paris not in St-Denis. Westminster was thus as much a capital as the city of London, or more so. Even today one speaks of the 'Cities of London and Westminster', two distinct 'cities'. Relations between Crown and abbey in St-Denis were not so continuous or so intense at the governmental rather than ritual level.[66]

Continuity of royal burial site is linked to the question of whether a kingdom had a capital. Although smaller than some other European kingdoms, Bohemia was marked out by the fact that it clearly had one.[67] Prague was not only the essential inauguration site but also the heart of the country, 'mistress of all Bohemia', in the phrase of Cosmas, first chronicler of the Bohemians.[68] Prague's central location, symbolic importance and economic preponderance mean that it can be called a capital without danger of the anachronism that might attach to a description of even London or Paris by that term. Indeed, when a thirteenth-century Bohemian chronicler called Prague castle 'the seat of the king of the Bohemians and of the whole kingdom', the phrase 'seat of the whole kingdom' is a perfect medieval counterpart to the modern 'capital city'.[69] It is perhaps only in the central cities of the Russian principalities that we find a close parallel to Prague at this time. Hence it is no surprise that, of the eighteen kings and dukes of Bohemia from the Premyslid dynasty whose burial places are definitely known, eight were buried in St Vitus' Cathedral in Prague (including one reinterment), while three others were buried elsewhere in Prague and another in Vysehrad, the fortress on the opposite bank of the river from the cathedral a mile or two upstream. This makes a total of twelve of the eighteen, that is, two-thirds. In addition, of those whose burial site is not known definitely, there are grounds for thinking at least another three were buried in Prague or Vysehrad.[70] The contrast with Germany, which had no capital and whose kings were buried in many different and far-flung places, is clear.

Actual changes in the size and shape of the kingdom might also have an impact on the choice of burial site. In 1199 Alfonso VIII of Castile and his wife Queen Eleanor formally granted the monastery of Las Huelgas, 'which we have founded near the city of Burgos and endowed with our own property', to the Cistercian Order. 'Moreover', they declared, 'we promise that we and our children who wish to abide by our counsel and command should be buried in the monastery.'[71] Alfonso, Eleanor and their young son Henry I (1214–17) were buried in Las Huelgas. Subsequently, however, as the kings of Castile expanded their frontiers spectacularly at the expense of the Muslim rulers to the south, Burgos became less central and new cities from the conquered regions were chosen for royal burials: between 1252 and 1350, Seville and Cordoba were selected for four royal burials out of the five that occurred.

When a new royal burial church replaced an old one there might be significant cultural implications. The dynasty that was eventually to produce the kings of Scots had its roots in Ireland and had spread from there to the northwestern seaboard of Britain. The most important monastery in the region was Iona, founded in 563 by St Columba on a small Hebridean island, and later king-lists claim that this was the traditional burial place of the kings of the dynasty of Kenneth Macalpine (d. 858) down to the time of Donald III (Domnall Bán), who died in 1097 or 1099.[72] The shift at that time to interment in the Benedictine abbey of Dunfermline, founded by Queen Margaret, who was of English descent, can be seen as marking a reorientation of the Scottish dynasty. Margaret herself, her husband Malcolm Canmore, and three of their sons who succeeded as kings of Scots were buried in Dunfermline. They continued their role as defenders of Scotland even after death, for in 1263, 170 years after the death of Margaret and Malcolm, they were seen, along with their three sons, coming out of the church of Dunfermline in order to fight a Norwegian army that had invaded the kingdom.[73] A total of eight kings of Scots were eventually buried in Dunfermline, the last of them, Robert Bruce (d. 1329), being a descendant of a Norman family invited to Scotland by one of Queen Margaret's sons. The shift of the royal burial church from Iona a hundred miles eastwards to Dunfermline had been part of a wider change in Scotland, away from its Gaelic roots and towards England and Europe.

The practice of the kings of Portugal also shows that different churches might be preferred as burial churches in different periods.[74] The first two kings of Portugal, Alfonso I (d. 1185) and

Sancho I (d. 1211), were buried in the priory of the Holy Cross in Coimbra, the most important Portuguese city at this time. The monastery had been founded with Alfonso's support and so had clear links with the new dynasty. The next king, Alfonso II (d. 1223), although he showed favour to the priory in Coimbra, desired to be buried in the monastery of Alcobaça, a Cistercian house halfway between Coimbra and Lisbon. Alfonso's successor, Sancho II of Portugal, was deposed and driven into exile in Castile by his brother Alfonso III, and, although Sancho stated in his will that he wished his body to be returned to Portugal for burial in Alcobaça, Alfonso was not willing to give him this legitimizing treatment and Sancho's remains still lie in Toledo Cathedral.

Alfonso III himself was buried in Alcobaça. His successor, however, King Denis (d. 1325), chose to be buried in St Denis of Odivelas, a short distance north of Lisbon. This was an unusual step in three ways: Odivelas was a nunnery, not a monastery of men; Denis' wife was not buried in the same church, unlike the other queens of Portugal; and the dedication to St Denis is unique in Portugal. An earlier version of Denis' will chose Alcobaça as his place of burial, so he had clearly made a considered change of opinion. He had founded the convent of St Denis and presumably had a say in choosing the dedication to a saint with his own, unusual, name. The next three kings of Portugal, Alfonso IV (d. 1357), Peter I (d. 1367) and Ferdinand I (d. 1383), were buried in Lisbon Cathedral, Alcobaça and the Franciscan church at Santarém respectively, so without a definite pattern. However, after the succession crisis of 1383–5, which ended with the accession of the illegitimate John I, an entirely new royal mausoleum was created. This was the monastery of Batalha (Santa Maria da Vitória), which was founded as a thanksgiving after the Battle of Aljubarrota, John I's victory over the Castilians in 1385 that confirmed him as king of Portugal. Late in his reign he founded a funerary chapel there. He and his wife, Philippa, share a joint tomb in Batalha with carefully carved effigies. John's successor, Edward (Duarte) (d. 1438), and his successor, Alfonso V (d. 1481), and his successor, John II (d. 1495), are also buried there, along with the four younger sons of John and Philippa with their wives. Batalha is a dynastic mausoleum in the fullest sense, providing a last resting place for wives and cadets of the royal family as well as kings, and commemorating in its very name the triumph of the old Portuguese royal lineage when faced with the threat of incorporation into Castile.

In Denmark, the Benedictine abbey of Ringsted, in the centre of the island of Zealand, was a royal burial site for many generations. A late medieval account, similar to the guide book to St-Denis, lists the royal burials there, the date and place of death, the length of reign of the kings, the family relationships and the location of the tomb. The first member of the ruling family to be buried in Ringsted was Canute Laward, duke of Schleswig, who was murdered in 1131. His son, Valdemar I, was able to secure his canonization, and the official translation of Canute's remains to the altar in 1170 marked the beginning of the church's dominant position as a royal mausoleum. The late medieval catalogue lists twenty royal burials, including six ruling kings of Denmark, from Valdemar I (d. 1182) to Erik VI (d. 1319), as well as queens, royal princes and the exiled king of Sweden, Birger Magnusson, whose wife's burial in 1341 is the latest recorded.[75] The first half of the fourteenth century saw Danish royal burials shift from Benedictine Ringsted to the Cistercian abbey of Sorø, also on Zealand. Interments took place here of kings who died in 1322, 1375 and 1387. Margaret, the effective ruler of Denmark, Norway and Sweden (d. 1412), was first buried at Sorø also, but in 1413 the bishop of Roskilde had her body transferred to the cathedral of Roskilde, despite the objections of the Cistercians of Sorø. Thereafter Roskilde became the usual burial place for Danish royalty, today claiming thirty-nine royal tombs.

It is hard to generalize about the history of dynastic mausolea. Even if they were established, as in the case of the Scottish kings at Iona (probably) and Dunfermline (definitely), they might not endure. The eleven kings of Scots who died between 1200 and 1500 were buried in nine different places, belonging to six different religious Orders. Only two were buried in churches of their own foundation. Nevertheless, looking across the wide range of evidence, it appears that kings preferred burial in monasteries to burial in secular churches, with exceptions such as the Premyslids in Prague and the Danish royal house from the fifteenth century; that there were some well-established Benedictine houses that had a long if not absolutely continuous history as burial churches,

St-Denis pre-eminently but also Westminster and Ringsted; and that the Cistercian Order was favoured in many places from the twelfth century onwards: Sorø in Denmark, Alcobaça in Portugal, Las Huelgas in Castile, Santes Creus and Poblet in Aragon, plus Royaumont for uncrowned Capetians in France. Of the thirteen kings of Aragon who ruled between the union of Aragon and Barcelona in the twelfth century and the end of the Middle Ages, eight are buried in Poblet, including every king after 1387. Peter IV, who died in that year, not only undertook a major rearrangement of the tombs in Poblet but made it a requirement that all future kings should promise to be buried there.[76] Occasionally burial church and coronation church coincided, at least on many occasions: this is true of Westminster in England and Székesfehérvár (Alba Regia) in Hungary. Burial of kings in Franciscan or Dominican churches was rare, the Dominican La Batalha in late medieval Portugal being an exception.

Even if continuity of burial church was maintained, as in France, there might be changes over time within the church. At St.-Denis, careful thought was given to the arrangement of the tombs. In 1263–4, under Louis IX, a new layout was introduced, with a clear rationale:

> At St.-Denis in France a simultaneous and joint relocation of the kings of the French buried in various places in that monastery was undertaken by the holy king Louis and Matthew, abbot of that monastery. Both the kings and the queens of the family descending from Charlemagne were placed together on the right side of the monastery, raised two and a half feet above the ground, with carved images, and the others, stemming from the family of king Hugh Capet, were placed on the left.[77]

Here, the recognized distinction between the 'second family' and the 'third family' of kings of France (see below, pp. 285–6) was being given striking visual form. At the same time as the tombs were rearranged, they were given statues of those within. Hence many of the Merovingian and Carolingian rulers in St.-Denis are depicted in the courtly costume of the mid thirteenth century.

St Louis certainly had strong views about royal burials. He thought only kings should be buried at St.-Denis and other members of the royal family should go to Royaumont, the Cistercian abbey founded by his mother, Blanche, in memory of his father. Louis had supposedly helped the monks build the walls of the abbey, carrying stones himself. As he lay dying outside the walls of Tunis on his second and ill-fated crusade, Louis was informed that his son, John Tristan, who was also in the army, had died: 'The king chose his burial at St.-Denis and the burial of his son in the church of Royaumont, because he was not willing that he should be buried in the church of St.-Denis, where only kings were buried.'[78] In Louis' view, there was a burial church for kings and another for members of the royal family, although this distinction was certainly not observed in practice.

Reinterment

Bodies did not always stay in the place where they were first buried. As soon as Leo VI became Byzantine emperor in 886, he had the body of Michael III exhumed from its tomb in Chrysopolis, on the Asian shore opposite Constantinople, had it dressed in imperial robes and reburied in honour in a marble sarcophagus in the Church of the Holy Apostles in Constantinople, the traditional burial place of the East Roman and early Byzantine emperors.[79] Michael had been assassinated in 867 by Leo's father Basil I, although there were rumours that Leo was actually Michael's son, not Basil's.[80] For those who believe that Leo was Michael's son, and that Leo knew this, his act was one of filial piety. For others, 'Leo was seeking to atone for the crime of his dynasty', that is, the usurpation and murder perpetrated by his father.[81] Exactly the same interpretation has been placed on the action of Henry V of England when he reinterred the body of Richard II in 1414. Richard had been deposed by Henry's father, Henry IV, in 1399 and murdered the following year. The dead king's body was not buried in the royal mausoleum at Westminster Abbey in 1400, despite his having prepared a tomb there for himself. The relocation of Richard's remains to the abbey in 1413 marked a greater sense of security on the part of the new regime, unafraid to acknowledge the royalty of their deposed victim, but also perhaps Henry V's 'desire to atone for his father's usurpation'.[82]

Reinterments could thus symbolize reconciliation, even if of a posthumous kind. A striking example is the transfer of the body of

Maria, widow of Alfonso XI of Castile, from its original resting place at Evora in Portugal to the royal chapel in Seville, to lie by the side of King Alfonso. This ceremony was initiated by her son, Peter I of Castile, but the reason Maria died in Portugal rather than in Castile was that she had fled there from Peter during the political and military struggles of the early years of his reign after he had had four of her supporters killed before her eyes. Nevertheless, in 1357 Peter sent the archbishop of Seville, other prelates and a chief officer of his household to collect his mother's body, received it in Seville surrounded by clergy and nobles, and celebrated a funeral service with great honour before interring the body next to Alfonso, her husband.[83] Peter's sense of dynastic fitness outweighed any memory of antagonism; what his mother would have thought we do not know.

Sometimes reinterments brought the dead ruler to the place of burial he had requested during his lifetime. The Frankish king Charles the Bald explicitly requested that his body be interred in the abbey of St.-Denis outside Paris; this was clear from at least 862, fifteen years before his death.[84] After he died in Italy in 877, his followers carried his body back to France but were overwhelmed by the stench of the corpse and interred it at the monastery of Nantua, west of Lake Geneva. A few years later, however, his bones were disinterred and taken 300 miles north for honourable burial in St.-Denis.[85] St Denis had been the king's particular patron and protector in life, and he now rested near the saint in death.

The emperor Henry V's reinterment of his father, Henry IV, at Speyer in 1111 is an example both of a posthumous reconciliation and of the fulfilment of the dead king's wishes about his burial place. The younger Henry had fled his father's court and rebelled in December 1104, gaining a considerable body of supporters among the German nobles. A year later he captured his father and, on 31 December 1105, forced him to abdicate. Nevertheless, the older Henry escaped and war continued between father and son, until the death of the old emperor on 7 August 1106 in Liège. Amongst his last requests was the plea 'to bury him alongside his ancestors in Speyer'.[86] Henry IV was well aware of the connection between the church of Speyer and his own dynasty. 'We especially revere the church of Speyer', he had written, 'which was gloriously constructed by our ancestors, the august emperor Conrad, that is, our grandfather, and the august emperor Henry, that is, our father, and by us.'[87] Henry thus wished to rest alongside his grandfather Conrad II and his father Henry III. However, the path of the dead emperor's body to final inhumation in Speyer Cathedral was not a simple one. The main problem was that Henry had died excommunicate because of his quarrel with the papacy and burial in consecrated ground was denied to excommunicates. So, although the loyal bishop of Liège buried Henry's body in his cathedral, it was dug up and placed on unconsecrated ground on an island in the Meuse. Even when Henry V agreed to have his father's coffin transported to Speyer, the bishop there refused to let it remain in the cathedral and it was placed in an adjacent unconsecrated chapel, where the inhabitants, conscious of the emperor's devotion to Speyer, frequently visited it. Only after five years, and very complicated dealings with the pope, was permission granted for the emperor to be buried in the cathedral. On 7 August 1111, in the presence of an assembly of bishops, abbots and nobles, Henry V celebrated a 'most magnificent anniversary' for the father he had deposed, and Henry IV was finally 'buried in the church alongside his ancestors'.[88]

A reinterment with a powerful, if complex, political message, was that of Sancho III 'the Great' of Navarre. He died in 1035 and was succeeded by his three sons, each of whom took a portion of the kingdom, Navarre going to García, Aragon to Ramiro and Castile to Ferdinand. Sancho was buried at San Salvador de Oña in Castile. Two years after his death, Ferdinand of Castile, who was married to Sancha, a sister of Vermudo III, the king of Leon, defeated and killed his brother-in-law and became king of Leon. It was supposedly at the suggestion of his wife that Ferdinand transferred the remains of his father from Oña to Leon 'and buried him with the other kings of Leon'.[89] Ferdinand's powerful father now lay in the same resting place as the earlier kings of Leon, including the last one, whom Ferdinand had killed. Ferdinand was claiming a position as both king of Leon and inheritor of his father's traditions, perhaps with an eye on his brothers, García of Navarre and Ramiro of Aragon.[90] The royal pantheon attached to the church of San Isidoro at Leon to which Sancho III's body was brought became an important mausoleum of both the Leonese and Castilian rulers. An account of the

here in the sixteenth century lists thirty-three, including
o III, his father, Alfonso V, and his grandfather, Vermudo II;
Sancho III of Navarre; Ferdinand I and his wife Sancha; their son, García
of Galicia; Queen Urraca, their granddaughter; and many queen consorts and royal children.[91]

Not all reinterments involved removal of bodies from one church to
another. It was also not uncommon for bodies to be moved around within
a church, as in the rather dramatic case of St.-Denis, just mentioned.
Such reinterments often involved transfer to a more honourable position, meaning, in Christian churches, a place closer to the high altar and
the east end of the church. For example, in 1286 Sancho IV of Castile
moved his distant ancestor, Alfonso VI (d. 1109), whose body lay in the
abbey of Sahagún in Leon 'at the foot of the church', implying it was in an
entrance area at the west end of the building (a narthex or porticus), to
'the chapel before the high altar', where it was placed 'in a green monument', between two of Alfonso's, many, wives who had also been moved
there. The motive is not clear, apart from general respect, but the
chronicler describing the relocation calls Alfonso 'the king who won
Toledo', so perhaps it was Alfonso's reputation as the king who had
conquered Toledo, capital of Spain in the Visigothic period, from the
Muslims in 1085 that earned him this special treatment. His descendant
thought it worth making the effort for this honourable gesture 177 years
after Alfonso's death.[92]

Tombs

Royal tombs were usually made of expensive materials, such as marble
and alabaster. The most exclusive material was porphyry, a hard, purple-
red rock from the deserts of Egypt that the Roman emperors had
employed for grand monuments. It was expensive and rare. The tombs
of the eastern Roman emperors of the fourth and first half of the fifth
century in the Church of the Holy Apostles in Constantinople were of
porphyry, but not those of later emperors.[93] Most examples of porphyry
in the medieval west were taken from ancient Roman sites to be reused.
Sometimes tubs from bathhouses, after being given suitable lids, were
employed as tombs. There is a porphyry tub in Ravenna that might have

been used for the tomb of Theodoric, king of Ostrogothic Italy (d. 526); this, at least, was local belief by the ninth century.[94] It is possible that the late Roman bath in porphyry now in the Louvre was acquired by Charles the Bald (d. 877) to serve as his tomb in St-Denis.[95] Among the most spectacular royal porphyry tombs from the Middle Ages are those of the emperors Henry VI and Frederick II in the cathedral at Palermo.[96] These are big, the former measuring 2.37 by 1.03 metres (7 feet 9 inches by 3 feet 5 inches), and each stands enclosed in a canopy supported by columns, the whole structure being about 3.7 metres (over 12 feet) high. The tombs were not ancient survivals but were made in the reign of Frederick's predecessor, Roger II of Sicily (d. 1154), perhaps from porphyry obtained from ancient structures in Rome, and were originally intended for that king himself, although not in fact used for his burial.[97] Frederick II specified in 1215 that these empty tombs should be brought to Palermo Cathedral, where his father Henry VI already lay.[98] Henry VI and Frederick II were, in their own eyes, Roman emperors, and their actual domains reached from Sicily to the Baltic, so these huge sarcophagi of imperial stone reflect very well their own conception of their position in the world. Quite exceptionally for the Iberian peninsula, Peter III of Aragon (d. 1285) was buried in a porphyry 'tub' (*alveus*) sarcophagus in the Cistercian church of Santes Creus. This may have come from a fourth-century imperial mausoleum in Centcelles nearby, although it has also been suggested that it was imported from Sicily.[99] Its construction was due to Peter's son, James II, and James' interest in porphyry is also shown by his unfulfilled request for porphyry from Greece for the tomb of his wife, Blanche.[100]

Kings were sometimes buried with the crowns, sceptres and orbs that had marked their sovereignty in life, or with the swords and spurs that reflected their warrior and knightly status.[101] This custom was, however, far from universal, and many rulers followed the austere practice that had come with Christianity, when grave goods were abandoned and even great men went to the next life without their horses, slaves, weapons and treasure. What Christian kings might have, which their pagan predecessors in the barbarian world usually did not, was a record written on or in the tomb, identifying them and sometimes doing much more. Royal tombs were by no means always marked out with words to identify them

Figure 9 The tomb of the Holy Roman Emperor, Frederick II (d. 1250), in the cathedral at Palermo, which emphasizes his imperial status both by its size and by its precious material, porphyry.
Realy Easy Star/Toni Spagone/Alamy.

or epitaphs to glorify those who lay there, and the Danish royal tombs at Ringsted, for example, are simple marble slabs without inscriptions. But some of these anonymous tombs carried a message within. The practice of placing sheets of lead, or other materials, within the tomb, inscribed with the name and sometimes an account of the activities of the dead ruler, became more common from the eleventh century onwards.[102] It implies either that the people (sons or clerics?) who placed these plaques within the tomb expected that the tombs would at some point be opened or, alternatively, that they were a message for the Last Judgment. A similar practice of internal, identifying labels was used for the relics of the saints.

In the tomb of Valdemar I of Denmark (d. 1182), which was opened in 1855, a lead plaque was found, telling of his deeds: 'Here lies Valdemar I, conqueror and dominator of the Slavs, liberator of his country, preserver of the peace. He was the son of St Canute and he conquered the men of Rügen and was the first to convert them to the faith of Christ.' Valdemar was the son of the canonized duke Canute Laward and had overthrown the last stronghold of West Slav paganism on the island of Rügen in 1168. The plaque also praises him for rebuilding in brick the Danewerk (Danevirke), 'the wall that defends the whole kingdom'.[103] Since Valdemar is called 'Valdemar I', the plaque must date from after 1202, when his son became king as Valdemar II, and hence it must have been inserted after the tomb had been opened. It is thus retrospective in a stronger sense than usual for epitaphs, and its audience was certainly not the living but either future generations or perhaps God and his angels.

Unusually, the Byzantine emperor Basil II (d. 1025) composed his own epitaph. He was a famously successful general and he chose to be buried, not in the Church of the Holy Apostles, but in a church just outside the walls of Constantinople, in the area where troops mustered for campaigns. In his epitaph he asked passers-by to pray for him, in return for his campaigning.[104] The tone of epitaphs was not exclusively glorification. William the Conqueror's tomb in the church he had founded, St Stephen's, Caen, carried an epitaph in gold, which did indeed praise his bold conquests and wide domains but also pointed out the contrast with what he was physically now, after death: 'The great king William lies in this small urn and this little house is enough for a great lord.'[105]

A new practice grew up: images of the dead rulers on their tombs. The ancient world, both Greek and Roman, had been full of such human figures, often life-size or larger, in stone or marble, but the Middle Ages came to the tradition slowly and hesitantly. An early example is the bronze plaque with his life-size figure in relief on the tomb of Rudolf of Rheinfelden in Merseburg Cathedral. Rudolf was, in the eyes of the supporters of the emperor Henry IV, an 'anti-king', raised up by German rebels with the backing of the Church party, eventually including the intransigent reformer Pope Gregory VII. He was crowned in 1077 but killed in battle against Henry's supporters in 1080 (see above, p. 245). He was buried soon afterwards under the gilded bronze plaque, 1.96 by 0.68 metres (6 feet 5 inches by 2 feet 2 inches), which bears his image, with crown, orb and sceptre. The inscription on the plaque describes him as 'the sacred victim of war' and asserts 'he died for the Church'.[106] It is not clear whether this unabashedly propagandistic tomb explains the fact that the German emperors, in reaction, did not put images on their

Figure 10 The image of the 'anti-king' Rudolf of Rheinfelden (d. 1080) in Merseburg Cathedral, one of the earliest royal tomb effigies. The inscription claims 'he died for the Church'.
Ullstein bild/Getty Images.

graves until the fifteenth century, but certainly Rudolf's tomb-image is exceptional.[107]

Elsewhere the practice blossomed in the late twelfth and thirteenth centuries and became relatively common. There are more than eighty surviving recumbent effigies (*gisants*) on royal tombs from medieval Europe, some of these representing kings of earlier centuries rather than contemporaries.[108] After Louis VII was buried at Barbeau, by the Seine above Paris, in 1180, his tomb was erected by his widow Adela of Champagne, who herself died in 1206. The tomb was described as 'constructed of stones, gold and silver with wonderful workmanship, decorated most elaborately with bronze and jewels'.[109] Above the tomb was a recumbent image of the king in high relief, depicted in a long mantle, crowned and holding a sceptre.[110] The recumbent statues of Ferdinand II of Leon (d. 1188) and his ancestor Raymond of Burgundy in Santiago, which were created in the period 1200–15, are the earliest royal tomb effigies in the Iberian peninsula.[111] The images of Henry II of England, his son Richard I and his wife Eleanor of Aquitaine on their tombs in Fontevrault are from about the same period. The elaborate tombs of late medieval rulers, with their rich materials, canopies, enclosing metalwork and delicate carvings, had many similarities with the shrines of the saints, and they may have been influenced by them in their design. Some royal tombs were in fact shrines, those of the saint-kings, such as Edward the Confessor in Westminster Abbey.

A striking innovation of the last centuries of the Middle Ages was the joint tombs of kings and queens with their effigies side by side. Prior to that period it had not been uncommon for rulers and their wives to be buried in the same church. Of the fifteen Merovingian queens about whose interment there is information, five were buried at St.-Germain-des-Prés in Paris, in each case alongside their husband.[112] Carolingian and early Capetian queens were less frequently buried with their husbands, and the custom of both king and queen of France being interred in St-Denis developed only slowly, with isolated individual cases in the ninth, eleventh and twelfth centuries and two in the late thirteenth, but was virtually unbroken from the time of Charles IV (d. 1328). Almost all Portuguese queens were buried in the same church as their husbands. Of

Figure 11 Tomb effigies of Henry II of England (d. 1189) and his wife Eleanor of Aquitaine (d. 1204) in Fontevrault Abbey. Their son Richard I was also interred here under an effigy. In choice of burial place, the family's roots in Anjou outweighed their English royal title. Dorling Kindersley Ltd/Alamy.

the Norman and Plantagenet kings of England, sixteen were married and exactly half of these were buried in the same church as their queen or one of their queens, and the tendency became more pronounced over time, with six of the eight instances being fourteenth- or fifteenth-century.

The joint tombs with effigies of kings and queens went beyond this simple pattern of burial in the same church to a shared space and style. The tomb of James II of Aragon (d. 1327) and his wife Blanche of Anjou (d. 1310) in Santes Creus, which is perhaps the earliest joint royal tomb, was conceived and constructed as a unit. As mentioned above, James tried, although unsuccessfully, to obtain some porphyry for this tomb, so was seeking the very best material. James' grandson, Peter IV, 'the Ceremonious', of Aragon (d. 1387), determined to be buried in Poblet, where two of his predecessors lay, and undertook a long, complex and expensive project of construction and reorganization, which resulted in a distinctive necropolis: alabaster effigies of uniform style for him and his predecessors with tombs placed, not on the floor of the church, but above arches in the transept, and not flat but at an angle, so they were visible to those walking below.[113] Peter is there with his three (successive) wives, and several of his successors, who were all buried in Poblet, lie alongside their wives.

There are two Portuguese examples of royal joint tombs with effigies. At Alcobaça Peter I (d. 1367) and Ines de Castro (d. 1355) lie side by side. The tombs were constructed at Peter's command in the years 1358–63 and Ines' body transferred there from her original resting place (see above, p. 164). The other example is the joint tomb of John I (d. 1433) and Philippa of Lancaster (d. 1415) at Batalha, constructed in the years 1426–34. In both these instances the initiative for the arrangement came from the king and in the case of Peter and Ines it was definitely a sign of special devotion and affection. The same seems to be true of the first royal tomb of this type in England, that of Richard II (d. 1400) and Anne of Bohemia (d. 1394) in Westminster Abbey. This is a fairly substantial monument, 3.84 metres long, 2.10 metres wide and 1.90 metres high (12 feet 7 inches by 6 feet 11 inches by 6 feet 3 inches). Richard had this constructed in the late 1390s and it reflects the well-attested depth of his affection for Anne. Richard's usurper and murderer Henry IV (d. 1413) and his second wife Joanna of Navarre (d. 1437) also have a joint tomb, in Canterbury Cathedral. This was commissioned by Joanna and erected around 1425, with her effigy being added after her death. The images of Richard and Anne are gilded copper, those of Henry and Joanna alabaster.

The contract between Richard II and the London coppersmiths employed to make the effigies in Westminster Abbey survives. The figures were to be 'of gilt copper and brass, crowned, with their right hands entwined, and holding sceptres in their left hands'; the decoration is carefully described, including the appropriate heraldry for each spouse; and the coppersmiths are to complete the work within two years and receive £400 (in fact they were paid an extra £300 for the gilding).[114] The instruction that the royal couple are to be holding hands can hardly be anything other than a reflection of Richard's feelings for Anne. The only medieval royal double grave in Germany is that of Rupert of the Palatinate (d. 1410) and his wife Elizabeth (d. 1411) in Heidelberg; although a spectacular one was commissioned in 1499 for the emperor Henry II and the empress Cunigunda in Bamberg, it was not completed

Figure 12 The tomb of Richard II of England (d. 1400) and his wife Anne of Bohemia (d. 1394) in Westminster Abbey. Richard commanded that they should be shown holding hands.
Courtesy of Westminster Abbey.

until 1513. Rupert was Elector Palatine before his contested election as king in 1400 and Heidelberg was the burial church of the electors, so his choice of burial place was in a family rather than in an imperial tradition. Joint royal tombs are thus very rare and can, in some cases at least, be interpreted as expressions of marital love.

Body Part Burial

Bodies were not always buried whole. If the corpse was to be transported a long distance, it might well be disembowelled to prevent the stench of the decomposing intestines becoming unbearable. These would then need to be deposited somewhere. The more extreme custom also arose of boiling all the flesh off the bones, then burying these soft remains before transporting the bones to a distant destination. Thus, when Conrad-Otto, duke of Bohemia, died in southern Italy in 1191, where he had gone as part of the invading army of the emperor Henry VI, 'his flesh was deposited in Monte Cassino but his bones were brought to

272

Figure 13 The tomb of Peter I of Portugal (d. 1367) at Alcobaça; he claimed to have married Ines de Castro, mother of four of his children, and had her body transferred to the royal mausoleum of Alcobaça, where he eventually came to rest by her side. DEA/G. DAGLI ORTI/De Agostini/Getty Images.

Prague'.[115] Separate burials of flesh and bones were, like disembowelling, primarily practical and hygienic measures. The importance attached to separate burial of the heart was more a matter of symbolism and sentiment. As the heart was increasingly identified as the home of love, both by theologians and romantic poets, choosing a separate location for its burial was a way of expressing devotion and attachment to a particular place.[116]

The way that the distribution of body parts could reflect dynastic sentiment is shown in three cases from the late twelfth and thirteenth centuries: Richard I 'the Lionheart' of England, Louis IX (St Louis) of France and Louis' brother, Charles of Anjou, king of Sicily. When Richard lay dying after being shot by a crossbow bolt during the siege of a southern French castle in April 1199, he commanded that 'his brain and blood and intestines should be buried at Charroux, his heart at

Figure 14 The tomb of Ines de Castro (d. 1355) at Alcobaça.
DEA/G. DAGLI ORTI/De Agostini/Getty Images.

Rouen, and his body at Fontevrault, at his father's feet'.[117] Charroux is about forty-five miles from where Richard died, Fontevrault another seventy miles or so to the north. St Louis died on crusade in Tunis in 1270. His flesh was boiled off his bones and, along with his intestines, was taken by his brother, Charles of Anjou, king of Sicily, to be interred in the cathedral of Monreale outside Palermo; his bones were taken back to St-Denis.[118] Fifteen years later, in 1285, Charles of Anjou himself died, in the town of Foggia in Apulia. This is where his intestines were buried; his bones were buried in the cathedral at Naples, the chief city of his kingdom; his heart eventually came to the Dominican church in Paris.[119]

In each of these cases, family connections were significant. Richard I's bones were buried alongside his father, Henry II, in the church where his mother, too, was later to be buried; his heart was placed in the chief city of his duchy of Normandy. Although Richard had been king of England, no part of him came to England. He came to rest, although in parts, as he was when alive, a member of a great French dynasty. St Louis, too, went home to the dynastic mausoleum of the Capetian dynasty at St-Denis outside Paris. But he was both king of his kingdom and a member of his dynasty in a way that Richard was not. The Capetians had managed to identify themselves with their realm, and their dynastic mausoleum was just outside what was, or was to become, the capital of France. This kind of identification of dynasty and kingdom was something that the English kings were to develop only during the thirteenth century and subsequently. St Louis' brother, Charles of Anjou, had managed to acquire, by conquest and by papal grant, the kingdom of Sicily, and attaining the soft parts of St Louis for the cathedral of Monreale brought a powerful dynastic token into his new kingdom: physical parts of his brother, the most renowned king in Christian Europe, now lay in the heart of Charles' realm. When Charles himself died, none of his remains could be buried in Monreale, or in Palermo, since the island of Sicily had rebelled (the so-called 'Sicilian Vespers') and was now outwith his control, but his body was transported about eighty miles across the Apennines to be buried in his chief mainland city, Naples, and an important part of him, his heart, eventually returned to France, to the chief capital of his birth-dynasty, Paris, where it rested a few miles from St Louis' tomb. Rulers did not forget which dynasty they stemmed from, wherever they ruled and wherever they might die.

It was generally recognized that one motive for multiple burial was the desire to multiply the prayers and offerings made for the dead: three churches were better than one. But there was something beyond this simple motive in requesting that your heart be taken to Jerusalem. From the twelfth century, all kings paid at least lip service to the idea that one of their most important duties was to go on crusade, and if they had failed to do this in their lifetime, which was true of most rulers, they could send this very significant part of their body after their death. In his will Alfonso X of Castile (d. 1284) asked that his entrails be interred in Santa María la Real in Murcia, and his body either there or in Seville Cathedral, where his parents were buried. He continues, 'we also command that, after we die, they should take out our heart and should take it to the Holy Land beyond the sea (*Ultramar*) and bury it in Jerusalem, in Mount Calvary, where some of our ancestors lie'.[120] In the end, however, this wish was not fulfilled and his heart was buried in Murcia also.

Robert I of Scotland, first of the Bruce dynasty, died on 7 June 1329. His last wishes were reported in a deathbed speech as follows:

> When I was in prosperity, my heart was fixed firmly on being saved of my sins by struggle against God's enemies, and since he now takes me to him, so that the body may no wise fulfil what the heart devised, I would that the heart that conceived that intention was sent thither. Therefore I pray every one of you to choose from among you one who is honourable, wise and brave, and a noble knight in the field, to bear my heart against God's enemies, when soul and body are separated, for I wish it to be brought there honourably, since God does not will that I should have power to go thither.[121]

Another account is briefer but more specific: 'he left his heart to be sent to Jerusalem and buried at the Lord's Sepulchre'.[122]

The noble knight chosen for the task was Sir James Douglas, one of Bruce's most loyal supporters. On 1 September 1329 Douglas was granted a letter of protection from Edward III of England when he was 'about to set out for the Holy Land with the heart of the late Robert, king of Scotland', and on the same day the English king also wrote to Alfonso XI of Castile, asking him to protect Douglas if his journey to the Holy Land took him through his domains, so a circuitous route to Palestine was already envisaged.[123] On 25 August 1330 James Douglas was killed fighting Muslims in Spain. One account has him throwing the casket with Bruce's heart deep among the enemy and then hacking his way to it. His followers recovered his body, along with the heart of King Robert, and, after disembowelling Douglas, separating his flesh from the bones, and burying the soft tissue in Spain, they took his bones, along with the royal heart, back to Scotland. Bruce's heart was buried in Melrose Abbey after its long journey, and, like Alfonso's heart, never reached Jerusalem. The Douglas family were granted the right to bear the king's heart for ever, on their coat-of-arms.[124]

After the pope had pronounced against the practice of multiple burial in 1299, deeming it a horrible custom, the conscientious would have to seek special permission to be allowed to continue it. In 1323 Isabella of

France, queen of Edward II of England, obtained papal permission to have her body divided and buried in three churches of her choice; twenty-two years later, in 1345, after she had secured the deposition and murder of her husband and had seen her lover captured and executed by her son and then spent fifteen years in retirement from politics, she decided to have that permission renewed, which it was.[125] Successive kings of France requested the same privilege, until, in 1351, the pope granted the right to all future kings and queens of France to have their bodies 'cut up, cooked, or divided in any other way, and buried in one or various churches or places, as your devotion persuades you'.[126] Multiple burial continued, like many other things, despite papal disapproval.

Monuments might be erected for each burial, entrails, heart and body. After the death of Eleanor of Castile, queen of Edward I of England, in 1290, her entrails were buried in Lincoln Cathedral, her heart in the Dominican church in London and her body in Westminster Abbey. Both the tombs at Lincoln and Westminster had recumbent effigies, the latter of which survives (the present effigy in Lincoln is a modern replica), a work of art in gilt bronze, while some details are recorded of the heart tomb in the Dominican church: payments are recorded for the making of small images, painting, ironwork and stonework there.[127] At the abbey of Maubuisson, north-west of Paris, the entrails tombs of Charles IV of France (d. 1328) and his wife, Joan of Evreux (d. 1371), are surmounted by their effigies in marble, each clutching their entrails to their chest. The statues were made in 1370–2, so more than forty years after Charles' death. Joan had clearly planned to rejoin her husband, both at St-Denis, where their bodies were buried, and at Maubuisson, where their entrails lay.

Damnatio Memoriae

If rulers wanted to be remembered, especially in prayer, then their enemies wanted to wipe out their memory. In ancient Egypt and imperial Rome this process, conventionally termed *damnatio memoriae* ('condemnation of memory or remembrance'), might involve the

Figure 15 The entrails tombs of Charles IV of France (d. 1328) and his wife Joan of Evreux (d. 1371) at Maubuisson, showing them clutching their entrails to their chests. These effigies were made more than forty years after Charles' death.
© RMN-Grand Palais (musée du Louvre) / Hervé Lewandowski.

destruction or relabelling of statues and erasure of inscriptions. Public statuary was less significant in the medieval world, but posthumous revenge could be taken on the body.[128] One way was simply to deny proper burial, as in the case of the tyrannical Byzantine emperor

Phocas, who was burned in 610 and his ashes thrown into a common grave.[129] If they had been buried, you could dig them up. After the veneration of icons was restored in the Byzantine empire in 843, the body of the iconoclast emperor Constantine V (741–75) was exhumed, beaten and burned by authority of Michael III or the regent Theodora.[130] How much of Constantine was left after seventy years is not clear.

In the case of Constantine, the motive for the exhumation was religious hatred, but other actions of this type were more purely dynastic, aimed at political rivals whose legitimacy was not recognized. One contemporary chronicler says that, in 1014, after Sven, king of Denmark, who had just conquered England, died and was buried in the north of England, his rival Æthelred returned to power and planned to disinter and destroy his enemy's corpse. However, an Englishwoman, whose motives are not reported, forestalled him and had Sven's body transported to Scandinavia.[131] Sven's grandson Harthacnut was more successful in his plans. He and his half-brother Harold Harefoot had disputed the succession to England after the death of their father Canute in 1035, but Harthacnut had stayed in Denmark, so Harold had been able to establish himself as king. After Harold's death in 1040, Harthacnut finally came to England, was acknowledged as king and 'had the dead Harold dug up and cast into a marsh'.[132]

After conquering the kingdom of Sicily in 1194, the emperor Henry VI dug up the bodies of King Tancred and his son Roger, whom he regarded as usurpers, and removed all their royal insignia.[133] Henry's grandson, Manfred, king of Sicily, faced the same posthumous disturbance. Manfred was killed in battle at Benevento in 1266, defending his kingdom against the invading forces of Charles of Anjou. Some of Charles' barons, on seeing Manfred's blood-stained corpse, begged Charles to give his dead enemy an honourable burial. Charles said he would have done so if Manfred had not died excommunicate, but he had him buried at the foot of the Benevento bridge and every one of his soldiers placed a stone upon the spot, creating a mighty cairn. Subsequently, however, at the pope's command, the bishop of Cosenza removed Manfred's remains and took them to the banks of the river Garigliano, which marked the boundary of the kingdom of Sicily, and buried them there. 'Now the rain washes them and the wind tosses them, outside the kingdom', as Manfred himself explains to Dante, meeting him in purgatory.[134] Henry VI wanted to deny the regality of Tancred and his son, while Charles of Anjou seems to have thought that the chivalrous impulses of his barons, to bury a dead enemy honourably, deserved consideration, but were, upon reflection, outweighed by the harder line of canon law. The popes were notoriously vicious in their pursuit of the Hohenstaufen dynasty, to which Manfred belonged, and this spite did not stop with the death of their enemy.

PART II

A SENSE OF DYNASTY

CHAPTER 8

Names and Numbering

Terminology

DYNASTIES, LIKE CENTURIES, GIVE HISTORIANS A HANDY tool for labelling large chunks of time and place. If we have a wall map with the title 'Europa zur Zeit der Staufer' ('Europe in the Age of the Staufer or Hohenstaufen'), we have a rough idea of what to expect: a map of Europe in the period 1150–1250. Or if we find a book titled Tudor England (there are more than twenty) we should know when and where we are. Some of these dynastic terms assume overtones of meaning well beyond mere time and place, as is also the case with adjectives derived from individual rulers. 'Victorian' is a good example of this, a word, incidentally, first used in 1839! So we have these useful labels: The Carolingian World, Spain under the Bourbons, and so forth. But are these terms simply retrospective classifications adopted for convenience by modern historians, teachers and publishers, or are they something that would have had significance for contemporaries? Did members of medieval dynasties think of themselves in this way? Was there something that could be called a sense of dynasty?

The label 'Plantagenet', for example, is a convenient term for the rulers of England between the twelfth and fifteenth centuries, and can be used as an adjective in many ways (Plantagenet coins, Plantagenet queens, Plantagenet England) but the name was not employed by any members of the family between its first user Geoffrey of Anjou, who died in 1151, and possibly his second son, another Geoffrey, who died in 1158,[1] and Richard, duke of York, who started using it around 1448 as part of his campaign for the throne.[2] In the intervening 290 years no one called themselves 'Plantagenet', so in this case the name had no role in creating family identity or a sense of dynasty.

If we want to explore medieval conceptions of dynasty, we can begin with the terminology. The word 'dynasty' itself, meaning a line of rulers, was coined by Manetho, an Egyptian priest writing in Greek around 300 BC: δυναστεία, derived from δυναστής, 'ruler'.[3] His division of the pharaohs into thirty dynasties is still the backbone of ancient Egyptian chronology, although the dynasties he lists are not always composed of members of the same family. In Latin form the word was used by St Jerome in his chronologies and thus came to the medieval west, but it is fairly rare there. In the Latin west, *dinastia* can sometimes mean simply 'power', but more usually refers specifically to the ancient ruling houses of Egypt, just as in the original coinage. Gregory of Tours, writing in the late sixth century, says that at the time of Abraham, 'among the Egyptians it was the time of the sixteenth ruling power (*potestas*), which they call dynasty in their language'.[4] The writers of universal histories, from the Carolingian period onwards, often used the term when writing about Egypt. There is occasional confusion, as in the case of Fredegar's chronicle, which takes *dinastia* to be the name of an Egyptian king,[5] but for the most part there is a clear but limited usage. Some authors attempted a definition or paraphrase of the term. Gervase of Tilbury, writing around 1200 and dealing with early Egyptian history, says 'Dynasties changed through different lines of kings (*per diversa regum genera*) down to Cambyses.'[6] *Genus regum*, 'a line of kings' or 'a family of kings', is a good definition of dynasty. Later in the thirteenth century Rodrigo Jiménez de Rada also gave a succinct definition: 'Dynasty is defined as ruling power remaining in some family (*domus*).'[7] *Domus*, originally and often meaning 'house' or 'household', also assumed the meaning 'family', especially with reference to important or ruling families. Thus, Pope Nicholas III, elected in 1277, is described as '*natione Romanus, de domo Ursinorum*', that is, a Roman by birth and a member of the Orsini family, or the house of Orsini.[8] A Spanish chronicler in the late fourteenth century calls the French ruling family 'the house of France (*la casa de Francia*)'; a Portuguese historian of the following generation identifies the rulers of England as 'the house of England (*casa de Imgraterra*)'.[9] 'House of' is still standard form for dynastic genealogies.[10]

Contemporaries did not apply the word 'dynasty' to the ruling families of medieval Europe. But, as we have just seen in the case of *genus regum*, 'line of kings', and *domus*, 'house', there were plenty of synonyms available. Others in Latin included *prolis, prosapia, familia* (which does not always mean household), *genealogia, generatio, stirps.* And similar terms arose in the vernaculars: '*maison*' and 'house' and 'Haus' underwent a similar extension of sense as Latin *domus,* so that by the fifteenth century German language sources can speak of 'the house of Austria'.[11] In his account of his own life, written in Catalan, James I of Aragon refers to his family as 'our lineage (*liynatge*)', a term used more than fifty times in the work for his and other powerful kindreds.[12] It was thus entirely possible to make statements referring to what we might call dynasties. Henry I of England, for example, was, according to one contemporary source, 'known to be the seventh of this dynasty (*prosapia*) from Rollo' (the Viking who settled in Normandy) – this is quite accurate – and the pope could flatter St Louis by referring to 'your most Christian house (*domus*)'.[13] Margaret of Burgundy, sister of Edward IV and Richard III, writing in 1495, referred to the Wars of the Roses as 'the discords and dissensions that were once so great between the houses of York and Lancaster'.[14]

Names of Dynasties

In some societies dynastic names have been important. The dynasties of imperial China had names, which were chosen consciously and were used officially when dating events. China had a 'historiography office' set up by the Tang emperors and there were official compositions such as the *New History of the Tang* of 1060.[15] Medieval Europe was different. We have already observed that the Plantagenets did not call themselves Plantagenets. Nor did their great rivals, the Capetian kings of France, identify themselves as such, although they knew they were descended from Hugh Capet, who ruled from 987 to 996, and so did the revolutionaries of the late eighteenth century, who tried and executed Louis XVI under the name 'Citizen Capet'. Looking back from later centuries, French chroniclers recognized the year 987 as a moment of dynastic change but did not give the new dynasty a family name, instead identifying it by simply numbering it. Around the middle of the eleventh century, a writer in Aquitaine described the way Hugh Capet had ousted the last Carolingians and concluded, 'thus, as the second line of the kings of the Franks failed, the kingdom was transferred to the third line' (*linea* is the word used).[16] Likewise, for a writer of the twelfth century, Hugh Capet and his descendants were 'the third family (*familia*) of kings of France'.[17] In this view, the Merovingians were the first, the Carolingians the second and the family of Hugh Capet the third dynasty. The *Grandes chroniques de France*, the great compendium of French history first assembled in the thirteenth century and written in French not Latin, explains that the work is divided into three chief sections, 'because three families (*generacions*) have been kings of France', identifying them as the family of Meroveus, of Pippin and of Hugh Capet.[18] And this schema was continued into the eighteenth century, when the editors of the ordinances of the Capetian kings, who began publishing in 1723, titled their work *Ordonnances des rois de France de la troisième race*, 'Ordinances of the Kings of France of the Third Race'. *Race*, 'race', is not a medieval word but, by this time, was being used as a term for a lineage or descent group. It was a word borrowed from horse breeding, is probably cognate with the modern French for a breeding stud (*haras*), and gave no hint of its ominous future.

Surnames

When Richard, duke of York, adopted the style 'Richard Plantagenet' or when the French revolutionaries tried Louis XVI as 'Citizen Capet', they were treating 'Plantagenet' and 'Capet' as if they were hereditary surnames, which was certainly not how they were used for most of the Middle Ages. There are of course royal dynasties that take their name from the surname of their ancestor. In English and Scottish history Tudor and Stuart are well-known examples, in each case the name of an aristocratic lineage that had risen to kingship. But, in general, ruling dynasties do not need surnames: 'Henry, king of the English' is a perfectly adequate identifier. And the very custom of having surnames was a latecomer to European naming practice. In most parts of Europe surnames are unheard of before the eleventh century and do not become general until the fourteenth, although they were certainly spreading in the twelfth and thirteenth centuries. Indeed, by the

1220s they were so common that there is an English royal messenger at that time known as 'Reynold Sanz-surnun', one of the best surnames ever recorded.[19]

It seems, curiously enough, that the first ruling classes to develop hereditary surnames were those of Byzantium and Ireland, two parts of Christian Europe about as distant as it is possible to be, geographically, socially and culturally. And in these two parts of Christendom, exceptionally, royal dynasties did come to identify themselves by surname. In the case of Byzantium, the tenth century seems to be the crucial period when family names amongst the high-born become common and hereditary.[20] In the ninth century even the greatest were usually identified by just a single name, sometimes with the addition of their office, but over the course of time, an additional designation became usual. An early example is Argyros, meaning 'silver'; Leo Argyros, active in the mid-ninth century, is reported as the first to take this name.[21] One trend was the increasing use of patronymics and other forms of individual identifier, but eventually it was the hereditary surname that came to designate the aristocratic lineage. The plural form, such as Martinakioi, was a name for the group, the singular, as in Theophano Martinakia, for the individual. And when members of such families attained the imperial throne, as they did from the eleventh century, they kept these surnames. In this period, imperial surnames appear on coins for the first time.[22] The wife of Alexius Comnenus proudly displayed her surname in the wording on her seal: 'Irene Doukaina, empress'.[23] The great Byzantinist Alexander Kazhdan pointed out that Byzantinists give the imperial dynasties down to the eleventh century geographical labels – Isaurian, Amorian, Macedonian – but that thereafter they are known by family names – Doukai, Comnenians, Angeloi, and so forth.[24] The former are modern constructs, the latter contemporary usage. No one can doubt that family loyalties and family identity mattered before the tenth century, but the group label is a new badge of shared distinctiveness. In Byzantium knowing someone's surname meant knowing a lot about them.

In Ireland, too, the tenth century was a crucial formative period for hereditary surnames.[25] These almost all designated a grandfather, either in the form *mac meic* ('son of the son of'), abbreviated to Mac, or in the direct form *ua* ('grandson of'), later written O, thus creating the familiar

Irish dynasties with names in Mac and O: the O'Rourkes of Breifne descend from Ruairc who died in 893, the O'Connors of Connacht from Conchobar, the king who died in 973. These names are the names of dynasties, indicating membership of a family with claims to rulership and enduring over many generations. The difference between usage in this matter in Ireland and in other parts of western Europe can be seen at a glance if one looks at the indexes of modern editions of the Irish annals and those of chronicles from England or France or Germany, the former listing all the kings of a kindred under the family name, the latter giving them separate entries under their forenames.

Collective names for aristocratic kindreds did exist elsewhere. In areas of Germanic speech, there is evidence for contemporary terms for families formed by an ancestral name plus -ing. The kings of Kent in the sixth, seventh and eighth centuries were descended from a ruler named Oisc and were hence called the Oisingas.[26] The early medieval dukes of Bavaria were recognized as Agilolfings.[27] Archbishop Unwan of Hamburg-Bremen (1013–29) is described as 'sprung from the illustrious kindred of the *Inmedingi*'. Inmed or Immed is recorded as a noble Saxon name.[28] The practice can be found in Italy, which had German aristocratic settlers in the early Middle Ages. For instance, a noble kin-group in the region of Lucca in north-west Italy took their name from one of their members, Soffredo, and crop up in a local chronicle as 'those of the house of the Soffredings (*de domo Soffredingorum*)' or 'the Soffreding house (*de domo Soffredinga*)'.[29] The suffix -*ing* could also function as part of a patronymic. William of Malmesbury observes that the Merovingian kings (*Merovingi*) took their name from their ancestor Meroveus, and adds, 'In this same way, too, the sons of the kings of the English took patronymics from their fathers, so that the son of Edgar would be called Edgaring and the son of Edmund Edmunding', noting the common Germanic ancestry of the Franks and the English.[30]

Learned authors could also use the fancy Greek suffix -*ides* to indicate parentage or descent. Thus, Louis the Stammerer, son of Charles the Bald, was 'Karolides Ludovicus', and Robert II of France, son of Hugh Capet, 'Hugonides Rotbertus'.[31] And this manner of speaking could be generalized: one thirteenth-century text describes the kings whom we call Capetians as 'the Hugonid kings (*Hugonidarum regum*)'.[32] In late-thirteenth-century Frisia a feud arose between two families. A leading figure on one side was called Ebbo Menalda. The learned chronicler describing this series of events terms his side both the *Menaldingi* and the *Ebbonides*.[33] The former is the ancient Germanic suffix for groups of people, the latter a borrowing from ancient Greek practice.

In the eleventh and twelfth centuries, aristocratic families in some countries began to adopt the names of their newly built castles as surnames. There is a good explicit example of this practice in the chronicle of Conrad of Scheyern, a local Bavarian chronicle written in the early thirteenth century, which gives details of the aristocratic families in the region around Munich. Introducing Scheyern itself, Conrad says, 'let us say something briefly about that castle and about the nobles who derived their name from it, and still have it'. One share in the castle was held by 'the nobles who were subsequently named after the castle of Dachau', another by 'the counts of Grub, who were afterwards named after the castle of Valley'.[34] So three aristocratic lineages are here forming, identified by the castles they possess. These lineages were 'of' somewhere, hence the common association in Germany and France of the name elements 'von' and 'de' with aristocracy. The Habsburgs are perhaps the most notable family to take their name from a castle, in this case *Habichtsburg*, 'Hawk Castle', in modern Switzerland, where the family are attested from the eleventh century. When they attained royal power, as they did intermittently from 1273 and permanently from 1438, they retained their surname. In general, however, with the exceptions already mentioned, the royal and imperial dynasties of the Middle Ages did not identify themselves through a surname or any general collective appellation.

Naming Patterns within Dynasties

Although rulers rarely expressed a sense of dynasty through a surname, they almost always did so through forenames. While surnames are a development of the Middle Ages, and were not common until their last centuries, forenames (first names, Christian names) were universal. They are individual identifiers but can also mark a family identity. Indeed, one of the most common and most public ways that a sense of family can be expressed is in the choice of such names, and even today it is a subject of interest and importance not only for new parents but also for grandparents and aunts and uncles, who can be flattered or offended by the names chosen. In some times and places there are norms and expectations that a child will be named after a particular relative, a first son after a grandfather, for example, while the importance of maternal kin can be recognized by the introduction of new names from their side of the family. All these things mattered as much, if not more, to rulers.

A debate over the choice of a royal name for the baby Ladislas Posthumus of Hungary at his baptism in 1440 is described by his nurse:

> he was named King Ladislas, which annoyed some who thought that they should have called him King Peter, because that was the name he had brought with him [meaning that the date of Ladislas' baptism, 22 February, was the feast of Saint Peter's Chair]. Some thought that they should have named him King Albert in accordance with the will of his father, who was truly a pious king. But my gracious lady [Elizabeth the mother] had made a vow to God and to the holy king, saint Ladislas.[35]

Here there are three quite distinct grounds advanced for choice of name: Ladislas, a traditional royal name in Hungary, the name of a saint-king and the subject of a vow by the mother; Peter, the saint on whose day the baptism took place; and Albert, name of the father and chosen in his will.

The custom of rulers and other members of the ruling class having streams of forenames begins only in the seventeenth century. Today, in some countries, these long sequences, sometimes topped off with double-barrelled surnames, are an almost certain indicator of class. The modern British royal family is quite moderate in this respect: the names of the children of Queen Elizabeth are Charles Philip Arthur George, Anne Elizabeth Alice Louise, Andrew Albert Christian Edward and Edward Antony Richard Louis, in each case four names. They certainly cannot compare with Albert II, the king of the Belgians who abdicated in 2013, who was christened Albert Félix Humbert Théodore Christian Eugène Marie (and his life was complicated further by having to have his names in French, Dutch and German forms). Medieval rulers were content with less, but their choices were still full of meaning.

Leitnamen

Recurrent names often characterized a family or expressed its connections. The Germans, as always, have a word for this: *Leitnamen*, 'leading names'.[36] And some of these names seem to have been so distinctive of a particular aristocratic kindred that when an individual with the name turns up in the early Middle Ages with no other context, many of those working on the period are willing to bet that he (or more rarely she) was a member of that kindred. Modern scholars of the early Middle Ages have even created collective terms for such kin-groups by adding a suffix to the leading name. So, from the clan that used the name Ekkehard we have the Ekkehardiner, from the one that preferred Poppo we have the Popponen, and for the one that was fated to favour Boso, the Bosoniden or Bosonids.[37]

These terms are convenient modern labels for historians. But there is evidence from the medieval period itself that contemporaries were aware of these *Leitnamen*, and especially of the way that they embodied not merely blood relationship but also claims to authority and territory. For example, one chronicler explained the naming pattern of the counts of Flanders, who mustered nine counts named Baldwin between the ninth and the thirteenth centuries, in the following way:

> In the county of Baldwin and his family it was a custom observed for many years and regarded as a perpetual law that one of the sons who pleased the father most should receive the father's name and obtain the rule of the whole of Flanders alone by hereditary succession.[38]

In this picture, it is unclear at what point the father made the decision as to which son pleased him most: at birth? after several boys had been born? when they were teenagers? It is likely, of course, that the chronicle account is simply a reflection of the choice of a recurrent name for the eldest son. The name William was so much identified with the counts of Poitou that two members of the dynasty who did not bear the name assumed it when they happened to succeed to the title unexpectedly: Peter (William VII, 1039–58) and Guy-Geoffrey (William VIII, 1058–86).[39] And rulers were so concerned to perpetuate certain names that they might re-use them for subsequent children after the death of an earlier bearer: Charles VI of

France (1380–1422) had three sons called Charles, Charles VIII (1483–98) had two.

The association of a name with rule of a particular territory is brought out vividly in the case of the son of Petronilla, queen of Aragon (mentioned above, p. 57). Petronilla was betrothed to Raymond Berengar of Barcelona in 1137, laying the foundations for a new composite state. They had several children and the oldest surviving son was clearly seen as their heir, even though it appears father and mother could not agree on his name, for he appears both as Raymond and as Alfonso, the former in contexts associated with his father, the latter with his mother. In his will of 1162, Raymond Berengar the father bequeathed his realms of Aragon and Barcelona to 'his oldest son, Raymond', while two years later Petronilla abdicated in favour of 'my beloved son Alfonso ... who is called Raymond in my husband's will'.[40] Alfonso was a royal name in Aragon, Raymond a recurrent name in the line of the counts of Barcelona. Your name was a claim.[41]

These *Leitnamen* could even be used as a shorthand for the dynasty itself. In Canto 20 of the *Purgatorio*, Dante encounters Hugh Capet, first king of the Capetian dynasty, but the poet does not use the name 'Capetian', identifying the French ruling family instead as 'the Philips and Louis' by whom France is ruled in recent times'.[42] This is literally exact, since for 256 years, from 1060 to 1316, every king of France was indeed called Philip or Louis. A pictorial family tree of the Carolingians which circulated in Germany in the twelfth and thirteenth centuries was labelled with a verse: 'While this family held the reins of the Frankish kingdom, it gave to Rome sceptre-bearing Charleses and Louis'.[43] This too is accurate, for it is the case that in the eighth and ninth centuries every person called Charles or Louis was a member of the Carolingian family, while of the male-line descendants of Charlemagne in the ninth and tenth centuries, twelve were called Louis and ten Charles.[44] The monk Notker, writing for the emperor Charles the Fat, and expressing his hope that the emperor might have a legitimate son, pictured 'a little Louis or Charles (*Ludowiculum vel Carolastrum*)'.[45] The emperor Frederick Barbarossa's uncle, Otto of Freising, calls the two great families of twelfth-century Germany, now known as the Staufer or Hohenstaufen and the Welfs, 'the Henries of Waiblingen and the Welfs of Altdorf', thus using both a *Leitname* and a family castle to identify them.[46] Barbarossa himself was supposedly proud of his descent from 'the royal stock of the Waiblingen, who had descended from two royal families, that is, the Cloviscs and the Charleses', meaning the Merovingians and the Carolingians.[47]

Alongside the recurrent *Leitname* is the recurrent name part. Germanic aristocratic names were usually made up of two elements which each had a meaning in everyday speech. For instance, the Merovingian royal name Theudebert, borne by two kings of the dynasty, is composed of *theod* meaning 'people' and *bert* meaning 'bright'. Because of this, variations could be played with, to express family relationships. Æthelwulf, king of Wessex (839–58), named his first four sons Æthelstan, Æthelbald, Æthelbert and Æthelred, before running out of imagination and calling the youngest one Alfred. *Æthel* means 'noble', like modern German *Adel,* while the second elements mean 'wolf', 'stone', 'bold' and 'counsel' respectively (Alfred means 'elf-counsel'). In this way, a common distinctive naming feature of the family (the first element *Æthel*) could be combined with individual naming. Since these elements had separate meaning, there was even room for punning: the unfortunate Æthelred the Unready, Æthelwulf's distant descendant, was given his nickname because he was Æthelred Unræd – 'noble-counsel bad-counsel'.[48] And the elements could be imaginatively inverted, as in the case of the aristocratic Frankish brothers Nithard and Hartnid.[49]

Contemporary Confusion over Homonyms

It is not only modern students and scholars who are sometimes overwhelmed by the repetition of names in the ruling families of the past. Conrad of Scheyern, mentioned above (p. 289), became a little testy when trying to disentangle the family history of the noble house of Scheyern. The recurrence of a limited number of names made it hard to identify individuals in the past. In the end he concludes

let us now turn our pen to the nobles of our time, for it seems difficult and unnecessary to write down the deeds of each individual, for, as we have said, not two or three of them, but many, were called nobles of Scheyern, who almost all, except a few, bore two names, namely Otto and Ekkehard.[50]

The chronicler Richer of Saint-Rémi, writing in the 990s, expressed a similar awareness of the dangers of confusion when dealing with these recurrent dynastic forenames. He knew that anyone reading Carolingian history would be struck by 'frequent mentions of a Charles or a Louis' (this is still a problem today) and recognized that error could result if 'the order of events was not given careful consideration'. But, by paying close attention to chronology, he says, 'the careful reader will distinguish the different kings with the same names'.[51] The monastic historian Aimoin of Fleury, writing his *History of the Franks* around the year 1000, was also conscious of this problem:

> The genealogies of the kings, which were truly jumbled up because of the similar names, I have distinguished, as far as I have been able, and differentiated each one either by giving the name of his father or by the labels 'senior' and 'junior'.[52]

One way of distinguishing rulers with the same name was to give them a nickname.[53] In his list of French kings, the chronicler Rigord, writing in 1186, often does not distinguish homonyms, but occasionally adds a nickname: Charlemagne is Charlemagne, i.e. 'Charles the Great'; his son is 'Louis the Pious'; his son 'Charles the Bald'. All these terms are still in use by modern historians. Likewise, the king who died in 929 is 'Charles the Simple'. Rigord reserves the name Hugh Capet for the father of the king who ascended the throne in 987, not the king himself; he was by no means alone in this.[54] Among the kings of Rigord's own century, we find 'Louis the Fat' (Louis VI), 'Louis the Pious' (Louis VII) and 'Philip Augustus' (Philip II), the first and third of these names still being standard but the middle one quite unknown in modern historical writing, which reserves it for the ninth-century Carolingian emperor.[55] Most of these nicknames were given years or even centuries after the deaths of the monarchs they became attached to. They are retrospective tools of chroniclers and other writers, not contemporary, official designations, although they might eventually creep into formal royal documents: Louis the Fat (Louis VI), for example, appears as such in the registers of his grandson Philip Augustus.[56] Unusually, the West Frankish king Louis the Stammerer (877–9) was called that by a contemporary chronicler.[57] Undoubtedly retrospective is the nickname of the Irish king Niall mac Aéda, known as Niall Caille ('of the Callan') because he drowned in the river Callan.[58]

The Term Carolingian

A good example of the way a leading name could become something like a collective label is provided by the dynasty that modern historians call Carolingian.[59] There is scarcely a medieval ruler who left a deeper imprint on memory than Charlemagne, a king of the Franks from 768 and emperor from 800. His death in 814 could be used as a marker in time, as in the case of the chronicler Fulcher of Chartres, reporting the capture of Jerusalem by the crusaders in 1099: 'It was 15 July, 285 years after the death of Charlemagne.'[60] It is remarkable that, almost three centuries after Charlemagne's death, it could be referred to in this way, and referred to accurately, as a recognizable indicator of place in time. And Charlemagne also made it to the stars. The constellation of Ursa Major had been called 'The Wagon' by ancient Akkadians and Greeks, but to the English it became more specifically 'Charles' Wagon' or 'Charlemagne's Wagon' as tribute to the famous emperor.[61]

His name, Charles, has an unusual history. Charles Martel, his grandfather, is the first person to bear the name Charles (Karl). He was illegitimate and the sources mention that his father chose this name for him. It is a single syllable, which is unusual for early high-status names, and it has an ordinary language meaning of 'man', or perhaps more specifically, 'free peasant man'.[62] Whether Charles Martel's father was being kind and prophesying that this son would be 'a real man', or whether there was a sardonic tone in giving him this flat and definitely unaristocratic sounding name, we do not know. In some later legends the illegitimacy of Charles Martel was attributed to his grandson and in the imaginative literature of the thirteenth century the story was told that Charlemagne was called Charles because he had been conceived on a cart (*char*).[63]

The military success and political power of Charles Martel meant the new name was now acceptably aristocratic and could be given to Charles' grandson, the future Charlemagne, who carried it to even higher levels of fame and glory. It was then borne by two of his ninth-century descendants who ruled as emperors, Charles the Bald and Charles the Fat. It thus became associated with the most powerful dynasty in western Europe. The *Vision of Charles the Fat* (discussed below, pp. 347–9) depicts Carolingians themselves referring simply to 'our royal family', 'our stock', 'our family' (*genus nostrum regale, nostra propago, nostra genealogia*), but those who were not members of the family would need some other way of referring to it. One way was to call them the second line or second family (after the Merovingians) (see above, pp. 285–6), but the name Charles was also developed for this purpose. In the middle of the tenth century the chronicler Widukind refers to Louis the Child, who ruled the East Franks 900–11, as 'the last of the Charleses ruling the East Franks'.[64] Since Louis' name was not Charles, Widukind is clearly using 'the Charleses', in the plural, as a label for the dynasty of which he was a member. This is a usage found also in later German chroniclers, some-times with an added term, such as 'the stock of the Charleses' or 'the ancient and glorious blood of the Charleses'.[65] Two other terms also developed based on the name Charles (*Karolus* in Latin): *Karlenses* and *Karolingi*. These are used both as the equivalent of the modern term 'Carolingian', as in 'the royal stock of the *Karlenses*', or 'the kingship of the *Karolingi* began with Pippin', and also as designations for the West Franks or French as a people, as in 'the king of the *Karlenses*' (for non-Carolingian as well as Carolingian kings) or 'his high-born parents, Lotharingian and *Karlenses*'.[66] The name Charles itself began to assume grand and elaborate associations and by the thirteenth century there was even a prophecy that 'from the *Karlingi*, that is, the stock of King Charles and of the house of the kings of France, an emperor will be raised up, Charles by name, who will be ruler and monarch of the whole of Europe and he will reform the Church and the empire, but after him no other will reign'.[67] The most striking development of Charles' name was its adoption as the ordinary word for 'king' in the Slavic and Baltic languages, as well as in Rumanian and Turkish, a parallel to the way the personal name 'Caesar' became 'Tsar'. In this way a name of obscure and possibly derogatory nature became a word for 'sovereign'.

New Names in Dynasties

New names were introduced into dynasties in various ways.[68] Maternal kin, especially if of high status, could be honoured by giving names from their side of the family. A good example is the way the name Duarte (Edward) entered the Portuguese royal dynasty, and subsequently the Portuguese world, through the wife of John I, who was herself the grand-daughter of Edward III of England. Valdemar I of Denmark (1157–82) was named after his maternal great-grandfather, Vladimir of Kiev, thus bringing this Russian name into the Danish royal dynasty. Naming after a maternal grandfather is explicitly noted in the case of Godila, a noblewoman who married Liuthar, margrave of the Saxon Nordmark (985–1003), and 'bore him a first born son, calling him by the name of her father, Werner'.[69] And, although the patriarchal nature of medieval society, and of genealogical conventions, obscures it, there were also recurrent names in mother–daughter lines, which by the nature of things would not be seen as recurring in the same paternal family. For instance, between Matilda, wife of Henry I of Germany (919–36), and her great-great-granddaughter Matilda of Swabia, who died in the early 1030s, there were five generations of women alternately named Matilda or Gerberga, a pattern so well established that it could even be used as a guideline by contemporaries when conducting genealogical research.[70]

Marriage was the most common path whereby unfamiliar names might be added to the family roll-call but there were others. Youngest sons of large families were sometimes given unusual names that were not part of family tradition. One chronicler, when listing the five sons of the emperor Frederick Barbarossa, gives them all landed titles except for the last: 'Philip the clerk'.[71] Philip was not a name that had been borne in the family before and it may well have been chosen because the youngest son was destined to be an ecclesiastic rather than a great lay noble, although events were to turn out differently and Philip had to re-enter the laity and eventually became king.

If, as in Philip's case, a youngest son unexpectedly succeeded to power, his name might then become entrenched. A classic example of both methods of transmission, through marriage and through novel names for younger sons, is provided by the Scottish royal house under Malcolm III (1057/8–93) and his queen Margaret. Margaret was a descendant of the old royal house of Wessex and her first four sons received the assertively Anglo-Saxon names Edward, Edgar, Edmund, Æthelred, names of tenth- and eleventh-century kings of England. Malcolm, the father, does not seem have asserted the claims of his own, Gaelic, naming tradition. Then, after these four sons with English names, perhaps feeling that duty to Margaret's ancestors had been satisfied, Margaret and Malcolm chose unprecedented names for their last two sons, Alexander and David. Neither choice can be explained with certainty. Completely unknown in Scotland before the late eleventh century, Alexander might be a reference to the ancient hero or to the pope at the time of the marriage of Malcolm and Margaret (Alexander II, 1061–73), while David might look to either the biblical king or the Welsh saint. In the event, both sons succeeded to the throne and their names entered the repertoire of royal and aristocratic nomenclature. Two subsequent Alexanders ruled Scotland (Alexander II, 1214–49; Alexander III, 1249–86) and one subsequent David (David II, 1329–71), while younger sons of the dynasty also often bore the name. Today 'Sandy', the short form for Alexander, is a stereotypical indication of Scottishness.

Also, ancient royal names might be revived. Edward I, son of Henry III, was the first Edward in the English royal house since the Norman Conquest, almost two centuries earlier. The choice is explained by the devotion that Henry III had towards Edward the Confessor, who was not only the last king of the Wessex line but also a canonized saint. Through Edward I, this Anglo-Saxon name was revived and naturalized; it is the most common name of English kings. Less influential was the unusual choice of the name Dagobert for a son of Louis VIII of France, born in 1222, the year before Louis succeeded to the throne. Dagobert was a royal name under the Merovingian kings, who had ruled the Franks until 751, but it was unknown among later dynasties until this son of Louis VIII. Dagobert I, who died in 638 or 639, was claimed as the founder of the abbey of St-Denis, which was the burial place of the Capetian kings of

France and also the home of the community of monks who wrote their history, so he had particular significance for the ruling dynasty. But this Capetian Dagobert died at the age of nine or ten and was buried in the abbey of Royaumont, which his mother, Queen Blanche, had founded, and the name never did revive. Moreover, it seems as if the young prince actually bore two names, one of them more familiar in the family: 'Dagobert, that is Philip'.[72]

Name Change

Cases of name change have already been mentioned, when women moved to foreign courts and adopted new names more familiar there (p. 28), or the counts of Poitou who took the traditional comital name of William (p. 291), but there are other examples that show the way that certain names were associated with certain dynasties and roles. For example, in 781 Charlemagne's third son Carloman, at that time four years old, was given the name Pippin, even though he had an older half-brother of the same name. Giving him this important family name, which was the name of Charlemagne's own father, was marking him for royal status and he was simultaneously anointed king of Italy.[73] The older Pippin is described as 'deformed by a hunch on the back' and this may have been a reason for his exclusion.[74] He rebelled in 792, was defeated and sent to a monastery. Having his name taken by a younger half-brother must have rankled. A different kind of substitution between brothers occurred among the sons of the emperor Frederick Barbarossa. His firstborn, called Frederick after his father, born in 1164, was created duke of Swabia when a baby, but died at the age of five. A younger brother, Conrad, was now made duke of Swabia and also adopted the name Frederick. He had stepped into his brother's shoes in the fullest possible sense of the phrase.[75] Every duke of Swabia since 1079, almost a century, had been called Frederick, and the name and the title were now approaching synonyms, a process fully realized in the case of Dolphinus and Dauphin (above, p. 208).

A name change that involved no substitution of siblings but rather a reorientation of dynastic ambition is found in the case of the celebrated Holy Roman Emperor Charles IV. This son of King John of Bohemia, born in Prague in 1316, was baptized Wenceslas, which was the name of Bohemia's most famous saint and also the name of the child's grandfather and deceased uncle, the last two rulers of Bohemia from the ancient Premyslid line. The name could not have been more royal and Bohemian. However, King John was in origin a great noble from Luxemburg, which lay on the western edge of the Holy Roman Empire and where both French and German were spoken. In 1323 he sent the young Wenceslas to the court of the French king, Charles IV. Writing years later, Wenceslas recalled the king with affection:

> my father sent me to the king of France when I was in the seventh year of my boyhood and the king of France had me confirmed by a bishop and he gave me his own name, that is, Charles, and he gave me as a wife the daughter of his uncle Charles, who was named Margaret but known as Blanche.[76]

Charles was not only the name of the young prince's French patron but also that of the most famous ruler of the Middle Ages, the founder of the Western Empire. Although he grew up to be a king of Bohemia who left a great mark on Prague, evidenced in the Charles University and the Charles Bridge, Charles' new name was a prognostic of his imperial destiny. After his election as king of the Romans (emperor-elect) in 1346, the pope, confirming the election, expressed the opinion that Charles would be a devout ruler:

> that he is to be so Catholic, so devout, so generous to the Church, is due not only to his ancestry, since it is known that he descends from holy parents who did such things, but also is due to his name, for he is called Charles. Who was more devout and generous to the Church than Charlemagne?[77]

Despite all this, Charles was determined to call his own firstborn son Wenceslas and, after the death of this child, the next son was given the same name.[78] He grew up to succeed his father both as king of Bohemia and king of the Romans, a unique case of father–son succession to the empire in this period. While Charles IV's father had wanted to change his son's name from one with purely Bohemian resonance to one with imperial echoes, Charles himself thought the traditional Bohemian name could be widened to embrace new horizons.

On his accession in 1390, John, oldest son of Robert II of Scotland, 'with the assent of the estates', took the name Robert and ruled as Robert III.[79] In the earliest source no reason is given either for the change of name or for the requirement for parliamentary assent, but in the early sixteenth century the Scottish historian and theologian John Mair advanced a theory about it: 'I suppose they changed the name because they suspected that kings called John would be unlucky, since they saw the French John captured by the English a few days before.'[80] The 'French John' is John II of France, captured in the Battle of Poitiers in 1356, so a little more than 'a few days before'! Mair's view was repeated by later writers but becomes no more convincing through repetition.[81] Perhaps it is obvious that someone would want the fine name of Robert.

Numbering of Monarchs

Confusion between rulers with the same name might also be avoided by giving them numbers, and this was not only retrospective and unofficial, like most nicknames, but could also be contemporary and official. We are all familiar with the practice of giving monarchs a number: Henry VIII, Louis XIV, Napoleon III. This practice is not neutral. To obtain an idea of how sensitive an issue the numbering of monarchs can be, all one has to do is read the accounts of the 'pillar box war' of 1953, when some Scots objected to the royal logo 'EIIR' on post boxes introduced after the accession of Queen Elizabeth, since she was the first, not the second, Elizabeth to rule Scotland. Some of these offensive pillar boxes were blown up, and the decision was soon made to remove the logo and replace it with the royal crown of Scotland, which is what you see on Scottish post boxes today.

So clearly these numbers are not simply a device for torturing school children, but represent a claim, an assertion of a place in a legitimate sequence. The most curious example of this is the case of Pope Benedict XIII, both of them. The first Benedict XIII was elected in 1394 during the Great Schism. His pre-papal name was Peter de Luna and he is often known colloquially as Papa Luna. Despite being deposed not once but twice by councils called to end the Schism, he insistently refused to accept his deposition and died in his home town of Peñiscola in Valencia in

1423. The second Benedict XIII was elected in 1724. At least that was what he eventually became. At first, perhaps being insufficiently informed of the deficiencies of his medieval predecessor, he styled himself Benedict XIV. Once the mistake was pointed out, however, the status of Papa Luna as an anti-pope meant that he did not count (literally), so the eighteenth-century pope went from being Benedict XIV to being Benedict XIII. The fact that his next successor but one was also Benedict, originally and always Benedict XIV, does not ease the confusion. This proliferation of Benedicts is not merely a quirky comedy but underlines the way that numbering implies legitimacy. There can only be one rightful pope at a time, and the early eighteenth-century Benedict, by reverting from the title Benedict XIV to Benedict XIII, was making a statement about the true line and dismissing the claims of the Spanish pretender three hundred years earlier.

Unlike the numbering of crusades, which is modern, retrospective, and primarily for scholarly and pedagogic purposes,[82] numbering of monarchs was a medieval practice. It seems to be the case that it originated with the papacy, but not in its earliest days. Under the Roman empire, there were scarcely any popes with the same name, and this situation did not change substantially until the seventh century.[83] Early popes were thus known simply by their name and title. When names did begin to recur, the later pope was often given the soubriquet 'the Younger (*iunior*)' to distinguish him, as in the case of Leo II and Benedict II in the 680s.[84] But when two popes with the same name reigned close in time, confusion might arise. In the case of the popes whom we call Gregory II (715–31), and his immediate successor Gregory III (731–41), the difficulty is reflected in the cumbrous circumlocutions found in the contemporary Life of St Boniface. There the earlier of these Gregories is referred to as 'Gregory, second after the first, and prior to the most recent one, who is called "the Younger" in the common language of the Romans', and later, when this 'Gregory II' dies, he is succeeded by 'Gregory the Younger', whom the author also calls 'Gregory the Younger the second', and finally there is reference to both 'Gregory the Younger, the second after the first', and his successor, 'Gregory the Younger to the second, the third from the first'.[85] This must all have made a simple sequential numbering system seem an attractive alternative, and, beginning from this very period, such a numbering system is found, in inscriptions, in synodal acts and eventually in documents. It does not occur in the *intitulatio*, the pope's name and title at the beginning of the document, but in the dating clauses toward the end, and later can be found on papal seals and inside the rota, the double circle and cross introduced into papal documents in the eleventh century.[86]

The numbering of rulers then passed to the secular world, being taken up by the western emperors in their documents from the later tenth century.[87] In that case, too, it seems to have been the succession of rulers with the same name (Otto I, Otto II, Otto III) that stimulated the practice. A parallel can be found in the documents of the dukes of Normandy in the early eleventh century, where the occasional use of numbering resulted from the succession of three Richards (942–96, 996–1026, 1026–7) to ducal authority.[88] A full study of the subject over the course of the Middle Ages would need to look at when and where numbering of rulers was employed, and in what contexts: charters, coins, seals, chronicles, etc. Such a study might conceivably be readable. It is clearly a complex story. While popes, as mentioned, employed numeration in official contexts from the tenth century, many secular rulers did not take it up until the fourteenth or fifteenth centuries. The practice of numbering kings in chronicles might precede official use by hundreds of years. Numbering on coins was a late medieval development. In the Iberian peninsula, for example, numbering of monarchs on coins is basically an innovation of the fifteenth century. Although numbering appears occasionally on the coins and seals of the Portuguese monarchs from the time of Alfonso III (1248–79), it is only frequent from the time of Alfonso V (1438–81). In Castile, it begins on the coins of John II (1406–54), and is more common, on both coins and seals, from the time of Henry IV (1454–74). In Navarre, the practice begins under the disputed rule of Charles, prince of Viana, who was titular Charles IV (1441–61), and in Catalonia it begins in the 1460s.[89]

Here the focus will be on a couple of distinctive systems of numbering that highlight the question of where does one start? The first example is from Germany in 1198. The initial step on the road to becoming Holy Roman Emperor was election by the German princes as 'king of the

Romans'. One of the two rival claimants elected king of the Romans in the disputed election of 1198 was Philip, duke of Swabia. His style as king is 'Philip II (*secundus*), king of the Romans'.[90] But who was Philip I? The answer is Philip the Arabian, the Roman emperor who ruled from 244 to 249. The passage of 949 years could not erode the idea that the German duke Philip of Swabia, chosen by a group of German nobles in two assemblies in Thuringia, which was never part of the Roman empire, was the heir of the Caesars. That mild ordinal *secundus* turns out to be a bold assertion of a pedigree, an entitlement, and a long view of history.

Universal chronicles provided lists of Roman emperors, starting with Augustus, continuing with the Byzantine emperors and then switching to the west with Charlemagne. Otto of Freising, great-uncle of Philip II, numbers the Roman emperors consecutively, from Augustus to his own time, and notes that there were alternative systems of numbering, depending on how one treated the obscure imperial claimants of the late ninth and early tenth century, so that Otto I, crowned in 962, could be called either the seventy-seventh or the eighty-fourth emperor.[91] But, whatever local uncertainties there might be in the details of the list, there was a continuous sequence of emperors, and it stretched from Augustus to the writer's own time.

Another feature of the system of numbering in the Holy Roman Empire springs from the fact, just mentioned, that it was customary for the new ruler to be elected and crowned king in Germany before seeking to be crowned emperor by the pope. Only under the Habsburgs did papal coronation cease to be an essential condition for adoption of the imperial title.[92] Since not every German king actually was crowned by the pope, either because of quarrels between king and pope or for purely circumstantial reasons, the numbering of kings and emperors in the Holy Roman Empire was not always identical. For example, the chronicler Burchard of Ursberg, writing around 1230 and describing the accession of Frederick Barbarossa's son Henry as Holy Roman Emperor in 1191 calls him 'Henry, sixth of this name, or, according to the calculation of the Romans, fifth, for they do not number the first Henry, father of Otto I, in the catalogue of emperors'.[93] This is meticulous. 'The first Henry', founder of the Ottonian dynasty, was elected king in 919 but was never crowned emperor, so when his great-grandson Henry became emperor in the early eleventh century, he was Henry I as emperor and Henry II as king. And, of course, even the rulers who were crowned by the pope were kings until their imperial coronation, so their title changed during the course of their reign. When, in 1076, Gregory VII deposed Henry IV, as modern historians call him, he was careful in his terms: 'I deprive king Henry, son of the emperor Henry, of the government of the whole of the kingdom of the Germans and of Italy.'[94] Since Henry IV had not yet been crowned emperor, he was 'King Henry', while his father, Henry III, who had been crowned emperor, was thus 'the emperor Henry'. Henry IV was eventually crowned emperor, not by Gregory VII but by a pope of his own making, an anti-pope in the eyes of the Gregorians. And, of course, the emperor Henry III was also King Henry IV and the emperor Henry IV was also King Henry V, which is the numbering used by modern historians.[95]

Modern historians label these Henries simply by their number as king, but in their own documents they were scrupulous in numbering themselves, so that charters issued by Henry III after his imperial coronation in 1046 are dated in such complex ways as 'in the seventeenth year of the reign as king and the ninth year of the reign as emperor of the lord Henry, the third as king, the second as emperor'.[96] The results can be curious: Conrad, first Hohenstaufen ruler, elected king of the Romans in 1138, appears in his own documents as 'Conrad II, by grace of God king of the Romans (*Conradus dei gratia Romanorum rex secundus*)' but the modern edition in which these are printed is titled *Charters of Conrad III*! The first German ruler called Conrad (911–18) was king of Germany (or the East Franks) and nothing else.

Another instructive curiosity of numbering can be found in later medieval England. The Norman and Plantagenet kings of England from the conquest of 1066 down to the accession of Edward I in 1272 had names that were different from those of any of the pre-conquest rulers of Anglo-Saxon England. They were William, Henry, and so forth, not Æthelred or Egbert. Edward I was the first post-conquest king to have a name also borne by an Anglo-Saxon king, but since the last Edward before him, Edward the Confessor, had ruled more than two centuries earlier there was little danger of confusion in referring to him simply as 'King Edward'. Edward I was succeeded by his son and namesake Edward II. A reference to 'King Edward son of King Edward' would suffice to identify him. It was the fact that he was followed in turn by his son, yet another namesake, that evidently made those responsible for drawing up official records think about this issue. 'King Edward son of King Edward son of King Edward' was not impossible, but rather long-winded. In the Parliament Rolls a different approach was adopted: Edward became 'King Edward, the third after the conquest (*le roi Edward, le tierz apres le conquest*)'.[97] This style enshrined a view of the past: the Norman Conquest of 1066 had been a decisive break, when the clock restarted. The Edwards who had ruled England before then, Edward the Elder, Edward the Martyr and Edward the Confessor, were confined to a misty prehistory. The 'certain men, wise in the ways of the world', who supposedly invented this new style for Edward III, were also subscribing to a view of history.[98]

This need not have happened. A text from the very early thirteenth century describes Edward the Confessor as 'St Edward, king of the English, the third of this name', while there are isolated references, from the year 1307, just after the death of Edward I, as we call him, to 'the lord of glorious memory, Edward the Fourth, king of the English' and to 'the passing of the great king, Edward the Fourth'.[99] These formulations must imply that the speakers counted Edward the Elder, Edward the Martyr and Edward the Confessor as Edward I, II and III, and hence did not envisage the thread of English history as having been snapped in 1066. But, apart from these few exceptions, Edward I did not in fact become Edward IV, and Edward III did not become Edward VI. And 'King Edward, the third after the conquest' was followed in the Rolls of Parliament, with no compelling logic, by 'King Richard, the second after the conquest' and 'King Henry, the fourth after the conquest', and so on. Since there were no Richards or Henries in Anglo-Saxon England, the clarifying suffix was unnecessary but became fixed form until the time of the Tudors. The way that this system of numbering involved a choice, adopting one approach rather than another, becomes clear if one compares it with the system used for the French kings. In that case, the general practice was to number kings called Louis from Louis the Pious, son of Charlemagne, who was deemed by later centuries to be the first king of France called Louis, but, in contrast, there is one set of genealogical diagrams of the Frankish and French kings, in which the numbering restarts with the arrival of the Capetian dynasty, so that the king we call Louis VI is Louis I and so forth. In this isolated example, the five Carolingian rulers called Louis were thus consigned to the same misty past as the Anglo-Saxon Edwards.[100]

The Holy Roman Empire and late medieval England represent two opposite ways that the numbering of monarchs could mark out the place of the dynasty in time. When Philip of Swabia or his advisers adopted the style 'Philippus secundus' they stressed continuity. The political conglomerate of the year 1200 that included Germany and north Italy was, they were saying, the very same thing as the empire of the Caesars. Such incidents as the abdication of the last western emperor in 476 or the coronation of Charlemagne in 800 did not disrupt that seamless history, a history which continued to flow down to the end of the empire in 1806, although it is significant that the emperor Francis II describes the crown that he laid down in that year as the crown of the *Deutsches Reich*: a reality was being recognized just as it ended.[101] The English situation was the opposite. When Edward III was called Edward III, the conquest of 1066 was being recognized as a determining event, a break in history that was embraced rather than hidden. William the Conqueror had made efforts to present himself as the legitimate successor of Edward the Confessor, last king of the house of Wessex, but his late medieval descendants were frank about the conquest. Not everyone was happy with this approach (see below, p. 386).

Even more frank were the kings of Jerusalem, rulers of the crusader state established in the aftermath of the Christian conquest of Jerusalem in 1099. The first king, Baldwin I, as he is known in modern history books, styled himself 'by grace of God king of the Jerusalemites of Latin Christendom (*Latinitatis*)',[102] thus stressing the western and colonial roots of his realm. Later kings used similar forms, numbering themselves by their place in the sequence from Baldwin I. Thus, Baldwin's successor, Baldwin II, was 'Baldwin by grace of God second king of the Latins of Jerusalem', his successor Fulk was 'Fulk by grace of God third king of the Latins of Jerusalem', and so on. The recurrence of the same personal name was not relevant, so the king we label 'Baldwin IV' is, in his own documents, 'the sixth king', the king we call Amalric II is 'the ninth king'. The practice continued down to the time of John of Brienne, 'through the grace of God tenth king of the Latins of Jerusalem'. John ruled from

1210 to 1225.[103] Hence the system of enumeration called attention to the founding of the kingdom by western knights and clerics at a moment in the heroic past. And similar conceptions can be found in England as early as the thirteenth century, for, while the idea of counting the kings from the Norman Conquest may have appeared officially only with Edward III, it had a history prior to that time. Matthew Paris, the famous artist-historian of St Albans, working in the middle years of the thirteenth century, depicted the eight kings since the conquest, labelling William the Conqueror, 'William, the first king of England after its conquest', and continuing with this style down to Matthew's contemporary, Henry III, labelled 'Henry, eighth king'.[104] This is precisely the system employed by the crusader kings of Jerusalem.

Since the practice of numbering monarchs began at different times and in different places, it was often necessary for a decision to be made about what number to start with, that is, how many predecessors with the same name there had already been. Historians today refer to Charles IV, king of France (1322–8), and Charles IV, Holy Roman Emperor (1346–78), rulers of different realms but both with titles implying three Charles before them (the emperor Charles styled himself Charles IV in official documents; Charles IV of France was so-called only in contemporary chronicles).[105] The royal name Charles had not been borne for some time. The Carolingian dynasty is known by that name because the members who made its fortune, Charles Martel and his grandson Charles the Great (Charlemagne), were called Charles (*Carolus* in Latin). But this name, Charles, was only borne by kings descended from Charlemagne for four generations before it went into abeyance for more than three hundred years. After the death of Charles the Simple in 929 there were no kings called Charles until the late thirteenth century. Indeed, one author, writing in England or Normandy at the very beginning of the twelfth century explicitly terms Charles the Simple 'the last of the Charleses'.[106] The name was not completely unknown in the ruling dynasty of France but none who bore it became king of France. Then, in 1322, a King Charles ascended the throne of France. But what number was he to take, bearing in mind that Charlemagne and his immediate successors had ruled an area covering Europe from the Atlantic to the Elbe and from the North Sea to central Italy? Could Charlemagne really be regarded as a previous king of France?

Or, for that matter, a king of Germany? Charlemagne's world is the world admirably summed up by the title of Patrick Geary's book on the period, *Before France and Germany* (which appeared in French translation as *Naissance de la France*). When the Charles who became king of France in 1322 was known as Charles IV, a view was being expressed about Carolingian history. Somehow, from the various rulers called Charles in the ninth and early tenth centuries, ruling disparate and varying territories, three had been picked out as precursors. Since it is quite certain that the area of the later kingdom of France had been ruled by four kings called Charles in the Carolingian period, obviously one of them did not count.[107] It appears that Charles the Fat, ruler of France (the kingdom of the West Franks) 885–7, had, despite his girth, slipped through the net. The emperor Charles IV, who was originally named Wenceslas but adopted at confirmation the name of his patron Charles IV of France (above, p. 300), had to look for imperial predecessors and found three Carolingians from that earlier period. He was the fourth emperor called Charles, after Charlemagne, Charles the Bald and Charles the Fat.[108] So these two approximate contemporaries of the fourteenth century both bore the title 'Charles IV' but to do so drew on some, but not all, of the same predecessors. The choice of the French was confirmed and settled for good by Charles V (1364–80) who did indeed call himself 'Charles V', as is witnessed by writings in his own hand. Subsequent Charleses were numbered accordingly. In the empire, the next Charles was the famous Charles V, opponent of Luther and ruler also of Spain and its New World territories.

A particularly complicated situation arose in the Iberian peninsula after the king of Castile whom we know as Alfonso X or Alfonso the Wise (1252–84) decided to introduce numbering of monarchs in the vernacular chronicles that he sponsored.[109] The problem came partly from the plethora of Alfonsos in Iberian history, and more specifically from two issues: the relationship of the kings of Leon and Castile to those of the Asturian kingdom that had preceded them, and how to deal with the period 1157–1230, when Leon and Castile were separate kingdoms, each for a time ruled by an Alfonso. Alfonso the Wise definitely saw himself in the line of the kings of Asturias and numbered the earliest Asturian Alfonso, who ruled 739–57, Alfonso I. He then continued the numbering through the kings of Asturias and Leon from 739 to 1037, and then beyond, ignoring the violent seizure of the throne by a different dynasty in 1037. The reign of a woman, Urraca, daughter of Alfonso VI, did not break the sequence, but since Alfonso the Wise included Alfonso the Battler, king of Aragon and Urraca's husband for a while, as a legitimate king of Leon and Castile, he numbered him Alfonso VII, a style modern historians reserve for Urraca's son and successor. He also dealt differently with the period of the divided kingdoms 1157–1230. Modern historians number the king of Castile from 1158 to 1214 Alfonso VIII and his cousin, king of Leon 1188–1230, Alfonso IX. This is illogical, since one did not succeed the other and they did not rule the same kingdom. Alfonso the Wise was more logical. Since he had an extra Alfonso in Alfonso the Battler, he numbered Urraca's son and successor Alfonso VIII, and the two cousins ruling the separated kingdoms Alfonso IX of Castile and Alfonso IX of Leon. He thus recognized a real disjuncture in the history of the dynasty, something that modern numbering practices seek to veil. As so often, a number for a monarch is far from a neutral tool of chronology.

CHAPTER 9

Saints, Images, Heraldry, Family Trees

Dynastic Saints

S O, CHOICE OF NAME AND SYSTEMS OF NUMBERING REVEAL something of how dynasties conceived of themselves. There are many other cultural expressions that also manifest a sense of dynasty. Some families had dynastic saints, either in the sense of a saint especially associated with the dynasty as its patron, like St Martin and the Frankish kings, or in the more literal sense of a saint from the dynasty, like the Bohemian dynasty's Wenceslas or the Capetians' St Louis. The rulers of the Macedonian dynasty, which came to power in Byzantium in 867, considered themselves under the patronage of St Elijah. In Byzantium, unlike in the west, many Old Testament figures were treated as saints. They also tried to promote the sanctity of one of their own members, Theophano, wife of Leo VI. Although Leo had discarded her, he 'put as much effort into getting her sanctified as he put into searching for substitutes for her'.[1]

Some royal saints were formally canonized by the pope, in the complex official process that took its final shape in the twelfth century. These included the emperor Henry II (d. 1024, canonized 1146), Edward the Confessor of England (d. 1066, canonized 1161) and Louis IX of France (d. 1270, canonized 1297). For others, attempts were made to attain canonization but unsuccessfully, although the collection of evidence for the subject's miracles shows that there were active cults. Richard II of England sought the canonization of his great-grandfather, Edward II, in the 1380s and 1390s, sending the pope a book of Edward's miracles, which does not survive, while both Henry VII and Henry VIII of England made repeated attempts to have Henry VI (d. 1471) canonized, and there is a surviving collection of 172 of the dead king's miracles.[2]

Prior to the twelfth century, saints were recognized, not by a decision of the pope, but by having an active cult, with miracles, liturgical commemoration and special treatment of the tomb. Saintly kings of the early Middle Ages of this kind were not uncommon, numbering some twenty or so, although some of them are very obscure and can hardly be said to have prominent or continuous cults. What is striking is how many of them met bloody deaths, in battle or through murder or execution: Sigismund of Burgundy (d. 524), Oswald of Northumbria (d. 642), Edmund of East Anglia (d. 869), Wenceslas of Bohemia (d. 935), Edward the Martyr of England (d. 978), Olaf of Norway (d. 1030), Canute II (or IV) of Denmark (d. 1086), and others. It is a pattern sufficiently noticeable to constitute a type, the 'martyr-king' of northern and eastern Europe.[3] In later centuries too, the supposedly violent death of a supposedly blameless royal victim continued to present a prima facie case for sanctity, as in the case of Edward II and Henry VI of England, just mentioned.

Saintly queens present an entirely different profile.[4] They were not canonized because of bloody deaths and many of them were recognized as saints after they had retired to the nunnery, like St Radegund (d. 587), a Thuringian princess and Frankish queen, or lived out a pious widowhood, like Matilda (d. 968), wife of Henry I of Germany. There is an exceptional cluster of saintly royal women in east central Europe in the thirteenth century: Andrew II of Hungary (1205–35) was the father of a female saint, the grandfather of three, the father-in-law of another, and the nephew of a sixth. Many of these women were closely involved with the Franciscan Order, especially its female branch, the 'Poor Clares'. Their royal relatives could enjoy the glory of being related to saints but the saints, or at least those who wrote about them, might glory in their relationship with royalty. The first chapter in the Life of St Cunigunda, one of King Andrew's grand-daughters, is 'Concerning her family and the magnificence of her lineage'.[5]

When he was lobbying for the canonization of Louis of Toulouse (d. 1297), Robert, king of Naples (1309–43), who was Louis' younger brother, could draw on the support of the Franciscans, to which Order Louis had belonged, and part of their argument was that Louis had saints on both sides of his family: his father was a nephew of St Louis, king of France, his mother a member of the Hungarian royal family, which had produced St Stephen of Hungary and other early royal saints, as well as St Elizabeth, the canonized daughter of Andrew II. There is something not entirely logical about this point since, of course, the same was true of King Robert as well. In any case, Louis was canonized in 1317, his head enshrined in Naples by his brother, and his cult was launched. Simone Martini, one of the greatest painters of the time, was commissioned to produce a painting of him, which shows Louis, enthroned and with angels holding a crown above his head, placing a crown on the head of the kneeling Robert. Robert had helped make Louis a saint and Louis in return is vindicating Robert's kingship.[6]

Louis and Robert were members of a junior branch of the Capetians, a dynasty rich in dynastic saints. Their consciousness of this fact was constantly reinforced. Louis, the young son of Charles VI of France, and Dauphin until his death at the age of eighteen in 1415, had a painting at the head of his bed depicting St Louis (Louis IX) and St Louis of Toulouse, who were not only his namesakes but also two saints from his own dynasty, St Louis being a direct ancestor, Louis of Toulouse a great-nephew of St Louis.[7] The heir to the throne of France would thus see his holy relatives every night and morning. When his sister, Mary, entered the convent at the age of four, the religious house chosen for her was the priory of St.-Louis-de-Poissy, dedicated to her ancestor and founded by another, St Louis' grandson, Philip IV.

An especially explicit example of the invocation of dynastic saints can be found in the Preface to the Life of Waltheof of Melrose by Jocelin of Furness, which is dedicated to William the Lion, king of Scots (1165–1214), his son, Alexander (later Alexander II), and William's brother, Earl David. Waltheof was related to the Scots royal family, since after his father's death his mother had married, as a second husband, David I, William the Lion's grandfather. Jocelin says that William and the other dedicatees can take pride in this relationship: 'you are granted the privilege of exulting in the common stock and descent you share'. The saintly heritage of the Scottish royal family goes far beyond this, however. They are descended from St Margaret (d. 1093), who, Jocelin claims, herself descended, on her mother's side, from the Holy Roman Emperors (he gives no details), while her father was 'nephew and legitimate heir of the most holy Edward the

Figure 16 A dynastic saint. This painting of St Louis of Toulouse (d. 1297) by Simone Martini, shows him placing a crown on the head of his younger brother, Robert, king of Sicily (Naples) (1309–43).
Courtesy of Museum Capodimonte.

Confessor, king of England'. The implication of this descent is radical, since it 'would have made you the sceptre-bearers of the kingdom of England by hereditary right, coming to you by the right and direct line of successive generations, if the violent plundering of the Normans had, by God's permission, not impeded it until the time ordained'. The kings of Scots are, therefore, the rightful kings of England.

Nor are Waltheof, Margaret and Edward the Confessor the only saintly relatives:

> Not only did the most powerful in that glorious lineage of the English kings stand out in wealth and glory in the kingdom but also, pleasing God by their holiness and great justice, they were gloriously renowned for many kinds of miracles, both in life and after death. For, from the holy king Æthelwulf, who assessed the whole of England for tithes and dedicated those tithes to God and the Church, nine saintly kings are numbered, the later of whom are recognized as having shone forth in the Christian religion equally or even more admirably. In the tenth, St Edward, the holiness of all his predecessors flowed together, as it were, and thus from him, as from a most lucid fountain, the stream of religious life flowed to St Margaret his great-niece, and from her into her son, King David, your grandfather, and from him into King Malcolm your brother.[8]

Here there is a line of saint-kings, starting with Æthelwulf (d. 858), who introduced tithes, continuing over the generations (it is not clear which nine kings Jocelin had in mind), increasing in holiness, with their blood and their sanctity finally flowing, via St Margaret, into the Scottish royal dynasty, rightful inheritors of the kingdom of England.

Public Images

Another way a sense of dynasty could be expressed was in the public images, painted and carved, that adorned the walls of the palaces and castles of kings, and the gateways of cities.[9] In the 820s, during the reign of Louis the Pious, the hall of his palace at Ingelheim near Mainz was decorated with wall-paintings of images of rulers. Some of these monarchs were from ancient history – Cyrus, Alexander and so on – but the culmination, probably in the apse of the hall, was a series of Christian rulers: Constantine, Theodosius the Great, Charles Martel, Pippin and Charlemagne. This sequence began with the first Christian Roman emperor and concluded with the most recent. Louis the Pious could thus look at a gratifying chain of rulers: good Christian rulers, including his father, grand father and great-grand father. His Merovingian predecessors are invisible.[10]

But those very Merovingians might, in the course of time, become valuable predecessors. Once their reality faded, and the Carolingian usurpation of the throne was no longer a vivid political issue, a line of distant forerunners, some with peculiar and exotic names, could give a depth and colour to French royalty. This could be expressed in stone as well as on parchment. During the reign of Philip IV of France (1285–1314), a great hall was constructed in the royal palace on the Ile de la Cité in Paris. It was enormous, 70 by 27 metres (230 by 89 feet), and was decorated with statues of the kings of France from the legendary Pharamund down to Philip's immediate predecessor. These were placed along the side walls and on the central columns of the room. Under each was an inscription identifying the king and adding brief information. The programme required decisions about who was to be included and what was to be said about them. The portrayal of the Merovingians was very selective, in an attempt to give the impression of a single line of rulers succeeding each other, which was far from the historical reality, and the forcible removal of the dynasty by the Carolingians is described in neutral terms: 'Childeric III, brother of Theuderic, reigned nine years and died without heirs. Pippin, son of Charles Martel, of the lineage of Clothar II, was elected king.'[11] The dynastic revolution of 751 is thus legitimized and normalized as a peaceful transition to a ruler with hereditary claims. Likewise, the next change of dynasty, to the Capetians in 987, is explained by the lack of heirs of the Carolingian Louis V (or Louis IV as the inscription calls him). In this case there is no attempt to assert a genealogical link to earlier rulers, simply a reference to the election of Hugh Capet.[12] What the statues did impress on anyone present in the great hall was the antiquity and continuity of the line of French kings: forty-one in all, surrounding the diners at banquets, ambassadors at receptions, courtiers and petitioners, litigants and lawyers, enclosing them within a small army of ancient French royalty.[13]

It may be that knowledge of the statues in Paris had come to Peter IV, 'the Ceremonious', of Aragon (1336–87) and was one stimulus to his own plan to have sculptures of his ancestors created for the Royal Palace of Barcelona, as is detailed in a document he issued in 1342. In this he commands payment to be made to 'our faithful Master Aloy' for bringing alabaster to the palace and from it

> to make and form nineteen images prepared with all the expedient and necessary work and as beautiful as he can and knows how to make them, of which eight will represent images of the eight kings who succeeded one another as kings of Aragon and counts of Barcelona, down to our own times, and the others the images of those eleven who were counts of Barcelona but did not have the royal title.[14]

Peter had a very clear idea of the past of his dynasty, who were counts of Barcelona for many generations before they acquired the royal title through marriage to the queen and heir of Aragon in the twelfth century. As he sat in his palace in Barcelona, he wanted to be able to look at his male-line ancestors, eight kings and eleven counts, going back to the ninth century.

Someone who was definitely familiar with the forty-one dynastic statues in the palace of the French kings was Charles IV, king of Bohemia and Holy Roman Emperor (1346–78), who spent his childhood from the age of seven at the French court. At that time the statues would be new. Perhaps they were in Charles' mind when he commissioned, for his grand castle of Karlštejn (Karlstein), fourteen miles south-west of Prague, a cycle of wall paintings showing his ancestors.[15] These were painted around the years 1356–7 and, although they do not survive, copies were made in a book in the later sixteenth century, so what they depicted can be known.[16]

Charles' genealogical vistas were wide: the series starts with Noah and his biblically reported descendants down to Nimrod, then moves to Belus, legendary first king of Assyria, who is identified as the son of Nimrod, and follows his descendants, including Saturn and Jupiter, down to Priam, king of Troy. Here we are on solid ground, and the line of Priam's descendants, down to the early Frankish kings, is straightforward. The sequence of historically attested Merovingians runs from Clovis to Clothar II (d. 629), but at this point the male line ceases to be followed, as the Carolingians need to be introduced. This was done by way of a fictitious daughter of Clothar, called Blithildis, who married the equally fictitious ancestor of the Carolingians; this part of the genealogy had been concocted as early as the reign of Charlemagne himself.[17] Their descendants include Arnulf, bishop of Metz, and his son Ansegisel, both historical characters (the painting in Karlštejn shows Arnulf dressed as a bishop but the accompanying text is very clear that Arnulf fathered Ansegisel before he became a cleric). Ansegisel married Begga, daughter of the mayor of the palace, Pippin (d. 640). Begga is described as 'duchess of Lotharingia and Brabant (*ducissa Lothoringiae et Brabanciae*)', which, since Lotharingia did not exist at this time, is somewhat anachronistic, but points forward to the way the blood line would be traced. The line continues through the Carolingian descendants of Ansegisel and Begga, through Charlemagne and Charles the Bald, with some streamlining, down to a King Louis, who was the father of Charles, duke of Lotharingia and Brabant. This must be Louis IV (936–54), father of King Lothar (954–86) and Charles of Lorraine, who was excluded from the succession by the Capetians in 987. Charles' daughter, Countess Gerberga, married Lambert, count of Louvain, and their descendants attained the title of dukes of Lotharingia (in reality this time) and of Brabant. After many generations, the daughter of John I, duke of Brabant, married Henry of Luxemburg, who became the emperor Henry VII and was the grandfather of Charles IV.

These wall paintings were in the grand hall of Charles' palace at Karlštejn and hence visible to visitors, including foreign embassies. They presented a grand panorama, with biblical, Trojan, Merovingian and Carolingian ancestors. No attempt was made to disguise descent through the female line, rather the reverse, since these moments are marked by images of women, sometimes face-to-face with husbands, as is also the case with the last image, Charles IV and his first wife, Blanche of Valois, enthroned, their faces turning towards each other. The forty-seven generations from Noah, the common ancestor of all humanity, to Charles IV, Roman emperor, builder of Karlštejn, patron of these paintings, are given concrete visible form.[18]

Figure 17 Wall paintings from Karlštejn Castle near Prague, as copied in a sixteenth-century manuscript, showing the Holy Roman Emperor Charles IV (1346–78) and his ancestors.
Vienna, Österreichische Nationalbibliothek, MS 8330, p. 126.

Figure 18 Charles' wife Blanche (d. 1348), from the same source.
Vienna, Österreichische Nationalbibliothek, MS 8330, page 127.

An ambitious counterpart to these painted images or statues was attempted by some Byzantine rulers on a much more restricted physical space, their coins. The likenesses on coins were the most common images in medieval society and rulers were well aware of the messages they might carry. Beginning with Constantine V, some emperors had images of their predecessors and ancestors on their money, as well as their own images. A particularly crowded example is the coinage of Constantine VI and Irene in the years 780–92, which shows, on the reverse, Constantine's father, grandfather and great-grandfather, Leo III (d. 741), Constantine V (d. 775) and Leo IV (d. 780), thus depicting every ruler of what modern scholarship calls the Isaurian dynasty.[19] Earlier coins of this dynasty had also shown emperors of several generations.[20] Byzantine coins showing co-emperors were not uncommon, but these showing dead ancestors were unusual and represented a strong sense of lineage. They have indeed been called 'a representation of the notion of dynasty in all its verticality'.[21] Such images on coins are not common, simply for practical reasons of space, but they are parallel to the paintings on the palace walls in Ingelheim and Karlštejn or the life-size statues in Paris and Barcelona: an instant visual expression of a sense of dynasty.

Heraldry

If surnames were very rarely a form of group identification in the royal and imperial dynasties of the Middle Ages, there was, in this period when pictures were as powerful as words, one visual language that developed as a potent expression of dynasty: heraldry. This new way of displaying family identity was vivid, visual and public. From the twelfth century, ruling families adopted hereditary symbols, which they bore on their shields and banners and which could decorate and identify their books or their tombs. These symbols were mainly either abstract geometrical designs, such as chevrons, crosses and diagonal bands, or stylized animals, notably the lion. Eventually complex rules developed about the transmission of heraldic arms, so that a trained observer could look at one of the intricate coats-of-arms of the late medieval or Early Modern period and deduce the bearer's family connections. It has been nicely

Figure 19 A dynasty depicted in miniature. Coins of the Byzantine rulers Constantine VI and Irene from 780–92 showing Constantine's father, grandfather and great-grandfather. © Dumbarton Oaks, Byzantine Collection, Washington, DC.

pointed out that subjects of a late medieval king 'could read a coat more easily than they could read a letter'.[22] Rulers were early enthusiasts for heraldic symbols and by the year 1200 the kings of England had their three lions and the kings of France their fleurs-de-lys. Sometimes the images they adopted had a direct reference to the realm, as in the case of the kings of Leon and Castile who bore a shield with images of a lion and a castle quartered.

Heraldry was well suited to express both general family affiliation and individual identities. For example, the Angevin dynasty that ruled the king-dom of Sicily from 1266 descended from Charles of Anjou, younger brother of St Louis of France. Charles had, from 1246, borne as his arms the gold fleurs-de-lys on a blue shield of the royal house of France, differentiated by a red label, a label being a narrow horizontal band at the top of the shield with pendants, five in this case.[23] Such a differentiating feature is known in the language of heraldry as a 'difference'. It would be clear to any heraldically literate observer that Charles was a member of a junior branch of the French royal family. His descendants and successors as kings of Sicily, Charles II and Robert, bore the same coat-of-arms. King Robert's younger brothers, Philip of Taranto and John of Durazzo, bore their own differentiated versions of these arms, the former with a silver bend (a diagonal band from the viewer's top left to bottom right, superimposed on the other features of the shield), the latter with a border of alternating silver and red squares (but without the label).[24] The grammar of heraldry could express a sense of dynasty very well.

It also carried political messages, sometimes controversial ones. In 1325 Henry, earl of Leicester, was charged with changing his own arms (the royal lions plus a blue bend) to those of his executed brother, Thomas of Lancaster (the royal lions with a blue label bearing the fleurs-de-lys of France). Henry replied that these were his father's arms and his by hereditary right.[25] No legal proceedings in fact took place, but the incident shows, in the words of one heraldic expert, 'the political importance that could be attached to the adoption of a particular coat'.[26] Thomas of Lancaster had been an arch-enemy of the king, Edward II, and a gesture that might suggest identification with him or sympathy for him was bound to arouse suspicions. Henry of Leicester's point was in fact a reasonable one since his father had borne those arms, although the king's suspicions were also reasonable: Henry played an important part in the deposition of Edward II and was rewarded with his dead brother's earldom of Lancaster.

More straightforward is the case of Peter, duke of Coimbra, uncle and former regent of Alfonso V of Portugal, who took up arms against the king in 1449, and carried into battle a banner with the royal arms without any difference. It was a clear statement that he was the man who would be king.[27] Eleven years later, when Richard, duke of York, decided to make his bid for the English Crown, he took exactly the same decisive step. Previously he had borne the royal arms of England, the three lions quartered with the lilies of France, differentiated. He now had banners made for his trumpeters without the differentiation: 'he gave them banners with the whole arms of England without any difference'.[28]

The fact that, by the time of Richard of York, the royal arms of England included the lilies of France is explained by another, earlier deployment of heraldry to make a claim. When, in January 1340, Edward III of England was proclaimed king of France, basing his claim on descent through his mother, Isabella, daughter of Philip the Fair, he also adopted the French arms, quartering the lilies with the lions or leopards of England. This was a public and visual means of pointing out his descent and his claims, and the lilies were not finally removed from the English royal arms until 1801, with the eventual abandonment of the claim. In the world of heraldry, the Hundred Years War was still being fought in the age of Napoleon. A contemporary chronicler tells a curious story about the reaction of the French king, Philip VI, to this move on Edward's part. He did not object, he said, to his cousin's quartering the arms of France and England, but he thought that the lilies of France should be in the first quarter, not the leopards of England, since that arrangement 'gives greater honour to the tiny island of England than to the great kingdom of France'.[29] In fact, Edward did not put the English arms in the first quarter but the French lilies, which is where they remained until the reordering of the royal arms necessitated by the Act of Union with Scotland in 1707.

The ruling classes took their coats-of-arms to the grave with them. They could exhibit their own arms, and also those of important relatives, on their tombs. An extreme example is the tomb of Philippa of Hainault, wife of Edward III of England, who died in 1369, which displays thirty-two coats-of-arms, drawn from Philippa's wide extended kin, not only those as close as father and mother, husband and children, but also brothers-in-law and sisters-in-law, a daughter-in-law, cousins, and even, it seems, a fiancé of a deceased daughter.[30] Philippa's place in the web of international royal and lordly families is here advertised in the special language of the upper class. And that function of heraldry, as a language, is revealed sharply by the fact that a tomb in the Franciscan church at Assisi has been identified from its heraldry alone, even though it bears no inscription, as that prepared for John of Brienne (d. 1237), titular king of Jerusalem and Latin emperor of Constantinople.[31]

The coat-of-arms of Margaret of Denmark, queen of James III of Scotland (1460–88), as shown on the Trinity Altarpiece by the Flemish master Hugo van der Goes, illustrates the way that layers of dynastic identity had been built up and enshrined in heraldry by the later Middle Ages. Margaret's arms impale those of her husband, i.e. they place them on the (viewer's) left side; these are the traditional arms of Scotland, a red lion rampant, with blue tongue and claws, on a gold background, surrounded by a flowery red border.[32] On the other side are Margaret's arms, a complex pattern of four quarterings separated by a cross, with a small quartered shield superimposed upon it, and an even smaller shield superimposed on that. She was the daughter of Christian I of Denmark and, at this time, he ruled, or claimed the right to rule, all three of the Scandinavian kingdoms (they had a common ruler for many periods in the years 1388–1523). The four quarters show the arms of the kingdoms of Sweden (three gold crowns on a blue field), Denmark (three crowned blue lions guardant, on a gold field scattered with red hearts), Norway (a gold lion rampant with an axe on a red field), as well as the golden wyvern on a blue field representing lordship over the Wends, that is, Baltic Slavs.[33] The superimposed smaller shield quarters the arms presumed to be those of Holstein (two crossed gold batons intertwined in a twisted wreath on a red field) in the first and fourth quarters with those of Schleswig (two blue lions guardant on a gold field) in the second and third. King Christian was also duke of Schleswig and count, later duke, of Holstein, through inheritance from his mother's family.[34] Finally, the small shield superimposed on the superimposed shield bears the arms of Oldenburg (two red bars on a gold field).[35] Christian had been count of Oldenburg before being elected to the vacant throne of Denmark. This small piece of painting thus condenses generations of dynastic information.[36]

This new way of expressing a sense of dynasty was projected into the past, for heraldry became such an established part of upper-class life that it was assumed that it had always been so, and coats-of-arms were devised for rulers of the distant, and pre-heraldic past, and even for Christ and the Trinity.[37] Edward the Confessor got his coat-of-arms, which Richard II of England, an ardent devotee, impaled with his own arms, as shown on the Wilton Diptych.[38] Charlemagne too acquired a coat-of-arms. But what arms was he to take? Did he belong to France or Germany? The heralds of the later Middle Ages were even-handed, in depicting

325

Charlemagne with an, entirely imaginary, coat-of-arms in which the French fleurs-de-lys were impaled with the imperial eagle of Germany.[39]

Family Trees

There are many manifestations of dynastic consciousness, but there is one particular form that is so familiar to us that we might forget to think about it, that is, the diagrammatic family tree.[40] This is a standard way of conveying information about family relationships and has certain conventions, which vary slightly from country to country, but are, in general, clear: the passage of time proceeds from the top of the page downwards, so successive generations are below each other; the link between siblings is a horizontal line, and siblings are placed along it in birth order from left to right, unless there is a good reason for not doing so; a vertical line links parents to their children; illegitimate descent may be signalled by a broken rather than a solid line; marriage is indicated by some symbol of bond or copula, often an 'equals' sign, although the German system prefers the sideways eight or infinity sign, perhaps over optimistically.

The language of family relationship is strongly characterized both by the imagery of plants growing and thriving – root, seed, stock and so on – and by the language of generation – offspring, progeny, descendants. The graphic family tree combines these two things very well, the vegetable imagery and the terminology of descent, since it is a tree and each level descends from the level before. The tree has indeed often been used, and is still often used, as the paradigm for a diagram. It should be mentioned, however, that most graphic family trees are inverted trees, in the sense that the branches grow downwards. The opposite is obviously also possible, starting the tree at the bottom and having it spread upwards, as is the case with most medieval depictions of the Tree of Jesse, which showed Christ's descent (or ascent!) from Jesse, father of King David, and there are examples of medieval draughtsmen preferring this approach in secular trees too. For instance, there is a widely copied family tree of the Carolingian dynasty which occurs almost invariably in the standard top-down form, but one example, from the Cistercian monastery of Heilsbronn in Franconia, has inverted it, so the name of Arnulf of Metz, the ancestor of the dynasty, is in a medallion at the bottom of the page, and the last Carolingians are at the top of the page.[41] The result is it looks much more like a tree! British Library manuscript Harley 7353, a fifteenth-century roll vindicating the right of Edward IV of England during the Wars of the Roses, has a family tree just like a Tree of Jesse, depicting a reclining Peter I of Castile and Henry III of England at the bottom, with curling arboreal lines emerging from the loins, the lines dotted with their numerous descendants emerging from what look like acorn cups.

Prior to graphic family trees of this type, there had been genealogies in prose from ancient times. Medieval Europe was perfectly familiar with these: the Old Testament is full of them, some running on for many verses, while the very first words of the New Testament are 'The Book of the Generation of Jesus Christ (*Liber generationis Iesu Christi*)'. And medieval societies produced genealogies of their own dynasties.[42] A short genealogy of Charlemagne, which was produced during his lifetime, has been called 'the first genealogy of a ruler in the Christian Middle Ages',[43] but this seems to ignore the vast amount of genealogical material from medieval Ireland. Although these Irish genealogies survive only in manuscripts from the twelfth century and later, there is scholarly agreement that the texts must have originated much earlier, and they are very extensive; the pre-twelfth-century material contains about 20,000 names.[44] It is clear that they had a practical function, including use in disputes, since an Irish legal treatise of possibly eleventh-century date lists some of the qualities of a bad judge: 'to be ignorant, without inspecting historical records or synchron-ism or genealogies of the family of father and grandfather or family trees of kings and overkings and bishops and masters and abbots'.[45] The implica-tion is that a good judge will inspect genealogies, including royal genealogies.

But a prose genealogy and a graphic family tree are different ways of presenting information. Only the latter can show everything at a glance. The problems of presenting multiple lines of descent in a prose geneal-ogy are apparent even in a text as clear as the so-called 'Genealogies of Foigny'.[46] This dates to the 1160s and gives the descent of several aristo-cratic families of northern France from the ninth century to its own time. Because it is in continuous prose, it has to follow one line of descent, then go back to take up the other lines: 'King Hugh the Pious was the father of

King Robert and a daughter named Hadwig, countess of Hainault'; the text then follows the descendants of King Robert before going back to Robert's sister: 'Hadwig, countess of Hainault, King Robert's sister, gave birth to Beatrice'; the text then talks about Beatrice's family before going back to King Robert's daughter Adela and her male descendants; then it turns to the daughters: 'the first of the daughters of this Adela ... the second daughter of this first Adela' (there was another in the family). Other markers follow: 'now let us return to Hugh the Great' (son of Henry I of France), 'now to the account of those we left out, that is, the (other) children of Hadwig, countess of Hainault'.[47] The author does his best, but this is hard work. Turning from this text to the article of 1978 by Bernard Guenée in which this information is presented in conventional graphic form, as a family tree in the modern sense, we can suddenly see the wood because of the tree. The invention of this kind of diagram marked the birth of a great tool of clarification.

The idea of presenting genealogical information in graphic form evolved only slowly. Nor was the tree the only such form available, and there are genealogies that use other pictorial devices, for example, the human body, with the succession of figures forming the torso but a human head, arms and feet,[48] or a building. One elaborate Carolingian geneal-ogy, from the twelfth century, consists of a turreted building with windows from which the members of the family look out, the main line staring out from windows with open shutters in the central line of the building, the relatives from the collateral branches visible through windows without shutters to the right and the left of them.[49] It was the tree, loosely defined, however, that became the common way of representing a dynasty as extended through time.

While there were precedents, in the form of diagrams to illustrate kinship terms and pictorial genealogies of Christ, especially in manuscripts of Beatus of Liébana,[50] the first family trees representing contemporary dynasties seem to have been drawn for various particular purposes in the tenth and eleventh centuries. Perhaps the very earliest is a late-tenth-century diagram from the important monastery of Saint-Gallen, showing a few generations of the Carolingian dynasty, with brief notes about them and their dealings with the monastery.[51] Religious houses were always interested in their founders and benefactors.

Figure 20 An experiment in family tree design. A twelfth-century depiction of the Carolingian dynasty in the form of a turreted building with family members in the windows. Berlin, Staatsbibliothek, MS lat. fol. 295, fol. 80v.

Another motive for drawing up family trees was to check how close the family relationship was between a prospective bride and groom. In this period, the Church underlined and insisted upon a very strict rule about choice of marriage partner (see above, pp. 43–5): you could not marry your first cousin, second cousin, third cousin, fourth cousin, fifth cousin or sixth cousin, an astonishingly wide definition of prohibited degrees. In the end, in 1215, the Church itself had to relax these strict rules, but prior to that date conscientious lay people needed to observe them. The first difficulty was knowing who your sixth cousins were, and one result of the Church's strict rules was to stimulate genealogical investigation. In the case of possible consanguinity, relatives were encouraged to produce pedigrees. Papal advice in such cases was that 'each person should take pains to know his or her genealogy, both by witnesses and charters and by the relation of their elders'.[52] The great canonist Ivo of Chartres, when protesting against the planned marriage of one of the illegitimate daughters of Henry I of England with a nobleman in his own diocese of Chartres, explained to the king, 'I have in my hands a written genealogy which noblemen of the same lineage caused to be written', and then gives the king the details that, in Ivo's opinion, made this projected union incestuous.[53] When the emperor Frederick Barbarossa sought the annulment of his marriage to Adela of Vohburg in 1153, a genealogy was drawn up to show how they were related. It demonstrated that Adela's great-great-great-grandmother was the sister of Frederick's great-great-grandfather, and hence their marriage was within the prohibited degrees.[54]

The move from written genealogies of this type to the graphic representation of family trees is a natural one in such a world and, from the late tenth century, references to them and actual surviving diagrams increase in number. Those opposed to the marriage of the emperor Henry III and Agnes of Poitou in 1043 brought Henry a *figura*, a diagram, with the names of his ancestors to make their point.[55] This original chart of 1043 does not survive but it formed the basis of later graphic and pictorial family trees of German rulers used in chronicles of the twelfth and thirteenth centuries, and hence far removed from its original purpose.[56] The detailed family trees of the north French dukes and counts that were drawn up in the abbey of St.-Aubin in Angers in the

1070s may well have been designed to show that a proposed marriage would be uncanonical.[57]

A different purpose seems to have inspired another early graphic family tree, which has survived. It shows the descent of the emperor Henry II (1002–24) and his wife Cunigunda. Comprising a single sheet, 20.3 by 17 cm (8 by 6.7 inches), and now detached from the book in which it was first written, this chart is likely to have been produced in Bamberg around the year 1015.[58] The names, and occasionally the images, of individuals are placed within circles, and linked by lines showing descent. The topmost figure is St Arnulf, the seventh-century bishop of Metz who was the forefather of the Carolingian dynasty, and the chart then traces a simple father–son line from him to Louis the Pious, Charlemagne's son and successor. Then it branches into the three offshoots represented by the three sons of Louis the Pious and their descendants, ruling the kingdom of the West Franks, the kingdom of the East Franks and the Middle Kingdom with Italy, as any Carolingian genealogy in a modern textbook would do. For the East Frankish kingdom, it is entirely accurate, ending with Louis (the Child), whose circle is annotated 'after whom no one of this family possessed the royal throne any more',[59] while the West Frankish and Middle Kingdom branches contain more inaccuracies. One purpose of the chart is made clear by the way it traces the Carolingian descent of the empress Cunigunda, showing only the essential links between her and the West Frankish king Louis, son of Charles the Bald, not any collaterals or even husbands: the line goes from Louis to his daughter Ermintrude to her daughter Cunigunda to her son Count Siegfried to his daughter Cunigunda the empress. This is all apparently entirely accurate. The family tree that shows the descent of her husband, Emperor Henry II, is given far less space, squeezed into the lower right-hand corner of the page and limited to just a few generations. One message of this figure is the simple one: Cunigunda has Carolingian blood. Whether it was based on earlier versions, perhaps with a different purpose, is a question that has been debated, but in its existing form it was obviously produced by those who revered the Carolingians and wished to enhance Cunigunda's prestige and standing by stressing her link with them.

Graphic family trees were thus created for more than one reason. Alongside the monastic houses preserving the memory of their patrons, and the conscientious or the meddlesome checking on the legitimacy of a proposed marriage, there was also the powerful force of dynastic pride. Family trees were indeed a natural product of the dynastic world, as is indicated by their independent invention under the Muslim dynasties of Asia in the thirteenth century.[60] The earliest of these are found in the *Shajara-yi ansāb* ('Tree of Genealogies') of Fakhr-i Mudabbir, who was active in the courts of the Islamic sultans in north India in the early part of the century. This contains 139 genealogical trees, as well as some reflections by the author on their form. He accepts both descending and ascending 'trees'. The technique was developed by Rashīd al-Dīn, vizier of the Ilkhan rulers of Persia (d. 1318), whose historical works contain numerous family trees, with the males in small squares and the females in circles. The form then proliferated in the Islamic world during the later Middle Ages and Early Modern times. Clearly, any society where rule is based on the claims of family would find the graphic genealogy an attractive tool.

The first graphic family trees in the west were written into books. If the line of descent was long, then it would have to continue from one page to the next, and could then go on indefinitely, but at the expense of no longer being graspable at a glance. This limitation was clearly felt by the designer or draughtsman of the family trees found in the so-called 'Golden Book of Prüm'.[61] These genealogical charts of the Carolingians and Ottonians were drawn up in that Rhineland abbey in the second half of the eleventh century, but, instead of being copied into the book, they were drawn on a large sheet of parchment twice the height of the book and two folios wide and then bound into it. The result is an insert that can be unfolded to give a much wider field for the two trees. The same urge for greater pictorial or graphic space lay behind the development of the genealogical roll in the thirteenth century. Among the earliest genealogies in the roll format were copies of Peter of Poitiers' *Compendium of History in the Form of a Genealogy of Christ* (*Compendium historiae in genealogia Christi*). This had been devised as a teaching tool in the Schools of Paris, where Peter was chancellor. The chronicler who recorded his death in 1205 thought it worth reporting that he 'considered the need of poor clerks and devised the plan of having trees of the histories of the Old Testament painted on parchment sheets'.[62] These were presumably put up in teaching rooms and meant the poor clerks could follow the lectures without needing to have books. The *Compendium*, which covers the New Testament as well as the Old, survives in many copies, some in book form, some in rolls. These rolls might be 3.5 metres or more in length (well over 11 feet) and contained tables, pictures and text, but their overarching unity was provided by the genealogical tree.[63] Once such a format had been devised, it could be adapted for secular and contemporary purposes.

Dozens of these secular genealogical rolls were produced in England, showing the succession of the kings from Anglo-Saxon times.[64] They were perhaps particularly popular there since English royal records, unusually, tended to be in the form of rolls rather than books.[65] They often have well over a hundred pictures of kings, starting usually with Egbert (802–39) and going down to the reigning monarch at the time of composition.[66] An example that has been published is the so-called Chaworth Roll.[67] This is 6.5 metres (21 feet) long and 24.5 cm (9.6 inches) wide, starts with Egbert and, when originally produced in the 1320s, came down to Edward II, but was later extended to Henry IV. The kings and their children are depicted inside medallions which are linked with thick green lines; alongside and around the medallions there is text in Anglo-Norman, the language of the upper class in England at this time, explaining briefly who these figures were and what they did, with the emphasis on family ties: 'This Thomas was earl of Lancaster and of Leicester and seneschal of England. And also he was earl of Derby and, through the countess Alice, his wife, he was earl of Lincoln and of Salisbury.'[68] The only female figures on the roll are the daughters of kings, with one exception, Matilda, wife of Henry I, who brought the blood of the old Anglo-Saxon royal dynasty back into the ruling family. This is stressed in the text, but in general there is little attempt to disguise breaks in dynastic continuity. The conquests by the Danish and Norman kings are marked by a hiatus in the scheme of connecting lines. Yet the overall visual effect provided by the central line, with its uniform iconography and colour, is of continuity. The succession of kings gives unity to English history; the inclusion in the roll of the children of those kings, most of whom did not succeed to the throne, makes it also a family history.

The very complex relationship between writing the history of a kingdom and writing the history of its ruling dynasties is brought out by looking at various attempts to combine the graphic family tree with historical text that were made in thirteenth- and fourteenth-century France. Giles of Paris, who wrote a long poem about Charlemagne, the *Karolinus*, which he presented to Prince Louis of France (later Louis VIII) in 1200, subsequently added some supplementary material to a copy of the text, and this includes a five-page genealogical diagram of the kings of France, with reasonably extensive narrative accounts fitted around it.[69] This works quite well for the early kings, since there is only one line of descent from the legendary Pharamund to Clovis, so there is a wide, equal margin on either side of the diagram to provide room for the text, but things become complex when Giles has to show several contemporary Merovingian kings of the same generation, especially as he adds the ancestors of the Carolingians also. As a consequence, text becomes cramped and has to be squeezed in where there is room. Giles was aware that the reader might appreciate some guidance through this complex material, so he devised a system of colour coding:

> In order to have greater clarity about the people described in the following pages, I state alongside in this place that I put the kings of France, whom I am specially writing about, in red letters, so that they can be perceived to be set off from the others. The queens, their wives, through lines of red ink within. We pick out other kings, or those who descended from royal stock but were not kings, through simple ink lines. Moreover, we distinguish those who were both kings and emperors, as being more worthy, through a double colour, reddish gold and vermilion. Those who were only emperors and not kings of France, we mark out with reddish gold letters. We mark out the good kings of France through lines of vermilion coloured reddish gold, but do this separately.[70]

This was a great age of innovation for indexes, tables, keys, alphabetization and other finding devices, and Giles' scheme is a good example of this search for graphic order.[71]

A slightly different approach to this problem of combining text and diagram was taken by William de Nangis, the archivist of the abbey of Saint-Denis during the second half of the thirteenth century. He composed, among other works, a short history of the kings of France 'in the form of a kind of tree'.[72] This 'tree' consists of a crudely drawn double line, running down the margin of his text, with the names of the kings, and sometimes some of their children, in circles on it. This gives him plenty of space for text in the body of the page, but, like Giles of Paris, William de Nangis had the problem of the Merovingian kings who ruled simultaneously. Since he gives each of them his own column, the page is sometimes divided into as many as five narrow columns, which makes reading the text difficult, since there may be only one or two words per line in each column (e.g. 'Hic instinctu ma/tris sue interfecit/ Sigimondum regem/Burgundionum/filium Gundebaldi/regis cum uxore/et liberis').[73]

One of the most successful graphic representations of dynastic history was that produced by Bernard Gui in the early fourteenth century. Bernard Gui, the southern French Dominican who died in 1331, is now best known as an inquisitor. His inquisitors' handbook offers a fascinating, if sometimes chilling, insight into the methods and mentalities of those professionals charged with hunting down and destroying heresy, and he made a memorable fictional appearance in this role in Umberto Eco's novel *The Name of the Rose* and also in the subsequent film. But he wrote much else besides the handbook, including large amounts of historical writing. In works such as *The Kings of the French* (*Reges Francorum*) or *The Tree of the Lineage of the Kings of the French* (*Arbor genealogiae regum Francorum*) he sets out a long-term picture of French dynastic history.[74] The two works are closely related, although they look very different on the page, since the latter is organized around a pictorial device, the tree, which extends from top to bottom at the centre of each page. This tree is not quite the same as the modern genealogical diagram called a 'family tree' since, although it shows biological descent, it does so only for those kings 'descending in the right line of the tree (*in recta linea arboris descendendo*)' or 'in the right line of the tree of royal lineage (*in recta linea arboris genealogie regalis*)'. *Recta* can mean 'straight', 'direct', 'correct', 'just' and 'lawful'. Other figures are shown by lines and pictures linked to those on the main trunk of the tree but not on it. This means that Gui has to pick out a 'main line' of descent, which is in almost every case that of father–son transmission. These kings of 'the right line' are numbered successively from the legendary Pharamund, the first king, down to Philip of Valois, the thirty-eighth king, who was reigning at the time Gui completed his final version of these works.

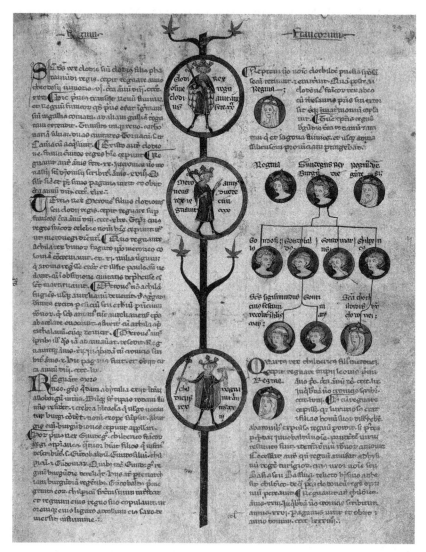

Figure 21 Bernard Gui's *The Tree of the Lineage of the Kings of the French*, an ambitious attempt to show biological descent and royal succession over more than thirty generations. Cambridge, Corpus Christi College, MS 45 34r.

This concept of a 'right line (*recta linea*)' means that Bernard Gui's tree is only partly a family tree of the modern kind, since it is concerned with succession as much as with descent.[75] Like the royal genealogical rolls of late medieval England, it is a 'combination of a royal genealogy and a regnal list'.[76] And the concept of the 'right line' as used by French chroniclers certainly implied direct biological descent, but had overtones of legitimacy too. A chronicler writing at Tours in the 1220s commented on Hugh Capet's usurpation of 987 that, although Hugh was descended from Charlemagne, 'this Hugh did not stem from the lineage of Charlemagne and the kings of France in the right line of descent' and described Hugh's rival, the last Carolingian claimant, as 'duke Charles, brother of Lothar, king of the French, who had descended from the lineage of kings in the right line'.[77] Here *recta linea* seems to be defined as unbroken male descent. The next major dynastic dislocation in France after that of 987 occurred in 1328, when Philip of Valois, a cousin of the previous king, succeeded. A contemporary chronicler wrote: 'Whence it seems clear that the right line of the kings of France failed and was transferred to the collateral line in him.'[78] Philip was descended from Hugh Capet in an unbroken male line, so here the phrase *recta linea* seems to mean direct descent from the previous king. The contemporary French translation of this passage has 'la droite ligne' and 'ligne transversale'.[79]

Bernard Gui gives marginal comments alongside the pictures of kings. He says, for example, that it was Pharamund, the first king, who decreed that the Franks should have long hair, to distinguish them from the natives of Gaul, who had short hair as a sign of their servitude to the Romans, and it was only in the time of Peter Lombard, bishop of Paris in the twelfth century, that this practice was given up.[80] Gui also explains that Hugh Capet was called Hugh Capet 'because when he was a boy he used to snatch off other boys' caps for a lark'.[81] But these snippets are not Gui's main purpose, which is to produce a right line (*recta linea*) embracing history from Pharamund to his own day. In the case of the Capetian kings this does not lead to many oddities, although Gui omits Hugh Capet, the first Capetian king, from both the tree and the numbered sequence since he regards him as a usurper, and he has no choice but to acknowledge the transmission of the crown to brothers in 1317 and 1322 and to a cousin in 1328, since he would otherwise have no 'right line' to trace. Most Capetians, however, followed their father on the throne. The situation regarding the two earlier lineages, the Merovingian and Carolingian, is more complicated. Gui knew that the Frankish realm was often divided between brothers and cousins in the Merovingian period, so that several kings would be ruling at the same time. He mentions these rival concurrent rulers, but still adheres to the strict concept of a 'right line', which he creates by tracing a succession of kings who were each descended from a predecessor. In this way, he carves out fourteen kings, from the legendary Pharamund to Theuderic IV, who died in 737, who represent a continuous male line of descent over fourteen generations. He has to ignore a lot to get this result, including the actual last Merovingian, the cousin of Theuderic IV, Childeric III, who was deposed in 751, but he gets his 'right line'. Those who designed the statues of the French kings in the royal palace in Paris (see above, p. 316), which were completed at precisely the time that Gui produced the first version of the *Tree of the Lineage of the Kings of the French*, also had to undertake a drastic pruning of the Merovingians to obtain a single line of kings, although they retained twenty-one rather than Gui's fourteen.

For the Carolingians, the results are not quite so arbitrary, but they still have peculiarities. The line from Pippin, first Carolingian king, down to his great-great-grandson, Louis the Stammerer, which covers the years 751 to 879, and that of the last three Carolingian rulers of France, from 936 to 987, are both cases of father–son descent. The complexity arises in the period between these two lines, when there were not only several non-Carolingian kings, whom Gui discusses but does not include in the 'right line', but also transmission of power between brothers within the Carolingian dynasty. Gui himself expresses confusion at this point. He wonders why Carloman, son of Louis the Stammerer, should be included in the 'right line' when he left no sons to succeed him, and the throne eventually came to his younger half-brother, Charles the Simple:

> I do not know, nor have I been able to find out, the cause for this Carloman being depicted in the right line of the tree, since the succession of the royal stock was not continued through him, unless perhaps because Charles the Simple, a legitimate son but a little boy, was not reigning at that time.[82]

Clearly, Gui was working with an earlier prototype, since he disclaims knowledge of why Carloman was 'in the right line of the tree'. Indeed, the error of making Carloman the father of Charles the Simple, and hence part of 'the right line', goes back as far as Richer, writing in the 990s.[83] Some thirteenth-century graphic genealogies, such as those of Giles of Paris and the so-called *Récit d'un ménestrel d'Alphonse de Poitiers*, place Carloman in the direct line in their diagrams.[84] Likewise, the *Grandes chroniques de France*, following the Continuation of Aimoin of Fleury, postulate a non-existent 'Louis Fainéant' as the son and successor of Carloman, succeeded in turn by his son, Charles the Simple. Carloman in fact left no son, and Charles the Simple was his half-brother.[85] Gui was trying his best to deal with discordant sources.

But he succeeded more than he failed in producing a continuous history, in which the three '*genealogiae*', the first, second and third, which we call Merovingian, Carolingian and Capetian, provide the guiding thread, and which can indeed be linked when marriage brings the blood of a former dynasty to the new one. A link of this kind is the Carolingians' supposed descent from an entirely legendary Blithildis or Blitilda, daughter of Clothar II (d. 629).[86] Another famous instance is the marriage of Philip Augustus to a woman of Carolingian descent, thus effecting the 'return to the stock (*reditus ad stirpem*)' of Charlemagne (see below, p. 350). Bernard Gui's graphic scheme was innovative but his purposes were traditional. Manetho, the Egyptian priest who invented the word 'dynasty' 1,600 years before Bernard Gui wrote, would have understood what he was doing: creating a history centred on, and structured by, a sense of dynasty.

CHAPTER 10

Responses to Dynastic Uncertainty: Prophecy and Astrology

I N 1490 OR THEREABOUTS HENRY VII OF ENGLAND ACQUIRED a large book (17 by 12 inches or 440 by 300 mm) of 291 folios, carefully written and illustrated.[1] It contained astronomical tables, a catalogue of stars with striking illustrations of the constellations (Draco, the dragon, is red, as was Henry VII's badge, and stands on a background of white and green, the Tudor colours), a lengthy astrological treatise, a treatise on geomancy, which was a technique for divination, the prophecies of Merlin, the political prophecies ascribed to John of Bridlington and others and the visions of St Birgitta of Sweden relating to the kingdoms of England and France. It is probable that Henry had commissioned this volume. It is a good example of the various ways people sought to find out about the future. Henry, who had won the throne by defeating and killing Richard III only five years before the book was made and had since then faced several serious challenges to his rule, knew very well about the uncertainties of political life and would value such a compendium as a guide to the future.

One of the deepest problems of a dynastic system is that one did not know what was going to happen next. There are some structural features that allow us to categorize dynasties and their dynamics and make some generalizations about them: age at marriage, average fertility, life expectancy, rules and customs regarding succession, etc. But the most fundamental feature of dynastic rule was unpredictability. At any moment, an unexpected death could turn the political world upside down. And whether a child was male or female, not something in this period that could be known until the birth itself, might shape the history of a state for generations. Sometimes a sudden descent into mental illness could unbalance the whole political world, like the paranoid mania that first seized Charles VI of France in 1392 or the catatonia that came upon Henry VI of England in the summer of 1453. In this insecure world, people sought out methods to diminish uncertainty and to have guidance for the future. The scientifically minded turned to the precise, technical forecasts of astrology, while others were fascinated by the more ambiguous glimpses of the future to be found in prophecy and vision.

Astrology

The idea that human life is influenced by the heavenly bodies can be traced back as far as the earliest historical records. Indeed, in the case of the sun and the moon, it is self-evident. For Europe, the important tradition in the interpretation of celestial influences was Babylonian, which was then taken up by the Greeks and Romans. Medieval astrology was raised on these foundations. The failure of attempts to christianize the heavens, by replacing the names of the zodiac with those of the biblical patriarchs or the old names of the stars with those of Christian saints, shows how deeply rooted the earlier traditions were.[2] If human life was shaped to some extent by the stars, then it made sense to study the stars to see what their influence was, to predict outcomes and perhaps guard against them. Horoscopes could be calculated for the moment of a person's birth or advice sought for the best time to undertake an activity. There was always a strand of Christian thinking opposed to the activity of the astrologers, especially if it showed any hint of the deterministic belief that humans were governed inescapably by the heavenly bodies, but there was also always a powerful countercurrent of those who thought that astrology and Christianity could be combined.[3]

The tradition of learned astrology grew faint in the Latin west in the early Middle Ages, but in the Greek east, with its continued access to the important Greek texts, there was more continuity with the ancient world. The vicissitudes of dynastic politics were among the most important subjects dealt with by astrology. The first question asked of a new astrologer arriving in Constantinople was when would the emperor die.[4] A seventh-century chronicle (surviving now only in an Ethiopian translation) tells how astrologers warned of a plot against the emperor Maurice (582–602):

a prefect who knew astrology came forward, and likewise another person named Leon, the logothete, and, observing a star which had appeared in the heaven, they said that this star which had appeared portended the assassination of the emperor. And they went and made this announcement to the empress Constantina and said unto her: 'Learn what thou shouldst do and take measures that thou and thy children may escape destruction; for this star which has appeared is a presage of a revolt against the emperor.'[5]

Astrologers gave advice on military matters, although not always success-fully. In the late eighth century the 'pseudoprophet and astrologer' Pankratios was killed in a battle between the Byzantines and Bulgars, a battle which he had predicted the emperor would win.[6]

The Byzantine emperor Manuel Comnenus (1143–80) firmly believed that human life was influenced by the movements of the heavenly bodies, as he argued in a defence of astrology that he composed.[7] He even postponed military operations if the astrological conditions were unfavourable. On one occasion he recalled a naval expedition because of a mistake made in drawing up the astrological calculations about its success. He had an astrologer attend at the birth of his son and when, late in his reign, astrologers predicted violent storms, he prepared caves as refuges and had all the glass removed from the imperial buildings.[8] Byzantine rulers continued to take an interest in the political and military uses of astrology down to the last century of the state, when, during his rebellion against his father John V in the 1370s, Andronicus IV obtained horoscopes for important events, such as his attack on Constantinople in 1376.[9]

The evidence for learned astrology in Latin Christendom is slight in the early Middle Ages but the influx of Arab astrological texts in Latin translation into Latin Christendom that marked the eleventh, twelfth and thirteenth centuries transformed the situation. Areas of contact between the Christian and Islamic worlds, such as Sicily and Spain, were important in this passage of knowledge. A contemporary illustration of the deathbed of William II of Sicily in 1189 shows him attended by an Arab astrologer, taking readings of the stars.[10] The impact that Arabic science had is echoed even today not only by our use of 'Arabic numerals' but also by Arabic names of stars like Aldebaran and Betelgeuse – it proved easier to accept Arabic names for the stars than to rebaptize them with Christian ones. The newly translated astrological texts were taught in universities and studied in courts and formed the basis for the widespread practice of astrology for a variety of purposes.

As in Byzantium, ruling dynasties in the west were very interested in the prospect of predicting the future.[11] Dynastic politics were so unpredictable and the stakes so high that a court astrologer was as common as a court doctor, and might indeed be the same man. A particularly celebrated court astrologer was Michael Scot, who was in the entourage of the emperor Frederick II in Italy. He was, as his name suggests, a Scot. Before joining Frederick's court he had worked in Toledo, the great centre of translation from Arabic into Latin, where, in 1217, he completed a translation of the most important astronomical work of Nur ad-Din al-Bitruji, a Spanish Muslim of the previous generation. Subsequently he moved to Italy and enjoyed the patronage of successive popes before entering the emperor's service in 1227 or 1228. He wrote an introduction to astrology, at the emperor's request, in which he was careful to avoid the charge of determinism, by stressing that 'the heavenly bodies are not the causes of what there is but only signs, just as the hoop hanging outside the tavern is not wine but the sign of wine'.[12] This by no means diminished the value of astrology: 'Know that from these two things, namely the twelve signs of the zodiac and the seven planets below the firmament, much can be known about the good and bad fortune of future times and of persons, from their birth to their end.'[13] He and Frederick had erudite discussions about subjects as diverse as how many heavens there are and why the sea is salt.[14] But some of the emperor's enquiries had a more immediate and practical application. As Frederick entered a long and bitter war with the cities of northern Italy, Michael predicted that the stars foretold his victory:

Thus it is, if the heavens do not lie and the stars have not gone mad and if the earth follows the heavenly bodies with their eternal motion, that the great wisdom of this ruler will bring to nothing the seditious wills and crush the rebel peoples and impose the unbreakable bridle of laws.[15]

Michael had a high reputation in his own time as 'observer of the stars, seer, prophet, another Apollo'.[16]

In the generation after Frederick II there was also a king renowned for his interest in astrology. This was Alfonso X of Castile (1252–84), whose court was a centre of translations from Arabic into Castilian, including astrological works, such as the *The Complete Book on the Judgments of the Stars* of the eleventh-century North African astrologer 'Aly Aben Ragel' (Abū l-Ḥasan 'Alī ibn Abī l-Rijāl). One section of this is devoted to questions concerning the length of a king's reign and the time of his death.[17] In the following century, payments for 'the emperor's astrologer' are recorded in the reign of the Holy Roman Emperor Louis the Bavarian (1314–47), while the famous writer Christine de Pisan, herself the daughter of an astrologer, praised Charles V of France as an 'astrologer king ... very expert and wise in this science of astrology'.[18] Charles' library did indeed contain seventy-five books of astrology, 8 per cent of the total 914 volumes.[19]

Actual horoscopes survive for many medieval rulers. There is one for Constantine Porphyrogenitus, Byzantine emperor 913–59, who was born on 3 September 905. This horoscope was almost certainly calculated soon after his birth since its predictions are generally wrong.[20] There are extant examples for every English king born between 1284 and 1470.[21] The French royal court was also deeply interested in what the stars had to say. In 1187 Philip Augustus of France had his court astrologer and physician, Roger de Furnival, cast a horoscope for the king's new-born son, Louis (later Louis VIII).[22] Horoscopes survive for Louis X, Charles V, Charles VI, Louis XI and Charles VIII.[23] When Charles VII of France was seriously ill in the winter of 1457–8, his estranged son, the Dauphin Louis, consulted astrologers as to whether he would recover, and received the comforting, but false, answer that the king would not.[24] Charles VII himself had a reputation for consulting astrologers. In a book addressed to his grandson, Charles VIII, the author praises 'all your predecessors, very Christian kings, who loved and cherished and held dear this science of astrology more than any other of the liberal arts', naming specifically Charlemagne, as supposed founder of the University of Paris, Charles V, who founded a college for the subject and donated books, globes and astrolabes, and 'Charles VII, your grandfather, who always had around him the most expert astrologers he could find'.[25] There are surviving astrological dossiers for the years 1407–8 and 1437 concerning the political situation in France.[26] The French astrologer Germain de Thibouville is said to have predicted the deaths of Charles VI and Henry V in 1422 correctly.[27]

The Holy Roman Emperor Frederick III (1440–93) had a reputation for taking astrology seriously. During a journey to meet the powerful Charles the Bold, duke of Burgundy, the German princes urged him to hasten, but the emperor rode slowly on the advice of his astronomer. Frederick consulted astronomers on what would befall his son, Maximilian, and was even sufficiently skilled to make some prognostications himself. He had a horoscope drawn up for his bride, Eleanor of Portugal, which specified the ideal time for their union and, it has been suggested, this might explain his well-attested delay in consummating their marriage after it had taken place in 1452.[28]

Frederick's contemporary and rival, Matthias Corvinus of Hungary (1458–90), also regarded astrology as a vital guide in the precarious business of political life. There were numerous astrological texts in his famous library and he put great faith in the advice of his astrologer, Martin Bylica. Bylica, who was Polish, studied at the universities of Cracow and Bologna, both of which had a professorial chair in astrology, and was then court astrologer to Cardinal Rodrigo Borgia (later to be Pope Alexander VI) before being recruited to the chair of astrology at the new Hungarian university of Bratislava. He cast the horoscope for the opening of the university on 5 June 1467. The following year he sent to Matthias Corvinus a detailed interpretation of the meaning of a comet that had just appeared and, after the virtual collapse of the university of Bratislava in 1471, he moved permanently to the royal court, giving astrological advice on the king's military undertakings and casting horoscopes for members of his family, as well as one for the emperor Frederick III, which gave the astrological explanation of why Frederick was a military failure. Bylica's last task for Matthias Corvinus was to give the astrological explanation for his death.[29]

Astrologers could give retrospective validation as well as prospective advice, for kings were happy to hear that their successes had been written in the stars. The astrologer William Parron wrote in his book on the influence of the stars, which was dedicated to Henry VII, that Henry's victory at Bosworth in 1485 had been determined by the stars. Parron was at this time receiving payments from the king's privy purse.[30] Astrologers also stressed how dangerous it was to ignore their advice. The story was told that, on the morning of his fatal battle with the Swiss, Charles the Bold, duke of Burgundy, was warned by his astrologer that he should not attack them and that if he did, 'unless God turned aside the heavenly influences', it would go badly for him. Charles boasted that 'the fury of his sword would conquer the course of heaven', went into battle and, concludes the story, 'things turned out for him as we know'.[31] His naked body was found some days after the battle.

Those opposed to astrology were irritated that the court found the subject so fascinating. 'Many rulers and great men, agitated by a harmful inquisitiveness, attempt by vain methods to find out hidden things and investigate the future', wrote Nicholas Oresme in his treatise against astronomers of the 1360s.[32] These critics told stories of the fatal errors into which such 'vain methods' might lead.

> They say that, when King James of Majorca wished to depart from Avignon, he had all the astrologers of the papal court summoned, to choose the hour of his departure, and he departed at the hour that had been selected and chosen by the unanimous agreement of all the astrologers, and, nevertheless, on that journey he lost his life and his kingdom too.[33]

This refers to James III of Majorca, who was attempting, with papal help, to regain his throne, from which he had been ejected, but was defeated and killed in the Battle of Lluchmajor in 1349.

Even when predictions appeared to have been proven false, however, there were ways for astrologers to salvage the reputation of their science. A celebrated astrologer predicted that the Byzantine rebel Alexius Branas would enter the city of Constantinople in 1187, but in fact he was killed by a sortie of loyal troops. Another astrologer pointed out, however, that Branas' head had been paraded through the streets of the city and hence the prediction was accurate.[34] And a common type of story concerned those who had misunderstood a prediction because of ambiguity of meaning. The duke of Suffolk was warned by an astrologer 'to beware of the tower', and had thus been relieved in 1450 when he was released after a term of imprisonment in the Tower of London, but, making his way overseas, he was killed on a ship called Nicholas of the Tower.[35] The astronomer who gave this advice to the duke was himself eventually to be a victim of his dangerous art. In 1477 he was accused of drawing up the horoscopes of the king, Edward IV, and his son, the Prince of Wales, and calculating their deaths, for which he was hanged.[36]

Prophecy

For its practitioners and those who believed them, astrology was a science. A different source of knowledge of the future was provided by dreams, visions and prophecies. These did not rest on the mathematical and empirical rules of science but on occult powers, individual experience or charisma. The prophecies might come from the mouth of living wise men or women or they might be found in the writings of ancient seers. Whether prophetic knowledge came in dream or vision or in ancient books, it frequently concerned itself with the fate of rulers and dynasties.[37]

An important example of a text reporting such a dynastic visionary experience is the *Vision of Charles the Fat*.[38] Charles the Fat was the son of Louis the German and the great-grandson of Charlemagne and the last Frankish ruler to govern the whole empire. In this account, which is in the first person, Charles reports how he was 'snatched away in spirit' after going to his bed one Sunday night. Lifted up by a gleaming white figure, he is taken to some deep valleys where fiery pools burned, in which he sees the bishops who had served his father and uncles, that is, the three sons of Louis the Pious who had fought for their father's inheritance throughout the middle decades of the ninth century. The bishops explain that they are being punished there because of the part they played in stirring up discord between the three brothers and warn him that his own bishops who behave in this way will also come to this place. Escaping the attacks of demons with the assistance of his heavenly guide, Charles now comes to some fiery mountains, bubbling with molten metal, where he finds the suffering souls of the nobles and followers of his father, Louis the German, and of Charles' own brothers. They suffer this punishment, they say, because 'while we lived, we loved to do battle and to commit homicide and to plunder, at your side, or at the side of your father, your brothers or your uncles, out of desire for earthly things'.[39] Those who had fostered the family dissensions and conflicts of the Carolingian rulers, be they ecclesiastical or lay, are here being given their punishment after death.

Going on, Charles is guided to a valley, one side of which is dark and fiery but the other side lovely beyond description. Here, he says, 'I saw some kings of my family in great torment', one of them being his father, Louis the German, standing up to his thighs in a barrel of boiling water. Louis greets his son and explains that he spends one day in the boiling water but the next is transferred to a barrel of cool water, and 'this is done through the prayers of St Peter and St Remigius, under whose patronage our royal family has so far ruled'.[40] Thanks to those two saints, he adds, his brother Lothar (who was emperor 840–55) and Lothar's son, Louis (who was emperor 855–75), have already gone from this place of punishment to the joys of paradise. Charles is now escorted to paradise to meet Lothar and Louis, his uncle and cousin, who are crowned and in glory. Lothar addresses him:

> Charles, my successor, now secure in the empire of the Romans, come to me. I know that you have passed through the place of punishment where your father, my brother, is placed in the hot waters prepared for him, but by God's mercy he will very soon be freed from those punishments, just as we have been freed by the merits of St Peter and the prayers of St Remigius, to whom God gave a great apostolate over the kings and the whole people of the Franks. Unless he helps and gives aid to the rest of our stock, our family will presently cease reigning and ruling. Know that the power of the empire will soon be taken from your hands and afterwards you will live a very short time.[41]

After this doleful prediction, Lothar's son, Louis, turns to Charles and tells him, 'Louis, the son of my daughter, should, by hereditary right, receive the Roman empire, which you have held until now.'[42] This young boy now seemed to appear before them. When Charles the Fat finally returns to himself after this vision, he recognizes this designation of the young Louis: 'Henceforth let everyone, willing or not, know, that the whole of the Roman empire will come back into his hands according to God's design.'[43]

The prominent place of St Remigius in this account suggests it may have been written by someone associated with the church of Rheims, whose patron Remigius was. The child Louis is the son of Boso and Ermengard, daughter of the emperor Louis, who was elected king of Provence in 890, crowned emperor in 901 but blinded by his opponents in 905. The text is intended to support his claim to the empire by 'hereditary right', that is, through his direct descent from earlier emperors, even if through the female line. It was obviously written after the death of Charles the Fat in 888, but how long after is less certain. Louis needed support to be accepted as king in 890 but he also needed it to become emperor in 901 and, even more so, afterwards when facing the challenge of a rival emperor. A prophetic vision, in which his Carolingian ancestors and predecessors expressly mark him out as their successor by hereditary right, argued that imperial power was his destiny.

Prophetic vision was also important for the dynasty that followed the Carolingians as rulers of France. By the middle of the eleventh century a prophecy attributed to the early medieval saint Valery was circulating about the Capetian kings. According to what is probably the earliest recorded version, Valery appeared in a dream to Hugh Capet, the first Capetian king, and told him to transfer his, Valery's, body and that of St Riquier to their original resting place, and, in return, 'through our prayers, you will be made king of France, and afterwards your heirs will have the government of the whole kingdom, down to the seventh generation'.[44] A slightly later version has the saint promising 'you will be king of the French, and your offspring, and your stock will hold the kingdom until the seventh succession'.[45] This prophecy would obviously be of great interest to the seventh Capetian king, Philip II Augustus, who came to the throne in 1180. It was, in fact, copied into one of his official registers.[46] During his reign, links between the Capetians and the previous Carolingian dynasty were pointed out in various ways. Philip himself had Carolingian blood and was repeatedly called *Karolides*, 'descendant of Charles', in the poem that William the Breton wrote praising the king's deeds.[47] Another approach stressed not Philip's descent but the fact that his wife, Elizabeth (Isabella) of Hainault, was of Carolingian descent and that therefore the child of Philip and Elizabeth would be a descendant of Charlemagne.[48] Perhaps those who stressed this were ignorant of Philip's own claim to such ancestry. In any case, the contemporary chronicler, Andrew of Marchiennes, referring to Philip's son, Louis (later Louis VIII), was of the opinion that, 'If he reigns after his father, it is agreed that the kingdom will have returned to the line of Charlemagne.'[49] Andrew knew the prophecy of St Valery and perhaps this is how he saw it being fulfilled. Later writers also took up this idea of the *reditus ad stirpem*, 'the return to the stock' of Charlemagne (see p. 384 below).

A time limit of seven generations was also given to the Norman dynasty.[50] Norman tradition had a strange story, which told how in the days of Rollo, the first duke of Normandy, as the inhabitants of Rouen were relaxing on the banks of the Seine one evening, they were amazed to see a horseman travelling across the water, just as if it were land. When he reached them, they asked who he was, and he reassured them that he was a human being. That morning, he said, he had been at Rennes in Brittany, so he had travelled the 200 miles (320 kilometres) to Rouen in just a day. When the duke was informed about this, he asked to see the man; the mysterious traveller said he would meet the duke 'at the first hour' next morning. But when the duke looked for him at that hour, he was informed the stranger had already gone on his way, and he concluded the man had lied and was some kind of illusory creature. But some people disagreed: when the stranger had said 'at the first hour', they suggested, he had meant *his* 'first hour', not *the duke's* 'first hour'. Obviously, for a man who could travel 200 miles in a day, time went faster. This is a remarkable conception, bordering on science fiction, or perhaps the theory of relativity.

But what is relevant to dynastic history is the conversation that the speedy traveller engaged in that night in his lodgings. His host, obviously presuming that a man who travelled through time at his own pace might know future things, asked him if Rollo's dynasty would continue long. He answered that 'it would last for a long time and its rule would endure in full strength down to the seventh generation'.[51] But when he was asked what would happen after that, all he would do was make lines in the ashes of the fire with a stick, and then, when pressed for an answer, stir up the ashes and obliterate the lines. This story was written down during the reign of Henry I, who was king of England from 1100 and duke of Normandy from 1106. And he was of the seventh generation from Rollo.[52] 'Who will possess these lands after him', the earliest version of the text comments, 'the generation that will be at the time will be able to see', but it presumed the stirring of the ashes signified either the end of the duchy or at least serious troubles.[53] A later version, copied after Henry's death, was more definite about these troubles: 'We who have outlived King Henry see these things fulfilled for the most part.'[54]

The prophecy of St Valery about the Capetians and this strange Norman tale both concern the succession of dynasties, pointing to one thing, how many generations a given family might hold on to power. There were also far more extensive prophetic texts, circulating in large numbers, that claimed to describe the destinies of kings and kingdoms over long periods of time. One favourite form was to encode predictions in animal imagery, the most successful example being the *Prophecies of Merlin* in Geoffrey of Monmouth's *History of the Kings of Britain*, a work written in the 1130s by a canon of Oxford. The style of these prophecies is terse, staccato and cryptic:

> The cubs of the ruler will awake and, setting aside the forests, will hunt within the walls of the cities. They will make no small slaughter of those who oppose them and they will cut out the tongues of the bulls. They will load with chains the necks of the roaring ones and renew the days of their grandfather. Then, from the first to the fourth, from the fourth to the third, from the third to the second, the thumb will be rolled in oil. The sixth will cast down the walls of Ireland and change the forests into a plain.[55]

Writers of the late twelfth and early thirteenth century saw the phrase about the cubs as a clear prediction of the rebellion of Henry II's sons against him in 1173–4.[56]

The allusiveness and ambiguity of the prophecy format allowed continual reinterpretation of the meaning of individual passages. There is a phrase in the *Prophecies of Merlin* – 'the lynx penetrating everything, who will be intent on the ruin of his own people'[57] – which occurs at a point in the *Prophecies* that would correspond in time to the reigns of the sons of Henry II, some sixty years after Geoffrey published the text. Rather remarkably, the lynx in the *Prophecies* is responsible for the termination of the union of Normandy and England, as actually was the case with King John (1199–1216). An early interpreter of the *Prophecies*, writing in the 1170s, thought the prophecy about the lynx meant that it was through the lynx that 'the domination of the Normans in the island of Britain would come to an end'.[58] Soon afterwards, an alternative explanation was advanced, that the lynx was Henry the Young King, son of Henry II, who died while in rebellion against his father.[59] After the loss of Normandy by King John, however, the true interpretation seemed obvious. William the Breton, the chronicler of John's conqueror, Philip Augustus of France, was quite clear that John was the lynx: 'Truly he is Merlin's allegorical lynx, of whom Merlin, speaking of his father, whom he compares to a lion, says, "From him will come forth a lynx, penetrating all, who will be intent on the ruin of his own people."'[60]

But there was enough leeway in the wording and structure of the *Prophecies* to allow other interpretations. For some, the lynx was not John, but his son, Henry III, although the grounds for the identification could vary. The chronicler Matthew Paris, writing during Henry's reign, thought the phrase referred to Henry's heavy taxation and exactions: 'Truly a penetrating lynx, since there was not a purse in England that he did not cut open and shake out the contents.'[61] A Dominican chronicler, writing nearly fifty years after the death of Henry III, had a different interpretation when he came to sum up the king's reign: 'he was physically strong but hasty in his actions, but, since these had a fortunate and happy final outcome, many people thought that he was the one indicated as "the lynx penetrating all" by the prophet Merlin'.[62]

Merlin's prophecies were thus a key to unlock the truth of past events as well as a guide to the future. A particularly arresting example concerns the death of William Rufus while hunting in the New Forest in 1100, which was usually described as an accidental shooting by one of his companions, Walter Tyrrel. However, a close reading of Merlin's prophecies led some later commentators to a different interpretation: 'It is the common and almost universal opinion that Walter did this unintentionally and by accident, but the oracle of Merlin which predicted "to be killed by the dart of envy" compels us to understand it differently.'[63] The phrase 'to be killed by the dart of envy' comes in Merlin's prophecies at a point that clearly corresponds to William's death, and suggests that whoever first composed these prophecies, whether Geoffrey of Monmouth or a source he used, believed that it was murder not accident.

Geoffrey of Monmouth's *History of the Kings of Britain* was an enormously successful book throughout the Middle Ages and in many countries, so the *Prophecies of Merlin* reached a wide audience. Quite often the *Prophecies* circulated separately from the *History*, there being more than seventy examples of such texts,[64] and they also stimulated other writers to produce their own imitations.[65] An important example of a collection of prophecies attributed to Merlin but quite separate from Geoffrey of Monmouth's is that under the name of 'Richard of Ireland'. This was in French but written, sometime in the 1270s, by a Venetian who supported the pro-Church party, the Guelfs, in the struggles between the Church and the Holy Roman Emperor. It is a very long work and combines prophecies of Merlin with narrative sections containing tales of Arthurian romance. Since there are at least thirteen manuscripts, as well as two of an Italian translation, and the text was printed in French in 1498 and in Italian in 1480, there was clearly a demand for this work.[66]

Such independent Merlin prophecies reached the Iberian peninsula, where they were cited during the civil war between Peter the Cruel of Castile and his half-brother Henry of Trastámara in the mid fourteenth century. According to the historian Pero López de Ayala, who had served Peter but had then gone over to Henry, a letter was found among Peter's documents after his murder, in which a learned Muslim from Granada had interpreted a prophecy of Merlin at the king's request. The prophecy is included in the letter:

> In the parts of the West, between the mountains and the sea, will be born a black bird, a great eater and predator, and he would like to welcome in him all the honeycombs of the world and to put in his stomach all the gold of the world; and he will suffer indigestion and he will turn back, and he will not perish immediately from this disease. His wings will fall and his feathers will dry in the sun, and he will go door to door and no one will welcome him, and he will enclose himself in a forest, and he will die there twice, once to the world and once before God.[67]

Ayala's chronicle gives the full content of the supposed interpretation provided in the Muslim sage's letter: the black bird is Peter; the eating and greed refers to his oppression of his subjects; his wings are the great nobles of Castile, who will abandon him; and 'the forest', the sage has found out, is the old name of the city of Montiel, the place where Peter was actually murdered by his half-brother.

There can be little doubt that the letter is an invention, either of Ayala himself or of someone upon whom the historian relied.[68] A wise Muslim informing Peter the Cruel of the location of his future murder, on the basis of a prophecy of Merlin that the king has sent him, has to be a story that circulated among supporters of Peter's enemy, Henry of Trastámara, in the years after the murder. Its purpose may be inferred: to justify the murder and Henry's usurpation of the Crown by presenting it as a long-foreseen part of prophetic history, that is, the course of history as revealed to the seers and wise men and women of a legendary past. Ancient prophecy was summoned to justify political revolution, or, as a Castilian knight of the following generation observed, 'as soon as a new king comes, they immediately make a new Merlin'.[69]

Kings were naturally very interested in the question of the succession and might turn to Merlin for help. Edward IV of England, whose father had been killed in an attempt to gain the throne, and who had himself seized it by force, been deposed and exiled and then returned to recover the king-dom, knew from experience that Fortune had her caprices. A story was told about him, which, although unlikely to be true, illuminates contemporary thinking about both the allure and the deceptions of political prophecy:

> Now he decided to look into the prophecies of Merlin to find out what would happen to his descendants, which is a superstition that has reigned in England since the time of King Arthur. Seeing these prophecies, by the interpretation made of them to him (for they are like the oracles of Apollo, since they can always be understood in two ways), it was found that one of his brothers, whose name began with the letter G, would take the crown out of the hands of his children.[70]

Inspired by this news, the king ordered the killing of his brother George, duke of Clarence, famously drowned in a barrel of malmsey wine. Now falsely secure, Edward should have thought more carefully: his brother Richard (later Richard III) was duke of Gloucester, and Gloucester begins with a G.

Throughout the later centuries of the Middle Ages, the events of dynastic history were constantly being seen through the lens of Merlin's prophecies. Gerald of Wales' account of the Anglo-Norman invasion of Ireland, originally composed in 1189, was called *The Prophetic History*, since Gerald presented the events as the fulfilment of prophecies of Merlin (or Merlins, since he thought there were two seers of that name).[71] The death of Simon de Montfort the elder, killed in 1218 by a stone thrown by the besieged inhabitants of Toulouse, was prophesied by Merlin, 'that good diviner'.[72] The Italian Franciscan, Salimbene, included in his chronicle prophecies of Merlin about the emperors Frederick I and Frederick II, verses of Merlin 'in which predictions about the cities of Lombardy, Tuscany, the Romagna and the Marche are fully and truthfully contained', as well as a long account of a debate about prophecy between a learned Franciscan and a learned Dominican, in which Merlin figures prominently as a disputed example.[73]

There were other prophets and other styles of prophecy. Sometimes prophecies were not ascribed to sages of the past but to living contemporaries, such as Abbot Joachim of Fiore, St Birgitta and the Scottish Thomas Rymer, 'that rural seer', who was credited with predicting the death of Alexander III, king of Scots, in 1286.[74] And an alternative to animal symbolism employed the letters of the alphabet as a cryptic key. In the twelfth century, for example, there was a prediction that the Comnenian family would rule the Byzantine empire in a succession of emperors indicated by the word AIMA (αἷμα), 'blood'. The first Comnenian emperor was Alexius, the second John (J=I), the third Manuel, so Manuel consciously chose for his son a name beginning with A, Alexius. Later in the century the tyrannous emperor Andronicus Comnenus was told that his successor's name would begin with an I (*iota*), so he looked out for a rival called Isaac, but identified the wrong one.[75] An Italian prophetic text of the thirteenth century reads,

The first F., in his hair a lamb, in his pelt a lion, will be a destroyer of towns. In pursuit of a just purpose, he will find his end between the raven and the crow. He will live on in H., who will perish in the gates of Melatium. But the second F., of unexpected and marvellous birth, will be a lamb to be torn to pieces among the goats, but not overwhelmed by them.[76]

This is an only thinly disguised history of the emperor Frederick I, who died on crusade, his son, Henry VI, who died in Sicily (Melatium is perhaps Milazzo, on the north-east coast of Sicily), and his son, Frederick II, whose wars dominated the history of Italy in the second quarter of the thirteenth century.

Like this one, many of the prophecies found in the texts of the Middle Ages are clearly written after the events they claim to be foretelling and simply create a cryptic disguise for known historical happenings. When Geoffrey of Monmouth, writing his *Prophecies of Merlin* in the 1130s, tells how Merlin predicted an invasion of Britain by 'a people dressed in wood and in iron coats', then the rule of two dragons, one of whom will be killed, then the reign of the Lion of Justice, and how then 'the lion's cubs will be turned into fish of the sea', the actual historical references are clear: the Norman Conquest of 1066, the reigns of William I and William II Rufus, the accession of Henry I and the death of his son William in the wreck of the White Ship in 1120.[77] This is prophecy only in the sense that Miss Pole in Mrs Gaskell's novel *Cranford* practised it: 'Miss Pole herself, who we looked upon as a kind of prophetess, from the knack she had of foreseeing things before they came to pass – although she did not like to disturb her friends by telling them her foreknowledge' (Chapter 12).

Some prophecies, however, turned out to have an unexpectedly prophetic nature. One such is the prophecy of the green tree. Its original form was an utterance ascribed to Edward the Confessor on his deathbed in 1066. He claimed to have been visited by two long-dead monks, who had told him that after his death, because of the wickedness of the English nobles and clergy, God would deliver the kingdom into the hands of the enemy and it would be devasted by fire and the sword. When Edward asked these spiritual visitors how long England would endure these tribulations, they replied,

> If a green tree should be cut in two in the middle and the part that has been cut off carried away the distance of three *iugera* [approximately 213 metres or 699 feet] from the trunk, when it rejoins the trunk by itself, without the help of human hands or any prop, and it begins again to grow green shoots and bear fruit from the original love in its coalescing sap, it is only then the end of such evils can be hoped for.[78]

This was written very soon after the Norman Conquest of 1066 and seems to suggest that it is an impossibility for the sufferings to come to an end. That was certainly how the passage was interpreted by writers of the following generations. In 1125 the historian William of Malmesbury, himself half English and half Norman, wrote that 'we experience the truth of this prophecy because England has become the dwelling place of outsiders and is under the domination of foreigners . . . nor is there any hope of an end to this misery'.[79] In the following decade, another writer, Osbert of Clare, also interpreted the prophecy as indicating the impossibility of any improvement in the lot of the English people: 'For nowadays we see no king or earl or bishop coming from that people, any more than a felled tree rejoining its trunk and producing leaves and fruit.'[80]

The next writer to address this issue, however, advanced a completely different interpretation. Aelred of Rievaulx, composing his Life of Edward the Confessor around 1163, was writing in the reign of Henry II. Henry was the son of Matilda, the daughter of Henry I and Queen Matilda, and Queen Matilda was herself of the old royal line of the Anglo-Saxon kings. Hence Henry II had the blood of both the Norman and the Anglo-Saxon kings. Aelred writes that 'it is the special glory of our Henry to trace his physical descent from his [Edward's] holy kindred'.[81] He gives his interpretation of the prophecy: the tree is England; it was divided when the kingdom was taken from the old royal stock; the three *iugera* represent the three kings who had no connection with the old line, Harold, William I and William II; Henry I, by marrying Matilda, 'united the seed of the kings of the Normans and English'; the tree flourished when their daughter Matilda was born and came to fruit when Henry 'joined the two people like a keystone'. 'Now,' he adds, 'England certainly has a king of English descent, and it has bishops and abbots of the same race, and it has nobles and fine knights born from a mingling of the seed of each, bringing honour to one and consolation to the other.'[82] So the prophecy of the green tree had finally come true. The dynastic reunion represented by the accession of Henry II in 1154 has some similarities with the *reditus ad stirpem*, the return of Carolingian blood in the person of Louis VIII of France, as discussed above (p. 350, see also p. 384 below). In both cases, apparent ruptures in dynastic history were being made good.

The atmosphere of dreams and prophecy that was woven through dynastic life comes out in a story about Peter I of Portugal (1357–67). The king had two illegitimate sons named John, by two different women. He had been foretold (it is not said by whom) that his son John would bring great glory to the kingdom of Portugal. Peter naturally wondered which John would do this, and had a preference that it be the elder. He was convinced that it would, in fact, be the younger after having a dream in which he saw all Portugal burning, and then his younger son John appeared with a stick and extinguished the flames. He consulted experts in dream interpretation who confirmed this.[83] John did indeed go on to defeat a Castilian invasion and himself become king of Portugal, encouraged by a prophecy given to him by a visionary hermit.[84]

Foreknowledge of the dynastic future could thus be sought by various means, through astrology, prophetic visons or books of prophecy. Some of these methods were dangerous, as Eleanor Cobham found out.[85] Eleanor married Humphrey, duke of Gloucester, uncle of the young and sickly Henry VI of England, in 1428. She had already been his mistress for some years, and once he had his first marriage annulled, she was able to become his wife. After the death of Humphrey's older brother in 1435, Humphrey himself was next in line for the throne. If the young, unmarried and childless Henry VI died, Humphrey would be king and Eleanor queen. She had the reputation of 'scheming for a long time to exalt herself to a higher position in the kingdom of England than she had had'.[86]

Eleanor was perhaps unwise. She consulted two learned churchmen, whose learning extended to astrology and magic, to see whether the young king would live. One of them, Roger Bultybrok (or Bolingbroke), supposedly made a 'figure (*figura*)' of the king, along with 'very many objects, images, vestments, circles and instruments', which he created by his magical and necromantic art, under the pretext of conducting legitimate astronomy.[87] His collaborator, Thomas Southwell, a canon of the royal chapel of St Stephen's, Westminster, assisted him by consecrating these objects and Roger's book of spells, as well as reciting masses, so that Roger 'could be safe within the circle and would be able to summon to him demons and other evil spirits that are in the air and the earth'.[88] Roger's magical and astrological efforts eventually bore fruit:

he knew well that the king would not live long but would die within a short time, and thus, through the discovery and dissemination of this matter, the king's people would withdraw their hearty love of him, and the king himself, through knowledge of this discovery and dissemination, namely that he would die within a short time, would conceive such sadness in his heart that he would die more quickly because of that sadness and grief.[89]

Roger thought it very probable that the king would die in late May or early June of 1441. The events of that summer were in fact very different. Duke Humphrey had his enemies, as well as his ambitions, and they saw their chance when they heard that his wife had been dabbling in magic and getting predictions of the king's illness or death. In July 1441 Roger, Thomas and Eleanor were arrested and tried on charges of necromancy. The charges included not only calculating the time of the king's death but also seeking to procure it through magic.[90] The dragnet also hauled in Margery Jourdemayne, the so-called 'Witch of Eye', a local wise woman whom Eleanor had supposedly consulted. Eleanor argued in her defence that the images and other magical equipment were not to cause the king's death but 'for to have borne a child by her lord, the duke of Gloucester' – she could be the mother of kings.[91] Roger Bultybrok said his necromancy had been undertaken at Eleanor's request and was solely to know 'what should befall her and to what estate she should come', although he confessed, as he faced execution, that 'he presumed too far in his cunning' (that is, his science).[92] Thomas Southwell died in the Tower of London, Roger was hanged, drawn and quartered, Margery Jourdemayne was burned alive. Eleanor herself had to do penance, walking through the streets of London on three occasions, bareheaded and carrying a large candle. She was divorced from Duke Humphrey and spent the remaining eleven years of her life a prisoner in remote and windy castles. She never was the mother of kings.

CHAPTER 11

Pretenders and Returners: Dynastic Imposters
in the Middle Ages

I N THE SPRING OF 1487, IN CHRIST CHURCH CATHEDRAL (HOLY
Trinity) in Dublin, the young Edward VI was crowned king of England
and France and lord of Ireland. A parliament was summoned and coins
were struck in his name. Soon after his coronation he sailed for England,
with an army provided by his aunt, Margaret of Burgundy, and his Irish
supporters, notably the earl of Kildare. His purpose was to remove the
usurper, Henry Tudor. But luck was not with him, his army was defeated,
and he was captured. Henry Tudor did not execute him but preferred to
maintain the story that this boy was not, as his supporters claimed,
a prince of the royal house of York, but an English plebeian with the
absurd name of Lambert Simnel.[1]

In the world of dynasties, which was the world of most of medieval
Europe, a political claim was primarily in the person and the blood, much
more than in election or divine commission. Hence a claim could be
made simply by asserting a certain personal identity, in the form 'I am X'.
This appears particularly clearly in the case of pretenders and returners,
those men and women who claimed to be, or were claimed to be, either
the children of royal dynasties or long-lost rulers themselves coming back
from obscurity.[2] Some stories concentrate simply on the pathos of
a famous ruler living on in humble anonymity: Harold, the last Anglo-
Saxon king, the Holy Roman Emperor Henry V, Edward II of England
and Wladyslaw III of Poland are all recorded, not dying as generally
reported, but as ending their days as obscure hermits. There is obviously
a perennial taste for the mystery of the supposedly dead or the disappeared who have actually lived on elsewhere, with a secret life and a new
identity. But more dramatic are the cases where the king returns to claim

his own. These supposed returning kings show the underlying assumptions about political legitimacy in a dynastic system: their claims are in their blood. And they are also ideal tools to be manipulated by factions and dissidents.

The stories of kings living on as hermits are simple survival legends, strange and poignant, but cases of those who try to return, or of those who claim to be the sons of past rulers, are a distinctive but not infrequent feature of dynastic politics. Examples can be found in the ancient world and in modern times, and also throughout the medieval period, all over Christendom. They include supposed Merovingian kings, Byzantine emperors and Holy Roman emperors. Two famous cases, from the thirteenth and fourteenth centuries respectively, are the apparent return of Baldwin, count of Flanders and Latin emperor of Constantinople, and the reappearance of Woldemar, margrave of Brandenburg, in each case after an absence of decades.[3] There are examples of returning pretenders from Spain and from Norway. And, at the end of the Middle Ages, the Tudor dynasty of England, which seized the throne in 1485, faced a series of challenges from young men claiming to be princes of the previous Yorkist dynasty, challenges that, as in the case of Lambert Simnel alias Edward VI, came close to success.

And this raises a problem for our analysis, since, if these young men had succeeded, then the official story would be, not that they were pretenders, but that they were dispossessed Yorkists expelling a usurper. We all know that history is written by the victors, but that is true especially starkly in the case of pretenders, because, simply by calling them that, we sign up with the winning side. It is rather like the anti-popes. Who is it who decides who is a pope and who an anti-pope? The answer is, the last pope standing. The label 'anti-pope' is that applied by the victorious, and hence official, pope. Nobody starts out with the intention of becoming an anti-pope or of being labelled a pretender. So, in any discussion of the subject, we must be aware that the history of pretenders is the history of failed pretenders.

It is not as if the idea of a ruler returning after many years is beyond the bounds of possibility, for sometimes rulers really did disappear and return after decades. One of the most remarkable cases is that of Henry I of Mecklenburg, who left his north German principality to go on pilgrimage to the Holy Land in 1271 and only returned home to his wife and land in 1298. Kidnapped in the Holy Land by Muslims, he was held in captivity in Cairo for decades. News of this came to his wife Anastasia in 1275 and she made serious but ill-fated efforts to ransom her husband. In the following decades Henry's son exercised authority in Mecklenburg and he slipped into the habit of referring to his father as 'of blessed memory'. Two imposters claiming to be Henry also turned up but were unmasked and executed. Finally the Mamluk Sultan of Egypt released Henry, along with his loyal squire, who had accompanied him all those years, and the pair eventually reached Mecklenburg again in the summer of 1298, twenty-seven years after their departure. Henry's wife and, with whatever emotions, his son met him. With a story as strange as this, it is less surprising that tales of returning rulers were so often found credible.[4]

There is no single set of circumstances that gives rise to stories of survivors and returners, but there are some recurrent patterns. One situation that might well generate rumours of survival was death in battle, for in the bloody chaos and carnage of hand-to-hand combat it was often uncertain who had lived and who had died. Some of these stories, as mentioned, concerned kings who escaped from disastrous defeats and lived quiet, anonymous lives thereafter: Harold Godwinson survived the Battle of Hastings and ended his days as a hermit in Chester;[5] Wladyslaw III of Poland had not been killed by the Ottoman Turks at the Battle of Varna in 1444 and likewise lived on as a hermit in Spain. There were rumours, too, that Olaf Tryggvason had not drowned at the great sea-battle of Svolde in the year 1000. In his *Heimskringla*, the thirteenth-century author Snorri Sturluson cites earlier poets on the subject. One of these was King Olaf's contemporary, Hallfredr Ottarsson, and Samuel Laing's translation of the *Heimskringla* from 1844 gives an appealing rhyming English version of what he wrote:

> Does Olaf live? or is he dead?
> Has he the hungry ravens fed?
> I scarcely know what I should say,
> For many tell the tale each way.[6]

Snorri's dry comment on this is, 'But howsoever that be, King Olaf Tryggvason never thereafter returned to his kingdom in Norway.'[7]

But more significant in dynastic politics were those pretenders who did come back to their kingdoms, actually made public their claims to have survived death in battle and sought to re-establish themselves in power. In the early 1090s, for example, a man claiming to be a son of the Byzantine emperor Romanos IV Diogenes (1068–71) turned up. This son had not died in fighting at Antioch seventeen years earlier, as had been thought, but had survived. His supposed wife, the sister of the current emperor, Alexius Comnenus, did not, however, acknowledge him, and he was captured and sent off to Cherson in the Crimea, the Byzantine equivalent of Alcatraz at this time. But he did not give up. In Cherson he was able to enter into dealings with the Cumans, a neighbouring tribe of steppe nomads, escaped to join them, was acknowledged as emperor by them and then invaded the empire in 1094. It was only after a long campaign in the Balkans that he was captured and blinded.[8] And it is important to remember, of course, that if he had been successful, our accounts of these events would have been quite different, and the triumphant report composed by Anna Comnena, Alexius' daughter, would not exist. And modern historians would find a place for this son of Romanos Diogenes in their books.

The case of Alfonso the Battler of Aragon is slightly more complex. The earliest sources are clear that he survived the bloody defeat of the Christians in the Battle of Fraga in 1134, but died soon afterwards.[9] There is even a document, issued in that year that is dated 'after the great and disastrous slaughter of the Christians at Fraga, in which almost all fell by the sword, but a very few just managed to escape, without their weapons, along with the king'.[10] But this version of the king's end did not provide a very satisfactory narrative: it is neither heroic nor tragic. So, it is understandable that, by the thirteenth century, there were different versions of the king's fate. The *Latin Chronicle of the Kings of Castile*, the first part of which was composed in the 1220s, says 'he is said to have been killed by the Moors. But the opinion of others was that he escaped from that disaster ... and it was said that after the passage of many years he came in our own time to Aragon.'[11] Rodrigo Jiménez de Rada, archbishop of Toledo, whose chronicle was completed in 1243, writes that some say he was killed at Fraga and his body was ransomed from the Muslims to be given Christian burial. Others say he survived the encounter and, 'unable to bear the confusion of battle, he showed himself to this world as a pilgrim, changed in likeness and dress'.[12] In any case, a man claiming to be Alfonso turned up some thirty years after the Battle of Fraga and caused concern to his great-nephew, the king of Aragon at that time.[13]

The fall of the Hohenstaufen dynasty in the middle decades of the thirteenth century also brought a particularly rich crop of pretenders. Manfred, the son of Frederick II and king of Sicily, killed in battle in 1266, and his nephew Conradin, killed two years later after being captured in battle, both reappeared very soon after their supposed deaths. The Franciscan chronicler Salimbene relates that after Charles of Anjou defeated and killed Manfred at the Battle of Benevento, not one, but several pretenders arose, claiming to be the fallen king. Charles was kept busy: 'he killed many such Manfreds in those days', says Salimbene.[14]

But there were other situations that formed the background story for pretenders. Deposition, especially if followed by imprisonment or by disappearance, was one: Michael VII Ducas, the Byzantine emperor deposed in 1078, and the late medieval English kings Edward II, Richard II and Edward V, are in this category. Occasionally one encounters tales of babies exchanged in the cradle, reminiscent of the famous 'warming pan baby' story, which claimed that the son of James II, the last Catholic king of England, Scotland and Ireland, was not his but had been slipped into his wife's bedchamber in a warming pan. Harold Harefoot, who succeeded Canute in England in 1035, claimed that he was the king's son by the English noblewoman Ælfgifu, but his enemies expressed doubts. The various versions of the Anglo-Saxon Chronicle report that 'Harold said he was Canute's son by Ælfgifu but it was not at all true', or that 'Some men said that Harold was the son of King Canute by Ælfgifu but many men thought this quite incredible.'[15] A few years after Canute's death an adherent of Ælfgifu's great rival, Queen Emma, wrote that the likely truth was that the child of a servant girl had been sneaked into the bedroom of Canute's concubine (i.e. Ælfgifu) and passed off as hers.[16] By the twelfth century the gossip had become more elaborate, with Harold and his brother being actually the sons of a cobbler and a priest's concubine respectively.[17]

Apart from babies being smuggled in, there are cases of babies being smuggled out. In the middle of the fourteenth century a Sienese merchant, Giannino, claimed to be the rightful king of France. He said that he was actually John I, the baby who had held the royal title from 15–19 November 1316, dying at less than a week old. Giannino claimed that the baby who had died in 1316 was not the royal prince but another, substituted for him, and that he, the real royal baby, had been smuggled out of the palace and come eventually to Italy, where, forty years on, his story had been revealed to him. Not everyone was convinced. In 1359 the General Council of the commune of Siena banned Giannino for life from holding public office because of the claims he was making to royal blood.[18] And the Dante scholar Benvenuto da Imola, writing a little later, used the case to illustrate a passage in the Divine Comedy where Dante speaks of the folly of the people of Siena: 'But what would our poet have said', asks Benvenuto, 'if he had seen, not long ago, Giannino of Siena, who allowed himself to be persuaded so easily and so foolishly that he was the king of France?'[19]

But the most recurrent returner, the Holy Roman Emperor Frederick II, who died in 1250, had neither been killed in battle nor been deposed, except in name only. His posthumous career rested instead on the real Frederick's charisma and his dramatic life, magnified by the way he had become the focus of apocalyptic predictions, which was not the case with most returning rulers.[20] Salimbene admitted, when he heard that Frederick had died, 'I myself for many days could scarcely believe that he was dead'; only when the pope himself affirmed it did he believe, but even then, 'I shuddered when I heard it and could scarcely believe it.'[21] Many people scarcely believed it, and many others did not believe it at all. Hence there arose a series of false Fredericks, some of them of significant impact, like the pretender in Sicily in 1261, or another in the Rhineland in 1284, both of whom required considerable military effort to suppress.

The only occasion on which there was a female pretender of importance seems to have been in 1300 in Norway, when a woman appeared claiming to be Margaret, the so-called 'Maid of Norway'.[22] Margaret was the daughter of Erik Magnusson, king of Norway (1280–99) and, through her mother (also called Margaret), she was the heir to the Scottish throne. She had died in 1290 on her way from Norway to her new kingdom. She had a plausible claim to be heir of Norway as well as Scotland, since King Erik had no sons and was succeeded by a brother. In the marriage treaty between King Erik and Margaret's mother, it was indeed stated that 'if the king of Norway should beget by this Margaret a daughter or daughters, they will succeed to everything that can come to them according to Norwegian laws and customs, even to the kingdom if that is the custom'.[23] This left it open whether it was the custom, of course, but the Margaret who appeared in 1300, a year after King Erik's death, would, as his daughter, have been the most credible challenger to Erik's newly crowned brother, and she supposedly claimed to be his 'lawful heir'.[24] It has been suggested that she was the tool of a group of dissident nobles.[25] If so, they seem to have chosen badly, for the woman who made these claims in 1300 was already grey-haired, while the real Margaret would have been only seventeen. This false Margaret was burned alive near Bergen, but even then continued to trouble the authorities, as she became the focus of a cult, with pilgrimages and invocation of her as a saint.[26]

The length of time between the death or disappearance of the ruler and his apparent re-emergence varied considerably, but was always biologically possible, except in the case of some supposed emperor Fredericks of the later Middle Ages. The longest gap, apart from these, is of thirty-eight years, and occurs in the very special case of John I of France, the one who, according to all accounts, died as a week-old baby in 1316, but by 1354 had supposedly turned up in Italy in the form of Giannino of Siena. Alfonso the Battler of Aragon and Woldemar of Brandenburg reappeared twenty-nine years after their apparent deaths, Baldwin of Flanders twenty years. In fact, the pseudo-Baldwin's supporters explained the fact that he seemed to be shorter than the ruler who had set off long ago on the Fourth Crusade as an effect of age.[27] But there are cases of a much swifter return. In the Byzantine empire Michael VII, who was deposed in 1078, and Alexius II, who was deposed and killed in 1183, supposedly were active again within a few years, two and six respectively. Conradin of Hohenstaufen was executed in 1268 but in the very next year some Germans in Italy were hailing a young man as the lost prince and a putative Richard II of England was winning recognition in some quarters just two years after the king's death in 1400.[28] The shorter the gap between disappearance and return, however, the more acute were questions of identification and resemblance (a subject discussed below).

When the pseudo-Frederick II appeared in Germany in 1284, 'many people asked, if he was the emperor, why had he lain hidden for such a long time'.[29] This is a natural enquiry. Especially in the case of a return after many years, the returners had to explain their absence. The missing years were often accounted for as a period of penitence. Pseudo-Baldwin, for example, explained that, after he had escaped from captivity among the Saracens, he had been enjoined seven years penance by the pope for abandoning the faith in that time. The seven years were now up, which is why he could return publicly to Flanders.[30] The false-Frederick II who turned up in Sicily in 1261 'declared that long ago, after being granted divine permission through an oracle, he had feigned his death and spent nine years on pilgrimage in expiation of his sins'.[31] The false Woldemar's situation was more complex. He had, he said, feigned his death, substituting another body, and left his principality of Brandenburg, for one cause alone: his marriage was within the prohibited degrees, and this was the only way he could obey his conscience and also preserve his wife's honour, since she would now be able to remarry.[32] In actual fact, Margrave Woldemar had married a cousin within the prohibited degrees, and she had indeed remarried after his death, or presumed death.

There were also other ways of explaining disappearance and survival. The false Margaret, Maid of Norway, said that during her voyage from Norway to Scotland she had been sold by one of her aristocratic ladies-in-waiting, and spirited away.[33] Perkin Warbeck, claiming to be the younger of the Princes in the Tower, son of Edward IV of England, explained that he had been spared and conducted abroad by the assassin sent by his wicked uncle Richard III, but that he had been made to promise on oath that he would not reveal his true identity 'for a certain period of years'.[34]

Whenever they appeared, these pretenders signified a challenge to the existing powers. Sometimes they were adopted by dissident factions within the country, sometimes used by foreign enemies, sometimes both. A good example of the way foreign enemies could try to use a pretender or returner is provided by the case of the Byzantine emperor Michael VII Ducas. In March 1078 Michael was forced to abdicate the imperial throne

367

and became a monk. About two years later, however, a figure appeared in southern Italy claiming to be the former emperor and won powerful backers in an attempt at restoration. Robert Guiscard, the Norman warrior who had carved out a conquest principality in the region, was willing to lead an army across the Adriatic against the Byzantine empire, with the supposed Michael VII in his train, while Pope Gregory VII commanded the bishops of Apulia and Calabria to offer absolution of their sins to those going on the expedition.[35]

There were doubters:

> There were at that time some men with the duke (i.e. Robert Guiscard) who had served in the palace in the time of the emperor Michael and said they knew his face and that this man did not resemble him in the least, but that he had come in the hope of getting some gift from the duke on false pretences.[36]

Guiscard was apparently indifferent to whether the man was genuine or not and was not dissuaded from launching his attack. The supposed Michael was with him when the Norman leader besieged the important Byzantine city of Dyrrachium in the summer of 1081. Guiscard's ploy was not a success. The inhabitants apparently said they would surrender if they could see the deposed emperor. Dressed in imperial robes and accompanied by a fanfare, the claimant was paraded before the walls, but the effect was disastrous. According to one account, the besieged citizens shouted that 'they did not recognize him at all', while, according to another, even more humiliatingly, they did identify the figure before them: 'This man used to bring jugs full of wine to the table and was one of the lower butlers!'[37]

Anna Comnena, one of the sources for this story, considered various theories about who the pretender was and who initiated the plot to put him forward, some of them seeing the pretender himself as the instigator, others attributing a far-reaching scheme to Robert Guiscard. Anna has obvious motives for ridiculing this attempt to give legitimacy to Guiscard's invasion, but Guiscard himself seems to have thought it worthwhile, and Gregory VII was convinced enough to give the expedition its proto-crusading status.

A surviving or returning king could indeed be a useful weapon for hostile neighbours. The pretender claiming to be the Byzantine emperor

Alexius II turned up at the court of the Sultan of Iconium, who always treated him as the genuine emperor and allowed him to recruit troops to attack the Byzantine cities along his frontier.[38] At the beginning of the fifteenth century Scotland harboured a supposed Richard II of England and at the end of the century a supposed Richard IV (Perkin Warbeck).[39] The former was a continuing challenge to the regime of the usurper Henry IV and the imposter did not in fact die until 1419, while the latter presented similar difficulties for the usurper Henry VII. This Richard IV was treated royally and used as a figurehead for Scottish incursions into England. In both instances there were links and contacts between the pretenders in Scotland and opponents of the government within England. In 1417, during his trial after the defeat of his rising against Henry V, Sir John Oldcastle refused to recognize the authority of the court since, he said, his liege lord, King Richard, was still alive in Scotland.[40]

A returner or pretender was in many ways a good tool for dissidents and rebels, since he simultaneously fitted the requirements of a dynastic system, that is, his claim was framed in genetic terms, and yet he was actually an absolute outsider, free of ties and obligations to any particular aristocratic faction or interest. In one sense, he was like a foreign queen, chosen to avoid the awkwardness of selecting a bride from any group among the indigenous nobility, but he also asserted that he was native, natural and had claims of blood. The pretender cannot in actual fact be a member of any aristocratic family for they are already known; hence the pretender has to be a 'nobody'. The advantages of this for the aristocratic rebels who patronized the pretender included control of their nominal leader and the possibility of forming alliances of various aristocratic factions, since the pretender is not in fact a representative of a specific family. He appears as a new player in the game, even though his claims are ancestral. Although there are some cases where the returning kings were associated with revolutionary upheaval, apocalypticism and prophecy, most of these returners were not of this type. They were dynastic pretenders and claimed their right as such: they presented themselves as lords denied their hereditary right. What they were demanding was exactly what the existing emperors, kings or lords had, namely a preeminent place in the social hierarchy justified by rights of blood.

In many cases, the evidence exists to identify the aristocratic and other oppositional groups who stood behind the pretender. In 675 a short-lived puppet king, Clovis, supposedly a Merovingian prince, was put forward by Ebroin, the mayor of the palace, in his attempt at a political come back after defeat by rivals. The Life of St Leger, who was one of his opponents, gives some details of the partisans of this 'Clovis, whom they had falsely made king'.[41] Likewise, the names of the Flemish nobles who gave their support to the false Baldwin are recorded, and in many cases we can deduce the grounds for their opposition to the rule of Countess Joan, daughter of the real Baldwin. In the case of the false Frederick II of 1261, the sources name a group of Sicilian dissidents, and in 1284 the support for the next false Frederick was associated particularly with the Rhineland towns hostile to the king, Rudolf of Habsburg. For some time Woldemar of Brandenburg had the backing, not of dissidents, but of the Holy Roman Emperor himself, Charles IV, an emperor who had only recently established his power against rivals, rivals who were the most determined opponents of the pretender.

The role of dissident aristocratic factions in the manufacture of pretenders is revealed particularly clearly in those cases where pretenders had to be argued into their role by their supposed partisans. Perkin Warbeck in his confession after capture gave a particularly detailed account of such pressure, which began when he arrived in Cork in Ireland in late 1491:

> They of the town, because I was arrayed with some cloths of silk of my said master's, came unto me and threaped (asserted) upon me that I should be the duke of Clarence's son that was before time at Dublin, and, for as much as I denied it, there was brought unto me the Holy Evangelist (the Gospels) and the cross by the mayor of the town, which was called John Lewellen, and there in the presence of him and others I took mine oath as the truth was that I was not the foresaid duke's son neither of none of his blood. And after this came unto me an Englishman whose name was Stephen Poytron, with one John Atwater, and said to me, in swearing great oaths, that they knew well I was King Richard's bastard son, to whom I answered with like oaths that I was not, and then they advised me not to be afeared but that I should take it upon me boldly and if I would do so they would aid and

assist me with all their power against the king of England, and not only they . . . and so against my will made me learn English and taught me what I should do and say, and after this they called me duke of York, the second son of King Edward IV, because King Richard's bastard son was in the hands of the king of England.[42]

The Yorkist plotters here are extremely persistent. First they insist that Warbeck is the duke of Clarence's son, that is, Edward, Earl of Warwick, the last surviving legitimate male of the house of York. He 'was before time at Dublin', as Warbeck's confession mentions, in 1487, when the pretender Lambert Simnel had claimed to be the earl and had been crowned in Dublin as Edward VI. Finding Warbeck obstinate on this point, they suggest that he is actually the illegitimate son of Richard III (Clarence's brother), John of Gloucester or Pontefract. Faced with the awkward problem that John was a captive of Henry Tudor, they finally decide that he is the younger of the missing Princes in the Tower, Richard, son of Edward IV. In a brisk sequence they have thus worked their way through the sons of all three of the Yorkist brothers, Clarence, Richard III and Edward IV. Warbeck stresses his initial obduracy and says he eventually collaborated 'against my will'. Well, he would wouldn't he? This is from a confession, although one that did not, in the end, save his neck.

But he is not the only pretender to paint such a picture. The pseudo-Baldwin of Flanders also had to be persuaded into his role. He was originally encountered early in 1224 as a pious hermit in the forests near Tournai, at a time when rumours of Baldwin's return were already circulating, and more and more people began to say he was Count Baldwin returned from captivity: 'Everywhere he was called "Count" by all, but he did not wish to reply anything to that, except that he was called "Christian".'[43] He compared those who said he was the count to the Bretons who awaited the return of King Arthur. They were not discouraged: 'But the more he denied it, each of them said, "You are the count."'[44] Eventually he gave way to this persistent pressure, was escorted in triumph to Valenciennes, where he was washed, shaved and dressed like a count ('*comme conte*').

It was important for the opponents of returning pretenders to deny their claims as vigorously as possible, and one way of doing this was to demonstrate that the ruler in question really had died. When the false

Maid of Norway turned up in 1300, those who disbelieved her claims made much of the evidence for the burial of the real Maid ten years earlier: her body had been brought back from Orkney, where she had died, to Bergen, where her father, King Erik, had opened her coffin and looked on her face, before burying her alongside her mother.[45] It might be thought that producing the body itself would clinch the case, but it did not always do so. When the deposed King Richard II was buried by the new regime in March 1400, his body was transported 200 miles to London before interment, and there 'he was above ground for two days, to show him to the people of London so that they would believe for certain that he was dead'.[46] The king's face was left uncovered so that 'men might see and know his person from all other'.[47] But seventeen years later, as we have seen, there were still those who were unconvinced.

Another way of undermining the pretender was to prove his genuine identity, especially if this could be done by asserting an alternative and humiliating identity. When the Merovingian king Guntram was facing the challenge of a man claiming to be the son of Guntram's father Clothar I, and hence his own half-brother, he refused even to refer to the pretender by the noble name he used, Gundovald, and, in an angry speech, spoke of 'this stranger, whose father ran a mill, and, to tell the truth, whose father was a wool-carder'.[48] It appears that he was so irate that he could not even settle on an abusive enough choice of paternal occupation. Later the same pretender was mocked by his enemies, who shouted at him, 'aren't you the painter who, in the time of King Clothar, used to go around the churches decorating the walls and arches?'[49] At the other end of the Middle Ages, this demeaning and patronizing rhetoric was also the response of Henry VII, the first Tudor king, when he faced the challenge of Perkin Warbeck, who, as we have seen, claimed to be Richard, duke of York, the younger of the Princes in the Tower. Henry referred to the young pretender as 'the childe', 'the garçon' or 'the feigned lad'.[50] Warbeck's real origins, in the city of Tournai, might also be mentioned. When the earl of Kildare wrote defending himself against charges of having supported the pretender, he denied having given any help to 'the French lad'.[51] And hostile chroniclers always attribute lowly origins to pretenders: as already mentioned, the false Michael VII was supposedly a lower-rank butler; Anna Comnena stresses the lowly origins of the false son of Romanos Diogenes; according to one source the pseudo-Alfonso the Battler was a smith, while the false Conradin was the son of a smith, the false Frederick of 1284 a peasant, Woldemar a peasant or a miller, and Lambert Simnel the son of an organ-maker.[52]

Opponents of the pretenders sometimes also drew on the terms that Christians had long used to decry pagan idolatry. The chronicler Saba Malaspina calls the false Frederick II of 1261 a '*simulachrum*' and an 'idol (*ydolum*)': disaffected exiles 'flocked to the *simulachrum*'; royal forces were sent 'to repress that idol and his worshippers'.[53] *Simulachrum* means image or semblance, and was often, like idol, used to describe effigies of the pagan gods. In a similar way, Thomas Warde of Trumpington, the false Richard II, was called by his opponents, not only a fool and a fake, but also an idol (*ydolum*) and 'mawmet'.[54] This last word, which derives from the name of the prophet Muhammad, also meant 'pagan idol'.[55] So the term usefully conveyed both the idea that reverence was being paid to a false object and the judgment that a bone-headed stupidity was involved – Christians from the time of the martyrs had stressed the foolishness of worshipping lifeless images of wood and stone. It was also possible to tar the pretender with the brush of heresy. This was a charge raised against the false Frederick of 1284, which is perhaps why he was burned rather than executed in some other way. And when, in 1406, the English Parliament condemned the heretical Lollards, they included a denunciation of the 'evil people (*mauveys hommes et femmes*)' who spread the rumour that Richard II was still alive.[56]

Recognition

Pretenders and their supporters and the existing rulers and their supporters engaged in political and military competition of the usual kind, the kind familiar between opponents when there was no question of a pretender, but, because of the special nature of the pretender's case, they were also involved in a conflict about questions of identity. Since the disputing sides were arguing about who someone was, one thing that these pretenders and returners illuminate is how identity was recognized, established and tested.

Pretenders were clad in royal or imperial robes, crowned, had seals, all the trappings of sovereignty. But while these things might be persuasive, for, as Polonius points out in *Hamlet*, 'the apparel oft proclaims the man', there was also the body beneath the clothes, and the kind of truth it carried. Modern states have often required information about such things as eye and hair colour, or height, to be specified in identity cards or passports, obviously as means of checking identity. British passports issued before 1988 had a space for entering height and for 'distinguishing marks'. Such distinguishing marks also excited attention in the stories of several of these returning rulers. For example, it was reported that the Pseudo-Baldwin 'had the same scars on his body that Baldwin had had'.[57] Wladyslaw III of Poland, the king who supposedly survived the Battle of Varna in 1444, was recognized living as a hermit in Spain twenty years later by the fact that his feet had six toes.[58] By a remarkable coincidence, the corpse of Henry II, duke of Silesia, who was killed in battle against the Mongols in 1241, had also been recognized by the six toes on his left foot.[59]

An especially elaborate case concerns the Holy Roman Emperor Henry V. There was a rumour that Henry had not died in 1125 but had gone as a penitent into exile, leaving a substitute body to be buried in his stead. According to one variant of the story, a figure very similar to the emperor had been received at the abbey of Cluny. One day a German visitor who had known the monarch came to the abbey and was asked by the abbot to see if he could identify the man he had taken into his abbey. The German immediately asserted that he was an imposter, not the emperor. The supposed emperor, however, was unruffled. He gave the visitor a slap and said to him:

> It is true you have been with me, but you were always a traitor, and when you were caught in one of your treacheries, although you escaped, one of my followers pierced your right foot with a spear, and the wound or scar will still be apparent. Servants, seize this trickster and you will see!

The scar was indeed found, but the visitor was not finished. 'My lord', he said, 'who this man is pretending to be, had a right arm so long that he could completely cover his right knee with it when standing upright.' The supposed emperor immediately did this without trouble. For a while, comments our source, he was treated with reverence but was eventually discovered to be an impostor.[60]

In this curious scene, the two protagonists engage in a kind of duel. Their weapons are distinguishing marks of a physical kind, either innate (a long arm) or acquired (a scar). The emperor claims to identify the German visitor by knowing that he has a scar on his foot, a place that would not be immediately visible. The visitor counter-attacks by appeal to a distinctive feature of the real emperor. It is clear from the story that the supposed emperor is at first sitting, since he has to rise to demonstrate that his arm is indeed long enough to cover his knee. He seems to be vindicated, both by knowing of the other's scar and by his own physiognomy. Unfortunately, we are not told how he was eventually unmasked.

Scars are witnesses, since they are traces of an event in life; they may be ineradicable; they can be seen and touched. Hence, from the time of doubting Thomas to that of modern detective fiction, they have been invoked as proof of identity. But there are other features, other 'distinguishing marks', that identify a person. One such emerges in the case of the man claiming to be the son of the Byzantine emperor Romanos Diogenes, who had found support among the nomadic Cumans. Anna Comnena says that during his campaign, when the Cumans were besieging Adrianople, the Byzantine general Nicephorus Bryennios, who had known Romanos' son, spoke with the pretender from the ramparts. 'Judging from the man's voice,' he concluded, 'he would not acknowledge him to be Romanos Diogenes' son.'[61] A century later, the pretender claiming to be the emperor Alexius II was more careful, imitating the young ruler's stammer (ψελλισμός), as well as matching his hair colour.[62]

In his discussion of the Merovingian pretender Gundovald, Marc Widdowson mentions the parallels with the famous case of Martin Guerre, a case that its most well-known narrator, Natalie Zemon Davis, says caused her 'to reflect upon the significance of identity in the sixteenth century'.[63] Widdowson remarks that the similarities between these cases is partly because in both sixth-century Gaul and sixteenth-century France there was a 'lack of basic technologies for establishing persistence of identity, like photography'. Likewise, in a pioneering article on imposture, Henri Platelle linked 'the problem of the identity of persons' with the 'technical deficiences' of the Middle Ages.[64] One cannot doubt that finger printing and DNA analysis have provided tools for establishing identity that the medieval world could not dream of, but what of the simpler issue of the ability to produce a likeness?

Standard histories of art assert or assume that realistic portraiture cannot be found in the Middle Ages prior to the late fourteenth or early fifteenth centuries. This may be debated, but, whether or not realistic portraits were painted before 1400, it is clear that some people thought that they could be. The historian William of Malmesbury, for example, explained that St Anselm could not take the direct route from Rome to Lyons in 1099 since his enemy, the anti-pope Guibert, had circulated his picture: 'it was said that Guibert had sent a painter to Rome to have his image painted on a panel, so that, in whatever costume he disguised himself, he could still not hide'.[65]

When the Muslim traveller Ibn Battuta came to China in 1345 he was struck by the Chinese 'mastery of painting' and noted with interest that 'if I visited one of their cities, and then came back to it, I always saw portraits of me and my companions painted on the walls and on paper in the bazaars ... the resemblance was correct in all respects'. This was done at the command of the government. 'It is their custom', Ibn Battuta says,

> to paint everyone who comes among them. They go so far in this that if a foreigner does something that obliges him to flee from them, they circulate his portrait throughout the country and a search is made for him. When someone resembling the portrait is found, he is arrested.[66]

Perhaps William of Malmesbury and Ibn Battuta were deluded, but there is no doubt they both thought that the wanted poster was part of medieval experience. Moreover, the portraits of prospective brides that were commissioned as part of marriage negotiations (see above, p. 34) suggest a belief in naturalistic portraiture.

Whether or not we believe that realistic portraiture of this kind was possible in the Middle Ages, it is certainly true that we are in an age before the mass production of likenesses. The vast majority of people would never have seen their ruler. But physical likeness was not the only criterion. In the absence of scars or extra toes, there were other ways to test the pretender's identity. One way was through probing what he knew. Those arguing for the genuineness of the pretender often pointed to the knowledge he had, private or secret, that supported his claimed identity. This issue of secret knowledge turns up in the account of the pseudo-Alfonso the Battler in the thirteenth-century chronicle by Rodrigo Jiménez de Rada. When, years after Alfonso's supposed death, a figure appeared claiming to be the king,

> The testimony of many people of Castile and Aragon asserted that it was he, people who had had familiar contact with him in those two kingdoms, and who recalled many secrets, which he remembered he had long ago shared with them.[67]

In a similar vein, the false Frederick in Sicily in 1261 not only 'seemed like the emperor in everything' but also 'had a very good knowledge of many of the circumstances of the kingdom and the empire and the royal court'.[68] In the case of both pseudo-Baldwin and the false Woldemar, chroniclers assert that the pretenders established their credentials by *intersigna*, a word meaning tokens, credentials or signs known only to the parties involved.[69] These two cases are far apart in time and space and it is striking that this same term should crop up.

But pretenders could also be caught out, revealed by gaps in their knowledge. The supposed Baldwin of Flanders was flummoxed when confronted by his sovereign, Louis VIII of France, who asked him where he had been married, where he had been knighted and where he had performed homage to Louis' father, King Philip. Giving no answers to these questions, the pretender found his support dissolving.[70] He was eventually captured by the countess of Flanders, daughter of the real Baldwin, and hanged. One feels that his adherents should have briefed him more fully.

As already pointed out, a history of pretenders is, almost by definition, a history of failed pretenders. Many of the returning rulers discussed here were eventually captured and killed by their enemies. A violent end befell the Merovingian pretender Gundovald, the earliest such figure in the Middle Ages, and the Plantagenet pretender Perkin Warbeck, the last. Several pretenders were hanged, receiving the punishment of commoners, to rub home the point.[71] This is what happened to those claiming to be Alfonso the Battler, Baldwin of Flanders, and Richard IV of England, i.e. Perkin Warbeck. Some, like the pseudo-Frederick II of 1284–5, Margaret the Maid of Norway, and a man claiming to be King Olaf of Denmark in

1402, were burned to death.[72] Others died obscure deaths. But, alongside this record of defeat, it is worth pointing out the remarkable success of some pretenders. In 1094 the false son of Romanos Diogenes led an army of invasion against the Byzantine empire. In 1225 the false Baldwin took control of much of Flanders and received some international recognition, including a letter from the government of Henry III of England expressing delight at his return and a wish that he might renew old alliances against the king of France.[73] The false Frederick II of 1261 and his successor of 1284–5 both presented real political threats to the established powers of Sicily and the Empire respectively and required armies to put them down. In 1487 Lambert Simnel was crowned king of England in Dublin as Edward VI and headed an invasion force that fought a major battle in the heart of England, while Perkin Warbeck, as Richard Plantagenet, was welcomed in Vienna, Antwerp and Edinburgh, and given a noble Scottish wife.

And even in the case of those who came to a violent end, there were voices that continued to maintain the genuineness of the pretenders even after they were swinging from the gallows or smouldering in ashes. The troubadour Bertran de Born found it useful to believe that the pseudo-Alfonso the Battler was the real thing, since it gave him a weapon against his enemy, the contemporary ruler of Aragon, also Alfonso. The poet accused this later Alfonso of having 'hanged his predecessor'.[74] Likewise, the countess of Flanders, daughter of Count Baldwin, was accused by many of 'parricide' for executing the pretender of 1225.[75]

Perhaps the most remarkable fortune was that of the false Woldemar of Brandenburg, who was accepted as the genuine margrave by the Holy Roman Emperor, received many of the ancestral lands and, although eventually dispossessed, died a natural death in 1356 and was buried in the Saxon town of Dessau honourably, 'as the margrave (*sicut marchio*)'.[76] Dessau was the chief centre of another branch of the family to which the margraves belonged. But, of course, as with all these pretenders, the last note has to be doubt. Looking back on the incident of the pseudo-Baldwin decades later, a German chronicler remarked, 'The Flemings dispute whether he was count Baldwin or not, and the case is still *sub judice*.'[77] And, as a contemporary of the false Woldemar commented, 'the story of this Woldemar was truly amazing and there are various opinions about him to this day'.[78]

CHAPTER 12

New Families and New Kingdoms

A TENTH-CENTURY JUDGE IN IRAN RECORDED A DISPUTE between two Arabs about which of them had the better pedigree; the clinching line was apparently 'My family line (*nasab*) begins with me; yours ends with you.'[1] It was better to be the vigorous founder of a dynasty than the effete twilight heir of one. New men could come in, new dynasties be founded. Since, as both Darwinians and creationists agree, humankind is of common descent, there are no 'new' families in a literal biological sense. But dynasties are not simple biological units. They are structures of power, self-identifying groups of relatives seeking to extend their dominance through time, and they have their history, their rise and fall.

This same tenth-century judge who recorded the anecdote about the two Arabs also told the story of a king who had seized power by force. Once he had established himself and won a high reputation for governing well, he summoned an assembly of wise men and asked them to tell him frankly if there were any faults or defects in his government, promising not to harm them whatever they said. They could only find fault with one thing, that this new ruler was not of royal blood.

> What, he asked, was the case with the king who preceded me? He was a king's son, they replied. And with his father? They said the same. He repeated the question till he had enumerated ten ancestors or more, receiving in each case the same answer, till he got to the last, of whom they said he was a conqueror. I then, am that last, and if my days be good, the sovereignty will remain with my children after me, and their descendants will have royal blood as good as that which my predecessor had.[2]

The point is quite clear. Ancient royalty is simply conquest that has endured.

This undeferential conception of kingship can also be found in the medieval west, sometimes expressed with pungency, as in the words of Gregory VII, the radical pope of the eleventh century:

> Who does not know that kings and dukes had their origin in men who disregarded God and, with blind desire and intolerable presumption, strove to dominate their equals, that is, other men, through pride, plunder, perfidy, homicides and every kind of crime, under the inspiration of the lord of this world, the devil?[3]

Not all new men were quite as dramatically bad as that, but they usually required force, and often perfidy, to remove established rulers and implant their own dynasty. Then, of course, if they endured, they would be ancient royalty.

Early Germanic kings were members of families that claimed divine descent, like the Amal dynasty of the Ostrogoths or the Anglo-Saxon kings who traced their ancestry back to Woden, but when these divine dynasties died out, they were replaced by families whose earthly origins were no secret. The most well known and most successful usurpers of the medieval period were the Carolingians and Capetians but other important royal dynasties came to power by military might and the displacement of predecessors, like the Normans in England and the Angevins in Sicily, both of these with papal approval. In contrast, there were no significant new dynasties in Ireland because the pool of potential kings in the dynasty was always so large. Hence the Irish dynasties of the earlier Middle Ages endured, in many cases down to the seventeenth century.

Not all new dynasties were established by usurpation. The Ottonians, who ruled Germany from 919, and subsequently attained Italy and revived the imperial title, before dying out in the male line in 1024, came to the throne by election when the succession was an open question, although they sometimes had to fight to get everyone to acknowledge their sovereignty. When, in 919, Henry, duke of Saxony, was elected king of Germany, his descent was well known, as a member of a prominent aristocratic family, and he had a chance to found a new ruling dynasty, which he did. In 1066 the same situation arose in

England, when Harold, one of the wealthiest earls, became king on the death of Edward the Confessor without children, but Harold, unlike Henry, was not able to found a new dynasty since he had the bad luck to face competition from Duke William and his Normans, a ruthless and successful war-leader with a determined and equally ruthless army behind him. The situations in Germany in 919 and England in 1066 were otherwise similar, with leading aristocrats taking the throne when the succession was unclear. It was the whirl of events that determined that Henry's Saxon dynasty would last 105 years and Harold's 280 days.

There are occasions when contemporaries were aware of the inception of a new dynasty. When Romanos III succeeded Constantine VIII on the Byzantine throne in 1028, the chronicler Michael Psellos reports that the new ruler supposedly believed that 'his reign was the beginning of a new period', since 'the imperial dynasty (βασίλειον γένος)' that descended from Basil the Macedonian had ended with Constantine. Romanos looked forward to 'a future line (γενεά)'.[4] In fact he died childless after six years, but Psellos' terminology shows that there is no anachronism in our speaking of a Macedonian dynasty, since that is how Romanos III himself pictured his predecessors.

Foundation Legends and Founding Figures

Some dynasties had their own foundation legends and founding figures. This is true of the Piasts of Poland and Premyslids of Bohemia (both of these dynastic designations are modern), in each case involving descent from a ploughman. The stories of these Polish and Bohemian founders were written down at almost exactly the same time, around 1120, and they place the founding figures many generations in the past, nine and fifteen respectively. In the Polish story, two mysterious and possibly angelic figures are turned away from the ruling duke's banquet but are given hospitality by a poor ploughman who lives outside the fortress. They ensure that the food and drink does not run out and they perform the symbolic rite of giving the first haircut to the ploughman's son, Siemowit. Siemowit grows up, increasing in strength and virtue 'until the King of Kings and Duke of Dukes ordained him duke of Poland with common assent'.[5] The Bohemian story is rather stranger. It is set in a time when

Bohemia was ruled by a prophetess, Libuše. The Bohemians, however, express a desire to have a duke. Libuše describes to them what they are asking for, the freedom they are surrendering, the servitude they seem voluntarily to be imposing on themselves: 'it is easy to appoint a duke but difficult to remove him once appointed'.[6] Nevertheless, she agrees to accept their decision and says she will reveal to them their new duke, who will also become her husband. She tells them where they will find the ploughman Premysl working and prophesizes that his descendants will rule the land for ever. He is fetched and marries Libuše. His humble cork shoes are preserved in the ducal chapel as a reminder to the Premyslids from whence they came. Both these legends trace the ruling dynasty well beyond any historically attested period into a misty past and give it some kind of validation, through supernatural or prophetic endorsement. The choice of a new ruler from among the rural labouring class might also have an echo of David being taken from his shepherding duties to become king of Israel.

Where an account of a dynasty chooses to start is a highly charged issue. In 1180 Adam of Dryburgh, a Premonstratensian canon from the abbey of Dryburgh in the Scottish borders, composed a work entitled *The Triple Tabernacle*. It is a work of elaborate symbolism, taking as its starting point the tabernacle of the Old Testament, that is, the sacred tent containing the Ark of the Covenant, which was the centre of the Israelite cult before the building of the Temple. Adam encourages his readers to picture the tabernacle in their mind's eye and he also furnishes it, in his imagination, with a series of pictures: '*depingo*', 'I paint', is the verb he uses of this word-painting. What is of relevance to dynastic history is the series of images of rulers that Adam summons up for his readers. Converting his imagined tabernacle into a kind of portrait gallery, Adam first depicts the Roman emperors. He starts with Constantine, then continues with images of the other Christian emperors, omitting Julian the Apostate, down to Constantine VI and Irene, who were reigning in Byzantium at the end of the eighth century when Charlemagne was crowned emperor in the west. He then backtracks to Clovis, first Christian king of the Franks, and continues to evoke images of the kings of the French down to his own time. Next, he deals with the kings of the English, starting from Alfred (871–99) and coming down to Henry the Young King, the son of Henry II crowned in 1170, whom Adam styles 'Henry III'. After that he moves on to the kings of Scots, starting with Malcolm Canmore in the later eleventh century. After a long account of the English and Scots kings, mostly borrowed from an earlier writer, Aelred of Rievaulx, he gives a list of the names of all the rulers who should be depicted in this house of the mind – the emperors from Constantine to Frederick Barbarossa, the kings of the French, the English and the Scots – and adds the concession that people in other regions reading his work could replace the kings of the English and the Scots with pictures of their own rulers.[7]

Three things could be pointed out about Adam's selection of ruler-images. First, he thinks that conversion marks a new start in history. He knows Constantine was not the first Roman emperor, nor Clovis the first king of the Franks, but his imaginary tabernacle starts the history of the empire and the history of the Franks with their conversions. Second, he chooses certain rulers as founding fathers, even if they are not the first of their dynasty. Alfred was not the first king of his line, nor Malcolm Canmore of his, but they are chosen to mark the point where the author sees that a continuous regnal tradition begins. Adam had precedents in conceptualizing English history in this way, since from at least the 1120s chronicles wrote of Alfred as 'the first of all kings to obtain the sole monarchy of the whole of England'.[8] And subsequent historians down to the present day have often chosen to start the history of England with Alfred and that of Scotland with Malcolm Canmore. Third, for this Anglo-Scottish writer, the emperors and the kings of the French were the essential core of the Christian community, to which lesser national traditions might be added as circumstance suggested: you could drop the kings of the English and the Scots if you lived elsewhere, but not the emperors or the kings of the French. Adam thus has strong views both on where dynastic histories should begin and on what is central and what peripheral.

Tellingly, when Adam writes about Edgar, the tenth-century king of England, whom he regards as 'shining like the morning star and like a full moon in his days', he adds 'he is no less memorable to the English than Cyrus is to the Persians, Charles (Charlemagne) to the French or Romulus to the Romans'.[9] This concept, that every people had its ancient hero-king, and this very phrasing, have a very long history and underwent noteworthy variations. The Melrose Chronicle, for example, expanded in a similar vein: 'Edgar, the peaceable king, was no less memorable to the English than Romulus to the Romans, Cyrus to the Persians, Alexander to the Macedonians, Charles the Great to the French, Arthur to the Britons.'[10] The phrase can be traced back to the ancient historian Justinus, who used it of the Parthian ruler Arsaces: 'Arsaces, who acquired and established the kingdom securely, is no less memorable to the Parthians than Cyrus to the Persians or Romulus to the Romans or Alexander to the Macedonians.'[11] Where we start a story partly determines what kind of story we tell, and these heroic figures represent one way of starting it. Medieval dynasties were eager to associate themselves with them, whatever the historical realities. Perhaps the most remarkable case is the adoption of Arthur, hero of the Britons and Welsh, by the Plantagenet kings of England, who had no connection with the ancient king at all, but embraced him as a central figure of court ceremony and court literature in the late Middle Ages. Edward I visited the supposed tomb of Arthur and Guinevere at Glastonbury and had his own Round Table made, which is still visible in Winchester Castle.[12]

Healing the Dynastic Rent

If kings, and the authors who wrote about them, might picture a founding figure at the head of the stream in which they swam, they might also be aware of uncomfortable gaps and breaks in transmission. The first Capetians knew that they did not descend in a direct male line from the Carolingians, the Norman kings claimed to be the lawful successors of Edward the Confessor but could not trace descent from that childless monarch. One way this rent in dynastic continuity could be healed was by the blood of a former dynasty being united with the current one through marriage. Such cases occur on more than occasion. A well studied example is the so-called *reditus regni ad stirpem Karoli Magni*, the 'return of the kingdom to the stock of Charlemagne', when the marriage of Philip Augustus brought Carolingian blood into the Capetian family (see above, p. 350). The *reditus* is illustrated in a fifteenth-century French history, which shows Charlemagne embracing Louis IX.[13] It was also the case that Philip already had Carolingian blood and this was pointed out by no less a figure than Pope Innocent III in a letter to the bishops of France, which mentions in passing Philip's Carolingian ancestry. Since this letter was incorporated into the Decretals of 1234, the standard canon law collection of the later Middle Ages, it is a claim that would be widely known, and was cited from this source ('as we read in the canons').[14] Other monarchs took pride in Carolingian ancestry. When the first German ruler of the Salian line, Conrad II, became king in 1024, contemporaries remarked upon the fact that his wife, Gisela, was of Carolingian descent.[15] This obviously meant that when the son of Conrad and Gisela, Henry III, succeeded in 1039, he too was of Carolingian descent. The great German chronicler Otto of Freising, writing a century later, made a point of this in his *History*: 'In him the imperial dignity, which for a long time past had been exiled from the seed of Charles, was brought back to the noble and ancient shoot of Charles.'[16] So it was worth claiming to be of the stock or seed of Charles. But the stock or seed of Charles was itself in need of tying to earlier rulers, and this had been done early, in the time of Charlemagne himself, by the creation of a fictitious 'Blithildis', a Merovingian princess who had married the ancestor of the Carolingians.[17] She is described as the daughter of King Clothar but later writers vacillate about which Clothar this was: Clothar I (d. 561) or Clothar II (d. 629). In the long run it did not matter, for she fulfilled her function either way, for 'the royal lineage was repaired in this way through the female line'.[18]

The marriage of Henry I of England, son of William the Conqueror, and Edith (renamed Matilda), a descendant of the old Wessex line, in 1100 united the blood of conqueror and conquered. The Anglo-Saxon Chronicle stresses her descent, calling her 'Matilda, daughter of King Malcolm of Scotland and the good queen Margaret, kinswoman of King Edward and of the right royal lineage of England'.[19] The prophecy of the green tree, already in circulation (see above, pp. 356–7), describing a seemingly impossible event, the reunion of a severed tree to its stump, was reinterpreted and applied to this mingling of the blood of the old and the new dynasty. When Henry II, grandson of Henry I and Matilda, became king in 1154, it was a cause for celebration of the union of the two seeds. This view became a standard feature of later English chroniclers, including those writing in the vernacular: 'Then this tree first struck again to its kind [or stock] once more.'[20]

A way of indicating a bond between one's own dynasty and the one that had preceded it was by adopting the names of that earlier family. The Carolingians and the Merovingians had quite distinct naming patterns up to the time of the dispossession of the latter by the former in 751. In that year Pippin (who had a distinctively Carolingian name) dethroned Childeric III (who had a distinctively Merovingian name). But, a generation later, Pippin's son Charlemagne gave his newly born twin boys the Merovingian names Chlodwig (Ludwig) and Clothar (Lothar). He was supposedly inspired 'by love of the kings of ancient times' in choosing these names.[21] Lothar soon died but his brother grew up to be known to historians as Louis the Pious. It is only the conventions of modern spelling that hide the fact that all the many kings called Louis and Ludwig look back to the Merovingians and to the founder of the Frankish empire, the first Chlodwig, known in French and English as Clovis.

When Henry III of England called his firstborn son 'Edward' in 1239, he did so out of respect for Edward the Confessor, who was both a saint and the last king of the house of Wessex (see p. 298). The old royal name thus came back, indeed going on to be the most common name of an English (subsequently British) king. The sumptuous shrine of Edward the Confessor in Westminster Abbey, coronation church of the kings of England, symbolized a view of English royalty in which the Anglo-Saxon kings played a full part. But this stress on continuity was not the only view and it sometimes had to be defended. When, under Edward III, as we call him, the kings of England adopted the practice of numbering themselves from the Norman Conquest (see pp. 305–6), critical voices were raised:

> This Edward had himself called Edward 'the third after the Conquest', that is to say after William the Bastard, in his letters and charters, and in the opinion of several people this was not at all to his or his ancestors' honour, since conquest by force never gives right; but it would be more fitting if he had had a right going back to before the Conquest, for otherwise he and all his successors would have been possessors in bad faith and intruders.[22]

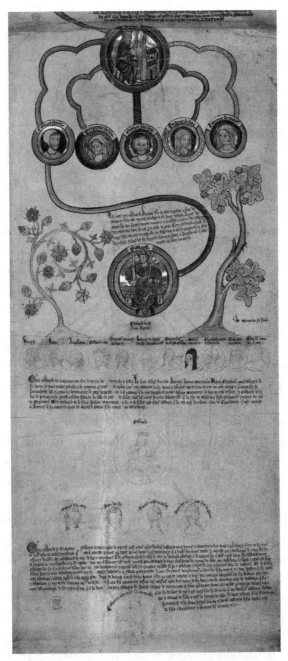

Figure 22 An English royal genealogical roll to which, around 1340, an addition has been made criticizing Edward III's adoption of the style 'third since the conquest'. BL, MS Royal 14 B VI, © The British Library.

The marriage of Henry I and Matilda and the adoption of the name and the cult of Edward the Confessor by Henry III represented two ways of establishing dynastic continuity, but the addition of a number 'since the conquest' to the royal style disregarded it completely. Seizing the throne by force was rarely celebrated in so many words. The successful contender would usually produce a justification, and the ousted dynasties might not go quietly.

Excluded Dynasts

The Capetian accession of 987 in France and the Norman Conquest of England in 1066 both took place when there were living members of the previous dynasty, Charles of Lorraine and Edgar Atheling, both of whom were actually acknowledged as king in the crisis year by sections of the ruling class. In both cases, force determined the issue. These representatives of the old dynasty, Charles and Edgar, had to work out a way of dealing with the new dispensation.

Charles of Lorraine was a younger son of Louis IV ('d'Outremer'), king of France. He was born in 953, one of twins. His twin brother died after a short while, but the baby Charles, who possessed 'natural strength and power', survived.[23] On his father's death the following year, Charles' older brother Lothar became king at the age of thirteen. In order to secure his accession, his mother, Queen Gerberga, needed the support of the most powerful noble in the kingdom, Hugh 'the Great'. Hugh's uncle and father had both been kings of the West Franks, in opposition to Louis IV's father, and he himself was of Carolingian descent on his mother's side. The price for his support was high. As a contemporary chronicler put it, 'the boy Lothar, the son of Louis, was consecrated king at St.-Remi, with the support of duke Hugh, archbishop Bruno, and the other bishops and chief men of France, Burgundy and Aquitaine. Burgundy and Aquitaine were given by him to Hugh.'[24]

The archbishop Bruno mentioned here was Gerberga's brother, the archbishop of Cologne, and her other brother was Otto I, king of the East Franks. In the mid-tenth century it was not clear that 'France' and 'Germany' were two distinct and permanently separated kingdoms, and, after the death of Hugh the Great in 956, Archbishop Bruno played an important part in running young Lothar's kingdom. For example, he probably arranged the king's marriage to Emma, stepdaughter of Otto I, at a great meeting in his episcopal city in 965, a meeting attended by Gerberga, King Lothar, his brother Charles, Otto I and other members of the East Frankish royal house.[25] Bruno actually died in France, at Rheims, later in that same year.

Charles grew up serving his brother but without a lordship of his own. In his early twenties, however, he tried to establish himself in Lotharingia (part of the kingdom of the East Franks), where he had family ties: his mother Gerberga had been married to the duke of Lotharingia before marrying Louis IV. He joined an expedition of 976 launched by some exiled Lotharingian nobles which led to a pitched battle at Mons. But it seems to have been around this time that relations between Charles and his brother, King Lothar, became hostile. Charles accused his sister-in-law Emma, Lothar's wife, of adultery with Bishop Adalbero of Laon (see above, p. 228). The charge was apparently deemed baseless and Charles was forced into exile. Charles later complained of 'having been expelled from the kingdom by his brother' and 'considered that he had been expelled by his brother at the instigation of queen Emma'.[26]

This estrangement of the brothers coincided with a new hostility between the kingdom of the West Franks and the kingdom of the East Franks, under its young ruler, Otto II, who was cousin of King Lothar and Charles. In 977 Otto II made Charles duke of Lower Lotharingia, an act explicitly aimed at his brother: 'duke Charles, brother of King Lothar, whom the emperor Otto had placed in charge of Lower Lotharingia under him so that he could resist his brother's actions more forcefully'.[27] In the following years there was open warfare between the two kingdoms, Lothar occupying Charlemagne's old capital of Aachen and Otto ravaging the outskirts of Paris. Peace was concluded in 980 but hostilities later flared up again.

Charles could well have continued in his somewhat anomalous state, brother of the king of the West Franks, great duke in the kingdom of the East Franks, and there are indications that he was reconciled to Lothar, but events in 986–7 changed the situation completely: Lothar died at the age of forty-four, and was succeeded by his son, Louis V, but the new king died in a hunting accident the following year. Instead of Charles, Duke

Hugh, son of Hugh the Great, known as Hugh Capet, was elected and crowned king in the summer of 987 and moved quickly to have his son Robert crowned joint king. Hugh had the support of Adalbero, archbishop of Reims, who supposedly argued that 'a kingdom is not acquired by hereditary right'.[28]

Charles was not willing to accept this situation, although he now had the disadvantage of confronting a crowned and anointed king. The struggle that followed was marked by some dramatic moments of betrayal. The first was Charles' capture of Laon with the assistance of some of the town's inhabitants who were hostile to its bishop. Charles' troops arrived outside the city at nightfall and entered it pretending to be townsmen. Charles' men and their allies within the town then took possession of it, also capturing Bishop Adalbero and Queen Emma, the couple Charles had accused of adultery a decade earlier. Hugh Capet made more than one attempt to recapture Laon but its hilltop position made attack very hard.

The next piece of treachery concerned Arnulf, illegitimate son of King Lothar and thus Charles' nephew. He was a cleric and he promised to abandon Charles' party and find a way to return Laon to Hugh, if Hugh granted him the archbishopric of Rheims, now vacant. This Hugh agreed to, and Arnulf swore obedience to him. Arnulf lamented the dilemma he confronted: 'On one side, we are impelled by the faith we have promised to the kings of the Franks, on the other, we are driven by the power of Duke Charles, who is determined to recover the kingdom for himself, either to change lords or become an exile.'[29] Arnulf decided the best way to resolve this dilemma was for him to hand over Rheims to Charles but to play-act resistance, 'so that the royal power would be weakened, his uncle's ability to rule would increase but he himself would not appear a deserter'.[30] With Laon and Rheims in his hands, Charles had established himself in the heart of the French royal domains.

The final act of treachery was undertaken by Bishop Adalbero of Laon, who had escaped from captivity in Laon. He contacted Arnulf and promised that he would secure Arnulf's reconciliation with Hugh Capet if he would reciprocate by reconciling him with Charles and obtaining restitution of his bishopric. Arnulf went to Charles, secured his agreement and arranged a meeting with Adalbero where the three of them swore oaths of mutual support. Meanwhile Adalbero kept King Hugh informed and arranged for him to make a show of accepting Arnulf's allegiance. Adalbero now returned to Laon and swore an oath of allegiance to Charles. That night they drank toasts to each other. Later, however, Adalbero removed their weapons from the side of the beds where Charles and Arnulf were sleeping, summoned his own men and seized them. Hugh Capet was informed, came quickly and imprisoned Charles, his wife, his two daughters and one of his sons, along with Arnulf, who was soon deposed from his archbishopric.

This was the end of Charles' attempt to reverse the accession of the Capetians. He had come quite close to success and there were some who called him king. In Catalonia, for example, which was at this time part of the kingdom of France, documents were sometimes dated by Charles' reign, such as a charter of 19 April 990, 'in the third year of the reign of King Charles, brother of Lothar'. Dating of this type continued occasionally until 992, 'the fifth year of the reign of King Charles'.[31] By this time in his ghost-reign Charles may already have died in captivity. Otto, Charles' son, was not captured with him and succeeded him as duke of Lower Lotharingia, dying, without children, in the early years of the eleventh century. Charles stressed his hereditary right to the kingship of the West Franks. As one of his spokesmen put it in 990, 'By what right is the legitimate heir disinherited, by what right is he deprived of the kingdom?'[32] Writing some decades later, an author at Sens summed up the significance of Hugh Capet's coronation: 'Here ended the kingship of Charlemagne.'[33] Charles of Lorraine went down fighting for his dynastic rights.[34]

Edgar Atheling (meaning 'prince') also had to decide whether to submit to a new dynasty or hold out for his birth-right. He had a remarkably varied and unpredictable life. Born in the 1050s, to the exiled son of King Edmund Ironside, and spending his early years in Hungary or Germany, Edgar came to England with his parents and sisters in 1057. Edgar's father died very soon after arrival, but the young Edgar and his family were taken under the protection of the king, his great-uncle, Edward the Confessor. In January 1066, after Edward's death, the teenage Edgar Atheling was passed over for the succession, perhaps because of his youth, and certainly because he lacked a power-base in England in any way comparable with that of Earl Harold Godwinson, who did become king. After Harold's death in October 1066 in battle against the invading army of William, duke of Normandy, Edgar was considered a serious candidate for the throne in opposition to William and had the backing of Archbishop Ealdred of York, but support was insufficient and in December 1066 both Edgar and Ealdred submitted to William.

According to a Norman source, William was good to Edgar: 'he enriched him with wide lands and held him as one of his dearest friends, because he was of the family of King Edward'.[35] William also made sure, however, that on his first visit back to Normandy after his coronation as king of England, he took Edgar with him. Whether he was a hostage or simply a dear friend is not clear. In 1068, however, Edgar and his family fled to Scotland, where they were received by Malcolm III, who married Edgar's sister, Margaret. In 1069–70 Edgar raided northern England in support of the great rebellion against William. In 1074 the king of France offered Edgar a base in France to harry William's Norman lands but this did not work out well, and Edgar eventually submitted to William again and was again well treated. His landholdings in England are listed in the Domesday Book of 1086.[36] In that same year, Edgar led 200 knights on an expedition to Apulia, another Norman conquest state, though what they did there is not known.[37]

After William the Conqueror's death in 1087, Edgar became very close to Robert, William's son and successor as duke of Normandy. He reportedly 'loved the duke, who was his own age, like a foster-brother'.[38] In 1091 William Rufus, who had succeeded his father as king of England, invaded his brother's duchy of Normandy and, when peace was made between them, one of its terms was that Edgar Atheling should be deprived of his Norman lands and expelled from the duchy.[39] Edgar sought refuge with his sister, Queen Margaret, in Scotland, but his exile did not last long. Later in 1091 William Rufus and his brother Robert, now allies, invaded Scotland and, at Robert's suggestion, Edgar was employed to negotiate terms between the kings of England and Scotland. Edgar was then reconciled with William Rufus and returned to Normandy with Robert. He continued to be active on both sides of the English Channel and in the autumn of 1097 he led an army from England into Scotland to depose the incumbent king, Donald, and put his nephew and namesake Edgar on the throne. Edgar Atheling also participated in the crusade, fighting in the Holy Land and returning through Byzantium and Germany.[40] After the death of William Rufus in 1100, Edgar continued his loyalty to Robert of Normandy in his struggles with the youngest brother, Henry I, and was captured fighting for Robert against Henry in the decisive Battle of Tinchebray in 1106, although he was soon released.

Writing in 1125, when Edgar must have been in his seventies, William of Malmesbury strikes an elegiac note: 'after being spun around by the varied sport of fortune, he now wastes away his grey hairs deep in the country, secluded and silent'.[41] Fortune's sport had taken him from central Europe to England to Normandy to Scotland to Italy to the Holy Land to Byzantium, and he had fought against the Normans and for them, his sister had become a queen but he had never become a king. Whenever new men arrived in the dynastic world, it was at the expense of old men. Charles of Lorraine and Edgar Atheling are classic examples, coming to terms with a new regime that denied them something that, in the words of the Anglo-Saxon Chronicle speaking of Edgar, 'was fully his by right of birth'.[42] The dynastic world was a fiercely competitive arena, with winners and losers, and required constant effort even to stay in the same place. Hugh Capet gave his name to the most long-lived dynasty in European history and William the Conqueror earned his nickname; they did so at the expense of ancient dynasties.

New Kingdoms

The most dramatic way a new dynasty could establish itself was by creating a new kingdom. In the year 1000, if one excludes the numerous small kingdoms of the Celtic world, there were eleven kingdoms in Latin Christian Europe.[43] Over the course of the next five hundred years this figure increased, sometimes by fissure, as when Castile split off from Leon, although the two kingdoms were permanently reunited in 1230, sometimes by the simple elevation of a ducal title into a royal one, as in the case of Poland and Bohemia, but also by conquest: Sicily, Jerusalem, Cyprus, Majorca. The kingdoms of Aragon and Portugal were the result of both fissure and conquest, first separating from their parent kingdoms of, respectively, Navarre and Leon, then expanding through warfare.

Fierce and fortunate families could take advantage of this multiplication of kingdoms: the descendants of Tancred de Hauteville, a Norman knight, ruled in magnificence in their royal capital of Palermo; the Lusignan family, named after their castle of Lusignan in Poitou, were kings, and on one occasion, a queen, of Cyprus for 277 years (1197–1474); the royal title of Jerusalem passed through the hands of several French aristocratic dynasties and those of the Hohenstaufen dynasty, before the Lusignans acquired it too.

Some of these new kingdoms were formally constituted by the papacy. In 1179 the pope granted to Alfonso of Portugal 'the kingdom of Portugal and the whole honour and dignity that pertain to kings'.[44] Alfonso had already been calling himself 'king' for forty years, but obviously thought ratification of his title by the papacy worth having. The most remarkable and enduring of these new papal kingships was Sicily. Famously, Metternich insisted that Italy was just a geographical term, that is, not a political one, and for 1,300 years, from the time of the Lombard invasion of 568 to the unification of 1870, the peninsula was indeed split into competing political units. Around the year 1000, the north comprised the kingdom of Italy, previously Lombard, subsequently Carolingian, now under the western (Holy Roman) Emperor, although sometimes disputed by local dynasties; the central region of Italy contained the papal domains, including Rome, and the duchy of Spoleto, which sometimes acknowledged the superiority of the western emperor; the south was divided between several Lombard duchies and principalities and the Byzantine empire, which controlled most of Apulia and Calabria; the island of Sicily was Muslim; important trading cities like Venice, Naples and Amalfi were independent or semi-independent.

In the early eleventh century warriors from northern France, Normans, arrived into this fragmented world, as pilgrims or mercenaries or both. In 1030 they established their first permanent base at Aversa, just north of Naples. The most famous of these northern warriors were the sons of Tancred de Hauteville, from whom the kings of Sicily descended. Tancred, who held a modest estate in the Cotentin peninsula in Normandy, had faced the problem of having twelve sons by sending the older ones out into the world to earn their living by fighting. Two of them, Robert Guiscard, who arrived in Italy around 1046/7, and Roger, who came a decade later, were able to create lordships for themselves in southern Italy. The Normans fought everybody, Lombards, Byzantines and Muslims, slowly establishing their own territories in the region. In 1059 the pope recognized realities and created Robert Guiscard duke of Apulia and Calabria, to be held as a papal fief, and also, with a breathtaking assurance, made him future duke of Sicily. In fact, the conquest of the island of Sicily took thirty years, from 1061 to 1091. Guiscard's brother Roger became count of Sicily. By the end of the eleventh century, the political geography of southern Italy had thus been transformed, with Norman lords ruling most of the region, although not as one united state, and both Byzantine and Muslim sovereignty had been brought to an end.

The unification of the Norman territories took place in the late 1120s. Robert Guiscard's grandson, William, duke of Apulia and Calabria, died childless in 1127. His inheritance was claimed by his cousin, Roger II, count of Sicily, and, after some difficulties, he obtained it. Sicily, Apulia and Calabria were now under one ruler, and in 1130 the Norman Prince of Capua also submitted to him. The next step was to turn this assemblage of conquest territories into a kingdom. On 27 September 1130 Anacletus II (condemned by his opponents as an antipope) granted the royal title to Count Roger of Sicily, and, after Anacletus' death in 1138, Roger ensured that he obtained a confirmation of his new status from the victorious pope, Innocent II.[45] Roger II reigned until his death in 1154, the first king of a state that lasted until 1860. The long-term consequences of the establishment of the new kingdom were religious and cultural as well as political. A region that had been Latin Christian, Greek Christian and Muslim eventually became overwhelmingly Catholic, a world where Greek, Arabic and variants of Romance were spoken eventually became overwhelmingly Italian-speaking. It is a classic example of the conquest states being created on the frontiers of Latin Christendom in this period and the family of Tancred de Hauteville a perfect illustration of how determination and military vigour could create a new ruling dynasty.

The Norman conquerors in southern Italy could advance two justifications for their new kingdom: it had been established, in part, by the conquest and subjugation of non-Christians, and it had been authorized by the pope. Likewise, the campaigns that led to the creation of the kingdom of Jerusalem, as well as the expansionary wars of the Iberian kingdoms, were justified as holy wars, and participants in them received special privileges from the pope. Here the dynastic interests of aggressive families and the aims of the high medieval Church coincided.

CHAPTER 13

Dynasties and the Non-Dynastic World

D YNASTIES WERE THE CHIEF POLITICAL FORM IN MEDIEVAL Europe but not the only one. Other systems, based on other principles, existed, and the dynastic rulers encountered them every day and had to take them into account. These included the Church, the town, the rare but sometimes powerful republics, not to mention the ruler's subjects, who might organize themselves into collective assemblies or imagine they formed a nation, a nation in some way not identical to the ruler's kingdom.

Elective Monarchy

Election, the selection of a candidate to rule, from a potential field, by authorized electors, was not unknown in the Middle Ages, but was rare. The most important examples of explicit and continuous elective constitutions are provided by the papacy and the republic of Venice. In both cases an increasingly clearly defined body of men chose a ruler for life, and hereditary succession was never established, despite the possibility of the Orseoli family becoming hereditary doges of Venice in the early eleventh century. Some popes were relatives of other popes (never sons of course) but no family ever came to dominate for long. The sequence of doges runs from a traditional real starting date of 811 to 1797, the sequence of popes from the first century AD to the present (there is a fuller discussion of the Venetian Republic at pp. 414–16, below).

Some kingdoms were elective, but, even when the principle of elective kingship was asserted, the reality might be different. During the negotiations leading up to the marriage of Erik, king of Denmark, Norway and

Sweden, and Philippa, daughter of Henry IV of England, in 1406, English envoys wrote a report for the English government on the succession practices of the three Scandinavian kingdoms:

> the kingdom of Denmark is transmitted by free election, but nevertheless those there are accustomed always to elect those who are nearest of the royal blood, and if there are several children they are accustomed at all events to elect the one of them who seems to the electors most suitable and capable ... the kingdom of Sweden is transmitted by election and not by succession and yet they are accustomed to elect the nearest of the royal blood or one of the children, just as was said of the kingdom of Denmark, but the kingdom of Norway is transmitted by succession and not by election.[1]

The theoretical distinction between elective Denmark and Sweden and non-elective Norway might therefore produce no real difference in the patterns of dynastic inheritance. Indeed, for three centuries, from the reign of Sven Estrithson (1047–74/6) down to 1375, all Danish kings, bar one, were male-line descendants of Sven.[2]

The most notable example of elective kingship in medieval Europe was the Empire, traditionally known as the Holy Roman Empire. This traces its origins to Christmas day 800, when Charlemagne, king of the Franks and the Lombards, was crowned emperor in Rome. The theory was that this was a continuation of the ancient Roman empire and its pretensions were enormous. Charlemagne's grandson, the emperor Charles the Bald, supposedly saw himself as 'emperor and Augustus of all kings this side of the sea'.[3] The territorial extent of the Empire varied considerably over the centuries, but, from the mid-tenth century, consisted basically of Germany and north Italy.

The elective nature of the Empire was made especially clear in the period after 1254, when the sequence of emperors from the Hohenstaufen dynasty, which had possessed the imperial throne virtually uninterrupted for a century, came to an end. Between 1254 and 1438 the German throne was held or claimed by members of seven different dynasties, and only once in those centuries did the throne pass from father to son. This was in 1376 when the powerful Charles IV secured the election of his son Wenceslas (Wenzel) during his lifetime. Otherwise, the elective nature of the Empire was illustrated vividly by the succession of a member of a different dynasty on the death of each emperor. After 1438 the situation changed and the Habsburgs managed to hold on to the Empire continuously, although keeping up the appearances of election.

The death of German rulers without clear male heirs in 911, 1024, 1125, 1137 and 1254 was, in every case, followed by an election, not by any prearranged succession, and biological chance thus contributed to the survival of elective kingship. The principle was stated unequivocally by Otto of Freising, uncle of the emperor Frederick Barbarossa. If, for Margaret of Burgundy (above, p. 5), royal succession should be determined by 'propagation of blood', Otto thought exactly the opposite: 'this is the crowning glory of the law of the Roman Empire, which it claims for itself as a special privilege, not to descend through propagation of blood but to have kings created by the election of the princes'.[4]

Because it was an established rule that the Holy Roman Emperor could only become emperor after coronation by the pope, and this might be delayed, and sometimes never happen, the election of the German ruler was seen as the first part of a two-stage process. After election and coronation in Aachen, the king bore the title 'king of the Romans', and this remained his title until imperial coronation. The king of Germany was thus king of the Romans. As the English chronicler Matthew Paris put it, 'the kingship of Germany is called the kingship of the Romans, because it is like a pledge for the acquisition of the Empire of the Romans'.[5] But coronation as emperor depended on circumstances, especially the willingness of the pope to cooperate and the confidence of the king of the Romans to leave Germany. In a remarkable period in the thirteenth century and early fourteenth century, there was actually a 92-year hiatus (1220–1312) in which no imperial coronation took place.

Despite this, there were, nevertheless, periods when the Empire looked very much like a hereditary monarchy, in practice if not in theory. German rulers were succeeded by their sons on three successive occasions in the tenth century, and on three successive occasions in the eleventh and early twelfth centuries. Ruling kings sought to ensure the succession of their sons, even very young ones, by securing oaths of allegiance to them or having them crowned in their father's lifetime. But the idea that the crown was dependent on election by the chief nobles and bishops (the 'princes') was resilient, and could be stated explicitly during moments of crisis or uncertainty.

An example occurred during the reign of Henry IV (1056–1105). Henry had succeeded his father, Henry III, who had succeeded his father, Conrad II, so he represented the third generation in the direct line, establishing a tradition of transmission of power from father to son. Henry stirred up a great deal of opposition amongst his own nobles, as well as from the papacy, and, in 1077, at a meeting in Forchheim, between Bamberg and Nuremberg, the rebel nobles opposed to him not only chose a king to replace him, but also determined to end the hereditary tendency for good:

> There it was approved, and confirmed by the authority of the Roman pontiff, that royal power should not come to anyone through inheritance, as was previously the custom, but the son of the king, even if he were truly worthy, should become king through free election rather than through line of descent; however, if the king's son should not be worthy, or if the people did not want him, the people should have the power to make king whomsoever they wanted.[6]

This endorsement of the elective principle was not immediately effective, since, although the dissidents elected an anti-king, Rudolf of Rheinfelden, and chose another after Rudolf's death, Henry IV reigned for more than a quarter of a century after the meeting at Forcheim and was succeeded by his son Henry V (although hardly voluntarily, since the younger Henry deposed him). It was only with the death of Henry V without children in 1125 that the great nobles of Germany could insist on a free election. Thereafter, no son succeeded a father until 1190, when Henry VI came to the throne of his father, Frederick Barbarossa.

Henry VI, as the son of the previous ruler, looked around him and saw that hereditary succession to royal power was the common practice in Latin Europe. He determined to bring the Empire into line. In the spring of 1196 Henry presided over an assembly at Würzburg, where he wished to ratify with his chief men a new and unheard-of decree concerning the Roman kingdom, namely, that in the Roman kingdom, just as in France and other kingdoms, kings should succeed by hereditary right; the chief men who were there consented to this and confirmed it with their seals.[7]

This agreement, however, did not endure. Henry was a terrifying man – 'most savage to rebels, invincible to enemies, stern to the insolent, merciless to traitors'[8] – and many of the German nobles gave their consent when in his presence, but a core of opposition formed. Eventually this attempt of Henry VI to secure 'the end of election and the beginning of hereditary office'[9] was defeated. However, although the plan was abandoned, Henry did succeed in having his infant son (later Frederick II) proclaimed king by the princes at an assembly in Frankfurt late in 1196.[10]

Understandably, the popes championed the elective principle. Innocent III, defending the election of the Welf Otto IV rather than a member of the Hohenstaufen dynasty, Henry's brother, as a successor to Henry VI, wrote:

We stand for the liberty of the princes, because we completely refuse any favour to whoever attempts to claim the Empire for himself by right of succession. For it would seem that the Empire was not conferred through election by the princes but obtained by succession of blood if, just as a son once succeeded a father, so now a brother were to succeed a brother or a son a father directly.[11]

Popes did not claim the right to choose the emperor-elect but the right to approve or disapprove the choice of the German princes, especially in the case of a disputed election, as in this case, and they always had the ultimate veto on whether to crown the candidate as emperor, rather than king of the Romans, the title he held until imperial coronation.

The Empire thus continued to be elective. The composition of the electoral body was only gradually formalized. The number of seven (the archbishops of Cologne, Mainz and Trier, the king of Bohemia, the margrave of Brandenburg, the duke of Saxony and the count palatine of the Rhine) appears for the first time in the thirteenth century, and was recognized in the Golden Bull of 1356, the fullest and most explicit legislation on the subject. This was intended, in the words of Charles IV, who issued it, 'to foster unity among the electors and encourage a unanimous election'.[12] There was now a clear category of 'prince elector (*princeps elector*)', separate from the other princes of the Empire. The electoral title continued to be highly valued down to the end of the Empire in 1806 and was extended only rarely to new recipients (Bavaria in 1623, Hanover in 1692).

The Empire had its enthusiastic champions, the most famous of them being Dante, whose *Monarchia* was written in the first quarter of the fourteenth century. The term *monarchia*, according to Dante, 'which they call the empire', means 'sole rule over everything that is in time', that is, universal temporal government.[13] There is indeed a translation of the work titled 'On World-Government'.[14] Dante regards universal peace as the greatest good, and argues that 'for the well-being of the world it is necessary for there to be a monarchy or empire'.[15] It was God's providence that created the Roman empire, and it is not accidental that the Son of God came to earth in the reign of Augustus, 'when there was a perfect monarchy and everywhere the world was quiet'.[16] The Roman empire does not depend for its authority on the pope or the Church, and the Roman emperor is 'rightly the monarch of the world'.[17] This exalted conception of universal monarchy found concrete embodiment, in Dante's eyes, in Henry VII, the first king of the Romans or Holy Roman Emperor to set foot in Italy for more than fifty years, whom Dante regarded as 'another Moses, who will snatch his people away from the oppression of the Egyptians and lead them to a land flowing with milk and honey'.[18] He urged Italy to rejoice 'because your bridegroom, the comfort of the world and the glory of your people, the most merciful Henry, divine Augustus Caesar, hastens to the wedding'.[19] Henry's early death ended these dreams, but Dante reserved a place in Paradise for 'lofty Henry, who will come to set Italy straight before she is prepared for it'.[20]

But early fourteenth-century Italy also heard voices arguing that the Empire was an anachronism. Robert the Wise, king of Naples, issued a manifesto addressed to the pope declaring that all political arrangements were subject to change and that the Empire had been created by force and violence and should not be regarded as an enduring part of the landscape. It had once had dominion over almost all the world but now it was 'diminished, mutilated, lacerated and occupied by many different rulers' and 'reduced to the tiniest number of subject territories'. Its rulers had been no friends either to the Church or to Italy and were now usually Germans, 'a coarse, wild race, that adheres to barbaric savagery more than to the Christian faith'. King Robert suggested that the pope give serious consideration to 'what good or benefit come to the world' from appointing an Emperor, and his underlying theme was that the emperor Henry VII, who had just died, in the summer of 1313, need not be replaced.[21] Henry had invaded Robert's kingdom of Naples, which might well explain some of his judgments, but people who have been invaded often have a point of view.

Some historians, and others, consider that Germany took a 'special path (*Sonderweg*)', different from other European, or west European, countries, especially in the way that it did not develop powerful central institutions in the late medieval or Early Modern period. One explanation for this might be the elective nature of the German monarchy, which hindered dynastic consolidation, although it has also been argued that elective monarchy had advantages as well as disadvantages.[22] Be that as it may, it stood out in a world of hereditary dynasties.

Dynasties and the Church

The tension between the Christian message and dynastic thinking was expressed quite sharply by Jesus himself: 'If any man come to me, and hate not his father, and mother, and wife, and children, and brethren, and sisters, yea, and his own life also, he cannot be my disciple' (Luke 14: 26). Such an uncompromising rejection of ordinary family feeling would seem to rule out any chance of Christians thinking or acting dynastically. Yet, as time went by, and the Church established itself as a dominant and propertied establishment, there came to be many ways whereby the Church could serve dynasticism and dynasticism serve the Church.

In one sense, the Church of the later medieval period was less dynastic and more like a modern state than any of the kingdoms of Europe. It had a complex, far-reaching and well-articulated organization, with legislative, executive and judicial parts and supposedly meritocratic criteria for appointment to office. It was highly bureaucratic, with use of the written word and record-keeping more extensive and sophisticated than any of the contemporary dynastic systems. The thing it lacked was physical force, although this could be summoned up, and to some degree directed, by alliances with secular powers. Dynastic kingdoms, run as family affairs, always interacted with this international institution, based as it was on transcendental and supernatural claims. One of the more obvious ways in which this happened was the practice of ruling families putting children into the Church, especially at its highest, richest and most powerful levels. They were thereby ensured an aristocratic way of life without placing a strain on family resources.

Royal Abbesses and Nuns

In particular, the Church offered a respectable station in life for royal women who were not destined for marriage, or who had survived it. In the first century of English Christianity, as recorded by Bede, there are many examples of royal abbesses, such as Etheldreda, daughter of the king of East Anglia and wife of the king of Northumbria, who became abbess of Ely, or Ebba, the half-sister of the Northumbrian kings Oswald and Oswiu, who was abbess of the double monastery (i.e. for men and women) of Coldingham.[23] The daughters of Carolingian kings frequently entered nunneries, sometimes as widows. There are some fourteen cases in the first century of the dynasty.[24] When Theodrada, daughter of Charlemagne, entered a nunnery after her father's death, she received a congratulatory letter from the Irish monk Dungal, praising her for her desire 'to spurn secular dress and put on the holy veil of Christ, to despise changing and perishable things and seek constant and eternal things, to renounce the devil and the world and its pomp and works and follow Christ'. He concludes with a little complimentary verse: 'This letter greets you, Theodrada, born of imperial seed, adorned with good manners and with beauty.'[25] There need be no doubt about Theodrada's religious motives, but there is also no question that to be the abbess of a wealthy religious house, as she was, gave her security, authority and a status matching her royal birth.

The royal nunnery of Shaftesbury was founded by Alfred the Great of Wessex, probably in the 880s, and he appointed his daughter Æthelgeofu as abbess, with 'many noble nuns' under her rule and large endowments of land and wealth.[26] It became the resting place of royal saints from the house of Wessex, Queen Ælfgifu in 944 and Edward the Martyr in 979, both of them performing miracles at their tombs.[27] At the time of the Domesday Survey of 1086 Shaftesbury was by far the richest nunnery in England. An illegitimate half-sister of Henry II was abbess from the 1170s or 1180s to 1216.[28] More than three centuries after its foundation, the nunnery was still providing a comfortable and secure position for women associated with the royal family.

The Saxon convent of Quedlinburg, which was founded to commemorate the first German king to come from Saxony, Henry I (d. 936), who was buried there, had royal abbesses, all of them daughters of kings and emperors, continuously for 130 years (966–1096). It thus maintained this royal tradition despite the change of dynasty, from Ottonian to Salian, in 1024. Nunneries could offer a secure life for both royal widows and young princesses. Eleanor of Provence, high-born queen of Henry III of England, and immensely wealthy, became a nun at Amesbury in 1286, after fourteen years of widowhood, and died and was buried there in 1291. Her granddaughter Mary was also a nun there, entering the convent at the age of seven. Mary's life was not strongly circumscribed by taking the veil. She had a grant of £100 per year from the royal treasury, later increased to £200, was frequently at court or on extensive pilgrimages, and built up considerable gambling debts.[29]

The new mendicant Orders of the thirteenth century also provided safe and suitable surroundings for royal women, for, although penniless wandering was prescribed for male friars, the female branches were enclosed and stable, like the existing nunneries. In central Europe a remarkable group of royal women supported or became 'Poor Clares', that is, members of the female branch of the Franciscans, and also won a reputation as saints.[30] The ruling dynasties of Bohemia, Poland and Hungary were interrelated by complex webs of marriage, as the lives of these women show. Agnes (d. 1282), a daughter of Premysl Otakar I of Bohemia, corresponded with Clare of Assisi, the founder of the Poor Clares, and herself founded a convent of the Order in Prague in

1234, which she entered. Her sister Anne (d. 1265) married Henry II of Silesia and bore him ten children. After Henry was killed in battle against the Mongols in 1241, Anne remained in Silesia and founded a convent of Poor Clares in Wroclaw in 1257, where she retired and was buried. Salome (d. 1268), daughter of the ruler of Cracow, married Coloman, brother of Bela IV of Hungary, but insisted on a chaste marriage, and after Coloman's death she returned to Cracow, where her brother, Boleslaw V, founded a convent of Poor Clares for her. Two daughters of Bela IV, Cunigunda (d. 1292) and Yolande (d. 1298), married Polish princes. Cunigunda married Boleslaw V but, like her sister-in-law Salome, insisted on a chaste marriage. She founded a convent of Poor Clares during her widowhood and joined the Order. Yolande married Boleslaw the Pious, a cousin of Boleslaw V, founded a convent of Poor Clares at Gniezno after his death and entered the Order.

All five of these women had a saintly reputation, although that of Yolande is late, and either entered the Order of Poor Clares or founded houses of the Order. They had the support of powerful and wealthy fathers and brothers. The chaste marriages were clearly 'undynastic' in the sense of ending the possibility of sons inheriting from their fathers, and indeed Boleslaw V was succeeded by a cousin, and Coloman left no children, although it may be that the story of chaste marriage sprang from the childlessness of these two rulers rather than explaining it. Nevertheless, the dense network of intermarriage, blood relationships and saintly emulation involved in the story of these five royal and saintly ladies can justify the label 'Dynastic Cults'.[31]

Younger Sons and the Church

Placing younger sons in the Church, which could provide them with a comfortable life and a high status, at the cost of at least theoretical celibacy, was a policy pursued by many aristocratic families but, perhaps surprisingly, not very much by royalty. Charles the Bald, 'alone among ruling Carolingians',[32] placed two of his four legitimate sons in the Church: Carloman (d. 876), abbot of St.-Médard, Soissons, who was blinded after a supposed conspiracy in 873,[33] and Lothar (d. 865), abbot of St.-Germain, Auxerre.

In some ways, this lack of younger sons going into the Church is unexpected, for it could be very useful for a king to have a son or brother in the ecclesiastical hierarchy, as is illustrated by the career of Bruno, archbishop of Cologne, who was a son of Henry I of Germany (919–36) and a younger brother of Otto I (936–73). He was given the best clerical education, served as Otto's chancellor and then, in 953, at the age of twenty-eight, was appointed archbishop of Cologne. Cologne was one of the most important cities in Lotharingia, the westernmost duchy of Germany and one with a tradition of separatism. Bruno's biographer, writing for his successor, depicts Lotharingia as a wild place: 'there the nobles are accustomed to violence and plunder, the populace is eager for rebellion, and everyone, intent on civil strife, desires to enrich himself from the misery of others'.[34] At the very time of his appointment, Bruno found a major rebellion in progress, one of the participants being the duke of Lotharingia. Otto decided the best policy was to make his brother 'the guardian, overseer and, so to speak, archduke of the West'.[35] For twelve years (953–65) Bruno served not only as the archbishop of an ancient and important city but also held a central political position in his brother's regime, securing Lotharingia, often by armed force, against rebellious aristocrats. He also played a major role in the neighbouring kingdom of the West Franks during the minority of its ruler, King Lothar, who was Bruno's nephew, and probably was responsible for arranging Lothar's marriage to Otto I's stepdaughter during an assembly held in Cologne (see above, p. 389). On more than one occasion he led an army into France to support Lothar against his enemies and rivals. During Otto's Italian expedition of 961–5, Bruno, and William, archbishop of Mainz, Otto's illegitimate son, acted as regents. So, for twelve years Otto I had a loyal brother guarding his left flank, and a brother, moreover, who would not have his own family interests to compete with Otto's.[36] The combination of 'priestly devotion and royal courage' that Otto supposedly praised in his brother could be a powerful dynastic instrument.[37]

Like the Carolingians, the Capetians, too, rarely placed younger sons in the Church, although Louis VI was an exception. Henry, one of Louis' younger sons, was tonsured when young, made abbot of numerous royal abbeys, then dramatically converted to the Cistercian Order in 1145. But he did not refuse election as bishop of Beauvais in 1149 and archbishop of Rheims in 1162, where he served until his death in 1175. He was an active bishop, defending the rights and property of his see, pursuing a policy of economic development and backing Pope Alexander III during the long papal schism of 1159–78. So, for much of the reign of Louis VII, a major prelate of the northern French Church was the king's brother. Another son of Louis VI, Philip, became archdeacon of Paris. No other Capetian kings, however, appear to have placed sons in the Church in this way.[38]

There are some isolated examples of Byzantine emperors appointing sons or brothers as patriarchs of Constantinople. Stephen, the third son of Basil I, became patriarch aged nineteen in 886, appointed by his brother, Leo VI; he died in 893. At Christmas 923, the emperor Romanos I Lekapenos, as well as having his two older sons crowned co-emperors, had his third son Theophylact tonsured as a cleric, although the boy was only ten years old; he had been castrated as a child. At the age of twenty, Theophylact became patriarch and held the office from 933 to 956. The patriarch Ignatius (formerly Niketas) (847–58, 867–77) was the son of the emperor Michael Rangabe but, far from being appointed through family influence, had been castrated and made a monk aged fourteen at the time of his father's deposition in 813. He had subsequently risen through the ecclesiastical hierarchy. In general, however, the function of the Church in the Byzantine dynastic system was not to provide an alternative path for younger sons but rather to be the destination of deposed emperors and their families, often combined with blinding.

In the west, there are several cases of illegitimate sons of kings becoming bishops or abbots, for instance, Rorico, bishop of Laon (949–76), son of Charles the Simple, king of the West Franks; William, archbishop of Mainz (954–68), son of Otto I of Germany; and Arnulf, an illegitimate son of King Lothar of France (954–86), who became a canon and then archbishop of Rheims (988–91, 999–1021). Of all the kings of England between 1066 and 1485, only two placed a son in the Church and, in each case, it was an illegitimate son: Gervase, abbot of Westminster, son of King Stephen, and Geoffrey, archbishop of York, son of Henry II. The standard practice in England was to endow younger sons with earldoms or, after 1337, dukedoms.

There were occasions when sons who had been placed in the Church had to be recalled on family grounds. Philip of Swabia, youngest son of the emperor Frederick Barbarossa, was given a clerical education and promoted to ecclesiastical offices while still only eleven or twelve. In 1191, at the age of fourteen, he was elected bishop of Würzburg. However, in 1192 or 1193, plans changed and he began a secular career, accompanying his brother, Henry VI, in Germany and Sicily, which Henry conquered in 1194, and being invested by him as duke of Tuscany in 1195. The clerical career was put irreversibly behind him when Philip married a Byzantine princess in 1197. The motives for the switch from clerical to lay in 1192 or 1193 are not made explicit but it is probably relevant that, although Frederick Barbarossa left five surviving sons on his death in 1190, none of them had sons before 1194 (and that son proved, in the event, to be the only one). So it may be that recalling Philip to lay estate was an attempt to increase the chances of male offspring in the dynasty. In fact, Philip himself only had daughters, but he proved a champion of his young nephew, Henry VI's son Frederick II, and was himself elected German king after Henry's death.

More spectacular was the case of Ramiro II of Aragon, often referred to as Ramiro el Monje, 'Ramiro the Monk', brother of Alfonso the Battler, king of Aragon (see p. 63). He was raised in a Benedictine monastery and served as abbot of two Spanish religious houses, as well as being elected but never consecrated as bishop of several sees. His brother died childless in 1134 and Ramiro was elected king by an assembly of Aragonese nobles. In quick succession, he married, fathered a child, Petronilla, who was then engaged to the powerful neighbouring ruler, Raymond Berengar of Barcelona, and, having fulfilled his dynastic duty, he retired to his monastery in 1137, leaving Raymond Berengar as de facto ruler of Aragon.

Sometimes the ruler's decision to place a child or a brother into the Church was viewed as a kind of sacrifice, in the sense both of an offering to God and of a loss for some greater good, which of course is what makes the offering of value to God. The chronicler Thietmar of Merseburg writes of the empress Theophanu, wife of Otto II, that 'from the fruit of her womb she offered as a tithe to God two daughters, one, Adelheid by name, to Quedlinburg, the other, who was called Sophia,

to Gandersheim'.[39] Both these princesses became abbesses and lived
into their sixties, but Thietmar's words suggest that offering them to
the monastic life still represented some kind of sacrifice on the part of
their mother: they were 'tithes'. The same idea of an offering to God is
found in the case of Margaret (d. 1270), daughter of Bela IV of
Hungary, who was promised to the Church before she was born. Her
mother was pregnant with her during the Mongol invasions of Hungary
in 1241–2 and she and her husband the king 'took a vow that, if
a daughter were to be born, they would make her a nun, for the
liberation of the mother and the country, as a kind of expiatory
offering'.[40] Margaret entered a Dominican house at the age of three.
A yet more explicit invocation of sacrifice is found in Leo VI's funeral
oration for his father, the Byzantine emperor Basil I, which says that
Basil's offering his son Stephen to the Church was like Abraham offering Isaac, except superior, since Abraham was acting on God's command but Basil's decision was his own initiative![41] This Stephen was
patriarch of Constantinople 886–93.

Dynasties and the Internationalism of the Church

The Church had an international hierarchy of its own which did not always
correspond to the boundaries of kingdoms, and this overlap of ecclesiastical and political units often resulted in friction or required readjustments. Within Britain, the two English archbishoprics, Canterbury and
York, both claimed that their authority extended beyond the kingdom of
England, Canterbury claiming a primacy over the whole island, York
insisting that the Scottish Church was subject to it. Canterbury's main
success was in establishing its authority over the Church in Wales, where
the eventual ecclesiastical geography was four bishoprics immediately
subject to Canterbury, despite spasmodic attempts to secure an independent Welsh archbishopric. Canterbury's victory was a direct consequence
of the Anglo-Norman conquest and settlement of most of Wales in the
twelfth and thirteenth centuries. In Scotland, neither Canterbury nor York
was able to make much headway because of the opposition of the Scottish
royal dynasty, although attempts to establish a Scottish archbishopric in
the twelfth century were also unsuccessful. In a highly unusual

arrangement, in 1192 the Scottish Church was placed directly under the papacy but without any archbishop: 'the Scottish Church ought to be subject to the apostolic see, whose special daughter she is, without any intermediary'.[42]

Ecclesiastical boundaries that cut across political ones were common in the Iberian peninsula. There, many bishoprics were established in places conquered from the Muslims, some on the basis of memories or records of the bishoprics of pre-Muslim times, but the hierarchy of archbishoprics was largely new. After Santiago de Compostella was raised to archiepiscopal status in 1120, it was eventually assigned the bishoprics of Zamora, Salamanca, Avila, Ciudad Rodrigo, Plasencia, Badajoz, Coria, Lamego, Idanha (Guarda), Lisbon and Evora. Of these eleven sees, five were in the kingdom of Leon, four in the kingdom of Portugal and two in the kingdom of Castile, which had separate rulers from Leon 1157–1230. Hence the bishop of Lisbon, an important city of the kings of Portugal, was ecclesiastically subordinate to an archbishopric in the neighbouring, and sometimes hostile, kingdom of Leon-Castile. Lisbon did not become an independent archbishopric until 1393, when Evora, Lamego, Guarda and Silves, the last taken from the archbishopric of Seville, were placed under it. It was now an entirely Portuguese archbishopric. Such tangled histories could be told of many Iberian dioceses. On two occasions younger sons of the kings of Aragon became archbishops of Toledo, the most important see in Castile, a situation hard to imagine in other countries, and a consequence of the lack of correspondence between ecclesiastical and political boundaries.[43]

Like the Church, from which they sprang, the crusading Orders, such as the Templars, Hospitallers (Knights of St John) and Teutonic Knights, were international and run by a hierarchy that was, in principle, celibate and non-dynastic, in the sense that office was by appointment rather than inheritance. From small beginnings in the early twelfth century, the Orders grew into institutions of enormous wealth and power, and always had to be considered by the dynasties of Christian Europe. They often played a major role in the politics of kingdoms and sometimes ruled states of their own: the Teutonic Knights established the largest, in Prussia and Livonia, while the Hospitallers conquered the island of Rhodes in 1306–10 and made it their headquarters, which it remained until 1522. In the crusading states of the eastern Mediterranean and in the Iberian peninsula, the armies of Christian kings were frequently supplemented by the forces of the Orders, although Alfonso the Battler's desire to leave his kingdom of Aragon to the military Orders was not fulfilled (see pp. 63–4 above).

The most dramatic clash between a dynasty and the Orders was Philip the Fair's destruction of the Templars in 1307–12. Events began with the king's officials arresting all the Templars in France, confiscating the Order's property and charging its members with heresy and sexual offences. The use of torture, or the threat of it, ensured that the prisoners confessed, however odd the charges might be – spitting on the cross, denying Christ, obscene kissing, even idol worship – but the king found that the pope, Clement V, was not inclined to be cooperative, and needed considerable pressure to go along with the prosecution. But Philip the Fair was a ruthless man and hastened the pace by a mass burning of Templars outside Paris in May 1310. Clement eventually yielded to pressure and suppressed the Order at the Council of Vienne in 1312. The bull suppressing the Order is dated 22 March 1312. King Philip, his brothers and sons, 'surrounded by a seemly and powerful retinue of many skilled nobles and great men', had arrived in Vienne on 20 March.[44] The property of the Templars was transferred to the Hospitallers, who had to agree to make a huge payment to the king. The royal house of France had destroyed an international religious Order.

The complex interplay between dynastic ambitions and the politics of the Church can be seen during the period of the Great Schism. The existence of two rival popes was not in itself unusual. The earliest case seems to have been in 217–35, and in the twelfth century there were rival popes in 1100–01, 1105–11, 1118–21, 1124, 1130–8, 1159–78 and 1179–80, so for forty-five years, almost half the century. What distinguished the so-called Great Schism of 1378–1417 was the entrenchment of two rival lines of popes in two important centres, Avignon and Rome, for almost forty years. The kings of Latin Europe had to take sides and their choices were often dictated as much by the choices of their dynastic rivals as by their own convictions. France tended to back the Avignon popes, which encouraged France's enemy, England, to back the Roman popes. This naturally led Scotland, France's ally and England's enemy, to back the Avignon popes.

The alignment of ecclesiastical and political loyalties was particularly clear in the Iberian peninsula during the crisis following the death of Ferdinand I of Portugal without sons in 1383. The Castilian king, John I, claimed the throne in the right of his wife, Ferdinand's daughter, but faced opposition within Portugal from various parties, not all of them allies. Castile recognized the Avignon pope, Portugal the Roman pope; this created a particular dilemma for clergy in the diocese of Tuy, which was partly in one kingdom, partly in the other. Naturally, the Avignon pope backed Castile and the Roman pope Portugal. The eventual victor in the struggle of 1383–5 was John of Avis, illegitimate half-brother of Ferdinand I of Portugal (see above, pp. 171–2).

When the Roman pope Boniface IX issued bulls legitimizing John of Avis, recognizing him as king and granting him dispensations for his earlier vows of poverty, chastity and obedience, he also gave a brief account of the Roman pope's view of the crisis of 1383–5: 'John, son of Henry [this is John I of Castile], of damned memory, at that time the occupier of the kingdoms of Castile and Leon, was attempting to devastate and take possession of the kingdoms of Portugal and the Algarve'; moreover, John had adhered to 'that son of perdition, Robert, once cardinal-priest of the basilica of the twelve apostles, then and now an antipope, who presumed and now presumes by sacrilegious audacity to call himself Clement VII'.[45] The succession crisis in Portugal had thus been given a sharper edge by the clash of popes. John I of Castile was not even given the dignity of the kingship of Castile, he is merely 'John, son of Henry', and also a 'son of perdition', while Clement VII, first of the Avignon popes of the Great Schism, is belittled by use of his given name. When John of Avis was looking for allies, England, with its hostility to Castile, was a natural choice, made easier, or perhaps even made possible, by the common adherence of Portugal and England to the Roman popes. Just like the Protestant Reformation, the Great Schism produced two hostile religious camps in Christendom and dynasties had to choose a side.

Republics

Most of medieval Europe was ruled by dynasties, but there were one or two areas where different forms of political organization survived or developed. Iceland and Venice are two, very different, examples of political societies completely independent of kings. The former was an empty land settled by Scandinavian, mainly Norwegian, farmers and fighters in the period 870–930. Many of them had left home in order to escape the authority of the Norwegian kings and had no desire either to submit to the rulers of their country of origin or to replicate royal government in their new land. The result was extremely unusual, a republic with sophisticated consultative and legal procedures but no king, aristocracy or powerful bishops. Outsiders were amazed at the way Icelanders organized their own affairs. One German cleric noted, with wonder and some admiration, 'they have no king, only law'.[46] But others were dismayed at their effrontery in completely disregarding the dynastic principle. After Cardinal William of Sabina had officiated at the coronation of King Haakon Haakonsson in 1247, the first coronation of a Norwegian king, he also supported Haakon's claim to rule over Iceland, 'for he called it unfair that that land should not be subject to some king like all others in the world'.[47] For the cardinal, rule by kings was the norm, the Icelandic republic an aberration. In fact, it was not until 1262–4 that the Icelanders formally submitted to the king of Norway (Haakon died in the middle of the process, in 1263). Henceforth Iceland had a king 'like all others in the world'. The Icelandic Commonwealth, or Free State, as it is sometimes called, lasted well over three centuries, and produced a body of literature in the vernacular that is among the greatest ever created in the Middle Ages, and one that throws a vivid light on the violent but self-regulating and non-dynastic world of this remarkable medieval republic.

Venice too provides an example of a medieval republic, but one about as different from Iceland as it is possible to be. Iceland was poor, remote, lacked towns and played a minimal part in European politics. Venice was one of the richest trading cities of medieval Europe, with a central role in Italian politics as well as a maritime empire in the Adriatic and Mediterranean. The origins of the city are to be sought during the invasions that marked the fall of the Western Roman Empire, and it was for a long time technically part of the Eastern Roman (or Byzantine) Empire. For example, when the Franks began to encroach on north-east Italy in the late eighth and early ninth century, Byzantine war fleets were sent to Venetian waters to assert the emperor's authority and in 810 Byzantine envoys came to Aachen, where Charlemagne acknowledged that Venice belonged to their emperor, not to the Franks.[48] The local representative of Byzantine power was known by the imperial title *dux* ('duke'), a term that eventually became worn down to the Venetian word *doge*.

Gradually Venice became detached from the Byzantine empire. This took a long time and did not usually involve clear-cut steps. Donald Nicol, in his influential book *Byzantium and Venice*, titled the first four chapters 'Venice: the Byzantine province', 'Venice: the Byzantine protectorate', 'Venice: the ally of Byzantium' and 'Venice: the partner of Byzantium', indicating the subtle change in the nature of the relationship between the Adriatic trading city and the imperial power. The documents record- ing the Venetians' trading privileges in Constantinople begin to read less like the grants of a sovereign than treaties between independent powers. One, issued by the co-emperors Basil II and Constantine VIII in 992, calls the Venetians 'outsiders' or 'foreigners' (*extranei*) and says how they have 'made a request to our empire' for preferential treatment; the emperors grant this but also specify that Venice must render military aid in certain circumstances.[49]

Eventually Venice became not a province or protectorate of Byzantium but its enemy and conqueror, picking up numerous territor- ial acquisitions after the fall of Constantinople to Venetian and crusad- ing forces in 1204. At the same time its own internal government developed. A tendency for the office of doge to become hereditary was checked. The office of doge was for life, but was attained through a complex process of election, not by dynastic right, in this respect resembling the papacy. A system of executive councils gave a large share of control to the richest and most powerful citizens of Venice, limiting the doge's authority. The end result was a secular republic, with an elected head, centred in a populous trading city and also controlling a maritime empire extending hundreds of miles into the eastern Mediterranean. In the fifteenth century Venice took over Cyprus, which had been ruled by a French dynasty for 292 years, an urban republic thus defeating a dynasty and bringing to an end a dynastic state. The title 'most serene' was commonly used for emperors and other rulers in medieval Europe; it is fitting that Venice is known as 'the most serene republic' – *La Serenissima*. It lasted until 1797.

Dynasties and Cities

Iceland and Venice were very unusual. But if sovereign republics were rare, there were many places in medieval Europe that obtained more limited forms of self-government, notably the towns. Wherever cities were populous, wealthy and self-confident, and in medieval Europe this meant primarily northern Italy and Flanders, they might find themselves in conflict with their supposed rulers. The Holy Roman Emperors battered the walls of Milan, but Milan battered back. The great cities of Flanders fought their sovereigns, that is, the counts of Flanders and their successors, the dukes of Burgundy, in a mortal contest that lasted centuries. In these two most highly urbanized parts of medieval Europe the cities struggled to free themselves from the world of dynasty. In northern Italy many of them were extremely successful in this effort and attained actual practical independence almost as great as that of Venice, although they were always theoretically subject to the Holy Roman Empire and many succumbed to local dynasties of their own in the later Middle Ages, the classic example being Florence, where the Medici family went from being ordinary citizens in the thirteenth and fourteenth centuries to being de facto rulers of the city throughout most of the fifteenth century, finally acquiring title, as dukes of Florence, in 1532.

One of the most long-lasting and disruptive conflicts between towns seeking autonomy and dynastic rulers was that between the towns of northern Italy and the Holy Roman Emperors who claimed to be their rulers. It was Charlemagne's conquest of the kingdom of the Lombards that first brought northern Italy under the authority of Frankish rulers based north of the Alps. Charlemagne's empire broke up in the time of his grandsons, but his claim to imperial authority, to being, in fact, the successor to the Roman emperors of antiquity, was eventually inherited by the Ottonian kings of Germany. Otto I re-established the link across the Alps by conquering northern Italy and, in 962, being crowned emperor in Rome. Thereafter German kings always aimed at controlling Italy and receiving the imperial title, although they were not always successful in doing so. Between 951, when Otto I first campaigned in Italy, and 1212, the accession of Frederick II, who was normally based in the peninsula, German kings led expeditions over the Alps on thirty-two occasions. Their purpose was always to secure recognition of their authority and often to defeat dangerous rivals. Sometimes this required long periods south of the Alps. Frederick Barbarossa (1152–90), for example, spent over one-third of his reign in Italy. The 'Italian expedition (*expeditio Italica*)' of the German kings was one of the most considerable military undertakings of the Middle Ages and might require up to two years of planning.[50]

As the north Italian cities grew in size, wealth and power in the eleventh and twelfth centuries, they not only developed new forms of self-government and imposed curbs on their local bishops and nobles but also often found themselves in opposition to their nominal rulers, the emperors. From the point of view of the emperors, Italy was part of their empire and, when they went there, they did so because Italy was theirs, but from the point of view of the north Italian cities, these unwelcome expeditions of German armies crossing the Alps might look more like invasions. In the reigns of both Frederick Barbarossa and his grandson, Frederick II (1212–50), the north Italian cities grouped themselves into a confederacy, the Lombard League, to resist imperial authority. Milan was one of the chief cities of the League, and hence a chief target of both Frederick Barbarossa and Frederick II. The great north Italian city had an anti-royalist reputation: 'this city is said to have been hostile to kings from of old'.[51] After a lengthy siege, Barbarossa conquered the city in 1162 and ordered it destroyed. There is a moving account of the evacuation of the inhabitants:

> Who is there who could keep back tears on seeing the lamentation and the sorrow and the mourning of the men and the women and especially of the sick, the pregnant and the children, going out and leaving their own homes?[52]

But the Milanese survived, revived, and eventually led their allies to a decisive victory over Barbarossa at the Battle of Legnano in 1176.

The struggle between the emperors and their north Italian opponents was a complicated one. First, by no means all the cities fought on one side. The smaller cities around Milan, for example, who felt the pressure of their large and threatening neighbour, were quite happy to join the emperor in attacking her. Second, the struggle between emperor and cities was always entangled with that between emperor and pope. Pope Alexander III was an ally of the Lombard League, which built a city named in his honour, Alessandria,[53] while Barbarossa maintained a rival line of popes for eighteen years. A third complication arose from an important dynastic marriage, between Barbarossa's son Henry and Constance, heir to the kingdom of Sicily. Although Henry had to fight for his right to succeed to Sicily, he did so successfully, and was from 1194 both Holy Roman Emperor and king of Sicily, a dual role eventually also held by his son Frederick II. The geopolitical consequences were enormous, since the pope and the Lombard League now confronted a power that claimed, and to some degree exerted, authority in Italy from the Alps to the Mediterranean.

These wars were not wars between dynasties but wars between a dynasty, on the one hand, the Hohenstaufen family of Barbarossa and Frederick II, and, on the other, an alliance of cities and popes. The conflict reached a height of intensity in the middle decades of the thirteenth century. Italy was polarized into supporters of the emperor, Ghibellines as they came to be called, and supporters of 'the Church', known as Guelfs.[54] For well over a century, political loyalties and alliances in Italy revolved around one's attitude to a particular imperial dynasty. Pope Innocent IV deposed Frederick II and aimed at excluding his dynasty from power: 'let it not be that the sceptre of rule over the Christian people should remain with him any longer, nor let it be transferred to any of his brood of vipers'.[55] The popes were eventually successful in their avowed aim of wiping out the dynasty completely, but, ironically, the only way they could do so was by calling on another dynasty, the Angevins, a branch of the Capetians, who established themselves as rulers of Sicily by defeating and killing the last of the Hohenstaufen. Meanwhile many of the north Italian cities developed into something like republican city-states.

There are many other examples of conflict between dynasties and the towns they claimed to rule, perhaps most notably that between the dukes of Burgundy and their towns, especially Ghent, which was not infrequently at war with its duke, but the case of Italy in the twelfth and thirteenth centuries is a clear enough example to illustrate the nature of these clashes. The wealth generated by trade and commerce, their populousness and their fortifications made the towns very desirable objects for kings and other dynastic rulers, but also gave them the possibility of resisting those rulers. Often kings and the ruling classes of the cities could ally. If the towns were willing to pay enough in taxes, then kings were willing to give them limited self-government. This might be particularly true of regions with small or middle-sized towns, like England or France (excluding Flanders). But the larger and wealthier cities, like Milan, Florence or Ghent, had the resources to resist their lords, even if not always with ultimate success. The Holy Roman Emperors, the dukes of Burgundy, and other dynasts sitting on such urban goldmines would understandably try to maintain their authority and the profits that flowed from them, and could often call on considerable military resources from their aristocratic followers. Hence, on occasion, the whiff of class war in these conflicts, as German dukes, counts and knights descended on the trading cities of Italy, or the knightly retainers of the dukes of Burgundy faced the urban militias of Flanders. One of the most spectacular clashes of this kind occurred in 1302, when French knights confronted the infantry of the Flemish towns at Courtrai and suffered a bloody defeat:

> And thus, in the face of the weavers, the fullers and the common Flemish footsoldiers, the skill of battle and the flower of knighthood came crashing down, with all the strength of their most magnificent steeds and warhorses, and the beauty and power of this most mighty army was turned into a dungheap and the glory of the French was made shit and worms.[56]

The note of class conflict is unmistakable.

Dynasty and the Kingdom

As the case of Flanders shows, royal dynasties often faced, and might have to fight, the non-dynastic world within the kingdoms they ruled. Though the identification of dynasty and kingdom could be achieved, it might turn instead into antagonism. This emerged especially in cases of dynasties ruling multiple kingdoms, for one consequence of the transmission of power through the dynastic system was the possibility of building up great territorial conglomerates through careful choices of bride. The most famous example in European history is provided by the Habsburgs, who went from being middle-ranking German counts in the twelfth century to rulers of the world's greatest empire in the sixteenth, almost entirely, as far as their European territories are concerned, by marriage and succession. One branch then continued its dominance of the Danubian region down to the First World War. Their dizzying list of titles underlines the way that their territory had been built up piecemeal. In the Peace of Westphalia of 1648, for example, Ferdinand III appears as

> Ferdinand III, elected Emperor of the Romans, forever august, king of Germany, Hungary, Bohemia, Dalmatia, Croatia, Slavonia, archduke of Austria, duke of Burgundy, Brabant, Styria, Carinthia, Carniola, margrave of Moravia, duke of Luxemburg, Upper and Lower Silesia, Württemberg and Teck, prince of Swabia, count of Habsburg, Tyrol, Kiburg and Gorizia, margrave of the Holy Roman Empire, Burgau, Upper and Lower Lausitz, lord of the Mark of Slavonia, Pordenone and Salins.[57]

Of modern European states, Spain and Great Britain both ultimately originated from dynastic marriages, and the same is true of important medieval political units that no longer exist, like Poland–Lithuania or the semi-regal Burgundian lands of the late Middle Ages. Modern commentators sometimes write as if the formation of some of these composite states was natural, while others, for example Austria–Hungary, are dismissed as archaic and unnatural, but they were all natural products of the dynastic system.

Because dynasties pursued power, prestige and territory for themselves, not for a 'state' or 'nation', their lands often transcended political boundaries. The counts of Flanders, for example, held lands both in the kingdom of France and in the Holy Roman Empire ('Imperial Flanders'). Hence, when Baldwin of Hainault succeeded to the county of Flanders in 1191, he had to do homage and swear fidelity to the king of France, which he did on 1 March 1192, and promise him the inheritance payment known as 'relief', and then the following month travel to Germany to do homage to the emperor.[58] The counts of Flanders saw no contradictions in this situation and they had no interest at all in tidying it up. Both their lands and the scope of their political ambitions were greater because they were vassals of both the king of France and the emperor.

A more complex situation was created when a king of one country held lands in another kingdom. The most intractable case of this type concerned the lands of the king of England in France. In 1066 the duke of Normandy, who recognized the suzerainty of the king of France, became king of England, and for the next 500 years, until the English loss of Calais in 1558, every English king held lands in France. These lands were not annexed to the kingdom of England, but, for most of the period, recognized as territories held from the king of France as superior lord. Only after Edward III claimed the French throne in 1340 did the quarrel assume a different constitutional form. Before then, the title of the kings of England always reflected this dual nature, monarch in one kingdom, great lord in another, even if their territories in France varied over time: William the Conqueror was 'king of the English and duke of the Normans', Henry II was 'king of the English and duke of the Normans and of the men of Aquitaine and count of the Angevins', Henry III, who acknowledged the loss of Normandy, was 'king of England, lord of Ireland and duke of Aquitaine'. The acknowledged superiority of the king of France regarding these lands meant that he could insist on homage from the king of England or could summon him to his court in the case of disputes over territories. Most controversially, the French king could claim appellate jurisdiction in cases involving the inhabitants of the king of England's French lands. In extreme situations, he could declare those lands forfeit, as happened, for instance, in 1202 and in 1294, on both occasions leading to years of war between the two kings. The Norman and Plantagenet kings of England were just as tenacious of their dynastic inheritance in France as they were of their kingdom of England.

Such situations were not uncommon elsewhere. The kings of Scots held lands in the kingdom of England and performed homage and swore fealty for them. The king of England claimed that the king of Scots owed homage for the kingdom of Scotland too, but was rarely able to insist on that. In 1278, for instance, Alexander III of Scotland came to Westminster and spoke before an assembly of Edward I and his chief men: 'I Alexander, king of Scotland, become the liegeman of the lord Edward, king of England, against all people.' Edward accepted this homage, 'reserving the right and claim of the king of England and his heirs for the homage of the king of Scotland and his heirs for the kingdom of Scotland, when they wish to discuss it.' The king of Scots then swore fealty to Edward, although he was allowed to swear through his representative Robert Bruce (father of the later King Robert), promising faithful service 'due from the lands and holdings that I hold from the king of England'.[59] The disputed issue, the independence or subordination of Scotland, was thus quite clear, but so too was the undisputed issue: the king of Scots was the liegeman of the king of England for his lands in England, just as the king of England was the liegeman of the king of France for his lands in France. Twenty-three years later, when the issue was being decided not by assemblies but by battle, the Scots claimed that 'the kingdom of Scotland was always completely free in relation to the king of England, since by general law an equal cannot command an equal and a king should not be subject to a king or a kingdom to a kingdom' and 'by general law no kingdom ought to be subject to another in any way', but this was an argument raised in the midst of war and hardly describes the complexities of dynastic relations in medieval Europe.[60]

Dynastic ambitions that transcended the frontiers of kingdoms also characterized the expansion of the house of Barcelona in the central Middle Ages. Technically part of the kingdom of France, the county of Barcelona was governed by a line of vigorous expansionist rulers in the eleventh and twelfth centuries. They expanded by conquest, notably at the cost of the neighbouring Muslim states, by marriage to female heirs and by becoming overlords of counts and other lords on both sides of the Pyrenees. These overlordships included, at various times, those of Carcassonne, Béziers, Narbonne and Montpellier, with their important cities, as well as the Pyrenean counties from Béarn to Roussillon. These areas were all under the nominal suzerainty of the distant kings of France, based 400 miles to the north, but in culture and language they had much in common with the Catalan lands of the counts of Barcelona. Through marriage to a female heir in 1112, the counts of Barcelona acquired most of Provence. This was not part of France at this time, but part of the Holy Roman Empire. Another marriage agreement with great consequences took place in 1137, when the count was betrothed to the female heir to the kingdom of Aragon, bringing to the dynasty the royal title and a territory quite outside any even theoretical French jurisdiction. A further symbolic step took place in 1180, when Catalan documents ceased using the regnal year of French kings in their dating formulae.[61] By 1200, the count-kings ruled, either directly or as overlords, an assemblage of lands that stretched from Zaragoza in the valley of the Ebro and Tortosa in southern Catalonia near the Mediterranean coast, through the southern lands of the kingdom of France and as far as Nice in Provence, in the Holy Roman Empire.

It is not impossible to imagine that these lands would form the core of a new state, Occitan in language, ruled by the count-kings and cutting off the kingdom of France from the Mediterranean. That this did not happen is partly due to the Albigensian Crusade (1209–29), which brought armies of northern French knights down into the south, blessed by the pope, to root out the heresy which the Church identified as a major problem there. One way they tried to do this was by sacking cities and dispossessing local lords. Peter II of Aragon inevitably became involved, not because his orthodox credentials were doubted (he was one of the leaders of the Christian army at the great victory of Las Navas in 1212) but because he was the suzerain of several of the southern French lords whom the crusaders had expelled from their lands. At the Battle of Muret in September 1213 Peter and his allies faced the crusaders under the command of the French noble Simon de Montfort, whose son and namesake was later famous in English history. The crusaders were victorious and Peter was killed in the battle, just fourteen months after he helped win the Battle of Las Navas against the Muslims. Dynastic power was great but there were other forces at work in medieval politics and the Church Militant was one of the most powerful of them. Peter's son and successor, James I, was just five years old at the time of Muret, but he went on to agree the Treaty of Corbeil in 1258, by which the king of France renounced all claims to the county of Barcelona and its surrounding territories, while James gave up his claims to overlordship in the south of France, with the exception of Montpellier, where he had been born.[62]

In the later Middle Ages the kings of Aragon continued to look for opportunities for expansion, and found many, so that they eventually had something like a Mediterranean empire, but the Treaty of Corbeil marked a sharp delimitation of their sphere of influence. The boundaries of dynastic power and the boundaries of the kingdom were being aligned. Barcelona, long an independent political unit, was now not even notionally part of the kingdom of France. Conversely, the king of Aragon no longer had any formal suzerainty over the lords of southern France, with the exception of Montpellier. This agreement did not create the modern boundary of France and Spain, since Roussillon, on the northern or 'French' side of the Pyrenees, did not come to the kingdom of France until 1659, but it was a clear attempt to make the territory ruled by a dynasty and the territory of the kingdom identical.

Dynastic lands that extended beyond the boundaries of a single kingdom could create divided loyalties. The kings of England who were also dukes of Normandy in the years 1066–1204 ruled over a cross-Channel territory with a cross-Channel aristocracy. The great aristocrats with lordships in Normandy and in England had as little interest as their rulers in giving any weight to the fact that their lands were in two kingdoms. The kings of France obviously thought differently, and the conquest of Normandy by the French king in 1204 made it untenable for the Anglo-Norman aristocracy to continue to hold lands on both sides of the Channel (with a few exceptions). In 1244 Louis IX of France issued an ultimatum to his subjects who held lands in England: 'since nobody can serve two lords properly, you must adhere fully and inseparably either to me or to the king of England'.[63] Some then chose to abandon their English lands, some to give up their French lands. Henry III of England responded by ordering the seizure of all lands in England held by subjects of the French king.[64] A similar fissure occurred after the outbreak of interminable warfare between England and Scotland in 1295 ended the two peaceful centuries when great nobles could happily hold lands in both kingdoms. As national antagonisms deepened in the later Middle Ages, the international networks of religious houses were also sometimes disrupted. In England 'alien priories', that is, smaller religious houses in England that were dependencies of abbeys in France, were repeatedly confiscated during war between the two countries, and by the early fifteenth century almost all had either been converted into independent

English houses or granted to native monasteries or colleges. The same ruptures affected ties between English and Scottish monasteries.

In addition to creating territories that comprised lands in more than one kingdom, dynastic transmission might bring in foreign rulers. If the throne passed to or through women, this could lead to the prospect of inheritance of the throne by a foreign husband or son. A famous example is the claim of Edward III of England to the throne of France, a claim transmitted through his mother, the French princess Isabella. A French writer expressed, in hypothetical terms, his view of foreign rulers coming to the French throne in such a way:

> Say, for example, that the king of France had an elder daughter and a son who was younger; this daughter was married to a son of the king of Hungary, and a son is born from that marriage; who would in reason love the people and the kingdom of France better, the younger son of the king, or the son of this older daughter? Without a doubt, the son of the king.[65]

Edward III's English subjects also had their reservations about having a ruler who was both king of England and king of France, and when he made his claim to the French throne he had to reassure them that 'the kingdom of England would in no way be subject to the kingdom of France'.[66]

Medieval aristocracies were extremely wary and distrustful about the prospect of their kingdom coming into the hands of a foreign ruler through marriage. When a marriage was negotiated between the heir to the kingdom of England and the heir to the kingdom of Scotland in 1290, the Scots lords secured explicit promises that 'the rights, laws, liberties and customs of the kingdom of Scotland ... shall be observed, whole and inviolable, for all time' and that 'the kingdom of Scotland shall remain separate and delimited from the kingdom of England, free in itself and without any subjection'; other commitments were precise, including provisions that no one would be summoned outside the kingdom for any crime committed within it and that the new royal seal of Scotland would be of exactly the same design as the old one.[67] The Scots thus accepted the prospect of a foreign ruler, but only with safeguards.

Similar documents spelling out the limits of personal union or pre-serving the position of native nobles can be found elsewhere when a foreign king seemed likely. In 1310, when John, count of Luxemburg, was attempting to win the crown of Bohemia, as husband of the sister of the last king of the native Premyslid dynasty, he made a series of promises designed to win the support of the Bohemian nobility. The nobles would not have to undertake military service beyond the frontiers of Bohemia and Moravia, unless they agreed and were paid to do so; the general tax called *berna* would be levied only for the king's coronation and the marriage of his daughters; the right of daughters to inherit estates in the absence of sons was recognized. Then follow clauses designed to prevent John bringing in and endowing his foreign followers:

> we will not appoint any foreigner as captain, burgrave or castellan in our castles, or as fief-holder or official in Bohemia or Moravia, or in our court, nor will we give, either in perpetuity or for a term, any estates, possessions, castles or offices to foreigners, nor allow them to inherit them in the kingdom of Bohemia in any way.[68]

John was crowned king of Bohemia soon after issuing this document and his male-line descendants bore the title down to 1437.

Rather similar terms were agreed by Louis the Great, king of Hungary, in 1355, when he wished to win the assent of the Polish nobility to his succession to the Polish throne after the death of its current incumbent; Louis was a grandson of the previous Polish king through his mother. He promised the Polish nobles that, if they accepted him as heir to their kingdom, he would impose no extraordinary taxation, as the current king and his father had done, he would not demand hospitality for his court when travelling, or, if this was unavoidable, he would pay for any-thing consumed, and that if a military expedition went beyond the borders of Poland, he would reimburse those who accompanied him.[69]

Resentment against foreign kings was expressed very explicitly by a Swedish cleric in the following century, after the death of King Christopher of Sweden, Norway and Denmark in 1448. Although Christopher was distantly descended from earlier Scandinavian mon-archs, he was the son of a German prince of the house of Wittelsbach and had been brought up at the court of the Holy Roman Emperor and he had employed German officials and advisers extensively during his reign. After his death, the Swedes chose a native nobleman, Charles Knutsson, as their king. An ecclesiastic at the cathedral of Strängnäs picked up his pen to record his feelings about this: 'It is not possible to measure how much damage the kingdom and Sweden and its inhabitants have suffered from a foreign king and the lordship and rule of foreigners. God preserve us, so that never shall foreign rulers be lords over us Swedes!'[70]

Native aristocracies thus sought ways to avoid their kingdoms being swallowed up in dynastic empires. Others, too, might have an interest in ensuring that the accidents of birth, marriage and death did not produce dangerous mega-states. A case of this type that was to dominate European politics for a century occurred in 1194, when, through inheritance backed by conquest, the emperor Henry VI acquired the kingdom of Sicily. From the point of view of the papacy, this produced a kind of threatening sandwich, with the Holy Roman Empire to the north of the papal lands and the kingdom of Sicily to the south in the same hands. Papal policy was thereafter governed by the need to keep these two realms separate, a goal made somewhat easier by the elective nature of the Empire. But the price of this policy was eternal vigilance. In 1209, for instance, Pope Innocent III was willing to crown Otto IV emperor in Rome, but then found that Otto planned to recreate the union of the Empire and Sicily, invading the kingdom and seeking to replace its young ruler, Frederick II, son of the emperor Henry VI. Innocent then switched his support to Frederick. In 1216 Frederick formally promised that, when he became emperor, he would hand over Sicily to his son Henry, 'lest it be thought there was any kind of union of kingdom and Empire'.[71]

The Hohenstaufen cause was inherited by the royal house of Aragon and when Pope Martin IV deprived Peter III of Aragon of his kingdom in 1283 and offered it to a son of the king of France, he specified that this son 'should not be the one who is to succeed him in the kingdom of France' and went on to make complex provisions aimed at avoiding any personal union of the two kingdoms, and, extending the prohibition further, ruled that Aragon 'should never at any time be united in the same person with the kingdoms of France or Castile or Leon or England'.[72] The combination of Sicily and the Empire in the hands of one ruler had been trouble enough, and all nightmare unions of this type were henceforth to be banned.

Relations between kings and those they ruled were shaped by their subjects' conceptions of the community or territory to which they belonged. The kings of medieval Europe did not always bother to specify what they were kings *of.* The title 'king' might serve quite well on its own. For example, the kings of Burgundy in the period of the independent kingdom (888–1032) normally appear in their documents in this simple form: 'Rudolf, by God's favour, king'.[73] But kings often did add a genitive noun to their title, and it is significant what that noun was. Were they kings of peoples, kingdoms, lands? There is a general tendency for royal titles to become territorial as the Middle Ages progress, earlier kings being kings of peoples, later ones kings of countries, although this was not a universal trend.[74] English kings were 'kings of the English' in their documents before the reign of John (1199–1216) but 'kings of England' from that time. In some cases the multiple titles of rulers indicate a recognition that their lands were a congeries of territories. The later charters of Ferdinand III (d. 1252), for example, give his title as 'by the grace of God, king of Castile, of Toledo, of Leon, of Galicia, of Seville, of Cordoba, of Murcia and of Jaén'.[75] The title makes no attempt to impose a unity on the lands he ruled as king. In contrast, the king of the French was usually just 'the king of the French (*rex Francorum*)'. An instructive exception is the way that Louis VII had become 'king of the French and duke of the Aquitanians (*rex Francorum et dux Aquitanorum*)' on marriage to Eleanor of Aquitaine, heir to the duchy. The implication of this title was that being king of the French did not make you ruler of Aquitaine. Later kings recognized that this point of view was unacceptable. When Louis' son, Philip Augustus, swallowed up Normandy in 1204, he did not become 'king of the French and duke of the Normans'. Philip and his successors regarded the title of 'king of the French' as encompassing the whole kingdom; they did not need special titles for different parts of it.[76] The dynasty was stressing the identity of the rulers, the kingdom and the inhabitants of the kingdom, what has been called 'regnal solidarity'.[77]

Conclusion

SO WHY DID THE DYNASTIC SYSTEM OF POLITICAL POWER come to an end? The first answer is that it didn't completely. Apart from the few remaining countries where hereditary monarchs still exercise real political power, there have also been some modern dictatorships where sons have been groomed to step into their father's shoes, as in the case of North Korea, and even in democracies there have been political dynasties producing recurrent presidents. Nevertheless, direct transmission of ruling power through inheritance has virtually disappeared. Office has been distinguished from property, the latter being quite legitimately transmitted on family lines, while the former cannot be. And this distinction was made during the period of the dynastic system. A French lawyer writing in 1419 puts it very clearly: 'The lordship that the king has in the kingdom is of a different kind from the lordship of property that is transmitted through family inheritance.'[1] So the monarch does not own the realm in the same way that a householder owns a house. Once this wedge had been inserted, there was plenty of learned theory to back the idea that kingship was an office not a piece of family property, and kings could be criticized for not fulfilling the duties of their office. The Church sometimes stressed the idea that kings had to be 'suitable', a usefully indeterminate quality that aggressive popes like Gregory VII (1073–85) actually did use to justify deposition and replacement of kings.[2] Legal experts spoke of the king being 'under the law'.

The idea that kingship was an office with duties as well as rights was embodied in the promises given at coronation. Before he could be anointed or crowned in 1189, Richard I of England had to swear on the gospels and on holy relics,

> that, all the days of his life, he would exhibit peace and honour and reverence towards God and Holy Church and her ordained clergy ... that he would exercise rightful justice and equity among the people entrusted to him ... that he would abolish bad laws and wicked customs if any had been introduced into his kingdom, and establish good laws and observe them without any deceit or bad intention.[3]

Similar sworn undertakings formed part of the coronation service in other countries.

In those kingdoms where the kingship was theoretically elective, it became the practice for newly chosen rulers to issue what have been called 'election charters' or 'coronation charters', with a series of provisions about how they would rule. In Scandinavia, the first such charter was issued by Erik V Klipping of Denmark in 1282 and subsequently became a standard feature of Danish political life, while the practice was adopted in Sweden in 1371 and Norway in 1449.[4] That issued by Christopher II of Denmark in 1320, amongst other things, abolished recently imposed taxes, specified that the king could only make war with the consent of the great men and prohibited him from employing Germans as officials or counsellors. All these oaths and undertakings suggest that the concept of monarchy as the inherited property of the ruler, with which he could do what he liked, was not the only one. Kingship could also be seen as entailing reciprocal obligations, answerable office and binding promises. In a charter of 1367, the king of France gave a long and detailed list of the privileges of the Dauphiné and then ruled that the inhabitants could refuse to do homage to a new Dauphin unless he first swore to uphold them.[5] If there was a contract of such kind between ruler and ruled, the question might arise of what to do if the ruler broke it.

If one believes that there are 'peoples', 'nations' or 'communities', then it is possible to claim that these entities have interests of their own, separate from and perhaps opposed to those of the rulers. A good example comes from Scotland in the early fourteenth century, a time when Robert Bruce was fighting to establish himself as king of an

independent Scotland in the face of determined English efforts to sub-
due the kingdom. In the Declaration of Arbroath of 1320, the leaders of
the Scots praised Robert Bruce for the way he had led the fight for
Scotland's independence, but added,

> But if he should give up what he has begun, seeking to subject us or our
> kingdom to the king of the English or the English, we would immediately
> strive to expel him as our enemy and a subverter of his right and ours, and
> we would make someone else our king.[6]

Their loyalty, they were saying, was to their kingdom first, to the
dynasty second.

In several ways, the relationship of the dynasty to the kingdom and its
inhabitants, perhaps conceived collectively as a nation, could become
difficult. National feeling could be harnessed by dynasties to reinforce
their power and authority but it could also fuel opposition to them.
A good example of the former case is England, where, from as early as
the tenth century, 'king, people and country formed the unity that was
England and the English people'.[7] In the thirteenth century England
also provides a good example of the latter, as the opponents of Henry III
were partly inspired by a hostility to his foreign relatives and favourites,
and reportedly demanded of the king 'that all foreigners should be
expelled from England and it should be governed by natives'.[8]

Royal families or families aspiring to royalty had to fight hard to
convince the inhabitants of the kingdom of the unity of 'king, people
and country'. Dynasties looked out for their family interests, not for those
of a nation or people, insofar as these can be said to have 'interests'.
Dynasties came from somewhere. Ruling families might well have
a regional power base. The Ottonians were a Saxon dynasty and had to
struggle to win recognition in Bavaria and Lotharingia. The Capetians
were for a long time limited to the Ile-de-France and its adjacent territories. When Philip Augustus came to Tournai in 1187, the local chronicler pointed out that 'it was unheard of that any of his predecessors had
ever come there'.[9] The successful dynasties, as the Capetians eventually
became, were the ones who convinced a large enough number of important people that the community they identified with, kingdom, country
or nation, was actually embodied in the ruling family: 'for king *and*

country' not 'for king *or* country'. When country and king parted ways, a new politics was born. As representative assemblies (estates, parliaments) became widespread and regular in the later Middle Ages, the question might arise, who speaks for the kingdom, the king or the estates? War between different claimants to the throne was commonplace in medieval Europe, but war between the king and those who claimed to represent the country or kingdom was another kind of conflict.

It was rare in the Middle Ages, or indeed in subsequent centuries, for opposition to the ruler to aim at putting an end to monarchy itself, although something like this happened in northern Italy and in Switzerland, but, more recently, European monarchies have frequently been formally abolished: in England, precociously but temporarily, in the years 1649–60; in France in 1792–1804, 1848–52, and finally in 1870; in Portugal in 1910; in Austria–Hungary (including Bohemia) and Germany after the First World War; in Greece in 1924–35, and definitively in 1973/4; in Spain in 1873–4 and in 1931, although, very unusually, the monarchy was restored in 1975; in Italy in 1946. The modern trend in Europe has been against dynasty. In 1900 every European state except France and Switzerland was a monarchy. In 2000 only seven were left (excluding mini-states) and in all of them the sovereign's power was purely ceremonial.

In medieval Europe, however, dynastic politics were the rule not the exception. It was a time, in the words of the historian of Lambert Simnel, Matthew Bennet, 'when the destinies of nations were tied to bloodlines'.[10] This resulted in a curious blend of certainty and uncertainty. Rudolf Schieffer, discussing the relationships between fathers and sons in the Carolingian dynasty, pointed out that, in this dynastic world, not only were marriages, births and deaths 'political events of the first importance', but 'personal changes at the top level became apparent on the horizon years or even decades before they happened in fact'.[11] This situation is what explains the combination of the known and the unknown in the political landscape. Everyone knew that the king would die; no one was sure when. Ambitious young nobles might be tempted to support a restless young prince, chafing at the bit to succeed his father, but what if the father lived for another ten or twenty years? Everyone is going to be alive one day and dead the next, but we do not know what days they will be. 'Nothing is more certain than death,' went the medieval saying, 'but nothing is more uncertain than the hour of death.'[12] Death could come at age two, at age twenty, at age forty, even at the age of a hundred, although there seem to be no examples of rulers dying at that age. And the same uncertain certainty was true of many other things in this world of family politics. Even apparently certain situations could change. Old childless kings were likely to die without sons, but who knew whether a late marriage to a young bride might alter everything?

Ruling dynasties were not biological units but political ones. Collateral branches might be excluded or pruned, the offspring of some sexual unions put on a different legal footing from others, females given the same rights of inheritance as males or not. Family structures varied across medieval Europe and over the course of time. Yet dynasties were political units governed by biological uncertainty in such crucial matters as the fertility of a bride, the sex of children and sudden death. 'The destinies of nations were tied to blood-lines', but blood-lines fail. Writing in the late 1050s, the intransigent cardinal Humbert of Silva Candida raged against the rulers of his time, who had dared to interfere in the business of the Church. He warned them that God can punish in this world as well as in the next, and, after pointing out as examples the wars, earthquakes, tempests, diseases and famines that were afflicting Christians, he added as especially relevant to them, the way that dynasties become extinct:

> Moreover, let them consider that, in the land of the French, where kings succeed though family relationship, which king for a hundred years and more can be recalled whose descendants ruled even to the fourth generation? The Ottos, who were worse intruders on the priestly office than any kings before them, scarcely attained the third generation. And, after them, the first Henry left no further generation. Anyone who investigates will be able to find out what has happened in other kingdoms and principalities.[13]

Humbert is referring to Otto I, Otto II and Otto III, whose direct line died out in 1002 and were succeeded by Henry II (titled Henry I as emperor), who died childless in 1024. And, at the time he was writing, no French family had held the throne for more than three successive generations without interruption for almost two hundred years. So his comments on the impermanence of dynasties are literally correct.

In this world biological luck had big consequences. The Norman Conquest of 1066, when a French-speaking aristocracy seized England and displaced its native ruling class, with all the political and cultural consequences that flowed from that, was only conceivable because of the succession crisis posed by the childlessness of its king. If Edward the Confessor had had a son, the English language spoken today would be very different, with far fewer words of French origin, and perhaps still with those bewildering endings that German has maintained. Much of this book has been about things that did not happen. Any study of a dynastic system is always throwing up such counterfactuals: there could have been a European state consisting of Castile and France; there could have been a big independent state between France and Germany; the Scandinavian kingdoms might all be one. In the present world, as mentioned, several states, such as Spain and the United Kingdom, are the result of dynastic marriages, of the fifteenth and sixteenth centuries respectively in these examples. Nationalists sometimes talk as if nations are primordial and perennial, but countries come and go, and nations with them. There were no Belgians in the Middle Ages.

Dynastic politics also meant that the place of passions was even more central than it is in modern democratic polities. Chastellain, the dry-eyed observer of late medieval power, sees the rivalry of rulers as natural, since 'rulers are men and their affairs are high and grave, and their nature is subject to many passions, such as hatred and envy, and their hearts are truly the habitation of such things because of their glory in ruling'.[14] Glory, hatred, envy. Many other things shaped the politics of medieval Europe – religious beliefs, personalities, class hatred, class pride, love of liberty, nationalism, xenophobia, economic interests – but, almost everywhere and almost always, a major part in the story was played by dynasticism, that is, the births, marriages and deaths of the rulers and the dynamics of their families – and their passions.

APPENDIX A

Main Dynasties

The Main Royal and Imperial Dynasties of Latin Christendom and Byzantium 500–1500

Aragon

The kingdom of Aragon was created in 1035 by Sancho III of Navarre for his illegitimate son Ramiro. The betrothal of Ramiro's great-granddaughter, Petronilla, queen of Aragon, and Raymond Berengar, count of Barcelona, in 1137 created a composite state ('The Crown of Aragon'), which was ruled by their male-line descendants until 1410; after a two-year interregnum, the crown then passed into the hands of a junior branch of the Castilian royal family (see above, pp. 74–6).

Bohemia

The native dynasty, the Premyslids, ruled as dukes or kings down to 1306. After a period of competition and uncertainty, the house of Luxemburg then ruled from 1311 to 1437.

Burgundy

There was an early medieval kingdom of the Burgundians, which was conquered by the Franks in 534; an independent kingdom of Burgundy 888–1032, ruled by the 'Rudolfinger' dynasty, subsequently a constituent part of the Holy Roman Empire; as well as the late medieval lands of the dukes of Burgundy, who aspired to an independent kingship.

Byzantium

Before the eleventh century, few dynasties continued for more than a generation or two. Exceptions are the Heraclian dynasty, 610–711 (with a hiatus from 695 to 705), and the Macedonian, 867–1056. The Comnenians reigned from 1081 to 1185 and the Angeloi from 1185 to 1204. After the Byzantines reconquered Constantinople from the westerners in 1261, the empire was ruled by the Palaeologan dynasty down to the conquest of Constantinople by the Turks in 1453.

Castile

See Leon-Castile.

Cyprus

The French Lusignan dynasty ruled Cyprus from 1197 to 1489, the last monarch being Catherine Cornaro, widow of James II of Lusignan.

Denmark

Descendants of Gorm the Old, sometimes called the house of Jelling, ruled Denmark from the middle of the tenth century until 1042; his descendants through the female line then reigned from Sven Estrithson (1047–74/6) until 1375 (with one female-line descendant 1137–46); in the later Middle Ages, the three Scandinavian kingdoms often had common rulers: Denmark and Norway had a common king from 1380; Denmark, Norway and Sweden from 1388 (*de iure*) and 1396 (de facto).

England

In the early Middle Ages Anglo-Saxon England was divided into numerous kingdoms, a system sometimes called the Heptarchy ('Seven Kingdoms'), an idealized and simplified concept that assumed the kingdoms were East Anglia, Essex, Kent, Sussex, Wessex, Mercia and Northumbria. All these except Wessex disappeared during the Viking invasions of the ninth century and the kings of Wessex united

England under their rule during the tenth. The Wessex kings ruled England until 1066, with gaps during the reigns of the Danish kings from 1013 to 1014 and from 1016 to 1042. The Norman kings reigned from 1066 to 1154, the Plantagenets from 1154 to 1485, with the Lancastrian branch reigning from 1399 to 1461 and 1470 to 1471, and the Yorkist branch 1461–70 and 1471–85. The Tudors reigned from 1485.

France

The kingdom of the West Franks, or France, emerged from the break-up of the Frankish kingdoms (q.v.) in 888. The last Carolingians ruled to 987, with gaps from 888 to 898 and 922 to 936, the Capetians from 987, with the Valois branch from 1328.

Frankish Kingdoms

The Frankish kingdoms were ruled by Merovingians from c. 500 to 751 and Carolingians from 751; the Frankish kingdom finally broke up in 888; thereafter see France and Germany. See also Holy Roman Empire.

Germany

The kingdom of the East Franks, or Germany, emerged from the break-up of the Frankish kingdoms (q.v.) in 888. The last Carolingians ruled to 911, the Ottonians 919–1024, the Salians 1024–1125, the Hohenstaufen 1138–1254; thereafter rulers from various dynasties (see p. 398 above) until 1438, when the Habsburgs established themselves. See also Holy Roman Empire.

Holy Roman Empire

Charlemagne, king of the Franks, was crowned Roman emperor on Christmas day 800. Thereafter, for more than a thousand years, this improbable title was an adjunct of rulers whose power was usually based north of the Alps. Charlemagne's direct descendants held it until 899, then, for a generation, it was contested between various Italian rulers; in

962 Otto I, king of the East Franks (Germany) was crowned emperor and thereafter the title was always linked with rule in Germany. Geographically, the Empire then consisted of, roughly, Germany and northern Italy. It was dissolved in 1806. In the period covered by this book, the title 'Holy Roman Empire' was not a contemporary term and is used here as a convenience.

Hungary

The native Arpad dynasty ruled from the tenth century until 1301 (with female-line descendants 1038–46); the Angevins 1310–95; the Hungarian noble Matthias Corvinus ruled from 1458 to 1490.

Ireland

Early medieval Ireland had 100 to 150 kings, of different rank and standing, from the *rí tuaithe*, a local king ruling an area of about 200 to 250 square miles, through overkings and provincial kings, to the *ard rí* or high king. Provincial dynasties of importance in the central and late Middle Ages included the O'Briens (Uí Briain) and MacCarthys (MacCarthaigh) of Munster, the O'Connors (Uí Conchobhair) of Connacht, the O'Neils (Uí Néill) of Ulster and the MacMurroughs (Mac Murchada) of Leinster.

Jerusalem

After the Christian conquest of Jerusalem in 1099, the crusaders elected Godfrey de Bouillon, a son of the count of Boulogne, as ruler but he did not take the title of king. On his death in 1100, his brother Baldwin became King Baldwin I and was succeeded by a distant cousin, Baldwin of Le Bourg, as Baldwin II. Among the descendants of Baldwin II the throne frequently passed through the female line (1131, 1185, 1186, 1190, 1205, 1212), in most cases with queens regnant whose husbands exercised royal authority and usually had the title of king. In this way the title came to the Hohenstaufen dynasty (see Germany) 1225–68. It then passed to the Lusignan kings of Cyprus, although there were other claimants. After the fall of the kingdom to the Muslims in 1291 it was a purely honorific title.

Leon-Castile

The kings of Asturias and Leon from 739 to 1037 were all male-line descendants of Peter, duke of Cantabria (with one exception, Silo, 774–83). Ferdinand of Castile, a younger son of the king of Navarre, seized the throne in 1037 and, after him, his sons ruled Leon and Castile until 1109, when the crown passed to his granddaughter Urraca, the first female sovereign in western Europe. Her descendants by her first husband, Raymond of Burgundy, ruled Leon and Castile until the reign of Isabella the Catholic (1474–1504). Leon and Castile were in the hands of different branches of the family 1157–1230, and an illegitimate male descendant, Henry of Trastámara, seized the throne in 1369, so late medieval Castilian monarchs are sometimes classified as 'the house of Trastámara'.

Lombards

The Lombards, a Germanic people, arrived in Italy in 568 and occupied large parts of the peninsula. Their kings, based in the north of the country, came from various different families and no long-lasting dynasty emerged. In 774 Charlemagne conquered the Lombards and took the title 'King of the Franks and the Lombards'.

Majorca

Conquered from the Muslims by the king of Aragon in the thirteenth century, it was ruled by its own kings, younger members of the Aragonese royal house, from 1276 to 1285 and 1298 to 1343; otherwise it was ruled by the kings of Aragon.

Naples

The revolt of 1282, called the Sicilian Vespers, split the kingdom of Sicily (see Sicily below) into an island half and a mainland half. The capital of the latter was the city of Naples. Here the descendants of Charles I of Anjou ruled down to 1435, though frequently with rivals, either from their own dynasty or from the so-called 'second house of Anjou' (sometimes, confusingly, called the 'third house of Anjou'!), which was descended from Louis of Anjou (d. 1384), younger brother of the king of France. Louis' grandson, René, was in effective control of Naples from 1435 to 1442, but the kingdom was then taken by Alfonso, king of Aragon and Sicily, and, after his death in 1458, was ruled by his descendants as a separate kingdom.

Navarre

Navarre (known as the kingdom of Pamplona until the twelfth century) emerged as a kingdom in the ninth century, was ruled by various branches of a native dynasty from 905 until 1234, then passed by marriage to the counts of Champagne. In the later Middle Ages Navarre was unusual in the number of queens-regnant it had (see p. 447). It therefore passed through several dynasties as calculated by male-line descent. It was in the hands of the Capetian kings of France, either as consorts or direct rulers from 1284 to 1328, then in the hands of a junior branch of the Capetians, again as consorts or direct rulers, from 1328 to 1425.

Norway

Information about the early kings of Norway, mainly drawn from the sagas, is uncertain. After the reign of Harald Hardrada (1046/7–66) most Norwegian kings either were or claimed to be his descendant, down to 1319. In the later Middle Ages, the three Scandinavian kingdoms often had common rulers: Norway had a common king with Sweden from 1319 to 1343 and from 1362 to 1364; Norway and Denmark had a common king from 1380; Norway, Denmark and Sweden from 1388 (*de iure*) and 1396 (de facto).

Poland

The native Piast dynasty ruled as dukes or kings down to 1370, with an interval of rule by the Premyslids of Bohemia 1300–1306, but for much of that period (1138–1295, 1296–1300 and 1306–20) Poland was divided into independent duchies with no king. Louis the Great of Hungary ruled as king from 1370 to 1382 and was succeeded in Poland by his daughter Hedwig (Jadwiga), who married Jagiello, prince of Lithuania; he and his descendants, the Jagiellonian dynasty, ruled down to 1572.

Portugal

Portugal emerged as a separate kingdom in the twelfth century. It was based on the county of the same name, part of the kingdom of Leon-Castile which Alfonso VI granted to his illegitimate daughter Teresa and her husband, the immigrant nobleman Henry of Burgundy. After the deaths of both Alfonso and Henry, Teresa began styling herself queen (see above, pp. 134–5). Her son Alfonso removed her from power in 1128 and assumed the royal title in 1139. This was formally recognized by the pope in 1179. All subsequent medieval kings and queens of Portugal descend from Alfonso I, after 1385 through the illegitimate John of Avis.

Scotland

The territory of modern Scotland was, in the early medieval period, divided between the Irish kingdom of Dalriada on the west coast ('Scots' originally meant 'Irish'), the kingdom or kingdoms of the Picts in the east and north and the kingdom of Strathclyde in the south-west. South-east Scotland (Lothian) was Anglo-Saxon, while Scandinavian settlements were established along the coasts and isles from the ninth century. The ruling dynasty of Dalriada gradually brought much of this area under its control. Kenneth Macalpine (Cináed mac Alpin) (d. 858) is traditionally regarded as first king of Picts and Scots and his male-line descendants ruled in Scotland until the eleventh century, when the kingship passed through the female line. This branch then ruled as kings of Scots continuously from 1057 to 1286. After a regency from 1286–92, John Balliol's brief reign (1292–6) and the English conquest, the Bruces reigned from 1306 to 1371, and the Stewarts inherited the throne through marriage in 1371.

Sicily

The kingdom was created by Norman conquerors, headed by the sons of Tancred de Hauteville, who established their authority over the island of Sicily and much of the south Italian mainland in the eleventh century. The royal title was conferred in 1130. In 1194, this Norman line was displaced by Henry VI, the Holy Roman Emperor, who had married Constance, last legitimate member of the royal family. Henry was a member of the Hohenstaufen dynasty, descendants of the dukes of Swabia, which is why Italian historians refer to Hohenstaufen rule in the kingdom of Sicily as *svevo* (e.g. 'lo stato normanno e svevo'). At the invitation of the papacy, Charles of Anjou conquered the kingdom in 1266, dispossessing the Hohenstaufen. But Charles, the first king of the Angevin line, lost the island of Sicily itself during the so-called Sicilian Vespers of 1282 (see Naples, above). From 1282 Sicily was ruled by members of the royal family of Aragon, sometimes by kings of Aragon (1282–5, 1291–5), otherwise by a junior branch. Sicily was in permanent union with Aragon after 1409.

Sweden

The twelfth and early thirteenth centuries were marked by rivalry between two dynasties, those of Erik and Sverker. From 1250 to 1364 the Folkungs, descendants of the strongman Birger Jarl and his wife, a member of the Erik dynasty, ruled. In the later Middle Ages, the three Scandinavian kingdoms often had common rulers: Sweden had a common king with Norway from 1319 to 1343 and 1362–4; Sweden, Norway and Denmark from 1388 (*de iure*) and 1396 (de facto).

Visigothic Kingdom

The Visigoths settled in southern Gaul in 418, then extended into the Iberian peninsula. Although they lost most of southern Gaul to the Franks in 507, they ruled their Iberian kingdom down to the time of the Muslim invasion of 711. They had native kings of various families, which sometimes held the throne for more than one generation, as in the periods 418–531 and 567–603.

Wales

Wales was divided into several principalities, the most important of which were Gwynedd in the north, Powys in the centre and Deheubarth in the south. Anglo-Norman conquest and settlement from the late eleventh century established Marcher lordships amongst these native principalities. The last native prince was killed in 1282 and his domains taken by the English Crown.

APPENDIX B

Minorities

Provisional List of Kings, Emperors and Queens Regnant Coming to the Throne Younger than 15 in Latin Christendom and Byzantium 500–1500. Ages Given are Often Approximations.

Name	Kingdom	Accession	Age
Athalaric	Ostrogoths	526	8
Theudebald	Franks	547	*parvulus*
Childebert II	Franks	575	5
Clothar II	Franks	584	0
Theudebert II	Franks	596	11
Theuderic II	Franks	596	10
Sigebert II	Franks	613	11
Adaloald	Lombards	616	14
Reccared II	Visigoths	621	*parvulus*
Sigebert III	Franks	633/4	3
Clovis II	Franks	639	6
Constans II	Byzantium	641	11
Clothar III	Franks	657	8
Childeric II	Franks	662	7
Garibald	Lombards	671	<8
Clovis III (IV)	Franks	690/1	13/14
Liutpert	Lombards	700	*puerilis aetatis*
Osred	Northumbria	705	8
Dagobert III	Franks	711	11–15
Constantine VI	Byzantium	780	9
Michael III	Byzantium	842	2
Charles of Provence	Provence	855	10
Carloman	West Franks	879	12
Louis the Blind	Provence	890	9
Louis the Child	East Franks	900	6
Constantine VII	Byzantium	913	8
García I Sánchez	Navarre	925	6
Lothar	West Franks	954	13

(cont.)

Name	Kingdom	Accession	Age
Edgar	Mercia	957	14
Edward the Martyr	England	975	13
Æthelred the Unready	England	978	10
Otto III	Germany	983	3
Alfonso V	Leon	999	5
Vermudo III	Leon	1028	11
Henry IV	Germany	1056	5
Philip I	France	1060	8
Sigurd Magnusson	Norway	1103	13/14
Olaf Magnusson	Norway	1103	4/5
Sigurd Haraldsson	Norway	1136	5
Inge Haraldsson	Norway	1136	3
Petronilla	Aragon	1137	1
Malcolm IV	Scotland	1153	12
Haakon Sigurdsson	Norway	1157	10
Alfonso VIII	Castile	1158	2
Magnus Erlingsson	Norway	1161	5
Alfonso II	Aragon	1164	7
Baldwin IV	Jerusalem	1174	13
Alexius II	Byzantium	1180	11
Baldwin V	Jerusalem	1185	7
Frederick II	Sicily	1198	2
Ladislas III	Hungary	1204	4
James I	Aragon	1213	5
Henry I	Castile	1214	10
Henry III	England	1216	9
Sancho II	Portugal	1223	13
Louis IX	France	1226	12
Alexander III	Scotland	1249	7
Theobald II	Navarre	1253	14
John IV	Byzantium	1258	7
Erik V Klipping	Denmark	1259	10
Joanna I	Navarre	1274	1
Wenceslas II	Bohemia	1278	6
Erik Magnusson	Norway	1280	12
Erik Menved	Denmark	1286	12
Birger Magnusson	Sweden	1290	10
Ferdinand IV	Leon-Castile	1295	9
Alfonso XI	Leon-Castile	1312	1
John I	France	1316	0
Magnus Eriksson	Norway/Sweden	1319	3
Edward III	England	1327	14
David II	Scotland	1329	5
John V	Byzantium	1341	9
Frederick III	Sicily	1355	13
Olaf	Denmark	1376	6
Richard II	England	1377	10

(cont.)

Name	Kingdom	Accession	Age
Maria	Sicily	1377	14
Charles VI	France	1380	11
Mary	Hungary	1382	12
Beatrice	Portugal	1383	10
Hedwig	Poland	1384	10
Henry III	Castile	1390	11
John II	Castile	1406	1
James I	Scotland	1406	11
Henry VI	England	1422	0
Wladyslaw III	Poland	1434	10
James II	Scotland	1437	6
Alfonso V	Portugal	1438	6
Ladislas Postumus	Hungary	1440	0
James III	Scotland	1460	9
Francis Phoebus	Navarre	1479	10
Edward V	England	1483	12
Charles VIII	France	1483	13
Catherine	Navarre	1483	14
James IV	Scotland	1488	15 *

* Although James was 15 at accession he is included here since he was treated as a minor.

APPENDIX C

Female Sovereigns

Provisional List of Queens Regnant and Empresses Regnant in Latin Christendom and Byzantium 500–1500

Irene of Byzantium (797–802)+#
Zoe of Byzantium (1042)+#
Theodora of Byzantium (1042, 1055–6)+#
Urraca of Leon-Castile (1109–26)+#
Teresa of Portugal (1116–28/30)
Melisende of Jerusalem (1131–52/61)
Petronilla of Aragon (1137–64)
Sybilla of Jerusalem (1186–90)
Isabella of Jerusalem (1190–1205)
Constance of Sicily (1194–8)+‡
Maria of Jerusalem (1205–12)
Isabella II (Yolande) of Jerusalem (1212–28)
Joanna I of Navarre (1274–1305)+
Joanna II of Navarre (1328–49)
Joanna I of Naples (1343–81)+‡
Margaret of Denmark (1375), Norway (1380) and Sweden (1389) (d. 1412)
Maria of Sicily (1377/92–1401)+‡
Mary of Hungary (1382–5, 1386–95)+
Beatrice of Portugal (1383–5)+
Hedwig (Jadwiga) of Poland (1384–99)+
Joanna II of Naples (1414–35)+
Blanca of Navarre (1425–41)‡
Charlotte of Cyprus (1458–60)+
Catherine Cornaro of Cyprus (1474–89)+#
Isabella of Castile (1474–1504)‡
Leonor of Navarre (1479)
Catherine of Foix of Navarre (1483–1517)‡

Queens with name+ or image# shown alone on coins; shown jointly ‡.

APPENDIX D: Family Trees

Balliol and Bruce

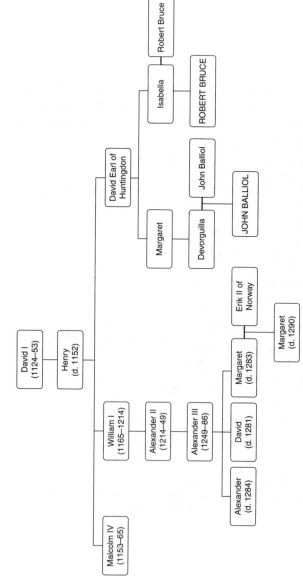

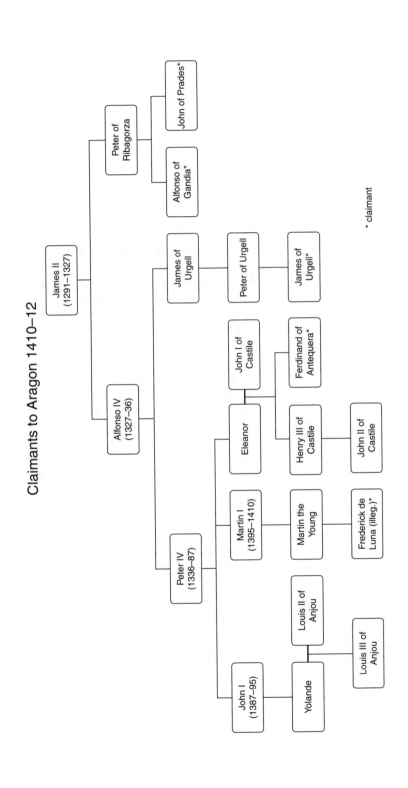

Claimants to Aragon 1410–12

* claimant

Notes

INTRODUCTION: ROYAL FAMILIES

1. 'Ad belli studium, ecce pater; circa Dei cultum, ecce mater': Raoul de Caen, *Gesta Tancredi*, p. 615.

2. 'Plerique colum et pensa sibi mutuo transmittebant innuentes occultius ut ad muliebres operas turpiter demigraret quisquis huius militiae inveniretur immunis': *Itinerarium peregrinorum*, 1. 17, ed. Stubbs, p. 33, ed. Mayer, p. 277 (after Henry II and Philip Augustus take the cross in January 1188).

3. 'a fin que la chose publique feust mieux et plus puissamment deffendue par les malles que par les fumelles': Taylor, 'The Salic Law and the Valois Succession to the French Crown', p. 363, citing Raoul de Presles' translation of the *City of God* in BnF, MS fr 22912–3, fol. 151 (this was composed in 1370–5 and presented to Charles V).

4. Compare the statistics in Lilie, 'Der Kaiser in der Statistik. Subversive Gedanken zur angeblichen Allmacht der byzantinischen Kaiser'; he deals with the whole Byzantine period down to 1453, and counts ninety-four emperors, basing his list on the eighty-eight in Ostrogorsky, *Geschichte des byzantinischen Staates*, p. 479, but adding Artabasdos and counting five emperors twice because they had two periods of rule (see his comments at p. 214 n. 10).

5. *Medieval Slavic Lives of Saints and Princes*, tr. Kantor, p. 45 (Slavonic Life of Constantine (Cyril), c. 9).

6. Aristakès of Lastivert, *Récit des malheurs de la nation Arménienne*, IX (46), p. 32; I am grateful to Tim Greenwood for valuable advice on the translations from this text.

7. There is a large bibliography. Important works that also point to further reading include Simms, *From Kings to Warlords: The Changing Political Structure of Gaelic Ireland in the Later Middle Ages*; Jaski, *Early Irish Kingship and Succession*; Byrne, *Irish Kings and High Kings*; Warntjes, 'Regnal Succession in Early Medieval Ireland'.

8. 'Suein et Harold a concubina geniti erant, qui, ut mos est barbaris, aequam tunc inter liberos Chnud sortiti sunt partem hereditatis': Adam of Bremen, *Gesta Hammaburgensis ecclesiae pontificum*, 2. 74, ed. Schmeidler, p. 134.

9. 'In sola mulierum copula modum nesciunt; quisque secundum facultatem suarum virium duas aut tres et amplius simul habet; divites et principes absque numero. Nam et filios ex tali coniunctione genitos habent legitimos': Adam of Bremen, *Gesta Hammaburgensis ecclesiae pontificum*, 4. 21, ed. Schmeidler, p. 251.

10. Bartlett, *Gerald of Wales 1146–1223*, pp. 38–45 (repr., 39–44).

11. 'In hoc regno, cujus non populi voto aut electione sed sanguinis propagatione, nec jure belli, rex dinoscitur constitui': *Memorials of King Henry VII*, ed. Gairdner, p. 397.

1 CHOOSING A BRIDE

1. Gautier d'Arras, *Eracle*, ed. Pratt, line 1267, p. 38, ed. Löseth, line 1275, p. 67.

2. 'exceptis eis rebus et negociis, sine quibus res publica terrena non subsistit, coniugio videlicet usuque armorum': Notker Balbulus, *Gesta Karoli magni imperatoris*, 2. 10, ed. Haefele, p. 66.

3. Gregory of Tours, *Libri historiarum decem*, 4. 26, ed. Krusch and Levison, pp. 157–9.

4. Fredegar, *Chronica*, 4. 35, ed. Krusch, p. 134, ed. Wallace-Hadrill, p. 22.

5. Fredegar, *Chronica*, 4. 58, ed. Krusch, p. 150, ed. Wallace-Hadrill, p. 49.

6. Wallace-Hadrill, *The Long-Haired Kings*, pp. 203–4. See Ewig, 'Studien zur merowingischen Dynastie', pp. 38–46; Dailey, *Queens, Consorts, Concubines: Gregory of Tours and Women of the Merovingian Elite*, pp. 80–117.

7. 'uxorem de militari ordine sibi imparem duxerit. Quomodo ergo magnus dux patietur de suis militibus feminam sumptam reginam fieri sibique dominari?': Richer of Saint-Rémi, *Historiae*, 4 .11, ed. Hoffmann, p. 238. See Van Winter, 'Uxorem de militari ordine sibi imparem'. Brühl, *Deutschland-Frankreich: die Geburt zweier Völker*, pp. 591–3, argues cogently that neither were these words uttered by Archbishop Adalbero of Rheims, as Richer claims, nor was Charles actually married to a woman significantly below him in status. This does not affect the point that Richer believed such a disparaging marriage *would have been* a powerful objection against Charles' candidacy.

8. 'Equidem multo saluberrimum iudicarim reipublicae, si principum affinitates intra regni fines continerentur': Erasmus, *Institutio principis christiani*, 9. 1, ed. Herding, p. 208.

9. Martin, *A Bride for the Tsar: Bride-Shows and Marriage Politics in Early Modern Russia*, p. 4.

10. Ross, *Edward IV*, pp. 84–103.

11. ὅτι τὲ ἐξ ἀλλοδαπῆς ἐστὶ καὶ συγγενῶν ὄχλος οὐ προσῆν αὐτῇ, δι' ὧν ὁ βασιλεὺς ὀχλοῖτο: Anna Comnena, *Alexias*, 3. 2. 3, ed. Reinsch and Kambylis, p. 91.

12. Hellmann, 'Die Heiraten der Karolinger'; Konecny, *Die Frauen des karolingischen Königshauses*; Kasten, *Königssöhne und Königsherrschaft: Untersuchungen zur Teilhabe am Reich in der Merowinger- und Karolingerzeit*, pp. 252–7; Pohl, 'Why Not to Marry a Foreign Woman: Stephen III's Letter to Charlemagne'.

13. MacLean, *Kingship and Politics in the Late Ninth Century: Charles the Fat and the End of the Carolingian Empire*, p. 2.

14. The sources call them both count and duke: Thegan, *Gesta Hludowici imperatoris*, 4, 26, ed. Tremp, pp. 178, 214; Astronomus, *Vita Hludowici imperatoris*, 8, 32, ed. Tremp, pp. 308, 392; *Annales regni Francorum*, s.a. 819, ed. Kurze, p. 150.

15. 'Volumus etiam ut, si alicui illorum post decessum nostrum tempus nubendi venerit, ut cum consilio et consensu senioris fratris uxorem ducat; illud tamen propter discordias

evitandas et occasiones noxias auferendas cavendum decernimus, ut de exteris gentibus nullus illorum uxorem accipere praesumat': *Capitularia regum Francorum*, 1, ed.
Boretius, no. 136, p. 272 (the 'Ordinatio Imperii').

16. Carloman married a daughter of the important Bavarian count and duke Ernst, Louis
the Younger married Liutgard, daughter of the Saxon count Liudolf, Charles the Fat
married Richardis, daughter of the Alsatian count Erchanger.

17. These statements are based on Werner, 'Die Nachkommen Karls des Grossen'.

18. Barlow, *The Godwins: The Rise and Fall of a Noble Dynasty*, p. 128.

19. Καὶ περὶ ταύτης τῆς ὑποθέσεως παραγγελία καὶ διάταξις φοβερὰ καὶ ἀπαραποίητος τοῦ
μεγάλου καὶ ἁγίου Κωνσταντίνου ἐναπογέγραπται ἐν τῇ ἱερᾷ τραπέζῃ τῆς καθολικῆς τῶν
Χριστιανῶν ἐκκλησίας τῆς Ἁγίας Σοφίας· τοῦ μηδέποτε βασιλέα Ῥωμαίων συμπενθεριάσαι
μετὰ ἔθνους παρηλλαγμένοις καὶ ξένοις ἔθεσι χρωμένου τῆς Ῥωμαϊκῆς καταστάσεως,
μάλιστα δὲ ἀλλοπίστου καὶ ἀβαπτίστου, εἰ μὴ μετὰ μόνων τῶν Φράγγων: Constantine
Porphyrogenitus, *De administrando imperio*, 13, ed. Moravcsik, p. 70.

20. 'Inaudita res est, ut porphyrogeniti porphyrogenita, hoc est in purpura nati filia in
purpura nata, gentibus misceatur': Liudprand of Cremona, 'Legatio', 15, in *Liudprandi
opera*, ed. Becker, p. 184.

21. Skylitzes, *Synopsis historiarum*, ed. Thurn, p. 336.

22. 'Ipso anno Erchanger cum rege pacificatus est, cuius sororem ... rex tanquam pacis
obsidem in matrimonium accepit': *Annales Alamannici, continuatio Sangallensis tertia*, s.a.
913, ed. Pertz, p. 56; 'ut aiunt, sororis sue filiam Karolus tanquam pacis obsidem
Widekindi filio dedit uxorem': *Vita Godefridi comitis Cappenbergensis prima*, ed.
Niemeyer and Ehlers-Kisseler, p. 157; see Althoff, 'Namengebung und adliges
Selbstverständnis', p. 134.

23. 'filia sua Gisla, quae esset vas pacis, pigneratrix federis': William of Malmesbury, *Gesta
regum Anglorum*, 2. 112, ed. Mynors et al., p. 170.

24. For a note about the empire ('Holy Roman Empire') see Appendix A; for comment on
the significance of the marriage in the eyes of the Hohenstaufen, see Weller, *Die
Heiratspolitik des deutschen Hochadels im 12. Jahrhundert*, pp. 192–5.

25. 'Quae cum pulcherrimae essent et ab eo plurimum diligerentur, mirum dictu, quod
nullam earum cuiquam aut suorum aut exterorum nuptum dare voluit, sed omnes
secum usque ad obitum suum in domo sua retinuit, dicens se earum contubernio
carere non posse': Einhard, *Vita Karoli Magni*, 19, ed. Holder-Egger, p. 25.

26. Dagron, *Emperor and Priest: The Imperial Office in Byzantium*, p. 33.

27. John's marriage to Isabella of Gloucester took place before he was king (or was
expected to be king) and was dissolved in the first year of his reign.

28. Margaret, wife of Harold Hen (1074–80); Bodil, wife of Erik Evergood (1095–1103);
Helwig, wife of Valdemar IV (1340–75). Helwig was the daughter of Duke Erik II of
Schleswig and hence a cousin of the king. See Skovgaard-Petersen, 'Queenship in
Medieval Denmark', with list on pp. 40–2.

29. See, for example, the imaginative maps of bride exchange in Spiess, 'Europa heiratet.
Kommunikation und Kulturtransfer im Kontext europäischer Königsheiraten des
Spätmittelalters'; also the thoughtful comments in Spiess, 'Unterwegs zu einem

fremden Ehemann: Brautfahrt und Ehe in europäischen Fürstenhäusern des Spätmittelalters'.

30. Justinian II and Theodora the Khazar, Constantine V and Irene the Khazar, Romanos II and Eudokia (Berta); see the convenient list of empresses in Garland, *Byzantine Empresses: Women and Power in Byzantium, AD 527–1204*, pp. 229–31. It should be noted that the marriage of Justinian II and Theodora, sister of the Khazar ruler, was entered into when Justinian was in exile, so is hardly the same as a marriage negotiated with a ruling emperor.

31. Macrides, 'Dynastic Marriages', p. 268 n. 26, lists ten negotiated and three achieved marriages between Byzantine and western ruling families of the eighth, ninth and tenth centuries; Schreiner, 'Die kaiserliche Familie: Ideologie und Praxis im Rahmen der internationalen Beziehungen in Byzanz', pp. 763–71, lists fifty-seven actual or projected foreign marriage projects from the sixth to the twelfth centuries, plus five doubtful cases.

32. Bryennios, *Historiae*, ed. Gautier, p. 77, says she was the eldest daughter of Samuel, Tsar of the Bulgarians: πρεσβυτέρᾳ τῶν βασιλέως Βουλγάρων Σαμουὴλ θυγατέρων Αἰκατερίνᾳ. Samuel was Tsar 997–1014. Skylitzes, *Synopsis historiarum*, ed. Thurn, p. 492, says she was the daughter of Ivan (John) Vladislav, Samuel's nephew, who conducted the last resistance of the Bulgars to Byzantine conquest in 1015–18: Αἰκατερίναν τὴν θυγατέρα τοῦ Βλαδισθλάβου τοῦ Βουλγαρίας βασιλέως. Scholars seem to accept that she was the daughter of Ivan Vladislav.

33. Some are discussed in Nicol, 'Mixed Marriages in Byzantium in the Thirteenth Century'.

34. 'in mores tamen tam recenter abhorruisti redire Latinos, Graece consuetudinis nimis procaciter emulatrix ... accepta benedictione Latina, susceptoque corpore Christi, Latinis traditionibus consecrato': Innocent III, *Epistolae* 8. 135 (134), *Die Register Innocenz' III.*, ed. Hageneder et al., 8, p. 249 (PL 215, col. 714); see Nicol, 'Mixed Marriages in Byzantium in the Thirteenth Century', pp. 162–3, for this and her later return to 'Greek custom'. For the name change, and the possibility that she reverted to Margaret, see Thoma, *Namensänderungen in Herrscherfamilien des mittelalterlichen Europa*, pp. 180–1.

35. Koran 5. 5; Friedmann, *Tolerance and Coercion in Islam: Interfaith Relations in the Muslim Tradition*, pp. 160–93, analyzes early Sunni tradition on this subject.

36. *Continuatio isidoriana hispana. Crónica mozárabe de 754*, 59, ed. López Pereira, pp. 232–4 (also in MGH, AA 11, p. 356); Ibn 'Abd al-Hakam, 'Narrative of the Conquest of al-Andalus', pp. 39–40; Barton, *Conquerors, Brides, and Concubines: Interfaith Relations and Social Power in Medieval Iberia*, pp. 15–17.

37. *Codex Carolinus*, ed. Gundlach, no. 95, p. 643 (dated to 785–91).

38. 'filiam suam dux Francorum nomine Eudo causa federis ei in coniugio copulandam ob persecutionem Arabum differendam iam olim tradiderat': *Continuatio isidoriana hispana. Crónica mozárabe de 754*, 79, ed. López Pereira, pp. 254–6 (also in MGH, AA 11, p. 361).

39. El-Hajji, 'Intermarriage between Andalusia and Northern Spain in the Umayyad Period'; Barton, *Conquerors, Brides, and Concubines: Interfaith Relations and Social Power in Medieval Iberia*, pp. 25–32.

40. 'Destruyó las murallas de Qastiliya, conquistó sus castellos y obligó a pactar a su rey, que le dio su hija en matrimonio': *Una descripción anónima de al-Andalus*, ed. Molina, 2, p. 198 (Spanish transl.); Barton, *Conquerors, Brides, and Concubines: Interfaith Relations and Social Power in Medieval Iberia*, p. 27; Molina, 'Las campanãs de Almanzor a la luz de un nuevo texto', pp. 246–7.

41. Barton, *Conquerors, Brides, and Concubines: Interfaith Relations and Social Power in Medieval Iberia*, pp. 123–8, summarizes the evidence and discusses the legend; see also the comments of González, *Repoblación de Castilla la Nueva*, 1, pp. 90–1.

42. Nicol, *The Last Centuries of Byzantium 1261–1453*, p. 74; Bryer, 'Greek Historians on the Turks: The Case of the First Byzantine-Ottoman Marriage', p. 481.

43. Ibn Battuta, *Travels*, tr. Gibb and Beckingham, 2 (117), pp. 488, 497–501; she would be a daughter of Andronicus III.

44. Bryer, 'Greek Historians on the Turks: The Case of the First Byzantine–Ottoman Marriage'; Nicol, *The Reluctant Emperor: A Biography of John Cantacuzene, Byzantine Emperor and Monk, c. 1295–1383*, pp. 76–8, 89.

45. Friedmann, *Tolerance and Coercion in Islam: Interfaith Relations in the Muslim Tradition*, p. 173, citing Ibn 'Abbas.

46. *Annales Bohemiae* (1196–1278), s.a. 1261, ed. Emler, p. 297.

47. See the comments of Van Houts, *Married Life in the Middle Ages, 900–1300*, pp. 162–3.

48. Eadhild to Hugh the Great 926, Edith to Otto (I) 929–30, (another) Eadgifu to Louis, brother of Rudolf II of Burgundy c. 930.

49. MacLean, 'Making a Difference in Tenth-Century Politics: King Athelstan's Sisters and Frankish Queenship', p. 169; see also Foot, *Æthelstan: The First King of England*, pp. 44–52.

50. 'lucidissimi tres radii alias et oppositas Europae partes illustraverint': Gerald of Wales, *Topographia Hibernica*, 3. 54, ed. Dimock, p. 202.

51. 'Inter hos itaque populos, victu, vestitu, moribus, habitatione tam remotos ab Anglia, filias regis Angliae commorantes, barbaries saxea Saxonum, dubius Hyspanorum cum Agarenis conflictus, tyrannis effera Siculorum, poterant in continuum horrorem inducere, nisi generositas aviae suae Matildis imperatricis et in ejus foemineo corpore virile pectus, neptibus suis tolerantiae semitas ... imitabiles praemonstrassent': Ralph de Diceto, *Ymagines historiarum*, ed. Stubbs, 2, p. 17.

52. See Ahlers, *Die Welfen und die englischen Könige 1165–1235*.

53. As suggested by Gillingham, *Richard Coeur de Lion: Kingship, Chivalry and War in the Twelfth Century*, pp. 70, 124–5.

54. 'rex Castellae ... laboravit ut haberet totam Vasconiam, quam sibi credebat de iure competere tanquam sibi promissam ab Henrico, rege Anglorum, socero suo. Duxerat quidem nobilis rex Castelle filiam dicti Henrici regis dominam Alienor ... cum qua sepe dictus rex Henricus dicebatur genero suo, regi Castelle, Vasconiam promisisse ... rex Castelle cum quibusdam de uassallis suis intrauit Vasconiam et fere totam occupauit preter Baionam et Burdegalim; habuit et Blayam et Borc, que sunt ultra Garonam, et terram que est inter duo maria, et sic reuersus est in regnum suum': *Chronica latina regum Castellae*, 17, ed. Charlo Brea, pp. 51–2; see González, *El*

reino de Castilla en la epoca de Alfonso VIII, 1, pp. 865–75. The Worcester Annals report that King John, during his French expedition of 1206, captured the castle of 'Mons Alba', which was garrisoned by the seneschal of the king of Spain, with 120 knights and 2,000 sergeants: *Annales Prioratus de Wigornia*, ed. Luard, p. 394; Wendover reports the capture of the castle on 1 August, with some details, but does not mention the seneschal of the king of Spain: Matthew Paris, *Chronica majora*, ed. Luard, 2, pp. 494–5. The most important southern French town called Montauban is in Tarn-et-Garonne, about 30 miles north of Toulouse. Warren, *King John*, p. 134, calls the castle that John captured 'Montauban (Bourg-en-Gironde)'. Bourg (the 'Borc' in the passage above) is 18 miles north of Bordeaux and also known as Bourg-sur-Gironde. However, in the second edition of 1978 (pp. 117–18) he identifies it as Montauban in Tarn-et-Garonne. The capture of 'Mons Alba' was important enough to be used as a legal dating point: Beverley, East Riding of Yorkshire Archives and Local Studies Service, DDCC/141/68/p41/b.

55. 'ratione donationis quam fecit, vel fecisse dicitur, dominus Henricus quondam rex Angl': *Foedera* (new edn.), 1. 1, p. 310 (the document is now TNA, E 30/1108).

56. 'devolutum est ius regni Angliae ad reginam Castellae et haeredes suos, quae sola tunc de omnibus fratribus et sororibus suis superstes fuit praeter dictum Johannem. Ipsa autem regina et haeredes sui ius quod habuerunt in regno nobis et filiae suae quam habemus uxorem liberaliter concesserunt': Thorne, *Chronica*, cols. 1868–9; *Foedera* (new edn.), 1. 1, p. 140 (from BL, MS Cotton Julius D II, a letter to St Augustine's Abbey, Canterbury).

57. *Gesta regis Henrici secundi Benedicti abbatis*, ed. Stubbs, 2, pp. 132–3; Roger of Howden, *Chronica*, ed. Stubbs, 3, pp. 29, 55, 66.

58. *The Records of the Parliaments of Scotland to 1707*, ed. Brown et al., 1428/7/4.

59. *Charters and Other Records of the City and Royal Burgh of Kirkwall with the Treaty of 1468 between Denmark and Scotland*, pp. 96–102; Crawford, 'The Pawning of Orkney and Shetland: A Reconsideration of the Events of 1460–9', pp. 37–8, 52–3. The Norwegians made several later efforts to pay the cash but were rebuffed.

60. 'Erat enim inter eos affinitatis vinculum, nam eorum uxores sorores erant, filie Berengarii senioris comitis de Sulcebach, magni et egregii principis et in regno Theutonicorum potentissimi: unde ampliore erga eum habundabat gratia et liberalitatem in eum et suos tenebatur, maxime interveniente imperatrice, effundere cumulatiorem': William of Tyre, *Chronicon*, 16. 23, ed. Huygens, 2, p. 749.

61. *Conradi III et filii eius Heinrici Diplomata*, ed. Hausmann, nos. 229, DDH. (VI.) 11, pp. 404–6, 531–2.

62. 'Hic [Charles the Simple] reliquit filium Ludovicum ex Eadgiva Anglorum regis filia susceptum. Qui calamitatis paternae procellis semet involvi metuens, ad Anglos Saxones maternae affinitatis invitatus gratia se contulit': *Chronicon sancti Benigni Divionensis*, col. 814.

63. His nickname certainly by the 1060s: 'Hludovicus transmarinus quia de Anglorum terra revocatus est': Gautier, 'Aux origines du dessin généalogique en France: l'exemple de l'abbaye Saint-Aubin d'Angers (XIe-XIIe siècle)', p. 12 (photograph of Angers,

Bibliothèque municipale, MS 58, fol. IIv). In the twelfth century, it is common: 'regnante Ludovico transmarino': Orderic Vitalis, *Historia ecclesiastica*, 5. 9, ed. Chibnall, 3, p. 80; 'Karolus Simplex genuit alium Ludovicum transmarinum': Ralph de Diceto, *Opuscula*, p. 219.

64. 'les aliances des mariages des belles dames nées du sang royal, de qui naîtra nouveaulz parens es estranges contrés et affinitez es nacions lointaines': Christine de Pisan, *Le livre des fais et bonnes meurs du sage roy Charles V*, 2. 17, ed. Solente, 1, p. 178.

65. 'Semper enim Romanae ecclesiae obedientiae iugo placuit nobis colla submittere, et nisi primo nobis ecclesia Romana defuerit, non erit ab ea nobis discendi voluntas': William of Æbelholt, *Epistolae*, 1. 30, ed. Christensen et al., p. 474.

66. 'conquestus est ei de Philippo rege Franciae, qui Botildam (*recte* Ingeburgam) sponsam suam, sororem illius, injuste relinquerat, et aliam loco ejus in uxorem duxerat': Roger of Howden, *Chronica*, ed. Stubbs, 4, pp. 85–6.

67. *Cronica et cartularium monasterii de Dunis*, ed. Van De Putte, pp. 530–1, nos. CCCCLXII (601), CCCCLXIV (604); Davidsohn, *Philipp II. August von Frankreich und Ingeborg*, p. 277.

68. 'Pergo ignota locis, trepidans quidnam antea discam:/ gentem, animos, mores, oppida, rura, nemus?/ Quem, precor, inveniam peregrinis advena terris, / quo mihi nemo venis civis, amice, parens?': Venantius Fortunatus, *Carmina*, 6. 5, 'De Gelesuintha', lines 111–14, ed. Reydellet, 2, p. 64 (MGH, AA 4.1, p. 139).

69. 'Filie regum et principum in deliciis a lacte nutrite, nichil scientes preter gloriam et felicitatem natalitie terre, nubunt in exteras nationes et aliena regna, barbaros mores et ignotas linguas disciture sevisque dominis ac repugnantibus a naturali usu legibus serviture': Goscelin of Saint-Bertin, *Liber confortatorius*, ed. Talbot, p. 41; see the comments of Van Houts, 'The Flemish Contribution to Biographical Writing in England in the Eleventh Century', p. 124.

70. κατέλιπον Ἐλισσαῖον τὸν εὐνοῦχον καὶ νοτάριον πρὸς τὸ διδάξαι αὐτὴν τά τε τῶν Γραικῶν γράμματα καὶ τὴν γλῶσσαν, καὶ παιδεῦσαι αὐτὴν τὰ ἤθη τῆς Ῥωμαίων βασιλείας: Theophanes, *Chronographia*, AM 6274 (AD 781/2), ed. de Boor, 1, p. 455.

71. Ekkehard IV, *Casus sancti Galli*, 90, ed. Haefele, p. 184; the text says she was betrothed to 'Constantino Graeco regi', which would suggest Constantine VII (913–59), but there seems to be agreement that the engagement was actually with Constantine's son Romanos, later Romanos II (959–63). He and Hadwig were of the same age. See Garland, *Byzantine Empresses: Women and Power in Byzantium, AD 527–1204*, p. 126.

72. 'Deinde consecratam reginam usque ad tempestivum tempus nuptiarum studiose nutriri precepit, in quo nutrimento et linguam addisceret et se secundum Teutonicos mores componeret': *Gesta Normannorum Ducum*, ed. Van Houts, 2, p. 218, for other details, and her age, see the notes to this passage; *Annales de Wintonia*, ed. Luard, p. 43; *Anglo-Saxon Chronicle* (E), s.a. 1110, ed. Plummer and Earle, p. 242; Chibnall, *The Empress Matilda: Queen Consort, Queen Mother and Lady of the English*, pp. 9, 22–5.

73. Thoma, *Namensänderungen in Herrscherfamilien des mittelalterlichen Europa*, pp. 169–201.

74. Constantine VII Porphyrogenitus, *De administrando imperio*, 26, ed. Moravcsik, p. 112; Liudprand of Cremona, 'Antapodosis', 5. 20, in *Liudprandi opera*, ed. Becker, p. 141.

75. There is a letter of Hildegard of Bingen to 'Bertha regina Graecorum': *Epistularium Hildegardis Bingensis*, classis 4, ep. 319, ed. Van Acker and Klaes-Hachmöller, p. 79. The other evidence that she was first called Berta comes from one local monastic chronicle and an entry in a necrology: 'Anno Domini MCXLII Chunradus rex sororem uxoris sue Berhtam filiam domini Perngeri comitis de Sultzpach domino Manueli Constantinopituno imperatori (deponsavit an. 1144) misit uxorem': *Lateinische Chronik des Klosters Kastl*, ed. Moritz, p. 106; cf. ibid., p. 148; there is record of the death on 28 September of 'Berhta imperatrix Grecorum': *Monumenta Necrologica Claustroneoburgensis*, ed. Fuchs, p. 60. On Berta, see Dendorfer, *Adelige Gruppenbildung und Königsherrschaft: die Grafen von Sulzbach und ihr Beziehungsgeflecht im 12. Jahrhundert*, pp. 98–102; Weller, *Die Heiratspolitik des deutschen Hochadels im 12. Jahrhundert*, pp. 59–67.

76. Choniates, 'De Manuele Comneno', in *Historia*, 1. 2, ed. Bekker, pp. 72–3, ed. van Dieten, pp. 53–4.

77. 'filio imperatoris Heinrico regi venit regina Cunihild nomine, quae ibidem in natali apostolorum regalem coronam accepit et mutato nomine in benedictione Cunigund dicta est': *Annales Hildesheimenses*, ed. Waitz, p. 40; the name forms Cunihild and Gunhild both occur: Thoma, *Namensänderungen in Herrscherfamilien des mittelalterlichen Europa*, pp. 196–7.

78. 'propter barbariem Danorum sive Nortmannorum nominum': Giesebrecht, *Geschichte der deutschen Kaiserzeit*, 2, p. 714 (a letter of Siegfried of Gorze from 1043, discussed on pp. 30–1.).

79. William of Malmesbury, *Gesta regum Anglorum*, 5. 394, ed. Mynors et al., p. 716; Orderic Vitalis, *Historia ecclesiastica*, 8. 22, ed. Chibnall, 4, p. 272; in the *Durham Liber Vitae*, she appears both as 'Magtild regina' (fol. 15v) and as 'Eadgith', along with her brothers (fol. 47), ed. Rollason and Rollason, 1, pp. 92, 138.

80. 'sa mere, qui estoit venue de Espaigne, n'avoit ne parens ne amis en tout le royaume de France': Jean de Joinville, *Vie de saint Louis*, 72, ed. Monfrin, p. 36; 'femme estrange', 'estrange femme': ibid., 72, 74, pp. 36, 38; Grant, *Blanche of Castile, Queen of France*, p. 82, says Joinville's claim is 'untrue' but she refutes it by referring to friends Blanche built up after her arrival in France.

81. 'exhilaravit': Adam of Eynsham, *Magna Vita sancti Hugonis*, 5. 13, ed. Douie and Farmer, 2, p. 156.

82. *The Court and Household of Eleanor of Castile in 1290: An Edition of British Library, Additional Manuscript 35294*, ed. Parsons, p. 12 n. 35; Parsons, *Eleanor of Castile: Queen and Society in Thirteenth-Century England*, p. 54; for other aspects of Eleanor's cultural influence in England see Tolley, 'Eleanor of Castile and the "Spanish" Style'.

83. 'Cibos quoque suos manibus non tangebat, sed ab eunuchis eius alimenta quaeque minutius concidebantur in frusta, quae mox illa quibusdam fuscinulis aureis atque bidentibus ori suo ligurriens adhibebat': Peter Damian, *Epistolae* 66 (*Institutio monialis*), ed. Reindel, 2, p. 270 (also in PL 145, col. 744, c. 11); the lady has been identified as Maria Argyropoula, sister of the Byzantine emperor Romanos III (1028–34) and wife of John Orseolo, son of (and co-ruler with) Doge Peter II Orseolo (991–1008): Ciggaar, *Western Travellers to Constantinople: The West and Byzantium, 962–1204*, p. 266. Herrin,

Byzantium: The Surprising Life of a Medieval Empire, pp. 203–11, 'Venice and the Fork', takes the passage as the starting point of a brief discussion of Byzantine–Western relations in the period.

84. 'Quia videlicet multa superflua et luxuriosa mulierum ornamenta, quibus Grecia uti solet, sed eatenus in Germanię Francięque provinciis erant incognita, huc primo detuli, memeque eisdem plus quam humanę naturę conveniret, circumdans et in huiusmodi habitu nocivo incedens alias mulieres similia appetentes peccare feci': Otloh of St. Emmeran, *Liber Visionum*, 17, ed. Schmidt, pp. 91–2 (written c. 1062).

85. 'coeperunt confluere gratia eiusdem reginae in Franciam atque Burgundiam, ab Arvernia et Aquitania, homines omni levitate vanissimi, moribus et veste distorti, armis et equorum faleris incompositi, a medio capitis comis nudati, histrionum more barbis rasi, caligis et ocreis turpissimi, fidei et pacis foedere omnino vacui': Rodulfus Glaber, *Historiarum libri quinque*, 3. 40, ed. France, p. 166. Glaber mistakenly thought that Queen Constance was the daughter of the duke of Aquitaine and hence identified her followers as Aquitainians, ibid., p. 107 n. 5. On Constance, see Woll, *Die Königinnen des hochmittelalterlichen Frankreich, 987–1237/38*, pp. 64–95.

86. 'Corpore perverso creat haec nunc vita tyrannos,/ Trunca veste viros, sine federe pacis ineptos./ Consilio muliebre gemit respublica laxa': Rodulfus Glaber, *Historiarum libri quinque*, 3. 40, ed. France, pp. 166–8.

87. The relationship is set out in a family tree in Parisse, 'Sigefroid, abbé de Gorze, et le mariage du roi Henri III', p. 553; see also p. 330.

88. 'honestas regni, quae temporibus priorum imperatorum veste et habitu nec non in armis et equitatione decentissime viguerat, nostris diebus postponitur, et ignominiosa Franciscarum ineptiarum consuetudo introducitur, scilicet in tonsione barbarum, in turpissima et pudicis obtutibus execranda decurtatione ac deformitate vestium mutisque aliis novitatibus': Giesebrecht, *Geschichte der deutschen Kaiserzeit*, 2, pp. 714–19. The letter is also printed, with French translation, in Parisse, 'Sigefroid, abbé de Gorze, et le mariage du roi Henri III', pp. 554–64.

89. *Chronica regia Coloniensis, continuatio secunda*, ed. Waitz, pp. 186–7 (s.a. 1210, although the event took place in 1213).

90. Rydén, 'The Bride-Shows at the Byzantine Court – History or Fiction?'; Afinogenov, 'The Bride-Show of Theophilos: Some Notes on the Sources'. Both scholars assume the bride shows are fictional. For a vigorous assertion of their historicity see Treadgold, 'The Bride-Shows of the Byzantine Emperors'; Treadgold, 'The Historicity of Byzantine Bride-Shows'. Dagron, *Emperor and Priest: The Imperial Office in Byzantium*, p. 47, simply says 'These accounts . . . seem to be largely true.'

91. Niketas, *The Life of St Philaretos the Merciful*, ed. Rydén, pp. 82–92; the *Life* was written around 821. There is a discussion in Herrin, *Women in Purple: Rulers of Medieval Byzantium*, pp. 132–8.

92. Hunger, 'Die Schönheitskonkurrenz in "Belthandros und Chrysantza" und die Brautschau am byzantinischen Kaiserhof', pp. 151–2 ('das idealisierte Porträt einer Kaiserin'); Rydén, 'The Bride-Shows at the Byzantine Court – History or Fiction?', p. 175; Kazhdan and Sherry, 'The Tale of a Happy Fool: The *Vita* of St. Philaretos the

Merciful (*BHG* 1511z-1512b)', p. 353 n. 7; Vinson, 'The Life of Theodora and the Rhetoric of the Byzantine Bride-show', p. 48 n. 50; Niketas, *The Life of St Philaretos the Merciful*, ed. Rydén, p. 89 n. 95.

93. Martin, *A Bride for the Tsar: Bride-Shows and Marriage Politics in Early Modern Russia*, pp. 55–6.

94. 'undecumque adductas procerum filias inspitiens': Astronomus, *Vita Hludowici imperatoris*, 32, ed. Tremp, p. 392; see 195–6 below.

95. *Vita S. Theophanonis Imperatricis*, 10, ed. Kurtz, p. 6.

96. 'Habet etiam in mandatis, quod videat pectus eius nudum. Nam secundum iudicia sibi data cognoscetur, an sit apta ad prolem, quam multum desiderat dominus rex': *Acta aragonensia*, 1, ed. Finke, no. 319, p. 479.

97. Ibid., p. 484.

98. 'la mandoe ad vedere dali duchi d'Orliens et Borbone et da madama di Borbone et cum loro andoe mons. d'Aubigny, quale è stato multo adoperato in questa praticha et tornoe ad fare la relatione de la conditione sua, perchè l'havevano vista nuda, et in effecto è un pocho zoppa': Labande-Mailfert, 'Le mariage d'Anne de Bretagne avec Charles VIII vu par Erasme Brasca', p. 26 n. 23, from the reports of the Milanese envoy Erasmus Brasca. The 'mons. d'Aubigny' is Bérault or Bernard Stuart, lord of Aubigny, on whom see Contamine, 'Stuart, Bérault (1452/3–1508), Soldier and Diplomat', *ODNB*, 53, pp. 134–5.

99. 'ut quae ab eis placuisset sibi in matrimonium elegisset': Æthelweard, *Chronicon*, Prologue, ed. Campbell, p. 2.

100. Meller et al., eds., *Königin Editha und ihre Grablegen in Magdeburg*, pp. 105–56, esp. p. 149.

101. *Official Correspondence of Thomas Bekynton*, ed. Williams, 2, p. 181 (modernized).

102. *Foedera* (original edition), 12, pp. 142–5.

103. Chaplais, *English Medieval Diplomatic Practice*, 1. i, p. 91, gives several examples, in his valuable discussion of 'viewing the bride' (pp. 88–93).

104. 'imaginem virginis, pictor eunuchus, domino mittendam uti simillime depingeret': Ekkehard IV, *Casus sancti Galli*, 90, ed. Haefele, p. 184.

105. Gregory of Tours, *Libri historiarum decem*, 4. 38; 5. 38, ed. Krusch and Levison, pp. 169–70, 243; John of Biclar, *Chronica*, ed. Cardelle de Hartmann, p. 61; see Nelson, 'A propos des femmes royales dans les rapports entre le monde wisigothique et le monde franc à l'époque de Reccared'; Hartmann, *Die Königin im frühen Mittelalter*, pp. 21–5.

106. 'Ipse quoque, acceptam soceri sui uxorem, Galliciensium regnum obtinuit': Gregory of Tours, *Libri historiarum decem*, 6. 43, ed. Krusch and Levison, p. 316; see also John of Biclar, *Chronica*, ed. Cardelle de Hartmann, p. 74: 'His diebus Audeca in Gallecia Suevorum regnum cum tirannide assummit et Sisegutiam relictam Mironis regis in coniugium accepit.'

107. 'Nec moratus Chlothacharius uxorem germani sui Guntheucam nomine sibi in matrimonio sociavit': Gregory of Tours, *Libri historiarum decem*, 3. 6, ed. Krusch and Levison, p. 103.

108. 'regnumque eius Chlothacharius rex accepit, copulans Vuldotradam, uxorem eius, stratui suo. Sed increpitus a sacerdotibus, reliquit eam, dans ei Garivaldum ducem, ... ': Gregory of Tours, *Libri historiarum decem*, 4. 9, ed. Krusch and Levison, p. 141.

109. 'rex propter coniugatione Brunichildis suspectum habere coepit Merovechum, filium suum': Gregory of Tours, *Libri historiarum decem*, 5. 2-3, ed. Krusch and Levison, pp. 195-6; 5. 14, 18, pp. 207-13, 222-4, for the persecution of Merovech and his death.

110. 'Regina vero Theudelinda quia satis placebat Langobardis, permiserunt eam in regia consistere dignitatem, suadentes ei, ut sibi quem ipsa voluisset ex omnibus Langobardis virum eligeret, talem scilicet qui regnum regere utiliter possit': Paul the Deacon, *Historia Langobardorum*, 3. 35, ed. Waitz, pp. 140-1.

111. 'per ipsam omnes Langobardi eum sublimavant in regno': Fredegar, *Chronica*, 4. 70, ed. Krusch, p. 156, ed. Wallace-Hadrill, p. 59.

112. 'ipsum coniugatum sublimarit in regnum': Fredegar, *Chronica*, 4. 51, ed. Krusch, p. 145, ed. Wallace-Hadrill, p. 42.

113. 'nil regi defuit absque nobilissima coniuge; quam ubique sibi iussit inquirere, ut inventam hanc legaliter adquireret, et adeptam imperii sui consortem faceret. Igitur per regna et per urbes discurritur, et regalis sponsa perquiritur; sed longe lateque quaesite, vix tandem digna repperitur ... Sed abnegat illa, se unquam Cnutonis sponsam fieri, nisi illi iusiurando affirmaret, quod numquam alterius coniugis filium post se regnare faceret nisi eius, si forte ille Deus ex eo filium dedisset ... Placuit ergo regi verbum virginis, et iusiurando facto virgini placuit voluntas regis, et sic Deo gratias domina Emma mulierum nobilissima fit coniunx regis fortissimi Cnutonis': *Encomium Emma Reginae*, 2. 16, ed. Campbell, p. 32.

114. 'fortasse vix aut numquam bellandi adesset finis, nisi tandem huius nobilissimae reginae iugali copula potiretur': *Encomium Emmae Reginae*, Argumentum, ed. Campbell, p. 6.

115. 'Chnud regnum Adelradi accepit uxoremque eius': Adam of Bremen, *Gesta Hammaburgensis ecclesiae pontificum*, 2. 54 (52), ed. Schmeidler, p. 114.

116. Leo the Deacon, *Historiae*, 3. 9, ed. Hase, pp. 49-50; Skylitzes, *Synopsis historiarum*, ed. Thurn, pp. 260-1.

117. ὀκνοῦσαν μέν, ὡς περιᾴδεται, τὴν συναφήν. Ἤδη γὰρ καὶ φρενῶν ὑπεπίμπλατο καὶ πεπειραμένη δὲ ἄλλως λειότητος ἐραστοῦ τὸν τραχὺν ἀπέστεργε. Καί ποτε, φασί, καθ᾽ὕπνους φαντασαμένη τὸν νεανίαν καὶ «ὦ Ἀλέξιε» ἀνακράξασα, οἷα ἔπαθεν οἶδεν αὐτή: Eustathios of Thessaloniki, *The Capture of Thessaloniki*, ed. Kyriakides, p. 52.

118. 'Defuncto autem Æthelwulfo rege, Æthelbald, filius eius, contra Dei interdictum et Christianorum dignitatem, necnon et contra omnium paganorum consuetudinem, thorum patris sui ascendens, Iuthittam, Karoli Francorum regis filiam, cum magna omnibus audientibus infamia, in matrimonium duxit': Asser, *De rebus gestis Aelfredi*, 17, ed. Stevenson, p. 16.

119. 'Talis fornicatio qualis nec inter gentes ita ut uxorem patris aliquis habeat': 1 Corinthians 5: 1.

120. Bede, *Historia ecclesiastica gentis Anglorum*, 2. 5, ed. Colgrave and Mynors, p. 150; 'Eadbold ... lifode on heðenum þeawe swa þ he heafde his feder lafe to wife': *Anglo-Saxon Chronicle* (E), s.a. 616, ed. Plummer and Earle, p. 23.

121. Bede, *Historia ecclesiastica gentis Anglorum*, 2. 6, ed. Colgrave and Mynors, p. 154.

122. Ibid., 1. 27, p. 84. The issue of whether these are authentic questions of Augustine of Canterbury does not affect the main point here.

123. *Paenitentialia minora Franciae et Italiae*, ed. Kottje, p. 191 (Paenitentiale Oxoniense II, c. 3); Kasten, 'Stepmothers in Frankish Legal Life', p. 57.

124. 'Uxorem patris si quis acciperit, mortis periculum incurrat': *Capitularia regum Francorum*, 1, ed. Boretius, no. 7, p. 15; *Pactus legis Salicae*, 'Capitula legi Salicae addita', 6. 1. 2, ed. Eckhardt, p. 267; *Lex Salica*, ed. Eckhardt, pp. 176–7.

125. 'Illicita etiam novercarum conjugia, similiter et uxorem fratris defuncti fratrem superstitem ducere, quæ ibi antea fiebant, nimis ostendit execranda, et a fidelibus velut ipsam mortem devitanda': Turgot, *Vita S. Margaretae Scotorum Reginae*, 8, ed. Hodgson Hinde, p. 245.

126. 'οἶμαι τοίνυν Οὐάρνοις ξυνοίσειν τὴν κηδείαν ἐς Φράγγους μᾶλλον ἢ ἐς τοὺς νησιώτας ποιεῖσθαι. Βρίττιοι μὲν γὰρ οὐδὲ ὅσον ἐπιμίγνυσθαι ὑμῖν οἷοί τέ εἰσιν, ὅτι μὴ ὀψέ τε καὶ μόλις· Οὔαρνοι δὲ καὶ Φράγγοι τουτὶ μόνον τοῦ Ῥήνου τὸ ὕδωρ μεταξὺ ἔχουσιν, ὥστε αὐτοὺς ἐν γειτόνων μὲν ὡς πλησιαίτατα ὄντας ὑμῖν, ἐς δυνάμεως δὲ κεχωρηκότας μέγα τι χρῆμα, ἐν προχείρῳ ἔχειν εὖ ποιεῖν τε ὑμᾶς καὶ λυμαίνεσθαι, ἡνίκα ἂν αὐτοῖς βουλομένοις εἴη· λυμανοῦνται δὲ πάντως, ἢν μὴ τὸ κῆδος αὐτοῖς ἐμπόδιον ἔσται: Procopius, *De bello Gothico*, 4. 20, ed. Dewing, 5, pp. 252–64 (*History of the Wars*, 8. 20). Taking the story as historically accurate, Eugen Ewig identifies the Frankish bride as Theudechild, sister of Theudebert I: 'Die Namengebung bei den ältesten Frankenkönigen und im merowingischen Königshaus', p. 51.

127. López de Ayala, *Crónica del Rey don Pedro*, 1 (1350), 13, ed. Orduna, 1, pp. 24–5.

128. See the remarkable first-hand account by Helene Kottannerin, *Die Denkwürdigkeiten der Helene Kottannerin (1439–1440)*, ed. Mollay, pp. 12–13, 22.

129. *Lexikon des Mittelalters*, 3, col. 1319, s.v. 'Dorothea'; *The Cambridge History of Scandinavia*, 1, pp. 742–4 ('In Denmark it was the goal of the council to nominate a princely candidate who would also be acceptable as a spouse for Queen Dorothea', p. 744).

130. 'quod si diabolus ipsum forsan temtaret, quod nollet nostram maiestatem ducere in uxorem, relinqueretis ipsum regem et adhaerere nostrae maiestati velitis' (she is addressing the chief men of Hungary): *Acta vitam Beatricis reginae Hungariae illustrantia*, ed. Berzeviczy, p. 221, no. 156.

131. 'el Re di Boemia essere stato electo Re de Hungaria et che ha pigliata la Regina per mogliere': *Acta vitam Beatricis reginae Hungariae illustrantia*, ed. Berzeviczy, p. 165, no. 115.

132. 'propter aliquid secretum impedimentum, quod habet rex in animo et nemini vult revelare': *Acta vitam Beatricis reginae Hungariae illustrantia*, ed. Berzeviczy, pp. 229–30, no. 156; the whole letter (pp. 219–31), from 1492, gives Beatrice's detailed account of events; there is some discussion of the case in d'Avray, *Papacy, Monarchy and Marriage 860–1600*, pp. 161–9, with p. 327–34.

133. 'La infelicissima regina de Hungaria', *Acta vitam Beatricis reginae Hungariae illustrantia*, ed. Berzeviczy, p. 438, no. 311.

134. 'ladite Dame ne convolera à autres nopces, fors avec le Roy futur, s'il lui plaist et faire se peut': Morice, *Mémoires pour servir de preuves à l'histoire ecclésiastique et civile de Bretagne*, 3, col. 717.

135. Nelson, 'Queens as Jezebels: The Careers of Brunhild and Balthild in Merovingian History', p. 7; Hartmann, *Die Königin im frühen Mittelalter*, p. 21: 'Nach Athanagilds Tod heiratete Goiswinth den neuen König Leowigild, der dadurch wohl sein Königtum zu stärken suchte.'

136. 'Beispielen … in denen die Ehe mit der Königswitwe als Hebel zur Erringung der Macht diente': Ubl, *Inzestverbot und Gesetzgebung: die Konstruktion eines Verbrechens (300–1100)*, p. 101.

137. Stafford, 'Charles the Bald, Judith and England', p. 151; cf. her remarks in *Queens, Concubines and Dowagers: The King's Wife in the Early Middle Ages*, pp. 49–50.

138. Herbert, 'Goddess and King: The Sacred Marriage in Early Ireland', p. 265; cf. 'The assumption of power was seen as a marriage with the local goddess of sovereignty': Simms, *From Kings to Warlords: The Changing Political Structure of Gaelic Ireland in the Later Middle Ages*, p. 11.

139. Chaney, *The Cult of Kingship in Anglo-Saxon England: The Transition from Paganism to Christianity*, p. 27.

140. *Fragmentary Annals of Ireland*, ed. Radner, p. 85.

141. *The Russian Primary Chronicle*, tr. Cross and Sherbowitz-Wetzor, pp. 91, 93.

142. 'Cupan voluit matrem Sancti Stephani regis sibi per incestuosum copulare connubium et Sanctum Stephanum occidere ducatumque eius sue subdere potestati': *Chronici Hungarici compositio saeculi XIV*, 64, ed. Domanovszky, p. 313.

143. 'Execrabile facinus et adsuetae [ad]modum iniquitatis est opus defunctis regibus suppre[sti]tis eius coniugis regale torum appetere, et horrendis pollutionum maculis sordidare. Quis enim christianorum aequanimiter ferat, defuncti regis coniugem alieno postmodum connubio uti aut sequuuturi principis libidini subiugari? … Nullus ergo licebit supprestitem reginam sibi in coniugio adducere, non sordidis contactibus maculare. Non hoc sequuuturis regibus licitum, non cuique hominum licebit esse permissum': *Concilios visigóticos e hispano-romanos*, ed. Vives, p. 421 (Thirteenth Council of Toledo, 683, cl. 5).

144. *Concilios visigóticos e hispano-romanos*, ed. Vives, pp. 479–80 (Third Council of Zaragoza, 691, cl. 5).

145. Two of the most insistent statements of the rigorist position from the middle decades of the eleventh century are Peter Damian's 'De parentelae gradibus', in *Die Briefe des Petrus Damiani*, 1, ed. Reindel, no. 19, pp. 179–99 (PL 145, cols. 191–204), and a letter of Pope Alexander II, *Epistolae*, no. 92, PL 146, cols. 1379–83, JL 4500, 'Ad sedem apostolicam', which was incorporated into Gratian's *Decretum*, 2. 35. 5. 2, ed. Friedberg, cols. 1271–4.

146. *Recueil des actes de Philippe 1er, roi de France*, ed. Prou, no. 16, pp. 47–9.

147. For her analysis of the Capetians' dilemmas see Bouchard, 'Consanguinity and Noble Marriages in the Tenth and Eleventh Centuries', pp. 273–9, and her conclusion, 'It [the definition of the prohibited degrees] kept the Capetians from marrying women from other royal families of western Europe, as they would have preferred' (p. 287).

148. Ubl, *Inzestverbot und Gesetzgebung: die Konstruktion eines Verbrechens (300–1100)*, pp. 117, 482.

149. 'statuimus ut nulli liceat christiano de propria consanguinitate sive cognatione uxorem accipere usque dum generatio recordatur, cognoscitur aut memoria retinetur': *Concilia aevi Karolini DCCCLX–DCCCLXXIV*, ed. Hartmann, pp. 130 (letter of Pope Nicholas I to the Council of Mainz, 861–3), 266–7 (Council of Worms, cl. 8 (32), 868). The clause was incorporated in later collections, including Gratian, *Decretum*, 2. 35. 2. 18, ed. Friedberg, col. 1268.

150. Ubl, I*nzestverbot und Gesetzgebung: die Konstruktion eines Verbrechens (300–1100)*, p. 85.

151. Tenbrock, *Eherecht und Ehepolitik bei Innocenz III.*; d'Avray, *Dissolving Royal Marriages: A Documentary History, 860–1600*, pp. 58–68, 69–75; d'Avray, *Papacy, Monarchy and Marriage 860–1600*, pp. 75–6, 80–5.

152. 'Sane in Oriente una duobus fuit incestuose coniuncta, in Occidente vero unus sibi duas presumpsit iungere per incestum': Innocent III, *Epistolae* 2. 72 (75), *Die Register Innocenz' III.*, ed. Hageneder et al., 2, p. 128 (PL 214: 611); cf. *Gesta Innocentii III*, 58, PL 214, col. CIV, ed. Gress-Wright, p. 79.

153. 'ut dicitur, minus legitime copulata': Innocent III, *Epistolae* 16. 149, PL 216, col. 940.

154. Davidsohn, *Philipp II. August von Frankreich und Ingeborg*; Gaudemet, 'Le dossier canonique du mariage de Philippe Auguste et d'Ingeburge de Denmark (1193–1213)'; Conklin, 'Ingeborg of Denmark, Queen of France, 1193–1223'; d'Avray, *Dissolving Royal Marriages: A Documentary History, 860–1600*, Chapter 6.

155. Sigebert of Gembloux, *Chronica: Continuatio Aquicinctina*, ed. Bethmann, p. 431.

156. *Les Registres de Philippe Auguste I: Texte*, ed. Baldwin, pp. 549–53; Davidsohn, *Philipp II. August von Frankreich und Ingeborg*, pp. 297–306, with the material in tabular form on pp. 42, 307–9.

157. 'ludibrii fabulam': Innocent III, *Epistolae* 2. 188 (197), *Die Register Innocenz' III.*, ed. Hageneder et al., 2, p. 360 (PL 214: 746).

158. 'superinductam preciperet a regis consortio tam localiter quam carnaliter removeri, ut non solum a regis amplexibus, verum etiam a regni finibus faceret illam excludi, et prefatam reginam ab ipso rege solemniter recipi, et regaliter pertractari': *Gesta Innocentii III*, 54, PL 214, col. C, ed. Gress-Wright, pp. 75–6; cf. Innocent III, *Epistolae*, 2. 188 (197), *Die Register Innocenz' III.*, ed. Hageneder et al., 2, p. 361 (PL 214: 747).

159. 'utilitati et necessitati regni Franciae': Innocent III, *Epistola*, 'Apostolica sedes', PL 214, cols. 1191–4; Cartellieri, *Philipp II. August, König von Frankreich*, 4, pp. 82–8 (2 Nov. 1201, Po. 1499).

160. Roger of Howden, *Chronica*, ed. Stubbs, 4, pp. 112–13; *Gesta Innocentii III*, 84, PL 214, col. CXXXV–CXXXVI, ed. Gress-Wright, p. 170.

161. 'recepit in gratiam et in coniugales affectus legitimam suam Ingelburgem reginam': Robert of Auxerre, *Chronicon (continuatio)*, ed. Holder-Egger, p. 279.

162. Notably the case of Premysl Otakar I of Bohemia.

163. 'venerunt Londonias nuncii dicti regis Castellae, ubi, duarum filiarum regis Angliae inspectione habita diligenti, dominam Johannem de Wodestok, minorem regis filiam, elegerunt, dicentes eam magis congruere aetati sui sponsi futuri': Murimuth, *Continuatio chronicarum*, ed. Thompson, p. 170; Joan is also known as Joan of the Tower, as was her more celebrated aunt, daughter of Edward II, who became queen of Scots.

164. For Joan's life, see Green, *Lives of the Princesses of England*, 3, pp. 229–60; on the Castilian marriage also see Russell, 'Una alianza frustrada. Las bodas de Pedro I de Castilla y Juana Plantagenet'.

165. 'ad tractandum et concordandum cum nobili et potente viro duce Austriae … super sponsalibus inter filium dicti ducis primogenitum et Johannam filiam nostram carissimam contrahendis': *Foedera* (new edn.), 2. 2 (1821), p. 915 (*Calendar of the Patent Rolls Preserved in the Public Record Office, Edward III A. D. 1334–1338*, p. 157).

166. 'Et pro expensis ipsius domine factis in Bavarr' per unum annum ut in esculentis et poculentis quando non habuerunt sufficenter de imperatore, xlvi li': TNA, E36/203 (Wardrobe accounts 12–14 Edward III), fol. 91v (p. 184); Green, *Lives of the Princesses of England*, 3, p. 238.

167. *Foedera* (new edn.), 2. 2, p. 1164 (*Calendar of the Close Rolls Preserved in the Public Record Office, Edward III, 6, A. D. 1341–1343*, p. 245).

168. TNA, SC1/37/182.

169. *Foedera* (new edn.), 3. 1, pp. 22–3.

170. *Foedera* (new edn.), 3. 1, p. 25 (*Calendar of Close Rolls Preserved in the Public Record Office, Edward III, 7, A. D. 1343–1346*, p. 484, 27 December 1344).

171. *Foedera* (new edn.), 3. 1, p. 46.

172. 'quant ils serront arivez a Burdeux, s'ils eient certeines novelles que le marriage de l'enfant d'Espaigne soit afferme aillours, la dite dame retournera en Engleterre sanz plus demourer': *Foedera* (new edn.), 3. 1, p. 153 (15 February 1348).

173. Green, *Lives of the Princesses of England*, 3, p. 249.

2 WAITING FOR SONS TO BE BORN

1. Hollingsworth, 'A Demographic Study of the British Ducal Families', p. 365.

2. 'inter principes vel magnos viros reconciliationis vel pacis causa': *Councils and Synods with Other Documents Relating to the English Church*, 1 (*871–1204*), ed. Whitelock et al., 2, p. 981 (Council of Westminster, 1175); cf. the exception 'pro bono pacis' in *Decretales Gregorii IX*, 4. 2. 2, ed. Friedberg, col. 673. In general, see Onclin, 'L'Age requis pour le mariage dans la doctrine canonique médiévale'.

3. 'cum adhuc essent pueruli in cunis vagientes': Roger of Howden, *Chronica*, ed. Stubbs, 1, p. 218.

4. Hathui, the niece of Queen Matilda, married a young Saxon noble 'in her thirteenth year (*in tertio decimo aetatis suae anno*)', while the Westphalian aristocrat Godila bore her first child by Margrave Liuthar of the Nordmark at the same age: Thietmar of Merseburg, *Chronicon*, 4. 39; 7. 3 (4), ed. Holtzmann, pp. 176, 400. In both cases 'in her thirteenth year' means, of course, at the age of twelve.

5. Parsons, 'Mothers, Daughters, Marriage, Power: Some Plantagenet Evidence, 1150–1500', pp. 66–7.

6. 'ita quod nullum ad eam rex Norwag' inhonestum accessum interim habeat vel carnalem': *The Acts of the Parliaments of Scotland*, 1, ed. Thomson and Innes, p. 422 (80).

7. 'Amor quoque coniugalis, eis pene nullus fuit. Nam cum ille adhuc pubesceret, illa vero anus foret, contrariis moribus dissentiebant. Cubiculum commune sibi, non patiebantur. ... Si quando colloquendum erat, locum sub divo habebant. ... Quorum mores usque adeo discordes fuere, ut non multopost sequeretur et divortium': Richer of Saint-Rémi, *Historiae*, 3. 94, ed. Hoffmann, p. 221; Brühl, *Deutschland-Frankreich: die Geburt zweier Völker*, p. 570, regards all this as as 'eine böswillige Erfindung Richers'.

8. Goldstone, *Joanna: the Notorious Queen of Naples, Jerusalem and Sicily*, p. 75.

9. 'Ve populis, quibus regnandi spes in subsecutura dominorum sobole non relinquitur': Thietmar of Merseburg, *Chronicon* 1. 19, ed. Holtzmann, p. 25.

10. 'quatenus a superna clementia pro continuanda regni pace imperatori filium dari secum implorarent': *Brunwilarensis monasterii fundatorum actus*, 27, ed. Waitz, p. 138 (1047).

11. 'Premerement de parler au Roy dangleterre de pourueoir a ses enfanz les quiex se il plest a dieu il aura de ma dame la Reynne fille du Roy de france / et fait a regarder ou cas la ou il aroit pluseurs fiex & filles comment il voudroit estre pourueu as fils puis nez & as filles / Jtem fait a regarder encor plus ou cas se ma dame moroit senz fils / et il i eust filles pluseurs / comment seroit pourueu aus puis nees / Jtem se la premiere estoit Reynne / Jtem fait encor [sic] a regarder / ou cas se ma dame moroit senz fil marler [sic] et il i auoit vne fille ou – pluseurs et li Rois dangleterre auoit fil marle de sa seconde femme qui seroit Rois / comment seroit pourueu / en ce cas a la fille ou as filles du premier marriage': Brown, 'The Political Repercussions of Family Ties in the Early Fourteenth Century: The Marriage of Edward II of England and Isabelle of France', p. 593, from AN, JJ 44, fol. 67, no. 103.

12. Loudon, *Death in Childbirth: An International Study of Maternal Care and Maternal Mortality 1800–1950*, p. 160; Schofield, 'Did the Mothers Really Die? Three Centuries of Maternal Mortality in "The World We have Lost"', pp. 259–60, suggests a lower rate of 10 maternal deaths per 1,000 births in Early Modern England. Rates of 40–50 per 1,000 births are recorded in late-eighteenth and early nineteenth-century lying-in hospitals in the British Isles and the continent: Loudon, *The Tragedy of Childbed Fever*, p. 61, table 5.1.

13. 'Mortua est Constantia, regina Franciae, labore partus, superstite filia, cujus causa mors sibi acciderat': Robert of Torigni, *Chronica*, ed. Howlett, p. 207; see also Suger (continuator), *De glorioso rege Ludovico, Ludovici filio*, 17, ed. Molinier, pp. 165–6.

14. 'laborans in partu': Ralph de Diceto, *Ymagines historiarum*, ed. Stubbs, 2, p. 77, wrongly calling her Margaret; 'mortua est autem de duobus geminis': *Flandria generosa*, 'Continuatio Claromariscensis', ed. Bethmann, p. 329.

15. 'Circa medium Quadragesimae, rege Karolo redeunte de partibus Tholosanis, cum apud Exoldunum (Issoudun) castrum cum uxore sua praegnante devienisset, gravata forte itinere, per mensem vel circiter ante tempus peperit masculum, qui baptizatus satis cito post modicum expiravit; et aliquibus diebus mater post filium decessit': *Continuatio Chronici Girardi de Fracheto*, ed. Guigniaut and de Wailly, p. 62.

16. Froissart, *Chroniques*, ed. Kervyn de Lettenhove, 9, p. 44.

17. Stürner, *Friedrich II.*, 2, pp. 142, 312.

18. 'Cum autem eadem domina regina Guta pia, inclita, invalescente morbo, quem in infantuli partu tunc noviter precedente contraxerat ex vehementibus doloribus velut ex certis mortis nuncciis cognosceret, quod ei ultimus vite terminus advenisset, sapienter de rebus et de domo sua incepit disponere et, que prodessent anime, cogitare': Peter of Zittau, *Chronicon Aulae Regiae*, 1. 65, ed. Emler, p. 79.

19. Ibid., 1. 7, 19, pp. 13–14, 25–6, for the date of her birth and marriage.

20. 'pro conservatione sanitatis et liberatione regine que gravida est'; 'duabus sororibus que detulerunt pallium beati Edmundi usque Westm' contra partum regine nostre': TNA, C62/21 (Liberate Roll 29 Henry III), membranes 16, 13: *Calendar of the Liberate Rolls Preserved in the Public Record Office*, 2, pp. 275, 284; the St Edmund in question was Edmund of Abingdon (d. 1240), whose cloak was preserved by the nuns of Catesby, Northamptonshire; see Creamer, 'St Edmund of Canterbury and Henry III in the Shadow of Thomas Becket', p. 130.

21. *Exchequer Rolls of Scotland, 5: 1437–54*, ed. Burnett, pp. 447, 512; *Accounts of the Lord High Treasurer of Scotland, 4: 1507–13*, ed. Paul, p. 334.

22. For other examples see Bartlett, *Why Can the Dead Do Such Great Things? Saints and Worshippers from the Martyrs to the Reformation*, pp. 246–7.

23. Grandeau, 'Les enfants de Charles VI. Essai sur la vie privée des princes et des princesses de la maison de France à la fin du Moyen Âge', p. 812.

24. 'ego Peronella, regina Aragonensis, iacens et in partu laborans apud Barchinonam . . .': *Liber feudorum major*, ed. Miquel Rosell, 1, no. 16, pp. 22–3.

25. 'infanti meo qui est ex utero meo, Deo volente, processurus . . . Si autem filia ex utero meo processerit . . .': ibid.

26. 'gubernacula . . . sub nomine regentis tenenda si puer masculus nasceretur usquequam ad intelligibilem etatem annorum quatuordecim pervenisset, si vero filia nasceretur ipse Philippus rex Francie fieret et regnaret': Bernard Gui, *Reges Francorum* and *Arbor genealogiae regum Francorum*, CCCC, MS 45, fols. 28v, 46 (identical text) (also in RHF, 21, pp. 725–6); this is confirmed by the wording of an oath Philip extracted in Nîmes on 18 July 1316: Brown, 'The Ceremonial of Royal Succession in Capetian France: The Double Funeral of Louis X', p. 245 and n. 76. For the provisions of 17 July 1316, see Lehugeur, *Histoire de Philippe le Long, roi de France 1316–1322. 1. Le règne*, pp. 37–41; Giesey, *Le Rôle méconnu de la loi salique. La succession royale (xive–xvie siècles)*, pp. 28–35, 271–4.

27. An identical situation occurred in 1328 during the two months between the death of Charles IV and the birth of his posthumous daughter.

28. *Regesta Imperii*, 12: *Albrecht II, 1438–1439*, ed. Hödl, no. 1178.

29. 'Quo casu deficiente sive aborsum edente': Bower, *Scotichronicon*, 11. 3, ed. Watt et al., 6, p. 10.

30. 'illa, astu femineo usa, impregnatam esse mentiebatur ... nec matronas admitteret honestas ad discernendum suum statum ... statuit perpetuo deludere populum supponendo sibi partum alienum ... recessit a terra cum verecundia': *Chronicon de Lanercost, 1201–1346*, ed. Stevenson, pp. 117–18: this part of the Chronicle was written by Richard of Durham. On him, see Gransden, *Historical Writing in England I: c.550–c.1307*, pp. 494–501.

31. See Duncan, 'The Community of the Realm of Scotland and Robert Bruce: A Review', pp. 187–8 (as part of a review of the first edition of Geoffrey Barrow's *Robert Bruce and the Community of the Realm of Scotland*); also his brief comment in Duncan, *The Kingship of the Scots, 842–1292: Succession and Independence*, pp. 175, 177–8.

32. 'Regina Francie Margarita, uxor Ludovici regis, primo habuit filiam, et non auderunt insinuare regi. Vocaverunt episcopum Guillelmum, ut ei nuntiaret': *Anecdotes historiques, légendes et apologues tirés du receuil inédit d'Etienne de Bourbon*, ed. Lecoy de la Marche, p. 388 n. 1, from an exempla collection in Tours, now MS 468.

33. 'Ex hoc iubet rex omnes e custodias relaxari, vinctos absolvi conpositionesque negligentum fisco debitas praecipit omnino non exigi': Gregory of Tours, *Libri historiarum decem*, 6. 23, ed. Krusch and Levison, p. 290. The language might suggest that those who were freed were imprisoned for debt or non-payment of fines or taxes rather than as criminals.

34. Constantine VII Porphyrogenitus, *Book of Ceremonies*, 2. 21, ed. Reiske, 2, pp. 615–19; cf. 1. 42, ed. Reiske, 1, pp. 216–17.

35. 'Ludovico regi Francorum circa foedera nuptiarum ultimis in diebus sors arrisit benignior ... ad suscipiendam in trigamia sobolem masculinam ... Rex igitur ex matrimonio tam primo quam secundo susceptis quatuor filiabus solummodo, tandem ex tertio ... multo felicius feliciter filium procreavit, desideratum a populis, a clero devotius et propensius expetitum': Ralph de Diceto, *Ymagines historiarum*, ed. Stubbs, 1, p. 438.

36. 'timebat ne regnum Francie ab herede qui de semine suo egrederetur gubernari desisteret': Suger (continuator), *De glorioso rege Ludovico, Ludovici filio*, 18, ed. Molinier, p. 166.

37. Petrus Riga, *Versus de gaudio filii regis*, ed. Delaborde, p. 125, line 37.

38. 'Nox erat, in partu celebri regina laborat;/ Urbs super hoc vigili te prece, Xriste, rogat./ Urbis prona marem mendicant vota futurum,/ De mare sollicitat flebilis aula Deum': ibid., p. 124, lines 5–8; see the comments on the poem by Jordan, '"*Quando fuit natus*": Interpreting the Birth of Philip Augustus'.

39. 'Quo rumore per urbem audito et cum gaudio suscepto, quale uel quantum lingua explicari non posset, statim campanarum omnium per urbis amplitudinem totam tantus undique sonus et clangor erupit, tantaque luminaria cerea fuerant per plateas

omnes accensa, quod sonitus tanti tantique tumultus insoliti, nec non et nocturni luminis tam immensi, causam ignorantes urbis incendium tunc imminere putabant. Vnde et auctor operis huius … a strata quo recubans sompnum carpere iam ceperat experrectus ad fenestram illico prosiliit, prospiciensque uidit in platea uetulas duas admodum pauperculas, manibus tamen faces cereas preferentes et tam uultu quam uocibus totoque gestu corporis exultantes passibusque properis, tanquam sibi inuicem obuiando et confligendo, cursitantes. Cumque causam tante commocionis et exultacionis ab eis inquisisset, earum una respiciens statim et respondens: "Regem", inquit, "habemus nobis a Deo nunc datum et regni heredem Deo donante perualidum"': Gerald of Wales, *De principis instructione*, 3. 25, ed. Bartlett, p. 674 (RS edn., pp. 292–3).

40. 'pre gaudio nativitatis illustrissimi pueri Philippi fillii domini regis': *Gallia christiana*, 8, instrumenta, col. 517, no. XLII.

41. Rigord, *Gesta Philippi Augusti*, prologue, ed. Carpentier et al., p. 116, calls his history of Philip Augustus 'liber gestorum regis Philippi Augusti a Deo dati'; later writers often give Philip the soubriquet 'Dieudonné'; see also Gerald of Wales, *De principis instructione*, 3. 25, ed. Bartlett, p. 674 (RS edn., pp. 291–2): 'puerum in cunis ab alto dilapsum et in Franciam demissum, Francisque regni heredem ualidum summo opere desiderantibus tanquam a Deo datum'.

42. *Chronique du religieux de Saint-Denys*, 12. 6, ed. Bellaguet, 1, p. 732.

43. 'pour le joyeux advenement et nativité de mons. le Dauphin': *Registre criminel du Châtelet de Paris, du 6 septembre 1389 au 18 mai 1392*, 1, p. 504; cf. p. 498. The similar reference on p. 491 is to the previous Dauphin Charles, who was born and died in 1386.

44. 'post obitum meum, heredem et successorem relinquo mei Sepulcrum Domini quod est Iherosolimis et eos qui observant et custodiunt illud et ibidem serviunt Deo et Ospitale pauperum quod Iherosolimis est et Templum Salomonis cum militibus qui ad defendendum christianitatis nomen ibi vigilant. His tribus totum regnum meum concedo … ut ipsi habeant et possideant per tres iustas et equales partes': *Colección diplomática de Alfonso I de Aragón y Pamplona, 1104–1134*, ed. Lema Pueyo, no. 241, pp. 356–66, quotation at pp. 359–60; also in *Liber feudorum major*, ed. Miquel Rosell, 1, no. 6, pp. 10–12; *El Gran Priorado de Navarra de la Orden de San Juan de Jerusalén; siglos XII–XIII*, ed. García Larragueta, 2, no. 10, pp. 15–18. See Forey, *The Templars in the Corona de Aragon*, pp. 17–23. For a debate on whether Alfonso intended his will to be taken seriously, see Lourie, 'The Will of Alfonso "El Batallador", King of Aragon and Navarre: A Reassessment'; Forey, 'The Will of Alfonso I of Aragon and Navarre'; Lourie, 'The Will of Alfonso I of Aragon and Navarre: A Reply to Dr. Forey'; Forey, 'A Rejoinder'.

45. *Cartulaire général de l'ordre du Temple, 1119?–1150*, ed. d'Albon, p. 373, 'Bullaire', no. 2 (Innocent II, 1135–7); *Papsturkunden in Spanien, 1*, ed. Kehr, no. 50, p. 318.

46. 'Hoc autem peccatum erat magnum coram Domino, sed Aragonenses, amisso charo domino, hoc ideo faciebant, ut filii suscitarentur ex semine regio': *Chronica Adefonsi imperatoris*, 1. 62, ed. Maya Sánchez, pp. 178–9.

47. *Procesos de las antiguas cortes y parlamentos de Cataluña, Aragon y Valencia*, 4, no. 32, pp. 70–5; *Liber feudorum major*, ed. Miquel Rosell, 1, nos. 10–12, pp. 15–19.

48. *Cartulaire général de l'ordre du Temple, 1119?-1150*, ed. d'Albon, no. 314, pp. 204–5.

49. *Procesos de las antiguas cortes y parlamentos de Cataluña, Aragon y Valencia*, ed. Mascaró, 4, no. 130, pp. 317–18 (Adrian IV, 1158); *Papsturkunden in Spanien*, 1, ed. Kehr, no. 81, pp. 364–5; *Liber feudorum major*, ed. Miquel Rosell, 1, no. 13, p. 19.

50. *Genealogia Welforum*, ed. Becher, 8; *Historia Welforum*, 12, ed. Becher, pp. 26, 46; see also the case of Hugh, Margrave of Tuscany (d. 1001), discussed in Ubl, 'Der kinderlose König. Ein Testfall für die Ausdifferenzierung des Politischen im 11. Jahrhundert', pp. 328–31 ('Die Kirche als Erbe').

51. Hudson, *The Oxford History of the Laws of England II: 871–1216*, pp. 656–7.

52. Eugenius III, *Epistolae*, 93, PL 180, cols. 118–19; Barlow, *Edward the Confessor*, app. D, pp. 323–4.

53. 'partiren-se per parentesch e no ach negun fiyl d'ell': James I, *Llibre dels fets del rei en Jaume*, 34, ed. Bruguera, 2, p. 43.

54. 'illa ... causante se monacho non regi nupsisse': William of Newburgh, *Historia rerum anglicarum*, 1. 31, ed. Howlett, 1, p. 93.

55. Robert of Torigni, *Chronica*, ed. Howlett, pp. 164–5; the sources are discussed by Duby, *Medieval Marriage: Two Models from Twelfth-Century France*, pp. 54–62.

56. 'þa forlet se cyng þa hlæfdian. seo wæs gehalgod him to cwene. 7 let niman of hire eall þæt heo ahte. on lande. 7 on golde. 7 on seolfre 7 on eallon þingon': *Anglo-Saxon Chronicle* (E), s.a. 1048 (*recte* 1051), ed. Plummer and Earle, p. 176; this source says Edith was sent to the nunnery of Wherwell, where Edward's sister was abbess; the *Vita Ædwardi regis*, 1. 3, ed. Barlow, p. 36, says she was sent to Wilton, where she had been brought up; see Stafford, *Queen Emma and Queen Edith: Queenship and Women's Power in Eleventh-Century England*, pp. 264–5.

57. 'reducitur regina, eiusdem ducis filia, ad thalamum regis': *Vita Ædwardi regis*, 1. 4, ed. Barlow, p. 44.

58. 'ob vinculum consanguinitatis': Otto of Freising, *Gesta Friderici I imperatoris*, 2. 11, ed. Waitz and von Simson, p. 111; on the family tree drawn up probably to demonstrate this relationship, see p. 330.

59. The sources are gathered in Simonsfeld, *Jahrbücher des Deutschen Reiches unter Friedrich I.*, 1 (1152–8), pp. 167–9, who doubts the report of some, perhaps later, chroniclers, that the grounds were adultery.

60. *Chancelaria de D. Afonso III*, ed. Ventura and Resende de Oliveira, index s.v.; on Beatrice see Resende de Oliveira, 'Beatriz Afonso, 1244–1300'.

61. 'pro ea contra eundem regem proposuit coram nobis, quod, cum dicta comitissa [Matilda] esset ipsius regis uxor legittima, idem rex cum filia ... regis Castelle ac Legionis illustris, matrimonium de facto, immo potius contubernium, manifeste contraxit': Reg. Vat. 24, fols. 187v–188, no. 357 (26 July 1256); *Les Registres d'Alexander IV*, ed. Bourel de la Roncière et al., 1, no. 1438, pp. 437–8.

62. 'quod olim, tempore quo regni Portugalie gubernacula suscepisti, propter necessitates urgentes, quibus tua sublimitas premebatur et propter vitanda gravia et manifesta pericula, que tibi et regno tuo cominus imminebant, ac etiam propter metum qui cadere poterat in constantem, vivente adhuc clare memorie Mattildi, ... uxore tua

legitima, cum nobili muliere Beatrice, nata carissimi in Christo filii nostri Alphonsi, illustris regis Castelle, … de facto matrimonium contraxisti': Reg. Vat. 27, fols. 104–v–105 (19 June 1263); *Les Registres d'Urbain IV*, ed. Guiraud and Clémencet, 1: *Registre dit Caméral*, pp. 103–4, no. 375, 'Qui celestia simul et terrena'; there is a translation of the letter in d'Avray, *Dissolving Royal Marriages: A Documentary History, 860–1600*, pp. 109–11, who, working from the published text, suggests emending the editor's 'statum' to 'constantem'; this is indeed the reading of the manuscript.

63. 'cum sobolem habere non possent': *Annales Admuntenses, Continuatio Garstensis*, ed. Waitz, p. 600.

64. 'sterilis regina sic repudiata': *Chronicon Rhythmicum Austriacum*, line 629, ed. Wattenbach, p. 363.

65. 'Cum autem sicut accepimus ex persistentia matrimonii taliter inter te ac dictam Kunigundim contracti pax in Ungarie atque Boemie regnis et aliis vicinis provinciis conservetur': Reg. Vat. 27, fol. 58v (20 April 1262, Po. 18277); calendared only in *Les Registres d'Urbain IV*, ed. Guiraud and Clémencet, 1: *Registre dit Caméral*, no. 228, p. 64.

66. πατὴρ ἀκοῦσαι παιδὸς γλιχόμενος ἄρρενος: Choniates, 'De Manuele', in *Historia, Comneno*, 3. 5, ed. Bekker, p. 151, ed. van Dieten, p. 115.

67. A crucial piece of evidence for Alfonso's wives is the passage in the *Chronicon regum Legionensium* of Pelayo, bishop of Oviedo, listing Alfonso's 'five legitimate wives' and 'two concubines', one of them Zaida-Elizabeth: *Crónica del Obispo Don Pelayo*, ed. Sánchez Alonso, pp. 86–7 (translated, with notes, in *The World of El Cid: Chronicles of the Spanish Reconquest*, pp. 87–8); for discussion, see Reilly, *The Kingdom of León-Castilla under King Alfonso VI, 1065–1109*, pp. 79–80, 105–10, 146–7, 192–3, 234–5, 247, 295–8, 338–40, 345–6.

68. For a succinct account, see Tougher, *The Reign of Leo VI (886–912): Politics and People*, pp. 133–63.

69. 'cogita te cottidie esse morituram, et numquam de secundis nuptiis cogitabis': Jerome, *Epistulae*, 54. 18, ed. Labourt, 3, p. 41 (PL 22, col. 560).

70. Ὁ δὲ δεύτερος γάμος, εἰ καὶ συγκεχώρηται, 'αλλ' ἐπιτετίμηται: Theodore the Stoudite, *Epistulae*, 50, ed. Fatouros, 1, p. 147; St Paul thought that a second marriage disqualified a man for office in the Church: 1 Timothy 3: 2; Titus 1: 6.

71. Symeon Magister et Logotheta, *Chronicon*, 132. 22; 133. 13, 22–3, 31–2, ed. Wahlgren, pp. 267, 274, 278–9, 282–3; *Vita Euthymii patriarchae*, 6–8, 10, ed. Karlin-Hayter, pp. 37–43, 45–9, 63.

72. Grierson et al., 'The Tombs and Obits of the Byzantine Emperors', p. 22.

73. Guilland, 'Les noces plurales à Byzance', with pp. 237–46 specifically on Leo VI.

74. Nicholas I, Patriarch of Constantinople, *Letters*, no. 32, ed. Jenkins and Westerink, p. 218.

75. Nicholas I, ibid., p. 230.

76. 'quaecunque sequuntur primas, secundae dicuntur, etiam si millesimae sint': Hostiensis, *Summa aurea*, IV, 'De secundis nuptiis', col. 1443.

77. Symeon Magister et Logotheta, *Chronicon*, 133. 39, 47, 49, 50, 59, ed. Wahlgren, pp. 285, 288–9, 292; *Vita Euthymii patriarchae*, 11–15, ed. Karlin-Hayter, pp. 71–103; Nicholas I, Patriarch of Constantinople, *Letters*, no. 32, ed. Jenkins and Westerink, pp. 214–44.

78. Tougher, *The Reign of Leo VI (886–912): Politics and People*, p. 163.

79. There is a very large bibliography. Examples include Duncan, *The Kingship of the Scots, 842–1292: Succession and Independence*, pp. 175–311; Barrow, *Robert Bruce and the Community of the Realm of Scotland*, pp. 3–99. See also Stones and Simpson, *Edward I and the Throne of Scotland, 1290–1296: An Edition of the Record Sources for the Great Cause*.

80. *The Acts of the Parliaments of Scotland*, 1, ed. Thomson and Innes, p. 424 (82); *Foedera* (new ed.), 1. 2, p. 638.

81. Unless Alexander's widow produced a child: see p. 59.

82. *Documents Illustrative of the History of Scotland from the Death of Alexander III to the Accession of Robert Bruce*, ed. Stevenson, 1, no. 108, pp. 162–73 (The Treaty of Birgham).

83. 'racione proximitatis in gradu': Stones (ed.), *Anglo-Scottish Relations 1174–1328: Some Selected Documents*, no. 19, p. 120 [60].

84. Ibid., no. 19, pp. 118–24 [59]–[62].

85. For the following, see Sesma Muñoz, *El Interregno (1410–1412): concordia y compromiso político en la Corona de Aragón*.

86. 'Quo finito sermone, dictus reverendus Magister Vincentius . . . publicationem de dicto nostro rege et domino . . . ibi publice alta et intelligibili voce coram dictis dominis ambaxiatoribus et populo ibidem congregato, legendo de verbo ad verbum unum ex instrumentis . . . confectis, solemniter publicavit. Et cum in publicatione predicta fuit in passu illo seu puncto in quo nomen excellentissimi ac magniffici principis et domini domni Ferdinandi nostri veri regis et domini exprimitur seu continetur, idem Magister Vincentius et et omnes desuper nominati et alii etiam ibidem presentes magnis et altis vocibus jocunditatem et gaudium denotantes exclamarunt dicentes repetitis vicibus per magnam pausam durantibus, "Viva, viva nostre rey e senyor don Ferrando!"': *Cortes de los antiguos reinos de Aragón y de Valencia y principado de Cataluña*, 10, pp. 491–2; *Parlamentos del Interregno (1410–1412)*, ed. Sesma Muñoz, 2, pp. 621–3.

87. The same point can be made about the ceremony of Ferdinand's coronation: Salicrú i Lluch, 'La coronació de Ferran d'Antequera: l'organització i els preparatius de la festa'.

88. 'don Hernando era más útil para el regimiento deste reino . . . pero . . . creía que el Duque de Gandía y el conde de Urgel como varones legítimos y descendientes por línea de varón de la prosapia de los reyes de Aragón eran mejores en derecho': Zurita, *Anales de la Corona de Aragón*, 11. 87, ed. Canellas López, 5, p. 270.

89. 'Et en este se acabó el linaje del Rey Felipe de Francia que dixieron el Grande, et llamabaule en Francia el Bel. Et algunos dixieron que aquella muerte del Rey Felipe, et otrosi el desfallecimiento de su linaje, veno, porque este Rey Felipe fizo prender al Papa. Et otros dixieron . . . porque este Rey Felipe en el su tiempo fizo grandes despechamientos en el regno de Francia . . . Et algunos dixieron . . . porque este Rey Felipe echó los Judios de todo su regno . . . pero la razon porque acaesció, Dios es sabidor': *Crónica del rey Don Alfonso el Onceno*, 173, ed. Rosell, p. 284.

90. 'in familiam nomenque adoptauit': Suetonius, *De uita Caesarum*, 'Diuus Iulius', c. 83.

91. See Levick, *Augustus: Image and Substance*, pp. 25–6, with notes on pp. 54–5, for discussion of the exact legal status of this provision of Julius Caesar's will.

92. Suetonius, *De uita Caesarum*, 'Diuus Augustus', c. 65; 'certum erat, uni spem successionis incumbere', ibid., 'Tiberius', c. 15.

93. For adoption in Byzantium, see Macrides, 'Kinship by Arrangement: The Case of Adoption', and 'Substitute Parents and their Children'; Pitsakis, 'L'adoption dans le droit byzantin'.

94. Nicholas I, Patriarch of Constantinople, *Letters*, no. 32, ed. Jenkins and Westerink, p. 216.

95. In general, see Hlawitschka, 'Adoptionen im mittelalterlichen Königshaus'; *Médiévales* 35 (1998): *L'adoption. Droits et pratiques*; Jussen, *Spiritual Kinship as Social Practice: Godparenthood and Adoption in the Early Middle Ages*; Di Renzo Villata, 'Adoption between *Ancien Régime* and Codification: Is it in Remission in a Changing World?'.

96. Santinelli, 'Continuité ou rupture? L'adoption dans le droit mérovingien'; for an example in English translation, with some comment, see *The Formularies of Angers and Marculf: Two Merovingian Legal Handbooks*, tr. Rio, pp. 196–7.

97. This is the case of 'Childebertus adoptivus' in the mid seventh century. See, for example, Wood, *The Merovingian Kingdoms 450–751*, p. 222–4; Becher, 'Der sogenannte Staatsstreich Grimoalds. Versuch einer Neubewertung'; Hamann, 'Zur Chronologie des Staatsstreichs Grimoalds', pp. 51–8. The case of the adoption of Theudebert I by Childebert I is described in Gregory of Tours, *Libri historiarum decem*, 3. 24, ed. Krusch and Levison, p. 123.

98. '"Evenit inpulso peccatorum meorum, ut absque liberis remanerem, et ideo peto, ut hic nepus meus mihi sit filius"': ibid., 5. 17, p. 216.

99. Usually interpreted as Guntram's own kingdom, but possibly Childebert's father's. This is the interpretation of 'cunctum ei regnum tradedit' by Santinelli, 'Continuité ou rupture? L'adoption dans le droit mérovingien', p. 15; the fullest discussion of the complexities of this transaction, and later dealings between Guntram and Childebert, is in Jussen, *Spiritual Kinship as Social Practice: Godparenthood and Adoption in the Early Middle Ages*; see also his 'Adoptiones franques et logique de la pratique. Remarques sur l'échec d'une importation juridique et les nouveaux contextes d'un terme romain'.

100. Childebert and his cousin, another nephew of Guntram's, occur as 'adoptivi filii', and 'filios … qui ei fuerant adoptati', Guntram says 'Non ego … alium filium praeter Childebertum habeo', and Gregory writes, correspondingly 'Childebertus rex alium patrem nisi patruum non habet': Gregory of Tours, *Libri historiarum decem*, 7. 8, 13; 8. 3, 13, ed. Krusch and Levison, pp. 331, 334, 373, 379.

101. '"Hoc est indicium, quod tibi omne regnum meum tradedi. … Nihil enim, facientibus peccatis, de stirpe mea remansit nisi tu tantum, qui mei fratris es filius. Tu enim heres in omni regno meo succede, ceteris exheredibus factis"': Gregory of Tours, *Libri historiarum decem*, 7. 33, ed. Krusch and Levison, p. 353.

102. Roumy, *L'adoption dans le droit savant du XIIe au XVIe siècle*, provides a full study.

103. 'les recherches entreprises pour étudier l'application pratique de l'adoption dans les sources judiciaires ou notariales n'ont rien donné': García Marsilla and Sansy,

'L'adoption dans les textes juridiques espagnols du XIIIe siècle', p. 67; *Las Siete Partidas*, 4. 16 ('de los fijos porfijados'), 3, pp. 91–9.

104. Bresc and Beatrice, 'Actes de la pratique, I – L'adoption en Sicile (XIVe–XVe siècles)'; Kuehn, 'L'adoption à Florence à la fin du Moyen Âge'; Aubenas, 'L'adoption en Provence au Moyen Âge (XIVe–XVIe siècles)'; Maurice, 'Actes de la pratique, II – L'adoption dans le Gévaudan (XVe siècle)'. There is an isolated but explicit case in Provence dating to 3 February 1257 (1256 old style): Aubenas, 'L'adoption en Provence au Moyen Âge (XIVe–XVIe siècles)', p. 704 n. 1; Roumy, *L'adoption dans le droit savant du XIIe au XVIe siècle*, p. 199.

105. 'ceste matiere chet plus en droict escrit qu'en coutume': Bouteiller, *Somme rural*, tit. 94, p. 535; Roumy, *L'adoption dans le droit savant du XIIe au XVIe siècle*, p. 188 n. 267, cites this passage from the 1611 printing as title 93. Bouteiller wrote in the late fourteenth century.

106. 'son fils substitué, et autres apres luy substituez, soient tenus de porter les nom, surnom, cry, et armes d'iceluy seigneur testateur': Du Bouchet, *Preuves de l'histoire de l'illustre maison de Coligny*, p. 1131 (Lourdin's will of 1441; his daughter was married to a Coligny); Roumy, *L'adoption dans le droit savant du XIIe au XVIe siècle*, p. 209. See also Maurel, 'Un artifice contre l'extinction des familles? La substitution de nom et d'armes à Marseille (fin XIVe–fin XVe siècle)'.

107. 'Mortuo itaque Buosone, parvulus erat ei filius de filia Hludowici Italici regis; obviam quem imperator ad Hrenum villa Chirihheim veniens honorifice ad hominem sibi quasi adoptivum filium eum iniunxit': 'Continuatio Ratisbonensis' in *Annales Fuldenses*, s.a. 887, ed. Kurze, p. 115; Hermann of Reichenau dropped the 'quasi': 'Mortuo Bosone, filius eius ex filia Ludowici Italiae imperatoris, puer Ludowicus, ad Karolum imperatorem veniens, benigne ab eo susceptus et in filium adoptatus est': Hermann of Reichenau, *Chronica*, s.a. 887, ed. Pertz, p. 109.

108. MacLean, *Kingship and Politics in the Late Ninth Century: Charles the Fat and the End of the Carolingian Empire*, p. 166. Timothy Reuter in his translation of the Annals of Fulda wrote, 'It is however unclear whether adoption in this sense was known to the Franks, and it could equally be that Charles was simply making his peace with the son of a man whom he and the other Carolingians had never accepted as a legitimate ruler [i.e. Boso]': *The Annals of Fulda*, tr. Reuter, p. 113 n. This Louis was the ruler later known as 'Louis the Blind', who died in 928. See also the discussion of the historiography of this subject in Offergeld, *Reges pueri. Das Königtum Minderjähriger im frühen Mittelalter*, pp. 472–88 ('Die Adoption Ludwigs von Vienne').

109. 'Stephanus bonae memoriae rex, avunculus ipsius, cum filius eius patre superstite esset mortuus, quoniam alium non habuit filium, hunc fęcit adoptivum ipsumque regni heredem locavit': *Annales Altahenses maiores*, s.a. 1041, ed. von Oefele, p. 24.

110. 'Sciatis quod ego rex Stephanus Henricum ducem Normannie post me successorem regni Anglie et heredem meum jure hereditario constitui ... Ego etiam securitatem sacramento duci feci quod ... sicut filium et heredem meum ... eum manutenebo': *Regesta regum Anglo-Normannorum, 1066–1154*, 3, ed. Cronne and Davis, no. 272, p. 97; 'Ipsum [Henry of Anjou] siquidem rex in filium suscepit adoptivum, et heredem

regni constituit': Henry of Huntingdon, *Historia Anglorum*, 10. 37 (8. 37 in the RS edition), ed. Greenway, p. 770; 'Stephani regis Anglie et Henrici ducis Normannie concors ad invicem facta est adopcio': Gerald of Wales, *Expugnatio Hibernica*, 1. 31, ed. Scott and Martin, p. 216; 'Henrico duce Normannorum, quem rex Stephanus adoptavit sibi in filium et constituit heredem et successorem regni': Roger of Howden, *Chronica*, ed. Stubbs, 1, p. 212.

111. Matthew Paris, *Chronica majora*, ed. Luard, 1, pp. 204–6; Matthew Paris, *Historia Anglorum*, ed. Madden, 1, pp. 294–5.

112. 'dominum Ludovicum ... in nostrum legitimum filium adoptaverimus, receperimus, admiserimus et ordinaverimus ... volentes ... quod ipse dominus Ludovicus noster legitimus filius omnibus et singulis privilegiis ... gaudeat et utatur quibus filii legitimi adoptivi uti et gaudere possunt et debent. Praeterea nos ipsum dominum Ludovicum ... nostrum legitimum filium adoptivum uberrimis ac maternis prosequentibus affectibus ... in regem futurum ... ipsum et eius posteros ... nominaverimus, pronutiaverimus, declaraverimus, fecerimus, instituerimus et ordinaverimus in heredem et successorem nostrum legitimum post decessum nostrum': *Thesaurus novus anecdotorum*, ed. Martène and Durand, 1, cols. 1580–1; the document is also printed elsewhere; the original is AN J//1043 no. 3. For the preliminary negotiations, see Jarry, 'Instructions secrètes pour l'adoption de Louis Ier d'Anjou par Jeanne de Naples (Janvier 1380)'.

113. Faraglia, *Storia della regina Giovanna II d'Angiò*, pp. 185 n. 1, 201, 249–52; Ryder, *Alfonso the Magnanimous: King of Aragon, Naples, and Sicily 1396–1458*, pp. 77–112.

114. James I of Aragon made an agreement of mutual adoption (*afillamiento*) with the king of Navarre in 1231 but nothing came of it: James I, *Llibre dels fets del rei en Jaume*, 139, 142, 146, ed. Bruguera, 2, p. 137–40; *Documentos de Jaime I de Aragón*, ed. Huici and Cabanes, 1, no. 147, pp. 264–6. Margaret, ruler of all three Scandinavian kingdoms, is said to have adopted her great-nephew Erik of Pomerania: Etting, *Queen Margrete I (1353–1412), and the Founding of the Nordic Union*, p. 65. The deposed Queen Charlotte of Cyprus is said to have adopted Alfonso, illegitimate son of Ferdinand of Naples, as her heir for Cyprus, plainly hoping in this way to acquire powerful backing for a restoration. Alfonso's career is traced in detail in Forcellini, 'Strane peripezie d'un bastardo di casa di Aragona'; he discusses the adoption at 38, pp. 442–3, citing as his primary source Navagero, *Storia Veneziana*, col. 1146. Navagero says that Charlotte 'addottò il figliuolo di detto Alonso', who has just been described as the 'figliuolo naturale' of Ferdinand of Naples. Presumably this is an error or misprint. Many other secondary sources report this adoption but without citing primary sources.

115. Goody, *The Development of the Family and Marriage in Europe*, p. 46.

116. Ibid., p. 95.

117. 'Quid quod nonnulli, filios non habentes, a respectu se tamen salutis suae et remedio peccatorum penitus auertunt, ac licet semine sanguinis sui careant, quaerunt tamen quoscumque alios, quibus substantiam propriae facultatis addicant, id est, quibus umbratile aliquod propinquitatis nomen inscribant, quos sibi quasi adoptiuos

imaginarii parentes filios faciant, et in locum eorum quae non sunt pignorum perfidia generante succedant?': Salvian, *Ad ecclesiam*, 3. 2, ed. Lagarrigue, p. 246.

118. 'ad ineundum vitae conjugalis ordinem nolite moras innectere … Festinate ergo ut de lumbis vestris exeat qui vanam spem tot ambitiosorum hominum destruat et ad unius spem mobilitatem reducat': Ivo of Chartres, *Epistolae* 239, PL 162: 247.

119. 'E nós haguem per muyler la reyna Dona Lionor per conseyl de nostres hòmens, que. ns conseylaven que pus nostre pare no havia pus fiyl sinó nós, que prenguéssem muyler estan jove, per ço car éls hanán gran regart de nostra vida … e que en totes guises volien que hereu romangués de nós per tal que el regno no exís de la natura': James I, *Llibre dels fets del rei en Jaume*, 18, ed. Bruguera, 2, pp. 21–2.

120. 'Quia vero nondum reginali conubio participarat, ueretur curie tota contio ne illo absque liberis de medio facto sub extraneo regimine redigatur. Unde regi dant consilium, dignitate regia dignam accipere in matrimonium': *Passio sancti Athelberhti regis et martiris*, 3, ed. James, p. 237 (this anonymous work survives in a manuscript of the early twelfth century).

121. This is deduced partly from William of Malmesbury's statement that he was 'more than forty (*maior quadragenario*)' when he died (*Gesta regum Anglorum*, 4. 333, ed. Mynors et al., p. 576), and partly from the birth order of William the Conqueror's other children.

122. 'curialis juventus ferme tota crines suos juvencularum more nutriebat': Eadmer, *Historia novorum*, ed. Rule, p. 48.

123. 'exsoletorum prostibulum': William of Malmesbury, *Gesta regum Anglorum*, 4. 314, ed. Mynors et al., p. 560; *exsoletus* seems to have several overtones: prostitution (i.e. paid sex), bisexuality, a passive role in homosexual sex. OMT translates as 'a brothel for perverts'.

124. 'Legitimam coniugem nunquam habuit sed obscenis fornicationibus et frequentibus moechiis inexplebiliter inhesit': Orderic Vitalis, *Historia ecclesiastica* 10. 2, ed. Chibnall 5, p. 202.

125. Barlow, *William Rufus*, pp. 101–10.

126. For discussion of Richard's sexuality, see Gillingham, 'Richard I and Berengaria of Navarre', pp. 133–6; Gillingham, *Richard I*, pp. 263–6.

127. 'De te … iam publicus rumor est quia nec proprie coniugi maritalis thori fidem conservas … ': Adam of Eynsham, *Magna vita sancti Hugonis*, 5. 6, ed. Douie and Farmer, 2, p. 104; '"Esto memor subversionis Sodomae, et ab illicitis te abstine" … praefatus rex … mulierem suam, quam a multo tempore non cognoverat, recepit, et abjecto concubitu illicito adhaesit uxori suae': Roger of Howden, *Chronica*, ed. Stubbs, 3, pp. 288–9.

128. 'In qua custodia cum idem Richardus peccata sua cuidam episcopo confessus, proposuisset se continere de caetero; non multo post quidam episcopus Angliae visitans eum, et gratiam ejus captans, suadet ei, quasi pro salute corporis conservanda … sicque miserum in sua nequitia confortavit': Helinand of Froidmont, *Chronica*, 49, ed. Tissier, p. 205 (PL 212, col. 1082).

129. 'similium convenienciam': Gerald of Wales, *De principis instructione*, 3. 30, ed. Bartlett, p. 728 (RS ed., p. 326).

130. 'ille parvos magna dulcedine fovit et adultos regni consortes faciens, nunquam eorum intuitu dare operam matrimonio curavit': William of Malmesbury, *Gesta regum Anglorum*, 2. 140, ed. Mynors et al., p. 228 (the reading of the B version).

131. Foot, *Æthelstan: The First King of England*, pp. 43, 56, 59–62.

3 FATHERS AND SONS

1. *Las Siete Partidas*, 2. 1. 9, ed. Real Academia de la Historia, 2, p. 10.

2. As lifetime titles for Poland in 1025 and 1076 and Bohemia in 1085 and 1158; in 1198, after Philip of Swabia was crowned king of the Romans (emperor elect), he then crowned Premysl Otakar, duke of Bohemia, as hereditary king of Bohemia; kingship was revived independently in Poland in 1295–6, 1300–6 and, more permanently, 1320.

3. 'Post excessum incliti regis Heinrici ductores primi conveniebant et de statu regni consilium habebant. Perplures diiudicabant Heinricum regno potiri, quia natus esset in aula regali; alii vero desiderabant Ottonem possidere principatus honorem, quia etate esset maior et consilio providentior': *Vita Mathildis reginae posterior*, 9, ed. Schütte, p. 161.

4. 'Rectumne patrem egisse rere regia tibi in dignitate genito non in eadem genitum praeponendo?': Liudprand, *Antapodosis*, 4. 18, in *Liudprandi opera*, ed. Becker, p. 114. Writing long after the event, Eadmer of Canterbury explained some of the opposition to the succession of Edward (the Martyr), son of King Edgar, in 975, and the preference for his younger half-brother, Æthelred, on the grounds that Edward's mother had not been consecrated queen (*in regnum ... sacratam*) but Æthelred's had: Eadmer, *Vita sancti Dunstani*, 59, ed. Turner and Muir, p. 144.

5. Clanchy, *From Memory to Written Record: England 1066–1307*.

6. 'he dyde þæt ealle þa heafodmæn on Normandig dydon manræden 7 holdaðas his sunu Willelme': *Anglo-Saxon Chronicle* (E), s.a. 1115, ed. Plummer and Earle, p. 246.

7. Dudo of Saint-Quentin, *De moribus et actis primorum Normanniae ducum*, 2. 34, 3. 58, 4. 67–8, 128, ed. Lair, pp. 173, 201–3, 220–2, 297; *Gesta Normannorum Ducum*, 6. 11 (12), ed. Van Houts, 2, p. 80; in general, see Garnett, '"Ducal" Succession in Early Normandy'.

8. 'Willelmum ... haeredem regni substituere sibi volebat ... Fide et sacramento professi sunt se et regnum et regni coronam ... in eum ... translaturos': Eadmer, *Historia novorum*, 5, ed. Rule, p. 237.

9. 'rex et dux iam designatus': Hugh the Chanter, *The History of the Church of York 1066–1127*, ed. Johnson, p. 164.

10. 'attulit ei praeceptum, per quod pater suus illi regnum ante mortem suam tradiderat, et spatam quae vocatur sancti Petri, per quam eum de regno revestiret, sed et regium vestimentum et coronam ac fustem ex auro et gemmis': *Annales Bertiniani*, s.a. 877, ed. Waitz, p. 138.

11. 'sentiens se mortem evadere non posse ... coronam et spatam ac reliquum regium apparatum filio suo Hludowico misit, mandans illis qui cum eo erant, ut eum in regem sacrari ac coronari facerent': *Annales Bertiniani*, s.a. 879, ed. Waitz, pp. 147–8.

12. There is a remarkable first-hand account: Helene Kottannerin, *Die Denkwürdigkeiten der Helene Kottannerin (1439–1440)*, ed. Mollay.
13. Thietmar of Merseburg, *Chronicon*, 8. 7 (5), ed. Holtzmann, p. 500 (1018).
14. 'ipse enim vere rex erit et imperator multorum populorum': Widukind of Corvey, *Res gestae saxonicae*, 1. 25, ed. Hirsch and Lohmann, pp. 37–8.
15. Richer of Saint-Rémi, *Historiae*, 3. 91, ed. Hoffmann, p. 220.
16. Brühl, *Deutschland-Frankreich: die Geburt zweier Völker*, p. 569; Bautier, 'Sacres et couronnements sous les Carolingiens et les premiers Capétiens: Recherches sur la genèse du sacre royal français', pp. 51–2.
17. 'regnante domno Lothario augusto serenissimo anno XXVII, filio vero ejus domno Ludovico, adolescenti egregio, regnante anno III': *Recueil des actes de Lothaire et de Louis V, rois de France (954–987)*, ed. Halphen, nos. 45–6, pp. 104, 107.
18. Lewis, 'Anticipatory Association of the Heir in Early Capetian France'; Louis issued charters as *rex designatus* in his father's reign and, when he attended the Christmas court of Henry I at London in 1100, he was called *electus rex Francorum*: *Recueil des actes de Louis VI, roi de France (1108–1137)*, ed. Bautier and Dufour, 1, nos. 7–8, pp. 10–14; Simeon of Durham, *Historia regum*, 182, ed. Arnold, p. 232.
19. Rigord, *Gesta Philippi Augusti*, 3, ed. Carpentier et al., p. 126.
20. Delisle, *Catalogue des actes de Philippe Auguste*, pp. lxix–lxxv.
21. 'coronam illi inposuit et imperialis nominis sibi consortem fecit': *Annales regni Francorum*, s.a. 813, ed. Kurze, p. 138; Einhard, *Vita Karoli Magni*, 30, ed. Holder-Egger, p. 34.
22. 'sicut Karolus pater eius fecerat ipsum': *Chronicon Moissiacense*, s.a. 817, ed. Pertz, p. 312.
23. There is a full list of Byzantine co-emperors from the eighth to the fifteenth centuries, with comment, in Ostrogorsky, 'Das Mitkaisertum im Mittelalterlichen Byzanz'; see also Dölger, 'Das byzantinische Mitkaisertum in den Urkunden'.
24. 'more Grecorum conregnantem instituere vultis?': *Die Briefsammlung Gerberts von Reims*, ed. Weigle, no. 26, p. 49 (Adalbero of Rheims to Egbert of Trier, 984).
25. *Catalogue of the Byzantine Coins in the Dumbarton Oaks Collection and in the Whittemore Collection*, 3. 2, pp. 478, 482, 484–5, 496–500, plates XXXI–XXXII.
26. Constantine was born on 3 September 905 and was crowned at Pentecost (Whitsun), 15 May 908: Pingree, 'The Horoscope of Constantine VII Porphyrogenitus'; Symeon Magister et Logotheta, *Chronicon*, 133. 59, ed. Wahlgren, p. 292.
27. τελευταῖος πάντων ὁ Κωνσταντῖνος. οὗτος τοίνυν ὁ Κωνσταντῖνος σχῆμα μόνον καὶ ὄνομα τῆς βασιλείας ἔχων: Skylitzes, *Synopsis historiarum*, ed. Thurn, p. 234.
28. Skylitzes, *Synopsis historiarum*, ed. Thurn, p. 248.
29. ἀπὸ μὲν γὰρ γεννήσεως ἄχρις εἰκοστοῦ χρόνου τῆς ἡλικίας αὐτοῦ τῷ τε πατρὶ καὶ τῷ Φωκᾷ Νικηφόρῳ καὶ τῷ μετ' ἐκεῖνον Ἰωάννῃ τῷ Τζιμισκῇ συνεβασίλευσεν ὑποκείμενος, εἶτα δὴ δύο πρὸς τοῖς πεντήκοντα ἔτεσι τὴν αὐτοκράτορα ἔσχεν ἀρχήν: Psellos, *Chronographia*, 1. 37, ed. Renauld, 1, pp. 23–4; ed. Reinsch, p. 23.
30. Skylitzes, *Synopsis historiarum*, ed. Thurn, p. 369; Cedrenus, *Historiarum compendium*, ed. Bekker, 2, p. 480.

31. 'pater dicti domini Thome fuit vocatus Willelmus de Cantilupo miles et baro qui fuit potens homo et magne auctoritatis et senescallus domini Henrici quarti regis Anglorum': BAV, MS Vat. lat. 4015, fol. 92v (testimony of Robert of Gloucester, chancellor of Hereford and a doctor of canon law, in the canonization process of Thomas de Cantilupe). Nicholas Trevet, writing his Anglo-Norman chronicle in the 1330s, and the author of the *Eulogium Historiarum*, writing in the 1360s, also call our Henry III 'Henry IV': Leiden, Universiteitsbibliotheek, MS VG G F 6, fol. 91v; *Eulogium historiarum*, ed. Haydon, 3, pp. 123, 137–9.

32. Bernard Gui, *Reges Francorum, Arbor genealogiae regum Francorum*, discussed further, pp. 335–9; on these works, see Delisle, 'Notice sur les manuscrits de Bernard Gui', pp. 245–52, 254–8; I cite from CCCC, MS 45; see fols. 16v, 17v, 26v, 27, 29, 33, 43v, 44, 45, 45v, 46v, 47, 48. Numbering the Philips in this way was not only a practice of Bernard Gui's; see, for example, Geoffroy de Courlon, *Chronique de l'abbaye de Saint-Pierre-le-Vif de Sens*, ed. Julliot, p. 564; Guillelmus Scotus, *Chronicon*, ed. Guigniaut and de Wailly, p. 202.

33. Otto II as king in 961 and as emperor in 967; Otto III as king in 983; Henry III in 1028; Henry IV in 1053; Conrad, son of Henry IV, in 1087; Henry V in 1098; Henry, son of Conrad III, in 1147; Henry VI as king in 1169 (the plan to have him made co-emperor was thwarted); Frederick II in 1196; Henry (VII) in 1220; Conrad IV in 1237; see Giese, 'Zu den Designationen und Mitkönigserhebungen der deutschen Könige des Hochmittelalters (936–1237)'.

34. 'Otto iunior … coimperator': *Ottonis II. et III. Diplomata*, ed. von Sickel, nos. 24–5, pp. 33–5 (972).

35. Lampert of Hersfeld, *Annales*, s.a. 1051, 1052, ed. Holder-Egger, p. 63; Hermann of Reichenau, *Chronica*, ed. Pertz, p. 133; *Heinrici III. Diplomata*, ed. Bresslau and Kehr, no. 330, p. 452, onwards.

36. 'Cum vero puer ipse tribus annis gereret, omnis populus necnon et sublimes una cum suo genitore ad principalem dignitatem eum videlicet asciverunt, atque eis iusiurandum iuraverunt': *Chronicon Salernitanum*, 159, ed. Westerbergh, p. 166; Loud, *Age of Guiscard*, p. 41.

37. Simms, *From Kings to Warlords: The Changing Political Structure of Gaelic Ireland in the Later Middle Ages*, p. 52.

38. 'in ecclesia Dominice Resurrectionis regia decoratus est unctione et sollempniter coronatus statimque sine dilatione exhibite sunt eidem puero universorum baronum cum solita iuramentorum forma manualiter fidelitates': William of Tyre, *Chronicon*, 22. 30 (29), ed. Huygens, 2, p. 1058.

39. 'principibus … filio Waldemari Kanuto regios honores decernere placuit, qui non solum paterne maiestatis futurus possessor, sed eciam presens dignitatis socius nosceretur': Saxo Grammaticus, *Gesta Danorum*, 14. 33. 1, ed. Friis-Jensen, 2, p. 1244.

40. *Danmarks middelalderlige annaler*, ed. Kroman, index entries under 'Valdemar (III)'.

41. 'Fieri quoque asserebat posse, rege interempto, et patria desolata, primatum discordiam, pravorum contra bonos tirannidem, et inde totius gentis captivitatem': Richer of Saint-Rémi, *Historiae*, 4. 12, ed. Hoffmann, p. 240.

42. The term is from Giese, 'Die designativen Nachfolgeregelungen der Karolinger 714–979', p. 497: 'Die Idee eines "Reservekönigs"'.

43. 'ad refellendum emulorum tumultum': Suger, *Vita Ludovici Grossi*, 32, ed. Waquet, p. 268.

44. 'In custamento militum et servientium ad custodiam patrie post mortem regis Richardi': *The Great Roll of the Pipe for the First Year of the Reign of King John*, ed. Stenton, p. 38; cf. pp. 71, 79, 87; 'universi . . . qui castella habebant munierunt illa hominibus et victu et armis': Roger of Howden, *Chronica*, ed. Stubbs, 4, p. 88.

45. 'quod post unius regnantis occasum interstitium temporis inter predecessoris obitum et plenum dominium successoris, quod interregnum veteres appellabant, grande possit imperio . . . afferre discrimen': *Historia Diplomatica Friderici II*, ed. Huillard-Bréholles, 5. 1, p. 31.

46. 'Rex obiit, nec rege carens caret Anglia pace./ Hec Henrice creas miracula, primus in orbe': Henry of Huntingdon, *Historia Anglorum*, 10. 40, ed. Greenway, p. 776.

47. Byrne, 'A Note on the Emergence of Irish Surnames', p. xxxix.

48. Smith, 'Dynastic Succession in Medieval Wales'; see also p. 203 herein.

49. Forey, *The Templars in the Corona de Aragon*, p. 64.

50. Gregory of Tours, *Libri historiarum decem*, 9. 20, ed. Krusch and Levison, p. 436; the so-called Treaty of Andelot, generally now dated to 586.

51. Giese, 'Die designativen Nachfolgeregelungen der Karolinger 714–979'.

52. 'regni successio indivisa et integra . . . iuxta generalem totius Ispanie consuetudinem aprobatam': AN, AE/III/165, Cote d'origine: J//601/25 (consulted online); it is printed in Piskorski, *Las Cortes de Castilla*, pp. 196–7, with a regularized spelling and one important misprint ('Iahennni' for 'duximus'); Daumet, *Mémoire sur les relations de la France et de la Castille de 1255 à 1320*, pp. 1–9.

53. 'affermons . . . ke coustume et vssaghes ont este tel ou roiaume Descoche de si lonch tans de coi il nest point de memoire e sont encore ke se fiez de roi Descoche et ses oirs malles a oirs de se proper char e muire cil fiex ainscois ki li rois ses pere li oir ki seront issu de cel fil demeurent e doiuent demourer airete del roiame. Dont sil auenoit chose ke chius Alixandres nos fiex et cele Margherite sasanbloient par mariaghe e eussent oirs malles de leur deus chars chil oir ki diaus deus seroient issu demouroient airete del roiaume Descoche selonch le coustume et lussaghe deuantdis': *The Acts of Alexander III, King of Scots, 1249–1286*, ed. Neville and Simpson, no. 133, pp. 165–8; see Duncan, *The Kingship of the Scots, 842–1292: Succession and Independence*, pp. 166–9.

54. 'tanquam vir strenuus et in actibus bellicis pro defensione juris et libertatis regni Scotie quam plurimum expertus': *The Records of the Parliaments of Scotland to 1707*, ed. Brown et al., 1315/1; *The Acts of Robert I, 1306–29*, ed. Duncan, no. 58, pp. 342–3; Bower, *Scotichronicon*, 12. 24, ed. Watt et al., 6, pp. 378–80; on this and the following paragraph, see the discussion in Penman, 'Diffinicione successionis ad regnum Scottorum: Royal Succession in Scotland in the Later Middle Ages', pp. 50–3.

55. *The Acts of Robert I, 1306–29*, ed. Duncan, p. 62.

56. 'Preterea cum aliquibus preteritis temporibus a quibusdam ... in dubium fuisset revocatum quo jure successio in regno Scotie si clara forsitan non extiterit decidi deberet et firmari, in eodem parliamento ... declaratum extitit ac diffinitum quod per consuetudinem in inferioribus feodis seu hereditatibus in regno observatam cum in successione regni aliqua talis consuetudo hactenus non fuit introducta, minime debuit seu in futurum debeat dicta successio terminari sed quod proximior masculus tempore mortis regis ex linea recta descendente, vel masculo deficiente proximior femella ex eadem linea, vel illa linea penitus deficiente, proximior masculus ex linea collaterali ... in regno debeat succedere. Quod jure imperiali satis consonum censetur': *The Records of the Parliaments of Scotland to 1707*, ed. Brown et al., 1318/30; *The Acts of Robert I, 1306–29*, ed. Duncan, no. 301, pp. 560–1.

57. See, for example, Kunisch (ed.), *Der dynastische Fürstenstaat: Zur Bedeutung von Sukzessionsordungen für die Entstehung des frühmodernen Staates*.

58. Duindam, *Dynasties: A Global History of Power, 1300–1800*, pp. 88–9.

59. Simms, *From Kings to Warlords: The Changing Political Structure of Gaelic Ireland in the Later Middle Ages*, pp. 54–7.

60. Dumville, 'The Ætheling: A Study in Anglo-Saxon Constitutional History'.

61. The title duke of Calabria was born by the following heirs: Robert, son of Charles II, from 1297; his son Charles (d. 1328); Robert's grand-daughter Joanna, with her husband Andrew of Hungary, who were invested with the duchy of Calabria and the principality of Salerno in 1333; Charles Martel, son of Joanna, in 1346; Otto of Brunswick, husband of Joanna, in 1375; Louis of Anjou, Joanna's adopted son, in 1380. The rival claimant, Louis of Hungary, styled himself prince of Salerno by 1348.

62. The agreement of 1349 is printed in Guiffrey, *Histoire de la réunion du Dauphiné à la France*, pp. 223–46; for the heraldry, Mérindol, 'L'héraldique des princes angevins', p. 286.

63. See the documents of 1367 printed in Guiffrey, *Histoire de la réunion du Dauphiné à la France*, pp. 306–13.

64. 'et pour ce estoit appellé monseigneur le dalphin': *Les Grandes chroniques de France: chronique des règnes de Jean II et de Charles V*, ed. Delachenal, 2, p. 66.

65. 'Como el linage humano sea inclinado, y apetezca, que los hombres deban desear pensar en el ensalzamiento del estado y honor de los hijos, y descendientes de ellos ... nuestro muy caro y muy amado nieto ... y habemos erigido y erigimos, por las presentes, nombre y título de Principado sobre las dichas villas y lugares, y le habemos dado, y damos título y honor de Príncipe': *Anales del Reino de Navarra*, 6, ed. Moret, pp. 261–2.

66. 'non valet privilegium principis ante coronationem': Accursius, *Glossa ordinaria* to Code 7. 37. 3, ad 'infulas', col. 1869; see the comment by Kantorowicz, *The King's Two Bodies*, p. 324, and, on interregna in general, pp. 317–36.

67. 'Scotorum autem principes, qui et reges dicuntur, sicut et Hispanie principes, qui nec coronari tamen consueuerant nec inungi': Gerald of Wales, *De principis instructione*, 1. 20, ed. Bartlett, p. 388 (RS edn., p. 138).

68. Petit-Dutaillis, *Étude sur la vie et le règne de Louis VIII (1187–1226)*, pp. xi–xii; Tessier, *Diplomatique royale française*, pp. 224–6.

69. 'Philippus Dei gratia Francorum Rex': *Ordonnances des roys de France de la troisième race*, 1, p. 295; Lewis, *Royal Succession in Capetian France: Studies on Familial Order and the State*, p. 150, says he was 'the first of his line' to entitle himself king 'before his coronation'.

70. 'coronatio nichil fecit quantum ad transmittendam successionem': Óváry, 'Negoziati tra il Re d'Ungheria e il Re di Francia per la successione di Giovanna I. d'Angiò', p. 142 (the opinion of Louis of Piacenza).

71. 'Alia est opinio quod rex hereditarie succedens non necessario accipit aliquam potestatem super temporalia ex eo quod coronatur a persona ecclesiastica, quamvis posset contingere quod ex hoc aliquam acciperet potestatem super temporalia': William of Ockham, *Octo quaestiones de potestate papae*, 5. 6, ed. Offler, p. 158; the work dates to 1341/2.

72. 'Rex hereditarie succedens nullam recepit potestatem super temporalia ex eo quod coronatur': *Somnium Viridarii*, 1. 170, ed. Schnerb-Lièvre, 1, p. 234; cf. the French version: 'Roy qui vient a un royaume par succession ne prent aucun novel pover pour rayson de son couronement': *Songe du Vergier*, 1. 78, ed. Schnerb-Lièvre, 1, p. 127. Both versions date to the 1370s.

73. Coke, *La sept part des reports Sr. Edvv. Coke Chiualer, chiefe Iustice del Common Banke*, fol. 10v.

74. On fathers and sons, see Schieffer, 'Väter und Söhne im Karolingerhause'; Kasten, *Königssöhne und Königsherrschaft: Untersuchungen zur Teilhabe am Reich in der Merowinger- und Karolingerzeit*; Krüger, 'Herrschaftsnachfolge als Vater-Sohn-Konflikt'; Weiler, 'Kings and Sons: Princely Rebellions and the Structures of Revolt in Western Europe, c. 1170–c. 1280'.

75. 'Enimvero quasi leo regna quae adhuc cepit, firmissime tenuit, neque mihi, quamvis filio, partem vel unam dedit': Ekkehard IV, *Casus sancti Galli*, 146, ed. Haefele, p. 284 (MGH, SS 2, p. 147).

76. Vale, *Charles VII*, p. 163.

77. 'de long temps il avoit eu désir de régner et d'avoir couronne en teste et encore plus maintenant pour cause que son père lui tenoit la main roide': Chastellain, *Chronique*, 4. 88, ed. Kervyn de Lettenhove, 3, p. 446.

78. 'In processu quoque temporis cum adolevisset, cernens se nil dominii rei peculiaris praeter victum et vestitum ex regno, unde coronatus fuerat, posse mandare, coepit corde tristari atque apud patrem ut ei quidpiam dominii largiretur conqueri … Ille vero cernens se non posse diutius talia aequanimiter tolerare, junctis secum aliquibus suae aetatis juvenibus, coepit infestari ac diripere ad libitum res genitorum. Tamen paulo post Dei nutu in se reversus, ad genitores rediens, humili eos satisfactione benevolos erga se reddidit. Tunc demum ab eisdem largitur illi, ut optimum decebat filium, jus ubique ac potestas regni. … repente illum mors invida mundo subripuit': Rodulfus Glaber, *Historiarum libri quinque*, 3. 32–3, ed. France, p. 152.

79. His life has been brilliantly illuminated by Strickland, *Henry the Young King, 1155–1183*.

80. Although Offa of Mercia had had his son consecrated king ('*to cyninge gehalgod*') during his lifetime: *Anglo-Saxon Chronicle* (A), s.a. 785 (*recte* 787), ed Plummer and Earle, p. 54.

81. 'suggerentes incongruum videri quibuslibet regem esse et dominationem regno debitam non exercere': Ralph de Diceto, *Ymagines historiarum*, ed. Stubbs, 1, p. 350.

82. 'tam infrunito factus est animo patricida, ut in summis desideriis mortem eius posuerit': Walter Map, *De nugis curialium*, 4. 1, ed. James et al., p. 282.

83. 'Dii boni! Si tanti fratres fraterno se inuicem federe filialique affectu patrem filii respexissent, duplicique tam beneuolencie quam nature, uinculo astricti fuissent, quanta et quam inestimabilis, quam inclita et incomparabilis in euum et patris fuisset gloria et prolis uictoria!': Gerald of Wales, *Topographia Hibernica*, 3. 52, ed. Dimock, p. 201; Gerald of Wales, *De principis instructione*, 2. 11, ed. Bartlett, p. 483 (RS ed., p. 179).

84. 'impie, inhumane et indigne'; 'cupiens nos privare regno et vita': Henry IV, *Die Briefe Heinrichs IV.*, ed. Erdmann, no. 37, pp. 47–9.

85. 'meum inquam Absalon dilectissimum': ibid., no. 39, p. 53.

86. He is labelled Henry (VII) to distinguish him from the later emperor Henry VII (1308–13). He was born early in 1211, elected king of the Romans in April 1220 and died in February 1242.

87. *Historia Diplomatica Friderici II*, ed. Huillard-Bréholles, 4. 1, p. 525.

88. Roland of Padua, *Chronica*, 3. 10, ed. Jaffé, p. 61.

89. 'In morte filii natura condoluit et paternos affectus eduxit in lacrimas quas offense filii denegabat': *Historia Diplomatica Friderici II*, ed. Huillard-Bréholles, 6. 1, p. 29; the fall of Henry (VII) is discussed by Weiler, *Kingship, Rebellion and Political Culture: England and Germany, c.1215–c.1250*.

90. Ralph de Diceto, *Ymagines historiarum*, ed. Stubbs, 1, pp. 355–66.

91. *Procès en nullité de la condamnation de Jeanne d'Arc*, ed. Duparc 1, p. 328.

92. 'ledit dampnable traittié fait a Troies': *Pour ce que plusieurs*, ed. Taylor, p. 82.

93. Kölzer, 'Das Königtum Minderjähriger im fränkisch-deutschen Mittelater: Eine Skizze'; Wolf, 'Königinwitwen als Vormünder ihrer Söhne und Enkel im Abendland zwischen 426 und 1056'; Offergeld, *Reges pueri. Das Königtum Minderjähriger im frühen Mittelalter*; Beem (ed.), *The Royal Minorities of Medieval and Early Modern England*; Ward, 'Child Kingship in England, Scotland, France and Germany, c. 1050–c. 1250'.

94. 'Gnedige fraw, Vnd hiett ainen Sun der Zehen Jar alt wĕr, wier nemen sein nicht auf zu ainem herren, Wenn er moecht uns den tuerkken nicht vorgesein': Kottannerin, *Die Denkwürdigkeiten der Helene Kottannerin (1439–1440)*, ed. Mollay, p. 22.

95. 'ille, qui ex prosapia imperiali prodiens bonae puer indolis iam coadolescebat; cuius etsi aetas idonea ad reprimendam barbarorum saevitiam minus sufficere videretur, tamen nobilium principum istius regni, quorum non parvus est numerus, consilio et fortitudine Deo iuvante comprimerentur': *Capitularia regum Francorum*, 2, ed. Boretius and Krause, no. 289, pp. 376–7 (*Hludowici regis Arelatensis electio*). For a birthdate of 881 for Louis, see Offergeld, *Reges pueri. Das Königtum Minderjähriger im frühen Mittelalter*, p. 474 n. 567.

96. Vogtherr, '"Weh dir, Land, dessen König ein Kind ist". Minderjährige Könige um 1200 im europäischen Vergleich', p. 293, estimates 'at least eighty cases' between 1100 and 1500, compared with the fifty-seven for that period in Appendix B (see pp. 444–6).

97. Constans II in 641, aged eleven; Constantine VI in 780, aged nine; Michael III in 842, aged two; Constantine VII in 913, aged eight; Alexius II in 1180, aged eleven; John IV in 1258, aged seven; John V in 1341, aged nine; see the comments of Lilie, 'Der Kaiser in der Statistik. Subversive Gedanken zur angeblichen Allmacht der byzantinischen Kaiser', pp. 218–20.

98. Gregory of Tours, *Libri historiarum decem*, 7. 7, ed. Krusch and Levison, p. 330.

99. His age is given as eight by Jordanes, *Romana*, 367, ed. Mommsen, p. 48, and Procopius, *De bello Gothico*, 1. 2, ed. Dewing, 3, p. 14 (*History of the Wars*, 5. 2), but as 'scarcely ten (*vix decennem*)' in Jordanes, *Getica*, 304, ed. Mommsen, p. 136.

100. Procopius, *De bello Gothico*, 1. 4, ed. Dewing, 3, pp. 34–40 (*History of the Wars*, 5. 4); Jordanes, *Getica*, 306, ed. Mommsen, p. 136.

101. Wolf, 'Königinwitwen als Vormünder ihrer Söhne und Enkel im Abendland zwischen 426 und 1056'; Offergeld, *Reges pueri. Das Königtum Minderjähriger im frühen Mittelalter*, pp. 182–293.

102. Martina for Constans II in 641 (in this case a stepmother), Irene for Constantine VI in 780, Theodora for Michael III in 842, Zoe Karbonopsina for Constantine VII in 913, Maria of Antioch for Alexius II in 1180 and Anna of Savoy for John V in 1341; the exception is John IV in 1258, whose mother was already dead.

103. 'Hec, quamvis sexu fragilis . . . egregie conversacionis fuit regnumque filii sui custodia virili servabat': Thietmar of Merseburg, *Chronicon*, 4. 10, ed. Holtzmann, pp. 142–3.

104. 'Bien est France abatardie, Signor baron entendes, Quant feme l'a en baillie': Hugh de la Ferté, 'En talent ai que je die', *Recueil de chants historiques français depuis le XIIIe siècle*, 1, ed. Le Roux de Lincy, p. 171.

105. Grant, *Blanche of Castile, Queen of France*, pp. 78–105.

106. Bagge, *From Viking Stronghold to Christian Kingdom: State Formation in Norway, c. 900–1350*, pp. 357–9.

107. Black-Veldtrup, *Kaiserin Agnes (1043–1077): quellenkritische Studien*, pp. 91–2, lists all the sources for the following event.

108. 'Summa tamen rerum et omnium quibus facto opus erat administratio penes imperatricem remansit, quae tanta arte periclitantis rei publicae statum tutata est, ut nihil in ea tumultus, nihil simultatis tantae rei novitas generaret': Lampert of Hersfeld, *Annales*, s.a. 1056, ed. Holder-Egger, p. 69; his tone changed later: see p. 79, s.a. 1062.

109. Gregory VII, *Registrum*, 4. 3, ed. Caspar, p. 299.

110. Lampert of Hersfeld, *Annales*, ed. Holder-Egger, s.a. 1062, p. 80.

111. Peter of Zittau, *Chronicon Aulae Regiae*, 1. 6–83, ed. Emler, pp. 12–105.

112. '[Fridericus] Heinrici filii sui eum constituens tutorem et totius regni Romani per Alemanniam provisorem': Caesarius of Heisterbach, *Vita, passio et miracula sancti Engelberti*, 1. 5, ed. Zschaeck, pp. 241–2.

113. 'Balium vero regni domino pape dimisit, ab omnibus iuramento firmandum, quoniam ad eum spectabat, tanquam ad dominum principalem . . . sicque debitum carnis exsolvit, rege pupillo in familiarium custodia derelicto': *Gesta Innocentii III*, 23, PL 214, col. XXXIX, ed. Gress-Wright, p. 20.

114. *Recueil general des anciennes lois françaises*, 5, nos. 546, 549–50, pp. 415–39.

115. 'Cum autem sibi nil desit quod deceat regiam majestatem, per sacramentum fidelitatis, quo astringor, ipsum assero deinceps tutela non indigere, sed per ipsum debere milicie domique negocia moderari': *Chronique du religieux de Saint-Denys*, 9. 10, ed. Bellaguet, 1, p. 558; the cardinal of Laon was Pierre Aycelin; he made his will 'lying sick in Rheims (*jacente infirmo Remis*)' on 7 November 1388: Félibien and Lobineau, *Histoire de la ville de Paris*, 5, pp. 675–7.

116. *Le Livre au roi*, 6, ed. Geilsammer, p. 148.

117. *Recueil general des anciennes lois françaises*, 5, no. 546, pp. 415–23.

118. Bisson, *The Medieval Crown of Aragon: A Short History*, p. 36.

119. Woodacre, *The Queens Regnant of Navarre: Succession, Politics, and Partnership, 1272–1512*, p. 64.

120. See the detailed study by Carpenter, *The Minority of Henry III*.

121. 'rector noster et regni nostri': *Patent Rolls of the Reign of Henry III (1216–32)*, 1, pp. 3–187 passim.

122. 'Sciatis quod provisum est per commune consilium regni nostri quod nulla carta, nulle littere patentes de confirmacione, alienacione, vendicione, vel donacione, seu de aliqua re que cedere possit in perpetuitatem, sigillentur magno sigillo nostro usque ad etatem nostram completam': *Patent Rolls of the Reign of Henry III (1216–32)*, 1, p. 177.

123. 'Vae tibi terra cuius rex est puer': Ecclesiastes 10: 16.

124. 'non regem sed puerum nominant deridendo': Carpenter, *The Minority of Henry III*, p. 161 n. 16, citing TNA, SC 1/1, no. 39.

125. 'Rex enim puer erat, mater vero utpote femina his et illis consiliantibus facile cedebat': *Annales Altahenses maiores*, s.a. 1060, ed. von Oefele, p. 56.

126. 'Sed maledicta terra ubi puer regnat et mulier principatum tenet; regnum non precibus uel blanditiis, sed legibus et inperio regendum est': *Historia Compostellana*, 1. 107, ed. Falque Rey, p. 183.

127. 'Nam rex puer erat, et pro suo velle sicut harundinem ad suum placitum agitabant': Andreas Marchianensis, *Historia regum Francorum*, 3. 27, ed. Waitz, p. 210.

128. Although the nickname first occurs only several generations after his reign: 'Lodewicus … qui cognominatus est Infans': *Gesta episcoporum Halberstadensium*, ed. Weiland, p. 82 (material perhaps originally put together in the 990s); Bührer, 'Studien zu den Beinamen mittelalterlicher Herrscher', p. 209; see also Widukind of Corvey, *Res gestae saxonicae*, 1. 22, ed. Hirsch and Lohmann, p. 34 (from the 960s): 'tempore Ludewici adolescentis'; Thietmar of Merseburg (d. 1018), *Chronicon*, 1. 6, ed. Holtzmann, p. 10: 'Conradus … Luthuwici successor pueri'.

129. 'Arnolfus imperator, habito conventu, nulli fidens, sacramentum fidelitatis denuo sibi et filio parvulo Ludowico a cunctis exigit': Hermann of Reichenau, *Chronica*, s.a. 897, ed. Pertz, p. 111; see also Dümmler, *Geschichte des Ostfränkischen Reiches*, 3, p. 457 n. 1.

130. Bresslau, 'Der angebliche Brief des Erzbischofs Hatto von Mainz an Papst Johann IX.', p. 27; Bresslau regarded this letter of Hatto of Mainz as a twelfth-century forgery, but its authenticity was defended by Beumann, 'Die Einheit des ostfränkischen Reichs

und der Kaisergedanke bei der Königserhebung Ludwigs des Kindes'; see Brühl, *Deutschland-Frankreich: die Geburt zweier Völker*, p. 390; Offergeld, *Reges pueri. Das Königtum Minderjähriger im frühen Mittelalter*, p. 529.

4 FEMALE SOVEREIGNS

1. There is a summary of her life in Hill, *Imperial Women in Byzantium 1025–1204: Power, Patronage and Ideology*, pp. 62–6.

2. 'Vnus igitur, loquens pro omnibus cunctis in idipsum consentientibus, ex persona populorum recognouit regnum Castelle deberi de iure regine domine Berengarie et quod eam omnes recognoscebant dominam et reginam regni Castelle. Verumptamen supplicauerunt omnes unanimiter ut regnum, quod suum erat iure proprietatis, concederet filio suo maiori, scilicet domino Fernando, quia, cum ipsa femina esset, labores regiminis regni tolerare non posset. Ipsa uero, uidens quod ardenti desiderio concupierat, petitis gratanter annuit et filio supradicto regnum concessit': *Chronica latina regum Castellae*, 35, ed. Charlo Brea, pp. 78–9.

3. Shadis, *Berenguela of Castile (1180–1246) and Political Women in the High Middle Ages*, esp. pp. 97–121, and Bianchini, *The Queen's Hand: Power and Authority in the Reign of Berenguela of Castile*, esp. pp. 140–79.

4. Shadis, *Berenguela of Castile (1180–1246) and Political Women in the High Middle Ages*, p. 6; Bianchini, *The Queen's Hand: Power and Authority in the Reign of Berenguela of Castile*, p. 19; there are many examples in *Documentos medievais portugueses. Documentos régios*, 1. 1, ed. Azevedo.

5. 'que se reginam appellari faciebat'; 'que se reginam nominari faciebat'; 'que se reginam nominabat'; 'dicta regina': Gislebert of Mons, *Chronicon Hanoniense*, 125, 167, 174, 178, ed. Vanderkindere, pp. 193, 249, 259, 263. Matilda was also called Teresa. She titles herself 'queen' in some of her charters: Nicolas, 'Countesses as Rulers in Flanders', p. 125.

6. 'Regina enim dicebatur, quia filia regis erat et pro fratre suo minus firmo regnum patris sui tenuerat in Hyspaniis': *Vita Alberti episcopi Leodiensis*, ed. Heller, p. 140.

7. General narratives in Garland, *Byzantine Empresses: Women and Power in Byzantium, AD 527–1204*, pp. 73–94; Herrin, *Women in Purple: Rulers of Medieval Byzantium*, pp. 51–129; there is a succinct summary in Whittow, 'Motherhood and Power in Early Medieval Europe, West and East: The Strange Case of the Empress Eirene', pp. 61–4, with bibliography. For the coins, see Kotsis, 'Defining Female Authority in Eighth-Century Byzantium: The Numismatic Images of the Empress Irene (797–802)'; for the laws, *Jus Graecoromanum*, ed. Ioannes and Panagiotes Zepos, 1, pp. 45, 49.

8. *Annales Laureshamenses*, s.a. 801, ed. Pertz, p. 38.

9. General narrative in Garland, *Byzantine Empresses: Women and Power in Byzantium, AD 527–1204*, pp. 136–57; on views of her many marriages, Laiou, 'Imperial Marriages and Their Critics in the Eleventh Century: The Case of Skylitzes'.

10. Psellos, *Chronographia*, 5. 22, ed. Renauld, 1, p. 99; ed. Reinsch, pp. 91–2.

11. Περιΐσταται οὖν ἡ βασιλεία ταῖς δυσὶν ἀδελφαῖς: Psellos, *Chronographia*, 6. 1, ed. Renauld, 1, p. 117; ed. Reinsch, p. 107.

12. Αἱ γοῦν ἀδελφαὶ μόναι τέως βασιλεύειν ἑλόμεναι: Psellos, *Chronographia*, 6. 2, ed. Renauld, 1, p. 117; ed. Reinsch, p. 107.

13. τὴν ἰσχὺν ἑαυτῇ ἐμνηστεύετο: Psellos, *Chronographia*, 6. 18, ed. Renauld, 1, p. 126; ed. Reinsch, p. 114.

14. γίνεται ταῦτα ταῖς μὲν βασιλίσσαις τέλος τοῦ δι᾽ ἑαυτῶν τί ποιεῖν καὶ αὐτοκρατεῖν ἐν τοῖς πράγμασιν, ἀρχὴ δὲ τῷ Μονομάχῳ Κωνσταντίνῳ καὶ πρώτη τῆς βασιλείας κατάστασις: Psellos, *Chronographia*, 6. 21, ed. Renauld, 1, p. 127; ed. Reinsch, pp. 115–16.

15. Described (by Henry Maguire) and illustrated in *The Glory of Byzantium: Art and Culture of the Middle Byzantine Era, A.D. 843–1261*, no. 145, pp. 210–12. There is debate about its authenticity. See also Kotsis, 'Mothers of the Empire: Empresses Zoe and Theodora on a Byzantine Medallion Cycle'.

16. On Theodora, see Garland, *Byzantine Empresses: Women and Power in Byzantium, AD 527–1204*, pp. 161–7; Todt, 'Die Frau als Selbstherrscher: Kaiserin Theodora, die letzte Angehörige der makedonischen Dynastie'.

17. τὴν αὐτοκράτορα Ῥωμαίων ἀρχὴν ἑαυτῇ ἀνατίθησιν: Psellos, *Chronographia*, 6. 204 (a 1), ed. Renauld, 2, p. 72; ed. Reinsch, p. 197.

18. ἀρρενώσασα: Psellos, *Chronographia*, 6. 205 (a 2), ed. Renauld, 2, p. 72; ed. Reinsch, p. 197.

19. Aristakès of Lastivert, *Récit des malheurs de la nation Arménienne*, XVIII (101), p. 92.

20. τότε πρῶτον ὁ καθ᾽ ἡμᾶς χρόνος τεθέαται γυναικωνίτιν μετασχηματισθεῖσαν εἰς βασιλικὸν βουλευτήριον: Psellos, *Chronographia*, 6. 1, ed. Renauld, 1, p. 117; ed. Reinsch, p. 107.

21. τὰ τῆς γυναικωνίτιδος παίγνια τοῖς βασιλικοῖς κατεκίρνων σπουδάσμασι: Psellos, *Chronographia*, 6. 5, ed. Renauld, 1, p. 119; ed. Reinsch, p. 109.

22. ἐπιστασίας ἀνδρὸς: Psellos, *Chronographia*, 6. 10, ed. Renauld, 1, p. 121; ed. Reinsch, p. 110.

23. Ὅτι μὲν οὖν ἀπρεπὲς ἔδοξε ξύμπασιν ἐξ ἀρρενωποτέρου φρονήματος ἐκθηλυνθῆναι τὴν Ῥωμαίων ἀρχὴν: Psellos, *Chronographia*, 6. 207 (a 4), ed. Renauld, 2, p. 73; ed. Reinsch, p. 198.

24. ἄρρενος, ἔφη, δεῖσθαι τὸ κράτος καὶ φρενὸς καὶ ψυχῆς: Psellos, *Ἐπιτάφιοι λόγοι εἰς τοὺς πατριάρχας Μιχαὴλ Κηρουλλάριον*, ed. Sathas, p. 358; see Todt, 'Die Frau als Selbstherrscher: Kaiserin Theodora, die letzte Angehörige der Makedonischen Dynastie', p. 157; cf. Psellos, *Chronographia*, 6. 220 (a 17), ed. Renauld, 2, p. 80; ed. Reinsch, p. 204.

25. ἅτε γυναῖκα καὶ κληρονόμον τοῦ κράτους: Psellos, *Chronographia*, 4. 22, ed. Renauld, 1, p. 67; ed. Reinsch, p. 63 (John the Orphanotrophus is speaking).

26. ποῦ ποτε ... ἢ τὸν κλῆρον τῆς βασιλείας ἐννομώτατα ἔχουσα: Psellos, *Chronographia*, 5. 26, ed. Renauld, 1, p. 102; ed. Reinsch, p. 94.

27. τὸ πᾶν κράτος περιέστη ὡς εἰς κληρονόμον τὴν βασιλίδα Ζωήν; Τὴν προγονικὴν δὲ παραλαβοῦσα βασιλείαν: Skylitzes, *Synopsis historiarum*, ed. Thurn, pp. 416, 479.

28. Aristakès of Lastivert, *Récit des malheurs de la nation Arménienne*, XVII (95), p. 88.

29. Psellos, *Chronographia*, 6. 206 (a 3), ed. Renauld, 2, p. 73; ed. Reinsch, p. 197.

30. δεύτερον αἷμα βασίλειον: Psellos, *Chronographia*, 5. 36, ed. Renauld, 1, p. 108; ed. Reinsch, p. 99.

31. Aristakès of Lastivert, *Récit des malheurs de la nation Arménienne*, IX (50), p. 39.

32. αἱ μάνναι ἡμῶν αἱ πορφυρογέννητοι: Skylitzes, *Synopsis historiarum*, ed. Thurn, p. 434.

33. Todt, 'Die Frau als Selbstherrscher: Kaiserin Theodora, die letzte Angehörige der Makedonischen Dynastie', p. 169; *Catalogue of the Byzantine Coins in the Dumbarton Oaks Collection and in the Whittemore Collection*, 3. 1, ed. Bellinger et al., p. 180; 3. 2, p. 753.

34. Psellos, *Chronographia*, 2. 5, ed. Renauld, 1, p. 28; ed. Reinsch, p. 27.

35. Ademar of Chabannes, *Chronicon*, 3. 32, ed. Bourgain, pp. 154–5; see Arbagi, 'The Celibacy of Basil II'.

36. Psellos, *Chronographia*, 3. 5, ed. Renauld, 1, p. 34; ed. Reinsch, p. 33. A marriage had been planned for Zoe when she was much younger, but with a western ruler, Otto III, not with a potential successor to the throne in Constantinople. Otto died before the wedding could take place: Dölger, *Regesten der Kaiserurkunden des oströmischen Reiches*, 1. 2: *Regesten von 867–1025*, no. 784, p. 196. Wolf, 'Zoe oder Theodora – Die Braut Kaiser Ottos III. 1001/2?', argues it was Theodora not Zoe who was the potential bride.

37. τὸν ἄζυγα βίον: Psellos, *Orationes panegyricae*, 11, ed. Dennis, p. 121.

38. Reilly, *The Kingdom of León-Castilla under Queen Urraca, 1109–1126*; her charters as queen are edited by Irene Ruiz Albi in *La reina doña Urraca (1109–1126), cancillería y colección diplomática*, ed. Ruiz Albi; for her coinage, see Crusafont, Balaguer and Grierson, *Medieval European Coinage, 6: The Iberian Peninsula*, pp. 225–34; Martin, *Queen as King: Politics and Architectural Propaganda in Twelfth-Century Spain*, for an argument about her architectural patronage. It is possible that the Anglo-Saxon queen Seaxburh ruled Wessex in her own right for a year in 672–3: Yorke, 'Seaxburh [Sexburga] (d. 674?), queen of the Gewisse', *ODNB*, XLIX, p. 616.

39. The *Chronicon Compostellanum*, ed. Falque Rey, p. 83, refers to Count Raymond, 'quem rex A. a Burgundia in Ispaniam venire fecerat, et cui totum suum regnum iureiurando pollicitus fuerat'.

40. The evidence for Sancho's designation as heir is a charter confirmation of 1107: 'Sancius puer filius regis regnum electus patrifactum conf.' This phrase is found only in one version of a later copy but was enough to convince Reilly that 'Sancho was formally recognized as heir to the kingdom': Reilly, *The Kingdom of León-Castilla under Queen Urraca, 1109–1126*, p. 42. *Tumbo A de la Catedral de Santiago*, ed. Lucas Alvarez, no. 77, pp. 167–9, prints the version without the phrase 'regnum electus patrifactum', which it gives in a note as a collation with the version in Tumbo C.

41. '... notum est et omnibus Hispanie regnum incolentibus quoniam pater meus imperator Adefonsus, appropinquante sui transitus hora, mihi apud Toletum regnum totum tradidit et filio meo Adefonso nepoti suo Gallitiam, si maritum susciperem': *Historia Compostellana*, 1. 64, ed. Falque Rey, p. 102; see also Alfonso's own words: 'totam ei [i.e Alfonso, Urraca and Raymond's son] Galletiam concedo, si eius mater Vrraca uirum ducere uoluerit': ibid., 1. 46, p. 84.

42. In the period between Raymond's death and the death of her father Alfonso, Urraca appears in documents as 'mistress of the whole of Galicia', or even 'empress of the

whole of Galicia': 'totius Gallecie domina': *Tumbo A de la Catedral de Santiago*, ed. Lucas Alvarez, no. 78, pp. 176–7 (13 December 1107); 'tocius Gallecie imperatrix': Reilly, *The Kingdom of León-Castilla under Queen Urraca, 1109–1126*, p. 50 (21 January 1108); both also in *Documentos medievales del Reino de Galicia: Doña Urraca (1095–1126)*, ed. Recuero Astray, no. 14, pp. 53–4, no. 17, pp. 56–7, but with the document dated by Reilly as 1108 there dated 21 January 1107 and hence before Raymond's death.

43. The argument that the marriage of Urraca and Alfonso of Aragon took place before the death of Alfonso VI was advanced in detail by Ramos y Loscertales, 'La sucesion del Rey Alfonso VI', but did not convince Reilly, *The Kingdom of León-Castilla under Queen Urraca, 1109–1126*, p. 52 n. 26.

44. 'ayuntáronse los nobles e condes de la tierra e fuéronse para la dicha doña Vrraca su fija diçiendole ansí: tu non podrás gouernar nin retener el reino de tu padre e a nosotros regir si non tomares marido': *Crónicas anónimas de Sahagún*, 18, ed. Ubieto Arteta, p. 26.

45. See especially *La reina doña Urraca (1109–1126), cancillería y colección diplomática*, ed. Ruiz Albi, no. 4, pp. 360–2, of December 1109; in certain circumstances a union of Aragon and Leon-Castile could have been the outcome. See the comments of Reilly, *The Kingdom of León-Castilla under Queen Urraca, 1109–1126*, pp. 63–4.

46. 'Urraka, Dei nutu totius Yspanie regina': *La reina doña Urraca (1109–1126), cancillería y colección diplomática*, ed. Ruiz Albi, no. 1, pp. 353–6; 'regnante Adefonso rege Aragoneni in Legione': Reilly, *The Kingdom of León-Castilla under Queen Urraca, 1109–1126*, p. 63.

47. 'non curo yo qué faga la mi hueste e mis guerreros': *Crónicas anónimas de Sahagún*, 20, ed. Ubieto Arteta, p. 34.

48. 'a manera de bárvaro cruel': ibid., pp. 32–3.

49. 'Nul prince chrétien n'avait plus que lui de courage, d'ardeur à incessamment combattre les musulmans, de force de résistance. Il dormait avec sa cuirasse et sans matelas; et comme un jour on lui demandait pourquoi il ne couchait pas avec les filles des chefs musulmans qu'il avait faites prisonnières: "Un véritable soldat", dit-il, "ne doit vivre qu'avec les hommes, et non avec les femmes!"': Ibn al-Athir, *Annales du Maghreb et de l'Espagne*, tr. Fagnan, p. 555 (AH 529). There is another translation in *Recueil des Historiens des Croisades, Historiens Orientaux*, 1, 414.

50. *Historia Compostellana*, 1. 64, ed. Falque Rey, p. 102.

51. 'Aragonensis tyrannus': *Historia Compostellana*, 1. 83, ed. Falque Rey, p. 131; this is a standard term for Alfonso the Battler in the *Historia Compostellana*.

52. 'como es costumbre de las lenguas lisonjeras, la dicha muger del conde era ya llamada reina de los sus domésticos e caualleros': *Crónicas anónimas de Sahagún*, 25, ed. Ubieto Arteta, p. 41.

53. *Papsturkunden in Portugal*, ed. Erdmann, no. 16, pp. 169–70 (18 June 1116, an original).

54. *Documentos medievais portugueses. Documentos régios*, 1. 1, ed. Azevedo, no. 48, pp. 59–60 ('ego regina Tarasia'), no. 49, pp. 60–2, ('ego infant domna Tarasia regina de Portugal'), both of 1117; the former is an original, the latter not. Earlier documentary references to her as queen are dubious: ibid., 1. 2, pp. 571–2; Reilly, *The Kingdom of León-Castilla under Queen Urraca, 1109–1126*, p. 117 n. 103. In 1121 a papal legate

addressed her as 'T. venerabili regine Portugalen (sium)': *Papsturkunden in Portugal*, ed. Erdmann, no. 24, pp. 180–1.

55. Cf. the pithy account in the *Chronica Adefonsi imperatoris*, 1. 73, ed. Maya Sánchez, p. 184; 'Ipsa autem Tarasia erat filia regis domni Adefonsi, sed de non legitima, ualde tamen a rege dilecta, nomine Xemena Munionis, quam rex dilectionis et honoris causa dedit maritatam Enrrico comiti et dotauit eam magnifice dans Portugalensem terram iure hereditario. Mortuo autem comite Enrrico, Portugalenses uocauerunt eam reginam; qua defuncta, filium suum regem, sicut et postea fuit, ad honorem nominis sui dixerunt.'

56. On her, see Chibnall, *The Empress Matilda: Queen Consort, Queen Mother and Lady of the English*.

57. Blackburn, 'Coinage and Currency', pp. 187–8.

58. See Mayer, 'Studies in the History of Queen Melisende of Jerusalem'; Hamilton, 'Women in the Crusader States: The Queens of Jerusalem (1100–1190)', pp. 147–57; Mayer, 'The Succession to Baldwin II of Jerusalem: English Impact on the East'. Her charters are in *Die Urkunden der lateinischen Könige von Jerusalem*, ed. Mayer, 1, nos. 152–204, pp. 341–86.

59. 'ei primogenita regis filia cum spe regni post regis obitum traderetur': William of Tyre, *Chronicon*, 13. 24, ed. Huygens, 1, p. 618.

60. 'regni curam et plenam eis tradidit potestatem': ibid., 13. 28, 1, p. 625.

61. 'idem comes cum predicta uxore . . . in ecclesia Dominici Sepulchri . . . sollempniter et ex more coronatus et consecratus est': ibid., 14. 2, 2, p. 634.

62. 'sollempniter inunctus, consecratus et cum matre coronatus est': ibid., 16. 3, 12, p. 717.

63. 'semper ad matris ubera dependere': ibid.

64. 'indignum esse ut femineo regeretur arbitrio': ibid., 17. 13, 2, p. 778.

65. Chibnall, *The Empress Matilda: Queen Consort, Queen Mother and Lady of the English*, p. 206.

66. *Chronicon Compostellanum*, ed. Falque Rey, p. 82.

67. 'comitem Larensem P. Gundisaluidem, qui cum matre ipsius regis [Alfonso VII] adulterine concubuerat et ex ipsa regina adulterinos filios et filias genuerat': *Historia Compostellana*, 3. 24, ed. Falque Rey, p. 458.

68. Orderic Vitalis, *Historia ecclesiastica*, 12. 7, ed. Chibnall, 6, pp. 406–8.

69. 'Animus mulieris infirmus est et instabilis et cito exorbitat, ut scriptum est: Melior est iniquitas uiri quam benefaciens mulier': *Historia Compostellana*, 1. 107, ed. Falque Rey, p. 181; the biblical citation is Ecclesiasticus 42: 14.

70. 'Quid non audet muliebris uecordia? Quid non presumit serpentis uersutia? Quid non aggreditur sceleratissima uipera? Quid audeant, quid presumant, quid aggrediantur muliebria figmenta, Eue prothoparentis nostre satis indicant exempla. Ruit in uetitum audacissima mens mulieris: sacrosancta uiolat fas que nefas que confundit': ibid., 2. 39, ed. Falque Rey, p. 284.

71. 'Erat autem mater mulier prudentissima, plenam pene in omnibus secularibus negociis habens experientiam, sexus feminei plane vincens conditionem, ita ut manum mitteret ad fortia': William of Tyre, *Chronicon*, 16. 3, ed. Huygens, 2, p. 717.

72. 'Hanc [sc. regni curam et administrationem] consilio principum regionis strenue et feliciter, vires et animum transcendens femineum, usque ad illum diem administraverat ...': ibid., 17. 13, 2, p. 777.

73. Ibid., 16. 3, 18. 27, 2, pp. 717, 850.

74. 'domina Milissendis regina, mulier provida et supra sexum discreta femineum, que regnum tam vivente marito quam regnante filio congruo moderamine annis triginta et amplius, vires transcendens femineas, rexerat ...': ibid., 18. 27, 2, p. 850.

75. 'manum suum misit ad fortia': Proverbs 31: 19, in midst of the eulogy of the strong woman.

76. 'oculi omnium in te respiciunt ... Opus est ut manum tuam mittas ad fortia, et in muliere exhibeas virum ... Ita prudenter et moderate oportet te cuncta disponere, ut omnes, qui te viderint, ex operibus regem te potius, quam reginam existiment ... Sed non sum, inquies, ad ista sufficiens ... Opera haec opera sunt viri; ego autem mulier sum, corpore debilis, mobilis corde, nec provida consilio, nec assueta negotiis': Bernard of Clairvaux, *Epistolae*, 354, ed. Leclerq and Rochais, 2 (8), pp. 297–8.

77. Arnulf of Lisieux, *Epitaphium Matildis Imperatricis*.

78. 'She was unpopular because she was a woman': Davis, *King Stephen, 1135–1154*, p. 13; 'To many of the political elite, Matilda was unsuitable because she was a woman': Stringer, *The Reign of Stephen: Kingship, Warfare, and Government in Twelfth-Century England*, p. 1; 'An even stronger objection to Matilda ... was that she was a woman': Bartlett, *England under the Norman and Angevin Kings 1075–1225*, p. 10. Even Marjorie Chibnall wrote of 'the reluctance of many magnates ... to accept a woman ruler': *The Empress Matilda: Queen Consort, Queen Mother and Lady of the English*, p. 96.

79. John of Salisbury, *Historia pontificalis*, 42, ed. Chibnall, pp. 83–6; William of Malmesbury, *Historia novella*, 1. 3, ed. King, p. 10.

80. 'que filio magis competunt, non debere filie regalia sceptra addici': Gilbert Foliot, *Letters and Charters*, ed. Morey and Brooke, no. 26, p. 61. The letter is discussed at length in Morey and Brooke, *Gilbert Foliot and his Letters*, Chapter 7, 'The Case for the Empress Matilda', pp. 105–23; see also Chibnall, *The Empress Matilda: Queen Consort, Queen Mother and Lady of the English*, pp. 85–7.

81. This is the case of the daughters of Zelophehad, which occurs in Numbers 27: 1–11 and 36: 1–13. The former passage contains God's injunction that daughters should inherit in the absence of sons, the latter the condition that they should not marry outside their tribe. Gilbert Foliot refers to 'the last chapter' of Numbers, and hence the latter passage, but must presumably also be invoking the earlier injunction. It has been argued that this condition for the daughters inheriting – that they should not marry outside their tribe – could be seen as relevant to Matilda's unpopular marriage with Geoffrey of Anjou: Crouch, 'Robert, Earl of Gloucester, and the Daughters of Zelophehad', pp. 232–3; Garnett, *Conquered England: Kingship, Succession, and Tenure 1066–1166*, p. 233 n. 839; see also Hudson, *The Oxford History of the Laws of England II: 871–1216*, p. 352.

82. Holt, 'Feudal Society and the Family in Early Medieval England: IV. The Heiress and the Alien', p. 5; 'asserens filiam nepoti in paterna hereditate praeferendam': John of

Salisbury, *Letters*, no. 131, ed. Millor et al., 1, p. 227. She lost her case but because she was deemed illegitimate not because she was female.

83. 'dexó el señorio de su reino a la dicha donna Hurraca su fixa': *Crónicas anónimas de Sahagún*, 16, ed. Ubieto Arteta, p. 25.

84. *La reina doña Urraca (1109–1126), cancillería y colección diplomática*, pp. 291–3 ('Intitulación'), 321–2 ('Los sincronismos de reinos').

85. 'dompna Urracha regina . . . decentis memorie domini Aldefonsi regis filia': *La reina doña Urraca (1109–1126), cancillería y colección diplomática*, no. 148, pp. 590–2.

86. 'fide et sacramento spoponderunt filie regis se totum regnum Anglorum illi contra omnes defensuros, si patrem suum superviveret': John of Worcester, *Chronicle*, 3, ed. McGurk, p. 166.

87. 'justam heredem regni Anglie': *Regesta regum Anglo-Normannorum, 1066–1154*, 3, ed. Cronne and Davis, no. 391, p. 150.

88. 'filia regis et regni Ierosolimitani haeres': *Die Urkunden der lateinischen Könige von Jerusalem*, ed. Mayer, 1, no. 109, p. 269.

89. For the late medieval examples, see Monter, *The Rise of Female Kings in Europe, 1300–1800*, esp. pp. 54–93; Woodacre, *The Queens Regnant of Navarre: Succession, Politics, and Partnership, 1272–1512*.

90. 'los homes sabios et entendudos . . . establescieron que si fijo varon hi non hobiese, la fija mayor heredase el regno': *Las Siete Partidas*, 2. 15. 2, 2, p. 133.

91. *Epistolae saeculi XIII e regestis pontificum Romanorum selectae*, ed. Rodenberg, 3, no. 646, p. 643, Clement IV, 'Constitui ab eo', Po. 19434, 4 November 1265, confirming the cardinals' arrangements of 28 June 1265.

92. 'Si vero solum feminini sexus liberos superesse contingat, succedat primogenita in eisdem': Reg. Vat. 41, fol. 162 v°, n° 7; *Les Registres de Martin IV (1281–1285)*, ed. Olivier-Martin, no. 455, pp. 191–2, 'Qui regna transfert', 27 August 1283, Po. 22061.

93. 'rectam heredem': *The Acts of the Parliaments of Scotland*, 1, ed. Thomson and Innes, p. 424 (82); *Foedera* (new ed.), 1. 2, p. 638.

94. See the comments in Duncan, *The Kingship of the Scots, 842–1292: Succession and Independence*, pp. 181–2. He is even more forthright in his article on Margaret in the *ODNB*: 'to see her as queen is misleading, and effectively connives at the manipulative insensitivity of those men, led by the English king, of whose ambition for political power she was the pathetic child victim': Duncan, 'Margaret [called the Maid of Norway] (1282/3–1290), queen-designate of Scots', *ODNB*, 36, p. 636.

95. *Foedera* (new edn.), 1. 2, p. 742.

96. 'Quod si forte, deficientibus masculis, contigerit feminam innuptam in regno succedere, illa maritabitur persone, que ad ipsius regni regimen et defensionem existat idonea, Romani tamen pontificis super hoc consilio requisite': *Epistolae saeculi XIII e regestis pontificum Romanorum selectae*, ed. Rodenberg, 3, no. 646, p. 644, Clement IV, 'Constitui ab eo', Po. 19434, 4 November 1265, confirming the cardinals' arrangements of 28 June 1265.

97. 'Elisabeth Regina uxorque dicti Regis Ludovici, una cum Maria filia ejus, regimen Hungariæ gubernabat, quæ quidem Maria appellabatur Rex Hungariæ . . . cum rege Maria . . . Rex autem Maria', etc.: Caresinus, *Chronica*, ed. Pastorello, pp. 67–8.

98. 'omnis vulgus concordi animo hanc virginem regem appellat'; 'cumulatis viribus plateas civitatis vagantur per omnes et regem regnare Mariam clamitant'; 'rex femineus': Thurocz, *Chronica Hungarorum*, 187–8, 194, ed. Galántai and Kristó, pp. 190–1, 203; a particular agility in reconciling feminine verb form and masculine noun is shown by Paulus de Paulo: 'Maria filia senior antedicti regis in civitate praedicta coronata fuit in regem': *Memoriale Pauli de Paulo patritii Iadrensis*, ed. Šišić, p. 5.

99. One chronicler reports that Louis had recognized her 'during his lifetime as his legitimate daughter', but this obviously implies a need to do so, and the existence of doubters: 'quam rex Ludovicus, dum viveret, pro filia legitima recognovit': John of Saint-Victor, *Memoriale historiarum*, ed. Guigniaut and de Wailly, p. 663; see also the report to the king of Aragon claiming the same thing: *Acta aragonensia*, 1, ed. Finke, no. 137, p. 211 ('quam ipse rex filiam recognovit'); see, in general, Brown, 'The Ceremonial of Royal Succession in Capetian France: The Double Funeral of Louis X'.

100. Fawtier, *The Capetian Kings of France: Monarchy and Nation, 987–1328*, p. 129.

101. 'proceribus et paribus regni (licet non omnibus) praesentibus': *Continuatio Chronici Girardi de Fracheto*, ed. Guigniaut and de Wailly, p. 47; *Continuatio Chronici Guillelmi de Nangiaco*, ed. Géraud, 1, p. 431.

102. 'Tunc etiam declaratum fuit quod ad coronam regni Franciae mulier non succedat': *Continuatio Chronici Girardi de Fracheto*, ed. Guigniaut and de Wailly, p. 47; *Continuatio Chronici Guillelmi de Nangiaco*, ed. Géraud, 1, p. 434. In his comment on the accession of Charles IV in 1322, Bernard Gui explains the exclusion of female candidates simply 'because one has never read that daughters succeeded to rule in the kingdom of France (*quia filie in regno Francie ad regnandum numquam leguntur successisse*)': *Reges Francorum, Arbor genealogiae regum Francorum*, CCCC 45, fols. 29, 47: also in RHF, 21, p. 732.

103. 'non aequanimiter ferentes subdi regimini Anglicorum': *Continuatio Chronici Guillelmi de Nangiaco*, ed. Géraud, 2, p. 83.

104. *Recueil general des anciennes lois françaises*, 5, no. 546, pp. 415–23.

105. Taylor, 'The Salic Law and the Valois Succession to the French Crown', pp. 362–4; Giesey, *Le Rôle méconnu de la loi salique. La succession royale (xive–xvie siècles)*, pp. 82–98.

106. See Taylor, 'The Salic Law and the Valois Succession to the French Crown'; Taylor, 'The Salic Law, French Queenship and the Defence of Women in the Late Middle Ages'.

107. Lewis, 'War Propaganda and Historiography in Fifteenth-Century France and England'; Contamine, '"Le royaume de France ne peut tomber en fille." Fondement, formulation et implication d'une théorie politique à la fin du Moyen Âge'.

108. *Pour ce que plusieurs*, ed. Taylor; Giesey, *Le Rôle méconnu de la loi salique. La succession royale (xive–xvie siècles)*, pp. 119–25.

109. Ibid., p. 58.

110. Ibid., p. 63.

111. 'car leurs pensees et leurs jugemens pourroient estre un pou trop soudains': ibid., p. 64.

112. Ibid.

113. Ibid., p. 65.

114. 'gener illius in regnum succederet': Simeon of Durham, *Historia regum*, 213, ed. Arnold, p. 282.

115. 'Angliam calumpniabantur sponsus et sponsa': Henry of Huntingdon, *Historia Anglorum*, 10. 5, ed. Greenway, p. 708.

116. 'sceptro regni transmaritimo … aspiravit': *Actus pontificum Cenomannis in urbe degentium*, ed. Busson and Ledru, p. 445. The new edition of this text by Weidemann does not include these later continuations.

117. 'Cui successit arbitrio et electione optimatum Thancredus nothus, cunctis Teutonicam aspernantibus ditionem, quippe Constantia defuncti regis amita, cui eo defuncto jus successionis competere videbatur, Henrico Frederici imperatoris Teutonici filio nupserat': William of Newburgh, *Historia rerum anglicarum*, 5. 7, ed. Howlett, 2, p. 429.

118. 'dicentes quod filiam suam non reciperent reginam, quia non erat consuetudo regni illius quod mulier regnum illud haberet quamdiu frater vel nepos esset in progenie qui regnum de jure habere posset': Roger of Howden, *Chronica*, ed. Stubbs, 3, p. 299.

119. 'statutum et ordinatio hujusmodi jus successionis eorundem filiorum nostrorum ac liberorum eorum, sexum excludendo feminium, nimium restringebat': *Parliament Rolls of Medieval England*, ed. Given-Wilson, 8, pp. 341–7, 354–61 (quote at pp. 359–60); Given-Wilson, *Henry IV*, pp. 294–5, 298; Bennett, 'Henry IV, the Royal Succession and the Crisis of 1406', pp. 16–27.

120. 'Lege divinitus Salphat data filiabus Usurpator iuris iusti probaris heredis': BL, MS Harley 7353.

121. *The Popular Songs of Ireland*, ed. Croker, p. 321 (from a manuscript, no longer extant, in the 'State Paper Office'); *Verse in English from Tudor and Stuart Ireland*, ed. Carpenter, p. 38; Robbins and Cutler, eds., *Supplement to the Index of Middle English Verse*, no. 2571.5. The poem is in the form of a letter sent to Walter, archbishop of Dublin, by the loyal city of Waterford at the time of the Warbeck rebellion.

122. 'qua lege quid iniquius dici aut cogitari possit, ignoro': Augustine, *De civitate Dei*, 3. 21, ed. Dombart and Kalb, 1, p. 90.

123. 'iure naturali pater plus tenetur cuilibet sue proli quam extraneo': François de Meyronnes, *Flores beati Augustini extracti per veritates ex libris De Civitate Dei extracti*, fol. 10v. A sixteenth-century printing of the work adds a mention of the Salic Law to this passage: *Flores d. Augustini ex suis libris De Civitate Dei excerpti* (Lyons, 1580), fol. 26v.

124. 'Sed oritur dubium quare in regnis que ex genere habent regnantes mulieres communiter non succedunt': François de Meyronnes, *Flores Augustini ex libris De Civitate Dei extracti*, fol. 10v.

125. 'regnum nedum est hereditas sed eciam dignitas pertinens ad totam rem publicam; nunc autem in dignitatibus non succedunt mulieres quia dignitatis capaces non sunt sicut hereditatis': ibid.

126. 'quod videtur iniquum valde in personis privatis quamvis rationabilis esse possit in personis publicis sicut in regibus et principis': Thomas Waleys, *Expositio super libros*

Augustini De Civitate Dei, 3. 21, cited from Utrecht, Universiteitsbibliotheek, MS 306 (3 C 3), fol. 48v.

127. Raoul de Presles' translation of the *City of God* in BnF, MS fr. 22912–3, fols. 150–1 (a presentation copy to Charles V, 1376); see Taylor, 'The Salic Law and the Valois Succession to the French Crown', pp. 362–3; Giesey, *Le Rôle méconnu de la loi salique. La succession royale (xive–xvie siècles)*, pp. 69–72.

128. 'ut exemplo Francorum legem statuerent, ne femina fieret heres regni': *Chronicon Angliae ab Anno Domini 1328 usque ad annum 1388*, ed. Thompson, p. 92; the accuracy of this account has been questioned, since the author was so hostile to Gaunt: Given-Wilson, 'Legitimation, Designation and Succession to the Throne in Fourteenth-Century England', pp. 91–2.

5 MISTRESSES AND BASTARDS

1. Duindam, *Dynasties: A Global History of Power, 1300–1800*, p. 122.
2. 'in concubinam accepit'; 'concubinam suam Richildem desponsatam atque dotatam in coniugem sumpsit': *Annales Bertiniani*, s.a. 869, 870, ed. Waitz, pp. 107–8; Nelson, *Charles the Bald*, pp. 221–2, calls the first event a 'betrothal' and interprets the use of the term 'concubine' as stemming from the annalist's hostility; Charles himself called the October event a '*conjunctio*': *Recueil des actes de Charles II le Chauve, roi de France*, ed. Tessier, 2, pp. 288–91, no. 355; he labelled his link with his first wife, Ermentrud, differently: '*uxoreo vinculo*', ibid., 2, p. 55, no. 246.
3. Mikat, *Dotierte Ehe, rechte Ehe: zur Entwicklung des Eheschliessungsrechts in fränkischer Zeit*; Hyam, 'Ermentrude and Richildis', p. 154, interprets '*desponsatam atque dotatam in coniugem sumpsit*' in the following sense: 'They were married on 22 January … Richildis was already *desponsata atque dotata*', rather than the whole phrase as describing a constituitive act.
4. Unless the use of the term 'concubine' is interpreted in this way.
5. *Digest* 20. 1. 8; 23. 2. 24; 23. 2. 41; 23. 2. 56; 24. 1. 3; 24. 1. 58; 24. 2. 11; 25. 2. 17; 25. 7 ('De Concubinis'); 31. 29; 32. 29; 32. 41; 31. 49; 33. 2. 24; 34. 1. 15; 34. 9. 16; 38. 1. 46; 38. 10. 7; 39. 5. 31; 42. 5. 38; 45. 1. 121; 48. 5. 14; 48. 5. 35; 50. 16. 144 ('quae uxoris loco sine nuptiis in domo sit').
6. 'Is, qui non habet uxorem, et pro uxore concubinam habet, a communione non repellatur: tamen ut unius mulieris, aut uxoris aut concubinae, sit coniunctione contentus … Christiano non dicam plurimas, sed nec duas simul habere licitum est, nisi unam tantum aut uxorem, aut certe loco uxoris (si coniux deest) concubinam': Gratian, *Decretum*, 1. 34. 4–5, ed. Friedberg, col. 126. The first canon is derived ultimately from the First Council of Toledo, c. 17 (*Concilios visigóticos e hispano-romanos*, ed. Vives, p. 24).
7. 'luxoriam super modum deditus tres habebat maxime ad instar reginas et pluremas concupinas. Reginae vero haec fuerunt: Nantechildis, Vulfegundis et Berchildis. Nomina concubinarum, eo quod plures fuissent, increvit huius chronice inseri': Fredegar, *Chronica*, 4. 60, ed. Krusch, p. 151, ed. Wallace-Hadrill, p. 50.

8. 'Praetermissis nunc generibus feminarum, regis vocantur liberi, qui de regibus fuerant procreati': Gregory of Tours, *Libri historiarum decem*, 5. 20, ed. Krusch and Levison, p. 228.

9. 'Si vero absque legitimis liberis aliquis eorum [i.e. his three sons] decesserit, potestas illius ad seniorem fratrem revertatur. Et si contigerit illum habere liberos ex concubinis, monemus ut erga illos misericorditer agat': *Capitularia regum Francorum*, 1, ed. Boretius, no. 136, cl. 15, p. 273 (the 'Ordinatio imperii' of 817).

10. 'consuetudo regni Norweiae est usque in hodiernum diem, quod omnis qui alicujus regis Norweiae dinoscitur esse filius, licet sit spurius, et de ancilla genitus, tantum sibi jus vendicat in regnum Norweiae, quantum filius regis conjugati, et de libera genitus': Roger of Howden, *Chronica*, ed. Stubbs, 3, p. 272.

11. 'In der Tat also bekannte sich das Norwegen der Sagas zu der "merowingischen" Auffasung, nach dem das väterliche Blut genügte, um Königsfähigkeit zu vermitteln': Rüdiger, *Der König und seine Frauen: Polygynie und politische Kultur in Europa (9.–13. Jahrhundert)*, p. 92.

12. 'Nam Carlomannus, filius magni Ludovici, filios non habuit nisi tantum unum nomine Arnulfum, ex nobilissima quidem femina sed non legaliter sibi desponsata conceptum': Erchanbert, *Breviarium regum Francorum, continuatio*, ed. Pertz, p. 330; Arnulf names her in his charters: *Arnolfi Diplomata*, ed. Kehr, nos. 87, 136, pp. 129, 204. 'Similiter Ludovicus rex Franciae habuit unum filium nomine Hug, bellissimum et bellicosissimum iuvenem, de concubina praecellentissimae generositatis': Erchanbert, *Breviarium regum Francorum, continuatio*, ed. Pertz, p. 330.

13. *Annales Laubacenses*, ed. Pertz, p. 15; *Annales Bertiniani*, s.a. 853, ed. Waitz, p. 43; *Lotharii I. et Lotharii II. Diplomata*, ed. Schieffer, no. 113, pp. 262–3.

14. Le Jan, *Famille et pouvoir dans le monde franc (VIIe–Xe siècle): essai d'anthropologie sociale*, p. 276 (the '6' by Lothar I is a misprint for '26'); Kasten, *Königssöhne und Königsherrschaft: Untersuchungen zur Teilhabe am Reich in der Merowinger- und Karolingerzeit*, p. 252.

15. *The Gesta Normannorum Ducum*, ed. Van Houts, 1, pp. xxxviii n. 91, 58, 68, 78, 128; 2, p. 268.

16. 'hoc nullatenus secundum scita canonum posse esse, ideo quod mater eius non fuisset desponsata': ibid. 2, p. 268; for comment, see Rüdiger, *Der König und seine Frauen: Polygynie und politische Kultur in Europa (9.–13. Jahrhundert)*, pp. 343–4, and Van Houts, *Married Life in the Middle Ages, 900–1300*, pp. 79–80; on Gunnor, see Van Houts, 'Countess Gunnor of Normandy'.

17. Génestal, *Histoire de la légitimation des enfants naturels en droit canonique*, pp. 147–9, thinks the latter.

18. Rodulfus Glaber, *Historiarum libri quinque*, 4. 20, ed. France, p. 204.

19. Esmyol, *Geliebte oder Ehefrau? Konkubinen im frühen Mittelalter*, pp. 142–3.

20. Konecny, *Die Frauen des karolingischen Königshauses*, pp. 54–6, 89, 118, 120; Konecny, 'Eherecht und Ehepolitik unter Ludwig dem Frommen', pp. 3, 12.

21. 'Am Beispiel Alpais' und Swanahilds wird deutlich, dass Erfolg oder Misserfolg der Söhne einer Frau, oder die Parteizugehörigkeit eines Historiographen oft darüber

entschied, ob eine Frau als "uxor" oder "concubine" bezeichnet wurde': Konecny, *Die Frauen des karolingischen Königshauses*, p. 26. The ambiguity in the classification is reflected in the interrogative titles chosen by some modern historians who discuss the issue, e.g. Esmyol, *Geliebte oder Ehefrau? Konkubinen im frühen Mittelalter*, Hartmann, 'Concubina vel regina? Zu einigen Ehefrauen und Konkubinen der karolingischen Könige'.

22. E.g. *Annales Bertiniani*, s.a. 862, ed. Waitz, p. 60; Nicolas I, *Epistolae*, nos. 46, 53, ed. Perels, pp. 325, 350.

23. 'id est meretrices, sumpto uocabulo a pollutione uel formositate suae pellis qua incautos inliciant': *Glossae biblicae*, ed. Vaciago, pp. 197, 354, 538.

24. Her father was Walter Clifford: *The English Register of Godstow Nunnery*, ed. Clark, 3, nos. 156, 200, pp. 135, 161.

25. 'pro amore Rosemunde filie sue': *Rotuli Hundredorum*, 2, pp. 93–4.

26. 'tumbam in medio chori ante altare, sericis pannis velatam, et lampadibus et cereis circumdatam': Roger of Howden, *Chronica*, ed. Stubbs, 3, pp. 167–8 (*Gesta regis Henrici secundi Benedicti abbatis*, ed. Stubbs, 2, pp. 231–2); for the king's grants to Godstow, *The Letters and Charters of Henry II King of England (1154–1189)*, ed. Vincent, nos. 1180–93.

27. 'Et porque el rey era muy acabado hombre en todos sus fechos, teníase por muy menguado porque no tenía fijos de la reina; et por esto cató manera cómo oviere fijos de otra parte': *Crónica del rey don Alfonso el Onceno*, 90, ed. Rosell, p. 227.

28. Daumet, *Étude sur l'alliance de la France et de la Castille au XIVe et au XVe siècles*, p. 143 (from AN J 602, no. 44).

29. López de Ayala, *Crónica del Rey don Pedro*, 2 (1351). 3, ed. Orduna, 1, p. 34.

30. Sitges, *Las mujeres del rey don Pedro*, assembles much of the relevant documentation in Castilian translation.

31. López de Ayala, *Crónica del Rey don Pedro*, 4 (1353). 2, 11–12, ed. Orduna, 1, pp. 84, 97–9.

32. 'E nunca jamas vio a la rreyna doña Blanca, su muger': López de Ayala, *Crónica del Rey don Pedro*, 4 (1353). 21, ed. Orduna, 1, p. 110.

33. 'E nunca vio jamas a doña Iohana de Castro': López de Ayala, *Crónica del Rey don Pedro*, 5 (1354). 10, 12, ed. Orduna, 1, pp. 139–40.

34. Estow, *Pedro the Cruel*, p. 211, for discussion of this issue.

35. Jones, *Blanche de Bourbon*, p. 9.

36. 'tu novissima tua faciens pejora prioribus, adultera non dimissa nec regina recepta predictis, quamdam superinduxisti aliam impudenter adulteram': Daumet, ed., *Innocent VI et Blanche de Bourbon: Lettres du Pape publiées d'après les Registres du Vatican*, p. 105 (Reg Vat. 236, fol. 91v, 12 May 1354); Daumet prints all of Innocent's relevant letters.

37. López de Ayala, *Crónica del Rey don Pedro*, 13 (1362). 7, ed. Orduna, 2, pp. 62–3; Sitges, *Las mujeres del rey don Pedro de Castilla*, p. 388 (a letter of the king from Archivo de la Corona de Aragón, R. 1. 178, fol. 130v).

38. The will is printed in *Crónicas de los reyes de Castilla*, ed. Rosell, 1, pp. 593–8; Sitges, *Las mujeres del rey don Pedro de Castilla*, p. 252.

39. Tuck, 'Vere, Robert de, ninth earl of Oxford, marquess of Dublin, and duke of Ireland (1362–1392), courtier', *ODNB*, 56 (2004), pp. 312–15, citing TNA: PRO, E 36/66.

40. 'His operibus feminæ deputabantur, quæ natu nobiles, et sobriis moribus probabiles, interesse reginæ obsequiis dignæ judicabantur. Nullus ad eas virorum introitus erat, nisi quos ipsa, cum interdum ad illas intraret, secum introire permittebat. Nulla eis inhonesta cum viris familiaritas, nulla unquam cum petulantia levitas': Turgot, *Vita S. Margaretae Scotorum Reginae*, 4, ed. Hodgson Hinde, p. 239; 'Domicellas suas vacare non pertulit, sed singulis singula iniungens opera, illam texere, illam nere, illam vero consuere doctrix sedula erudivit': Peter of Zittau, *Chronicon Aulae Regiae*, 1. 20, ed. Emler, p. 27.

41. George Akropolites, *Historia*, 52, ed. Heisenberg, pp. 103–4; see the comments in the translation by Macrides, pp. 274–6; for the empress' red shoes, see Macrides, Munitiz and Angelov, *Pseudo-Kodinos and the Constantinopolitan Court: Offices and Ceremonies*, pp. 267, 354.

42. López de Ayala, *Crónica del Rey don Pedro*, 4 (1353). 26; 11 (1360). 14, ed. Orduna, 1, p. 117; 2, pp. 19–20; Lopes, *Crónica do Rei D. Pedro I*, 27, 31, 44, ed. Macchi, tr. Steunou, pp. 158–60, 180–4, 244–6.

43. Tompkins, 'The Uncrowned Queen: Alice Perrers, Edward III and Political Crisis in Fourteenth-Century England, 1360–1377', pp. 13–40, establishes her origins for the first time, building on the work of Mark Ormrod.

44. Henzler, *Die Frauen Karls VII. und Ludwigs XI.: Rolle und Position der Königinnen und Mätressen am französischen Hof (1422–1483)*, pp. 21–3, 30–1, 38–41, 56–62, 66–7, 83–4, 102–4, 133–43, 189–90, 201–2, 215–16; Champion, *La dame de Beauté Agnès Sorel*.

45. 'sibi data fuit in concubinam quedam pulcherrima, delectabilis et placens juvenis … vulgariter vocabatur palam et publice parva regina': *Chronique du religieux de Saint-Denys*, 43. 5, ed. Bellaguet, 6, pp. 486–8; see Autrand, *Charles VI: la folie du roi*, pp. 415–18.

46. Gray, *Scalacronica*, ed. Stevenson, pp. 196–7; Bower, *Scotichronicon*, 14. 24, ed. Watt et al., 7, pp. 318–20; Penman, *David II, 1329–71*, pp. 242–53.

47. 'Only two bastards are recorded for the fourteen kings of the dynasty' (i.e. the direct line from Hugh Capet to 1328): Fawtier, *The Capetian Kings of France: Monarchy and Nation, 987–1328*, p. 53; for a list of Henry I's illegitimate children, see *The Complete Peerage*, 11, Appendix D, pp. 105–21; Thompson, 'Affairs of State: The Illegitimate Children of Henry I', Appendix A.

48. González, *Alfonso IX*, 1, pp. 309–21; Calderón Medina, 'Las otras mujeres del rey: El concubinato regio en el reino de León (1157–1230)'.

49. 'Habuerat tamen ex concubina filium, qui Tancredus vocatus fuit, et fuerat ipsa concubina filia comitis Licii': *Breve chronicon de rebus Siculis*, ed. Stürner, pp. 50–2.

50. 'ex concubina natus': Adam of Clermont, *Flores historiarum* (*Excerpta*), ed. Holder-Egger, p. 592; there are many other examples of this phrase applied to Manfred.

51. 'Nothus dicitur, qui de patre nobili et de matre ignobili gignitur, sicut ex concubina … Huic contrarius spurius, qui de matre nobili et patre ignobili nascitur': Isidore of Seville, *Etymologiae*, 9. 5. 20.

52. E.g. 'spurius est qui patre ignobili sed nobili est matre generatus, sicut e contra nobili patre sed matre procreatus ignobili nothus consuete uocatur': Bede, *In primam partem Samuhelis libri iv*, 3. 17, ed. Hurst, pp. 147–8; 'Spurius et hybrida ignobilis ex parte patris,

sicut manzer et nothus ex parte matris dicitur': Andrew of St Victor, *Expositio hystorica in librum Regum*, in Reg. 1. 17, ed. Van Liere, p. 58: 'spurius et hibida [hibrida] dicitur ignobilis ex patre, manzer et nothus ex matre': Rodrigo Jiménez de Rada, *Breviarium historie catholice*, 4. 80, ed. Fernández Valverde, 1, p. 250. Isidore's distinction is the guiding thread of the argument in McDougall, *Royal Bastards: The Birth of Illegitimacy, 800–1230*. Another way of describing these children was that they were 'of oblique blood (*obliquo sanguine*)': *Vita Ædwardi regis*, ed. Barlow, p. 32 (Harold Harefoot); Adam of Bremen, *Gesta Hammaburgensis ecclesiae pontificum*, 3. 52 (51), ed. Schmeidler, p. 197 (William the Conqueror). Sara McDougall interprets Adam's phrase as indicating William had 'mixed blood ... his combination of high and low status blood', 'his high status father and low status mother' (*Royal Bastards*, pp. 46–7, 118). The classical usage, as in Lucan, is to indicate 'collateral descent'; 'ex obliquo' in Gratian's *Decretum* means collateral descent.

53. Génestal, *Histoire de la légitimation des enfants naturels en droit canonique*, p. 157.

54. *Oxford English Dictionary*, s.vv 'bastard', 'bast'; this etymomogy is far from being generally agreed: see Wartburg, *Französisches Etymologisches Wörterbuch*, 1, pp. 276–7, s.v. 'bastardus'; *Le Trésor de la langue française*, 4, p. 264, s.v. 'bâtard'.

55. *Domesday Book*, ed. Farley, 1, fol. 113b (Devon 29).

56. 'Heinrici quondam regis Anglorum filius sed bastardus': John of Worcester, *Chronicle*, 3, ed. McGurk, p. 268.

57. E.g. in the testament of James II of Cyprus (1473): Mas Latrie, *Histoire de l'isle de Chypre sous le règne des princes de la maison de Lusignan*, 3, pp. 345–7.

58. 'qui abastardatus est in curia christianitatis': *The Great Roll of the Pipe for the First Year of the Reign of King John*, p. 152.

59. 'saniori ... consilio': *Gesta Stephani*, ed. Potter, p. 12.

60. This interpretation is much contested by McDougall, *Royal Bastards: The Birth of Illegitimacy, 800–1230*, pp. 4, 16, 125–8, 137.

61. Sickel, 'Das Thronfolgerecht der unehelichen Karolinger'; MacLean, *Kingship and Politics in the Late Ninth Century: Charles the Fat and the End of the Carolingian Empire*, pp. 129–34; Hagn, *Illegitimität und Thronfolge: zur Thronfolgeproblematik illegitimer Merowinger, Karolinger und Ottonen*, pp. 144–64.

62. 'Imperator cum suis apud Franconofurt colloquium habuit missisque Romam nuntiis Hadrianum pontificem invitavit in Franciam. Voluit enim, ut fama vulgabat, quosdam episcopos inrationabiliter deponere et Bernhartum filium suum ex concubina haeredem regni post se constituere; et hoc, quia per se posse fieri dubitavit, per pontificem Romanum quasi apostolica auctoritate perficere disposuit. Cuius fraudulenta consilia Dei nutu dissipata sunt; nam pontifex Romanus ab urbe digressus et Heridano flumine transito vitam praesentem finivit sepultusque est in monasterio Nonantulas. Quod cum imperator comperisset, contristatus est valde, eo quod in tali negotio voti compos effici non potuit': 'Continuatio Mogontiacensis' in *Annales Fuldenses*, s.a. 885, ed. Kurze, p. 103.

63. Génestal, *Histoire de la légitimation des enfants naturels en droit canonique*, p. 181 (referring it mistakenly to Charlemagne).

64. 'Siquidem ab illo genealogia regum caelitus provisa per intervalla temporum secundis incrementorum successibus coepit exuberare, quousque in magno Carolo summum imperii fastigium non solum Francorum, verum etiam diversarum gentium regnorumque obtineret. Post cuius decessum variante fortuna rerum gloria, quae supra vota fluxerat, eodem, quo accesserat, modo cępit paulatim diffluere, donec deficientibus non modo regnis, sed etiam ipsa regia stirpe partim inmatura aetate pereunte partim sterilitate coniugum marcescente hic solus de tam numerosa regum posteritate idoneus inveniretur, qui imperii Francorum sceptra susciperet': Regino of Prūm, *Chronicon*, s.a. 880, ed. Kurze, pp. 116–17.

65. 'eo tamen modo, ut si de legali sua uxore heres ei non produceretur': 'Continuatio Ratisbonensis' in *Annales Fuldenses*, s.a. 889, ed. Kurze, p. 118; 'Luduwicus filius eius, qui unicus tunc parvulus de legali uxore natus illi erat, in regnum successit': 'Continuationes Altahenses' in *Annales Fuldenses*, s.a. 900, ed. Kurze, p. 134.

66. Cramp, 'Aldfrith (d. 704/5), King of Northumbria', in *ODNB*, 1, pp. 618–19.

67. 'frater eius [sc. of Ecgfrith] nothus', Bede, *Vita sancti Cuthberti* (prose), 24, ed. Colgrave, p. 238.

68. 'quia nothus erat': William of Malmesbury, *Gesta regum Anglorum*, 1. 51–2, ed. Mynors et al., pp. 78–80.

69. 'in ordinatione regum nullus permittat pravorum praevalere assensum, sed legitime reges a sacerdotibus et senioribus eligantur, et non de adulterio vel incoestu procreati, quia sicut nostris temporibus ad sacerdotium secundum canones adulter pervenire non potest, sic nec christus Domini esse valet et rex totius regni et haeres patriae, qui ex legitimo non fuerit connubio generatus': *Councils and Ecclesiastical Documents Relating to Great Britain and Ireland*, ed. Haddan and Stubbs, 3, p. 453 (cl. 12); Alcuin, *Epistolae*, no. 3, ed. Dümmler, pp. 23–4; the translation of *adulter* as 'bastard' is supported by the usage in cl. 16, ed. Haddan and Stubbs, p. 455, ed. Dümmler, p. 25: 'Adulterinos namque filios ... spurios et adulteros iudicamus.'

70. 'iste Willelmus quem Franci Bastardum vocant': Adam of Bremen, *Gesta Hammaburgensis ecclesiae pontificum*, 2. 54 (52), ed. Schmeidler, p. 115; for the date, see the editorial comment on p. lxvi.

71. 'nobilibus indigenis et maxime ex Ricardorum prosapia natis despectui erat utpote nothus': *Gesta Normannorum Ducum*, 7. 3, ed. Van Houts, 2, p. 96.

72. 'me nothum degeneremque et principatu indignum detestatus indicavit ... me velut nothum contempserunt': Orderic Vitalis, *Historia ecclesiastica*, 7. 15, ed. Chibnall, 4, pp. 82–4. George Garnett notes 'there is no hint to this effect in contemporary sources': '"Ducal" Succession in Early Normandy', p. 108 n. 156. As is often the case with information in Orderic, one can either dismiss it as uncorroborated or accept it and recognize that corroboration is unlikely, given the state of the surviving sources.

73. 'eo quod spurius sit, natus scilicet ex nobili patre et matre ignobili quae lanas carpere, dum viveret ipsa, non cessaret': Galbert of Bruges, *De multro, traditione et occisione gloriosi Karoli comitis Flandriarum*, 47, ed. Rider, p. 97. McDougall, *Royal Bastards: The Birth of Illegitimacy, 800–1230*, pp. 150, 152, cites this passage but then goes on to say, 'we do not know for certain that William was, in fact, the son of a low

status mother'. Suger calls him 'Guilelmus Bastardus', an appellation more commonly applied to William the Conqueror: Suger, *Vita Ludovici Grossi regis*, 30, ed. Waquet, p. 248.

74. Sancho III 'dedit Ramiro, quem ex concubina habuerat, Haragon, quandam semotim regni sui particulam, scilicet ne fratribus, eo quod materno genere inpar erat, quasi hereditarius regni videretur': *Historia Silensis*, 29, ed. Estévez Sola, p. 201.

75. 'constituit Constantiam amitam suam, uxorem Henrici regis Alemannorum, haeredem regni Siciliae; et fecit omnes primates regni sui jurare fidelitates praedictae amitae, ut ipsi illam in dominam et reginam susciperent si ille sine prole decessisset': *Gesta regis Henrici secundi Benedicti abbatis*, ed. Stubbs, 2, pp. 202–3; cf. Richard of San Germano, *Chronica*, ed. Garufi, p. 6. See Fröhlich, 'The Marriage of Henry VI and Constance of Sicily: Prelude and Consequences', and, in general on Tancred, Reisinger, *Tankred von Lecce. Normannischer König von Sizilien 1190–1194*.

76. For the place, see *Annales Casinenses*, ed. Pertz, p. 314: 'Tancredus comes Licii, qui apud Troiam cum quibusdam aliis iuraverat fidelitatem Constantiae uxori Henrici regis Theutonicorum et filiae quondam regis Roggerii'; for the date, Baaken, 'Unio regni ad imperium. Die Verhandlungen von Verona 1184 und die Eheabredung zwischen König Heinrich VI. und Konstanze von Sizilien', pp. 277–9.

77. 'intelligens ac mecum reputans quantum hec rerum mutatio calamitatis afferret, quantum illius regni quietissimum statum, vel hostilis incursus procella concuteret, vel gravis sedictionum turbo subverteret, repente consternatus animo cepta deserui ... Intueri michi iam videor turbulentas barbarorum acies eo quo feruntur impetu irruentes, civitates opulentas et loca diuturna pace florentia metu concutere, cede vastare, rapinis atterere et fedare luxuria': *Epistola ad Petrum Panormitane Ecclesie Thesaurarium de calamitate Sicilie*, pp. 169–70; there is a translation in *A History of the Tyrants of Sicily by 'Hugo Falcandus'*, tr. Loud and Wiedemann, pp. 252–63, which also sets out very clearly the grounds for the dating, at pp. 36–7 n. 91; Clementi, 'The Circumstances of Count Tancred's Accession to the Kingdom of Sicily, Duchy of Apulia and the Principality of Capua', p. 72 n. 59, argues that the letter must date from 1194 not 1190; see also the comments of Reisinger, *Tankred von Lecce. Normannischer König von Sizilien 1190–1194*, pp. 185–7.

78. 'fedissime gentis ... pueri puelleque barbare lingue stridore perterriti ... gens dura et saxea ... nepharium esset et monstro simile [for Palermo] ... barbarorum ingressu pollui': *Epistola ad Petrum Panormitane Ecclesie Thesaurarium de calamitate Sicilie*, pp. 170–2.

79. 'Utrumne regem sibi creandum existiment et collectis viribus contra barbaros dimicandum? An vero ... malint quodlibet durum servitutis iugum suscipere quam fame et dignitati sue et patrie libertati consulere?': *Epistola ad Petrum Panormitane Ecclesie Thesaurarium de calamitate Sicilie*, p. 172.

80. 'Disce prius mores Augusti, disce furorem!/ Teutonicam rabiem quis tolerare potest?/ ... pueri tibi more licebit / Discere barbaricos barbarizare sonos?': Petrus de Ebulo, *Liber ad honorem Augusti sive de rebus Siculis*, lines 120–3, ed. Kölzer and Stähli, p. 53.

81. Lopes, *Crónica do Rei D. Pedro I*, 1, 43, ed. Macchi, tr. Steunou, pp. 22, 238–42.

82. On this, see Monteiro, 'The Battle of Aljubarrota (1385): A Reassessment'.

83. *Monumenta Portugaliae Vaticana*, 2, ed. Costa, CXII-CXV, CVIII-CXI (Boniface IX, 27–28 January 1391); also in Portuguese in Lopes, *Crónica del Rei Dom João I*, 2. 125–6, in *The English in Portugal, 1367–1387*, pp. 316–29.

84. There are translated excerpts from the main chronicle source for his regency and reign, Fernão Lopes, *Crónica del Rei Dom João I*, in Lopes, *The English in Portugal, 1367–1387*.

85. Woodacre, *The Queens Regnant of Navarre: Succession, Politics, and Partnership, 1272–1512*, p. 80.

86. 'prolem de legali conubio non habuerat … sed Normanni Eustachium de concubina filium eius susceperunt, quia compatriotam nothum quam Britonem seu Burgundionem liberum praeesse sibi maluerunt': Orderic Vitalis, *Historia ecclesiastica*, 11. 4, ed. Chibnall 6, p. 40.

87. 'Si ne purroit consentir/ Un bastard roialme tenir'; 'vous deveroiez bien sentir/ En vostre coer qe ceo n'est pas droitz/ Q'un bastard deust estre rois': Chandos Herald, *La vie du Prince Noir*, lines 1803–4, 2928–30, ed. Tyson, pp. 97, 129.

88. 'Et mist li sains Peres tout le royaumme d'Espagne en le main de Henry frere bastart à ce roy Piere et le legitima à tenir royaumme et hiretage': Froissart, *Chroniques*, 1. 113. 691, ed. Diller, 3, p. 365; cf. *Chroniques*, ed. Kervyn de Lettenhove, 7, pp. 83, 87.

89. Lopes, *The English in Portugal, 1367–1387*, p. vi (from a document of 1434).

90. Rodríguez, 'Pero López de Ayala and the Politics of Rewriting the Past'.

91. Ryder, *Alfonso the Magnanimous: King of Aragon, Naples, and Sicily 1396–1458*, p. 239.

92. Boustronios, *Chronicle*, 161, 206, tr. Dawkins, pp. 41, 48; Alfonso's career is traced in detail in Forcellini, 'Strane peripezie d'un bastardo di casa di Aragona'.

93. Mas Latrie, *Histoire de l'isle de Chypre sous le règne des princes de la maison de Lusignan*, 3, pp. 345–7; Boustronios, *Chronicle*, 98, tr. Dawkins, p. 33.

94. 'Sub eadem quoque tempestate Iacobus Ioannis Cypri regis e pellice filius defuncto patre regno potitur; hunc pater intellexerat imperandi cupidissimum, utpote qui egregia forma, procera statura corporis, magna eloquentia et singulari ingenio preditus regio se honore dignum reputabat': Antonius de Bonfinis, *Rerum Ungaricarum decades*, 3. 8. 362, ed. Fogel et al., 3, p. 204.

95. 'Alii filii mei se revera bastardos, iste vero solus se legitimum et verum esse probavit': Gerald of Wales, *Vita Galfridi archiepiscopi Eboracensis*, 1. 3, ed. Brewer, p. 368.

96. 'Cum summa, dilecti filii nostri bastardi, Johannis de Gloucestria, ingenii vivacitas, membrorum agilitas et ad omnes bonos mores pronitas, magnam et indubiam nobis de futuro eius servitio bono spem, gratia divina, promittant': *Foedera*, ed. Thomas Rymer (original edn.), 12, p. 265.

97. 'quem de Alayta nobili muliere Theotonica soluta dudum suscepimus non soluti': Winkelmann, 'Zum Leben König Enzio's', pp. 311–12 (from BAV, MS Pal. lat. 272, fols. 77-77v).

98. 'ex matre infami et ignobili': Thomas Tuscus, *Gesta imperatorum et pontificum*, ed. Ehrenfeuchter, p. 515.

99. Werner, 'Die Nachkommen Karls des Grossen', p. 418.

100. Airlie, 'Private Bodies and the Body Politic in the Divorce Case of Lothar II', pp. 17–18; note the reservations of Hagn, *Illegitimität und Thronfolge: zur Thronfolgeproblematik illegitimer Merowinger, Karolinger und Ottonen*, pp. 165–9, who recognizes 'eine gewisse Tendenz . . . jedoch kein völlig festgefügtes System'.

101. Kasten, 'Chancen und Schicksale "unehelicher" Karolinger im 9. Jahrhundert', pp. 48–9.

102. Gentile, 'Les bâtards princiers piémontais et savoyards', pp. 392–3.

103. Narbona Cárceles, 'Les bâtards royaux et la nouvelle noblesse de sang en Navarre (fin XIV siècle–début XVe siècle)', pp. 425, 429; Harsgor, 'L'essor des bâtards nobles au XV e siècle', p. 322.

104. Hicks, 'The Royal Bastards of Late Medieval England', pp. 377–8; *The Complete Peerage of England, Scotland, Ireland, Great Britain and the United Kingdom*, 6, pp. 138–9.

105. 'en aucuns pays, lez bastars portent lez armes du lygnage duquel ilz descendent, aveques aucune differance, laquelle coustume est assez raysonnable': *Songe du Vergier*, 1. 148. 18, ed. Schnerb-Lièvre, 1, p. 292.

106. 'sunt qui signum bastardiae portant et tales portant arma suorum parentum integra cum quadam benda ex traverso': Johannes de Bado Aureo, *Tractatus de armis*, ed. Jones, p. 138 (the work was commissioned by the queen, Anne of Bohemia).

107. Duerloo, 'Marks of Illegitimacy in the Southern Netherlands', p. 36 n. 6; Norton, 'The Heraldry of the Illegitimate Children of the Nobility', p. 76.

108. Johannes de Bado Aureo, *Tractatus de armis*, ed. Jones, p. 138; Boudreau, 'Théories et discours des anciens sur les brisures de bâtardise (XIVe–XVIIIe siècles)', p. 90 n. 16.

109. Hablot, 'L'emblématique des bâtards princiers au XVe siècle', p. 443.

110. BL, MS Yates Thompson 3, fol. 1.

111. 'Johannes bastardus Burgundie': Maillard-Luypaert, 'Jean de Bourgogne, bâtard de Jean Sans Peur, évêque de Cambrai de 1439 à 1480', pp. 12–13, 45.

112. 'Ii in illis regionibus in nullo probro habentur, veluti apud nos . . . Eam consuetudinem habent reges et principes aliqui ut pellices in suis arcibus alant. Earum filiis, quot ex eis sustulerint, vita incolumi ditiones aliquas attribuunt. Has eis, patre vita defunto, filii justi non adimunt': Leo of Rozmital, *De Leonis a Rosmital nobilis Bohemi itinere per partes Germaniae, Belgii, Britanniae, Franciae, Hispaniae, Portugalliae atque Italiae, annis MCCCCLXV–VII*, pp. 28–9; there is an English translation, *The Travels of Leo of Rozmital*, tr. Letts, p. 40.

113. Marchandisse, 'Corneille, Bâtard de Bourgogne (ca 1426–1452)', p. 55.

114. Aurell, *Les noces du comte: mariage et pouvoir en Catalogne (785–1213)*, pp. 445, 481.

115. 'In regnum vero et terram predictam nullus succedet, qui non fuerit de legitimo matrimonio procreatus': *Epistolae saeculi XIII e regestis pontificum Romanorum selectae*, ed. Rodenberg, 3, no. 646, p. 644, Clement IV, 'Constitui ab eo', Po. 19434, 4 November 1265, confirming the cardinals' arrangements of 28 June 1265.

116. Génestal, *Histoire de la légitimation des enfants naturels en droit canonique*.

117. 'divinis et humanis legibus detestabile': *Epistolae pontificum romanorum ineditae*, ed. Loewenfeld, *Epistola* 106, pp. 52–53 (from the Collectio Britannica, BL, MS Add. 8873, fol. 45). The grandee was judge Orzocco Torchitorio.

118. *Conciliorum oecumenicorum decreta*, 4, cl. 51, ed. Alberigo et al., p. 258; *Decretales Gregorii IX*, 4. 3. 3, ed. Friedberg, cols. 679–80.

119. 'Qui filii sint legitimi': *Decretales Gregorii IX*, 4. 17, ed. Friedberg, col. 709.

120. *Decretales Gregorii IX*, 4. 17. 2, ed. Friedberg, col. 710; 4. 17. 4, col. 711; 'Tanta est vis matrimonii ut qui antea sunt geniti post contractum matrimonium legitimi habeantur': 4. 17. 6, col. 712, Alexander III, *Tanta est vis*, JL 13917. See Lefebvre-Teillard, *Autour de l'enfant: du droit canonique et romain médiéval au code civil de 1804*, pp. 275–373, 'La légitimation de l'enfant naturel'.

121. Glanvill, *The Treatise on the Laws and Customs of England Commonly Called Glanvill*, 6. 17, ed. Hall, p. 68.

122. 'ut qui ex ambobus nati erant legitimi haberentur et in bona paterna successionis plenum ius obtinerent': William of Tyre, *Chronicon*, 19. 4, ed. Huygens, 2, p. 869.

123. 'ne quis tibi geniture defectum possit obicere': Reg. Vat. 18, fol. 16 (20 April 1235, Po. 9883); Alfonso in fact predeceased his father.

124. 'Robertus et Elizabeth diu cohabitantes prolis utriusque sexus multitudinem procrearunt … proles … regi Scotie … et ipsius regis regno Scotie subsidia non modicum sperantur verisimiliter profutura': *Vetera monumenta Hibernorum et Scotorum historiam illustrantia*, ed. Theiner, no. 577, pp. 289–90; *Calendar of Entries in the Papal Registers Relating to Great Britain and Ireland: Papal Letters*, 3 (1342–1362), ed. Bliss and Twemlow, p. 265; Bower, *Scotichronicon*, 11. 13, 14. 54, ed. Watt et al., 6, p. 36; 7, p. 446; Fordun, 'Gesta Annalia', 77, in *Chronica gentis Scotorum*, ed. Skene, 1, p. 317.

125. Glanvill, *The Treatise on the Laws and Customs of England Commonly Called Glanvill*, 7. 15; 7. 13, ed. Hall, pp. 88, 87.

126. 'Ac rogaverunt omnes episcopi magnates ut consentirent quod nati ante matrimonium essent legitimi, sicut illi qui nati sunt post matrimonium, quantum ad successionem hereditariam, quia ecclesia tales habet pro legitimis; et omnes comites et barones una voce responderunt quod nolunt leges Anglie mutare': *Statutes of the Realm*, 1, p. 4 (Statute or Provisons of Merton).

127. 'Quoniam … Philippus rex Francorum, praeter primogenitum suum, quem de conjuge prima suscepit, aliorum prolem non habet nisi puerum et puellam quos ei nobilis mulier quondam filia nobilis viri ducis Meraniae peperit nuper defuncta, de sua posteritate provide cogitans a nobis humiliter postulavit ut eos legitimare per favorem sedis apostolicae curaremus … ut … utilitati et necessitati regni Franciae provide consulamus': Innocent III, *Epistola* 'Apostolica sedes', PL 214: 1191–4; Cartellieri, *Philipp II. August, König von Frankreich*, 4, pp. 82–8 (2 Nov. 1201, Po. 1499).

128. 'auctoritate apostolica decernentes, ut si ex tam incestuosa et dampnata copula proles est vel fuerit quecumque suscepta, spuria et illegitima penitus habeatur, que secundum statuta legitima in bonis paternis nulla prorsus ratione succedit': Innocent III, *Die Register Innocenz' III.*, ed. Hageneder et al., 2, no. 72 (75), p. 133 (PL 214, col. 614) (25 May 1199, Po. 716).

129. 'cum prolem ex huiusmodi copula incestuosa susceptam denuntiaverimus spuriam et secundum constitutiones legitimas in bona paterna nullo unquam tempore successuram, tu, de quo miramur non modicum, callide procurasti ut ei pene penitus totum

regnum Legionense iuraret': Innocent III, *Epistolae* 6. 80, *Die Register Innocenz' III.*, ed. Hageneder et al., 6, no. 80, pp. 126–7 (PL 215, col. 83) (5 June 1203, Po. 1932).

130. Reg. Vat. 25, fol. 260 (21 October 1260, Po. 17956–7).

131. 'Nous ne yrons, ne vendrons en nulle place où elle soit; car ce nous tourneroit à trop grant blasme que une telle duchesse qui vient de basse lignie et qui a esté concubine du duc ung trop long temps en ses mariages, se ores qu'elle est mariée, alloit, ne passoit devant nous. Les coeurs nous devroient crever de dueil et à bonne cause': Froissart, *Chroniques*, ed. Kervyn de Lettenhove, 15, p. 240.

132. *Calendar of Entries in the Papal Registers Relating to Great Britain and Ireland: Papal Letters*, 4 (1362–1404), p. 545; *Parliament Rolls of Medieval England*, ed. Given-Wilson et al., 7, pp. 322–3; Walsingham, *The St Albans Chronicle*, ed. Taylor et al., 2, p. 52; Goodman, *John of Gaunt: The Exercise of Princely Power in Fourteenth-Century Europe*, pp. 363–4; Goodman, *Katherine Swynford*.

133. Pollard, *The Reign of Henry VII from Contemporary Sources*, 2, pp. 8–9, no. 5.

134. See Helmholtz, 'The Sons of Edward IV: A Canonical Assessment of the Claim that They Were Illegitimate'.

135. *The Saga of Hacon*, 14, 41–6, tr. Vigfusson and Dasent, pp. 22, 42–5.

136. 'ut huiusmodi non obstante defectu ad regalis solii dignitatem ... admittaris, nec non quod heredes tui legitimi tibi in dominio et honore succedant': *Diplomatarium Norvegicum*, 1. 1, no. 38, pp. 29–30, 8 November 1246, from Reg. Vat. 21, no. 221, fol. 340 (Po. 12350).

137. *Diplomatarium Norvegicum*, 1. 1, no. 32, pp. 26–7, 3 November 1246, from Reg. Vat. 21, no. 31, fol. 419v (Po. 12340).

138. *Landrecht des Königs Magnus Hakonarson*, Christenrecht 5, ed. Meissner, pp. 38–9.

139. Jochens, 'The Politics of Reproduction: Medieval Norwegian Kingship'; Rüdiger, *Der König und seine Frauen: Polygynie und politische Kultur in Europa (9.–13. Jahrhundert)*, pp. 58–9.

6 FAMILY DYNAMICS

1. Schultze, *Die Mark Brandenburg 1: Entstehung und Entwicklung unter den askanischen Markgrafen (bis 1319)*; other branches of the family, descended from Albert the Bear's younger sons, continued.

2. 'Quia me mea fata vocant et atra mors iam pre oculis volat, volo vobis assignare et vestre fidei commendare, qui post me debeat rem publicam gubernare. Vos scitis, quia nostra principalis genealogia partim sterilitate partim pereuntibus in inmatura etate me usque ad unum fuit redacta. Nunc autem, ut ipsi cernitis, sunt mihi a Deo dati quinque nati, inter quos dividere regnum Boemie non videtur mihi esse utile, quia omne regnum in se ipsum divisum desolabitur. Quia vero ab origine mundi et ab initio Romani imperii et usque ad hec tempora fuerit [fratrum] gratia rara, testantur nobis exempla rata. Nam Cain et Abel, Romulus et Remus et mei attavi Bolezlaus et sanctus Wenczelaus si spectes quid fecerint fratres bini, quid facturi sunt quini?': Cosmas of Prague, *Chronica Boemorum*, 2. 13, ed. Bretholz, p. 102.

3. 'quatinus inter meos natos sive nepotes semper maior natu summum ius et solium obtineat in principatu': ibid., 2.13, p. 102.

4. 'secundum patrie morem debitum': ibid., 3. 15, p. 177.

5. *The Russian Primary Chronicle*, tr. Cross and Sherbowitz-Wetzor, pp. 142–3; Vincent Kadlubek, *Chronica Polonorum*, 3. 26, ed. Plezia, pp. 118–19.

6. 'par nobile fratrum': Cosmas of Prague, *Chronica Boemorum*, 2. 1, ed. Bretholz, p. 82 (the phrase is from Horace).

7. 'Ve tibi Boemia, que non adeo nimis ampla,/ Cum sis communis dominis subiectaque multis,/ Herili de stirpe sati sexuque virile/ Iam sunt bis deni, nisi fallor ego, dominelli': ibid., 3. 29, p. 198.

8. 'Per morsum mortis regum generacio fortis/ Sic est devicta, stirps mascula nulla relicta': Peter of Zittau, *Chronicon Aulae Regiae*, 1. 85, ed. Emler, p. 109.

9. *Chronicon de Lanercost, 1201–1346*, ed. Stevenson, pp. 40–1.

10. 'Post cuius tempora longo seculorum intervallo filius patri nullus in regno successit, sed (filiarum) nepotes, altera nempe parte regali stirpe editi': Sven Aggesen, *Brevis historia regum Dacie*, 4, ed. Gertz, pp. 106–7. Gertz's suggested addition of *filiarum* is described as 'unwarranted' by Eric Christiansen in his translation, *The Works of Sven Aggesen*, p. 113 n. 50.

11. There is a particularly acute analysis of fraternal relations at the level of the great dukes and counts of Germany in Lyon, *Princely Brothers and Sisters: The Sibling Bond in German Politics, 1100–1250*.

12. Jaski, *Early Irish Kingship and Succession*, p. 152, with other comparable examples.

13. Duindam, *Dynasties: A Global History of Power, 1300–1800*, pp. 110–11.

14. 'regalia funera fraterno sanguine maduerunt': Rodrigo Jiménez de Rada, *Historia de rebus Hispaniae*, 6. 14, ed. Fernández Valverde, pp. 194–5.

15. 'Tanta fuit discordia fratrum cupiditate dominandi . . . Scrutare sedulo regum gesta et inuenies quia sociis in regno fere nunquam pax diuturna fuit. Porro Yspanici reges tante ferocitatis dicuntur fuisse, quod cum ex eorum stirpe quilibet regulus adulta etate iam arma primo sumpserit, siue in fratres siue in parentes, si superstites fuerint, ut ius regale solus obtineat, pro iuribus contendere parat': Luke of Tuy, *Chronicon mundi*, 4. 61, ed. Falque Rey, p. 296, based on *Historia Silensis*, 7, ed. Estévez Sola, p. 140.

16. Fredegar, *Chronica*, 4. 27, 37–8, ed. Krusch, pp. 131, 138–40, ed. Wallace-Hadrill, pp. 18, 30–2; Jonas, *Vita Columbani*, 1. 28, ed. Krusch, pp. 217–19.

17. *The Chronicle of Duke Erik: A Verse Epic from Medieval Sweden*, tr. Carlquist and Hogg, quotations from pp. 195, 198, 203.

18. 'Adefonsus . . . Garsiam minimum fratrem cepit, cui in uinculis presto posito, preter licentiam inperitandi omnis regius honor exhibebatur. Considerabat namque Adefonsus hunc interim salva pace post se regnaturum': *Historia Silensis*, 9, ed. Estévez Sola, pp. 143–4.

19. John of Worcester, *Chronicle*, 3, ed. McGurk, p. 212, with n. 1.

20. *Historia et Cartularium Monasterii Sancti Petri Gloucestriae*, ed. Hart, 1, pp. 110–11.

21. *Historia Silensis*, 9, ed. Estévez Sola, p. 144.

22. 'nichil preter solitudinem passus sit mali, si solitudo dici potest ubi . . . iocorum . . . et obsoniorum non deerat frequentia': William of Malmesbury, *Gesta regum Anglorum*, 4. 389, ed. Mynors et al., p. 706; cf. Orderic Vitalis, *Historia ecclesiastica*, 12. 24, ed. Chibnall, 6, p. 286.

23. The arrangement is set out in the 'Ordinatio Imperii', in *Capitularia regum Francorum*, 1, ed. Boretius, no. 136, pp. 270–3.

24. 'Karolo quidem nato . . . quid huic faceret ignorabat': Nithard, *Historiarum libri IIII*, 1. 3, ed. Müller, p. 3.

25. 'ceteri filii ob hoc indignati sunt': Thegan, *Gesta Hludowici imperatoris*, 21, ed. Tremp, p. 210.

26. Ibid., 35, p. 220.

27. 'Quo peracto imperator inspectis plerisque nobilium filiabus Huelpi comitis filiam nomine Iudith duxit uxorem': *Annales regni Francorum*, s.a. 819, ed. Kurze, p. 150.

28. 'Qua tempestate monitu a suorum uxoriam meditabatur inire copulam; timebatur enim a multis, ne regni vellet relinquere gubernacula. Sed compellebatur tandemque eorum voluntati satisfatiens et undecumque adductas procerum filias inspitiens, Iudith filiam Uuelponis nobilissimi comitis in matrimonium iunxit': Astronomus, *Vita Hludowici imperatoris*, 32, ed. Tremp, p. 392. This passage is analysed in detail by De Jong, 'Bride Shows Revisited: Praise, Slander and Exegesis in the Reign of the Empress Judith'; she argues for the fictional nature of this account and the importance of the Esther story as a model.

29. See the comments of De Jong, *The Penitential State: Authority and Atonement in the Age of Louis the Pious, 814–840*, p. 31.

30. 'Nato siquidem regi filio ex moderno coniuge, ferebatur eidem puero rex regnum suum promittere, quod olim . . . Liudolfo delegaverat, et magnates suos eidem promittere fidelitatem jurejurando fecerat': Flodoard, *Annales*, s.a. 953, ed. Lauer, p. 135. This child was Henry, who died young. The later life of Bruno of Cologne, which was composed in the twelfth century, gives the same explanation of Liudolf's rebellion but calls the child Otto: 'Interea dominus rex, uxore priore defuncta, ex regina, quam ab Ytalia duxerat, filium equivo cum suscepit, quem sibi successorem regali benedictione consecrari disponebat. Quo comperto filius eius Ludolfus maior natu, qui plurimo iam tempore spei huius detinebatur cupiditate, dampnum hoc irrecuperabile duxit intolerabile, adeo ut paterne vite sive saluti discrimen meditaretur in temptare': *Vita Brunonis altera*, 8, ed. Pertz, p. 276. This could not be Otto II, who was born in 955.

31. 'adolescens acer et fortis': Widukind of Corvey, *Res gestae saxonicae*, 2. 33, ed. Hirsch and Lohmann, p. 94.

32. 'so war es vielleicht für ihn wie für das Reich ein Gluck, dass ihm ein längeres Wirken nicht beschieden ward': Köpke and Dümmler, *Kaiser Otto der Grosse*, p. 291.

33. For the terms of the Treaty of Montmirail of January 1169, in which this arrangement was made, see John of Salisbury, *Letters*, no. 288, ed. Millor et al., 2, pp. 636–8; Robert of Torigni, *Chronica*, ed. Howlett, p. 240; Gervase of Canterbury, *Chronica*, ed. Stubbs, 1, pp. 207–8. Geoffrey was engaged to the heir of Brittany. Henry confirmed the division in 1170: *Gesta regis Henrici secundi Benedicti abbatis*, ed. Stubbs, 1, pp. 6–7.

34. 'Johannes minor filius regis Anglorum, quem vocant Sine Terra, quamvis multas et latas habeat possessiones et multas comitatus, transivit in Hiberniam': Robert of Torigni, *Chronica*, ed. Howlett, pp. 311–12.

35. 'quartum natu minimum Johannem Sine Terra agnominans': William of Newburgh, *Historia rerum anglicarum*, 2. 18, ed. Howlett, 1, p. 146.

36. 'Antea quam fato fieres ludente monarcha, / Patris ab ore tui Sine-terra nomen habebas': William the Breton, *Philippis*, 6, lines 591–2, ed. Delaborde, p. 175.

37. *Gesta regis Henrici secundi Benedicti abbatis*, ed. Stubbs, 1, pp. 35–43; Roger of Howden, *Chronica*, ed. Stubbs, 2, pp. 41–6; *The Letters and Charters of Henry II King of England (1154–1189)*, ed. Vincent, no. 1779; Strickland, *Henry the Young King, 1155–1183*, pp. 120–2.

38. 'quae ad communem utilitatem vel ad perpetuam pacem pertinent': *Capitularia regum Francorum*, 1, ed. Boretius, no. 136, pp. 270–3 (the 'Ordinatio Imperii').

39. 'ne posset inter eos discordia suboriri': *Layettes du Trésor des Chartes*, ed. Teulet et al., 2, no. 1710, p. 55.

40. *Actes et lettres de Charles Ier, roi de Sicile, concernant la France (1257–1284)*, ed. de Boüard, nos. 810–11, 854, 913, 932, 1044–6, pp. 234–6, 250–1, 277, 286–7, 332–7; *Actes du Parlement de Paris*, ed. Boutaric, 1, appendix, no. 537, pp. 388–9; Wood, *The French Apanages and the Capetian Monarchy 1224–1328*, p. 41.

41. Gregory of Tours, *Libri historiarum decem*, 3. 1; 4. 22, ed. Krusch and Levison, pp. 97, 155. Widdowson, 'Merovingian Partitions: A "Genealogical Charter"?', argues that Gregory had his own reasons for presenting these divisions as legitimate and equitable but they were in fact 'more contested than traditionally acknowledged' (p. 21).

42. *Francorum regum historia* (continuation of Ado of Vienne), ed. Pertz, p. 325; Erchanbert, *Breviarium regum Francorum, continuatio*, ed. Pertz, p. 329.

43. 'Hludowici regis filii in pago Retiense convenientes paternum inter se regnum diviserunt et sibi invicem fidelitatem servaturos esse sacramento firmaverunt. Cuius sacramenti textus theutonica lingua conscriptus in nonnullis locis habetur': 'Continuatio Mogontiacensis', in *Annales Fuldenses*, s.a. 876, ed. Kurze, p. 89.

44. 'Her Eadgar æþeling feng to Myrcna rice': *Anglo-Saxon Chronicle* (B and C), s.a. 957, ed. Plummer and Earle, p. 113. The Life of Dunstan, a source hostile to Eadwig, says 'rex . . . a brumali populo relinqueretur contemptus' and specifices that the frontier between the two kings' territories was 'the famous river Thames': 'B.', *Vita sancti Dunstani*, 24, ed. Winterbottom and Lapidge, p. 74.

45. 'feng þa Eadmund cing to Weast Seaxan and Cnut to Myrcean', *Anglo-Saxon Chronicle* (E), s.a. 1016, ed. Plummer and Earle, p. 153; 'feng tha Eadmund cyng to West Sexan and Cnut to þam norð dælae': *Anglo-Saxon Chronicle* (D), s.a. 1016, ed. Plummer and Earle, p. 152.

46. 'regnum sorte dividitur Anglie': John of Worcester, *Chronicle*, 2, ed. Darlington and McGurk, p. 520.

47. *Anglo-Saxon Chronicle* (A, C, D, E), s.a. 1035–7, ed. Plummer and Earle, pp. 158–61.

48. Some kind of division of the kingdom of the West Franks was planned by Louis IV in 953 but did not take effect: Brühl, 'Karolingische Miszellen III: Ein westfränkisches Reichsteilungsprojekt aus dem Jahre 953'.

49. 'regnum Scocie non est partibile': Stones (ed.), *Anglo-Scottish Relations 1174–1328: Some Selected Documents*, no. 19, p. 122 [61].

50. 'David rex Scotorum dedit terram de Torphigan. Feregus rex Galwitensium dedit terram de Galvyte': Dugdale, *Monasticon*, 6. 2, p. 838, from London, College of Arms, MS L. 17, fols. 141–156v, a sixteenth-century copy of records of Hospitaller property made by John Stillingwell in 1434 (including properties previously held by the Templars); the places are Torphichen in Lothian and Galtway in Galloway; see the comments of Oram, *The Lordship of Galloway*, p. 62.

51. Chaplais, 'Un message de Jean de Fiennes à Edouard II et le projet de démembrement du royaume de France (janvier 1317)'.

52. Smith, 'Dynastic Succession in Medieval Wales', argues that there was no rule or law of partible inheritance applying to the Welsh principalities in the twelfth and thirteenth centuries, although disputed successions might well produce divisions of the principality.

53. 'ut post obitum suum, si fieri posset, quietam inter se duceret vitam'; 'Adefonsum itaque, quem pre omnibus liberis carum habebat': *Historia Silensis*, 43, ed. Estévez Sola, p. 227.

54. See the careful analysis by Spiess, 'Lordship, Kinship, and Inheritance among the German High Nobility in the Middle Ages and Early Modern Period'.

55. 'Hoc scilicet fiebat, ne in plures divisa provincia claritas illius familiae per inopiam rei familiaris obsoleret': Lampert of Hersfeld, *Annales*, s.a. 1071, ed. Holder-Egger, p. 121.

56. 'Si vero aliquis illorum decedens legitimos filios reliquerit, non inter eos potestas ipsa dividatur; sed potius populus pariter conveniens unum ex eis, quem Dominus voluerit, eligat': *Capitularia regum Francorum*, 1, ed. Boretius, no. 136, cl. 14, p. 272 (the 'Ordinatio imperii' of 817).

57. Nelson, 'A Tale of Two Princes: Politics, Text and Ideology in a Carolingian Annal', p. 109.

58. 'Non ut confuse atque inordinate vel sub totius regni denominatione iurgii vel litis controversiam eis relinquamus, sed trina portione totum regni corpus dividentes, quam quisque illorum tueri vel regere debeat porcionem describere et designare fecimus': *Capitularia regum Francorum*, 1, ed. Boretius, no. 45, Preface, p. 127 (the *Divisio regnorum* of 806).

59. Ibid., pp. 126–30 ; there is a large literature, which can be approached through Giese, 'Die designativen Nachfolgeregelungen der Karolinger 714–979', pp. 453–4 n. 65.

60. Sumption, *Trial by Battle (The Hundred Years War I)*, pp. 170–3.

61. Ganshof, 'On the Genesis and Significance of the Treaty of Verdun (843)'.

62. 'propter nomen imperatoris … et propter dignitatem imperii': Nithard, *Historiarum libri IIII*, 4. 3, ed. Müller, p. 43.

63. It was divided 870–80, part of the East Frankish kingdom 880–911, part of the West Frankish kingdom 911–25.

64. See Brühl, *Deutschland-Frankreich: die Geburt zweier Völker*.

65. It is first recorded in Spanish texts, before entering English in the fifteenth century; when Innocent III urged the knights of Calatrava to join Peter of Aragon in war against

the Muslims, exhorting them 'to come to his frontier and manfully conquer those Saracens there (*quatinus in ipsius fronteriam veniretis et ibidem Sarracenos eosdem curaretis viriliter expugnare*)', he clearly had a harsh and dangerous borderland in mind: Innocent III, *Epistolae* 8. 97 (96), *Die Register Innocenz' III*, ed. Hageneder et al., 8, pp. 175–6 (PL 215: 667) (16 June 1205, Po. 2558).

66. Simon (Symon) de Phares, *Recueil des plus célèbres astrologues et quelques hommes doctes*, ed. Wickersheimer, p. vii, n. 1.

67. 'pro regno fragmina regni': Florus of Lyons, *Querela de divisione imperii*, line 76, ed. Dümmler, p. 561.

68. 'hoc nomen, videlicet regnum Francorum, quandoque large quandoque stricte accipitur: large quando Franci ubicumque manerent … stricte vero regnum Francorum accipitur quando sola Gallia Belgica regnum Francorum vocatur, que est infra Renum, Mosam et Ligerim coartata, quam Galliam appropriato vocabulo, moderni Franciam vocant': Delaborde, 'Notice sur les ouvrages et sur la vie de Rigord moine de Saint-Denis', p. 604, from Soissons, Bibliothèque municipale, MS 129 (120).

69. See the brief but lucid comments of Guenée, 'Les limites de la France'.

70. *Über die Grundung des deutschen Reiches durch den Vertrag von Verdun*: Brühl, *Deutschland-Frankreich: die Geburt zweier Völker*, p. 8; Bresslau, *Das tausendjährige Jubiläum der deutschen Selbständigkeit*, gives a detailed account of the celebrations organized in 1843; his own title argues for the accession of Conrad I in 911 as the defining moment.

71. Lot, *La naissance de la France*.

72. Zatschek, *Wie das erste Reich der Deutschen entstand* (Zatschek was a member of the Nazi party).

73. 'Pas plus qu'on ne visa à Verdun à détruire à jamais l'unité du monde chrétien, on ne crut que les frontières ainsi définies dureraient longtemps. En fait, le traité détermina pour tout le Moyen Age, et même au delà, la géographie politique de la France et, dans une moindre mesure, celle de la future Allemagne. Personne ne s'attendait à ces résultats': Lot, *La naissance de la France*, p. 389.

74. 'le traité de Verdun constitue comme une prefiguration de la carte politique de l'Europe occidental': Depreux, 'Le partage de l'Empire à Verdun (843) et les conditions d'exercice du pouvoir au haut Moyen-Age', p. 18.

75. 'Nec mora, adpraehensum Chlothacharius puerum seniorem brachium elesit in terra, defixumque cultrum in ascella, crudiliter interfecit … "Aut eiece eum a te, aut certe pro eo morieris" … Quibus interfectis, Chlothacharius, ascensis equitibus, abscessit, parvi pendens de interfectione nepotum': Gregory of Tours, *Libri historiarum decem*, 3. 18, ed. Krusch and Levison, pp. 117–19.

76. 'Cum rex Johannes cepisset Arthurum eumque aliquamdiu in carcere vivum tenuisset, in turre tandem Rothomagensi, feria quinta ante Pascha, post prandium, ebrius et daemonio plenus, propria manu interfecit, et grandi lapide ad corpus ejus alligato, projecit in Secanam; quod reti piscatorio, id est, sagena, inventum est, et ad littus tractum, cognitum; et in prioratu Becci … occulte sepultum propter metum tyranni': *Annales de Margam*, ed. Luard, p. 27; the source is probably Arthur's captor, William de Briouse.

77. 'Patrue, clamabat, parvi miserere nepotis;/ Patrue, parce tuo, bone patrue, parce nepoti;/ Parce tuo generi; fraterne parcito proli'; William the Breton, *Philippis*, 6, lines 558–60, ed. Delaborde, pp. 173–4.

78. Holt, 'The *Casus Regis*: The Law and Politics of Succession in the Plantagenet Dominions, 1185–1247'; Holt, 'The *Casus Regis* Reconsidered'.

79. 'Cum quis vero moritur habens filium postnatum et ex primogenito filio premortuo nepotem, magna quiden iuris dubitatio solet esse uter illorum preferendus sit alii in illa successione, scilicet utrum filius an nepos': Glanvill, *The Treatise on the Laws and Customs of England Commonly Called Glanvill*, 7. 3, ed. Hall, p. 77.

80. 'Filius, licet postgenitus, heres propinquior est hereditatis patris quam nepotes, filii fratris sui primogeniti': *Le Très Ancien Coutumier de Normandie*, 12. 1, ed. Tardif, pp. 12–13; it is possible, however, that this text postdates 1200.

81. 'notandum quod hec inquisicio facta fuit per preceptum domini regis non per consideracionem curie vel secundum consuetudinem regni': *Rotuli curiae regis (1194–1200)*, ed. Palgrave, 2, p. 189.

82. 'Sine die quia iudicium pendet ex voluntate domini regis': *Pleas before the King or his Justices, 1198–1202*, 2, ed. Stenton, nos. 484, 528, pp. 126–7, 144.

83. Bracton, *De legibus et consuetudinibus Angliae*, ed. Woodbine, 3, pp. 284–5, 320; 4, p. 46.

84. *Acta aragonensia*, 1, ed. Finke, no. 216, p. 323.

85. Goldstone, *Joanna: The Notorious Queen of Naples, Jerusalem and Sicily*, p. 145.

86. See the discussion in Léonard, *La Jeunesse de la reine Jeanne*, pp. 111–24 ('La question hongroise'), where several of the following sources are cited.

87. 'quaeritur quis debeat praeferri in successione dicti regni, an scilicet dictus filius ex propria persona, an dictus nepos ex persona patris ... expedit regi a seniori ... et id apostolicus videtur cogitasse ... nepos non potest dici primogenitus, nisi ficte et improprie, cum sit contra naturales terminos veritatis, sed nos non debemus attendere fictionem': Baldus de Ubaldis, *Commentaria in sextum Codicis librum*, 6. 30. 19, 'De jure deliberandi', 'Cum antiquioribus'.

88. 'Is autem de predictis liberis primogenitus intelligatur et in eodem regno tibi sit successor et heres, quem mortis tue tempore priorem gradu et maiorem natu reperiri continget': Reg. Vat. 48, fol. 269v; calendared in *Les Registres de Boniface VIII (1294–1303)*, ed. Digard et al., 1, no. 1977, col. 757 (Po. 24473); the Register reads 'de predictis liberis primogenitis', which Léonard, surely rightly, corrects silently to 'de predictis liberis primogenitus': Léonard, *La Jeunesse de la reine Jeanne*, p. 113 n. 1.

89. 'Instituimus haeredem et universalem successorem nostrum in regnis nostris ... Robertum primogenitum nostrum ... relinquimus ... Carolo, nepoti nostro, primo-genito quondam primogeniti nostri regis Hungariae, duo millia unciarum auri': *Codex Italiae diplomaticus*, 2, ed. Lünig, cols. 1066–8. The king of Hungary mentioned here is Canrobert's father, Charles Martel, who had assumed the title in 1292 but had never made it a reality.

90. Léonard, *La Jeunesse de la reine Jeanne*, pp. 119–21.

91. 'Vulgaris et communis opinio [*not* operis] est quod filius filii primogeniti intelligatur primogenitus in successione et preferatur patruo': Óváry (ed.), 'Negoziati tra il Re

d'Ungheria e il Re di Francia per la successione di Giovanna I. d'Angiò', pp. 141–2 (the opinion of Louis of Piacenza).

92. 'li 'nganni/ che ricever dovea la sua semenza': Dante, *Paradiso* 9, lines 2–3, in *La Commedia*, ed. Petrocchi, 4, p. 137.

93. 'se il y euist ung bon roy à chief en Angleterre qui la guerre désirast et son héritage à recouvrer, ... il trouveroit cent mille archiers et six mille hommes d'armes qui le serviroient ... Je suis le darrain né de tous les enffans d'Angleterre mais ... je seroie le premier à renouveller les guerres': Froissart, *Chroniques*, ed. Kervyn de Lettenhove, 16, p. 3.

94. Given-Wilson (tr.), *Chronicles of the Revolution 1397–1400*, p. 2.

95. 'Ait dux: "Gratiose agatis mecum, saluando vitam meam." Cui rex: "Illam gratiam habebis quam prestitisti Symoni de Burley"': *Continuatio Eulogii: The Continuation of the Eulogium Historiarum, 1364–1413*, ed. Given-Wilson, p. 74.

96. 'pour la très-singuliere, parfaitte loyal et vraye amour qu'il a toujourz eu à Nous et à noz Enfanz ... nostre dit Frere d'Anjou ait le gouvernement de nostre Royaume ... Noz très chiers et très amez Freres Phelippes Duc de Bourgoigne et Loys Duc de Bourbon soïent Tuteurs et Gouverneurs de noz diz Enfanz': *Ordonnances des roys de France de la troisième race*, 6, pp. 46, 50.

97. 'velut vir non sane mentis, verbis fatuis utendo, gestus eciam majestatem regiam dedecentes exercuerat ... quemdam abjectissimum virum obvium habuit, qui eum terruit vehementer ... "Non progrediaris ulterius, insigne rex, quia cito prodendus est!" ... Cujus fragore rex furore subito commotus est, et quasi alienatus a sensibus servientem ense vibrato interfecit ... "Sum ego adversariis tradendus"': *Chronique du religieux de Saint-Denys*, 13. 5, ed. Bellaguet, 2, pp. 18–20.

98. Ibid., 13. 6, ed. Bellaguet, 2, p. 24.

99. Froissart, *Chroniques*, ed. Kervyn de Lettenhove, 15, pp. 35–45.

100. 'existimabat nonnumquam se vitreum esse nec tangi patiebatur, virgas ferreas vestimentis inserebat': Pius II, *Commentarii rerum memorabilium*, 6, ed. Meserve and Simonetta, 3, p. 208.

101. 'Magnates regni Castelle et Legione et Gallecie adque Lusitanie fecerunt omagium domino Sancio filio illustris regis Alfonsi Castelle': *Anales toledanos III*, ed. Floriano, p. 173.

102. 'fijo mayor heredero': *Crónica de Alfonso X*, ed. González Jiménez, p. 186; González Jiménez, 'Sancho IV, infante', p. 153; Ballesteros-Beretta, *Alfonso X el Sabio*, p. 824; Salvador Martínez, *Alfonso X, the Learned: A Biography*, pp. 365–6.

103. 'los homes sabios et entendudos ... mandaron que si el fijo mayor moriese ante que heredase, si dexase fijo ó fija que hobiese de su muger legítima, que aquel ó aquella lo hobiese, et non otro ninguno': *Las Siete Partidas*, 2. 15. 2, ed. Real Academia de la Historia, 2, p. 133.

104. For events in Castile 1275–84, González Jiménez, 'Sancho IV, infante'; Salvador Martínez, *Alfonso X, the Learned: A Biography*, pp. 369–523.

105. 'Et por esto el regno pasó mucho mal et mucho daño': *Crónica del rey Don Alfonso el Onceno*, 92, ed. Rosell, p. 228 (recounting the final settlement of 1331).

106. Although the illegitimate Trastámara branch did use their de la Cerda descent through the female line as an argument for their rightful possession of the throne in 1386, according to the chronicler Fernão Lopes: Lopes, *Crónica del Rei Dom João I*, 2. 85, in *The English in Portugal, 1367–1387*, pp. 200–1.

107. Davies, *Conquest, Coexistence and Change: Wales 1063–1415*, pp. 60–1, 240 (diagrams 1–2, 5).

108. Lecuppre-Desjardin, *Le royaume inachevé des ducs de Bourgogne: XIVe–XVe siècles.*

109. 'qu'il yroit et actendroit telle adventure qu'il plairoit à Dieu de lui envoyer … "Veez cy en qui je me fie" … "Il est temps!"': this account follows Monstrelet, *Chronique*, 1. 212, ed. Douët d'Arcq, 3 (SHF 99), pp. 338–46; Vaughan, *John the Fearless*, pp. 274–86, lists and assesses the various contemporary sources.

110. *Les grands traités de la guerre de Cent ans*, ed. Cosneau, pp. 116–51.

111. 's'il lui plaisoit estre roy et prendre couronne au tiltre d'aucun de ses pays, come de Frise, qui de ancien temps a estré royaume, ou de Brabant, qui est la plus ancienne et excellent duchié de toute la chrétienneté': Bonenfant and Bonenfant, 'Le projet d'érection des États bourguignons en royaume en 1447', p. 12.

112. 'Le duc … n'oblia pas de parler du royaume de Bourgoingne, que ceulx de France ont longtemps a usurpé': Paravicini, 'Theatre of Death. The Transfer of the Remnants of Philip the Good and Isabel of Portugal to Dijon, November 1473–February 1474', p. 57 n. 139.

113. Stein, 'Un diplomate bourguignon de XVe siècle, Antoine Haneron', pp. 339–41.

114. Vaughan, *Charles the Bold*, pp. 145–55, describes these events.

115. Bührer-Thierry, 'La reine adultère'.

116. See, for instance, McCracken, *The Romance of Adultery: Queenship and Sexual Transgression in Old French Literature.*

117. Thegan, *Gesta Hludowici imperatoris*, 26, ed. Tremp, p. 214. For a detailed account of events, see Dohmen, *Die Ursache allen Übels. Untersuchungen zu den Unzuchtsvorwürfen gegen die Gemahlinnen der Karolinger*, pp. 109–80.

118. 'asserentes etiam eum – quod dictu nefas est – thori incestatorem paterni; patrem porro adeo quibusdam elusum praestigiis, ut haec non modo vindicare, sed nec advertere posset': Astronomus, *Vita Hludowici imperatoris*, 44, ed. Tremp, p. 456; for Bernard's relationship with Louis, see Thegan, *Gesta Hludowici imperatoris*, 36, ed. Tremp, p. 222; see the comments of Koch, *Kaiserin Judith: eine politische Biographie*, pp. 103–20; De Jong, *The Penitential State: Authority and Atonement in the Age of Louis the Pious, 814–840*, pp. 195–200.

119. 'Richgarda imperatrix adulterii cum Liutwardo Vercellensi episcopo, qui apud eam et imperatorem familiariter in palatio vigebat, ab imperatore et aliis incusata …': Hermann of Reichenau, *Chronica*, ed. Pertz, p. 109; cf. Regino of Prüm, *Chronicon*, s.a. 887, ed. Kurze, p. 127. For a detailed account of events, see Dohmen, *Die Ursache allen Übels. Untersuchungen zu den Unzuchtsvorwürfen gegen die Gemahlinnen der Karolinger*, pp. 242–87.

120. Richer of Saint-Rémi, *Historiae*, 3. 66, ed. Hoffmann, p. 205; for the identity of the accuser, *Die Briefsammlung Gerberts von Reims*, ed. Weigle, no. 31, pp. 54–7 (Dietrich of

Metz to Charles of Lorraine, 984). For a detailed account of events, see Dohmen, *Die Ursache allen Übels. Untersuchungen zu den Unzuchtsvorwürfen gegen die Gemahlinnen der Karolinger*, pp. 312–34.

121. 'Ad ignominiam meam et totius generis mei nefandissima in Laudunensem confinxerunt episcopum': ibid., no. 97, pp. 126–7. See the comments of Dufour, 'Emma II, femme de Lothaire, roi de France', pp. 219–21.

122. *Annales de Wintonia*, ed. Luard, pp. 20–5.

123. Choniates, 'De Alexio Isaacii Angeli fratro', in *Historia*, 2 (1). 2–3, ed. Bekker, pp. 641–7, ed. van Dieten, pp. 484–9. See the comments of Garland, 'Morality Versus Politics at the Byzantine Court: The Charges against Marie of Antioch and Euphrosyne', pp. 286–92; Garland, *Byzantine Empresses: Women and Power in Byzantium, AD 527–1204*, pp. 210–24.

124. *Continuatio Chronici Girardi de Fracheto*, ed. Guigniaut and de Wailly, pp. 40–1; *Continuatio Chronici Guillelmi de Nangiaco*, ed. Géraud, 1, p. 404–6.

125. 'omnes tres captae sunt et in quadrigis coopertis de nigro ductae ad loca fortia, custodiendo portatae': *Ex anonymo regum Franciae chronico*, ed. de Wailly and Delisle, p. 17 (from BnF, MS lat. 5689C).

126. Maurer, *Margaret of Anjou: Queenship and Power in Late Medieval England*, pp. 46–8, 176–8; Geaman, 'A Bastard and a Changeling? England's Edward of Westminster and Delayed Childbirth'.

127. 'Rex noster stupidus est et mente captus; regitur non regit; apud uxorem, et qui regis thalamum foedant, imperium est': Pius II, *Commentarii rerum memorabilium*, 3. 41, ed. Meserve and Simonetta, 2, p. 178.

128. *Calendar of State Papers and Manuscripts, Existing in the Archives and Collections of Milan*, 1, ed. Hinds, no. 38, p. 27 (translated from the Italian).

129. 'qui fecit Billas dicentes quod Edwardus princeps non fuit filius regine': *John Benet's Chronicle for the Years 1400 to 1462*, ed. Harriss and Harriss, p. 216.

130. *An English Chronicle of the Reigns of Richard II., Henry IV., Henry V. and Henry VI.*, ed. Davies, p. 79 (spelling modernized).

131. Flodoard, *Annales*, s.a. 951, ed. Lauer, p. 132; Richer of Saint-Rémi, *Historiae*, 2. 101, ed. Hoffmann, p. 169; see the comments by MacLean, 'Making a Difference in Tenth-Century Politics: King Athelstan's Sisters and Frankish Queenship', pp. 183, 185–6.

132. 'Regina enim nostra Comiti Radulpho nupsit, quod factum Rex noster quam maxime dolet': Gervase of Rheims, *Epistola ad Alexandrum II papam*.

133. Griffiths, 'Queen Katherine of Valois and a Missing Statute of the Realm'.

134. *La reina doña Urraca (1109–1126), cancillería y colección diplomática*, ed. Ruiz Albi, nos. 1–2, pp. 355, 357 (*armiger regine*), no. 138, p. 576 (*venerabilis comes domnus Petrus de Lara*); *Diplomatario de la Reina Urraca de Castilla y León (1109–1126)*, ed. Monterde Albiac, lists considerably more than 149 documents but includes mentions, lost documents, etc.

135. Reilly, *The Kingdom of León-Castilla under Queen Urraca, 1109–1126*, pp. 216–17; Reilly, *The Kingdom of León-Castilla under King Alfonso VII, 1126–1157*, pp. 31–2; Barton, *The*

Aristocracy in Twelfth-Century León and Castile, pp. 113, 280; *Chronica Adefonsi imperatoris*, 1. 18, ed. Maya Sánchez, pp. 158–9.

136. 'Hunc si vidisses, fore regem iam putavisses': *Praefatio de Almaria*, line 77, ed. Gil, p. 257.

137. 'Siquidem fama refert, quadam die in ecclesia Visiensi, eo predicante, memoratam reginam, et consulem Fernandum, qui eo tempore contubernalis eius, non vir legitimus erat, rubore verecundie suffusos de ecclesia festinanter exisse': *Vita sancti Theotonii*, 5, ed. Herculano, p. 81.

138. Reilly, *The Kingdom of León-Castilla under Queen Urraca, 1109–1126*, p. 153; Barton, *The Aristocracy in Twelfth-Century León and Castile*, p. 241.

139. 'Sepe caret victu . . . Contritis pannis ibi mansit pluribus annis . . . et lineis vestibus sibi denegatis, solis laneis contentatur. Inruptis calciis frequenter apparuit, quia pro emendacione eorundem dare nummisma non habuit': Peter of Zittau, *Chronicon Aulae Regiae*, 1. 10, ed. Emler, p. 16.

140. 'Quanto putas cor regis . . . turbacionis pungatur aculeo, qui regnum suum penitus desolatum invenit': ibid., 1. 15, p. 21.

141. Pangerl, 'Zawisch von Falkenstein'.

142. 'Sed quia de facili mutatur mens mulieris, regina, ut aiunt, quibusdam artis magice ab ipso illusa fallaciis, ipsum arccius amans, sibi mox complacere studuit . . . Zewissius in oculis regine se graciam invenisse considerans ampliora appeciit et regine animum in amorem suum, quibusdam nigromancie conatibus ipsam circumveniens, provocavit. Diabolus igitur . . . inter reginam et Zewissium illicitarum nupciarum commercium consumari paranimphus subdolus procuravit': Peter of Zittau, *Chronicon Aulae Regiae*, 1. 16, ed. Emler, pp. 22–3.

143. 'Sawischius mundam sic prostituit Chunigundam,/ Defunctique thorum maculat regis Bohemorum': ibid., p. 23.

144. 'Rex Chunegundam matrem iubet esse iocundam,/ Sic puer in matre letatur, qui sine patre,/ Vixerat in penis prius in terris alienis': ibid., 1. 17, p. 23.

145. 'Sewischius pueriles ludos regem exercere docuit, quatenus eo ludente statum regni pro propria utilitate disponeret': ibid., 1. 18, p. 24.

146. 'Vivas tranquille iuvenis rex': ibid., 1. 25, p. 33.

147. See the relevant sections of Phillips, *Edward II*, and Ormrod, *Edward III*.

148. Phillips, *Edward II*, pp. 3, 24, 25–6, 28–9, 97–103.

149. 'Beal fitz, beal fitz, eiez pitie de gentil Mortymer': Baker, *Chronicon*, ed. Thompson, p. 46.

150. 'aliam duxit uxorem, quae valide contra filium eius, *sicut novercarum mos est*, malignari ac scandalizare coepit. Unde factum est, ut una solemnitatum die, cum puer super eam vestimenta matris agnusceret, commotus felle diceret ad eam: "Non enim eras digna, ut haec indumenta tua terga contegerent, quae dominae tuae, id est matre meae, fuisse nuscuntur"': Gregory of Tours, *Libri historiarum decem*, 3. 5, ed. Krusch and Levison, pp. 100–1; see Kasten, 'Stepmothers in Frankish Legal Life'; Kasten, 'Noverca venefica. Zum bösen Ruf der Stiefmütter in der gallischen und fränkischen Gesellschaft'.

151. 'super amisso care genitricis amore/ Ex egri latebris ducens suspiria cordis': Hroswitha, *Gesta Ottonis*, lines 742–3, in Hrotsvit, *Opera omnia*, ed. Berschin, p. 301; on Hroswitha's attitude to Liudolf, see Sonnleitner, 'Der Konflikt zwischen Otto I. und seinem Sohn Liudolf als Problem der zeitgenössischen Geschichtsschreibung'.

152. Suger, *Vita Ludovici Grossi regis*, 14, 18, ed. Waquet, pp. 84, 124; Orderic Vitalis, *Historia ecclesiastica*, 11. 9, ed. Chibnall, 6, pp. 50–4.

153. 'Erant enim quidam regni perturbatores, qui ad haec omni studio vigilabant, ut aut regnum in aliam personam transferretur, aut non mediocriter minueretur': Ivo of Chartres, *Epistolae* 189, PL 162: 193.

154. 'Quapropter exitium illi magnopere peroptaverat, et multis conatibus per plurimos iniquitatis complices procuraverat, ut et ipsa ... in principatu gloriaretur, et filios suos, Philippum et Florum, si ille moreretur, in regni solio securior intronizare moliretur. ... quidam hirsutus de Barbarie venit, ... Hic nimirum inter ethnicos diu conversatus fuerat, et profunda physicae secreta subtiliter a didascalis indagaverat': Orderic Vitalis, *Historia ecclesiastica*, 8. 20, 11. 9, ed. Chibnall, 4, pp. 260–2, 6, pp. 50–4.

155. αὖτε γὰρ ἀποπνιγομένη μικροῦ τῷ τὴν πατρῴαν κοίτην ἀνοσίως ὑπὸ τοῦ πρωτοσεβαστοῦ ἐρευνᾶσθαι, καὶ ἄλλως δὲ θερμουργίαν ἀσπαζομένη καὶ ἀνδρικὴ τὸ φρόνημα οὖσα, προσκτωμένη δὲ καὶ τὸ φύσει πρὸς τὴν μητρυιὰν βαρύζηλον: Choniates, 'Alexius Manuelis Comneni filius', in *Historia*, 4, ed. van Dieten, p. 230; the text in Bekker's edition, p. 300, has a different reading. On these incidents, see Garland, 'Morality Versus Politics at the Byzantine Court: The Charges against Marie of Antioch and Euphrosyne', pp. 271–86; Garland, *Byzantine Empresses: Women and Power in Byzantium, AD 527–1204*, pp. 201–3, 206–8.

156. τὸ γένος οἱ ἐντεῦθεν ἐπιθολοῦν: Choniates, 'Alexius Manuelis Comneni filius', in *Historia*, 5, ed. Bekker, p. 302, ed. van Dieten, p. 232.

157. ψεκάδι τοῦ μητρικοῦ διεντυπούμενος αἵματος: ibid., ed. Bekker, p. 347, ed. van Dieten, p. 268.

7 ROYAL MORTALITY

1. Hollingsworth, 'A Demographic Study of the British Ducal Families', pp. 360–1.

2. Whether Berenguela should be included in the list or not is debateable. She has been excluded here.

3. Suger, *Vita Ludovici Grossi regis*, 32, ed. Waquet, p. 266.

4. 'Sed quia iuvenis erat, quandam puellam, filiam cuiusdam Germundi, insecutus est; illa in domo paterno fugiens, rex equo sedens iocando eam insecutus scapulas superliminare et pectus sella equi attrivit eumque valide confregit': *Annales Vedastini*, s.a. 882, ed. von Simson, p. 52; there is no mention of the incident in the account of Louis' death in the *Annales Bertiniani*, s.a. 882, ed. Waitz, p. 152.

5. 'el rey ... cabalgó en un caballo ruano castellano ... E salió fuera de la villa por la puerta que dicen de Burgos, é en un barbecho dió el rey de las espuelas al caballo en que iba, é en medio de la carrera estropezó el caballo, é cayó con el rey, en manera que

le quebró todo por el cuerpo': López de Ayala, *Crónica del rey don Juan primero de Castilla é de Leon*, 10 (1390). 20, ed. Rosell, 2, p. 143.

6. 'elle chevauchoit ung aubin ardent ... Ledict seigneur [Louis] me compta ces nouvelles et en eut tres grand joye': Commynes, *Mémoires*, 6. 6. 2, ed. Blanchard, p. 453.

7. 'Rex autem, arrepta lancea, ut eundem leporem insectaretur sinistro actus casu equum ad illas cepit urgere partes et cursui vehementer instare. Tandem inconsulte festinans, equus in preceps agitur corruensque in terram regem dedit precipitem iacentique pre casus dolore attonito, sella caput obtrivit, ita ut cerebrum tam per aures quam per nares etiam emitteretur': William of Tyre, *Chronicon*, 15. 27, ed. Huygens, 2, p. 710.

8. Fredegar, *Chronica, Continuatio*, 39, ed. Krusch, p. 186, ed. Wallace-Hadrill, p. 108.

9. 'Karolus iuvenis rex Galliae in quadam venatione ictibus cuiusdam apri fertur occisus; re autem vera a suo satellite in eadem venatione non sponte vulneratus occubuit', 'Continuatio Mogontiacensis', in *Annales Fuldenses*, s.a. 884, ed. Kurze, p. 101.

10. William of Malmesbury, *Gesta regum Anglorum*, 3. 275, ed. Mynors et al., pp. 502–4; Orderic Vitalis, *Historia ecclesiastica*, 10. 14, ed. Chibnall, 5, pp. 282–4; John of Worcester, *Chronicle*, 3, ed. McGurk, p. 92. Richard, second son of William the Conqueror, collided with a branch while chasing an animal in the New Forest according to Orderic Vitalis, *Historia ecclesiastica*, 5. 11, ed. Chibnall, 3, p. 114; William of Malmesbury says he died from the bad air during a stag hunt.

11. *Chronica Sealandie*, ed. Kroman, p. 114; *Tabula Ringstadiensis*, ed. Gertz, p. 85.

12. Guilland, 'La destinée des empereurs de Byzance', pp. 11–12 (Theodosius II, Basil I, John II Comenus).

13. Flodoard, *Annales*, s.a. 954, ed. Lauer, p. 138; Richer of Saint-Rémi, *Historiae*, 2. 103, 4. 5, ed. Hoffmann, pp. 170, 234.

14. *Anales toledanos II*, s.a. 1220, ed. Porres Martín-Cleto, p. 191.

15. Eisner, 'Killing Kings: Patterns of Regicide in Europe, AD 600–1800', p. 563.

16. For Byzantium, Lilie, 'Der Kaiser in der Statistik. Subversive Gedanken zur angeblichen Allmacht der byzantinischen Kaiser', p. 214.

17. Guilland, 'La destinée des empereurs de Byzance'; for the uncertainty whether Constantine VI died very soon after or some years after blinding, see Theophanes, *The Chronicle of Theophanes the Confessor*, tr. Mango and Scott, pp. 649–50.

18. Ralph de Diceto, *Ymagines historiarum*, ed. Stubbs, 1, p. 440.

19. 'Hii uero, serie hereditaria semper et iure naturali regna paterna consecuti, ... et decurso demum uite temporalis spacio, fine beato decedentes et eternam in celis retribucionem de tam pio iustoque regimine recipientes, filiis suis et heredibus sua feliciter regna contradunt': Gerald of Wales, *De principis instructione*, 3. 30, ed. Bartlett, p. 718 (RS ed., p. 320).

20. Suger, *Vita Ludovici Grossi regis*, 14, 18, ed. Waquet, pp. 84, 124; Ivo of Chartres, *Epistolae* 189, PL 162: 193; Orderic Vitalis, *Historia ecclesiastica*, 11. 9, ed. Chibnall, 6, pp. 50–4; see above, pp. 237–8.

21. William, *Sugerii Vita*, 3, ed. Lecoy de la Marche, pp. 396–7.

22. Theophanes, *Chronographia*, AM 6303, ed. de Boor, 1, p. 491.

23. 'dignissimam periurii vindictam': *Vita Heinrici IV. imperatoris*, 4, ed. Eberhard, p. 19.

24. Matthew Paris, *Chronica majora*, ed. Luard, 5, p. 550.

25. 'Sumpserant enim Gothi hanc detestabilem consuetudinem, ut, si quis eis de regibus non placuisset, gladio eum adpeterent, et qui libuisset animo, hunc sibi statuerent regem': Gregory of Tours, *Libri historiarum decem*, 3. 30, ed. Krusch and Levison, p. 126.

26. 'interficiens omnes illos qui regis [sic] interemere consueverant, non relinquens ex eis mingentem ad parietem': Gregory of Tours, *Libri historiarum decem*, 4. 38, ed. Krusch and Levison, p. 170; the phrase is biblical, 3 Kings (1 Kings), 16: 11.

27. 'Quippe, ut dicitur, a centum retro annis, et eo amplius, cum regum ibidem numerosa successio fuerit, nullus eorum senio aut morbo vitam finivit, sed omnes ferro interiere; suis interfectores tanquam legitimis successoribus, regni fastigium relinquentes': William of Newburgh, *Historia rerum anglicarum*, 3. 6, ed. Howlett, 1, p. 228.

28. Bagge, *From Viking Stronghold to Christian Kingdom: State Formation in Norway, c. 900–1350*, p. 287.

29. As pointed out by Bagge, *Cross and Scepter: The Rise of the Scandinavian Kingdoms from the Vikings to the Reformation*, p. 51.

30. *Capitularia regum Francorum*, 1, ed. Boretius, no. 45, c. 18, pp. 129–30 (the *Divisio regnorum*).

31. Lydon, 'A Land of War', p. 249.

32. Pollock and Maitland, *The History of English Law before the Time of Edward I*, 2, p. 506.

33. νήπιος, ὃς πατέρα κτείνας παῖδας καταλείπει: Stasinus, *Cypria*, fragment, cited by Clement of Alexandria, *Stromateis*, 6. 19. 1, in *Greek Epic Fragments*, ed. West, p. 106.

34. Theophylact Simocatta, *Historiae*, 8. 11, ed. de Boor, p. 305; *Chronicon Paschale*, s.a. 602, ed. Dindorf, 1, pp. 693–4; Theophanes, *Chronographia*, AM 6094, ed. de Boor, 1, pp. 289–90.

35. Nikephoros of Constantinople, *Breviarium historicum*, 45, ed. Mango, p. 112; Theophanes, *Chronographia*, AM 6203, ed. de Boor, 1, p. 380.

36. 'Filius eius nomen Merovius parvolus iusso Theuderici adprehensus, a quidam per pede ad petram percutitur, cerebrum eius capite aeruptum, amisit spiritum': Fredegar, *Chronica*, 4. 38, ed. Krusch, pp. 139–40, ed. Wallace-Hadrill, p. 32.

37. *Theophanes continuatus*, 1. 10; 2. 1, ed. Bekker, pp. 20, 41; ed. Featherstone, pp. 32, 64.

38. Psellos, *Chronographia*, 5. 42, ed. Renauld, 1, p. 111; ed. Reinsch, p. 102.

39. Theophanes, *Chronographia*, AM 6284, ed. de Boor, 1, p. 468; they had all been forcibly tonsured some years earlier: Theophanes, AM 6273, ed. de Boor, 1, p. 454.

40. *Annales regni Francorum*, s.a. 818, ed. Kurze, p. 148; *Annales Bertiniani*, s.a. 873, ed. Waitz, p. 122; *Annales Xantenses*, s.a. 873, ed. von Simson, p. 32; 'Continuatio Mogontiacensis', in *Annales Fuldenses*, s.a. 873, ed. Kurze, p. 78; see Nelson, 'A Tale of Two Princes: Politics, Text and Ideology in a Carolingian Annal'; 'Continuatio Mogontiacensis', in *Annales Fuldenses*, s.a. 885, ed. Kurze, p. 103.

41. Liudprand, *Antapodosis*, 2. 35–41, ed. Becker, pp. 53–6.

42. 'Ilicet admissi penetrant miserabile templum,/ Quo Ludovicus erat, subito rapiuntque ligantque/ Et pulchros adimunt oculos. Securus in aula/ Forte sedebat enim, idcirco

pia munera lucis/ Perdidit, obsessus tenebris quoque solis in ortu': *Gesta Berengarii imperatoris*, 4, lines 61–5, ed. Dümmler, p. 128 (also in MGH, Poetae, 4. 1, p. 397).

43. *Annals of Ulster (to A.D. 1131)*, ed. Mac Airt and Mac Niocaill, pp. 430–529 *passim.*

44. *Annals of Ulster (Annála Uladh)*, ed. Hennessy and MacCarthy, 3, p. 153.

45. *Brut y Tywysogyon or The Chronicle of the Princes: Red Book of Hergest Version*, s.a. 1175, ed. Jones, p. 163.

46. Gillingham, 'Killing and Mutilating Political Enemies in the British Isles from the Late Twelfth to the Early Fourteenth Century: A Comparative Study', p. 122; see also Gillingham, 'Conquering the Barbarians: War and Chivalry in Twelfth-Century Britain'.

47. *Brut y Tywysogyon or The Chronicle of the Princes: Red Book of Hergest Version*, ed. Jones, pp. 163, 175.

48. Roger of Howden, *Chronica*, ed. Stubbs, 3, p. 270.

49. *Chronici Hungarici compositio saeculi XIV*, 150, 157–8, 160, ed. Domanovszky, pp. 430, 443–4, 446–7.

50. Promis, *Monumenta historiae patriae: Scriptores*, 1, cols. 666–70; Butaud and Piétri, *Les Enjeux de la généalogie (XIIe–XVIIIe s.): pouvoir et identité*, p. 21.

51. 'in venatione occisus': Munich, Bayerische Staatsbibliothek, clm 29880/6 (the 'Bamberger Tafel'); on this, see p. 331 'a porco interfectus': Bernard Gui, *Arbor genealogiae regum Francorum*, CCCC 45, fol. 43v (cf. fol. 16v).

52. 'Cujus corpus gloriose sepultum fuit in ecclesia Sancte Marie de Barbael quam ipse fundavit: Ubi ad honorem Domini nostri Jhesu Christi et beate Dei Genitricis et Virginis Marie et omnium sanctorum die et nocte a sanctis et religiosis viris divina celebrantur officia pro anima ipsius et omnium predecessorum suorum et pro statu regni Francorum': Rigord, *Gesta Philippi Augusti*, 10, ed. Carpentier et al., p. 142.

53. 'sepulturam meam et sucessorum meorum': *Tumbo A de la Catedral de Santiago*, ed. Lucas Alvarez, no. 130, p. 264.

54. Brown, 'Death and the Human Body in the Later Middle Ages: The Legislation of Boniface VIII on the Division of the Corpse', p. 251.

55. Grierson et al., 'The Tombs and Obits of the Byzantine Emperors'.

56. Gregory of Tours, *Libri historiarum decem*, 2. 43, ed. Krusch and Levison, p. 93; Erlande-Brandenburg, *Le roi est mort: étude sur les funérailles, les sépultures et les tombeaux des rois de France*, p. 50; Périn, 'The Undiscovered Grave of King Clovis I (+511)'.

57. Yorke, 'The Burial of Kings in Anglo-Saxon England', pp. 243, 247–8, 251.

58. Taking Louis XII as the last medieval king; the exceptions were Philip I, Louis VII and Louis XI; royal burial at St-Denis continued to be the rule after the medieval period.

59. 'a sepultura patrum suorum regum, que in ecclesia Beati Dionisii quasi jure naturali habetur, se absentari deliberaverat': Suger, *Vita Ludovici Grossi regis*, 13, ed. Waquet, p. 84.

60. '"Francorum" inquit "regum sepulturam apud sanctum Dionisium esse scio, sed quia me nimium esse peccatorem sentio, secus tanti martiris corpus sepeliri non audeo"': Orderic Vitalis, *Historia ecclesiastica*, 11. 34, ed. Chibnall 6, p. 154.

61. Conrad III at Bamberg, Frederick I at Tyre, Henry VI at Palermo, Philip of Swabia at Speyer (transferred from Bamberg), Frederick II at Palermo, Henry (VII) at Cosenza, Conrad IV at Messina.

62. Conrad II, Henry III, Henry IV, Henry V (1039–1125); Philip of Swabia (d. 1208, buried at Speyer 1213); Rudolf of Habsburg (1291); Adolf of Nassau (d. 1298) and Albert I (d. 1308) were both transferred to Speyer in 1309.

63. This was Philip of Swabia, whose body was transferred to Speyer from Bamberg by his nephew Frederick II in 1213, five years after his death: *Annales Marbacenses*, ed. Bloch, p. 78; Burchard of Ursperg, *Chronicon*, ed. Holder-Egger and von Simson, p. 91.

64. 'ubi etiam eorum quilibet mausoleum habuerit': Delaborde, 'Notice sur les ouvrages et sur la vie de Rigord moine de Saint-Denis', p. 600, from Soissons, Bibliothèque municipale, MS 129 (120).

65. 'Pour ce que moult de gent et meismememt li haut homme et noble qui souvent viennent en liglise monsegnour saint Dyonise de France ou partie de vallans roys de France gisent en sepouture, desirent cognoistre et savoer la nessance et la descendue de leur très haute generacion et les mervellous faiz qui sunt raconté e publié par maintes terres des devans diz roys de France, je frere Guillaume, diz de Nangis, moine de la devant dite eglise Saint Dyonise, ay translaté du latin en franceys a la requeste de bonnes gens, pour ce que cil qui latin nentendent puissent savoer e cognoistre dont si noble gent e si beneureuse descendit e vint premierement': William de Nangis, *Chronique abrégée des rois de France*, p. 649. The French translation went on to be a popular text and was continued by later writers: Guyot-Bachy, 'La *Chronique abrégée des rois de France* de Guillaume de Nangis: trois étapes de l'histoire d'un texte'; Guyot-Bachy, 'La *Chronique abrégée des rois de France* et les *Grandes chroniques de France*: concurrence ou complémentarité dans la construction d'une culture historique en France à la fin du Moyen Age?'.

66. For a comparison, see Jordan, *A Tale of Two Monasteries: Westminster and Saint-Denis in the Thirteenth Century*; note also the reflections of Genet, 'Londres est-elle une capitale?'.

67. See Wolverton, *Hastening Toward Prague: Power and Society in the Medieval Czech Lands*, esp. pp. 82–5.

68. 'tocius Boemie domnam': Cosmas of Prague, *Chronica Boemorum*, 1. 9, ed. Bretholz, p. 19.

69. 'sedes regis Bohemorum et totius regni': *Annales de rebus gestis post mortem Przem. Otakari regis (II)*, s.a. 1279, ed. Emler, p. 347.

70. See the list in Wolverton, *Hastening Toward Prague: Power and Society in the Medieval Czech Lands*, p. 95, supplemented by information on the last four Premyslid rulers.

71. 'monasterium ... quod prope civitatem que dicitur Burgis construximus et de propriis bonis ditavimus ... Preterea, promisimus ... quod nos et filii nostri, qui consilio et mandato nostro acquiescere voluerint, in supra dicto monasterio ... sepeliamur': *Documentación del monasterio de Las Huelgas de Burgos (1116–1230)*, ed. Lizoain Garrido, no. 52, p. 93.

72. Anderson, *Kings and Kingship in Early Scotland*, pp. 266–8, 273–6, 279, 282–4, 288–91.

73. *Miracula sancte Margarite Scotorum regine*, 7, ed. Bartlett, pp. 86–8; Bower, *Scotichronicon*, 10. 15, ed. Watt et al., 5, pp. 336–8.

74. Vasconcelos Vilar, 'Lineage and Territory: Royal Burial Sites in the Early Portuguese Kingdom', p. 165.

75. *Tabula Ringstadiensis*, ed. Gertz.

76. Klein, 'Comment parler des arts au XIVe siècle? La genèse du panthéon aragonais-catalan à Poblet à l'époque du roi Pierre le Cérémonieux', p. 94.

77. 'Apud Sanctum-Dionysium in Francia facta est regum Francorum in monasterio illo per diversa loca quiescentium, per sanctum regem Franciae Ludovicum et Mathaeum abbatem illius monasterii, simul adjuncta translatio; et qui erant tam reges quam reginae de genere Magni Karoli descendentes simul in dextera parte monasterii per duos pedes et dimidium super terram caelatis imaginibus elevati positi sunt, et alii procedentes de genere regis Hugonis Capucii in sinistra': William of Nangis, *Chronicon*, ed. Géraud, 1, pp. 232–3, s.a. 1267; see Wright, 'A Royal Tomb Programme'; Erlande-Brandenburg, *Le roi est mort: étude sur les funérailles, les sépultures et les tombeaux des rois de France*, pp. 81–3; Meier, *Die Archäologie des mittelalterlichen Königsgrabes im christlichen Europa*, p. 333, fig. 165.

78. 'Elegerat autem dominus rex sepulturam suam apud sanctum Dionysium et sepulturam filii sui . . . in ecclesia Regalis-montis quod nolebat quod sepultus esset in ecclesia beati Dionysii, in qua sepulti erant soli reges': Achery, *Veterum scriptorum spicilegium*, 3, p. 667 (a letter of 1270 from Peter de Condé, probably the later archdeacon of Soissons, to the treasurer of the royal church of St-Frambaud de Senlis, who is not named but was Philip de Chaorse, one of the king's executors, as bishop-elect of Evreux); for Louis carrying stones, William de Saint-Pathus, *Vie de saint Louis*, 9, ed. Delaborde, p. 71.

79. *Theophanes continuatus*, 6. 1, ed. Bekker, p. 353; Symeon Magister et Logotheta, *Chronicon*, 133. 2, ed. Wahlgren, pp. 270–1.

80. Symeon Magister et Logotheta, *Chronicon*, 131.45, ed. Wahlgren, p. 255; see the discussion in Tougher, *The Reign of Leo VI (886–912): Politics and People*, pp. 42–67.

81. Ibid., p. 62, citing the view of 'several Byzantinists'.

82. Saul, *Richard II*, p. 428.

83. Lopes, *Crónica do Rei D. Pedro I*, 2, 16, ed. Macchi, tr. Steunou, pp. 24–6, 100–2.

84. *Recueil des actes de Charles II le Chauve, roi de France*, ed. Tessier, 2, nos. 246, 379, pp. 53–6, 347–50.

85. Regino of Prüm, *Chronicon*, s.a. 877, ed. Kurze, p. 113.

86. 'rogans, eum etiam Spire iuxta parentes suos sepelire': *Annales Hildesheimenses*, ed. Waitz, p. 57.

87. 'precipue autem ecclesiam Spiremsem a nostris parentibus Cûnrado imperatore augusto, avo videlicet nostro, et Heinrico imperatore augusto, patre videlicet nostro, et a nobis gloriose constructam veneramur': *Heinrici IV. Diplomata*, ed. von Gladiss and Gawlik, 2, no. 489, p. 666.

88. 'anniversarium permagnifice celebrat . . . iuxta maiores suos in aecclesia sepelitur': *Frutolfi et Ekkehardi Chronica necnon Anonymi Chronica imperatorum*, ed. Schmale and Schmale-Ott, pp. 304–6; ibid., p. 239 (Ekkehard III) (MGH SS 6, pp. 245, 239);

Annales Hildesheimenses, ed. Waitz, pp. 57, 62; *Annales Patherbrunnenses eine verlorene Quellenschrift des zwölften Jahrhunderts*, ed. Scheffer-Boichorst, p. 115.

89. 'Regina etiam Sancia postulante patrem suum regem Sancium a monasterio Oniensi transtulit et cum aliis regibus Legione sepeliuit': Luke of Tuy, *Chronicon mundi*, 4. 56, ed. Falque, p. 292; followed by Rodrigo Jiménez de Rada, *Historia de rebus Hispaniae*, 6. 12, ed. Fernández Valverde, p. 192.

90. Dectot, *Les tombeaux des familles royales de la péninsule ibérique au Moyen Age*, pp. 183, 193.

91. Ibid., p. 213.

92. 'el rey don Alfonso, que gano a Toledo . . . a los pies de la iglesia . . . la capilla ante el altar mayor . . . en un monumento verde': *Crónica del rey don Sancho el Bravo*, 3, ed. Rosell, pp. 73–4.

93. Grierson et al., 'The Tombs and Obits of the Byzantine Emperors'.

94. 'Theodoricus . . . mortuus est sepultusque est in mausoleum, quod ipse aedificare iussit extra portas Artemetoris, quod usque hodie vocamus Ad Farum, ubi est monasterium sanctae Mariae quod dicitur Ad memoria regis Theodorici. Sed, ut michi videtur, ex sepulcro proiectus est, et ipsa urna, ubi iacuit, ex lapide porfiretico valde mirabilis, ante ipsius monasterii aditum posita est': Agnellus of Ravenna, *Liber pontificalis ecclesiae Ravennatis*, 39, ed. Mauskopf Deliyannis, p. 197; ed. Holder-Egger, p. 304; see Ambrogi, *Vasche di età romana in marmi bianchi e colorati*, pp. 109–11, with photo on p. 123 (B. I. 32).

95. Montesquiou-Fezensac, 'Le tombeau de Charles le Chauve à Saint-Denis'; Erlande-Brandenburg, *Le roi est mort: étude sur les funérailles, les sépultures et les tombeaux des rois de France*, p. 39 and fig. 31.

96. Deér, *The Dynastic Porphyry Tombs of the Norman Period in Sicily*; the scientific analysis of Frederick's tomb undertaken in the 1990s is described in *Il sarcofago dell'imperatore. Studi, ricerche e indagini sulla tomba di Federico II nella Cattedrale di Palermo 1994–1999*.

97. *Rogerii II regis Diplomata Latina*, ed. Brühl, no. 68, p. 199 (1145); Roger intended to be buried in one of the porphyry sarcophagi in Cefalù; his daughter, the Empress Constance, recognized this original intention in a document of 1198 for Cefalù: *Constantiae imperatricis Diplomata*, ed. Kölzer, no. 56, p. 176.

98. Deér, *The Dynastic Porphyry Tombs of the Norman Period in Sicily*, p. 18; *Historia Diplomatica Friderici II*, ed. J.-L.-A. Huillard-Bréholles (6 vols. in 12, Paris, 1852–61) 1. 2, pp. 426–7 (the status and nature of this document is not quite clear).

99. The various arguments are set out in Johnson, 'The Porphyry Alveus of Santes Creus and the Mausoleum at Centcelles'.

100. Nickson, 'The Royal Tombs of Santes Creus. Negotiating the Royal Image in Medieval Iberia', p. 7.

101. There is an extremely thorough analysis of this topic in Meier, *Die Archäologie des mittelalterlichen Königsgrabes im christlichen Europa*.

102. Ibid., pp. 167–211.

103. 'Hic iacet Danorum rex Waldemarus primus, Sclauorum expugnator et dominator, patrie liberator, pacis conservator. Qui filius sancti Kanuti Rugianos expugnavit et ad fidem Christi primus convertit . . . Murum quoque ad tocius regni presidium, qui wlgo

Danewerch dicitur, ex lateribus coctis primus construxit': *Scriptores minores historiae Danicae*, ed. Gertz, 2, pp. 87–8 (the first comma should be after, not before, 'primus', as in Gertz; this is clear from the inscription on the reverse, 'rex Waldemarus primus, sancti Kanuti filius').

104. Rapp, 'Death at the Byzantine Court: The Emperor and his Family', pp. 278–9.

105. 'Rex magnus parva iacet hac Guillelmus in urna/ Sufficit et magno parva domus domino': Orderic Vitalis, *Historia ecclesiastica*, 8. 1, ed. Chibnall, 4, p. 110.

106. 'sacra victima belli … ecclesiae cecidit': Schramm and Mütherich, *Denkmale der deutschen Könige und Kaiser I: Ein Beitrag zur Herrschergeschichte von Karl dem Grossen bis Friedrich II. 768–1250*, p. 176.

107. Meier, *Die Archäologie des mittelalterlichen Königsgrabes im christlichen Europa*, pp. 242–3; the effigy of Rudolf I (d. 1291) in Speyer was not originally associated with his tomb.

108. Meier, *Die Archäologie des mittelalterlichen Königsgrabes im christlichen Europa*, pp. 306–7, fig. 158.

109. 'fecit construi sepulchrum miro artificio compositum ex lapidibus, auro et argento et ere et gemmis subtilissime decoratum': Rigord, *Gesta Philippi Augusti*, 10, ed. Carpentier et al., p. 142.

110. It was destroyed during the French Revolution, but antiquarian drawings survive: Erlande-Brandenburg, *Le roi est mort: étude sur les funérailles, les sépultures et les tombeaux des rois de France*, pp. 161–2, figs. 37–8.

111. Dectot, *Les tombeaux des familles royales de la péninsule ibérique au Moyen Age*, p. 89.

112. Hartmann, *Die Königin im frühen Mittelalter*, pp. 214–16; the statement that Fredegund and Chilperic I were buried in St-Denis (ibid., p. 208) must be a slip.

113. Klein, 'Comment parler des arts au XIVe siècle? La genèse du panthéon aragonais-catalan à Poblet à l'époque du roi Pierre le Cérémonieux.'

114. 'de coper et laton endorrez, coronez, ajonauntz et cloisauntz ensemble lour meyns dextres, et tenantz septres en lour meyns senestres': *Foedera* (original edn.), 7, pp. 797–8; *Age of Chivalry: Art in Plantagenet England, 1200–1400*, ed. Alexander and Binski, no. 446, pp. 393–4 (with photograph of the contract for the marble tomb); both contracts are in TNA, E 101/473/7; see also Duffy, *Royal Tombs of Medieval England*, pp. 163–73.

115. 'mortuus est predictus dux Boemiae Cunradus in Apulia circa Neapolim, cuius carnes in monte Cassino positae, sed ossa Pragam sunt deportata': Gerlach of Mühlhausen, *Chronicon*, ed. Wattenbach, p. 706, ed. Emler, p. 509.

116. Brown, 'Death and the Human Body in the Later Middle Ages: The Legislation of Boniface VIII on the Division of the Corpse'; Gaude-Ferragu, *D'or et de cendres. La mort et les funérailles des princes dans le royaume de France au bas Moyen Âge*, pp. 313–44; Bande, *Le Coeur du roi. Les Capétiens et les sepultures multiples XIIIe–XVe siècles*; Warntjes, 'Programmatic Double Burial (Body and Heart) of the European High Nobility, c. 1200–1400. Its Origins, Geography, and Functions'.

117. 'praecepit rex, ut cerebrum suum et sanguis ejus et viscera sua sepelirentur apud Charrou, et cor suum apud Rothomagum, et corpus suum apud Frontem Ebraudi, ad pedes patris sui': Roger of Howden, *Chronica*, ed. Stubbs, 4, p. 84.

118. William de Nangis, *Gesta Philippi tertii regis Franciae*, pp. 466–8, 486–8.

119. Enderlein, *Die Grablegen des Hauses Anjou in Unteritalien. Totenkult und Monumente (1266–1343)*, pp. 33–5.

120. 'Otrosí mandamos que luego que muriéremos, que nos saquen el coraçón e quel lieuen a la sancta Terra de Ultramar e quel sotierren en Jherusalem en Monte Calvar, allí do yazen algunos de nuestros auuelos': *Diplomatario andaluz de Alfonso X*, ed. González Jiménez, no. 521, p. 559.

121. 'And myn hart fichyt sekyrly was/ Quhen I wes in prosperité/ Off my synnys to sauffyt be/ To travaill apon Goddis fayis,/ And sen he now me till him tayis/ Sua that the body may na wys/ Fullfill that the hart gan devis/ I wald the hart war thidder sent/ Quharin consavyt wes that entent./ Tharfor I pray you everilkan/ That ye amang you ches me ane/ That be honest wis and wicht/ And off his hand a noble knycht/ On Goddis fayis my hart to ber/ Quhen saule and cors disseveryt er,/ For I wald it war worthily / Brocht thar, sen God will nocht that I/ Haiff power thidderwart to ga': Barbour, *The Bruce*, 20, lines 182–99, ed. Duncan, pp. 751–3.

122. 'legavit suum cor mitti Jerusolimis, et recondi apud Sepulcrum Domini': Bower, *Scotichronicon*, 12. 19, ed. Watt et al., 7, p. 64.

123. 'nobilis vir, Jacobus dominus de Douglas in Scotia, versus Terram Sanctam, in auxilio Christianorum contra Sarracenos, cum corde domini R. Regis Scotiae, nuper defuncti, sit profecturus': *Foedera* (new edn.), 2. 2, pp. 770–1 (*Calendar of Documents Relating to Scotland*, ed. Bain, 3, nos. 990–1, p. 179; *Calendar of the Patent Rolls Preserved in the Public Record Office, 1327–30*, p. 436; *Calendar of the Close Rolls Preserved in the Public Record Office, 1327–30*, p. 568).

124. Fordun, *Chronica gentis Scotorum*, ed. Skene, 1, pp. 353–4, *Gesta Annalia* 144; Barbour, *The Bruce*, 20, lines 309–600, ed. Duncan, pp. 759–73; Bower, *Scotichronicon*, 13. 20, ed. Watt et al., 7, pp. 66–70; Brown, *The Black Douglases: War and Lordship in Late Medieval Scotland, 1300–1455*, p. 27.

125. *Calendar of Entries in the Papal Registers Relating to Great Britain and Ireland: Papal Letters*, 2 (1305–1343), p. 235; 3 (1342–1362), p. 168.

126. 'scindendis, decoquendis, vel alias quomodolibet dividendis, ac in una, vel diversis ecclesiis, sive locis, prout devotio vobis suaserit, tumulandis': *Privilèges accordés à la couronne de France par la Saint-Siége*, ed. Tardif, no. 270, p. 245 (Clement VI for John II, 20 April 1351); for earlier, individual privileges, see Brown, 'Death and the Human Body in the Later Middle Ages: The Legislation of Boniface VIII on the Division of the Corpse', pp. 254–61.

127. Hunter, 'On the Death of Eleanor of Castile, Consort of King Edward the First, and the Honours Paid to her Memory', pp. 186–7; *Age of Chivalry: Art in Plantagenet England, 1200–1400*, ed. Alexander and Binski, no. 379, pp. 365–6 (drawing of c. 1641).

128. Elliott, 'Violence against the Dead: The Negative Translation and *damnatio memoriae* in the Middle Ages'.

129. Theophanes, *Chronographia*, AM 6102, ed. de Boor, 1, p. 299; Grierson et al., 'The Tombs and Obits of the Byzantine Emperors', p. 47.

130. Symeon Magister et Logotheta, *Chronicon*, 131. 44, ed. Wahlgren, p. 255; this happened 'at some time (which can no longer be accurately identified)', Skylitzes, *A Synopsis of Byzantine*

History 811–1057, tr. Wortley, p. 107 n. 99. Judith Herrin argues that the removal of his tomb gave a space for the reinterment of the remains of the empress Irene: Herrin, 'Moving Bones: Evidence for Political Burials from Medieval Constantinople', pp. 288–90.

131. Thietmar of Merseburg, *Chronicon*, 7. 37, ed. Holtzmann, p. 444; see also *Encomium Emmae Reginae*, 2. 3, ed. Campbell, p. 18. According to Simeon of Durham, *Historia regum*, 125, ed. Arnold, p. 146, and Gaimar, *Estoire des Engleis*, line 4162, ed. Short, p. 226, Sven was buried at York; there is a full discussion in Marafioti, *The King's Body: Burial and Succession in Late Anglo-Saxon England*, pp. 198–206.

132. 'He let dragan up þæne deadan Harald 7 hine on fen sceotan': *Anglo-Saxon Chronicle* (C), s.a. 1040, ed. Plummer and Earle, p. 162; discussed in Marafioti, *The King's Body: Burial and Succession in Late Anglo-Saxon England*, pp. 125–7, 144–60.

133. Roger of Howden, *Chronica*, ed. Stubbs, 3, p. 270.

134. 'Or le bagna la pioggia e move il vento/ di fuor dal regno': Dante, *Purgatorio* 3. 130–1, ed. Petrocchi, 3, p. 51; Villani, *Nuova Cronica*, 8. 9, ed. Porta, 1, pp. 423–4.

8 NAMES AND NUMBERING

1. 'Gaufridum, qui cognominatus est Plantegenest (sic)': William of Tyre, *Chronicon*, 14. 1, ed. Huygens, 2, p. 632; 'Gaufridus Plantagenet ... ab Henrico frater suo comite Andegavensi invaditur': *Chronicon Turonense magnum*, ed. Martène and Durand, col. 1015; ed. Salmon, p. 136, s.a. 1152. These two sources, one distant and one late, may have confused father and son.

2. Wolffe, *Henry VI*, pp. 35 n. 26, 323 n. 48; the earliest reference to him as 'Richard Plantagenet' seems to be in a chronicle entry describing events of that year: Gregory, *Chronicle of London*, ed. Gairdner, p. 189.

3. There is debate about whether Manetho was actually a historical figure.

4. 'apud Aegyptios autem sexta decima erat potestas, quam sua lingua dinastiam vocabant': Gregory of Tours, *Libri historiarum decem*, 1. 17, ed. Krusch and Levison, p. 16.

5. 'In Ebreis Lepdon iudex erat, et in Aegypto dinastia rex erat': Fredegar, *Chronica*, 2. 8, ed. Krusch, p. 47.

6. 'Variate autem sunt dinastie per diversa regum genera usque ad hunc Cambisem': Gervase of Tilbury, *Otia Imperialia*, 2. 15, ed. Banks and Binns, p. 364. Gervase is slightly recasting his source, Peter Comestor: 'Variatae quoque sunt dynastiae de generibus quorumdam regum ad alia saepe transeuntes, usque ad Cambysem', *Historia scholastica*, Genesis 64, col. 1109.

7. 'Dinastia autem dicitur principatus qui durat apud aliquam domum': Rodrigo Jiménez de Rada, *Breviarium historie catholice*, 2. 60, ed. Fernández Valverde, 1, p. 101.

8. 'Nicolaus tertius, natione Romanus de domo Ursinorum': *Annales Sanctorum Udalrici et Afrae Augustenses*, ed. Jaffé, p. 433.

9. López de Ayala, *Crónica del Rey don Pedro*, 18 (1367). 30, ed. Orduna, 2, p. 231; Lopes, *Crónica del Rei Dom João I*, 2. 80, 81, pp. 186, 188.

10. Moeglin, 'Les dynasties princières allemandes et la notion de maison à la fin du Moyen-Age'; Carozzi, 'Familia-domus: étude sémantique et historique'.

11. 'das haws von Osterreich': *Die Stadtrechte von Bremgarten und Lenzburg*, ed. Merz, p. 63. In the late fourteenth and early fifteenth century such phrases expanded their meaning to describe also the lands and territories of the dynasty, and even the inhabitants of their lands: Moeglin, 'Les dynasties princières allemandes et la notion de maison à la fin du Moyen-Age'.

12. James I, *Llibre dels fets del rei en Jaume*, 9, ed. Bruguera, 2, p. 14; 1, p. 255, for the frequency of the term, in various spellings.

13. 'qui huius prosapie [sc. from Rollo] loco .vii. fuisse dinoscitur': 'Additamenta', in *Gesta Normannorum Ducum*, ed. Van Houts, 2, p. 284; 'tueque christianissime domui': Reg. Vat. 28, fol. 107v, no. 95 (3 May 1264); *Les Registres d'Urbain IV*, ed. Guiraud and Clémencet, 2, no. 809, p. 396.

14. 'discordias et dissensiones quae olim inter illustres Eboracensem et Lancastriae domos viguerant': *Memorials of King Henry VII*, ed. Gairdner, p. 396.

15. Hartman and DeBlasi, 'The Growth of Historical Method in Tang China', pp. 18, 21.

16. 'Ita Francorum regum secunda deficiente linea, regnum in tertiam translatum est': *Miracula sancti Genulfi*, 26, ed. Holder-Egger, p. 1213; this was copied in the early twelfth century by Hugh of Fleury, *Modernorum Francorum regum actus*, 7, ed. Waitz, p. 384 (the manuscript of the *Miracula sancti Genulfi* was at Fleury).

17. 'tercia familia regum Francie': *Gesta Normannorum Ducum*, 8. 26, ed. Van Houts, 2, p. 244 (Robert of Torigny).

18. 'pour ce que III generacions ont esté des rois de France': *Les Grandes chroniques de France*, Prologue, ed. Viard, 1 (SHF 395), p. 3.

19. *Calendar of the Liberate Rolls (1226–72)*, 1, p. 53.

20. Patlagean, 'Les débuts d'une aristocratie byzantine et le témoinage de l'historiographie: système des noms et liens de parenté aux IXe–Xe siècles'; for the appearance of such names on seals, and a hypothesis about the reasons, see Stephenson, 'A Development in Nomenclature on the Seals of the Byzantine Provincial Aristocracy in the Late Tenth Century'.

21. *Theophanes continuatus*, 6. 27, ed. Bekker, p. 374; Skylitzes, *Synopsis historiarum*, ed. Thurn, p. 189.

22. *Catalogue of the Byzantine Coins in the Dumbarton Oaks Collection and in the Whittemore Collection*, 3. 1, ed. Bellinger et al., p. 180.

23. Zacos and Veglery, *Byzantine Lead Seals*, 1. 1, no. 103, p. 92; Garland, *Byzantine Empresses: Women and Power in Byzantium, AD 527–1204*, p. 286 n. 111.

24. Kazhdan, 'The Formation of Byzantine Family Names in the Ninth and Tenth Centuries', p. 90.

25. 'Most royal surnames derive from a tenth-century ancestor': Byrne, 'A Note on the Emergence of Irish Surnames', p. xxxiv.

26. Bede, *Historia ecclesiastica gentis Anglorum*, 2. 5, ed. Colgrave and Mynors, p. 150.

27. 'De genealogia qui vocantur Hosi, Drazza, Fagana, Hahilinga, Anniona, isti sunt quasi primi post Agilolfingos qui sunt de genere ducali': *Lex Baiwariorum*, 3. 1, ed. Schwind, pp. 312–13; 'quidam ex procerebus de gente nobile Ayglolfingam nomen

Chrodoaldus': Fredegar, *Chronica*, 4. 52, ed. Krusch, p. 146, ed. Wallace-Hadrill, p. 42.

28. 'clarissimo genere Inmedingorum oriundus': Adam of Bremen, *Gesta Hammaburgensis ecclesiae pontificum*, 2. 47 (45), ed. Schmeidler, p. 108. For nobles named Immed, see, for example, Widukind of Corvey, *Res gestae saxonicae*, 1. 31; 3. 28, ed. Hirsch and Lohmann, pp. 44, 117 (in both cases there are manuscripts having 'Inm-' rather than 'Imm-').

29. Ptolemy of Lucca, *Annales*, ed. Schmeidler, pp. 71, 76, 97, 98.

30. 'Meroveus, a quo omnes post eum reges Merovingi vocati sunt. Eodem modo et filii regum Anglorum a patribus patronimica sumpserunt, ut filius Edgari Edgaring, filius Edmundi Edmunding vocentur': William of Malmesbury, *Gesta regum Anglorum*, 1. 68, ed. Mynors et al., p. 98.

31. *Sermo in tumulatione Sanctorum Quintini, Victorici, Cassiani*, ed. Holder-Egger, p. 271; *Miracula sancti Benedicti*, 3. 8 (Aimoin of Fleury), ed. de Certain, p. 148.

32. *Genealogia ducum Brabantiae ampliata*, ed. Heller, p. 395.

33. *Chronicon Werumensium: Continuatio* (a. 1276–1280), ed. Weiland, pp. 565, 568; for a detailed discussion of the Frisian *cognationes* as *Fehdeverbände*, see Schmidt, 'Eine Friesische Fehde: Die "Menalda-Fehde" von 1295'.

34. 'Nunc de eodem castro … et de principibus, qui inde nomen traxerunt et adhuc habent, aliqua compendiose dicamus … partem unam principes, qui et postea de Dachawe castro dicti sunt possederant … Aliam partem comites de Grube habebant, qui et postea de castro Valeie nuncupati sunt': Conrad of Scheyern, *Chronicon Schirense*, 15, 17, ed. Jaffé, pp. 620–1.

35. 'der ward genannt Kung Lassla, das tet ettleichen zaren vnd maynten, man salt in Kung Peter haben genant, darumb daz er den nam mit im pracht hiet. So maynaten ettlich, man solt in Kung Albrecht haben gehaissen durch seins vaters willen, der so gar ain frumer Kunig ist gewesen. Aber meiner frau gnad het das verhaissen got und dem heiligen Kung sand Lassla': Helene Kottannerin, *Die Denkwürdigkeiten der Helene Kottannerin (1439–1440)*, ed. Mollay, p. 21.

36. For a good case-study of such names, see Le Jan, *Famille et pouvoir dans le monde franc (VIIe–Xe siècle): essai d'anthropologie sociale*, pp. 179–223.

37. Karl Schmid, the great historian of medieval German aristocratic families, calls such labels '*Hilfsnamen*': 'Zur Problematik von Familie, Sippe und Geschlecht, Haus und Dynastie beim mittelalterlichen Adel', p. 13 (repr. in Schmid, *Gebetsgedenken und adliges Selbstverständnis im Mittelalter*, p. 195).

38. 'In comitatu Balduwini eiusque familia id multis iam seculis servabatur quasi sancitum lege perpetua, ut unus filiorum, qui patri potissimum placuisset, nomen patris acciperet et tocius Flandriae principatum solus hereditaria successione optineret': Lampert of Hersfeld, *Annales*, s.a. 1071, ed. Holder-Egger, p. 121.

39. Richard, *Histoire des comtes de Poitou*, 1, pp. 237–40, 266–7.

40. *Liber feudorum maior*, ed. Miquel Rosell, 1, no. 494, p. 533: 'filio suo maiori Raimundo'; ibid., p. 24, no. 17: 'dilecto filio meo Ildefonso … qui in testamento eiusdem viri mei vocaris [sic] R(aimundus)'.

41. Curiously, Alfonso/Raymond's younger brother, who bore the name Peter, a royal name in Aragon and a version of Petronilla's, subsequently seized the opportunity to change his name to Raymond Berengar when he obtained the county of Provence, whose rulers had often borne that name. In his will of 1162, Raymond Berengar refers to 'alio filio suo Petro', granting him the county of Cerdaña and the *senioraticum* of Carcasonne: *Liber feudorum maior*, ed. Miquel Rosell, 1, no. 494, p. 533. This was Raymond Berengar IV (III), count of Provence 1168/73–81.

42. 'i Filippi e i Luigi/ per cui novellamente è Francia retta': Dante, *Purgatorio*, 20, lines 50–1, ed. Petrocchi, 3, p. 336.

43. 'Hec stirps francigenam regni dum strinxit habenam Rome sceptrigenos Karolos dedit ac Ludovicos': Schmid, 'Ein verlorenes *Stemma Regum Franciae*', p. 217.

44. Althoff, *Family, Friends and Followers*, p. 18; Werner, 'Die Nachkommen Karls des Grossen', p. 418.

45. Notker Balbulus, *Gesta Karoli magni imperatoris*, 2. 11, 14, ed. Haefele, pp. 68, 78.

46. 'Duae ... famosae familiae ... una Heinricorum de Gueibelinga, alia Gwelforum de Aldorfo': Otto of Freising, *Gesta Friderici I imperatoris*, 2. 2, ed. Waitz and von Simson, p. 103.

47. 'At ipse potius gloriabatur se de regia stirpe Waiblingensium progenitum fuisse, quos constat de duplici regia prosapia processisse, videlicet Clodoveorum ... et Carolorum': Burchard of Ursberg, *Chronicon*, ed. Holder-Egger and von Simson, pp. 24–5; see the comments of Schmid, '"De regia stirpe Waiblingensium". Bemerkungen zum Selbstverständnis der Staufer'.

48. Attested as early as the twelfth century: Walter Map, *De nugis curialium*, 5. 3, ed. James et al., p. 412.

49. Nithard, *Historiarum libri IIII*, 4.5, ed. Müller, p. 48.

50. 'Nunc ad principes nostri temporibus stilum vertamus quia difficile et superfluum videtur singulorum scribere facta. Nam ut supra diximus, non duo vel tres, sed plurimi erant principes Schyrenses dicti, qui fere omnes, exceptis paucis, duobus nominibus vocati sunt, videlicet Otto et Ekkehardus': Conrad of Scheyern, *Chronicon Schirense*, 18, ed. Jaffé, p. 621.

51. 'Et hoc inquam, ne Karolorum aliorumque frequens in utroque opere repetitio, operis utriusque ordinem turbet. Ubi enim rerum ordo non advertitur, tanto nitentem error confundit, quanto a serie ordinis errantem seducit. Unde cum hic atque illic sepe Karoli, sepe Ludouici notę offeruntur pro tempore auctorum prudens lector reges ęquivocos pernotabit': Richer of Saint-Rémi, *Historiae*, Prologue, ed. Hoffmann, p. 35 (Richer is referring here to his use of the earlier history of Hincmar); this did not prevent him confusing the relationship between Carlomann and Charles the Simple (see p. 339).

52. 'Genealogias quoque regum, quae propter similitudines nominum valde confusae erant, quanta potui diligentia distinxi, unumquemque vel patris nomine, vel Senioris Juniorisve appellatione ab altero distinguens, quemadmodum diligens lector in suis animadvertere potest locis': Aimoin of Fleury, *Historia Francorum*, Preface, PL 139: 628; RHF 3, p. 22.

53. Lehmann, 'Mittelalterliche Beinamen und Ehrentitel'; Bührer, 'Studien zu den Beinamen mittelalterlicher Herrscher'; Morby, 'The Sobriquets of Medieval European Princes'; Schieffer, 'Ludwig "der Fromme"'. Zur Entstehung eines karolingischen Herrscherbeinamens'; Brühl, 'Herrscherbeinamen', in *Deutschland-Frankreich: die Geburt zweier Völker*, pp. 142–4.

54. For example, Ademar of Chabannes, *Chronicon*, 3. 22, 30 (β and γ versions), ed. Bourgain, pp. 143, 150.

55. Rigord, *Gesta Philippi Augusti*, 41, ed. Carpentier et al., pp. 202–10; for the date of composition, see the editorial comment on p. 75; Louis VII is also called 'Louis the Pious' in the *Historia Francorum usque ad annum 1214*, ed. Molinier, p. 395, and in the *Chronique des rois de France*, ed. Delisle, p. 754 (the 'Anonymous of Béthune'), which, for Louis' reign, is based on it; it is also his style in Alberic of Trois-fontaines, *Chronica*, ed. Scheffer-Boichorst, pp. 848, 854, 856.

56. *Les Registres de Philippe Auguste I: Texte*, ed. Baldwin, pp. 550–1, 553.

57. 'qui Balbus appellabatur': Regino of Prüm, *Chronicon*, s.a. 878, ed. Kurze, p. 114.

58. Byrne, *Irish Kings and High Kings*, p. 221.

59. See Lot, 'Origine et signification du mot "Carolingien"'.

60. Fulcher of Chartres, *Historia Hierosolymitana*, 1. 30 (variant reading), ed. Hagenmeyer, p. 307.

61. West, *The East Face of Helicon: West Asiatic Elements in Greek Poetry and Myth*, pp. 29–30; *Iliad*, 18. 487; *Odyssey*, 5. 273; Ælfric, *De temporibus anni*, 9. 6, ed. Henel, p. 68; Trevisa, *On the Properties of Things*, 8. 23, ed. Seymour et al., 1, p. 502; the Ælfric reference, 'Carles wæn', may mean 'churl's wagon' but Trevisa's 'Cherlemaynes Wayne' is explicit.

62. Nonn, 'Karl Martell: Name und Beiname'.

63. Boutet, 'Bâtardise et sexualité dans l'image littéraire de la royauté (XIIe–XIIIe siècles)', p. 60.

64. 'Ultimus vero Karolorum apud orientales Francos imperantium': Widukind of Corvey, *Res gestae saxonicae*, 1. 16, ed. Hirsch and Lohmann, p. 25.

65. E.g. 'Karolorum stirpe': Ekkehard of Aura, *Chronicon universale*, s.a. 919, ed. Waitz, p. 175 (Frutolf); 'de antiquo et glorioso Karolorum sanguine': Otto of Freising, *Chronica sive Historia de duabus civitatibus*, 6. 28, ed. Hofmeister, p. 291.

66. 'Karlensium regia ... prosapia': *Chronicon Vedastinum*, ed. Waitz, p. 692; 'Hic Merovingorum regno in Hilderico finito, Karolingorum a Pippino ... inicium sumpsit': *Annales sancti Trudberti*, s.a. 753, ed. Pertz, p. 285; in the *Gesta episcoporum Cameracensium* (an original composition of 1025) both Lothar (d. 986) and Robert II (d. 1031) are 'rex Karlensium', and Gerard, bishop of Cambrai (1012–51), springs from 'non infimis parentibus Lothariensium atque Karlensium': 1. 97, 105, 114; 3. 1, ed. Bethmann, pp. 440, 444, 452, 465.

67. 'Dicunt preterea aliud ibidem esse vulgare propheticum, quod de Karlingis, id est de stirpe regis Karoli et de domo regum Francie, imperator suscitabitur Karolus nomine, qui erit princeps et monarcha totius Europe et reformabit ecclesiam et imperium, sed post illum nunquam alius imperabit': Alexander von Roes, *Memoriale*, 30, ed. Grundmann and Heimpel, pp. 136–7.

68. For a long and learned, if not entirely conclusive, discussion of the introduction of the unprecedented name Philip into the Capetian dynasty in the person of Philip I (1060–1108), see Dunbabin, 'What's in a Name? Philip, King of France'.

69. 'quae peperit ei ... primogenitum, patris sui nomine appellans Wirinharium': Thietmar of Merseburg, *Chronicon*, 4. 39, ed. Holtzmann, p. 176.

70. The chain runs: Matilda, wife of Henry I; Gerberga, her daughter, wife of Louis IV of France; Matilda, her daughter, second wife of Conrad, king of Burgundy; Gerberga, her daughter, wife of Hermann (II), duke of Swabia; Matilda of Swabia, her daughter. See Giesebrecht, *Geschichte der deutschen Kaiserzeit*, 2, p. 715, a letter of Siegfried of Gorze from 1043, arguing from the 'feminarum ... equivocatio' that the second Gerberga could not be a child of King Conrad's first marriage but must be a child of Matilda.

71. 'Philippum clericum': Gislebert of Mons, *Chronicon Hanoniense*, 54, ed. Vanderkindere, p. 94.

72. Alberic of Trois-fontaines, *Chronica*, ed. Scheffer-Boichorst, pp. 919, 930; *Abbreviationes gestorum Franciae regum*, RHF 17, p. 433; *Genealogia regum Franciae tertiae stirpis*, RHF 17, p. 434; 'Dagobertum, id est Philippum': *Chronicon Turonense magnum* (excerpts), RHF 18, p. 317. His birth, as 'Philip', on 20 February 1222 is recorded in 'Annales de Saint-Denis généralement connues sous le titre de Chronicon Sancti Dionysii ad Cyclos Paschales', ed. Berger, p. 280 (s.a. 1221, with Easter reckoning). Berger, *Histoire de Blanche de Castille, reine de France*, p. 207, expresses doubts about the date given for his death, because of mention of a *dominus Dagobertus* in the royal household accounts for 1234 (RHF 21, p. 240), but this is simply a reference to a *capellanus qui fuit ad dominum Dagobertem*. An earlier son of Louis, also called Philip, was born in September 1209 and died in 1218 or 1219: *Les Registres de Philippe Auguste I: Texte*, ed. Baldwin, p. 545; Baldwin, *The Government of Philip Augustus*, pp. 270, 536 n. 53. After he succeeded to the throne Louis endowed a chantry for this child: Dubois, *Historia ecclesiae Parisiensis*, 2, p. 309.

73. *Chronicon Moissiacense*, s.a. 781, ed. Pertz, p. 297; *Annales regni Francorum*, s.a. 781, ed. Kurze, p. 57.

74. 'gibbo deformis': Einhard, *Vita Karoli Magni*, 20, ed. Holder-Egger, p. 25; although one source does term him 'rex': Airlie, 'Earthly and Heavenly Networks in a World in Flux: Carolingian Family Identities and the Prague Sacramentary'.

75. Baaken, 'Die Altersfolge der Söhne Friedrich Barbarossas und die Königserhebung Heinrichs VI', explores the complex evidence.

76. 'misitque me meus pater iam dictus ad dictum regem Francie, me existente in septimo anno puericie mee, fecitque me dictus rex Francorum per pontificem confirmari et imposuit michi nomen suum equivocum, videlicet Karolus, et dedit michi in uxorem filiam Karoli, patrui sui, nomine Margaretam, dictam Blancza': Charles IV, *Karoli IV Imperatoris Romanorum Vita ab eo ipso conscripta*, 3, ed. Nagy and Schaer, p. 22.

77. 'quod ipse sit ita katholicus, ita devotus, ita ecclesie munificus, non solum sibi debetur ex successione, quia a sanctis parentibus et consimilia facientibus noscitur descendisse, sed etiam debetur sibi ex nomine, quia Karolus. Quis autem magis devotus et munificus

ecclesie quam Karolus Magnus fuit?': *Constitutiones et acta publica imperatorum et regum*, 8, no. 100, p. 146; see the discussion in Schneider, 'Karolus, qui et Wenceslaus'.

78. Beneš Krabice of Weitmile, *Cronica ecclesiae Pragensis*, pp. 517, 527.

79. 'de consensu statuum vocatus est abhinc rex Robertus tercius': Bower, *Scotichronicon*, 15. 1, ed. Watt et al., 8, p. 2, and note on p. 149.

80. 'Nomen, ut auguror, propterea mutarunt quia Iohannes infaustos reges suspicabantur cum ad paucos ante dies Iohannem Francum ab Anglis captum viderunt': Mair, *Historia Maioris Britanniae*, 6, c. 6, fol. 122.

81. For example, 'Sed quoniam Ioannes inauspicatum videbatur nomen propter Ioannem regem Franciae captum, commutato vocabulo Robertus appellatus est, patris nomen accipiens': Boece, *Scotorum Historia*, 16, fol. 347 ('an vnchancy name' in John Bellenden's translation of 1531: *Chronicles of Scotland*, 2, p. 354).

82. Constable, 'The Numbering of the Crusades'.

83. For the following see Rabikauskas, 'Papstname und Ordnungszahl. Über die Anfänge des Brauches, gleichnamige Päpste durch eine Ordnungszahl zu unterscheiden'.

84. *Liber pontificalis*, ed. Duchesne, 1, pp. 359, 363.

85. 'Gregorium a primo secundum et novissimo priorem ... (qui et vulgarica Romanorum lingua dicitur iunior); defuncto ... Gregorio secundo ... et Gregorio iuniore ... praesidente; Gregorio iuniore secundo; a ... Gregorio iuniore, a primo secundo, et a Gregorio a secundo iuniore, cum primo tertio': Willibald, *Vita Bonifatii*, 5–8, ed. Levison, pp. 21, 34, 36, 42.

86. Hartmann, 'Über die Entwicklung der Rota'.

87. Erben et al., *Urkundenlehre*, pp. 312–13 and 317–18.

88. E.g. *Recueil des actes des ducs de Normandie (911–1066)*, ed. Fauroux, nos. 34, 36, 44, 53, 55, 93, pp. 131, 141, 151, 171, 176, 244, all from the period 1017–40.

89. Crusafont, Balaguer and Grierson, *Medieval European Coinage, 6: The Iberian Peninsula*, pp. xxviii–xxix.

90. *Philippi regis Diplomata*, ed. Rzihacek and Spreitzer, pp. lxxvii–lxxviii.

91. Otto of Freising, *Chronica sive Historia de duabus civitatibus*, 6. 22, ed. Hofmeister, p. 285; cf. ibid., 6. 13, p. 273, where the Italian emperors of the tenth century '*confuse regnarunt*'; and the catalogue of emperors at the end of Book 7, pp. 382–3.

92. And even then, their official title was *imperator electus*.

93. 'Hainricus huius nominis sextus vel secundum cronicam Romanorum quintus – ipsi namque Hainricum primum, patrem Ottonis primi, non connumerant in katalogo imperatorum': Burchard of Ursberg, *Chronicon*, ed. Holder-Egger and von Simson, p. 70.

94. 'Heinrico regi, filio Heinrici imperatoris, ... totius regni Teutonicorum et Italie, gubernacula contradico': Gregory VII, *Registrum*, 3. 10a, ed. Caspar, 1, p. 270.

95. Otto of Freising calls the same rulers Henry III, Henry IV and Henry V in the body of his text but Henry II, Henry III and Henry IV in the catalogue of emperors appended to Book 7: Otto of Freising, *Chronica sive Historia de duabus civitatibus*, 6. 32, 34; 7. 13, ed. Hofmeister, pp. 297, 302, 324, 384–5.

96. 'anno autem domni Henrici tertii regis imperatoris autem secundi ... regni quidem XVII, imperii vero VIIII': *Heinrici III. Diplomata*, ed. Bresslau and Kehr, no. 351, p. 478.

97. The first occurrence is in the records of the Parliament of December 1332: *Parliament Rolls of Medieval England*, ed. Given-Wilson, 4, p. 182. A very early example of the style in historical writing is found in Nicholas Trevet's Anglo-Norman chronicle: 'Edward le second apres le conquest de William Bastard', Cambridge, Trinity College, MS O. 4. 32, fol. 100; Leiden, Universiteitsbibliotheek, MS VG G F 6, fol. 91. This work was written for Mary, daughter of Edward I, who died in 1332, but since it says John XXII (1316–34) held the papacy for 19 years, Nicholas must have continued it or revised it: *Calendar of the Close Rolls Preserved in the Public Record Office, Edward III, A. D. 1330–1333*, p. 511; Cambridge, Trinity College, MS O. 4. 32, fol. 100v; Leiden, Universiteitsbibliotheek, MS VG G F 6, fol. 91v.

98. 'Anno Domini milllesimo CCC^{mo}XXVII . . . et regis Edwardi tertii a conquaestu primo – et nota quod hoc verbum, "a conquaestu", a quibusdam mundi sapientibus est inventum ad denotandum tertium Edwardum, eo quod duo ejusdem nominis eum praecesserant post Willelmum conquaestorem, scilicet avus suus et pater; quorum primus vocabatur Edwardus de Wyntonia, secundus de Carnervan, a locis in quibus nati fuerunt': Murimuth, *Continuatio chronicarum*, ed. Thompson, p. 55. See Ormrod, *Edward III*, p. 4.

99. 'Hec prophetia Merlini Silvestris Anglorum Eadwardo regi sancto nominis huius tercio revelata fuit': BL, MS Cotton Faustina A VIII, fol. 116 (the prophecy of the green tree, discussed pp. 356–7); 'seneschallus regis Henrici tercii patris inclite memorie domini Edwardi quarti regis Anglorum': BAV, MS Vat. lat. 4015, fol. 76 (testimony in the canonization process of Thomas de Cantilupe given on 29 August 1307, less than 8 weeks after Edward's death); 'transitu magni regis Edwardi quarti': *Commendatio lamentabilis in transitu magni regis Edwardi*, ed. Stubbs, p. 3.

100. Melville, 'Geschichte in graphischer Gestalt. Untersuchungen zu einem spätmittelalterlichen Darstellungsprinzip', pp. 88–90, citing BAV, MS Reg. lat. 518, fols. 75v–78v.

101. *Corpus juris confoederationis Germanicae*, ed. Meyer, pp. 90–2; though the term *Heiliges römisches Reich deutscher Nation* had been current for three centuries by that time.

102. 'dei gratia Latinitatis Iherosolimorum rex': *Die Urkunden der lateinischen Könige von Jerusalem*, ed. Mayer, 1, no. 64, p. 197 (1115).

103. *Die Urkunden der lateinischen Könige von Jerusalem*, ed. Mayer, 1, p. 46, and passim; the kings of Cyprus recommenced the practice when they acquired the title king of Jerusalem in 1269, although their system of numbering seems to have been eccentric!

104. BL, MS Royal 14 C VII, fols. 8v–9 (the *Historia Anglorum*); the form *post conquisiconem eius* is unusual, or a mistake.

105. See, for example, *Constitutiones et acta publica imperatorum et regum*, 11, ed. Schwalm, for documents of the emperor Charles IV from 1354–6; Bernard Gui, *Reges Francorum*, *Arbor genealogiae regum Francorum*, CCCC 45, fols. 29, 47, for 'Charles IV' of France.

106. 'ultimus fuit Karolorum': *Quedam exceptiones de hystoria Normannorum et Anglorum*, 1, ed. Van Houts, p. 293.

107. This observation was the starting point for the investigations of Lévy, *Louis I, II, III . . . XIV . . . : l'étonnante histoire de la numérotation des rois de France*, the work of an amateur historian but full of insight.

108. See, for example, the list of emperors in Otto of Freising, *Chronica sive Historia de duabus civitatibus*, appendix to Book 7, ed. Hofmeister, pp. 381–2; Regino of Prüm calls Charles the Fat 'Carolus imperator, tertius huius nominis et dignitatis', *Chronicon*, s.a. 888, ed. Kurze, p. 128.

109. For the following, see Gimeno Casalduero, 'Sobre las numeraciones de los reyes de Castilla'.

9 SAINTS, IMAGES, HERALDRY, FAMILY TREES

1. Dagron, *Emperor and Priest: The Imperial Office in Byzantium*, p. 203.

2. Phillips, *Edward II*, pp. 604–5; for the book of Edward's miracles, *Issues of the Exchequer, Being a Collection of Payments Made Out of His Majesty's Revenue from King Henry III to King Henry VI*, ed. Devon, p. 259; Wolffe, *Henry VI*, pp. 351–8; *Henrici VI Angliae regis miracula postuma*, ed. Grosjean.

3. Folz, *Les saints rois du moyen âge en Occident (VIe–XIIIe s.)*, pp. 23–67; Vauchez, *Sainthood in the Late Middle Ages*, pp. 158–67.

4. Folz, *Les saintes reines du Moyen Age en Occident*.

5. 'De eius genealogia et stirpis magnificentia': *Vita et miracula sanctae Kyngae ducissae Cracoviensis*, 1, ed. Kętrzyński, p. 683. See, in general, Klaniczay, *Holy Rulers and Blessed Princesses: Dynastic Cults in Medieval Central Europe*.

6. Ibid., pp. 304–9.

7. Grandeau, 'Les enfants de Charles VI. Essai sur la vie privée des princes et des princesses de la maison de France à la fin du Moyen Âge', p. 825.

8. 'exultationis praerogativa vobis attribuitur in communione generis et germine nativae propagationis'; 'nepos et heres legitimus sanctissimi confessoris Edwardi regis Angliae, jure hereditario Anglici regni, per lineas rectas et directas successivae generationis in vos devoluto, vos sceptrigeros effecisset, nisi Normannorum violenta direptio, Deo permittente, usque ad tempus praefinitum praepedisset. Nec solum in illo glorioso stemmate regum Anglicorum in divitiis et gloria in regno potentissimi praefulserunt, sed etiam in sanctitate et justitia magna Deo placentes, in vita et post mortem miraculis multimodis magnifice claruerunt. A sancto namque rege Adwolfo, qui totam Angliam decimans, decimam Deo et Ecclesiae consecravit, novem numerantur reges sancti, quorum posterior par vel praestantior in Christiana religione micuisse dignoscitur: in decimo vero S. Edwardo cunctorum praedecessorum sanctitas quasi transfusa confluxit, et sic ex illo, tamquam fonte lucidissimo, vitae religiosæ rivulus in S. Margaritam proneptem ejus, et ex illa in filium suum regem David avum vestrum, et ex eo in Malcolmum regem fratrem vestrum emanavit': Jocelin of Furness, *Vita sancti Walthenis abbatis*, pp. 248–9.

9. In general on this topic, Holladay, *Genealogy and the Politics of Representation in the High and Late Middle Ages*.

10. Lammers, 'Ein karolingisches Bildprogramm in der Aula Regia von Ingelheim'; the verses of Ermoldus Nigellus that describe the pictures can be found, with English translation, in Godman (ed.), *Poetry of the Carolingian Renaissance*, pp. 254–5.

11. 'Childeric troisiesme, frere de Thedoric, regna neufs ans, et mourut sans hoirs. Pepin fils de Charles Martel de la lignee de Clotaire second, fut esleu Roy': Corrozet, *Les antiquitez, histoires, croniques et singularitez de la grande et excellente cite de Paris*, fol. 99.

12. Ibid., fol. 99v.

13. Bennert, 'Art et propagande politique sous Philippe IV le Bel: le cycle des rois de France dans la Grand'salle du palais de la Cité'; Holladay, 'Kings, Notaries, and Merchants: Audience and Image in the Grand'Salle of the Palace at Paris'; the sequence of statues was continued for later kings, down to the sixteenth century; there were eventually fifty-eight statues: Guerout, 'Le Palais de la Cité, des origines à 1417. Essai topographique et archéologique', 2, pp. 132–5.

14. 'ex ipsis ibi facere et formare decem et novem ymagines ab omni expedienti et necessario opere expeditas et quantoque potuerit et sciverit pulcriores, quarum octo representabunt effigies octo regum qui fuerunt unus post alium successive usque ad nostra tempora reges Aragonum et Barchinone comites inclusive, et cetere effigies illorum undecim qui fuerent tum comites Barchinone, titulum regium non habentes': *Documents per l'història de la cultura catalana mig-eval*, ed. Rubió i Lluc, 1, pp. 124–5, no. 112, from Archivo de la Corona de Aragón, Reg. 1. 305, fol. 92v.

15. The similarities between the two projects are pointed out by Žůrek, 'Godfrey of Viterbo and his Readers at the Court of Emperor Charles IV', p. 98.

16. Vienna, Österreichische Nationalbibliothek, MS 8330, fols. 6–59; also, copied from there, Prague, Archiv der Nationalgalerie, AA 2015, Codex Heidelbergensis.

17. *Genealogiae Karolorum: Commemoratio genealogiae Karoli imperatoris*, ed. Waitz; Oexle, 'Die Karolinger und die Stadt des heiligen Arnulf', pp. 252–62; see also pp. 339, 385.

18. The paintings are numbered 1 to 56 but that includes several of husbands and wives numbered separately.

19. *Catalogue of the Byzantine Coins in the Dumbarton Oaks Collection and in the Whittemore Collection*, 3. 1, ed. Bellinger, pp. 337–8, 340–1, 344 ('Class I').

20. Ibid., pp. 292–3, 300, 325–6, 328–33.

21. Dagron, *Emperor and Priest: The Imperial Office in Byzantium*, p. 32.

22. Clarke, 'The Wilton Diptych', p. 283.

23. D'azur, semé de fleurs-de-lys d'or, au lambel de gueules.

24. Mérindol, 'L'héraldique des princes angevins', pp. 281–6.

25. *Vita Edwardi Secundi*, ed. Denholm-Young, rev. Childs, pp. 232–4.

26. Ailes, 'Heraldry in Medieval England: Symbols of Politics and Propaganda', p. 88.

27. Costa-Gomes, 'Alfarrobeira: The Death of the Tyrant?', p. 157.

28. 'he gave them baners with the hole armys of Inglonde with owte any dyversyte': Gregory, *Chronicle of London*, ed. Gairdner, p. 208.

29. 'videntes quod parvam insulam Anglie magno regno Francie preiudicet honorandam': Geoffrey le Baker, *Chronicon*, ed. Thompson, pp. 66–7; Michael, "The Little Land of England is Preferred before the Great Kingdom of France": The Quartering of the Royal Arms by Edward III'; Ailes, 'Heraldry in Medieval England: Symbols of Politics and Propaganda', pp. 88–94; Hinkle, *The Fleurs de Lis of the Kings of France, 1285–1488*.

30. Morganstern, *Gothic Tombs of Kinship in France, the Low Countries, and England*, pp. 95–102 and Appendix VI, pp. 179–85, 'The Program of the Tomb of Philippa of Hainault, Queen of England (d. 1369)'; Fehrmann, *Grab und Krone: Königsgrabmäler im mittelalterlichen England und die posthume Selbstdarstellung der Lancaster*, pp. 60–6.

31. Wiener, *Das Grabmal des Johann von Brienne: Kaiser von Konstantinopel und König von Jerusalem*.

32. Or a lion rampant gules armed and langued azure within a double tressure flory-counter-flory of the second.

33. Azure, three open crowns or; Or, semé of hearts gules, three lions passant guardant in pale azure, crowned or; Gules, a lion rampant or, holding a long-handled axe argent; Azure a wyvern or.

34. Gules, two batons crossed in saltire enfiled by a twisted wreath or; Or, two lions passant guardant in pale azure.

35. Or, two bars gules.

36. Thompson and Campbell, *Hugo van der Goes and the Trinity Panels in Edinburgh*, p. 32; alternative versions of the arms exist.

37. For example, in the fifteenth-century Wernigeroder (Schaffhausensches) Wappenbuch (Bayerische Staatsbibliothek, Cod. icon. 308 n), fols. 1v–2 (available online).

38. Clarke, 'The Wilton Diptych', p. 284.

39. See, for example, Wyss, 'Die neun Helden: eine ikonographische Studie', pp. 98–102.

40. General bibliography on medieval family trees in graphic form can be approached through Melville, 'Geschichte in graphischer Gestalt. Untersuchungen zu einem spätmittelalterlichen Darstellungsprinzip'; Melville, 'Vorfahren und Vorgänger. Spätmittelalterliche Genealogien als dynastische Legitimation zur Herrschaft'; Schmid, 'Ein verlorenes *Stemma Regum Franciae*'; Klapisch-Zuber, *L'ombre des ancêtres: essai sur l'imaginaire médiéval de la parenté*; Norbye, 'Genealogies in Medieval France'; Laborderie, *Histoire, mémoire et pouvoir. Les généalogies en rouleau des rois d'Angleterre (1250–1422)*; Salonius and Worm (ed.), *The Tree: Symbol, Allegory, and Mnemonic Device in Medieval Art and Thought*; Norbye, '"Iste non ponitur in recta linea arboris genealogie." Graphische Darstellung und Legitimität in französischen Königsgenealogien'; Holladay, *Genealogy and the Politics of Representation in the High and Late Middle Ages*; Greer, 'All in the Family: Creating a Carolingian Genealogy in the Eleventh Century'.

41. Universitätsbibliothek Erlangen, MS 406; see Schmid, 'Ein verlorenes *Stemma Regum Franciae*', p. 218, with figure 7b (Plate XI).

42. See, for example, Sisam, 'Anglo-Saxon Royal Genealogies'; Duby, 'Remarques sur la littérature généalogique en France aux XIe et XIIe siècles'; Genicot, *Les généalogies*; Dumville, 'Kingship, Genealogies and Regnal Lists'; Croenen, 'Princely and Noble Genealogies, Twelfth to Fourteenth Century: Form and Function'; Butaud and Piétri, *Les Enjeux de la généalogie (XIIe–XVIIIe s.): pouvoir et identité*; Radulescu and Kennedy, eds., *Broken Lines: Genealogical Literature in Late-Medieval Britain and France*.

43. *Genealogiae Karolorum: Commemoratio genealogiae Karoli imperatoris*, ed. Waitz; 'die erste Herrschergenealogie des christlichen Mittelalters': Oexle, 'Die Karolinger und die

Stadt des heiligen Arnulf', p. 252. Helmut Reimitz seems more justified in calling it the 'älteste überlieferte Karolingergenealogie': Reimitz, 'Anleitung zur Interpretation: Schrift und Genealogie in der Karolingerzeit', p. 170.

44. Ó Corráin, 'Creating the Past: The Early Irish Genealogical Tradition', p. 180; for a guide to this material and a survey of the state of scholarship, see Ó Muraílele, 'The Irish Genealogies: An Overview and Some Desiderata'.

45. Ó Corráin, 'Creating the Past: The Early Irish Genealogical Tradition', p. 190; for the date of the text (*Urcuilte Brethemain*), Kelly, *A Guide to Early Irish Law*, p. 250.

46. They are in BnF, MS lat. 9376 (a miscellany), fols. 1–12v (which is available online) and edited by Waitz as *Genealogiae scriptoris Fusniacensis*. There is an extensive discussion in Guenée, 'Les généalogies entre l'histoire et la politique: la fierté d'être Capétien, en France, au Moyen Âge'.

47. 'Hugo Pius rex genuit Robertum regem et filiam Hadevidem nomine comitissam Hainonensium ... Hadevidis comitissa Hainonensium, soror Roberti regis, peperit Beatricem ... Prima filiarum predicte Ale ... Altera filia prime Ale ... Nunc ad Hugonem Magnum revertamur ... Nunc ad narrationem eorum quos superius obmisimus, liberorum scilicet Hadevidis comitisse Hainonensium ... ': BnF, MS lat. 9376, fols. 2v–5; *Genealogiae scriptoris Fusniacensis*, ed. Waitz, pp. 252–3.

48. As in BnF, MS fr. 13565, pp. 201–3, the so-called *Récit d'un ménestrel d'Alphonse de Poitiers* of 1250–70.

49. Berlin, Staatsbibliothek, MS lat. fol. 295, fol. 80v (Ekkehard of Aura, *Chronicon*); the genealogies of the Saxon and Salian kings on the following pages use architectural elements too, but not to the same degree.

50. Schadt, *Die Darstellungen der Arbores consanguinitatis und der Arbores affinitatis: Bildschemata in juristischen Handschriften*; Klapisch-Zuber, *L'ombre des ancêtres: essai sur l'imaginaire médiéval de la parenté*, pp. 61–7, 75–82; Williams, *The Illustrated Beatus: A Corpus of the Illustrations of the Commentary on the Apocalypse*, passim, with a list of the manuscripts which have these diagrams at 1, pp. 179–80.

51. BAV, MS Reg. lat. 339, fol. 7 (olim fol. 32); *Genealogiae Karolorum*, VII, ed. Waitz.

52. 'unusquisque suam genealogiam cum testibus et chartis, tum etiam ex recitatione maiorum scire laborat': Gratian, *Decretum*, 2. 35. 6, ed. Friedberg, col. 1278; *Decretales Gregorii IX*, 4 .18. 3, ed. Friedberg, cols. 718–19; this is attributed both to Celestine II (1142–3) and Clement III (1187–91).

53. 'prae manibus habemus scriptam genealogiam, quam scribi fecerunt nobiles viri de eadem tribu progeniti': Ivo of Chartres, *Epistolae* 261, PL 162: 265–6.

54. Wibald of Stablo, *Das Briefbuch Abt Wibalds von Stablo und Corvey*, ed. Hartmann, 3, no. 385 (J408), pp. 812–13; Hlawitschka, 'Weshalb war die Auflösung der Ehe Friedrich Barbarossas und Adelas von Vohburg möglich?', doubts that Wibald's chart was used for this purpose.

55. 'figuram quandam facere curavimus ... hanc ... regi ostendite ... cum ibi parentum suorum nomina invenerit': ed. Giesebrecht, *Geschichte der deutschen Kaiserzeit*, 2, p. 716; see also pp. 30–1.

56. Gädeke, *Zeugnisse Bildlicher Darstellung der Nachkommenschaft Heinrichs I*.

57. As argued by Gautier, 'Aux origines du dessin généalogique en France: l'exemple de l'abbaye Saint-Aubin d'Angers (XIe–XIIe siècle)', pp. 19–28. These family trees are to be found in BAV, MS Reg. lat. 1283A, fol. 65v, and are reproduced in Gautier's article at p. 20. They were first published by Poupardin, 'Généalogies Angevines du XIe siècle'.

58. Munich, Bayerische Staatsbibliothek, clm 29880/6 (the 'Bamberger Tafel'); see Gädeke, *Zeugnisse Bildlicher Darstellung der Nachkommenschaft Heinrichs I*, pp. 221–5; Schmid, 'Ein verlorenes *Stemma Regum Franciae*'; Margue, 'Bamberger Tafel', pp. 216–18; Jackman, *Studia Luxembourgensia*.

59. 'post quem nullus prosapie istius regale solium ultra possedit'.

60. Binbas, 'Structure and Function of the Genealogical Tree in Islamic Historiography'.

61. *Liber aureus Prumiensis* (SB Trier, HS 1709), a sheet between fols. 73v and 74; Schmid, 'Ein verlorenes *Stemma Regum Franciae*', plate III.

62. 'qui pauperibus clericis consulens excogitavit arbores historiarum veteris Testamenti in pellibus depingere': Alberic of Trois-fontaines, *Chronica*, ed. Scheffer-Boichorst, p. 886.

63. See Panayotova, 'Peter of Poitiers' *Compendium in genealogia Christi*: The Early English Copies'.

64. Laborderie, 'Les généalogies des rois d'Angleterre sur rouleaux manuscrits (milieu XIIIe siècle–début XVe siècle): conception, diffusion et fonctions'; Laborderie, 'A New Pattern for English History: The First Genealogical Rolls of the Kings of England'; Laborderie, *Histoire, mémoire et pouvoir. Les généalogies en rouleau des rois d'Angleterre (1250–1422)*; Laborderie, 'The First Manuals of English History: Two Late Thirteenth-Century Genealogical Rolls of the Kings of England in the Royal Collection'.

65. Clanchy, *From Memory to Written Record: England 1066–1307*, pp. 137–46.

66. Laborderie, 'The First King of England? Egbert and the Foundations of Royal Legitimacy in Thirteenth-Century Historiography'.

67. *The Chaworth Roll: A Fourteenth-Century Genealogy of the Kings of England*, ed. Bovey.

68. 'Cestui Thomas fut counte de Lancastre e de Leycestre e seneschal d'Engletere. E si fut counte de Derby e par la contesse Aleyse, sa compaigne, il fut counte de Nicol e de Saleburi': ibid., p. 46.

69. Colker, 'The "Karolinus" of Egidius Parisiensis', with some of the additional narrative material edited on pp. 238–41 (from BnF, MS lat. 6191, fols. 46v–48v); the text is discussed by Lewis, 'Dynastic Structures and Capetian Throne-Right: The Views of Giles of Paris', with two photographs and some edited text (from both BnF, MS lat. 6191 and Bern, Burgerbibliothek, MS 22); in contrast to the traditional view, that the genealogical material was added between 1216 and 1223, Lewis thinks it was incorporated much earlier, in 1200 or 1201.

70. 'Ad habendam maiorem evidenciam in personis que in sequentibus describuntur, hoc secus in hoc loco dicimus quod reges Franc', quos specialius describimus, litteris rubricatis damus intelligi ab aliis discernendos. Reginas uxores eorum per lineas de incausto interius rubricatas. Alios reges sive eos qui de regum prosapia descenderunt nec reges fuerunt per simplices lineas de incausto seponimus. Porro eos qui reges fuerunt et imperatores tanquam digniores duplici colore adonio minioque distinguimus. Eos qui tantum imperatores fuerunt et non reges Franc' per litteras de adonio

depromimus. Reges Franc' bonos per lineas de minio adoniatas sed hoc secretius designamus': BnF, MS lat. 6191, fol. 46v; Lewis, 'Dynastic Structures and Capetian Throne-Right: The Views of Giles of Paris', pp. 228–9 n. 15, reading 'non secus'; translation of colour terms is notoriously tricky.

71. See, for example, Rouse and Rouse, 'Statim invenire: Schools, Preachers, and New Attitudes to the Page'; Clanchy, *From Memory to Written Record: England 1066–1307*, pp. 174–86.

72. 'sub quadam arboris formula': BnF, MS lat. 6184, fol. 1. On this text, see Lamarrigue, 'La rédaction d'un catalogue des rois de France. Guillaume de Nangis et Bernard Gui'; Guyot-Bachy, 'La *Chronique abrégée des rois de France* de Guillaume de Nangis: trois étapes de l'histoire d'un texte'; Guyot-Bachy, 'La *Chronique abrégée des rois de France* et les *Grandes chroniques de France*: concurrence ou complémentarité dans la construction d'une culture historique en France à la fin du Moyen Age?'.

73. BnF, MS lat. 6184, fol. 3 ('At the instigation of his mother, he killed Sigismund, king of the Burgundians, son of King Gundebald, along with his wife and children').

74. For the manuscripts of the *Arbor genealogiae* see Delisle, 'Notice sur les manuscrits de Bernard Gui', pp. 245–8; Kaeppeli, *Scriptores ordinis praedicatorum medii aevi*, 1, pp. 218–19, no. 620; for discussion, see Lamarrigue, 'La rédaction d'un catalogue des rois de France. Guillaume de Nangis et Bernard Gui'; Lamarrigue, *Bernard Gui, 1261–1331: un historien et sa méthode*, esp. pp. 52–3, 320, 439–47; Norbye, '*Arbor genealogiae*: Manifestations of the Tree in French Royal Genealogies', pp. 80–3; Norbye, '"Iste non ponitur in recta linea arboris genealogie." Graphische Darstellung und Legitimität in französischen Königsgenealogien', pp. 341–4. I cite from CCCC, MS 45, which is online.

75. Cf. the comment of Bernard Guenée: 'Une généalogie des rois de France a moins pour but de faire apparaître la famille des rois que leur succession': 'Les généalogies entre l'histoire et la politique: la fierté d'être Capétien, en France, au Moyen Âge', p. 466; for comment on the concept of *recta linea*, see also Schneidmüller, 'Constructing the Past by Means of the Present: Historiographical Foundation of Medieval Institutions, Dynasties, Peoples, and Communities', pp. 169–72.

76. Laborderie, 'The First Manuals of English History: Two Late Thirteenth-Century Genealogical Rolls of the Kings of England in the Royal Collection', p. 17.

77. 'iste Hugo recta linea generationis de Caroli et regum Francorum progenie non descendit … Carolus dux frater Lotharii regis Francorum, qui recta linea de prole regum descenderat': *Chronicon Turonense magnum*, ed. Martène and Durand, col. 993 (RHF, 10, p. 281).

78. 'Unde apparet liquide quod recta linea regum Franciae defecit, et in isto translatus est (*var.* translatum est regnum) ad lineam transversalem': *Continuatio Chronici Guillelmi de Nangiaco*, ed. Géraud, 2, p. 86.

79. *Les Grandes chroniques de France*, ed. Viard, 9, p. 75.

80. Bernard Gui, *Arbor genealogiae regum Francorum*, CCCC, MS 45, fol. 33v (cf. fol. 2).

81. 'ex eo quod pueris ipse puer capucia ludo auferre solebat': Bernard Gui, *Arbor genealogiae regum Francorum*, CCCC, MS 45, fol. 41v; this explanation first occurs in the supplementary notes that Giles of Paris added to his *Karolinus* in the years 1216–23: 'Pater huius

Hugo cognominatus est Chapeth eo quod puer\<is\> ipse puer capas suas ludo auferre soleb\<at\>': BnF, MS lat. 6191, fol. 48v; Colker 'The "Karolinus" of Egidius Parisiensis', p. 240; Lewis, 'Dynastic Structures and Capetian Throne-Right: The Views of Giles of Paris', plate opposite p. 241.

82. 'Iste Karlomannus in recta linea arboris depingitur cuius causam nescio nec inveni cum per ipsum regalis prosapie successio non fuerit continuata nisi forte quia tunc Karolus simplex legitimus sed parvulus non regnabat': Bernard Gui, *Reges Francorum, Arbor genealogiae regum Francorum*, CCCC, MS 45, fol. 40 (cf. fol. 13v).

83. Richer of Saint-Rémi, *Historiae*, 1. 4, ed. Hoffmann, p. 39.

84. BnF, MS lat. 6191, fol. 48; BnF, MS fr. 13565, p. 202, the former dating to 1216–23, the latter to 1250–70.

85. *Les Grandes chroniques de France*, ed. Viard, 4, pp. 300–3; Continuation of Aimoin, BnF, MS lat. 12711, fols. 161v–r.

86. Bernard Gui, *Reges Francorum* and *Arbor genealogiae regum Francorum*, CCCC, MS 45, fols. 6v, 36; see also pp. 318, 385.

10 RESPONSES TO DYNASTIC UNCERTAINTY

1. BL, MS Arundel 66 (available online); it is described and analysed in depth in Fronska, 'The Royal Image and Diplomacy: Henry VII's Book of Astrology (British Library, Arundel 66)'.

2. McCluskey, 'Gregory of Tours, Monastic Timekeeping, and Early Christian Attitudes to Astronomy', pp. 16–18; Dagron, 'Das Firmament soll christlich werden: Zu zwei Seefahrtskalendern des 10. Jahrhunderts'.

3. Smoller, 'The Medieval Debate about Astrology', in *History, Prophecy, and the Stars: The Christian Astrology of Pierre d'Ailly, 1350–1420*, pp. 25–42, provides a summary; for Byzantium see Magdalino, *L'orthodoxie des astrologues: la science entre le dogme et la divination à Byzance, VIIe–XIVe siècle*; Magdalino, 'Astrology'.

4. Anna Comnena, *Alexias*, 6. 7. 5, ed. Reinsch and Kambylis, p. 182.

5. John, Bishop of Nikiu, *Chronicle*, 95. 18–19, tr. Charles, pp. 153–4.

6. ψευδοπροφήτην καὶ ἀστρονόμον: Theophanes, *Chronographia*, AM 6284 (AD 792), ed. de Boor, 1, p. 468.

7. Magdalino, *L'orthodoxie des astrologues: la science entre le dogme et la divination à Byzance, VIIe–XIVe siècle*, pp. 109–32, esp. 113–22.

8. Choniates, 'De Manuele Comneno', in *Historia*, 2. 7; 5. 2, 8; 7. 7, ed. Bekker, pp. 126–7, 199–200, 219–20, 286–8, ed. van Dieten, pp. 95–6, 154, 169, 220–1.

9. Pingree, 'The Astrological School of John Abramius'.

10. Petrus de Ebulo, *Liber ad honorem Augusti sive de rebus Siculis*, ed. Kölzer and Stähli, p. 43 (fol. 97).

11. Mentgen, *Astrologie und Öffentlichkeit im Mittelalter*, pp. 159–273; Boudet, *Entre science et nigromance. Astrologie, divination et magie dans l'Occident médiéval (xiiᵉ–xvᵉ s.)*; Boudet et al., eds., *De Frédéric II à Rodolphe II. Astrologie, divination et magie dans les cours (XIIIe–XVIIe siècle)*.

12. 'Ergo ista corpora superiora non sunt causa eorum quae sunt sed signa tantum veluti est circulus pendens ad tabernam, quia non est idem vinum sed signum vini': Michael Scot, *Liber introductorius*, ed. Edwards, p. 5.

13. 'Sciendo quod per predicta duo, scilicet 12 signa posita in zodiaco et per planetas 7 sub firmamento, potest multum cognosci fortuna et infortunium temporis futuri et personarum a principia sui ortus usque in finem': ibid., p. 12.

14. Haskins, *Studies in the History of Medieval Science*, p. 293.

15. 'Sed sic est – celum si non mentitur, et astra/ Si non delirant, et mobilitate perhenni/ Corpora si sequitur supracelestia mundus – :/ Excellens alias prudencia principis hujus/ Cisma voluntatum dirimet, populosque rebelles/ Conteret et legum dabit irresecabile frenum': Winkelman (ed.), 'Drei Gedichte Heinrichs von Avranches an Kaiser Friedrich II.', p. 486 (from Cambridge, University Library, Dd. XI. 78) ('Cisma' does seem to be accusative here).

16. 'A Michaele Scoto me percepisse recordor,/ Qui fuit astrorum scrutator, qui fuit augur,/ Qui fuit ariolus, et qui fuit alter Apollo': ibid.

17. Aly Aben Ragel, *El libro conplido en los iudizios de las estrellas. Partes 6 a 8. Traducción hecha en la corte de Alfonso el Sabio*, ed. Hilty, pp. 256–68.

18. Mentgen, *Astrologie und Öffentlichkeit im Mittelalter*, pp. 201–2; 'Cy dit comment le roy estoit astrologien ... tres expert et sage en ycelle ... celle science d'astrologie': Christine de Pisan, *Le Livre des fais et bonnes meurs du sage roy Charles V*, 3. 4, ed. Solente, 2 (SHF 444), pp. 15–19.

19. Boudet, *Entre science et nigromance. Astrologie, divination et magie dans l'Occident médiéval (xiie–xve s.)*, p. 304.

20. Pingree, 'The Horoscope of Constantine VII Porphyrogenitus'.

21. North, 'Scholars and Power: Astrologers at the Courts of Medieval Europe', p. 23 n. 38.

22. Poulle, 'La date de la naissance de Louis VIII'; Juste, *Les manuscrits astrologiques latins conservés à la bibliothèque nationale de France à Paris*, pp. 236–7 (BnF, MS lat. 16208).

23. Boudet and Poulle, 'Les jugements astrologiques sur la naissance de Charles VII', pp. 169–70; Juste, *Les manuscrits astrologiques latins conservés à la Bibliothèque nationale de France à Paris*, pp. 224 (with plate 8) (BnF, MS lat. 15971), 254–5 (BnF, MS n.a.l. 398).

24. Chastellain, *Chronique*, 4. 88, ed. Kervyn de Lettenhove, 3, pp. 446–7.

25. 'tous voz predecesseurs, roys tres crestiens, qui ont aymee et eue cherie et affectionee plus ceste science de astrologie que nulle des autres science liberalles ... Charles VIIe, vostre grand pere, qui tousjours a eu a l'entour de lui les plus expers astrologiens qu'il povoit finer': Simon de Phares, *Le Recueil des plus celebres astrologues*, Prologue, 11–14, ed. Boudet, 1 (SHF 515), pp. 21–3.

26. Juste, *Les manuscrits astrologiques latins conservés à la bibliothèque nationale de France à Paris*, pp. 162–7 (BnF, MS lat. 7443).

27. Simon de Phares, *Le Recueil des plus celebres astrologues*, 11. 38, ed. Boudet, 1 (SHF 515), pp. 552–3.

28. Pangerl, 'Sterndeutung als naturwissenschaftliche Methode der Politikberatung. Astronomie und Astrologie am Hof Kaiser Friedrichs III. (1440–1493)'.

29. Hayton, 'Martin Bylica at the Court of Matthias Corvinus: Astrology and Politics in Renaissance Hungary'.

30. Carlin, 'Parron, William (b. before 1461, d. in or after 1503), astrologer', in *ODNB*, 42, pp. 861-2.

31. 'conseillé par ... son astrologien, de nom aller contre les Suisses et que d'y aller, si Dieu ne destournoit les influences celestes, il lui en prendroit mal, respondit ces propres motz, que la fureur de son espee vainqueroit le cours du ciel, et lors y alla et lui en print comme l'on scet': Simon de Phares, *Le Recueil des plus celebres astrologues*, prologue, 38, ed. Boudet, 1 (SHF 515), p. 33.

32. 'Multi principes et magnates, noxia curiositate solliciti, vanis nituntur artibus occulta perquirere et investigare futura': Oresme, *Tractatus contra judiciarios astronomos*, ed. Coopland, p. 123.

33. 'Derechief, l'en raconte que le roy Jacques de Maillogues, quant il vault departir d'Avingnon, fist appeler tous lez astrologiens de court de Rome pour eslire l'eure de son department, lequel se departi en telle heure, laquelle fust prise et esleüe par conmun acort de tous lez astrologyens et, neantmoins, en celle veage, il perdy la vie et son royaume aussi': *Songe du Vergier*, 1. 184. 11, ed. Schnerb-Lièvre, 1, p. 405; the Latin version is much shorter: *Somnium Viridarii*, 2. 356. 11, ed. Schnerb-Lièvre, 2, p. 238.

34. Choniates, 'De Isaacio Angelo' in *Historia*, 1. 8, ed. Bekker, p. 506, ed. van Dieten, p. 388.

35. *An English Chronicle of the Reigns of Richard II., Henry IV., Henry V. and Henry VI.*, ed. Davies, p. 69.

36. *Third Report of the Deputy Keeper of the Public Records*, Appendix 2, pp. 213-14, on the trial of John Stacy, astrologer, in 1477; Kittredge, *Witchcraft in Old and New England*, pp. 138-9, 227-8.

37. Coote, *Prophecy and Public Affairs in Later Medieval England*, with a list of more than 150 English manuscripts of political prophecies, pp. 239-80; Daniel, *Les prophéties de Merlin et la culture politique (xiie-xvie s.)*.

38. The *Visio Caroli Grossi* is found in Hariulf, *Chronicon Centulense*, 3. 21, ed. Lot, pp. 144-50; *The Annals of St Neots*, ed. Dumville and Lapidge, pp. 86-94; William of Malmesbury, *Gesta regum Anglorum*, 2. 111, ed. Mynors et al., pp. 162-8; and numerous subsequent historical works. See Levison, 'Die Politik in Jenseitsvisionen des frühen Mittelalters'; Dutton, *The Politics of Dreaming in the Carolingian Empire*, Chapter 8. There is an English translation in Le Goff, *The Birth of Purgatory*, pp. 118-21.

39. 'Dum viximus, amavimus tecum et cum patre tuo et cum fratribus tuis et cum avunculis tuis facere praelia et homicidia et rapinas pro cupiditate terrena': *Visio Caroli Grossi*, in Hariulf, *Chronicon Centulense*, ed. Lot, p. 146.

40. 'vidique ibi aliquos reges generis mei esse in magnis suppliciis ... hocque fit precibus sancti Petri sanctique Remigii, cuius patrociniis hactenus genus nostrum regale regnavit': ibid., pp. 146-7.

41. 'Karole, successor meus nunc tutius in imperio Romanorum, veni ad me; sapio quoniam venisti per poenalem locum, ubi est pater tuus fraterque meus positus in thermis sibi destinatis, sed per misericordiam Dei citissime liberabitur de illis poenis, sicut et

nos liberati sumus meritis sancti Petri sanctique precibus Remigii, cui Deus magnum apostolatum super reges et super omnem gentem Francorum dedit. Qui nisi reliquias nostrae propaginis suffragatus fuerit et adiuverit, iam deficiet nostra genealogia regnando et imperando. Unde scito quoniam tolletur ocius potestas imperii de manu tua, et postea parvissimo vives tempore': ibid., pp. 147–8.

42. 'Imperium Romanorum quod hactenus tenuisti, iure haereditario, debet recipere Hludogvicus filius filiae meae': ibid., p. 148.

43. 'Denique sciant omnes, velint an nolint, quoniam secundum destinationem Dei in manu illius revertetur totum imperium Romanorum': ibid.

44. 'Per nostras enim orationes rex efficieris Galliae, et postea heredes tui usque ad septimam generationem possidebunt gubernacula totius regni': *Historia relationis sancti Walarici*, 4, ed. Holder-Egger, p. 695; dated 'probably before 1050' by Lewis, *Royal Succession in Capetian France: Studies on Familial Order and the State*, p. 36.

45. 'promitto tibi . . . te fore regem prolemque tuam Francigenarum stirpemque tuam regnum tenere usque ad septem successiones': Hariulf, *Chronicon Centulense*, 3. 23, ed. Lot, p. 154; the work was completed in 1088, as the author himself states (ibid., 4. 36, pp. 283–4).

46. Spiegel, 'The *Reditus regni ad stirpem Karoli Magni*: A New Look', p. 166.

47. William the Breton, *Philippis*, Preface, line 28; 1, line 351; 2, line 485; 3, lines 188, 427, 643; 4, lines 439, 528; 7, line 86; 10, line 99, ed. Delaborde, pp. 3, 21, 58, 72, 81, 89, 115, 118, 179, 285.

48. Werner, 'Die Legitimität der Kapetinger und die Entstehung des "Reditus regni Francorum ad stirpem Karoli"'; Spiegel, 'The *Reditus regni ad stirpem Karoli Magni*: A New Look'; Brown, 'La généalogie capétienne dans l'historiographie de Moyen Âge. Philippe le Bel, le reniement du *reditus* et la création d'une ascendence carolingienne pour Hugues Capet'.

49. 'Si iste post patrem regnaverit, constat regnum reductum ad progeniem Karoli Magni': ed. Brown, 'Vincent de Beauvais and the *reditus regni Francorum ad stirpem Caroli imperatoris*', p. 190.

50. For the following, see *Brevis relatio de Guillelmo nobilissimo comite Normannorum*, 12, 15, ed. Van Houts, pp. 39, 43–4; 'Additamenta', in *Gesta Normannorum Ducum*, ed. Van Houts, 2, pp. 284–6.

51. 'respondit illam diutius manere illudque imperium usque ad septimam generationem viriliter durare': *Brevis relatio de Guillelmo nobilissimo*, 15, ed. Van Houts, pp. 43–4; 'Additamenta', in *Gesta Normannorum Ducum*, ed. Van Houts, 2, p. 284–6.

52. Rollo, William Longsword, Richard I, Richard II, Robert I, William the Conqueror, Henry I.

53. 'Quis vero post eum has terras possidebit et possessas gubernavit generatio que tunc erit videre poterit': *Brevis relatio de Guillelmo nobilissimo*, 12, ed. Van Houts, p. 39.

54. 'Quod nos iam ex magna parte impletum videmus, qui Henrico regi . . . superviximus': 'Additamenta', in *Gesta Normannorum Ducum* ed. Van Houts, 2, p. 284.

55. 'Evigilabunt regentis catuli et postpositis nemoribus infra moenia civitatum venabuntur. Stragem non minimam ex obstantibus facient et linguas taurorum abscident. Colla

rugientium onerabunt catenis et avita tempora renovabunt. Exin de primo in quartum, de quarto in tercium, de tercio in secundum rotabitur pollex in oleo. Sextus Hibernie moenia subvertet et nemora in planiciem mutabit': Geoffrey of Monmouth, *Historia regum Britannie*, 7. 3 (114. 15–17), ed. Reeve, p. 149.

56. *Gesta regis Henrici secundi Benedicti abbatis*, ed. Stubbs, 1, pp. 42–3; Roger of Howden, *Chronica*, ed. Stubbs, 2, p. 47; Alanus de Insulis, *Explanatio in Prophetia Merlini Ambrosii*, 3. 34–8, ed. Wille, 1, pp. 166–7; Walter of Coventry, *Memoriale*, ed. Stubbs, 2, pp. 213–14 (the 'Barnwell Chronicle').

57. 'linx penetrans omnia, quae ruinae propriae gentis imminebit': Geoffrey of Monmouth, *Historia regum Britannie*, 7. 3 (115. 18), ed. Reeve, p. 149.

58. 'per illam dominatus Normannorum in insula Britannie finem accipiet': Alanus de Insulis, *Explanatio in Prophetia Merlini Ambrosii*, 3. 45, ed. Wille, 1, p. 171.

59. Walter Map, *De nugis curialium*, 4. 1, ed. James et al., p. 282.

60. 'Vere ipse est linx typica Merlini, de qua idem Merlinus de patre eius, quem leoni comparaverat, loquens: Ex eo, inquit, procedet linx penetrans omnia, que ruine proprie gentis imminebit': William the Breton, *Gesta Philippi Augusti*, ed. Delaborde, p. 293.

61. 'Vere linx penetrans, quia non est crumena in Anglia quam non perforet et contenta excutiat': Matthew Paris, *Chronica majora*, ed. Luard, 5, p. 451.

62. 'robustus viribus sed praeceps in factis, in quibus tamen, quia fortunatos et felices exitus habuerit, putant eum multi apud Merlinum fatidicum per lyncem designatum omnia penetrantem': Trevet, *Annales sex regum Angliae, 1135–1307*, ed. Hog, p. 280.

63. 'Hoc Galterium inscium et casu fecisse uulgaris et pene omnium una opinio est. Sed Merlini oraculum, quod spiculo inuidię suffocandum predixit, aliud nos intelligere cogit': Alanus de Insulis, *Explanatio in Prophetia Merlini Ambrosii*, 2. 45, ed. Wille, 1, pp. 149–50.

64. They are listed in Crick, *The Historia Regum Britanniae of Geoffrey of Monmouth, 3: A Summary Catalogue of the Manuscripts*, pp. 330–2.

65. See Daniel, *Les prophéties de Merlin et la culture politique (xiie–xvie s.)*.

66. *Les Prophécies de Merlin, edited from the ms. 593 in the Bibliothèque municipale of Rennes*, ed. Paton; for a study of this text, see Koble, *Les Prophéties de Merlin en prose. Le roman arthurien en éclats*.

67. 'En las partidas de Oçidente entre los montes e la mar nasçera un ave negra, comedora, e rrobadora, e todos los panares del mundo querria acoger en si, e todo el oro del mundo ençerrara en su estomago; e despues gomarlo ha e tornara atras, e non peresçera luego por esta dolençia ... caersele ante las alas, e secarsele han las plumas al sol, e andara de puerta en puerta, e non le querra acoger, e ençerrarse ha en selva, e morra ý dos vezes, una al mundo e otra ante Dios': López de Ayala, *Crónica del rey don Pedro*, 20 (1369). 3, ed. Orduna, 2, pp. 270–1.

68. Alvar, 'The Matter of Britain in Spanish Society and Letters', p. 247, is more definite: 'López de Ayala did not invent the letters'. See in general Jardin, 'Les prophéties dans la chronique de Pierre Ier de López de Ayala: respect et manipulation du temps'.

69. 'como viene rey nuevo, luego fazen Merlín nuevo': Díaz de Games, *El Victorial*, ed. Beltrán Llavador, p. 325.

70. 'Or est-il qu'il eut opinion de veoir les propheties de Merlin, pour sçavoir ce qu'il devoit advenir à sa postérité, qui est une superstition laquelle regne en Angleterre dez le temps du roy Arthus. Voyant lesdites propheties, par l'interprétation qui luy en fut faicte (car ce sont comme les oracles d'Apollo, où il y a tousjours double intelligence), fut trouvé que l'un de ses freres, duquel le nom se commenceroit par un G, osteroit la couronne hors des mains de ses enfans': Du Bellay, *Mémoires*, ed. Bourrilly and Vindry, 1, p. 42.

71. Gerald of Wales, *Expugnatio Hibernica*, 2, Preface, explicit; 3, Introduction, ed. Scott and Martin, pp. 134, 252–6; Bartlett, 'Political Prophecy in Gerald of Wales'.

72. 'Merlis, que fo bos devinaire': *La chanson de la croisade albigeoise*, 150, lines 43–6, ed. Martin-Chabot, 2, p. 76.

73. 'aliquos versus, in quibus futura praesagia civitatum Lombardie, Tuscie, Romagnole et Marchie pleniter et veraciter continentur': Salimbene de Adam, *Cronica*, ed. Scalia, 1, pp. 61, 361–85; 2, pp. 549–50, 811, 813–16.

74. 'ille vates ruralis': Bower, *Scotichronicon*, ed. Watt et al., 5, pp. 426–9.

75. Choniates, 'De Manuele Comneno' and 'De Andronico Comneno', in *Historia*, 5.8, 1. 5; 2. 9, ed. Bekker, pp. 220, 379, 442–4, ed. van Dieten, pp. 169, 293, 339–41. See Shukurov, 'AIMA: The Blood of the Grand Komnenoi'.

76. 'Primus F., in pilis agnus, in villis leo, erit depopulator urbium. In iusto proposito terminabit inter corvum et cornicem. Vivet in H., qui occidet in portis Melatii. Secundus autem F. insperati et mirabilis ortus, inter capras agnus laniandus, non absorbendus ab eis': Holder-Egger, 'Italienische Propheteen des 13. Jahrhunderts', pp. 175–6; Salimbene cites this prophecy but substitutes names for initials: Salimbene de Adam, *Cronica*, ed. Scalia, 2, pp. 549–50.

77. 'Populus namque in ligno et ferreis tunicis superveniet … Catuli leonis in aequoreos pisces transformabuntur': Geoffrey of Monmouth, *Historia regum Britannie*, 7. 3 (112. 9–12), ed. Reeve, p. 147.

78. 'Si arbor viridis a medio sui succidatur corpore et pars abscisa trium iugerum spatio a suo deportetur stipite, cum per se et absque humana manu vel quovis amminiculo, suo connectetur trunco, ceperitque denuo virescere et fructificare ex coalescentis suci amore pristino, tunc primum tantorum malorum sperari poterit remissio': *Vita Ædwardi regis*, 2. 11, ed. Barlow, p. 118.

79. 'Huius ergo vaticinii veritatem nos experimur, quod scilicet Anglia exterorum facta est habitatio et alienigenarum dominatio … nec ulla spes est finiendae miseriae': William of Malmesbury, *Gesta regum Anglorum*, 2. 227, ed. Mynors et al., pp. 414–16.

80. 'Neque enim hodie regem aut ducem aut pontificem ex eadem gente cernimus aliter originem ducere quam arborem succisam ut reuirescat et fructum proferat suo stipiti denuo coherere': Osbert of Clare, *Vita sancti Edwardi confessoris*, 22, ed. Bloch, p. 109.

81. 'de sancta eius progenie traxisse carnis originem Henrici nostri specialis est gloria': Aelred of Rievaulx, *Vita sancti Ædwardi regis et confessoris*, Prologue, ed. Marzella, p. 88.

82. 'semen regum Normannorum et Anglorum coniungens … noster Henricus … quasi lapis angularis utrumque populum copulavit. Habet nunc certe de genere Anglorum Anglia regem, habet de eadem gente episcopos et abbates, habet et principes, milites

etiam optimos, qui ex utriusque seminis coniunctione procreati aliis honori sunt, aliis consolationi': ibid, 30, pp. 154–5.

83. Lopes, *Crónica do Rei D. Pedro I*, 1, 43, ed. Macchi, tr. Steunou, pp. 22, 238–40.

84. Lopes, *Crónica del Rei Dom João I*, 1. 23–4, summarized in *The English in Portugal, 1367–1387*, p. 166.

85. Kittredge, *Witchcraft in Old and New England*, pp. 416–17 n. 40, gives a long list of sources for this notorious case; the indictments themselves are in TNA, KB9/72/1–6, 9, 11, 14; there is a detailed study by Griffiths, 'The Trial of Eleanor Cobham: An Episode in the Fall of Duke Humphrey of Gloucester'; Carey, *Courting Disaster: Astrology at the English Court and University in the Later Middle Ages*, pp. 138–53, concentrates on the technical astrological aspects; the main chronicle sources are *The Brut or The Chronicles of England*, ed. Brie, 2, pp. 478–82; *An English Chronicle of the Reigns of Richard II, Henry IV, Henry V and Henry VI*, ed. Davies, pp. 56–60; *A Chronicle of London, from 1089 to 1483* (ed. Tyrrell and Nicolas), pp. 128–30.

86. 'a diutino tempore iam preterito se ad alciorem statum in regno Anglie quam habuerat exaltare machinans': TNA, KB9/72/5–6, 9, 14.

87. 'quandam figuram de dicto rege ac quamplurima alia res, ymagines, vestimenta, circulos et instrumenta per artem magicam et nigromanticam colore astronomie subdole figurarum fecit': TNA, KB9/72/1–4.

88. 'ut idem Rogerus ... in circulo securus esse poterit et ad ipsum demones et alios malignos spiritus in aiero et in terra existentes convocare possit': ibid.

89. 'bene scivit quod idem rex non diu viveret set infra breve obiret et sic ut per detextionem et huiusmodi materie manifestacionem populus ipsius regis maius ab eo cordialem amorem retraherent ac idem rex per noticiam huiusmodi detectionis et manifestacionis, videlicet quod ipse sic ut promittitur infra breve obiret, caperet talem tristiciam in corde suo quod per illam tristiciam ac dolorem citius moreretur': ibid.

90. TNA, KB9/72/11; this is the only document among the indictments not to be in quadruplicate, and hence probably did not stem from the four simultaneous inquests mentioned in the Brut: *The Brut or The Chronicles of England*, ed. Brie, 2, p. 479.

91. *The Brut, or The Chronicles of England*, ed. Brie, 2, p. 480 (modernized).

92. *An English Chronicle of the Reigns of Richard II, Henry IV, Henry V and Henry VI*, ed. Davies, pp. 58, 60.

11 PRETENDERS AND RETURNERS

1. Bennett, *Lambert Simnel and the Battle of Stoke*.

2. See, in general, Platelle, 'Erreur sur la personne. Contribution à l'histoire de l'imposture au Moyen Âge'; Evans, *The Death of Kings: Royal Deaths in Medieval England*, pp. 147–73; Lecuppre, *L'imposture politique au Moyen Âge: la seconde vie des rois*; Menzel, *Falsche Könige zwischen Thron und Galgen: Politische Hochstapelei von der Antike zur Moderne*. There are references to four Byzantine cases, ranging from the seventh to the thirteenth centuries, in Dagron, *Emperor and Priest: The Imperial Office in Byzantium*,

p. 15. For useful Early Modern comparisons, Bercé, *Le roi caché: sauveurs et imposteurs: mythes politiques populaires dans l'Europe modern*; Perrie, *Pretenders and Popular Monarchism in Early Modern Russia: The False Tsars of the Time of Troubles*. A famous twentieth-century case concerned the supposed return, in 1920, of the Kumar of Bhawal, an Indian prince reported to have died in 1909.

3. Wolff, 'Baldwin of Flanders and Hainault, First Latin Emperor of Constantinople: His Life, Death and Resurrection, 1172–1225', pp. 294–301; Tschirch, 'Der falsche Woldemar und die märkischen Städte'; Strück, 'Märkische Urkunden aus der Zeit des falschen Woldemar im Anhaltischen Staatsarchiv Zerbst'; Schultze, *Die Mark Brandenburg 2: Die Mark unter Herrschaft der Wittelsbacher und Luxemburger (1319–1415)*, pp. 75–109; Schwinges, 'Verfassung und kollektives Verhalten. Zur Mentalität des Erfolges falscher Herrscher im Reich des 13. und 14. Jahrhunderts'.

4. Mayer, 'Two Crusaders Out of Luck'.

5. Thacker, 'The Cult of King Harold at Chester'.

6. Snorri Sturluson, *Heimskringla*, tr. Laing, 1, p. 483.

7. Snorri Sturluson, *Heimskringla*, tr. Hollander, p. 242.

8. Anna Comnena, *Alexias*, 10. 2. 2–4. 5, ed. Reinsch and Kambylis, pp. 283–93. Anna Comnena calls him Leo but this is an error and he probably claimed to be Constantine, the son who died at Antioch in 1073: Mathieu, 'Les faux Diogènes', pp. 134–5.

9. *Chronica Adefonsi imperatoris*, 1. 58, ed. Maya Sánchez, p. 177; Orderic Vitalis, *Historia ecclesiastica*, 13. 10, ed. Chibnall, 6, pp. 412–18; Ibn al-Athir, *Chronicle*, tr. Richards, p. 323.

10. 'post illam multam et malam mactationem christianorum in Fraga, in qua fere omnes gladio ceciderunt, perpauci vero vix inermes per fugam evaserunt cum rege': Lacarra, *Documentos para el estudio de la reconquista y repoblación del Valle del Ebro*, 1, no. 236, pp. 239–40.

11. 'dicitur a Mauris fuisse interfectus. Aliorum uero fuit opinio quia tunc euaserat de infortunio illo ... Qui post multa annorum curricula temporibus nostris uenisse dicebatur in Aragoniam': *Chronica latina regum Castellae*, 4, ed. Charlo Brea, p. 38.

12. 'ab aliis dicitur uiuus a prelio euasisse, et confusionem prelii nequiens tolerare peregrinum se exibuit huic mundo effigie et habitu inmutatus': Rodrigo Jiménez de Rada, *Historia de rebus Hispaniae*, 7. 3, ed. Fernández Valverde, p. 224.

13. The date of Alfonso's return depends on that of a letter of Alfonso II describing the case. See Lecuppre, *L'imposture politique au Moyen Âge: la seconde vie des rois*, pp. 88–9 n. 1, on the date of the letter, preferring 1162–3; one later source places the emergence of the pseudo-Alfonso in 1181: Floriano, 'Fragmento de unos viejos anales (1089–1196)', p. 153. See the brief but cogent comments of Bisson, 'The Rise of Catalonia: Identity, Power and Ideology in a Twelfth-Century Society', pp. 146–7.

14. 'Et multos tales diebus illis occidit Manfredos': Salimbene de Adam, *Cronica*, ed. Scalia, 1, p. 264 (cf. 2, p. 714) (MGH, SS 32, p. 174).

15. 'Harold, þe sæde þæt he Cnutes sunu wære 7 þære oðre Ælfgyfe, þeh hit na soð nære'; 'Sume men sædon be Harolde þæt he wære Cnutes sunu cynges. 7 Ælfgiue Ælfelmes dohtor ealdormannes. ac hit þuhte swiðe ungeleaflic manegum mannum': *Anglo-Saxon Chronicle* (C), s.a. 1035, (E), s.a. 1036, ed. Plummer and Earle, pp. 158, 161.

16. *Encomium Emmae Reginae*, 3. 1, ed. Campbell, pp. 38–40.

17. John of Worcester, *Chronicle*, 2, ed. Darlington and McGurk, p. 520.

18. di Carpegna Falconieri, *The Man Who Believed He Was King of France: A True Medieval Tale*, p. 122. This book contains a full account of the case, along with a careful analysis of the amount of trust one can place in the fifteenth-century *Istoria di re Giannino*, which some regard as entirely fictional. The story features in Maurice Druon's famous series of historical novels, *Les rois maudits* (1955–77).

19. 'Sed quid dixisset poeta noster, si vidisset, non est diu, Zaninum senensem, qui permisit sibi persuaderi tam facile, quam vane, quod erat rex Franciae?': Benvenuto da Imola on *Purgatorio* 13. 151–4, *Comentum super Dantis Aldigheris comoediam*, ed. Lacaita, 3, p. 372.

20. Cohn, *The Pursuit of the Millennium*, Chapter 6; Struve, 'Die falschen Friedriche und die Friedenssehnsucht im Mittelalter'; Lerner, 'Frederick II, Alive, Aloft and Allayed, in Franciscan-Joachite Eschatology'; Möhring, *Der Weltkaiser der Endzeit: Entstehung, Wandel und Wirkung einer tausendjährigen Weissagung*, pp. 209–68; Lecuppre, *L'imposture politique au Moyen Âge: la seconde vie des rois*, pp. 357–64.

21. 'Nam et ego ipse usque ad multos dies vix potui credere quod mortuus esset, nisi cum auribus meis ab ore Innocentii pape quarti audivi ... Horrui, cum audirem, et vix potui credere': Salimbene de Adam, *Cronica*, ed. Scalia, 1, p. 264 (MGH, SS 32, pp. 173–4).

22. The primary source for this event is a letter of 1 February 1320 printed in *Diplomatarium Norvegicum*, 6. 1, no. 100, pp. 104–5; there is discussion, along with a translation of this letter, in Anderson, 'Notes of Some Entries in the Iceland Annals Regarding the Death of the Princess "The Maiden of Norway", in A.D. 1290, and "The False Margaret", who was Burned at Bergen in A.D. 1301'; the continuing cult of the false Margaret is mentioned in another letter of 1320: *Diplomatarium Norvegicum*, 8. 1, no. 67, pp. 88–9; see also Lecuppre, *L'imposture politique au Moyen Âge: la seconde vie des rois*, p. 127; Menzel, *Falsche Könige zwischen Thron und Galgen: Politische Hochstapelei von der Antike zur Moderne*, pp. 168–9.

23. 'si dictus rex Norwag' de dicta Margareta filiam vel filias procreaverit succedent in omnibus que ipsam vel ipsas contingere possunt secundum leges et consuetudines Norichanas eciam in regno si consuetudo fuerit': *Acts of the Parliaments of Scotland*, 1, ed. Thomson and Innes, p. 422 (80) (25 July, 1281).

24. 'lofflige arffuingie': *Diplomatarium Norvegicum*, 6. 1, no. 100, p. 104.

25. Anderson, 'Notes of Some Entries in the Iceland Annals Regarding the Death of the Princess "The Maiden of Norway", in A.D. 1290, and "The False Margaret", who was Burned at Bergen in A.D. 1301', pp. 413–15.

26. Miracles were also reported at the site of the execution of pseudo-Baldwin: *Annales de Dunstaplia*, ed. Luard, p. 95.

27. Albert of Stade, *Annales Stadenses*, ed. Lappenberg, p. 358.

28. Gregory VII, *Registrum*, 8.6, ed. Caspar, pp. 523–4; *Notae Weingartenses*, ed. Waitz, p. 831; McNiven, 'Rebellion, Sedition and the Legend of Richard II's Survival in the Reigns of Henry IV and Henry V'.

29. 'Pluribus autem querentibus, si ipse esset imperator, cur tanto tempore latuerit': John of Vikting, *Liber certarum historiarum*, 2. 11, ed. Schneider, 1, p. 245.

30. Albert of Stade, *Annales Stadenses*, ed. Lappenberg, p. 358; there is a much more melodramatic version in Matthew Paris, *Chronica majora*, ed. Luard, 3, pp. 90–1.

31. 'indicat se olim obitu simulato de divine permissionis oraculo ad expianda delicta nonum annum in peregrinationis exercicio peregisse': Malaspina, *Chronicon*, 2. 6, ed. Koller and Nitschke, p. 132.

32. *Gesta archiepiscoporum Magdeburgensium*, ed. Schum, p. 436.

33. Anderson, 'Notes of Some Entries in the Iceland Annals regarding the Death of the Princess "The Maiden of Norway", in A.D. 1290, and "The False Margaret", who was Burned at Bergen in A.D. 1301', pp. 411–12.

34. 'usque in annos certos': Madden, 'Documents Relating to Perkin Warbeck, with Remarks on his History', pp. 199–200, with translation at pp. 156–8. This is Warbeck's letter of 1493 to Isabella the Catholic (BL, MS Egerton 616). There is a photograph of the letter in Arthurson, *The Perkin Warbeck Conspiracy 1491–1499*, p. 49.

35. Gregory VII, *Registrum*, 8.6, ed. Caspar, pp. 523–4; Guiscard's daughter was married to the (real) Michael VII's son: Falkenhausen, 'Olympias, eine normannische Prinzessin in Konstantinopel'.

36. 'Erant autem tunc etiam quidam cum duce, qui, in palatio tempore Michaelis imperatoris servientes, faciem eius se novisse et hunc similem illi minime, vel in modico, assimilari dicerent, sed fraudulenter hunc spe alicuius a duce accipiendi muneris advenisse': Malaterra, *De rebus gestis Rogerii Calabriae et Siciliae comitis et Roberti Guiscardi ducis fratris eius*, 3. 13, ed. Pontieri, p. 65.

37. μὴ ἐπιγινώσκειν αὐτὸν ὅλως διισχυριζόμενοι: Anna Comnena, *Alexias*, 4. 1. 3, ed. Reinsch and Kambylis, p. 121; 'Iste solebat/ Crateras mensis plenos deferre Lieo,/ Et de pincernis erat inferioribus unus': William of Apulia, *La Geste de Robert Guiscard*, 4, lines 269–71, ed. Mathieu, p. 218.

38. Choniates, 'De Isaacio Angelo' in *Historia*, 3. 1, ed. Bekker, pp. 549–53, ed. van Dieten.

39. McNiven, 'Rebellion, Sedition and the Legend of Richard II's Survival in the Reigns of Henry IV and Henry V'; Bower, *Scotichronicon*, 15. 9, 19, 31, ed. Watt et al., 8, pp. 28, 64, 114; Arthurson, *The Perkin Warbeck Conspiracy 1491–1499*.

40. 'respondit se non habere iudicem inter eos, vivente ligeo domino suo in regno Scocie, rege Ricardo': Walsingham, *The St Albans Chronicle: the Chronica maiora of Thomas Walsingham*, ed. Taylor et al., 2, p. 728; cf. p. 720 for his attempt to bring the pseudo-Richard into England.

41. 'Chlodoveum, quem falso regem fecerant': *Passio Leudegarii*, 23, ed. Krusch, p. 305 (19–20, pp. 300–1, for other details and names of some of the main supporters).

42. *The Great Chronicle of London*, ed. Thomas and Thornley, p. 285 (spelling modernized).

43. 'Partout fu quens nommés de tos,/ Mais il n'i vot respondre à rien,/ Fors c'on l'apieloit Crestiien': Philippe Mouskes, *Chronique rimée*, ed. de Reiffenberg, 2, p. 456, lines 24614–16 (MGH SS 26, p. 769).

44. 'Et quant il plus s'escondissoit,/ "Vous iestes quens" cascuns dissoit': ibid., 2, p. 457, lines 24629–30 (MGH SS 26, p. 770).

45. Anderson, 'Notes of Some Entries in the Iceland Annals regarding the Death of the Princess "The Maiden of Norway", in A.D. 1290, and "The False Margaret", who was Burned at Bergen in A.D. 1301', p. 418.

46. 'La fu il deux jours sur terre pour le monstrer a ceulx de Londres afin que ilz creussent pour certain quil fust mort': *Chronicque de la traïson et mort de Richart Deux Roy Dengleterre*, ed. Williams, p. 103.

47. *An English Chronicle of the Reigns of Richard II, Henry IV, Henry V and Henry VI*, ed. Davies, p. 21 (spelling modernized).

48. 'advena, cuius pater molinas gobernavit, et ut vere dicam, pater eius pectinibus insedit lanasque conposuit': Gregory of Tours, *Libri historiarum decem*, 7. 14, ed. Krusch and Levison, p. 336. On the alternative name of the pretender, Ballomer, see Widdowson, 'Gundovald, "Ballomer" and the Problems of Identity', with older literature cited at p. 609 n. 9.

49. 'Tune es pictur ille, qui tempore Chlothacharii regis per oraturia parietis adque camaras caraxabas?': Gregory of Tours, *Libri historiarum decem*, 7. 36, ed. Krusch and Levison, p. 357. There is a tendency to translate *caraxare* as 'daub' or an equivalent ('barbouillait': Viollet-le-Duc, *Dictionnaire raisonné de l'architecture française du XIe au XVIe siècle*, 7, p. 56; 'slap whitewash', Gregory of Tours, *History of the Franks*, tr. Thorpe, p. 419), but the word seems to mean the more neutral 'write' or 'paint', deriving from a Greek word with implications of scratching or inscribing. The *Dictionary of Medieval Latin from British Sources* defines *charaxare* simply as 'to write'; the glossary to Krusch and Levison's edition of Gregory gives both *scribere* and *pingere* as equivalents (p. 582).

50. Arthurson, *The Perkin Warbeck Conspiracy 1491–1499*, p. 23.

51. Ibid., p. 46.

52. Anna Comnena, *Alexias*, 10. 2. 2, ed. Reinsch and Kambylis, pp. 283–4; Floriano, 'Fragmento de unos viejos anales (1089–1196)', p. 153 ('*hun ferrero*'); *Notae Weingartenses*, ed. Waitz, p. 831; *Vita Henrici archiepiscopi Treverensis altera*, ed. Waitz, p. 462; *Gesta archiepiscoporum Magdeburgensium*, ed. Schum, p. 436; Bennett, *Lambert Simnel and the Battle of Stoke*, p. 121.

53. 'ad simulacrum … concurrunt … ad subvertendum ydolum et cultores eius': Malaspina, *Chronicon*, 2. 6, ed. Koller and Nitschke, pp. 132–3.

54. Walker, 'Rumour, Sedition and Popular Protest in the Reign of Henry IV', p. 59.

55. Both the *Middle English Dictionary*, s.v. maumet, and the *Oxford English Dictionary*, s.v. mammet, give 'a puppet, tool' as one meaning of the word, but their citations do not always make this sense certain.

56. *Parliament Rolls of Medieval England*, 8, p. 326.

57. 'Cicatrices in corpore habuit quas habuerat Baldewinus': Albert of Stade, *Annales Stadenses*, ed. Lappenberg, p. 358; cf. *Annales de Dunstaplia*, ed. Luard, p. 94.

58. Leo of Rozmital, *De Leonis a Rosmital nobilis Bohemi itinere per partes Germaniae, Belgii, Britanniae, Franciae, Hispaniae, Portugalliae atque Italiae, annis MCCCCLXV–VII*, pp. 74–6; Leo of Rozmital, *The Travels of Leo of Rozmital*, tr. Letts, pp. 97–9.

59. Długosz, *Annales seu Cronicae incliti regni Poloniae*, ed. Dąbrowski et al., 4, p. 25.

60. "'Tu mecum fuisti uere, sed semper proditor, et in una prodicionum tuarum inter-
ceptus, euasisti, sed tibi quidam satellitum pedem dextrum spiculo misso perforauit,
unde uulnus adhuc aut cicatrix apparet. Comprehendite, famuli, tricatorem, et
uidebitis!" Et apparuit cicatrix; at iuuenis ait: "Domino meo, quem iste se fingit
singularis erat in brachio dextro proceritas, ut stans extentus posset palma genu
dextrum operire". Quod ipse surgens statim impleuit': Walter Map, *De nugis curialium*, 5. 6, ed. James et al., pp. 480–2; the story that a man impersonating Henry had
retired to Cluny can also be found in Richard of Poitiers, *Chronica*, ed. Waitz, p. 80,
and Sigebert of Gembloux, *Chronica: Continuatio Praemonstratensis*, ed. Bethmann,
p. 451.

61. ὅσα γε ἀπὸ τῆς φωνῆς τοῦ ἀνδρὸς τεκμαιρόμενος ἔλεγε μήτε υἱὸν αὐτὸν ἐπιγινώσκειν
Ῥωμανοῦ τοῦ Διογένους: Anna Comnena, *Alexias*, 10. 3. 4, ed. Reinsch and Kambylis,
p. 289.

62. Choniates, 'De Isaacio Angelo', in *Historia*, 3. 1, ed. Bekker, p. 549, ed. van Dieten,
p. 420.

63. Widdowson, 'Gundovald, "Ballomer" and the Problems of Identity', p. 622; Davis, *The
Return of Martin Guerre*, p. viii.

64. 'Le problème . . . de l'identité des personnes . . . des insuffisances techniques': Platelle,
'Erreur sur la personne. Contribution à l'histoire de l'imposture au Moyen Âge', p. 145.

65. 'quod ferebatur Wibertus pictore Romam misso imaginem eius in tabula pingi fecisse,
ut quocumque se habitu effigiaret, non lateret': William of Malmesbury, *Gesta pontificum Anglorum*, 1. 55, ed. Winterbottom, 1, p. 160. Rodney Thomson comments, 'At
a time when realistic portraiture was not current, accurate multiple copying and its
rapid and widespresad distribution impossible, it is difficult to imagine that this really
happened' (ibid., 2, p. 68).

66. Ibn Battuta, *Travels*, tr. Gibb and Beckingham, 4 (178), p. 892.

67. 'annis aliquot interpositis quispiam se ostendit qui se eundem publice fatebatur, et
multorum Castelle et Aragonie id ipsum testimonia affirmabant, qui cum eo in utroque
regno fuerant familiariter conuersati, et ad memoriam reducebant secreta plurima, que
ipse olim cum eis habita recolebat': Rodrigo Jiménez de Rada, *Historia de rebus Hispaniae*, 7.
3, ed. Fernández Valverde, p. 224.

68. 'imperatori similis in omnibus videbatur, et multas conditiones regni et imperii cur-
ieque regalis peroptime noverat': Salimbene de Adam, *Cronica*, ed. Scalia, 1, p. 263
(MGH, SS 32, pp. 173–4).

69. *Chronicon Turonense magnum* (excerpts), ed. Holder-Egger, p. 470; Alberic of Trois-
fontaines, *Chronica*, ed. Scheffer-Boichorst, p. 915; *Annales de Dunstaplia*, ed. Luard,
p. 94; Heinricus Surdus de Selbach, *Chronica*, ed. Bresslau, p. 91. The word also occurs
in a passage describing the case of a man claiming in 1344 to be Alexander Bruce,
(illegitimate) nephew of King Robert Bruce of Scotland: Bower, *Scotichronicon*, 13. 50,
ed. Watt et al., 7, p. 158.

70. Philippe Mouskes, *Chronique rimée*, ed. de Reiffenberg, 2, p. 471, lines 24961–9 (MGH
SS 26, p. 773); Albert of Stade, *Annales Stadenses*, ed. Lappenberg, p. 358; Robert of
Auxerre, *Chronicon* (*additamentum*), ed. Holder-Egger, pp. 286–7.

71. See the list in Lecuppre, *L'imposture politique au Moyen Âge: la seconde vie des rois*, p. 311 n. 2.
72. For Oluf, see Etting, *Queen Margrete I (1353–1412), and the Founding of the Nordic Union*, pp. 135–8; she gives the main chronicle source in English translation.
73. *Foedera* (new edn.), 1. 1, p. 177; TNA C54/34 part 2 (Close Rolls 9 Henry III), m. 17d.
74. 'E pendet son ancessor': Bertran de Born, *The Poems of the Troubadour Bertran de Born*, ed. Paden et al., p. 331: *Molt m'es dissendre car col*, verse 5, line 39 (*Bibliographie des Troubadours*, ed. Pilet and Carstens, 80, 28); see Riquer, 'La littérature provençale à la cour d'Alphonse II d'Aragon', p. 193.
75. *Chronicon Turonense magnum* (excerpts), ed. Holder-Egger, p. 471.
76. *Gesta archiepiscoporum Magdeburgensium*, ed. Schum, p. 436.
77. 'Utrum comes Baldewinus fuerit nec ne, Flamingi certant, et adhuc sub iudice lis est': Albert of Stade, *Annales Stadenses*, ed. Lappenberg, p. 358.
78. 'Mirabile valde fuit de isto homine Woldemaro, et usque in hodiernum diem sunt de eo opiniones': *Gesta archiepiscoporum Magdeburgensium*, ed. Schum, p. 436.

12 NEW FAMILIES AND NEW KINGDOMS

1. Cited by Mottahedeh, *Loyalty and Leadership in An Early Islamic Society*, p. 100; there is a translation of this text: Al-Tanukhi, *The Table-talk of a Mesopotamian Judge*, tr. Margoliouth; the quote is at p. 63.
2. Al-Tanukhi, *The Table-talk of a Mesopotamian Judge*, tr. Margoliouth, p. 62.
3. 'Quis nesciat reges et duces ab iis habuisse principium, qui Deum ignorantes superbia rapinis perfidia homicidiis postremo universis pene sceleribus mundi principe diabolo videlicet agitante super pares, scilicet homines, dominari cęca cupidine et intollerabili presumptione affectaverunt?': Gregory VII, *Registrum*, 8. 21, ed. Caspar, 2, p. 552.
4. Οὗτος τοίνυν ὁ Ῥωμανὸς, ὥσπερ ἀρχὴν περιόδου τὴν ἡγεμονίαν οἰηθεὶς, ἐπειδὴ ἐς τὸν πενθερὸν Κωνσταντίνον τὸ βασίλειον γένος ἀπετελεύτησεν ἐκ Βασιλείου τοῦ Μακεδόνος ἠργμένον, εἰς μέλλουσαν ἀπέβλεπε γενεάν: Psellos, *Chronographia*, 3. 1, ed. Renauld, 1, p. 32; ed. Reinsch, p. 31.
5. 'eotenus quod rex regum et dux ducum eum Polonie ducem concorditer ordinavit': *Gesta principum Polonorum*, 3, ed. Maleczynski, p. 22 (this text was traditionally known as Gallus Anonymus).
6. 'facile est ducem ponere, sed difficile est positum deponere': Cosmas of Prague, *Chronica Boemorum*, 1. 5, ed. Bretholz, p. 14.
7. Adam of Dryburgh, *De tripartito tabernaculo*, 2. 13 (108–24), cols. 712–27; 2. 6 (87), col. 692, for 1180 as the date of composition.
8. Orderic Vitalis, *Historia ecclesiastica*, 4, ed. Chibnall, 2, p. 340.
9. 'quasi stella matutina et quasi luna plena in diebus suis luxit. Ipse Anglis non minus memoralis quam Cyrus Persis, Carolus Francis, Romulusve Romanis': Adam of Dryburgh, *De tripartito tabernaculo*, 2. 13, col. 719; this is borrowed from Aelred of Rievaulx, *De genealogia Henrici regis*, 8, ed. Pezzini, p. 38. The first part is biblical (Ecclesiasticus 50: 6–7) and liturgical.

10. 'pacificus rex Edgarus, non minus memorabilis Anglis, quam Romulus Romanis, Cirus Persis, Alexander Macedonibus, Karolus magnus Francis, Arcturus Britannis': *Chronica de Mailros*, ed. Stevenson, p. 34.

11. 'Sic Arsaces quaesito simul constitutoque regno non minus memorabilis Parthis quam Persis Cyrus, Macedonibus Alexander, Romanis Romulus': Justinus, *Epitoma historiarum Philippicarum Pompei Trogi*, 41. 5. 5, ed. Seel, p. 280.

12. Biddle, *King Arthur's Round Table: An Archaeological Investigation*.

13. Oxford, Bodleian Library, MS Bodley 968 (*Mirouer historiale abregie*), fol. 175; Daly, 'A Rare Iconographic Theme in a Bodleian Library Manuscript: An Illustration of the *Reditus regni ad stirpem Karoli Magni* in MS. Bodley 968'; Huth, 'Erzbischof Arnulf von Reims und der Kampf um das Königtum im Westfrankenreich', p. 87 (re identification as Louis IX not Louis VIII).

14. 'Carolus . . . de cuius genere rex ipse noscitur descendisse': Innocent III, *Epistolae* 7. 43 (42), *Die Register Innocenz' III.*, ed. Hageneder et al., 7, p. 73 (PL 215: 326); *Decretales Gregorii IX*, 2. 1. 13, ed. Friedberg, col. 243 ('Novit ille'); the French royal lawyer Pierre Dubois wrote, 'rex a tempore Karoli Magni sui (sic) de cuius genere descendit, ut in canone legitur': Dupuy, *Histoire du différend d'entre le pape Boniface VIII et Philippes le Bel*, p. 45; see Brown, 'La généalogie capétienne dans l'historiographie du Moyen Âge. Philippe le Bel, le reniement du reditus et la création d'une ascendance carolingienne pour Hugues Capet', p. 205 n. 45.

15. Wipo, *Gesta Chuonradi imperatoris*, 4, ed. Breslau, p. 24.

16. 'In ipsoque dignitas imperialis, quae per longum iam tempus a semine Karoli exulaverat, ad generosum et antiquum germen Karoli reducta est': Otto of Freising, *Chronica sive Historia de duabus civitatibus*, 6. 32, ed. Hofmeister, p. 297.

17. *Genealogiae Karolorum: Commemoratio genealogiae Karoli imperatoris*, ed. Waitz, pp. 245–6; Oexle, 'Die Karolinger und die Stadt des heiligen Arnulf', pp. 252–62; see also above, pp. 318, 339.

18. 'Post hos per muliebrem lineam reparatum est genus regium hoc modo': Ralph Niger, *Chronicon II*, ed. Anstruther, p. 146.

19. 'Mahalde . . ., Malcolmes cynges dohter of Scotlande & Margareta þære goda cwæne Eadwardes cynges magan. 7 of þan rihtan Ængla landes kyne kynne': *Anglo-Saxon Chronicle* (E), s.a. 1100, ed. Plummer and Earle, p. 236.

20. 'Þo smot uerst þis tre aȝen · to is kunde more': Robert of Gloucester, *Metrical Chronicle*, line 7255, ed. Wright, 1, p. 524.

21. Paul the Deacon, *Liber de episcopis Mettensibus*, ed. Kempf, p. 76 (MGH, SS 2, p. 265); Paul the Deacon, *Carmina*, ed. Dümmler, no. 39, pp. 71–3, 'Epitaphium Chlodarii', lines 29–30: 'Priscorum nimium regum devictus amore/ Hlutharium genitor nomen habere dedit'; Astronomus, *Vita Hludowici imperatoris*, 3, ed. Tremp, pp. 288–90; Jarnut, 'Chlodwig und Chlothar. Anmerkungen zu den Namen zweier Söhne Karls des Grossen', discusses theories about this choice of names and points to the particular circumstances of 778, when the twins were born.

22. 'Ceti Edward se fit apeler Edward le tierz apres le conquest, cest a dire apres William bastard, en se(s) lettres et chartres, et fut avis a plusours que ceo ne fu mie al honur de ly

ne de ses ancestres pur ceo que conquest par force ne done iames dreit, mes covendreit que il hust hu dreit devant le conquest, car autrement li et tuz ses successours huissent este possessours de male foy et entrusours': BL, MS Royal 14 B VI, membrane 7, an addition of the 1340s to a royal genealogy; see Laborderie, 'La mémoire des origines normandes des rois d'Angleterre dans les généalogies en rouleau des XIIIe et XIVe siècles', p. 215; Laborderie, 'The First Manuals of English History: Two Late Thirteenth-Century Genealogical Rolls of the Kings of England in the Royal Collection', pp. 24–5.

23. 'cum naturali virium robore': Richer of Saint-Rémi, *Historiae* 2. 102, ed. Hoffmann, p. 169.

24. 'Lotharius puer, filius Ludowici, apud Sanctum Remigium rex consecratur . . . favente Hugone principe ac Brunone archiepiscopo ceterisque praesulibus ac proceribus Franciae, Burgundiae atque Aquitaniae. Burgundia quoque et Aquitania Hugoni dantur ab ipso': Flodoard, *Annales*, s.a. 954, ed. Lauer, p. 139.

25. Böhmer and von Ottenthal, *Die Regesten des Kaiserreichs unter den Herrschern aus dem Sächsischen Hause 919–1024*, 1, no. 386, pp. 181–2.

26. 'Licet enim a fratre de regno pulsus sim'; 'Emmam quoque reginam cuius instinctu sese repulsum a fratre arbitrabatur': Richer of Saint-Rémi, *Historiae* 4. 9, 16, ed. Hoffmann, pp. 236, 243.

27. 'Karolum ducem regis Lotharii fratrem, quem Otto imperator multis beneficiis conductum, ut fraternis motibus secum fortior resisteret, citeriori Lotharingiae sub se prefecerat': *Gesta episcopum Cameracensium*, 1. 101, ed. Bethmann, p. 443.

28. 'nec regnum iure hereditario adquiritur': Richer of Saint-Rémi, *Historiae* 4. 11, ed. Hoffmann, p. 238.

29. 'Hinc fide promissa regibus Francorum urgemur, hinc potestati principis K. regnum ad se revocantis addicti permutare dominos aut exules fieri cogimur': *Die Briefsammlung Gerberts von Reims*, ed. Weigle, no. 168, p. 196 (Arnulf to Egbert of Trier, 990).

30. 'ut et regia potestas infirmaretur, et patruo virtus dominandi augesceret, nec ipse desertor videretur': Richer 4. 33, MGH SS 38, p. 253.

31. 'XIII kalendas. Madii. anno. III. regnante Karulus rex frater Leutarius'; 'anno V regnante Carulo rege': Zimmermann, 'La datation des documents catalans du IXe au XIIe siècle: un itinéraire politique', p. 360 and n. 77.

32. 'Quo iure legitimus heres exheredatus est, quo iure regno privatus?': *Die Briefsammlung Gerberts von Reims*, ed. Weigle, no. 164, p. 193 (Gerbert to Adalbero of Laon, 990); Gerbert was only a spokesman for Charles temporarily.

33. 'Hic deficit regnum Karoli Magni': *Historia Francorum Senonensis*, ed. Waitz, p. 368.

34. Carozzi, 'Le dernier des Carolingiens: de l'histoire au mythe', discusses the representation of Charles and his fate.

35. 'Adelinum . . . amplis terris ditavit, atque in carissimis habuit eum, quia regis Edwardi genus contigerat': William of Poitiers, *Gesta Guillelmi ducis Normannorum*, 2. 35, ed. Davis and Chibnall, p. 162.

36. *Domesday Book*, ed. Farley, 1, fol. 142a (Hertfordshire 38).

37. John of Worcester, *Chronicle*, 3, ed. McGurk, p. 44.

38. 'ducemque sibi coevum et quasi collactaneum fratrem diligebat': Orderic Vitalis, *Historia ecclesiastica*, 10. 12, ed. Chibnall, 5, p. 272.

39. *Anglo-Saxon Chronicle* (E), s.a. 1091, ed. Plummer and Earle, p. 226; John of Worcester, *Chronicle*, 3, ed. McGurk, p. 58.

40. Orderic Vitalis, *Historia ecclesiastica*, 10. 12, ed. Chibnall, 5, pp. 270–1, says Edgar was with a body of English crusaders who occupied Latakia in Syria during the Muslim siege of Antioch (June 1098). William of Malmesbury, *Gesta regum Anglorum*, 3. 251, ed. Mynors et al., p. 466, says Edgar went to Jerusalem at the time the Turks were besieging King Baldwin in Ramleh (May 1102). Both statements may be true, of course.

41. 'diverso fortunae ludicro rotatus, nunc remotus et tacitus canos suos in agro consumit': William of Malmesbury, *Gesta regum Anglorum*, 3. 251, ed. Mynors et al., p. 466.

42. 'eall swa him wel ge cynde waes': *Anglo-Saxon Chronicle* (D), s.a. 1066, ed. Plummer and Earle, p. 199.

43. Leon, Navarre, France, Burgundy, the Empire (Germany and northern Italy), England, Scotland, Denmark, Norway, Sweden, Hungary (although it is probably an oversimplification to assume the unitary nature of Scotland and Sweden); the rulers of Poland and Bohemia were dukes, not kings, at this time.

44. 'regnum Portugalense cum integritate honoris et dignitate quae ad reges pertinent': Alexander III, *Epistolae*, no. 1424, PL 200, col. 1237, JL 13420, 'Manifestis probatum'; the original is available online.

45. Deér, *Das Papsttum und die süditalienischen Normannenstaaten, 1053–1212*, pp. 62–4, 74–5; Hoffmann, 'Langobarden, Normannen, Päpste. Zum Legitimitätsproblem in Unteritalien', pp. 173–8; Innocent II, *Epistola* 416, PL 179, cols. 478–9; both pope's privileges are translated in Loud, *Roger II and the Making of the Kingdom of Sicily: Selected Sources*, pp. 304–6, 310–12.

13 DYNASTIES AND THE NON-DYNASTIC WORLD

1. 'regnum Dacie transit per eleccionem liberam set tamen consueuerunt ibidem semper eligere regales proximiores in sanguine, et si fuerint plures liberi consueuerunt saltem unum eorum eligere qui ipsis eligentibus uidetur esse utilior et sufficientior ... Swecie regnum transit per eleccionem et non per successionem set consueuerunt eligere proximiorem regalem aut unum de liberis, ut supra de regno Dacie dictum est, set regnum Norwegie transit per successionem et non per eleccionem': *Diplomatarium Norvegicum*, 19. 2, no. 650, pp. 791–5, from BL, MS Cotton Nero B III, fol. 13.

2. The exception was Erik III the Lamb (1137–46), the son of a daughter of Erik I.

3. 'se imperatorem et augustum omnium regum cis mare consistentium appellare praecepit': 'Continuatio Mogontiacensis', in *Annales Fuldenses*, s.a. 876, ed. Kurze, p. 86.

4. 'id iuris Romani imperii apex, videlicet non per sanguinis propaginem descendere, sed per principum electionem reges creare, sibi tamquam ex singulari vendicat prerogative': Otto of Freising, *Gesta Friderici I imperatoris*, 2. 1, ed. Waitz and von Simson, p. 103.

5. 'regnum Alemanniae, quod regnum Romanorum, eo quod sit quasi arra ad imperium Romanorum adquirendum, dicitur': Matthew Paris, *Chronica majora*, ed. Luard, 5, p. 624.

6. 'Hoc etiam ibi consensu communi comprobatum, Romani pontificis auctoritate est corroboratum, ut regia potestas nulli per hereditatem, sicut ante fuit consuetudo, cederet, sed filius regis, etiam si valde dignus esset, potius per electionem spontaneam quam per successionis lineam rex proveniret; si vero non esset dignus regis filius, vel si nollet eum populus, quem regem facere vellet, haberet in potestate populus': Bruno, *De Bello Saxonico Liber*, 91, ed. Lohmann, p. 85.

7. 'imperator habuit curiam Herbipolis circa mediam quadragesimam, in qua plurimi signum dominice crucis acceperunt. Ad eandem curiam imperator novum et inauditum decretum Romano regno voluit cum principibus confirmare, ut in Romanum regnum, sicut in Francie vel ceteris regnis, iure hereditario reges sibi succederent, in quo principes qui aderant assensum ei prebuerunt et sigillis suis confirmaverunt': *Annales Marbacenses*, ed. Bloch, p. 68; the subject had already been broached at an assembly in Mainz some months earlier: *Cronica Reinhardbrunnensis*, ed. Holder-Egger, p. 556; for general discussion, see Schmidt, *Königswahl und Thronfolge im 12. Jahrhundert*, pp. 231–55; Csendes, *Heinrich VI*, pp. 171–8.

8. 'apud rebelles atrocissimus, hostibus invictus, contumacibus severus, proditoribus immisericors': Gervase of Tilbury, *Otia Imperialia*, 2. 19, ed. Banks and Binns, p. 462.

9. 'terminus ... electionis principiumque successive dignitatis': ibid., p. 462.

10. *Cronica Reinhardbrunnensis*, ed. Holder-Egger, p. 558 (Frederick was called Constantine at this time).

11. 'In eo quoque stamus pro principum libertate quod ei favorem penitus denegamus qui sibi iure successionis imperium nititur vindicare. Videretur enim imperium non ex principum electione conferri, sed sanguinis successione deberi, si, prout olim patri filius, sic nunc fratri frater vel natus patri nullo succederet mediante': *Regestum Innocentii III papae super negotio Romani imperii*, ed. Kempf, no. 55, p. 149 (PL 216: 1057); cf. no. 29, p. 83 (PL 216: 1028).

12. 'ad unitatem inter electores fovendam et electionem unanimem inducendam': *Bulla Aurea Karoli IV. Imperatoris*, ed. Fritz, p. 45.

13. 'Est ergo temporalis monarchia, quam dicunt imperium, unicus principatus et super omnes in tempore': *Monarchia*, 1. 2, ed. Chiesa and Tabarroni, pp. 6–8.

14. Dante, *On World Government or De Monarchia*, tr. Schneider.

15. 'Et sic patet quod ad bene esse mundi necesse est monarchiam esse sive imperium': *Monarchia*, 1. 5, ed. Chiesa and Tabarroni, p. 28 (and repeatedly).

16. 'non inveniemus nisi sub divo Augusti, monarcha existente monarchia perfecta mundi undique fuisse quietum': ibid., 1. 16, p. 68.

17. 'auctoritas monarche Romani, qui de iure monarchia mundi est': ibid., 3. 1, p. 154.

18. 'Moysen alium ... qui de gravaminibus Egiptiorum populum suum eripiet, ad terram lacte ac melle manantem perducens': Dante, *Epistola* 5. 1, ed. Pastore Stocchi, p. 30.

19. 'quia sponsus tuus, mundi solatium et gloria plebis tue, clementissimus Henricus, divus et Augustus et Cesar, ad nuptias properat': ibid., 5. 2, p. 30.

20. 'alto Arrigo, ch'a drizzare Italia/ verrà in prima ch'ella sia disposta': Dante, *Paradiso* 30, lines 137–8, in *La Commedia*, ed. Petrocchi, 4, p. 507.

21. 'diminutum, mutilatum, laceratum et occupatum a pluribus et diversis principibus . . . ad brevissimum terrarum subiectarum sibi numerum est redacta . . . gentem acerbam et intractabilem, que magis adheret barbarice feritati quam Christiane professioni . . . quod bonum aut utile contingat mundo': *Constitutiones et acta publica imperatorum et regum*, 4. 2, ed. Schwalm, no. 1253, pp. 1369–73.

22. For a lively argument of this type, see Gillingham, 'Elective Kingship and the Unity of Medieval Germany'.

23. See, in general, Yorke, *Nunneries and the Anglo-Saxon Royal Houses*.

24. They are listed in Hartmann, *Die Königin im frühen Mittelalter*, pp. 203–4 (the number of fourteen excludes those prior to the family's accession to the throne and those categorized only as *Inhaberin*).

25. 'contempto habitu seculari, sacrum Christi velamen induere voluistis, . . . fluxa et caduca spernere, certa aeternaque requirere, abrenuntiare diabolo et seculo et pompae et operibus eius, et sequi Christum . . . Haec te caesareo generatam semine karta,/ Moribus et specie ornatam, Theodrada, salutat': Dungal, *Epistolae*, 7, ed. Dümmler, pp. 581–2.

26. 'multae nobiles moniales': Asser, *De rebus gestis Aelfredi*, 98, ed. Stevenson, p. 85.

27. Æthelweard, *Chronicon*, 4. 6, ed. Campbell, p. 54; *Anglo-Saxon Chronicle* (E), s.a. 980, ed. Plummer and Earle, pp. 123–5; Byrhtferth of Ramsey, *Vita sancti Oswaldi*, 4. 21, ed. Lapidge, p. 144.

28. *The Heads of Religious Houses: England and Wales 1 (940–1216)*, ed. Knowles et al., p. 219.

29. Prestwich, 'Mary [Mary of Woodstock] (1278–c. 1332)', *ODNB*, 36, pp. 66–7; Bartlett, *Why Can the Dead Do Such Great Things? Saints and Worshippers from the Martyrs to the Reformation*, pp. 438–9.

30. Klaniczay, *Holy Rulers and Blessed Princesses: Dynastic Cults in Medieval Central Europe*, pp. 195–294.

31. Klaniczay, *Holy Rulers and Blessed Princesses: Dynastic Cults in Medieval Central Europe*.

32. 'als einziger regierender Karolinger': Schieffer, 'Väter und Söhne im Karolingerhause', p. 157.

33. *Annales Bertiniani*, s.a. 873, ed. Waitz, p. 122; *Annales Xantenses*, s.a. 873, ed. von Simson, p. 32; 'Continuatio Mogontiacensis', in *Annales Fuldenses*, s.a. 873, ed. Kurze, p. 78; see Nelson, 'A Tale of Two Princes: Politics, Text and Ideology in a Carolingian Annal'.

34. 'Ibi principes vi et rapto assueti, populi rerum novarum cupidi, civilibus omnes cladibus intenti aliorum ditescere miseriis preoptabant': Ruotger, *Vita Brunonis Archiepiscopi Coloniensis*, 10, ed. Ott, p. 11.

35. 'fratrem suum Brunonem occidenti tutorem et provisorem, et, ut ita dicam, archiducem, in tam periculoso tempore misit': ibid., 20, p. 19.

36. For a story of Bruno once contemplating betrayal of Otto, see Thietmar of Merseburg, *Chronicon*, 2. 23, ed. Holtzmann, pp. 66–7, although the confused details make it doubtful.

37. 'In te namque et sacerdotalis religio et regia pollet fortitudo': Ruotger, *Vita Brunonis Archiepiscopi Coloniensis*, 20, ed. Ott, p. 19.

38. Although Charles of Anjou, the youngest son of Louis VIII, was intended for the Church until his elder brother John died, something pointed out by an anonymous reader of this book for Cambridge University Press.

39. 'De fructu vero ventris sui decimas Deo obtulit filias suas, I. ad Quidilingeburg Aethelheidam nomine, alteram ad Gonnesheim, quae Sophia dicitur': Thietmar of Merseburg, *Chronicon*, 4. 10, ed. Holtzmann, p. 142.

40. 'pro liberatione sua et regni ... quasi piaculum quoddam, si filia nasceretur, ut sanctimonialem eam facerent, devoverunt (*emended from* devenerunt)': *Vita beatae Margaritae de Hungaria*, 2, ed. Csepregi et al., p. 44.

41. Leo VI, *Oraison funèbre de Basile I par son fils Léon VI le Sage*, p. 64.

42. 'Scotticana ecclesia apostolicae sedi, cujus filia specialis existit, nullo mediante debeat subjacere': *Gesta regis Henrici secundi Benedicti abbatis*, ed. Stubbs, 2, p. 234 (there ascribed to Clement III, but in fact issued by Celestine III).

43. Sancho, youngest son of James I of Aragon and Yolande of Hungary, became archbishop of Toledo in 1266 at the age of sixteen; he was killed by Muslims in 1275. John, a younger son of James II of Aragon, was archbishop of Toledo 1319–28.

44. 'multorum peritorum nobilium ac magnatum decenti pariter ac potenti comitiva vallatus': *Continuatio Chronici Guillelmi de Nangiaco*, ed. Géraud, 1, p. 389; Barber, *The Trial of the Templars*, p. 228.

45. 'Quia damnate memorie Johannes Henrrici, tunc Castelle et Legionis regnorum detentor, ipsa Portugalie et Algarbii regna devastare et occupare nitebatur ... filio perditionis Roberto olim basilice duodecim Apostolorum presbytero cardinali, tunc et nunc antipape, qui se Clementem VII ausu sacrilego nominare presumebat, prout et nunc presumit': *Monumenta Portugaliae Vaticana*, 2, ed. Costa, CXII–CXV, CVIII–CXI (Boniface IX, 27–28 January 1391).

46. 'Apud illos non est rex, nisi tantum lex': Adam of Bremen, *Gesta Hammaburgensis ecclesiae pontificum*, Scholion 156 (150) to 4. 36 (35), ed. Schmeidler, p. 273.

47. *The Saga of Hacon*, 257, tr. Vigfusson and Dasent, p. 262.

48. *Annales regni Francorum*, s.a. 810, ed. Kurze, p. 133.

49. 'praecationem ad nostrum fecerunt imperium': Tafel and Thomas, ed., *Urkunden zur älteren Handels- und Staatsgeschichte der Republik Venedig*, 1, no. 17, pp. 36–9.

50. E.g. at the court held at Würzburg in October 1152, 'expeditio Italica ... paulo minus quam ad duos annos iurata est': Otto of Freising, *Gesta Friderici I imperatoris* 2. 7, ed. Waitz and von Simson, p. 108; the phrase *expeditio Italica* is a standard term.

51. 'civitas haec inimica regibus ab antiquo fuisse dicatur': Rahewin, *Gesta Friderici I imperatoris*, 3. 37, ed. Waitz and von Simson, p. 210.

52. 'Et quis esset, qui posset lacrimas retinere, qui videret planctum et luctum atque merorem marium et mulierum et maxime infirmorum et feminarum de partu et puerorum egredientium et proprios lares relinquentium?': *Narratio de Longobardie obpressione*, ed. Schmale, pp. 276–8 (MGH, SRG 27, p. 53).

53. Raccagni, *The Lombard League 1167–1225*, pp. 113–18.

54. A late medieval chronicler says these names arose from the war-cries of the Hohenstaufen and their rivals, the Welfs, with 'Ghibelline' being derived from Waiblingen, the place where Barbarossa's father had been raised: Andrew of Regensburg, *Cronica de principibus terrae Bavarorum*, ed. Leidinger, pp. 538–9.

55. 'Absit enim, ut in populo Christiano sceptrum regiminis ulterius maneat apud illum vel in viperam eius propaginem transferatur': *Epistolae saeculi XIII e regestis pontificum Romanorum selectae*, ed. Rodenberg, 2, no. 585, p. 416, 30 August 1248 (Po. 13007).

56. 'sicque ... coram textoribus, fullonibus et vulgaribus Flamingis et peditibus ... corruit ars pugne, flos militie cum electissimorum equorum et dextrariorum fortitudine; et pulcritudo ac potentia validissimi exercitus conversa est in sterquilinium factaque est ibi [gloria] Francorum stercus et vermis': *Annales Gandenses*, ed. Johnstone, p. 30.

57. 'dominum Ferdinandum tertium, electum Romanorum imperatorem, semper augustum, Germaniae, Hungariae, Bohemiae, Dalmatiae, Croatiae, Sclavoniae regem, archiducem Austriae, ducem Burgundiae, Brabantiae, Styriae, Carinthiae, Carniolae, marchionem Moraviae, ducem Luxemburgiae, Superioris ac Inferioris Silesiae, Württenbergae et Teckae, principem Sueviae, comitem Habsburgi, Tyrolis, Kyburgi et Gorritiae, marchionem Sacri Romani Imperii, Burgoviae ac Superioris et Inferioris Lusatiae, dominum Marchiae Sclavonicae, Portus Naonis et Salinarum': *Acta Pacis Westphalicae, Serie III Abteilung B: Verhandlungsakten 1: Die Friedensverträge mit Frankreich und Schweden 1: Urkunden*, ed. Oschmann, pp. 3–4.

58. Gislebert of Mons, *Chronicon Hanoniense*, 186, 188, 190, ed. Vanderkindere, pp. 275, 276, 277.

59. '"Ego Alexander rex Scocie devenio ligeus homo domini Edwardi regis Anglie contra omnes gentes'" ... salvo jure et clamio ejusdem regis Anglie et heredum suorum de homagio predicti regis Scocie et heredum suorum de regno Scocie, cum inde loqui voluerint ... servicia debita de terris et tenementis que teneo de rege Anglie': Stones (ed.), *Anglo-Scottish Relations 1174–1328: Some Selected Documents*, no. 12 (a), pp. 78–80 [39]–[40].

60. 'quia regnum ipsum Scocie ... de jure communi per quod par in parem non haberet imperium, et per quod rex regi non subest vel regnum regno ... quo ad ipsum regem Anglie fuit semper omnino liberum': Bower, *Scotichronicon*, 11. 48, ed. Watt et al., 6, p. 138; 'par droit commun que un roialme ne deit mye estre sugiet a un autre': *Chronicon de Lanercost, 1201–1346*, ed. Stevenson, p. 517, 'Illustrative Documents', no. 40 (from BL, MS Cotton Vespasian F VII).

61. Zimmermann, 'La datation des documents catalans du IXe au XIIe siècle: un itinéraire politique'.

62. The text of the Treaty is in *Layettes du Trésor des Chartes*, ed. Teulet et al., no. 4411, 3, pp. 405–8.

63. 'cum nequeat quis competenter duobus dominis servire, vel penitus mihi vel regi Angliae inseparabiliter adhaereat': Matthew Paris, *Chronica majora*, ed. Luard, 4, p. 288.

64. *Book of Fees*, 2, pp. 1142–3.

65. 'Mettons par exemple que le roy de France ait une fille ainsnee et un filz mainsné; ceste fille est mariee au filz du roy de Honguerie, duquel marriage est né un filz; lequel, par rayson, devera miex amer le pueple et le royaume de France, ou le filz mainsné du Roy, ou le filz de celle fille aisnee? Certes ... le filz du Roy': *Songe du Vergier*, 1. 142. 8, ed. Schnerb-Lièvre, 1, p. 250.

66. 'quod regnum Angliae in nullo regno Franciae subjiceretur': *Chronicon de Lanercost, 1201–1346*, ed. Stevenson, p. 333 (s.a. 1340); *Parliament Rolls of Medieval England*, ed. Given-Wilson, 4, p. 268, no. 9.

67. 'jura, leges, libertates et consuetudines ejusdem regni Scotiae ... integre et inviolabiliter perpetuis temporibus observentur ... regnum Scotiae remaneat separatum et divisum et liberum in se sine subjectione a regno Angliae': *Documents Illustrative of the History of Scotland from the Death of Alexander III to the Accession of Robert Bruce*, ed. Stevenson, 1, no. 108, pp. 162–73 (The Treaty of Birgham).

68. 'nullum capitaneum, nullum purcravium vel castellanum in castris nostris, nullum beneficiarium vel officialem aliquem in Boemia vel Moravia, vel in curia nostra ponemus alienigenam, nec bona, possessiones vel castra, vel officia aliqua alienigenis ipsis in perpetuum vel ad tempus dabimus, nec eos hereditare in regno Boemiae aliqualiter admittemus': *Regesta diplomatica nec non epistolaria Bohemiae et Moraviae*, 2, ed. Emler, no. 2245, pp. 973–5.

69. Długosz, *Annales seu Cronicae incliti regni Poloniae*, ed. Dąbrowski et al., 5, pp. 273–6.

70. 'Sed quantum dampnum regnum Swecie et indigine pertulerunt propter regem extraneum et dominum [dominium?] et principatum extraneorum sane mentis poterit estimare. Deus custodiet nos ne umquam dominentur nobis Sweivis principes extranei!': Paulsson, 'Studier i "Strängnäsmartyrologiet"', p. 33, from the Strängnäs Martyrology (Stockholm, National Library, MS A 28).

71. 'ne ... aliquid unionis regnum ad imperium quovis tempore putaretur habere': *Friderici II. Diplomata*, 2, ed. Koch, no. 369, p. 396 (1 July 1216).

72. 'de illo ex ejusdem regis Francie filiis quem ad hoc ipse rex elegerit, alio tamen ab eo qui sibi est in dicto regno Francie successurus ... Eadem insuper regnum et comitatus in eandem personam cum Francie vel Castelle seu Legionis aut Anglie regnis aliquo umquam tempore non concurrant': Reg. Vat. 41, fol. 162 v., n. 7; *Les Registres de Martin IV (1281–1285)*, ed. Olivier-Martin, no. 455, pp. 191–2, 'Qui regna transfert', 27 August 1283, Po. 22061.

73. *Regum Burgundiae e Stirpe Rudolfina Diplomata et Acta*, ed. Schieffer (1977), p. 77; this example, 'Rodulfus divina favente clementia rex', is no. 3, p. 97 (an original of 888).

74. For a refutation of the common assertion that French kings were 'kings of the French' in their documents before the reign of Philip Augustus (1180–1223), and 'kings of France' from that time, see Schneidmüller, 'Herrscher über Land oder Leute? Der kapetingische Herrschertitel in der Zeit Philipps II. August und seiner Nachfolger (1180–1270)'.

75. *Reinado y diplomas de Fernando III*, ed. González, 1, p. 518.

76. See the comments of Schneidmüller, 'Herrscher über Land oder Leute? Der kapetingische Herrschertitel in der Zeit Philipps II. August und seiner Nachfolger (1180–1270)', pp. 134–6.

77. Reynolds, *Kingdoms and Communities in Western Europe, 900–1300*, pp. 261–98, passim; Davies, 'The Peoples of Britain and Ireland 1100–1400 II: Names, Boundaries and Regnal Solidarities'.

CONCLUSION

1. 'Dominium quod rex habet in regno est alterius specie a dominio rerum quae patrimonialiter succedentur': Joannes de Terra Rubea (Terrerouge), *Contra rebelles suorum regum*, 1. 1. 13, fol. 15; for a summary of this author's views, see Giesey, 'The Juristic Basis of Dynastic Right to the French Throne', pp. 12–17; Giesey, *Le Rôle méconnu de la loi salique. La succession royale (xive–xvie siècles)*, pp. 129–35.

2. Robinson, *The Papacy 1073–1198: Continuity and Innovation*, pp. 312–18, on *idoneitas*.

3. 'juravit quod ipse omnibus diebus vitae suae pacem et honorem atque reverentiam Deo et Sanctae Ecclesiae et ejus ordinatis portaret. Deinde juravit, quod rectam justitiam et aequitatem exerceret in populo sibi commisso. Deinde juravit quod malas leges et consuetudines perversas, si quae sunt in regno suo inductae sunt, deleret et bonas leges conderet et sine fraude et malo ingenio eas custodiret': Roger of Howden, *Chronica*, ed. Stubbs, 3, p. 10; cf. *Gesta regis Henrici secundi Benedicti abbatis*, ed. Stubbs, 2, pp. 81–2.

4. Bagge, *Cross and Scepter: The Rise of the Scandinavian Kingdoms from the Vikings to the Reformation*, pp. 149–50.

5. *Recueil general des anciennes lois françaises*, 5, no. 411, p. 291; Carlyle and Carlyle, *A History of Medieval Political Theory in the West*, 6, pp. 67–8.

6. 'Quem si ab inceptis desisteret, regi Anglorum aut Anglicis nos aut regnum nostrum volens subicere, tanquam inimicum nostrum et sui nostrique iuris subversorem statim expellere niteremus et alium regem nostrum … faceremus': *Acts of the Parliaments of Scotland*, 1, ed. Thomson and Innes, p. 475 (115); an original survives in the National Records of Scotland in Edinburgh.

7. Davies, 'The Peoples of Britain and Ireland 1100–1400 II: Names, Boundaries and Regnal Solidarities', p. 11.

8. 'quod, alienigenis ab Anglia remotis, per indigenas gubernetur': *Annales Londonienses*, ed. Stubbs, p. 61.

9. 'Inauditum enim erat, quod aliquis antecessorum suorum umquam illuc venisset': Gislebert of Mons, *Chronicon Hanoniense*, 137, ed. Vanderkindere, p. 204.

10. Bennett, *Lambert Simnel and the Battle of Stoke*, p. 17.

11. 'Dies bedeutet eben nicht nur, dass Eheschliessungen, Geburten und Todesfälle zu politischen Vorgängen ersten Ranges werden, sondern auch dass sich personelle Veränderungen an der Spitze schon Jahre oder gar Jahrzehnte vor ihrer tatsächlichen Wirksamkeit sichtbar am Horizont abzeichnen': Schieffer, 'Väter und Söhne im Karolingerhause', p. 149.

12. 'Nihil certius morte, nihil incertior hora mortis'; the phrase is proverbial; see, e.g., Anselm (attrib.), *Meditatio VII*, col. 741; Peter Comestor, *Sermones*, 9, col. 1748; *Bracton's Notebook*, ed. Maitland, 1, pp. xix, 93.

13. 'Super haec attendant, quia cum in Francorum terra reges ex genere prodeant, quis regum a centum et amplius annis recolitur in filiis suis vel usque in quartam generationem regnasse? Siquidem Ottones, prae omnibus ante se regibus sacerdotalis officii praesumptores, vix attigere tertiam. Post quos primus Heinricus nullam. Quod et in aliis regnis et principatibus contigisse, qui disquisierit, invenire poterit': Humbertus of Silva Candida, *Adversus Simoniacos*, 3. 15, ed. Thaner, p. 217. Here I have taken

'Francorum' to refer to the French, i.e. the West Franks, which harmonizes with the use of the title 'rex Francorum' for Henry I of France elsewhere in the text (3. 7, p. 206), but if '*siquidem*' is taken strongly, as indicating the grounds for the previous statement, the '*Francorum terra*' would mean the land of the East Franks. If so, the implication would be that Humbert thinks East Frankish kingship hereditary. 'In Francorum regno reges ex genere prodeunt' is a quotation from Gregory I, *Homilia in evangelia*, 1. 10. 5, ed. Etaix, p. 69.

14. 'puisque les princes sont hommes, et leurs affaires sont haulx et agus, et leurs natures sont subgettes à passions maintes comme à haine et envie ... et sont leurs coeurs vray habitacle d'icelles à cause de leur gloire en régner': Chastellain, *Chronique*, 4. 6, ed. Kervyn de Lettenhove, 3, p. 30.

Bibliography of Works Cited

Manuscripts (including those consulted online)

Berlin, Staatsbibliothek, MS lat. fol. 295 (Ekkehard of Aura, *Chronicon*)

Beverley, East Riding of Yorkshire Archives and Local Studies Service, DDCC/141/68/ p41/b (document dated by the capture of 'Mons Alba', 1206)

Cambridge, CCCC, MS 45 (Bernard Gui, *Reges Francorum, Arbor genealogiae regum Francorum*) Trinity College, MS O. 4. 32 (Nicholas Trevet's Anglo-Norman chronicle)

Leiden, Universiteitsbibliotheek, MS VG G F 6 (Nicholas Trevet's Anglo-Norman chronicle)

London, BL, MS Arundel 66 ('Henry VII's Book of Astrology')

    BL, MS Cotton Faustina A VIII (prophecies)

    BL, MS Harley 7353 (genealogy of Edward IV)

    BL, MS Royal 14 B VI (genealogical roll)

    BL, MS Royal 14 C VII (Matthew Paris, *Historia Anglorum*)

    BL, MS Yates Thompson 3 (Dunois Hours)

    TNA, C62/21 (Liberate Roll 29 Henry III)

    TNA, E36/203 (Wardrobe accounts 12–14 Edward III)

    TNA, KB9/72/1–6, 9, 11, 14 (indictments against Eleanor Cobham)

    TNA, SC1/37/182 (letter of Frederick of Habsburg)

Munich, Bayerische Staatsbibliothek, clm 29880/6 (the 'Bamberger Tafel')

    Bayerische Staatsbibliothek, Cod. icon. 308 n (Wernigeroder or Schaffhausensches Wappenbuch)

Oxford, Bodleian Library, MS Bodley 968 (*Mirouer historiale abregie*)

Paris, AN, AE/III/165, Cote d'origine: J//601/25 (marriage agreement between Berengaria of Castile and Louis of France, 1255)

    BnF, MS fr. 13565 (*Récit d'un ménestrel d'Alphonse de Poitiers*)

    BnF, MS fr. 22912–3 (Raoul de Presles' translation of the *City of God*)

    BnF, MS lat. 6184 (William de Nangis, short history of the kings of France)

    BnF, MS lat. 6191 (Giles of Paris, *Karolinus*)

    BnF, MS lat. 9376 ('Genealogies of Foigny')

Prague, Archiv der Nationalgalerie, AA 2015, Codex Heidelbergensis (sixteenth-century copies of the Karlštejn wall paintings)

Utrecht, Universiteitsbibliotheek, MS 306 (3 C 3) (Thomas Waleys, *Expositio super libros Augustini De Civitate Dei*)

Vatican City, BAV, MS Reg. lat. 339 (genealogy from St.-Gallen)

    BAV, MS Reg. lat. 1283A (genealogy from Angers)

BAV, MS Vat. lat. 4015 (canonization process of Thomas de Cantilupe)
Reg. Vat. 18, 21, 24, 25, 27, 28, 41, 48
Vienna, Österreichische Nationalbibliothek, MS 8330 (sixteenth-century copies of the Karlštejn wall paintings)

Original sources

Abbreviationes gestorum Franciae regum, RHF 17 (1878), pp. 432–3.
Accounts of the Lord High Treasurer of Scotland, 4: 1507–13, ed. James Balfour Paul (Edinburgh, 1902).
Accursius, *Glossa ordinaria*, in *Corpus iuris civilis, 4, Codicis* (Lyon, 1627).
Achery, Luc d', *Veterum scriptorum spicilegium* (new edn., 3 vols., Paris, 1723).
Acta aragonensia, 1, ed. Heinrich Finke (Berlin and Leipzig, 1908).
Acta Pacis Westphalicae, Serie III Abteilung B: Verhandlungsakten 1: Die Friedensverträge mit Frankreich und Schweden 1: Urkunden, ed. Antje Oschmann (Münster, 1998).
Acta vitam Beatricis reginae Hungariae illustrantia, ed. Albert Berzeviczy, *Monumenta Hungariae Historica, Diplomataria*, 39 (Budapest, 1914).
Actes du Parlement de Paris, ed. E. Boutaric (2 vols., Paris, 1863–7).
Actes et lettres de Charles Ier, roi de Sicile, concernant la France (1257–1284), ed. A. de Boüard (Paris, 1926).
The Acts of Alexander III, King of Scots, 1249–1286, ed. Cynthia Neville and Grant Simpson (Regesta regum Scottorum, 4. 1, Edinburgh, 2012).
The Acts of Robert I, 1306–29, ed. A. A. M. Duncan (Regesta regum Scottorum 5, Edinburgh, 1987).
The Acts of the Parliaments of Scotland, 1, ed. Thomas Thomson and Cosmo Innes (Edinburgh, 1844).
Actus pontificum Cenomannis in urbe degentium, ed. G. Busson and A. Ledru (Archives historiques du Maine, 2, Le Mans, 1902); ed. Margarete Weidemann, *Geschichte des Bistums Le Mans von der Spätantike bis zur Karolingerzeit: Actus Pontificum Cenomannis in urbe degentium und Gesta Aldrici* (3 vols., Mainz, 2000), 1, pp. 31–114.
Adam of Bremen, *Gesta Hammaburgensis ecclesiae pontificum*, ed. Bernhard Schmeidler (MGH, SRG 2, 1917).
Adam of Clermont, *Flores historiarum (Excerpta)*, ed. Oswald Holder-Egger, MGH, SS 26 (1882), pp. 591–2.
Adam of Dryburgh, *De tripartito tabernaculo*, PL 198, cols. 609–792.
Adam of Eynsham, *Magna vita sancti Hugonis: The Life of Hugh of Lincoln*. ed. Decima Douie and D. Hugh Farmer (2 vols., London, 1961–2, repr. OMT, 1985).
Ademar of Chabannes, *Chronicon*, ed. P. Bourgain (CCCM 129, 1999).
Ælfric, *De temporibus anni*, ed. Heinrich Henel (Early English Text Society, original series, 213, 1942 for 1940).
Aelred of Rievaulx, *De genealogia Henrici regis*, ed. Domenico Pezzini, *Aelredi Rievallensis opera omnia 6: Opera historica et hagiographica* (CCCM 3, 2017), pp. 22–56.
Vita sancti Ædwardi regis et confessoris (BHL 2423), ed. Francesco Marzella, *Aelredi Rievallensis opera omnia 7: Opera historica et hagiographica* (CCCM 3A, 2017).
Æthelweard, *Chronicon*, ed. A. Campbell (Nelson's Medieval Texts, 1962).
Agnellus of Ravenna, *Liber pontificalis ecclesiae Ravennatis*, ed. Oswald Holder-Egger, MGH, Scriptores rerum Langobardicarum et Italicarum saec. VI–IX (1878), pp. 278–391; ed. Deborah Mauskopf Deliyannis (CCCM 199, 2006).
Aimoin of Fleury, *Historia Francorum*, PL 139, cols. 387–414, 627–870; RHF 3 (1869), pp. 21–143.

Akropolites, George, *Historia,* ed. A. Heisenberg (Stuttgart, 1903).
The History, tr. Ruth Macrides (Oxford, 2007).
Alanus de Insulis, *Explanatio in Prophetia Merlini Ambrosii,* ed. Clara Wille, *Prophetie und Politik: die Explanatio in Prophetia Merlini Ambrosii des Alanus Flandrensis: Edition mit Übersetzung und Kommentar* (2 vols., Bern, 2015).
Alberic of Trois-fontaines, *Chronica,* ed. Paul Scheffer-Boichorst, MGH, SS 23 (1874), pp. 631–950.
Albert of Stade, *Annales Stadenses,* ed. J. M. Lappenberg, MGH, SS 16 (1859), pp. 271–379.
Alcuin, *Epistolae,* ed. Ernst Dümmler, MGH, Epistolae 4 (Karolini aevi 2) (1895), pp. 1–481.
Alexander II, *Epistolae et decreta,* PL 146, cols. 1279–1430.
Alexander III, *Epistolae et privilegia,* PL 200.
Alexander von Roes, *Memoriale,* ed. Herbert Grundmann and Hermann Heimpel, *Die Schriften des Alexander von Roes und des Engelbert von Admont* (MGH, Staatsschriften des späteren Mittelalters, 1. 1, 1958), pp. 91–148.
Aly Aben Ragel, *El libro conplido en los iudizios de las estrellas. Partes 6 a 8. Traducción hecha en la corte de Alfonso el Sabio,* ed. Gerold Hilty (Barcelona, 2005).
Anales del Reino de Navarra, 6, ed. José de Moret (Tolosa, 1891).
Anales toledanos II, ed. Julio Porres Martín-Cleto, *Los Anales Toledanos I y II* (Toledo, 1993).
Anales toledanos III, ed. Antonio C. Floriano, *Cuadernos de historia de España,* 43–4 (1967), pp. 154–87.
Andreas Marchianensis, *Historia regum Francorum,* ed. Georg Waitz, MGH, SS 26 (1882), pp. 204–12.
Andrew of Regensburg, *Cronica de principibus terrae Bavarorum,* ed. Georg Leidinger, *Andreas von Regensburg. Sämtliche Werke* (Quellen und Erörterungen zur bayerischen Geschichte, Neue Folge, 1, 1903), pp. 503–687.
Andrew of St Victor, *Expositio hystorica in librum Regum,* ed. F. A. Van Liere (CCCM 53A, 1996).
Anecdotes historiques, légendes et apologues tirés du receuil inédit d'Etienne de Bourbon, ed. A. Lecoy de la Marche (SHF 185, 1877).
Anglo-Saxon Chronicle, ed. Charles Plummer and John Earle, *Two of the Saxon Chronicles Parallel* (2 vols., Oxford, 1892–9) (vol. 1 text).
Anna Comnena, *Alexias,* ed. Diether R. Reinsch and Athanasios Kambylis (2 vols., Berlin, 2001) (vol. 1 text).
Annales Admuntenses, ed. Georg Waitz, MGH, SS 9 (1851), pp. 569–600.
Annales Alamannici, ed. Georg Heinrich Pertz, MGH, SS 1 (1826), pp. 22–30, 40–4, 47–60.
Annales Altahenses maiores, ed. Edmund von Oefele (MGH, SRG 4, 1890).
Annales Bertiniani, ed. Georg Waitz (MGH, SRG 5, 1883).
Annales Bohemiae (1196–1278), ed. Josef Emler, Fontes rerum Bohemicarum, 2 (Prague, 1874), pp. 282–303.
Annales Casinenses, ed. Georg Heinrich Pertz, MGH, SS 19 (1866), pp. 303–20.
Annales de Dunstaplia, ed. Henry R. Luard, *Annales monastici* (5 vols., RS, 1864–9), 3, pp. 1–420.
Annales de Margam, ed. Henry Richards Luard, *Annales Monastici* (5 vols., RS, 1864–9), 1, pp. 1–40.
Annales de rebus gestis post mortem Przem. Otakari regis, ed. Josef Emler, Fontes rerum Bohemicarum, 2 (Prague, 1874), pp. 335–70.
'Annales de Saint-Denis généralement connues sous le titre de Chronicon Sancti Dionysii ad Cyclos Paschales', ed. Élie Berger, *Bibliothèque de l'École des chartes,* 40 (1879), pp. 261–95.
Annales de Wintonia, ed. Henry R. Luard, *Annales monastici* (5 vols., RS, 1864–9), 2, pp. 1–125.
Annales Fuldenses, ed. Friedrich Kurze (MGH, SRG 7, 1891).
Annales Gandenses, ed. Hilda Johnstone (Nelson's Medieval Classics, 1951).
Annales Hildesheimenses, ed. Georg Waitz (MGH, SRG 8, 1878).

Annales Laubacenses, ed. Georg Heinrich Pertz, MGH, SS 1 (1826), pp. 7, 9, 10, 12, 15, 52–5.

Annales Laureshamenses, ed. Georg Pertz, MGH, SS 1 (1826), pp. 22–39.

Annales Londonienses, ed. William Stubbs, *Chronicles of the Reigns of Edward I and Edward II* (2 vols., RS, 1882–3), 1, pp. 1–251.

Annales Marbacenses, ed. Hermann Bloch (MGH, SRG 9, 1907).

Annales Patherbrunnenses, eine verlorene Quellenschrift des zwölften Jahrhunderts, ed. Paul Scheffer-Boichorst (Innsbruck, 1870).

Annales Prioratus de Wigornia, ed. Henry R. Luard, *Annales Monastici* (5 vols., RS, 1864–9), 4, pp. 352–564.

Annales regni Francorum, ed. Friedrich Kurze (MGH, SRG 6, 1895).

Annales sancti Trudberti, ed. Georg Heinrich Pertz, MGH, SS 17 (1861), pp. 285–94.

Annales Sanctorum Udalrici et Afrae Augustenses, ed. Philipp Jaffé, MGH, SS 17 (1861), pp. 429–36.

Annales Vedastini, ed. Bernhard von Simson, *Annales Xantenses et Annales Vedastini* (MGH, SRG 12, 1909), pp. 40–82.

Annales Xantenses, ed. Bernhard von Simson, *Annales Xantenses et Annales Vedastini* (MGH, SRG 12, 1909), pp. 1–39.

The Annals of Fulda, tr. Timothy Reuter (Manchester, 1992).

The Annals of St Neots, ed. David Dumville and Michael Lapidge, *The Annals of St Neots with Vita Prima Sancti Neoti* (*The Anglo-Saxon Chronicle: A Collaborative Edition*, 17, 1983).

Annals of Ulster (Annála Uladh), ed. William M. Hennessy and Bartholomew MacCarthy (4 vols., Dublin, 1887–1901).

Annals of Ulster (to A.D. 1131), ed. Seán Mac Airt and Gearóid Mac Niocaill (Dublin, 1983).

Anselm (attrib.), *Meditatio VII*, PL 158, cols. 741–5.

Antonius de Bonfinis, *Rerum Ungaricarum decades*, ed. I. Fogel et al. (4 vols., Leipzig and Budapest, 1936–76).

Aristakès of Lastivert, *Récit des malheurs de la nation Arménienne*, tr. Marius Canard and Haïg Berbérian (Brussels, 1973).

Arnolfi Diplomata, ed. Paul Kehr (MGH, DD regum Germaniae ex stirpe Karolinorum 3, 1940).

Arnulf of Lisieux, *Epitaphium Matildis Imperatricis*, PL 201, col. 199.

Asser, *De rebus gestis Aelfredi*, ed. William Henry Stevenson, *Asser's Life of King Alfred* (Oxford, 1904).

Astronomus, *Vita Hludowici imperatoris*, ed. Ernst Tremp (MGH, SRG 64, 1995).

Augustine, *De civitate Dei*, ed. Bernhard Dombart and Alphonse Kalb (2 vols., CCSL 47–8, 1955).

B., *Vita sancti Dunstani* (BHL 2342), ed. Michael Winterbottom and Michael Lapidge, *The Early Lives of St Dunstan* (OMT, 2012), pp. 3–108.

Baker, Geoffrey le, *Chronicon* ed. Edward Maunde Thompson (Oxford, 1889).

Baldus de Ubaldis, *Commentaria in sextum Codicis librum* (Lyons, 1585).

Barbour, John, *The Bruce*, ed. A. A. M. Duncan (Edinburgh, 1997).

Bede, *Historia ecclesiastica gentis Anglorum: Ecclesiastical History of the English People*, ed. Bertram Colgrave and R. A. B. Mynors (OMT, 1969).

In primam partem Samuhelis libri iv, ed. David Hurst, CCSL 119 (1962), pp. 5–272.

Vita sancti Cuthberti (BHL 2021), ed. Bertram Colgrave, *Two Lives of Cuthbert* (Cambridge, 1940), pp. 142–306.

Beneš Krabice of Weitmile, *Cronica ecclesiae Pragensis*, ed. Josef Emler, *Fontes rerum Bohemicarum*, 4 (Prague, 1884), pp. 459–548.

Benvenuto da Imola, *Comentum super Dantis Aldigheris comoediam*, ed. J. P. Lacaita (5 vols., Florence, 1887).

Bernard of Clairvaux, *Epistolae*, ed. Jean Leclerq and Henri-Marie Rochais, *Sancti Bernardi opera* (8 vols., Rome, 1957–78), 7–8.

Bertran de Born, *The Poems of the Troubadour Bertran de Born*, ed. William D. Paden Jr. et al. (Berkeley, 1986).

Boece, Hector, *The Chronicles of Scotland, Compiled by Hector Boece, Translated into Scots by John Bellenden 1531*, ed. R. W. Chambers et al. (2 vols., Scottish Text Society, 3rd series, 10, 15, 1938–41).

Scotorum Historia (Paris, 1527).

Book of Fees (2 vols. in 3, London, 1920–31).

Boustronios, George, *The Chronicle of George Boustronios 1456–1489*, tr. R. M. Dawkins (University of Melbourne Cyprus Expedition Publication No. 2, 1964).

Bouteiller, Jean, *Somme rural* (Paris, 1603).

Bower, Walter, *Scotichronicon*, ed. Donald Watt et al. (9 vols., Aberdeen and Edinburgh, 1987–98).

Bracton, Henry de, *De legibus et consuetudinibus Angliae*, ed. G. E. Woodbine (4 vols., Cambridge, Mass., 1968–77, tr. S. E. Thorne).

Bracton's Notebook, ed. F. W. Maitland (3 vols., London, 1887).

Breve chronicon de rebus Siculis, ed. Wolfgang Stürner (MGH, SRG 77, 2004).

Brevis relatio de Guillelmo nobilissimo comite Normannorum, ed. Elisabeth Van Houts, Camden Fifth Series, 10 (1997), pp. 5–48.

Die Briefsammlung Gerberts von Reims, ed. Fritz Weigle (MGH, Die Briefe der deutschen Kaiserzeit 2, 1966).

Bruno, *De bello Saxonico liber*, ed. Hans-Eberhard Lohmann (MGH, Deutsches Mittelalter 2, Leipzig, 1937).

Brunwilarensis monasterii fundatorum actus, ed. Georg Waitz, MGH, SS 14 (1883), pp. 121–46.

The Brut or The Chronicles of England, ed. Friedrich W. D. Brie (2 parts, Early English Text Society, original series 131 and 136, 1906–8).

Brut y Tywysogyon or The Chronicle of the Princes: Red Book of Hergest Version, ed. Thomas Jones (Cardiff, 1955).

Bryennios, Nicephorus, *Historiae*, ed. Paul Gautier (Brussels, 1975).

Bulla Aurea Karoli IV. Imperatoris, ed. Wolfgang D. Fritz (MGH, Fontes iuris Germanici antiqui in usum scholarum, 11, 1972).

Burchard of Ursberg, *Chronicon*, ed. Oswald Holder-Egger and Bernhard von Simson (2nd edn., MGH, SRG 16, 1916).

Byrhtferth of Ramsey, *Vita sancti Oswaldi* (BHL 6374), ed. Michael Lapidge, *Byrhtferth of Ramsey: The Lives of St Oswald and St Ecgwine* (OMT, 2008), pp. 1–202.

Caesarius of Heisterbach, *Vita, passio et miracula sancti Engelberti* (BHL 2546–8), ed. Fritz Zschaeck, in *Die Wundergeschichten des Caesarius von Heisterbach*, 3, ed. A. Hilka (Bonn, 1937), pp. 223–328.

Calendar of Documents Relating to Scotland, ed. Joseph Bain (4 vols., Edinburgh, 1881–8).

Calendar of Entries in the Papal Registers Relating to Great Britain and Ireland: Papal Letters, ed. W. H. Bliss and J. A. Twemlow (14 vols., London, 1893–1960).

Calendar of State Papers and Manuscripts, Existing in the Archives and Collections of Milan, 1, ed. Allen B. Hinds (London, 1912).

Calendar of the Close Rolls Preserved in the Public Record Office, Edward III, A. D. 1327–1330 (London, 1896).

Calendar of the Close Rolls Preserved in the Public Record Office, Edward III, A. D. 1330–1333 (London, 1898)

Calendar of the Close Rolls Preserved in the Public Record Office, Edward III, A. D. 1341–1343 (London, 1902).

Calendar of the Close Rolls Preserved in the Public Record Office, Edward III, A. D. 1343–1346 (London, 1904).

Calendar of the Liberate Rolls (1226–72) (6 vols., London, 1916–64).

Calendar of the Patent Rolls Preserved in the Public Record Office, Edward III A. D. 1327–1330 (London, 1891).

Calendar of the Patent Rolls preserved in the Public Record Office, Edward III A. D. 1334–1338 (London, 1895).

Capitularia regum Francorum 1, ed. Alfred Boretius (MGH, 1883).

Capitularia regum Francorum 2, ed. Alfred Boretius and Victor Krause (MGH, 1897).

Caresinus, Raphael, *Raphayni de Cresinis cancellarii Venetiarum Chronica*, ed. Ester Pastorello (Rerum Italicarum scriptores, new ed., 12. 2, 1923).

Cartulaire général de l'Ordre du Temple, 1119?-1150, ed. Marquis d' Albon (Paris, 1913).

Cedrenus, George, *Historiarum compendium*, ed. Immanuel Bekker (2 vols., Bonn, 1838–9).

Chancelaria de D. Afonso III, ed. Leontina Ventura and António Resende de Oliveira (3 vols., Coimbra, 2006–11).

Chandos Herald, *La vie du Prince Noir*, ed. Diana B. Tyson (Tübingen, 1975).

La chanson de la croisade albigeoise, ed. Eugène Martin-Chabot (3 vols, Paris, 1931–61).

Charles IV, *Karoli IV Imperatoris Romanorum Vita ab eo ipso conscripta*, ed. Balázs Nagy and Frank Schaer (Budapest, 2001).

Charters and Other Records of the City and Royal Burgh of Kirkwall with the Treaty of 1468 between Denmark and Scotland, ed. John Mooney (Third Spalding Club, 1952).

Chastellain, Georges, *Chronique*, ed. J. Kervyn de Lettenhove, *Oeuvres de Georges Chastellain*, 1–5 (Brussels, 1863–4).

The Chaworth Roll: A Fourteenth-Century Genealogy of the Kings of England, ed. Alixe Bovey (London, 2005).

Choniates, Niketas, *Historia*, ed. Immanuel Bekker (Bonn, 1835); ed. Jan-Louis van Dieten (Berlin and New York, 1975).

Christine de Pisan, *Le Livre des fais et bonnes meurs du sage roy Charles V*, ed. Suzanne Solente (2 vols., SHF 437, 444, 1936–40).

Chronica Adefonsi imperatoris, ed. Antonio Maya Sánchez, *Chronica Hispana saeculi XII. Pars I* (CCCM 71, 1990), pp. 149–248.

Chronica de Mailros, ed. Joseph Stevenson (Bannatyne Club, 49, 1835).

Chronica latina regum Castellae, ed. Luis Charlo Brea, *Chronica Hispana saeculi XIII* (CCCM 73, 1997), pp. 35–118.

Chronica regia Coloniensis, continuatio secunda, ed. Georg Waitz (MGH, SRG 18, 1880).

Chronica Sealandie, ed. Erik Kroman, *Danmarks middelalderlige annaler* (Copenhagen, 1980), pp. 106–44.

Chronici Hungarici compositio saeculi XIV, ed. Alexander Domanovszky, *Scriptores rerum Hungaricarum*, 1 (Budapest, 1937), pp. 217–505.

The Chronicle of Duke Erik: A Verse Epic from Medieval Sweden, tr. Erik Carlquist and Peter C. Hogg (Lund, 2012).

A Chronicle of London, from 1089 to 1483 (ed. Edward Tyrrell and N. H. Nicolas) (London, 1827).

Chronicon Angliae ab Anno Domini 1328 usque ad annum 1388, ed. Edward Maunde Thompson (RS, 1874).

Chronicon Compostellanum, ed. Emma Falque Rey, *Habis* 14 (1983), pp. 73–83.

Chronicon de Lanercost, 1201–1346, ed. Joseph Stevenson (Bannatyne Club 65 and Maitland Club 46, Edinburgh, 1839).

Chronicon Moissiacense, ed. Georg Pertz, MGH, SS 1 (1826), pp. 282–313.

Chronicon Paschale, ed. Ludwig Dindorf (2 vols., Bonn, 1832).

Chronicon Rhythmicum Austriacum, ed. Wilhelm Wattenbach, MGH, SS 25 (1880), pp. 349–68.

Chronicon Salernitanum, ed. Ulla Westerbergh (Acta Universitatis Stockholmiensis, Studia Latina Stockholmiensia 3, Stockholm/Lund, 1956).

Chronicon sancti Benigni Divionensis, PL 162, cols. 755–848.

Chronicon Turonense magnum, ed. Edmond Martène and Ursin Durand, *Veterum Scriptorum Monumentorum Amplissima Collectio* (9 vols., Paris, 1724–33), 5, cols. 917–1072.

Chronicon Turonense magnum (excerpts), ed. André Salmon, *Recueil des chroniques de Touraine* (Tours, 1854), pp. 64–161; RHF 18 (1879), pp. 290–320; ed. Oswald Holder-Egger, MGH, SS 26 (1882), pp. 468–76.

Chronicon Vedastinum, ed. Georg Waitz, MGH, SS 13 (1881), pp. 674–709.

Chronicon Werumensium: Continuatio (a. 1276–1280), ed. Ludwig Weiland, MGH, SS 23 (1874), pp. 561–72.

Chronicque de la traïson et mort de Richart Deux Roy Dengleterre, ed. Benjamin Williams (London, 1846).

Chronique des rois de France, ed. Léopold Delisle, RHF 24 (1904), pp. 750–75.

Chronique du religieux de Saint-Denys, ed. Louis Bellaguet (6 vols., Paris, 1839–52).

Codex Carolinus, ed. Wilhelm Gundlach, MGH, Epistolae Merowingici et Karolini aevi (I) (1892), pp. 469–657.

Codex Italiae diplomaticus, 2, ed. Johann Christian Lünig (Frankfurt, 1726).

Coke, Edward, *La sept part des reports Sr. Edvv. Coke Chiualer, chiefe Iustice del Common Banke* (1608).

Colección diplomática de Alfonso I de Aragón y Pamplona, 1104–1134, ed. José Angel Lema Pueyo (San Sebastián, 1990).

Commendatio lamentabilis in transitu magni regis Edwardi, ed. William Stubbs, *Chronicles of the Reigns of Edward I and Edward II* (2 vols., RS, 1882–3), 2, pp. 1–21.

Commynes, Philippe de, *Mémoires*, ed. Joël Blanchard (2 vols., Geneva, 2007) (vol. 1 text).

Concilia aevi Karolini DCCCLX–DCCCLXXIV, ed. Wilfried Hartmann (MGH, Concilia 4, 1998).

Conciliorum oecumenicorum decreta, ed. Giuseppe Alberigo et al. (3rd. edn., Bologna, 1973).

Concilios visigóticos e hispano-romanos, ed. José Vives (Barcelona and Madrid, 1963).

Conrad of Scheyern, *Chronicon Schirense*, ed. Philipp Jaffé, MGH, SS 17 (1861), pp. 615–23.

Conradi III et filii eius Heinrici Diplomata, ed. Friedrich Hausmann (MGH, DD regum et imperatorum Germaniae 9, 1969).

Constantiae imperatricis Diplomata, ed. Theo Kölzer (MGH, DD 11. 3, 1990).

Constantine VII Porphyrogenitus, *Book of Ceremonies*, ed. J. J. Reiske (2 vols., Canberra, 2012, tr. Anna Moffat and Mexeme Tall).

De administrando imperio, ed. G. Moravcsik (2nd. edn., Washington, DC, 1967).

Constitutiones et acta publica imperatorum et regum, 4. 2, ed. Jakob Schwalm (MGH, 1909–11).

Constitutiones et acta publica imperatorum et regum, 8 (1345–1348), ed. Karl Zeumer and Richard Salomon (MGH, 1910–26).

Constitutiones et acta publica imperatorum et regum, 11 (1354–1356), ed. Wolfgang D. Fritz (MGH, 1978–92).

Continuatio Chronici Girardi de Fracheto, ed. Joseph-Daniel Guigniaut and Natalis de Wailly, RHF 21 (1855), pp. 1–70.

Continuatio Chronici Guillelmi de Nangiaco, ed. H. Géraud, *Chronique de Guillaume de Nangis et de ses continuateurs* (2 vols., SHF, 1843).

Continuatio Eulogii: The Continuation of the Eulogium Historiarum, 1364-1413, ed. Chris Given-Wilson (OMT, 2019).

Continuatio isidoriana hispana. Crónica mozárabe de 754, ed. José Eduardo López Pereira (2nd edn., Fuentes y Estudios de Historia Leonesa 127, Leon, 2009).

Corpus juris confoederationis Germanicae, ed. Guido von Meyer (Frankfurt, 1822).

Corrozet, Gilles, *Les antiquitez, histoires, croniques et singularitez de la grande et excellente cite de Paris* (Paris, 1577).

Cortes de los antiguos reinos de Aragón y de Valencia y principado de Cataluña, 10 (Real Academia de la Historia, Madrid, 1906).

Cosmas of Prague, *Chronica Boemorum*, ed. Berthold Bretholz (MGH, SRG, n.s. 2, Berlin, 1923).

Councils and Ecclesiastical Documents Relating to Great Britain and Ireland, ed. Arthur West Haddan and William Stubbs (3 vols. in 4, Oxford, 1869–78).

Councils and Synods with Other Documents Relating to the English Church, 1 *(871–1204)*, ed. D. Whitelock et al. (2 vols., Oxford, 1981).

The Court and Household of Eleanor of Castile in 1290: An Edition of British Library, Additional Manuscript 35294, ed. John Carmi Parsons (Toronto, 1977).

Crónica de Alfonso X, ed. Manuel González Jiménez (Murcia, 1998).

Crónica del Obispo Don Pelayo, ed. Benito Sánchez Alonso (Madrid, 1924).

Crónica del rey don Alfonso el Onceno, ed. Cayetano Rosell, *Crónicas de los reyes de Castilla* (3 vols., Biblioteca de autores españoles 66, 68, 70, Madrid, 1875–8), 1, pp. 171–392.

Crónica del rey don Sancho el Bravo, ed. Cayetano Rosell, *Crónicas de los reyes de Castilla* (3 vols., Biblioteca de autores españoles 66, 68, 70, Madrid, 1875–8), 1, pp. 67–90.

Cronica et cartularium monasterii de Dunis, ed. Ferdinand Van De Putte (Bruges, 1864).

Cronica Reinhardsbrunnensis, ed. Oswald Holder-Egger, MGH, SS 30. 1 (1896), pp. 490–656.

Crónicas anónimas de Sahagún, ed. Antonio Ubieto Arteta (Textos medievales 75, Zaragoza, 1987).

Crónicas de los reyes de Castilla, ed. Cayetano Rosell (3 vols., Biblioteca de autores españoles 66, 68, 70, Madrid, 1875–8).

Danmarks middelalderlige annaler, ed. Erik Kroman (Copenhagen, 1980).

Dante Alighieri, *La Commedia secondo l'antica vulgata*, ed. Giorgio Petrocchi (Le Opere di Dante Alighieri: edizione nazionale a cura della Società Dantesca Italiana, 7, 4 vols., rev. edn., Florence, 1994).

    Epistole, ed. Manlio Pastore Stocchi, *Epistole; Ecloge; Questio de situ et forma aque et terre* (Rome, 2012).

    Monarchia, ed. Paolo Chiesa and Andrea Tabarroni (Le opere, 4, Rome, 2013).

    On World Government or De Monarchia, tr. Herbert W. Schneider (New York, 1949).

Daumet, Georges, ed., *Innocent VI et Blanche de Bourbon: Lettres du Pape publiées d'après les Registres du Vatican* (Paris, 1899).

Decretales Gregorii IX, ed. Emil Friedberg (Corpus iuris canonici, 2, Leipzig, 1881), cols. 1–928.

Una descripción anónima de al-Andalus, ed. Luis Molina (2 vols., Madrid, 1983).

Díaz de Games, Gutierre, *El Victorial*, ed. Rafael Beltrán Llavador (Salamanca, 1997).

Diplomatario andaluz de Alfonso X, ed. Manuel González Jiménez (Seville, 1991).

Diplomatario de la Reina Urraca de Castilla y León (1109–1126), ed. Cristina Monterde Albiac (Zaragoza, 1996).

Diplomatarium Norvegicum, 1. 1, ed. C. A. Lange and Carl R. Unger (Christiania [Oslo], 1847); 6. 1, ed. Carl R. Unger and H. J. Huitfeldt (Christiania [Oslo], 1863); 8. 1, ed. Carl R. Unger and H. J. Huitfeldt (Christiania [Oslo], 1871); 19. 2, ed. Alexander Bugge (Kristiania [Oslo], 1914).

Długosz, Jan, *Annales seu Cronicae incliti regni Poloniae*, ed. Jan Dąbrowski et al. (11 vols., Warsaw and Cracow, 1964–2005).

Documentación del monasterio de Las Huelgas de Burgos (1116–1230), ed. José Manuel Lizoain Garrido (Burgos, 1985).

Documentos de Jaime I de Aragón, ed. Ambrosio Huici and Maria Cabanes (5 vols., Valencia and Zaragoza, 1976–82).

Documentos medievais portugueses. Documentos régios, 1, ed. Rui de Azevedo (2 vols., Lisbon, 1958–62).

Documentos medievales del Reino de Galicia: Doña Urraca (1095–1126), ed. Manuel Recuero Astray (Santiago de Compostella, 2002).

Documents Illustrative of the History of Scotland from the Death of Alexander III to the Accession of Robert Bruce, ed. Joseph Stevenson (2 vols., Edinburgh, 1870).

Documents per l'història de la cultura catalana mig-eval, ed. Antoni Rubió i Lluc (2 vols., Barcelona, 1908–21).

Dölger, Franz, *Regesten der Kaiserurkunden des oströmischen Reiches*, 1. 2: *Regesten von 867–1025* (2nd edn., Munich, 2003).

Domesday Book, ed. Abraham Farley (2 vols., London, 1783, supplementary vol. ed. H. Ellis, 1816).

Du Bellay, Martin, *Mémoires*, ed. V. L. Bourrilly and F. Vindry (4 vols., SHF 338, 350, 356, 387, 1908–19).

Du Bouchet, Jean, *Preuves de l'histoire de l'illustre maison de Coligny* (Paris, 1662).

Dudo of Saint-Quentin, *De moribus et actis primorum Normanniae ducum*, ed. Jules Lair (Mémoires de la Société des Antiquaires de Normandie, 3rd series, 3, Caen, 1858–65).

Dugdale, William, ed., *Monasticon anglicanum* (ed. John Caley et al., 6 vols. in 8, London, 1846).

Dungal, *Epistolae*, ed. Ernst Dümmler, MGH, Epistolae 4 (Karolini aevi 2) (1895), pp. 568–85.

Dupuy, Pierre, *Histoire du différend d'entre le pape Boniface VIII et Philippes le Bel* (Paris, 1655).

Durham Liber Vitae, ed. David Rollason and Lynda Rollason (3 vols., London, 2007).

Eadmer, *Historia novorum*, ed. Martin Rule (RS, 1884).

Vita sancti Dunstani, ed. Andrew J. Turner and Bernard J. Muir, *Lives and Miracles of Saints Oda, Dunstan and Oswald* (OMT, 2006), pp. 44–158.

Einhard, *Vita Karoli Magni*, ed. Oswald Holder-Egger (MGH, SRG 25, 1911).

Ekkehard IV, *Casus sancti Galli*, ed. Hans F. Haefele (Ausgewählte Quellen zur deutschen Geschichte des Mittelalters, 10, Darmstadt, 1980).

Ekkehard of Aura, *Chronicon universale*, ed. Georg Waitz, MGH, SS 6 (1844), pp. 33–265.

Encomium Emmae Reginae, ed. Alistair Campbell (Camden Third Series, 72, 1949, repr. with a supplementary introduction by Simon Keynes, Cambridge, 1998).

An English Chronicle of the Reigns of Richard II, Henry IV, Henry V and Henry VI, ed. John Silvester Davies (Camden Soc. 64, 1856).

The English Register of Godstow Nunnery, ed. Andrew Clark (3 vols., Early English Text Society, original series 129, 130, 142, 1905–11).

Epistola ad Petrum Panormitane Ecclesie Thesaurarium de calamitate Sicilie (formerly attributed to Hugo Falcandus), ed. G. B. Siragusa, *La Historia o Liber Regni Sicilie e la Epistola ad Petrum Panormitane Ecclesie Thesaurarium di Ugo Falcando* (Fonti per la storia d'Italia, 22, Rome, 1897), pp. 169–86.

Epistolae pontificum romanorum ineditae, ed. Samuel Loewenfeld (Leipzig, 1885).

Epistolae saeculi XIII e regestis pontificum Romanorum selectae, ed. Karl Rodenberg (3 vols, MGH, 1883–94).

Erasmus, *Institutio principis christiani*, ed. Otto Herding, *Opera omnia Desiderii Erasmi*, 4. 1 (Amsterdam, 1974), pp. 95–219.

Erchanbert, *Breviarium regum Francorum, continuatio*, ed. Georg Heinrich Pertz, MGH, SS 2 (1829), pp. 329–30.

Eugenius III, *Epistolae et privilegia*, PL 180, cols. 1013–606.

Eulogium historiarum, ed. Frank Scott Haydon (3 vols., RS, 1858–63).

Eustathios of Thessaloniki, *The Capture of Thessaloniki*, ed. Stilpon Paraskeua Kyriakides (reprint, with translation by John R. Melville Jones, Canberra, 1988).

Ex anonymo regum Franciae chronico, ed. Natalis de Wailly and Léopold Delisle, RHF 22 (1860), pp. 16–20.

Exchequer Rolls of Scotland, 5: 1437–54, ed. George Burnett (Edinburgh, 1882).

Flandria generosa, ed. D. L. C. Bethmann, MGH, SS 9 (1851), pp. 313–34.

Flodoard, *Annales*, ed. Philippe Lauer (Paris, 1905).

Floriano, Antonio C., 'Fragmento de unos viejos anales (1089–1196)', *Boletín de la Real Academia de la Historia*, 94 (1929), pp. 133–62.

Florus of Lyons, *Querela de divisione imperii*, ed. Ernst Dümmler, MGH, Poetae latini aevi Carolini 2 (1884), pp. 507–66.

Foedera, conventiones, litterae et ... acta publica, ed. Thomas Rymer (original edn., 20 vols., London, 1704–35); (new edn., 4 vols. in 7 parts, Record Commission, 1816–69).

Fordun, John of, *Chronica gentis Scotorum*, ed. W. F. Skene (Historians of Scotland 1 and 4, 2 vols., Edinburgh, 1871–2).

The Formularies of Angers and Marculf: Two Merovingian Legal Handbooks, tr. Alice Rio (Liverpool, 2008).

Fragmentary Annals of Ireland, ed. Joan Newlon Radner (Dublin, 1978).

François de Meyronnes (Franciscus de Mayronis), *Flores beati Augustini extracti per veritates ex libris De Civitate Dei extracti* (Cologne, 1473; titled *Flores d. Augustini ex suis libris De Civitate Dei excerpti*) Lyons, 1580).

Francorum regum historia, ed. Georg Heinrich Pertz, MGH, SS 2 (1829), pp. 324–5.

Fredegar, *Chronica*, ed. Bruno Krusch, MGH, Scriptores rerum Merovingicarum, 2 (1888), pp. 1–193.

    Chronica, ed. J. M. Wallace-Hadrill, *The Fourth Book of the Chronicle of Fredegar with its Continuations* (Nelson's Medieval Classics, 1960).

Friderici II. Diplomata, 2, ed. Walter Koch (MGH, DD regum et imperatorum Germaniae, 14. 2, 2007).

Froissart, Jean, *Chroniques. Livre I: le manuscrit d'Amiens, Bibliothèque municipale no 486*, ed. George T. Diller (5 vols., Geneva, 1991–8).

    Oeuvres de Froissart. Chroniques, ed. J. Kervyn de Lettenhove (25 vols., Brussels, 1867–77).

Frutolfi et Ekkehardi Chronica necnon Anonymi Chronica imperatorum, ed. Franz-Josef Schmale and Irene Schmale-Ott (Ausgewählte Quellen zur deutschen Geschichte des Mittelalters, 15, Darmstadt, 1972).

Fulcher of Chartres, *Historia Hierosolymitana*, ed. Heinrich Hagenmeyer (Heidelberg, 1913).

Gaimar, Geffrei, *Estoire des Engleis*, ed. Ian Short (Oxford, 2009).

Galbert of Bruges, *De multro, traditione et occisione gloriosi Karoli comitis Flandriarum*, ed. Jeff Rider, *Histoire du meurtre de Charles le Bon* (CCCM 131, 1994).

Gallia christiana, 8 (Paris, 1744).

Gautier d'Arras, *Eracle*, ed. E. Löseth, *Oeuvres de Gautier d'Arras* (2 vols., Paris, 1899), 1; ed. Karen Pratt (London, 2007).

Genealogia ducum Brabantiae ampliata, ed. Johannes Heller, MGH, SS 25 (1880), pp. 391–9.

Genealogia regum Franciae tertiae stirpis, RHF 17 (1878), pp. 433–4.

Genealogia Welforum, ed. Matthias Becher, *Quellen zur Geschichte der Welfen und die Chronik Burchards von Ursberg* (Ausgewählte Quellen zur deutschen Geschichte des Mittelalters 18b, Darmstadt, 2007), pp. 24–6.

Genealogiae Karolorum, 7, ed. Georg Waitz, MGH, SS 13 (1881), p. 248.

Genealogiae Karolorum: Commemoratio genealogiae Karoli imperatoris, ed. Georg Waitz, MGH, SS 13 (1881), pp. 245–6.

Genealogiae scriptoris Fusniacensis, ed. Georg Waitz, MGH, SS 13 (1881), pp. 251–6.

Geoffrey of Monmouth, *Historia regum Britannie*, ed. Michael D. Reeve (Arthurian Studies 69, Woodbridge, 2007).

Geoffroy de Courlon, *Chronique de l'abbaye de Saint-Pierre-le-Vif de Sens*, ed. M. G. Julliot (Sens, 1876).

Gerald of Wales (Giraldus Cambrensis), *De principis instructione*, ed. Robert Bartlett (OMT, 2018).

    Expugnatio Hibernica: The Conquest of Ireland, ed. A. B. Scott and F. X. Martin (Dublin, 1978).

    Topographia Hibernica, ed. James F. Dimock, *Giraldi Cambrensis opera*, 5 (RS, 1867), pp. 1–204.

    Vita Galfridi archiepiscopi Eboracensis, ed. J. S. Brewer, *Giraldi Cambrensis opera*, 4 (RS, 1873), pp. 355–431.

Gerlach of Mühlhausen, *Chronicon*, ed. Wilhelm Wattenbach, MGH, SS 17 (1861), pp. 683–710; ed. Josef Emler, *Fontes rerum Bohemicarum*, 2 (Prague, 1874), pp. 461–516.

Gervase of Canterbury, *Chronica*, ed. William Stubbs, *The Historical Works of Gervase of Canterbury* (2 vols., RS, 1879–80), 1.

Gervase of Rheims, *Epistola ad Alexandrum II papam*, ed. Léopold Delisle, RHF 11 (1876), p. 499.

Gervase of Tilbury, *Otia Imperialia*, ed. S. E. Banks and J. W. Binns (OMT, 2002).

Gesta archiepiscoporum Magdeburgensium, ed. Wilhelm Schum, MGH, SS 14 (1883), pp. 361–486.

Gesta Berengarii imperatoris, ed. Ernst Dümmler (Halle, 1871).

Gesta episcoporum Cameracensium, ed. L. C. Bethmann, MGH, SS 7 (1846), pp. 393–525.

Gesta episcoporum Halberstadensium, ed. Ludwig Weiland, MGH, SS 23 (1874), pp. 73–123.

Gesta Innocentii III, PL 214, cols. XV–CCXXVIII; ed. David Richard Gress-Wright (PhD thesis, Bryn Mawr College, 1981).

The Gesta Normannorum Ducum of William of Jumièges, Orderic Vitalis and Robert of Torigni, ed. Elisabeth Van Houts (2 vols., OMT, 1992–5).

Gesta principum Polonorum: The Deeds of the Princes of the Poles, ed. Karol Maleczynski et al. (Budapest and New York, 2003).

Gesta regis Henrici secundi Benedicti abbatis, ed. William Stubbs (2 vols., RS, 1867) (now attributed to Roger of Howden).

Gesta Stephani, ed. K. R. Potter (OMT, 1955, rev. edn. 1976).

Gilbert Foliot, *Letters and Charters*, ed. Adrian Morey and C. N. L. Brooke (Cambridge, 1967).

Gislebert of Mons, *Chronicon Hanoniense*, ed. Léon Vanderkindere (Commission Royale d'Histoire, Brussels, 1904).

Given-Wilson, Chris (tr.), *Chronicles of the Revolution 1397–1400* (Manchester Medieval Sources, 1993).

Glossae biblicae, ed. C. Vaciago (CCCM 189B, 2004).

Godman, Peter, ed., *Poetry of the Carolingian Renaissance* (London, 1985).

Goscelin of Saint-Bertin, *Liber confortatorius*, ed. C. H. Talbot, *Analecta monastica*, 3 (Studia Anselmiana 37) (1955), pp. 1–117.

El Gran Priorado de Navarra de la Orden de San Juan de Jerusalén, siglos XII–XIII, ed. Santos A. García Larragueta (2 vols. Pamplona, 1957).

Les Grandes chroniques de France, ed. Jules Viard (10 vols., SHF 395, 401, 404, 415, 418, 423, 429, 435, 438, 457, 1920–53).

Les Grandes chroniques de France: chronique des règnes de Jean II et de Charles V, ed. Roland Delachenal (4 vols. in 3, SHF 348, 375, 391–2, 1910–20).

Les grands traités de la guerre de Cent ans, ed. Eugène Cosneau (Paris, 1889).

Glanvill, *The Treatise on the Laws and Customs of England Commonly Called Glanvill*, ed. G. D. H. Hall (London, 1965, rev. edn. 1993).

Gratian, *Decretum*, ed. Emil Friedberg (Corpus iuris canonici, 1, Leipzig, 1879).

Gray, Thomas, *Scalacronica*, ed. Joseph Stevenson (Maitland Club, Edinburgh, 1836).

The Great Chronicle of London, ed. A. H. Thomas and I. D. Thornley (London, 1938).

The Great Roll of the Pipe for the First Year of the Reign of King John, ed. Doris M. Stenton (Pipe Roll Soc. 48 (n.s. 10), 1933).

Greek Epic Fragments, ed. Martin L. West (Cambridge, Mass., 2003).

Gregory I, *Homilia in evangelia*, ed. Raymond Etaix (CCSL 141, 1999).

Gregory of Tours, *History of the Franks*, tr. Lewis Thorpe (Penguin Classics, 1974).

Libri historiarum decem, ed. Bruno Krusch and Wilhelm Levison (MGH, Scriptores rerum Merovingicarum, 1. 1 (1937–51).

Gregory VII, *Registrum*, ed. Erich Caspar, MGH, Epistolae selectae, 2 (2 parts, Berlin, 1920–3).

Gregory, William, *Chronicle of London*, ed. James Gairdner, *The Historical Collections of a Citizen of London in the Fifteenth Century* (Camden Soc. n.s. 17, 1876), pp. 55–239.

Guillelmus Scotus, *Chronicon*, ed. Joseph-Daniel Guigniaut and Natalis de Wailly, RHF 21 (1855), pp. 201–11.

Hariulf, *Chronicon Centulense*, ed. Ferdinand Lot, *Chronique de l'abbaye de Saint-Riquier* (Paris, 1894).

Heinrici III. Diplomata, ed. Harry Bresslau and Paul Kehr (MGH, DD regum et imperatorum Germaniae, 5, 1931).

Heinrici IV. Diplomata, ed. Dietrich von Gladiss and Alfred Gawlik (3 vols., MGH, DD regum et imperatorum Germaniae, 6, 1941–78).

Heinricus Surdus de Selbach, *Chronica*, ed. Harry Bresslau (MGH, SRG, n.s. 1, 1922).

Helinand of Froidmont, *Chronica*, ed. Bertrand Tissier, *Bibliotheca Patrum Cisterciensium*, 7 (Bonnefont, 1669), pp. 72–205.

Henrici VI Angliae regis miracula postuma (BHL 3816 r), ed. Paul Grosjean (Subsidia Hagiographica 22, Brussels, 1935).

Henry IV, *Die Briefe Heinrichs IV.*, ed. Carl Erdmann (MGH, Deutsches Mittelalter 1, 1937).

Henry of Huntingdon, *Historia Anglorum: The History of the English People*, ed. Diana Greenway (OMT, 1996).

Hermann of Reichenau, *Chronica*, ed. Georg Pertz, MGH, SS 5 (1844), pp. 67–133.

Hildegard of Bingen, *Epistularium Hildegardis Bingensis*, ed. L. Van Acker and M. Klaes-Hachmöller (CCCM 91B, 2001).

Historia Compostellana, ed. Emma Falque Rey (CCCM 70, 1988).

Historia Diplomatica Friderici II, ed. J.-L.-A. Huillard-Bréholles (6 vols. in 12, Paris, 1852–61).

Historia et Cartularium Monasterii Sancti Petri Gloucestriae, ed. William Henry Hart (3 vols., RS, 1863–7).

Historia Francorum Senonensis, ed. Georg Waitz, MGH, SS 9 (1851), pp. 364–9.

Historia Francorum usque ad annum 1214, ed. Auguste Molinier, MGH, SS 26 (1882), pp. 394–6.

Historia relationis sancti Walarici (BHL 8763), ed. Oswald Holder-Egger, MGH, SS 15. 2 (1888), pp. 693–6.

Historia Silensis, ed. Juan A. Estévez Sola (*Chronica Hispana saeculi XII. Pars III*, CCCM 71B, 2018).

Historia Welforum, ed. Matthias Becher, *Quellen zur Geschichte der Welfen und die Chronik Burchards von Ursberg* (Ausgewählte Quellen zur deutschen Geschichte des Mittelalters 18b, Darmstadt, 2007), pp. 34–86.

A History of the Tyrants of Sicily by 'Hugo Falcandus', tr. Graham Loud and Thomas Wiedemann (Manchester, 1998).

Holder-Egger, Oswald, 'Italienische Prophetieen des 13. Jahrhunderts', *Neues Archiv*, 15 (1890), pp. 141–78.

Hostiensis (Henry de Segusio), *Summa aurea* (Venice, 1574).

Hrotsvit, *Opera omnia*, ed. Walter Berschin (Munich, 2001).

Hugh the Chanter, *The History of the Church of York 1066–1127*, ed. Charles Johnson (OMT, rev. edn., 1990).

Hugh of Fleury, *Modernorum Francorum regum actus*, ed. Georg Waitz, MGH, SS 9 (1851), pp. 376–95.

Humbertus of Silva Candida, *Adversus Simoniacos*, ed. F. Thaner, MGH, Libelli de lite imperatorum et pontificum 1 (1891), pp. 95–253.

Ibn 'Abd al-Hakam, 'Narrative of the Conquest of al-Andalus', tr. David A. Cohen, *Medieval Iberia: Readings from Christian, Muslim, and Jewish Sources*, ed. Olivia Remie Constable (2nd edn., Philadelphia, 2012), pp. 36–40.

Ibn al-Athir, *Annales du Maghreb et de l'Espagne*, tr. Edmond Fagnan (Algiers, 1898).

The Chronicle of Ibn Al-Athir for the Crusading Period from Al-Kamil Fi'L-Ta'Rikh, Part I: The Years 491–541/1097–1146, tr. D. S. Richards (Farnham, 2005).

Ibn Battuta, *Travels*, tr. H. A. R. Gibb and C. F. Beckingham (4 vols., Hakluyt Soc., 2nd series, 110, 117, 141, 178, 1958–94).

Innocent II, *Epistolae et privilegia*, PL 179, cols. 53–658.

Innocent III, *Die Register Innocenz' III.*, ed. Othmar Hageneder et al. (Rome and Vienna, 1964–).

Isidore of Seville, *Etymologiae*, ed. W. M. Lindsay. 2 vols., Oxford, 1911, unpaginated.

Issues of the Exchequer, Being a Collection of Payments Made out of His Majesty's Revenue from King Henry III to King Henry VI, ed. Frederick Devon (London, 1837).

Itinerarium peregrinorum, ed. Hans Eberhard Mayer, *Das Itinerarium peregrinorum. Eine zeitgenössische englische Chronik zum dritten Kreuzzug in ursprünglicher Gestalt* (MGH, Schriften 18, 1962).

Itinerarium peregrinorum et gesta regis Ricardi, ed. William Stubbs, *Chronicles and Memorials of the Reign of Richard I*, 1 (RS, 1864).

Ivo of Chartres, *Epistolae*, PL 162, cols. 11–296.

Jaffé, Philipp, *Regesta pontificum romanorum ab condita ecclesia ad annum post Christum natum MCXCVIII* (2nd edn., ed. S. Löwenfeld, F. Kaltenbrunner, P. Ewald, 2 vols., Leipzig, 1888).

James I, *Llibre dels fets del rei en Jaume*, ed. Jordi Bruguera (2 vols., Barcelona, 1991).

Jean de Joinville, *Vie de saint Louis*, ed. Jacques Monfrin (Paris, 1995).

Jerome, *Epistulae*, ed. Jérôme Labourt, *Saint Jérôme. Lettres* (8 vols., Paris, 1949–63).

Joannes de Terra Rubea (Terrerouge), *Contra rebelles suorum regum* (Lyons, 1526).

Jocelin of Furness, *Vita sancti Walthenis abbatis* (BHL 8783), *Acta Sanctorum, Augusti 1* (Antwerp, 1733), pp. 248–76.

Johannes de Bado Aureo, *Tractatus de armis*, ed. E. J. Jones, *Medieval Heraldry: Some Fourteenth Century Heraldic Works* (Cardiff, 1943), pp. 95–212.

John Benet's Chronicle for the Years 1400 to 1462, ed. G. Harriss and M. Harriss, Camden Fourth Series, 9 (1972), pp. 151–233.

John, Bishop of Nikiu, *Chronicle*, tr. R. H. Charles (London, 1916).

John of Biclar, *Chronica*, ed. Carmen Cardelle de Hartmann, *Victoris Tunnunensis chronicon cum reliquiis Consularibus Caesaraugustanis et Iohannis Biclarensis chronicon* (CCSL, 173A, 2001), pp. 59–83.

John of Saint-Victor, *Memoriale historiarum*, ed. Joseph-Daniel Guigniaut and Natalis de Wailly, RHF 21 (1855), pp. 630–75.

John of Salisbury, *Historia pontificalis*, ed. Marjorie Chibnall (OMT, 1986).

Letters, ed. W. J. Millor et al. (2 vols., OMT, 1979–86).

John of Vikting, *Liber certarum historiarum*, ed. Fedor Schneider (2 vols., MGH, SRG 36. 1–2, 1909–10).

John of Worcester, *Chronicle*, 2, ed. R. R. Darlington and P. McGurk (OMT, 1995).

Chronicle, 3, ed. P. McGurk (OMT, 1998).

Jonas, *Vita Columbani* (BHL 1898), ed. Bruno Krusch, *Ionae Vitae Sanctorum Columbani, Vedastis, Iohannis* (MGH, SRG 37, 1905), pp. 148–224.

Jordanes, *Romana et Getica*, ed. Theodor Mommsen (MGH, AA 5. 1, 1882).

Jus Graecoromanum, ed. Ioannes Zepos and Panagiotes Zepos (8 vols., Athens, 1931).

Justinus, *Epitoma historiarum Philippicarum Pompei Trogi*, ed. Otto Seel (Stuttgart, 1972).

Kottannerin, Helene, *Die Denkwürdigkeiten der Helene Kottannerin (1439–1440)*, ed. Karl Mollay (Vienna, 1971).

Lacarra, José María, ed., *Documentos para el estudio de la reconquista y repoblación del Valle del Ebro* (2 vols., Textos medievales 62–3, Zaragoza, 1982–3).

Lampert of Hersfeld, *Annales*, ed. Oswald Holder-Egger (MGH, SRG 38, 1894).

Landrecht des Königs Magnus Hakonarson, ed. Rudolf Meissner (Weimar, 1941).

Las Siete Partidas (Real Academia de la Historia, 3 vols., Madrid, 1807).

Lateinische Chronik des Klosters Kastl, ed. Joseph Moritz, *Stammreihe und Geschichte der Grafen von Sulzbach* (Abhandlungen der Königlich Bayerischen Akademie der Wissenschaften, Historische Classe 1, 2, 1833), pp. 104–16.

Layettes du Trésor des Chartes, ed. Alexandre Teulet et al. (5 vols., Paris, 1863–1909).

Leo of Rozmital, *De Leonis a Rosmital nobilis Bohemi itinere per partes Germaniae, Belgii, Britanniae, Franciae, Hispaniae, Portugalliae atque Italiae, annis MCCCCLXV–VII* (Stuttgart, 1843).

The Travels of Leo of Rozmital, tr. Malcolm Letts (Hakluyt Soc. 2nd series, 108, 1957 for 1955).

Leo the Deacon, *Historiae*, ed. C. B. Hase (Bonn, 1828).

Leo VI, *Oraison funèbre de Basile I par son fils Léon le Sage*, ed. A. Vogt and I. Hausherr, *Orientalia Christiana*, 77 (1932), pp. 1–79.

The Letters and Charters of Henry II King of England (1154–1189), ed. Nicholas Vincent et al. (Oxford, forthcoming).

Lex Baiwariorum, ed. Ernst von Schwind (MGH, Leges nationum Germanicarum 5. 2, 1926).

Lex Salica, ed. Karl August Eckhardt (MGH, Leges nationum Germanicarum 4. 2, 1969).

Liber feudorum maior, ed. Francisco Miquel Rosell (2 vols., Barcelona, 1945–7).

Le Liber pontificalis, ed. Louis Duchesne (rev. edn., 3 vols., Paris, 1955–7).

Liudprand of Cremona, *Liudprandi opera*, ed. Joseph Becker (MGH, SRG 41, 1915).

Le Livre au roi, ed. Auguste-Arthur Beugnot, *Recueil des historiens des croisades. Lois, 1: Assises de Jérusalem* (Paris, 1841), pp. 607–44; ed. Myriam Geilsammer (Paris, 1995).

Lopes, Fernão, *Crónica del Rei Dom João I*, tr. Derek W. Lomax and R. J. Oakley, *The English in Portugal, 1367–1387. Extracts from the Chronicles of Don Fernando and Don João* (Warminster, 1988).

Crónica do Rei D. Pedro, in *Chronique du roi D. Pedro*, ed. Giuliano Macchi (French tr. Jacqueline Steunou) (Paris, 1985).

López de Ayala, Pero, *Crónica del rey don Juan primero de Castilla é de Leon*, ed. Cayetano Rosell, *Crónicas de los reyes de Castilla* (3 vols., Biblioteca de autores españoles 66, 68, 70, Madrid, 1875–8), 2, pp. 65–144.

Crónica del Rey don Pedro, ed. Cayetano Rosell, *Crónicas de los reyes de Castilla* (3 vols., Biblioteca de autores españoles 66, 68, 70, Madrid, 1875–8), 1, pp. 399–593.

Crónica del rey don Pedro y del rey don Enrique, su hermano, hijos del rey don Alfonso onceno, ed. Germán Orduna (2 vols., Buenos Aires, 1994–7).

Lotharii I. et Lotharii II. Diplomata, ed. Theoder Schieffer (MGH, DD Karolinorum 3, 1966).

Loud, Graham A. (tr.), *Roger II and the Making of the Kingdom of Sicily: Selected Sources* (Manchester, 2012).

Louis VI, *Recueil des actes de Louis VI, roi de France (1108–1137)*, ed. Robert Henri Bautier and Jean Dufour (Chartes et diplômes relatifs à l'histoire de France, 4 vols., Paris, 1992–4).

Luke of Tuy, *Chronicon mundi*, ed. Emma Falque Rey (CCCM 74, 2003).

Macrides, Ruth J., J. A. Munitiz, and Dimiter Angelov (tr.), *Pseudo-Kodinos and the Constantinopolitan Court: Offices and Ceremonies* (Farnham, 2013).

Madden, Frederic, 'Documents Relating to Perkin Warbeck, with Remarks on his History', *Archaeologia*, 27 (1837), pp. 153–210.

Mair, John, *Historia Maioris Britanniae* (Paris, 1521).

Malaspina, Saba, *Chronicon*, ed. Walter Koller and August Nitschke (MGH, SS 35, 1999).

Malaterra, Geoffrey, *De rebus gestis Rogerii Calabriae et Siciliae comitis et Roberti Guiscardi ducis fratris eius*, ed. Ernesto Pontieri (Rerum italicarum scriptores, n.s., 5. 1, Bologna, 1928).

Map, Walter, *De nugis curialium*, ed. M. R. James et al. (revised edn., OMT, 1983).

Matthew Paris, *Chronica majora*, ed. Henry R. Luard (7 vols., RS, 1872–84).

Historia Anglorum, ed. Frederic Madden (3 vols., RS, 1866–9).

Medieval Slavic Lives of Saints and Princes, tr. Marvin Kantor (Ann Arbor, 1983).

Memorials of King Henry VII, ed. James Gairdner (RS, 1858).

Michael Scot, *Liber introductorius*, ed. Glenn Michael Edwards (PhD Thesis, University of Southern California, 1978).

Miracula sancte Margarite Scotorum regine, ed. Robert Bartlett, *The Miracles of St Æbbe of Coldingham and St Margaret of Scotland* (Oxford, 2003), pp. 70–144.

Miracula sancti Benedicti (BHL 1123–9), ed. E. de Certain, *Miracles de S. Benôit* (SHF 96, 1858).

Miracula sancti Genulfi (BHL 3359), ed. Oswald Holder-Egger, MGH, SS 15. 2 (1888), pp. 1204–13.

Monstrelet, Enguerran de, *Chronique*, ed. Louis Douët d'Arcq (6 vols., SHF, 91, 93, 99, 105, 108, 113, 1857–62).

Monumenta Necrologica Claustroneoburgensis, ed. Adalbertus Franciscus Fuchs, MGH, Necrologia Germaniae, 5, Dioecesis Pataviensis, Pars altera, Austria inferior (1913), pp. 3–105.

Monumenta Portugaliae Vaticana, 2, ed. António Domingues de Sousa Costa (Braga, 1970).

Morice, Hyacinthe, *Mémoires pour servir de preuves à l'histoire ecclésiastique et civile de Bretagne*, 3 (Paris, 1746).

Murimuth, Adam, *Continuatio chronicarum*, ed. Edward Maunde Thompson (RS, 1889).

Narratio de Longobardie obpressione, ed. Franz-Josef Schmale, *Italische Quellen über die Taten Kaiser Friedrichs I. in Italien und der Brief über den Kreuzzug Kaiser Friedrichs I.* (Ausgewählte Quellen zur deutschen Geschichte des Mittelalters 17a, Darmstadt, 1986), pp. 240–94.

Navagero, Andrea, *Storia Veneziana*, ed. L. Muratori, *Rerum Italicarum Scriptores*, 23 (Milan, 1733), cols. 919–1216.

Nicholas I, Patriarch of Constantinople, *Letters*, ed. R. J. H. Jenkins and L. G. Westerink (Washington, DC, 1973).

Nicolas I, *Epistolae*, ed. E. Perels, MGH, Epistolae 6 (Karolini aevi 4) (1925), pp. 257–690.

Nikephoros of Constantinople, *Breviarium historicum*, ed. Cyril Mango, *Nikephoros of Constantinople: Short History* (Washington, DC, 1990).

Niketas, *The Life of St Philaretos the Merciful*, ed. Lennart Rydén (Uppsala, 2002).

Nithard, *Historiarum libri IIII*, ed. Ernst Müller (MGH, SRG 44, 1907).

Notae Weingartenses, ed. Georg Waitz, MGH, SS 24 (1879), pp. 830–3.

Notker Balbulus, *Gesta Karoli magni imperatoris*, ed. Hans F. Haefele (MGH, SRG, n.s. 12, 1959).

Official Correspondence of Thomas Bekynton, ed. George Williams (2 vols., RS, 1872).

Orderic Vitalis, *Historia ecclesiastica: The Ecclesiastical History*, ed. Marjorie Chibnall (6 vols., OMT, 1968–80).

Ordonnances des roys de France de la troisième race, 1 (Paris, 1723); 6 (Paris, 1741).

Oresme, Nicholas, *Tractatus contra judiciarios astronomos*, ed. G. W. Coopland, *Nicholas Oresme and the Astrologers* (Liverpool, 1952), pp. 23–41.

Osbert of Clare, *Vita sancti Edwardi confessoris* (BHL 2422), ed. Marc Bloch, 'La vie de S. Edouard le Confesseur par Osbert de Clare', *Analecta Bollandiana* 41 (1923), pp. 5–131.

Otloh of St. Emmeran, *Liber Visionum*, ed. Paul Gerhard Schmidt (MGH, Quellen zur Geistesgeschichte des Mittelalters, 1989).

Otto of Freising, *Chronica sive Historia de duabus civitatibus*, ed. Adolf Hofmeister (MGH, SRG 45, 1912).

Gesta Friderici I imperatoris, ed. Georg Waitz and Bernhard von Simson, *Ottonis et Rahewini Gesta Friderici I imperatoris* (MGH, SRG 46, 1912), pp. 1–161.

Ottonis II. et III. Diplomata, ed. Theodor von Sickel (MGH, DD regum et imperatorum Germaniae, 2, 1888–93).

Óváry, L., 'Negoziati tra il Re d'Ungheria e il Re di Francia per la successione di Giovanna I. d'Angiò', *Archivio storico per le province napoletane*, 2 (1877), pp. 107–57.

Pactus legis Salicae, ed. Karl August Eckhardt (MGH, Leges nationum Germanicarum, 4. 1, 1962).

Paenitentialia minora Franciae et Italiae, ed. Raymund Kottje (CCSL 156, 1994).

Papsturkunden in Portugal, ed. Carl Erdmann (Abhandlungen der Akademie der Wissenschaften in Göttingen, Philologisch-Historische Klasse, Neue Folge 20. 3, 1927).

Papsturkunden in Spanien: vorarbeiten zur Hispania Pontificia: I. Katalanien, ed. Paul Kehr (Abhandlungen der Akademie der Wissenschaften in Göttingen, Philologisch-Historische Klasse, Neue Folge 18. 2, 1926).

Parisse, Michel, 'Sigefroid, abbé de Gorze, et le mariage du roi Henri III avec Agnès de Poitou (1043). Un aspect de la réforme lotharingienne', *Revue du Nord*, 2004/3–4 (356–357) (2004), pp. 543–66.

Parlamentos del Interregno (1410–1412), ed. José Ángel Sesma Muñoz (2 vols., Acta curiarum Regni Aragonum 7. 1–2, Zaragoza, 2011).

Parliament Rolls of Medieval England, ed. Chris Given-Wilson et al. (16 vols., Woodbridge, 2005).

Passio Leudegarii I (BHL 4849b), ed. Bruno Krusch, MGH, Scriptores rerum Merovingicarum, 5 (1910), pp. 282–322.

Passio sancti Athelberhti regis et martiris, ed. Montague R. James, 'Two Lives of St. Ethelbert, King and Martyr', *English Historical Review*, 32 (1917), pp. 214–44.

Patent Rolls of the Reign of Henry III (1216–32) (2 vols., London, 1901–3).

Paul the Deacon, *Carmina*, ed. Ernst Dümmler, MGH, Poetae latini aevi Carolini 1 (1881), pp. 27–86.

   Historia Langobardorum, ed. Georg Waitz (MGH, SRG 48, 1878).

   Liber de episcopis Mettensibus, ed. Damien Kempf (Louvain, 2013).

Paulo, Paulus de, *Memoriale Pauli de Paulo patritii Iadrensis*, ed. Ferdo Šišić (Zagreb, 1904).

Peter Comestor, *Historia scholastica*, PL 198, cols. 1053–1644.

   Sermones, PL 198, cols. 1721–1844.

Peter Damian, *Epistolae*, ed. Kurt Reindel, *Die Briefe des Petrus Damiani* (4 vols., MGH, Die Briefe der deutschen Kaiserzeit 4, Munich, 1983–93).

Peter of Zittau, *Chronicon Aulae Regiae*, ed. Josef Emler, *Fontes Rerum Bohemicarum*, 4 (Prague, 1884), pp. 1–337.

Petrus de Ebulo, *Liber ad honorem Augusti sive de rebus Siculis. Eine Bilderchronik der Stauferzeit aus der Burgerbibliothek Bern*, ed. Theo Kölzer and Marlis Stähli (Sigmaringen, 1994).

Petrus Riga, *Versus de gaudio filii regis*, ed. H.-François Delaborde, 'Un poème inédit de Pierre Riga sur la naissance de Philippe-Auguste', *Notices et documents publiés pour la Société de l'histoire de France à l'occasion du cinquantième anniversaire* (Paris, 1884), pp. 121–7.

Philippe Mouskes, *Chronique rimée*, ed. Baron de Reiffenberg (2 vols., Brussels, 1836–8).

Philippi regis Diplomata, ed. Andrea Rzihacek and Renate Spreitzer (MGH, DD regum et imperatorum Germaniae, 12, 2014).

Pius II (Enea Silvio Piccolomini), *Commentarii rerum memorabilium*, ed. Margaret Meserve and Marcello Simonetta (3 vols. to date, Cambridge, Mass., 2003–18).

Pleas before the King or his Justices, 1198–1202, 2, ed. Doris Stenton (Selden Society 68, 1952 for 1949).

Pollard, A. F., *The Reign of Henry VII from Contemporary Sources* (3 vols., London, 1913–14).

The Popular Songs of Ireland, ed. Thomas Crofton Croker (London, 1839).

Potthast, August, ed., *Regesta pontificum Romanorum (1198–1304)* (2 vols., Berlin, 1874–5).

Pour ce que plusieurs, ed. Craig Taylor *Debating the Hundred Years War*, (Camden 5th series, 29, 2006), pp. 53–134.

Praefatio de Almaria, ed. Juan Gil, *Chronica Hispana saeculi XII. Pars I* (CCCM 71, 1990), pp. 249–67.

Privilèges accordés à la couronne de France par la Saint-Siège, ed. Adolphe Tardif (Paris, 1855).

Procès en nullité de la condamnation de Jeanne d'Arc, ed. Pierre Duparc (5 vols., SHF, 1977–89).

Procesos de las antiguas cortes y parlamentos de Cataluña, Aragon y Valencia, ed. Próspero de Bofarull y Mascaró, *Colección de documentos inéditos del Archivo General de la Corona de Aragon*, 4 (1849).

Procopius, *De bello Gothico*, ed. H. B. Dewing, *History of the Wars* (7 vols., Cambridge, Mass., 1914–40), 3–5.

Promis, Domenico, *Monumenta historiae patriae: Scriptores*, 1 (Turin, 1840).

Les Prophécies de Merlin, edited from the ms. 593 in the Bibliothèque municipale of Rennes, ed. Lucy Allen Paton (2 vols., New York and London, 1926–7).

Psellos, Michael, *Chronographia*, ed. Émile Renauld (2 vols., Paris, 1926); ed. Diether R. Reinsch (Millennium-Studien 51, 2 vols, Berlin, 2014) (text vol. 1).

Ἐπιτάφιοι λόγοι εἰς τοὺς πατριάρχας Μιχαὴλ Κηρουλλάριον, ed. K. N. Sathas, *Μεσαιωνική Βιβλιοθήκη*, 4 (Athens, 1874), pp. 303–87.

Orationes panegyricae, ed. George T. Dennis (Stuttgart, 1994).

Ptolemy of Lucca, *Annales*, ed. Bernhard Schmeidler (MGH, SRG, n.s. 8, 1930).

Quedam exceptiones de hystoria Normannorum et Anglorum, ed. Elisabeth Van Houts, *The Gesta Normannorum Ducum of William of Jumièges, Orderic Vitalis and Robert of Torigni* (2 vols., OMT, 1992–5), 2, pp. 290–304.

Rahewin, *Gesta Friderici I imperatoris*, ed. Georg Waitz and Bernhard von Simson, *Ottonis et Rahewini Gesta Friderici I imperatoris* (MGH, SRG 46, 1912), pp. 162–346.

Ralph de Diceto, *Opuscula*, ed. William Stubbs, *Opera historica* (2 vols., RS, 1876), 2, pp. 177–285.

Ymagines historiarum, ed. William Stubbs, *Opera historica*, RS, 1876), 1, pp. 289–440; 2, pp. 1–174.

Ralph Niger, *Chronicon II*, ed. Robert Anstruther, *The Chronicles of Ralph Niger* (Caxton Soc., 1851), pp. 105–91.

Raoul de Caen, *Gesta Tancredi*, *Recueil des historiens des croisades. Historiens occidentaux*, 3 (Paris, 1866), pp. 587–716.

The Records of the Parliaments of Scotland to 1707, ed. Keith M. Brown et al. (St Andrews, 2007–17).

Recueil de chants historiques français depuis le XIIIe siècle, 1, ed. Antoine-Jean-Victor Le Roux de Lincy (Paris, 1841).

Recueil des actes de Charles II le Chauve, roi de France, ed. Georges Tessier (Chartes et diplômes relatifs à l'histoire de France, 3 vols., Paris, 1943–55).

Recueil des actes de Lothaire et de Louis V rois de France (954–987), ed. Louis Halphen (Chartes et diplômes relatifs à l'histoire de France, Paris, 1908).

Recueil des actes de Louis VI, roi de France (1108–1137), ed. Robert Henri Bautier and Jean Dufour (Chartes et diplômes relatifs à l'histoire de France, 4 vols., Paris, 1992–4).

Recueil des actes de Philippe Ier, roi de France (1059–1108), ed. Maurice Prou (Chartes et diplômes relatifs à l'histoire de France, Paris, 1908).

Recueil des actes des ducs de Normandie (911–1066), ed. Marie Fauroux (Caen, 1961).

Recueil des Historiens des Croisades, Historiens Orientaux, 1 (Paris, 1877).

Recueil general des anciennes lois françaises, 5, ed. François-André Isambert et al. (Paris, 1824).

Regesta diplomatica nec non epistolaria Bohemiae et Moraviae, ed. K. J. Erben and J. Emler et al. (7 vols. to date, Prague, 1854–).

Regesta Imperii, 12: *Albrecht II, 1438–1439*, ed. Günther Hödl (Vienna, 1975).

Regesta regum Anglo-Normannorum, 1066–1154, 3, ed. H. A. Cronne and R. H. C. Davis (Oxford, 1968).

Regestum Innocentii III papae super negotio Romani imperii, ed. Friedrich Kempf (Miscellanea historiae pontificiae, 12, Rome, 1947).

Regino of Prüm, *Chronicon*, ed. Friedrich Kurze (MGH, SRG 50, 1890).

Registre criminel du Châtelet de Paris, du 6 septembre 1389 au 18 mai 1392, ed. Henri Duplès-Agier (2 vols., Paris, 1861–4).

Les Registres d'Alexander IV, ed. Charles Bourel de la Roncière et al. (3 vols., Paris, 1902–59).

Les Registres d'Urbain IV, ed. Jean Guiraud and Suzanne Clémencet (4 vols., Paris, 1901–58).

Les Registres de Boniface VIII (1294–1303), ed. Georges Digard et al. (4 vols., Paris, 1884–1939).

Les Registres de Martin IV (1281–1285), ed. François Olivier-Martin (Paris, 1901–35).

Les Registres de Philippe Auguste, 1: *Texte*, ed. John W. Baldwin (RHF, Documents financiers et administratifs, 7, 1992).

Regum Burgundiae e Stirpe Rudolfina Diplomata et Acta, ed. Theodor Schieffer (MGH, DD, 1977).

La reina doña Urraca (1109–1126), cancillería y colección diplomática, ed. Irene Ruiz Albi (Leon, 2003).

Reinado y diplomas de Fernando III, ed. Julio González (3 vols., Cordoba, 1980–6).

Richard of Poitiers, *Chronica*, ed. Georg Waitz, MGH, SS 26 (1882), pp. 74–82.

Richard of San Germano, *Chronica (Ryccardi de Sancto Germano notarii Chronica)*, ed. Carlo Alberto Garufi (Rerum Italicarum Scriptores, 7. 2, Bologna, 1938).

Richer of Saint-Rémi, *Historiae*, ed. Hartmut Hoffmann (MGH, SS 38, Hanover, 2000).

Rigord, *Gesta Philippi Augusti*, ed. Elisabeth Carpentier et al., *Histoire de Philippe Auguste* (Paris, 2006).

Robert of Auxerre, *Chronicon*, ed. Oswald Holder-Egger, MGH, SS 26 (1882), pp. 219–76.

Robert of Gloucester, *Metrical Chronicle*, ed. W. A. Wright (2 vols., RS, 1887).

Robert of Torigni, *Chronica*, ed. Richard Howlett, *Chronicles of the Reigns of Stephen, Henry II and Richard I* (4 vols., RS, 1882–9), 4.

Rodrigo Jiménez de Rada, *Breviarium historie catholice*, ed. Juan Fernández Valverde (2 vols., CCCM 72A-B, 1992).

    Historia de rebus Hispaniae, ed. Juan Fernández Valverde (CCCM 72, Turnhout, 1987).

Rodulfus Glaber, *Historiarum libri quinque*, ed. John France, *Opera* (OMT, 1989).

Roger of Howden, *Chronica*, ed. William Stubbs (4 vols., RS, 1868–71).

Rogerii II regis Diplomata Latina, ed. Carlrichard Brühl (Cologne and Vienna, 1987).

Roland of Padua, *Chronica*, ed. Philipp Jaffé, MGH, SS 19 (1866), pp. 32–147.

Rotuli curiae regis (1194–1200), ed. Francis Palgrave (2 vols., London, 1835).

Rotuli Hundredorum (2 vols., Record Commission, London, 1812–18).

Ruotger, *Vita Brunonis Archiepiscopi Coloniensis*, ed. Irene Ott (MGH, SRG n.s. 10, 1951).

The Russian Primary Chronicle, tr. Samuel Cross and Olgerd Sherbowitz-Wetzor (Cambridge, Mass., 1953).

The Saga of Hacon, tr. Gudbrand Vigfusson and George Dasent, *Icelandic Sagas* (4 vols., RS, 1887–94) 4.

Salimbene de Adam, *Cronica*, ed. Giuseppe Scalia (2 vols., CCCM, 125-125A, 1998–9).

Salvian, *Ad ecclesiam*, ed. Georges Lagarrigue (Sources chrétiennes 176, 1971).

Saxo Grammaticus, *Gesta Danorum*, ed. Karsten Friis-Jensen (2 vols., OMT, 2015).

Scriptores minores historiae Danicae, ed. M. C. Gertz (2 vols., Copenhagen, 1917–22).

Sermo in tumulatione Sanctorum Quintini, Victorici, Cassiani, ed. Oswald Holder-Egger, MGH, SS 15. 1 (1887), pp. 271–3.

Sigebert of Gembloux, *Chronica: Continuatio Aquicinctina*, ed. Ludwig Bethmann, MGH, SS 6 (1844), pp. 405–38.

    Chronica: Continuatio Praemonstratensis, ed. Ludwig Bethmann, MGH, SS 6 (1844), pp. 447–56.

Simeon of Durham, *Historia regum*, ed. Thomas Arnold, *Symeonis monachi opera omnia* (2 vols., RS, 1882–5), 2, pp. 3–283.

Simon (Symon) de Phares, *Le Recueil des plus celebres astrologues*, ed. Jean-Patrice Boudet (2 vols., SHF 515, 519, 1997–9).

    Recueil des plus célèbres astrologues et quelques hommes doctes, ed. Ernest Wickersheimer (Paris, 1929).

Skylitzes, John, *A Synopsis of Byzantine History 811–1057*, tr. John Wortley (Cambridge, 2010).
Synopsis historiarum, ed. Hans Thurn (Berlin and New York, 1973).
Snorri Sturluson, *Heimskringla*, tr. Samuel Laing (3 vols., London, 1844); tr. Lee M. Hollander (Austin, 1964).
Somnium Viridarii, ed. Marion Schnerb-Lièvre (2 vols., Paris, 1993).
Songe du Vergier, ed. Marion Schnerb-Lièvre (2 vols., Paris, 1982).
Die Stadtrechte von Bremgarten und Lenzburg, ed. Walther Merz (Sammlung schweizerischer Rechtsquellen, Abt. 16, Die Rechtsquellen des Kantons Argau, Teil 1, Stadtrechte, 4, Aarau, 1909).
Statutes of the Realm (11 vols., Record Commission, 1810–28).
Stones, E. L. G., ed., *Anglo-Scottish Relations 1174–1328: Some Selected Documents* (rev. edn., OMT, 1970).
Stones, E. L. G., and Grant G. Simpson, *Edward I and the Throne of Scotland, 1290–1296: An Edition of the Record Sources for the Great Cause* (Oxford, 1978).
Suger, *Vita Ludovici Grossi regis*, ed. Henri Waquet (Paris, 1929).
Suger (continuator), *De glorioso rege Ludovico, Ludovici filio*, ed. Auguste Molinier, *Suger, Vie de Louis le Gros, suivie de l'histoire du roi Louis VII* (Paris, 1887), pp. 156–78.
Sven Aggesen, *Brevis historia regum Dacie*, ed. M. C. Gertz, *Scriptores minores historiae Danicae* (2 vols., Copenhagen, 1917–22), 1, pp. 94–141.
The Works of Sven Aggesen, tr. Eric Christiansen (Viking Society for Northern Research. Text Series 9, 1992).
Symeon Magister et Logotheta, *Chronicon*, ed. Staffan Wahlgren (Berlin and New York, 2006).
Tabula Ringstadiensis, ed. M. C. Gertz, *Scriptores minores historiae Danicae* (2 vols., Copenhagen, 1917–22), 2. 1, pp. 82–6.
Tafel, G. L. F., and G. M. Thomas, eds., *Urkunden zur älteren Handels- und Staatsgeschichte der Republik Venedig* (3 vols., Fontes rerum austriacarum II, 12–14, Vienna, 1856–7).
Tanukhi, Al-, *The Table-talk of a Mesopotamian Judge*, tr. D. S. Margoliouth (London, 1922).
Thegan, *Gesta Hludowici imperatoris*, ed. Ernst Tremp (MGH, SRG 64, 1995).
Theodore the Stoudite, *Epistulae*, ed. Georgios Fatouros (2 vols., Berlin, 1992).
Theophanes, *The Chronicle of Theophanes the Confessor*, tr. Cyril Mango and Roger Scott (Oxford, 1997).
Chronographia, ed. C. de Boor (2 vols., Leipzig, 1883–5) (text vol. 1).
Theophanes continuatus, ed. Immanuel Bekker, *Theophanes continuatus, Ioannes Cameniata, Symeon Magister, Georgius monachus* (Bonn, 1838), pp. 1–481.
Chronographiae quae Theophanis Continuati nomine fertur Libri I–IV, ed. Jeffrey Michael Featherstone (Berlin, 2015).
Theophylact Simocatta, *Historiae*, ed. C. de Boor (Leipzig, 1887).
Thesaurus novus anecdotorum, ed. Edmond Martène and Ursin Durand (5 vols., Paris, 1717).
Thietmar of Merseburg, *Chronicon*, ed. Robert Holtzmann (MGH, SRG, n.s. 9, 1935).
Third Report of the Deputy Keeper of the Public Records (London, 1842).
Thomas Tuscus, *Gesta imperatorum et pontificum*, ed. Ernst Ehrenfeuchter, MGH, SS 22 (1872), pp. 483–528.
Thorne, William, *Chronica*, ed. R. Twysden, *Historiæ Anglicanæ scriptores X* (London, 1652), cols. 1753–2296.
Thurocz, Johannes de, *Chronica Hungarorum*, ed. Elisabeth Galántai and Julius Kristó (Budapest, 1985).
Le Très Ancien Coutumier de Normandie, ed. Ernest-Joseph Tardif (Coutumiers de Normandie, 1, Rouen, 1881).
Trevet, Nicholas, *Annales sex regum Angliae, 1135–1307*, ed. Thomas Hog (English Historical Society, 6, 1845).
Trevisa, John, *On the Properties of Things: John Trevisa's Translation of Bartholomaeus Anglicus De proprietatibus rerum: A Critical Text*, ed. M. C. Seymour et al. (2 vols., Oxford, 1975).

Tumbo A de la Catedral de Santiago, ed. Manuel Lucas Alvarez (Santiago, 1998).

Turgot, *Vita S. Margaretae Scotorum Reginae* (BHL 5325), ed. James Raine, in *Symeonis Dunelmensis opera et collectanea*, 1; ed. J. Hodgson Hinde (Surtees Society, 51, 1868), pp. 234–54.

Die Urkunden der lateinischen Könige von Jerusalem, ed. Hans Eberhard Mayer (4 vols., MGH, Diplomata regum Latinorum Hierosolymitanorum, 2010).

Venantius Fortunatus, *Carmina*, ed. Marc Reydellet (3 vols., Paris, 1994–2004).

Verse in English from Tudor and Stuart Ireland, ed. Andrew Carpenter (Cork, 2000).

Vetera monumenta Hibernorum et Scotorum historiam illustrantia, ed. Augustin Theiner (Rome, 1864).

Villani, Giovanni, *Nuova Cronica*, ed. Giuseppe Porta (3 vols., Parma, 1990–1).

Vincent Kadlubek, *Chronica Polonorum*, ed. Marian Plezia, *Mistrza Wincentego zwanego Kadlubkiem Kronika polska* (Pomniki dziejowe Polski, seria II, vol. 11, Cracow, 1994).

Vita Ædwardi regis (BHL 2421), ed. Frank Barlow (2nd. edn., OMT, 1992).

Vita Alberti episcopi Leodiensis, ed. Johannes Heller, MGH, SS 25 (1880), pp. 135–68.

Vita beatae Margaritae de Hungaria, ed. Ildikó Csepregi et al., *The Oldest Legend: Acts of the Canonization Process, and Miracles of Saint Margaret of Hungary* (Budapest, 2018).

Vita Brunonis altera, ed. Georg Pertz, MGH, SS 4 (1841), pp. 275–9.

Vita Edwardi Secundi, ed. N. Denholm-Young and rev. Wendy Childs (OMT, 2005).

Vita et miracula sanctae Kyngae ducissae Cracoviensis (BHL 4666–7), ed. Wojciech Kętrzyński, *Monumenta Poloniae historica*, 4 (Lwów, 1884), pp. 682–744.

Vita Euthymii patriarchae, ed. Patricia Karlin-Hayter (Brussels, 1970).

Vita Godefridi comitis Cappenbergensis prima (BHL 3575–6), ed. Gerlinde Niemeyer and Ingrid Ehlers-Kisseler (MGH, SRG 74, 2005).

Vita Heinrici IV. imperatoris, ed. Wilhelm Eberhard (MGH, SRG 58, 1899).

Vita Henrici archiepiscopi Treverensis altera, ed. Georg Waitz, MGH, SS 24 (1879), pp. 456–63.

Vita Mathildis reginae posterior (BHL 5684), ed. Bernd Schütte, *Die Lebensbeschreibungen der Königin Mathilde* (MGH, SRG 66, 1994), pp. 143–202.

Vita S. Theophanonis Imperatricis (BHG 1794), ed. Eduard Kurtz, *Zwei griechische Texte über die hl. Theophano, die Gemahlin Kaisers Leo VI.* (Mémoires de l'Académie impériale des sciences de Saint-Pétersbourg, VIIIe série, classe historico-philologique, III, 2, St Petersberg, 1898).

Vita sancti Theotonii, ed. Alexandre Herculano, *Portugaliae monumenta historica: Scriptores*, 1 (Lisbon, 1856), pp. 79–88.

Walsingham, Thomas, *The St Albans Chronicle: The Chronica maiora of Thomas Walsingham*, ed. John Taylor et al. (2 vols., OMT, 2003–11).

Walter of Coventry, *Memoriale*, ed. William Stubbs (2 vols., RS, 1872–3).

Wibald of Stablo, *Das Briefbuch Abt Wibalds von Stablo und Corvey*, ed. Martina Hartmann (3 vols., MGH, Die Briefe der deutschen Kaiserzeit 9, 2012).

Widukind of Corvey, *Res gestae saxonicae*, ed. Paul Hirsch and H.-E. Lohmann (MGH, SRG 60, 1935).

William, *Sugerii Vita*, ed. A. Lecoy de la Marche, *Oeuvres complètes de Suger* (Paris, 1867), pp. 375–411.

William de Nangis, *Chronicon*, ed. H. Géraud, *Chronique de Guillaume de Nangis et de ses continuateurs* (2 vols., SHF, 1843).

    Chronique abrégée des rois de France, ed. P. C. F. Daunou, RHF 20 (1840), pp. 649–55.

    Gesta Philippi tertii regis Franciae, ed. P. C. F. Daunou, RHF 20 (1840), pp. 466–539.

William de Saint-Pathus, *Vie de saint Louis*, ed. H.-François Delaborde (Paris, 1899).

William of Æbelholt, *Epistolae*. ed. C. A. Christensen et al., *Diplomatarium Danicum*, 1. 3. 2 (Copenhagen, 1977).

William of Apulia, *La Geste de Robert Guiscard*, ed. Marguerite Mathieu (Palermo, 1961).

William of Malmesbury, *Gesta pontificum Anglorum*, ed. Michael Winterbottom (2 vols., OMT, 2007) (text vol.1).

Gesta regum Anglorum, ed. R. A. B. Mynors et al. (2 vols., OMT, 1998–9) (text vol. 1).

Historia novella, ed. Edmund King (rev. edn., OMT, 1998).

William of Newburgh, *Historia rerum anglicarum*, ed. Richard Howlett, *Chronicles of the Reigns of Stephen, Henry II and Richard I* (4 vols., RS, 1884–9), 1–2.

William of Ockham, *Octo quaestiones de potestate papae*, ed. H. S. Offler, *Guillelmi de Ockham Opera Politica*, 1 (2nd edn., Manchester, 1974), pp. 1–217.

William of Poitiers, *Gesta Guillelmi ducis Normannorum*, ed. R. H. C. Davis and Marjorie Chibnall (OMT, 1998).

William of Tyre, *Chronicon*, ed. R. B. C. Huygens (2 vols, CCCM 63–63A, 1986, paginated continuously).

William the Breton, *Gesta Philippi Augusti*, ed. H.-F. Delaborde, *Oeuvres de Rigord et de Guillaume le Breton* (2 vols., SHF, 210, 224, 1882–5), 1, pp. 168–333.

Philippis, ed. H.-F. Delaborde, *Oeuvres de Rigord et de Guillaume le Breton* (2 vols., SHF, 210, 224, 1882–5), 2.

Willibald, *Vita Bonifatii* (BHL 1400), ed. Wilhelm Levison, *Vitae sancti Bonifatii* (MGH, SRG 57, 1905), pp. 1–58.

Winkelman, Eduard, 'Drei Gedichte Heinrichs von Avranches an Kaiser Friedrich II.', *Forschungen zur deutschen Geschichte*, 18 (1878), pp. 482–92.

Wipo, *Gesta Chuonradi imperatoris*, ed. Harry Breslau (MGH, SRG 61, 1915).

The World of El Cid: Chronicles of the Spanish Reconquest, tr. Simon Barton and Richard Fletcher (Manchester, 2000).

Zurita, Jerónimo, *Anales de la Corona de Aragón*, ed. Angel Canellas López (8 vols., Zaragoza, 1967–77).

Secondary literature

Académie Internationale d'Héraldique. VIII Colloquium. Canterbury 29th August–4th September 1993. Proceedings (Canterbury, 1995).

Afinogenov, D., 'The Bride-show of Theophilos: Some Notes on the Sources', *Eranos*, 95 (1997), pp. 10–18.

Age of Chivalry: Art in Plantagenet England, 1200–1400, ed. Jonathan Alexander and Paul Binski (London, 1987).

Ahlers, Jens, *Die Welfen und die englischen Könige 1165–1235* (Hildesheim, 1987).

Ailes, Adrian, 'Heraldry in Medieval England: Symbols of Politics and Propaganda', in *Heraldry, Pageantry and Social Display in Medieval England*, ed. Peter Coss and Maurice Keen (Woodbridge, 2002), pp. 83–104.

Airlie, Stuart, 'Earthly and Heavenly Networks in a World in Flux: Carolingian Family Identities and the Prague Sacramentary', in *The Prague Sacramentary: Culture, Religion, and Politics in Late Eighth-Century Bavaria*, ed. Maximilian Diesenberger et al. (Turnhout, 2016), pp. 203–23.

'Private Bodies and the Body Politic in the Divorce Case of Lothar II', *Past & Present*, 161 (1998), pp. 3–38.

Allirot, Anne-Hélène, 'Les mariages royaux à la cour de France, entre faste et discretion (du règne de Saint Louis à celui de Charles V)', in *La cour du prince: cour de France, cours d'Europe, XIIe–XVe siècle*, ed. Murielle Gaude-Ferragu et al. (Paris, 2011), pp. 231–42.

Althoff, Gerd, *Family, Friends and Followers: Political and Social Bonds in Early Medieval Europe* (Eng. tr., Cambridge, 2004).

'Namengebung und adliges Selbstverständnis', in *Nomen et gens: zur historischen Aussagekraft frühmittelalterlicher Personennamen,* ed. Dieter Geuenich et al. (Berlin, 1997), pp. 127–39.

Alvar, Carlos, 'The Matter of Britain in Spanish Society and Letters', in *The Arthur of the Iberians,* ed. David Hook (Cardiff, 2015), pp. 187–270.

Ambrogi, Annarena, *Vasche di età romana in marmi bianchi e colorati* (Rome, 1985).

Anderson, Joseph, 'Notes of Some Entries in the Iceland Annals Regarding the Death of the Princess "The Maiden of Norway", in A.D. 1290, and "The False Margaret", who was Burned at Bergen in A.D. 1301', *Proceedings of the Society of Antiquaries of Scotland,* 10 (1872–4), pp. 403–19.

Anderson, Marjorie O., *Kings and Kingship in Early Scotland* (Edinburgh and London, 1973).

Arbagi, Martin, 'The Celibacy of Basil II', *Byzantine Studies,* 2. 1 (1975), pp. 41–5.

Arthurson, Ian, *The Perkin Warbeck Conspiracy 1491–1499* (Stroud, 1994).

Aubenas, Roger, 'L'adoption en Provence au Moyen Âge (XIVe–XVIe siècles)', *Revue historique de droit français et étranger,* 13 (1934), pp. 700–26.

Aurell, Martin, *Les Noces du comte: mariage et pouvoir en Catalogne (785–1213)* (Paris, 1995).

ed., *Les Stratégies matrimoniales (IXe–XIIIe siècle)* (Turnout, 2013).

Autrand, Françoise, *Charles VI: la folie du roi* (Paris, 1986).

Baaken, Gerhard, 'Die Altersfolge der Söhne Friedrich Barbarossas und die Königserhebung Heinrichs VI', *Deutsches Archiv für Erforschung des Mittelalters,* 24 (1968), pp. 46–78.

'Unio regni ad imperium. Die Verhandlungen von Verona 1184 und die Eheabredung zwischen König Heinrich VI und Konstanze von Sizilien', *Quellen und Forschungen aus italienischen Archiven und Bibliotheken,* 52 (1972), pp. 219–97.

Bagge, Sverre, *Cross and Scepter: The Rise of the Scandinavian Kingdoms from the Vikings to the Reformation* (Princeton, 2014).

From Viking Stronghold to Christian Kingdom: State Formation in Norway, c. 900–1350 (Copenhagen, 2010).

Baldwin, John W., *The Government of Philip Augustus* (Berkeley and Los Angeles, 1986).

Ballesteros-Beretta, Antonio, *Alfonso X el Sabio* (Barcelona, 1963).

Bande, Alexandre, *Le Coeur du roi. Les Capétiens et les sepultures multiples XIIIe–XVe siècles* (Paris, 2009).

Barber, Malcolm, *The Trial of the Templars* (Cambridge, 1978).

Barlow, Frank, *Edward the Confessor* (London, 1970).

The Godwins: The Rise and Fall of a Noble Dynasty (Harlow, 2002).

William Rufus (new edn., New Haven and London, 2000).

Barrow, Geoffrey, *Robert Bruce and the Community of the Realm of Scotland* (4th edn., Edinburgh, 2005).

Bartlett, Robert, *England under the Norman and Angevin Kings 1075–1225* (Oxford, 2000).

Gerald of Wales 1146–1223 (Oxford, 1982, repr., with new pagination and supplementary bibliography, as *Gerald of Wales: A Voice of the Middle Ages,* Stroud, 2006).

'Political Prophecy in Gerald of Wales', in *Culture politique des Plantagenêt,* ed. Martin Aurell (Poitiers, 2003), pp. 303–11.

Why Can the Dead Do Such Great Things? Saints and Worshippers from the Martyrs to the Reformation (Princeton and Oxford, 2013).

Barton, Simon, *Conquerors, Brides, and Concubines: Interfaith Relations and Social Power in Medieval Iberia* (Philadelphia, 2015).

The Aristocracy in Twelfth-Century León and Castile (Cambridge, 1997).

La Bâtardise et l'exercice du pouvoir en Europe du XIIIe au début du XVIe siècle, ed. Éric Bousmar et al. (*Revue du Nord,* Hors série. Collection Histoire no. 31, 2015).

Bautier, Robert-Henri, 'Sacres et couronnements sous les Carolingiens et les premiers Capétiens: recherches sur la genèse du sacre royal français', in *Recherches sur l'Histoire de la France Médiévale: Des Merovingiens aux Premiers Capétiens* (Aldershot, 1991), pp. 7–56 (no. II).

Becher, Matthias, 'Der sogenannte Staatsstreich Grimoalds. Versuch einer Neubewertung', in *Karl Martell in seiner Zeit*, ed. Jörg Jarnut et al. (Beihefte der Francia 37, 1994), pp. 119–47.

Beem, Charles, ed., *The Royal Minorities of Medieval and Early Modern England* (New York and Basingstoke, 2008).

Bennert, Uwe, 'Art et propagande politique sous Philippe IV le Bel: le cycle des rois de France dans la Grand'salle du palais de la Cité', *Revue de l'Art*, 97 (1992), pp. 46–59.

Bennett, Michael, 'Henry IV, the Royal Succession and the Crisis of 1406', in *The Reign of Henry IV: Rebellion and Survival, 1403–1413*, ed. G. Dodd and D. Biggs (York, 2008), pp. 9–27.

Lambert Simnel and the Battle of Stoke (Gloucester, 1987).

Bercé, Yves-Marie, *Le roi caché: sauveurs et imposteurs: mythes politiques populaires dans l'Europe modern* (Paris, 1990).

Berger, Élie, *Histoire de Blanche de Castille, reine de France* (Paris, 1895).

Beumann, Helmut, 'Die Einheit des ostfränkischen Reichs und der Kaisergedanke bei der Königserhebung Ludwigs des Kindes', *Archiv für Diplomatik*, 23 (1977), pp. 142–63, repr. in Helmut Beumann, *Ausgewählte Aufsätze* (Sigmaringen, 1987), pp. 44–65.

Bianchini, Janna, *The Queen's Hand: Power and Authority in the Reign of Berenguela of Castile* (Philadelphia, 2012).

Bibliographie des Troubadours, ed. Alfred Pilet and Henry Carstens (Halle, 1933).

Bibliotheca Hagiographica Latina (2 vols., Subsidia Hagiographica 6, 1898–1901; *Novum Supplementum*, ed. H. Fros, Subsidia Hagiographica 70, 1986).

Biddle, Martin, *King Arthur's Round Table: An Archaeological Investigation* (Woodbridge, 2000).

Binbas, Ilker Evrim, 'Structure and Function of the Genealogical Tree in Islamic Historiography', in *Horizons of the World. Festschrift for Isenbike Togan*, ed. Ilker Evrim Binbas and Nurten Kiliç-Schubel (Istanbul, 2011), pp. 468–82.

Bisson, Thomas N., *The Medieval Crown of Aragon: A Short History* (Oxford, 1986).

'The Rise of Catalonia: Identity, Power and Ideology in a Twelfth-Century Society', in *Medieval France and Her Pyrenean Neighbours* (London, 1989), pp. 125–52, originally published in French in *Annales* 39 (1984), pp. 454–79.

Black-Veldtrup, Mechthild, *Kaiserin Agnes (1043–1077): quellenkritische Studien* (Cologne, 1995).

Blackburn, Mark, 'Coinage and Currency', in *The Anarchy of King Stephen's Reign*, ed. Edmund King (Oxford, 1994), pp. 145–205.

Böhmer, Johann Friedrich, and Emil von Ottenthal, *Die Regesten des Kaiserreichs unter den Herrschern aus dem Sächsischen Hause 919–1024*, 1 (Innsbruck, 1893).

Bonenfant, A. M., and P. Bonenfant, 'Le projet d'érection des États bourguignons en royaume en 1447', *Le Moyen Age*, 45 (1935), pp. 10–23.

Bouchard, Constance B., 'Consanguinity and Noble Marriages in the Tenth and Eleventh Centuries', *Speculum*, 56 (1981), pp. 268–87.

Boudet, Jean-Patrice, *Entre science et nigromance. Astrologie, divination et magie dans l'Occident médiéval (xiie–xve s.)* (Paris, 2006).

Boudet, Jean-Patrice, Martine Ostorero and Agostino Paravicini Bagliani, eds., *De Frédéric II à Rodolphe II. Astrologie, divination et magie dans les cours (XIIIe–XVIIe siècle)* (Micrologus Library 85, Florence, 2017).

Boudet, Jean-Patrice, and Emmanuel Poulle, 'Les jugements astrologiques sur la naissance de Charles VII', in *Saint-Denis et la royauté: études offertes à Bernard Guénée* (Paris, 1999), pp. 169–79.

Boudreau, Claire, 'Théories et discours des anciens sur les brisures de bâtardise (XIVe–XVIIIe siècles)', in *Académie Internationale d'Héraldique. VIII Colloquium. Canterbury 29th August–4th September 1993. Proceedings* (Canterbury, 1995), pp. 81–96.

Boulton, D'Arcy Jonathan Dacre, 'Dynasties, Domains and Dominions: The Use and Non-Use of Dominional Arms by Subordinate Princes in the Kingdom of France, 1200–1500', in *Académie Internationale d'Héraldique. VIII Colloquium. Canterbury 29th August–4th September 1993. Proceedings* (Canterbury, 1995), pp. 39–74.

Boutet, Dominique, 'Bâtardise et sexualité dans l'image littéraire de la royauté (XIIe–XIIIe siècles)', in *Femmes: mariages-lignages, XIIe–XVIe siècles: mélanges offerts à Georges Duby* (Brussels, 1992), pp. 55–68.

Bresc, Henri, and Pasciuta Beatrice, 'Actes de la pratique, I – L'adoption en Sicile (XIVe–XVe siècles)', in *Médiévales, 35: L'adoption. Droits et pratiques*, ed. Didier Lett and Christopher Lucken (1998), pp. 93–9.

Bresslau, Harry, *Das tausendjährige Jubiläum der deutschen Selbständigkeit* (Schriften der wissenschaftlichen Gesellschaft in Strassburg 14, Strassburg, 1912).

'Der angebliche Brief des Erzbischofs Hatto von Mainz an Papst Johann IX', in *Historische Aufsätze Karl Zeumer . . . dargebracht* (Weimar, 1910), pp. 9–30.

Brown, Elizabeth A. R., 'Death and the Human Body in the Later Middle Ages: The Legislation of Boniface VIII on the Division of the Corpse', *Viator*, 12 (1981), pp. 221–70.

'La généalogie capétienne dans l'historiographie du Moyen Âge. Philippe le Bel, le reniement du reditus et la création d'une ascendance carolingienne pour Hugues Capet', in *Religion et culture autour de l'an Mil. Royaume capétien et Lotharingie*, ed. Dominique Iogna-Prat and Jean-Charles Picard (Paris, 1990), pp. 199–214.

'The Ceremonial of Royal Succession in Capetian France: The Double Funeral of Louis X', *Traditio*, 34 (1978), pp. 227–71.

'The Political Repercussions of Family Ties in the Early Fourteenth Century: The Marriage of Edward II of England and Isabelle of France', *Speculum*, 63 (1988), pp. 573–95.

'Vincent de Beauvais and the *reditus regni Francorum ad stirpem Caroli imperatoris*', in *Vincent de Beauvais. Intentions et réceptions d'une œuvre encyclopédique au Moyen Âge*, ed. Serge Lusignan et al. (Paris, 1990), pp. 167–96.

Brown, Michael, *The Black Douglases: War and Lordship in Late Medieval Scotland, 1300–1455* (East Linton, 1998).

Brühl, Carlrichard, *Deutschland-Frankreich: die Geburt zweier Völker* (2nd edn., Cologne, 1995)

'Karolingische Miszellen III: Ein westfränkisches Reichsteilungsprojekt aus dem Jahre 953', *Deutsches Archiv für Erforschung des Mittelalters*, 44 (1988), pp. 385–9.

Brundage, James, *Law, Sex and Christian Society in Medieval Europe* (Chicago, 1987).

Bryer, Anthony, 'Greek Historians on the Turks: The Case of the First Byzantine–Ottoman Marriage', in *The Writing of History in the Middle Ages: Essays Presented to Richard William Southern*, ed. R. H. C. Davis and J. M. Wallace-Hadrill (Oxford, 1981), pp. 471–93.

Bührer, Peter, 'Studien zu den Beinamen mittelalterlicher Herrscher', *Schweizerische Zeitschrift für Geschichte*, 22 (1972), pp. 205–36.

Bührer-Thierry, Geneviève, 'La reine adultère', *Cahiers de civilisation medieval*, 35 (1992), pp. 299–312.

Butaud, Germain and Valérie Piétri, *Les Enjeux de la généalogie (XIIe–XVIIIe s.): pouvoir et identité* (Paris, 2006).

Byrne, Francis J., 'A Note on the Emergence of Irish Surnames', in *Irish Kings and High Kings* (2nd edn., Dublin, 2001), pp. xxxi–xliii.

Irish Kings and High Kings (2nd edn., Dublin, 2001).

Calderón Medina, Inés, 'Las otras mujeres del rey: El concubinato regio en el reino de León (1157–1230)', *Seminário Medieval* (2009–2011), pp. 255–89.

The Cambridge History of Scandinavia, 1, *Prehistory to 1520*, ed. Knut Helle (Cambridge, 2003).

Carey, Hilary M., *Courting Disaster: Astrology at the English Court and University in the Later Middle Ages* (Basingstoke, 1992).

Carlin, Martha, 'Parron, William (b. before 1461, d. in or after 1503), Astrologer', in *ODNB*, 42 (2004), pp. 861–2.

Carlyle, R. W. and A. J., *A History of Medieval Political Theory in the West* (6 vols., Edinburgh and London, 1903–36; 2nd edn. of vol. 1).

Carozzi, Claude, 'Familia-domus: étude sémantique et historique', in *Famille et parenté dans la vie religieuse du Midi (XIIe–XVe siècle)* (Cahiers de Fanjeaux 43, 2008), pp. 15–30.

'Le dernier des Carolingiens: de l'histoire au mythe', *Le Moyen Age*, 82 (1976), pp. 453–76.

Carpenter, David, *The Minority of Henry III* (London, 1990).

Cartellieri, Alexander, *Philipp II. August, König von Frankreich* (4 vols. in 5, Leipzig, 1899–1922).

Catalogue of the Byzantine Coins in the Dumbarton Oaks Collection and in the Whittemore Collection, ed. Alfred R. Bellinger et al. (5 vols. in 9, Washington, DC, 1966–99).

Champion, Pierre, *La dame de Beauté Agnès Sorel* (Paris, 1931).

Chaney, William A., *The Cult of Kingship in Anglo-Saxon England: The Transition from Paganism to Christianity* (Manchester, 1970).

Chaplais, Pierre, *English Medieval Diplomatic Practice*, 1. i. (London, 1982).

'Un message de Jean de Fiennes à Edouard II et le projet de démembrement du royaume de France (janvier 1317)', *Revue du Nord*, 43 (1961), pp. 145–8, repr. in Pierre Chaplais, *Essays in Medieval Diplomacy and Administration* (London, 1981), X, with same pagination.

Chibnall, Marjorie, *The Empress Matilda: Queen Consort, Queen Mother and Lady of the English* (Oxford, 1991).

Ciggaar, Krijnie N., *Western Travellers to Constantinople: The West and Byzantium, 962–1204* (Leiden, 1996).

Clanchy, Michael, *From Memory to Written Record: England 1066–1307* (3rd edn., Oxford and Malden, Mass., 2013).

Clarke, M. V., 'The Wilton Diptych', *The Burlington Magazine for Connoisseurs*, 58, no. 339 (June 1931), pp. 283–94.

Clementi, Dione, 'The Circumstances of Count Tancred's Accession to the Kingdom of Sicily, Duchy of Apulia and the Principality of Capua', in *Mélanges Antonio Marongiu* (Palermo, 1967), pp. 57–80.

Cohn, Norman, *The Pursuit of the Millennium* (rev. edn., London, 1970).

Colker, Marvin L., 'The "Karolinus" of Egidius Parisiensis', *Traditio*, 29 (1973), pp. 199–325.

The Complete Peerage of England, Scotland, Ireland, Great Britain and the United Kingdom, ed. G. E. C[okayne] (rev. edn., 13 vols. in 14, London, 1910–59).

Conklin, George, 'Ingeborg of Denmark, Queen of France, 1193–1223', in *Queens and Queenship in Medieval Europe*, ed. Anne J. Duggan (Woodbridge, 1997), pp. 39–52.

Constable, Giles, 'The Numbering of the Crusades', in *Crusaders and Crusading in the Twelfth Century* (Farnham and Burlington, Vt., 2008), pp. 353–6 (Appendix B).

Contamine, Philippe, '"Le royaume de France ne peut tomber en fille." Fondement, formulation et implication d'une théorie politique à la fin du Moyen Âge', *Perspectives médiévales*, 13 (1987), pp. 67–81.

'Stuart, Bérault (1452/3–1508), soldier and diplomat', in *ODNB*, 53 (2004), pp. 134–5.

Coote, Lesley, *Prophecy and Public Affairs in Later Medieval England* (York, 2000).

Costa-Gomes, Rita, 'Alfarrobeira: The Death of the Tyrant?', in *Death at Court*, ed. Karl-Heinz Spiess and Immo Warntjes (Wiesbaden, 2012), pp. 135–58.

Cramp, Rosemary, 'Aldfrith (d. 704/5), King of Northumbria', in *ODNB*, 1 (2004), pp. 618–19.

Crawford, Barbara, 'The Pawning of Orkney and Shetland: A Reconsideration of the Events of 1460–9', *The Scottish Historical Review*, 48 (1969), pp. 35–53.

Creamer, Joseph, 'St Edmund of Canterbury and Henry III in the Shadow of Thomas Becket', *Thirteenth Century England*, 14 (2011), pp. 129–39.

Crick, Julia, *The Historia Regum Britanniae of Geoffrey of Monmouth*, 3: *A Summary Catalogue of the Manuscripts* (Woodbridge, 1989).

Croenen, Godfried, 'Princely and Noble Genealogies, Twelfth to Fourteenth Century: Form and Function', in *The Medieval Chronicle* (1), ed. Erik Kooper (Amsterdam, 1999), pp. 84–95.

Crouch, David, 'Robert, Earl of Gloucester, and the Daughters of Zelophehad', *Journal of Medieval History*, 11 (1985), pp. 227–43.

Crusafont, Miquel, Anna M. Balaguer and Philip Grierson, *Medieval European Coinage, with a Catalogue of the Coins in the Fitzwilliam Museum, 6: The Iberian Peninsula* (Cambridge, 2013).

Csendes, Peter, *Heinrich VI* (Darmstadt, 1993).

d'Avray, David, *Dissolving Royal Marriages: A Documentary History, 860–1600* (Cambridge, 2014).

Papacy, Monarchy and Marriage 860–1600 (Cambridge, 2015).

Dagron, Gilbert, 'Das Firmament soll christlich werden: Zu zwei Seefahrtskalendern des 10. Jahrhunderts', in *Fest und Alltag in Byzanz*, ed. Günter Prinzing and Dieter Simon (Munich, 1990), pp. 145–56, 210–15.

Emperor and Priest: The Imperial Office in Byzantium (tr. Jean Birrell, Cambridge, 2003).

Dailey, E. T., *Queens, Consorts, Concubines: Gregory of Tours and Women of the Merovingian Elite* (Leiden, 2015).

Daly, Kathleen, 'A Rare Iconographic Theme in a Bodleian Library Manuscript: An Illustration of the *Reditus regni ad stirpem Karoli Magni* in MS. Bodley 968', *Bodleian Library Record*, 11 (1982–5), pp. 371–8.

Daniel, Catherine, *Les prophéties de Merlin et la culture politique (xiie–xvie s.)* (Turnhout, 2006).

Daumet, Georges, *Étude sur l'alliance de la France et de la Castille au XIVe et au XVe siècles* (Paris, 1898).

Mémoire sur les relations de la France et de la Castille de 1255 à 1320 (Paris, 1913).

Davidsohn, Robert, *Philipp II. August von Frankreich und Ingeborg* (Stuttgart, 1888).

Davies, Rees, *Conquest, Coexistence and Change: Wales 1063–1415* (Oxford, 1987, reissued as *The Age of Conquest*, 1992).

'The Peoples of Britain and Ireland 1100–1400, II: Names, Boundaries and Regnal Solidarities', *Transactions of the Royal Historical Society*, 6th series, 5 (1995), pp. 1–20.

Davis, Natalie Zemon, *The Return of Martin Guerre* (Cambridge, Mass., 1983).

Davis, R. H. C., *King Stephen, 1135–1154* (3rd edn., London, 1990).

De Jong, Mayke, 'Bride Shows Revisited: Praise, Slander and Exegesis in the Reign of the Empress Judith', in *Gender in the Early Medieval World: East and West, 300–900*, ed. Leslie Brubaker and Julia M. H. Smith (Cambridge, 2004), pp. 257–77.

The Penitential State: Authority and Atonement in the Age of Louis the Pious, 814–840 (Cambridge, 2009).

Dectot, Xavier, *Les tombeaux des familles royales de la péninsule ibérique au Moyen Age* (Turnhout, 2009).

Deér, Josef, *The Dynastic Porphyry Tombs of the Norman Period in Sicily* (Cambridge, Mass., 1959).

Das Papsttum und die süditalienischen Normannenstaaten, 1053–1212 (Göttingen, 1969).

Delaborde, Henri-François, 'Notice sur les ouvrages et sur la vie de Rigord moine de Saint-Denis', *Bibliothèque de l'École des Chartes*, 45 (1884), pp. 585–614.

Delisle, Léopold, *Catalogue des actes de Philippe Auguste* (Paris, 1856).

'Notice sur les manuscrits de Bernard Gui', *Notices et extraits des manuscrits de la Bibliothèque Nationale*, 27. 2 (1879), pp. 169–455.

Dendorfer, Jürgen, *Adelige Gruppenbildung und Königsherrschaft: die Grafen von Sulzbach und ihr Beziehungsgeflecht im 12. Jahrhundert* (Munich, 2004).

Depreux, Philippe, 'Le partage de l'Empire à Verdun (843) et les conditions d'exercice du pouvoir au haut Moyen-Age', in *L'écrit et le livre peint en Lorraine*, ed. Anne-Orange Poilpré (Turnhout, 2014), pp. 17–41.

di Carpegna Falconieri, Tommaso, *The Man Who Believed He Was King of France: A True Medieval Tale* (tr. William McCuaig, Chicago, 2008).

Di Renzo Villata, Maria Gigliola 'Adoption between Ancien Régime and Codification: Is it in Remission in a Changing World?', in *Family Law and Society in Europe from the Middle Ages to the Contemporary Era*, ed. Di Renzo Villata (Studies in the History of Law and Justice 5, 2016), pp. 51–92.

Dictionary of Medieval Latin from British Sources (17 fascicules, Oxford University Press for the British Academy, 1975–2013).

Dohmen, Linda, *Die Ursache allen Übels. Untersuchungen zu den Unzuchtsvorwürfen gegen die Gemahlinnen der Karolinger* (Ostfildern, 2017).

Dölger, Franz, 'Das byzantinische Mitkaisertum in den Urkunden', in *Byzantinische Diplomatik* (Ettal, 1956), pp. 103–29 (originally published as a review in *Byzantinische Zeitschrift*, 36 (1936), pp. 123–45).

Dubois, Gérard, *Historia ecclesiae Parisiensis*, 2 (Paris, 1710).

Duby, Georges, *Medieval Marriage: Two Models from Twelfth-Century France* (Eng. tr., Baltimore, 1991).

'Remarques sur la littérature généalogique en France aux XIe et XIIe siècles', in *Comptes rendus de l'Académie des Inscriptions et Belles-Lettres* (1967), pp. 333–45, tr. as 'French Genealogical Literature: The Eleventh and Twelfth Centuries', in Duby, *The Chivalrous Society* (Berkeley and Los Angeles, 1977), pp. 149–57.

Duerloo, Luc, 'Marks of Illegitimacy in the Southern Netherlands', in *Académie Internationale d'Héraldique. VIII Colloquium. Canterbury 29th August–4th September 1993. Proceedings* (Canterbury, 1995), pp. 31–8.

Duffy, Mark, *Royal Tombs of Medieval England* (Stroud, 2003).

Dufour, Jean, 'Emma II, femme de Lothaire, roi de France', in *Kaiserin Adelheid und ihre Klostergründung in Selz*, ed. Franz Staab (Seyer, 2005), pp. 213–27.

Duindam, Jeroen, *Dynasties: A Global History of Power, 1300–1800* (Cambridge, 2016).

Dümmler, Ernst, *Geschichte des Ostfränkischen Reiches* (2nd edn., 3 vols., Leipzig, 1887–8).

Dumville, David, 'Kingship, Genealogies and Regnal Lists', in *Early Medieval Kingship*, ed. P. H. Sawyer and I. N. Wood (Leeds, 1977), pp. 72–104.

'The Ætheling: A Study in Anglo-Saxon Constitutional History', *Anglo-Saxon England*, 8 (1979), pp. 1–33.

Dunbabin, Jean, 'What's in a Name? Philip, King of France', *Speculum*, 68 (1993), pp. 949–68.

Duncan, A. A. M., 'Margaret [Called the Maid of Norway] (1282/3–1290), Queen-Designate of Scots', in *ODNB*, 36 (2004), p. 636.

'The Community of the Realm of Scotland and Robert Bruce: A Review', *The Scottish Historical Review*, 45 (1966), pp. 184–201.

The Kingship of the Scots, 842–1292: Succession and Independence (Edinburgh, 2002).

Duplessy, Jean, *Les monnaies françaises royales: de Hugues Capet à Louis XVI (987–1793)*, 1 (Paris, 1988).

Dutton, Paul Edward, *The Politics of Dreaming in the Carolingian Empire* (Lincoln, Neb., 1994).

Earenfight, Theresa, *Queenship in Medieval Europe* (Basingstoke and New York, 2013).

Eisner, Manuel, 'Killing Kings: Patterns of Regicide in Europe, AD 600–1800', *The British Journal of Criminology*, 51 (2011), pp. 556–77.

El-Hajji, Abdurrahman Ali, 'Intermarriage between Andalusia and Northern Spain in the Umayyad Period', *Islamic Quarterly*, 11 (1967), pp. 3–7.

Elliott, Dyan, 'Violence against the Dead: The Negative Translation and *Damnatio Memoriae* in the Middle Ages', *Speculum*, 92 (2017), pp. 1020–55.

Enderlein, Lorenz, *Die Grablegen des Hauses Anjou in Unteritalien. Totenkult und Monumente (1266–1343)* (Worms, 1997).

Erben, Wilhelm, Ludwig Schmitz-Kallenberg and Oswald Redlich, *Urkundenlehre* (Munich and Berlin, 1907).

Erlande-Brandenburg, Alain, *Le roi est mort: étude sur les funérailles, les sépultures et les tombeaux des rois de France jusqu'à la fin du 13e siècle* (Geneva, 1975).

Esmyol, Andrea, *Geliebte oder Ehefrau? Konkubinen im frühen Mittelalter* (Cologne, 2002).

Estow, Clara, *Pedro the Cruel* (Leiden, 1995).

Etting, Vivian, *Queen Margrete I (1353–1412), and the Founding of the Nordic Union* (Leiden, 2004).

Evans, Michael, *The Death of Kings: Royal Deaths in Medieval England* (London, 2003).

Ewig, Eugen, 'Die Namengebung bei den ältesten Frankenkönigen und im merowingischen Königshaus', *Francia*, 18 (1991), pp. 21–67.

'Studien zur merowingischen Dynastie', *Frühmittelalterliche Studien*, 8 (1974), pp. 15–59.

Facinger, Marion F., 'A Study of Medieval Queenship: Capetian France 987–1237', *Studies in Medieval and Renaissance History*, 5 (1968), pp. 1–48.

Falkenhausen, Vera Von, 'Olympias, eine normannische Prinzessin in Konstantinopel', in *Bisanzio e l'Italia: Raccolta di studi in memoria di Agostino Pertusi* (Milan, 1982), pp. 56–72.

Faraglia, Nunzio Federigo, *Storia della regina Giovanna II d'Angiò* (Lanciano, 1904).

Fawtier, Robert, *The Capetian Kings of France: Monarchy and Nation, 987–1328* (Eng. tr., London, 1960).

Fehrmann, Antje, *Grab und Krone: Königsgrabmäler im mittelalterlichen England und die posthume Selbstdarstellung der Lancaster* (Munich, 2008).

Félibien, Michel, and Guy Lobineau, *Histoire de la ville de Paris* (5 vols., Paris, 1725).

Folz, Robert, *Les saints rois du moyen âge en Occident (VIe–XIIIe s.)* (Subsidia hagiographica 68, Brussels, 1984).

Les saintes reines du Moyen Age en Occident (Subsidia hagiographica 76, Brussels, 1992).

Foot, Sarah, *Æthelstan: The First King of England* (New Haven, 2011).

Forcellini, Francesco, 'Strane peripezie d'un bastardo di casa di Aragona', *Archivio storico per le province napoletane*, 37 (1912), pp. 553–63; 38 (1913), pp. 87–114, 441–82; 39 (1914), pp. 172–214, 268–98, 459–94, 767–87.

Forey, Alan J., 'A Rejoinder (to Elena Lourie, q. v.)', *Durham University Journal*, 77 (n.s. 46) (1984–5), pp. 173.

The Templars in the Corona de Aragon (Oxford, 1973).

'The Will of Alfonso I of Aragon and Navarre', *Durham University Journal*, 73 (n.s. 42) (1980–1), pp. 59–65.

Friedmann, Yohanan, *Tolerance and Coercion in Islam: Interfaith Relations in the Muslim Tradition* (Cambridge, 2003).

Fröhlich, Walter, 'The Marriage of Henry VI and Constance of Sicily: Prelude and Consequences', *Anglo-Norman Studies*, 15 (1993), pp. 99–115.

Fronska, Joanna, 'The Royal Image and Diplomacy: Henry VII's Book of Astrology (British Library, Arundel 66)', *Electronic British Library Journal* (2014), pp. 1–28 (article 7).

Gädeke, Nora, *Zeugnisse Bildlicher Darstellung der Nachkommenschaft Heinrichs I* (Arbeiten zur Frühmittelalterforschung 22, Berlin, 1992).

Ganshof, F. L., 'On the Genesis and Significance of the Treaty of Verdun (843)', in *The Carolingians and the Frankish Monarchy* (London, 1971), pp. 289–302.

García Marsilla, Juan Vicente, and Danièle Sansy, 'L'adoption dans les textes juridiques espagnols du XIIIe siècle', in *Médiévales*, 35: *L'adoption. Droits et pratiques*, ed. Didier Lett and Christopher Lucken (1998), pp. 61–8.

Garland, Lynda, *Byzantine Empresses: Women and Power in Byzantium, AD 527–1204* (London and New York, 1999).

'Morality Versus Politics at the Byzantine Court: The Charges against Marie of Antioch and Euphrosyne', *Byzantinische Forschungen*, 24 (1997), pp. 259–95.

Garnett, George, *Conquered England: Kingship, Succession, and Tenure 1066–1166* (Oxford, 2007).

'"Ducal" Succession in Early Normandy', in *Law and Government in Medieval England and Normandy: Essays in Honour of Sir James Holt*, ed. George Garnett and John Hudson (Cambridge, 1994), pp. 80–110.

Gaude-Ferragu, Murielle, *D'or et de cendres. La mort et les funérailles des princes dans le royaume de France au bas Moyen Âge* (Lille, 2005).

Queenship in Medieval France, 1300–1500 (Eng. tr., New York, 2016).

Gaudemet, Jean, 'Le dossier canonique du mariage de Philippe Auguste et d'Ingeburge de Denmark (1193–1213)', *Revue historique de droit français et étranger*, 4th series, 62 (1984), pp. 15–29.

Gautier, Marc-Édouard, 'Aux origines du dessin généalogique en France: l'exemple de l'abbaye Saint-Aubin d'Angers (XIe–XIIe siècle)', *Archives d'Anjou: mélanges d'histoire et d'archéologie angevines*, 11 (2007), pp. 5–33.

Geaman, Kristen, 'A Bastard and a Changeling? England's Edward of Westminster and Delayed Childbirth', in *Unexpected Heirs in Early Modern Europe: Potential Kings and Queens*, ed. Valerie Schutte (Basingstoke, 2017), pp. 11–33.

Génestal, Robert, *Histoire de la légitimation des enfants naturels en droit canonique* (Bibliothèque de l'École des Hautes-Études, sciences religieuses, 18, Paris, 1905).

Genet, Jean-Philippe, 'Londres est-elle une capitale?', in *Les villes capitales au Moyen Âge* (Paris, 2006), pp. 155–85.

Genicot, Léopold, *Les généalogies* (Typologie des sources du Moyen Age occidental 15, Turnhout, 1975).

Gentile, Luisa Clotilde, 'Les bâtards princiers piémontais et savoyards', in *La Bâtardise et l'exercice du pouvoir en Europe du XIIIe au début du XVIe siècle*, ed. Éric Bousmar et al. (*Revue du Nord*, Hors série. Collection Histoire no. 31, 2015), pp. 387–410.

Giese, Wolfgang, 'Die designativen Nachfolgeregelungen der Karolinger 714–979', *Deutsches Archiv für Erforschung des Mittelalters*, 64 (2008), pp. 437–511.

'Zu den Designationen und Mitkönigserhebungen der deutschen Könige des Hochmittelalters (936–1237)', *Zeitschrift der Savigny-Stiftung für Rechtsgeschichte: Germanistische Abteilung*, 92 (1975), pp. 174–83.

Giesebrecht, Wilhelm, *Geschichte der deutschen Kaiserzeit*, 2 (5th edn., Leipzig, 1885).

Giesey, Ralph E, *Le Rôle méconnu de la loi salique. La succession royale (xive–xvie siècles)* (Paris, 2007).

'The Juristic Basis of Dynastic Right to the French Throne', *Transactions of the American Philosophical Society*, 51, no. 5 (1961), pp. 3–47.

Gillingham, John, 'Conquering the Barbarians: War and Chivalry in Twelfth-Century Britain', *The Haskins Society Journal*, 4 (1992), pp. 67–84, repr. in John Gillingham, *The English in the Twelfth Century. Imperialism, National Identity and Political Values* (Woodbridge, 2000), pp. 41–58.

'Elective Kingship and the Unity of Medieval Germany', *German History*, 9 (1991), pp. 124–35.

'Killing and Mutilating Political Enemies in the British Isles from the Late Twelfth to the Early Fourteenth Century: A Comparative Study', in *Britain and Ireland 900–1300*, ed. Brendan Smith (Cambridge, 1999), pp. 114–34.

Richard I (New Haven and London, 1999).

'Richard I and Berengaria of Navarre', in *Richard Coeur de Lion: Kingship, Chivalry and War in the Twelfth Century* (London and Rio Grande, Ohio, 1994), pp. 119–39, originally published in *Bulletin of the Institute of Historical Research*, 53 (1980), pp. 157–73.

Richard Coeur de Lion: Kingship, Chivalry and War in the Twelfth Century (London and Rio Grande, Ohio, 1994).

Gimeno Casalduero, Joaquín, 'Sobre las numeraciones de los reyes de Castilla', *Nueva Revista de Filología Hispánica*, 14, no. 3/4 (1960), pp. 271–94.

Given-Wilson, Chris, *Henry IV* (New Haven and London, 2016).

'Legitimation, Designation and Succession to the Throne in Fourteenth-Century England', in *Building Legitimacy: Political Discourses and Forms of Legitimacy in Medieval Societies*, ed. Isabel Alfonso et al. (Leiden, 2004), pp. 89–105.

The Glory of Byzantium: Art and Culture of the Middle Byzantine Era, A.D. 843–1261, ed. Helen C. Evans and William D. Wixom (New York, 1997).

Le Goff, Jacques, *The Birth of Purgatory* (Eng. tr., London, 1984).

Goldstone, Nancy, *Joanna: The Notorious Queen of Naples, Jerusalem and Sicily* (London, 2010).

González, Julio, *Alfonso IX* (2 vols., Madrid, 1944).

El reino de Castilla en la epoca de Alfonso VIII (3 vols., Madrid, 1960).

Repoblación de Castilla la Nueva (2 vols., Madrid, 1975–6).

González Jiménez, Manuel, 'Sancho IV, infante', *Historia. Instituciones. Documentos*, 28 (2001), pp. 151–216.

Goodman, Anthony, *John of Gaunt: The Exercise of Princely Power in Fourteenth-Century Europe* (Harlow, 1992).

Katherine Swynford (Lincoln, 1994).

Goody, Jack, *The Development of the Family and Marriage in Europe* (Cambridge, 1983).

Grandeau, Yann, 'Les enfants de Charles VI. Essai sur la vie privée des princes et des princesses de la maison de France à la fin du Moyen Âge', *Bulletin philologique et historique du Comité des travaux historiques et scientifiques*, année 1967, 2 (1969), pp. 809–49.

Gransden, Antonia, *Historical Writing in England I: c.550–c.1307* (London, 1974).

Grant, Lindy, *Blanche of Castile, Queen of France* (New Haven and London, 2016).

Green, Mary Anne Everett, *Lives of the Princesses of England*, 3 (London, 1851).

Greer, Sarah, 'All in the Family: Creating a Carolingian Genealogy in the Eleventh Century', in *Using and Not Using the Past after the Carolingian Empire, c. 900–c. 1050*, ed. Sarah Greer et al. (Abingdon, 2019), pp. 166–88.

Grierson, Philip, Cyril Mango and Ihor Ševčenko, 'The Tombs and Obits of the Byzantine Emperors (337–1042), With an Additional Note', *Dumbarton Oaks Papers*, 16 (1962), pp. 1–63.

Griffiths, Ralph A., 'Queen Katherine of Valois and a Missing Statute of the Realm', *Law Quarterly Review*, 93 (1977), pp. 248–58, repr. in Ralph A. Griffiths, *King and Country: England and Wales in the Fifteenth Century* (London, 1991), pp. 103–13.

'The Trial of Eleanor Cobham: An Episode in the Fall of Duke Humphrey of Gloucester', *Bulletin of the John Rylands University Library*, 51 (1968–9), pp. 381–99, repr. in Ralph A. Griffiths, *King and Country: England and Wales in the Fifteenth Century* (London, 1991), pp. 223–52.

Guenée, Bernard, 'Les généalogies entre l'histoire et la politique: la fierté d'être Capétien, en France, au Moyen Âge', *Annales*, 33 (1978), pp. 450–77.

'Les limites de la France', in *La France et les Français*, ed. Michel François (Paris, 1972), pp. 50–69, repr. in Bernard Guenée, *Politique et histoire au Moyen Age* (Paris, 1981), pp. 73–92.

Guerout, Jean, 'Le Palais de la Cité, des origines à 1417. Essai topographique et archéologique', *Mémoires de la Fédération des sociétés historiques et archéologiques de Paris et de l'Ile-de-France*, 1 (1949), pp. 57–212; 2 (1950), pp. 21–204; 3 (1951), pp. 7–101.

Guiffrey, J. J., *Histoire de la réunion du Dauphiné à la France* (Paris, 1868).

Guilland, Rodolphe, 'La destinée des empereurs de Byzance', in *Études byzantines* (Paris, 1959), pp. 1–32.

'Les noces plurales à Byzance', in *Études byzantines* (Paris, 1959), pp. 233–61.

Guyot-Bachy, Isabelle, 'La *Chronique abrégée des rois de France* de Guillaume de Nangis: trois étapes de l'histoire d'un texte', in *Religion et mentalités au Moyen Âge. Mélanges en l'honneur d'Hervé Martin*, ed. Sophie Cassagnes-Brouquet et al. (Rennes, 2003), pp. 39–46.

'La *Chronique abrégée des rois de France* et les *Grandes chroniques de France*: concurrence ou complémentarité dans la construction d'une culture historique en France à la fin du Moyen Age?', *The Medieval Chronicle*, 8 (2013), pp. 205–32.

Hablot, Laurent, 'L'emblématique des bâtards princiers au XVe siècle', in *La Bâtardise et l'exercice du pouvoir en Europe du XIIIe au début du XVIe siècle*, ed. Éric Bousmar et al. (*Revue du Nord*, Hors série. Collection Histoire no. 31, 2015), pp. 439–50.

Hagn, Hans, *Illegitimität und Thronfolge: zur Thronfolgeproblematik illegitimer Merowinger, Karolinger und Ottonen* (Neuried, 2006).

Hamann, Stefanie, 'Zur Chronologie des Staatsstreichs Grimoalds', *Deutsches Archiv für Erforschung des Mittelalters*, 59 (2003), pp. 49–96.

Hamilton, Bernard, 'Women in the Crusader States: The Queens of Jerusalem (1100–1190)', in *Medieval Women*, ed. Derek Baker (Studies in Church History, Subsidia, 1, 1981), pp. 143–74.

Harsgor, Mikhaël, 'L'essor des bâtards nobles au XVe siècle', *Revue Historique*, 253 (1975), pp. 319–54.

Hartman, Charles, and Anthony DeBlasi, 'The Growth of Historical Method in Tang China', in *The Oxford History of Historical Writing*, 2, ed. Sarah Foot and Chase Robinson (Oxford, 2012), pp. 17–36.

Hartmann, Heinz, 'Über die Entwicklung der Rota', *Archiv für Urkundenforschung*, 16 (1942), pp. 385–412.

Hartmann, Martina, 'Concubina vel regina? Zu einigen Ehefrauen und Konkubinen der karolingischen Könige', *Deutsches Archiv für Erforschung des Mittelalters*, 63 (2007), pp. 545–67.

Die Königin im frühen Mittelalter (Stuttgart, 2009).

Haskins, Charles Homer, *Studies in the History of Medieval Science* (2nd. edn., Cambridge, Mass., 1924).

Hayton, Darin, 'Martin Bylica at the Court of Matthias Corvinus: Astrology and Politics in Renaissance Hungary', *Centaurus*, 49 (2007), pp. 185–98.

The Heads of Religious Houses: England and Wales 1 (940–1216), ed. David Knowles et al. (2nd edn., Cambridge, 2001).

Hellmann, Siegmund, 'Die Heiraten der Karolinger', in *Ausgewählte Abhandlungen zur Historiographie und Geistesgeschichte des Mittelalters*, ed. Helmut Beumann (Darmstadt, 1961), pp. 293–91, originally published in *Festgabe Karl Theodor von Heigel zur Vollendung seines sechzigsten Lebensjahres* (Munich, 1903), pp. 1–99.

Helmholtz, R. H., 'The Sons of Edward IV: A Canonical Assessment of the Claim That They Were Illegitimate', in *Richard III: Loyalty, Lordship and Law*, ed. P. W. Hammond (London, 1986), pp. 91–103.

Henzler, Christine Juliane, *Die Frauen Karls VII. und Ludwigs XI.: Rolle und Position der Königinnen und Mätressen am französischen Hof (1422–1483)* (Cologne, 2012).

Herbert, Máire, 'Goddess and King: The Sacred Marriage in Early Ireland', in *Women and Sovereignty*, ed. Louise Olga Fradenburg (Edinburgh, 1992), pp. 264–75.

Herrin, Judith, *Byzantium: The Surprising Life of a Medieval Empire* (Princeton and London, 2007).

'Moving Bones: Evidence for Political Burials from Medieval Constantinople', in *Mélanges Gilbert Dagron* (Travaux et Mémoires 14, 2002), pp. 287–94.

Women in Purple: Rulers of Medieval Byzantium (Princeton, 2001).

Hicks, Michael, 'The Royal Bastards of Late Medieval England', in *La Bâtardise et l'exercice du pouvoir en Europe du XIIIe au début du XVIe siècle*, ed. Eric Bousmar et al. (*Revue du Nord*, Hors série. Collection Histoire no. 31, 2015), pp. 369–86.

Hill, Barbara, *Imperial Women in Byzantium 1025–1204: Power, Patronage and Ideology* (Harlow, 1999).

Hinkle, W. H., *The Fleurs de Lis of the Kings of France, 1285–1488* (Carbondale, Ill., 1991).

Hlawitschka, Eduard, 'Adoptionen im mittelalterlichen Königshaus', in *Beiträge zur Wirtschafts- und Sozialgeschichte des Mittelalters. Festschrift für Herbert Helbig zum 65. Geburtstag*, ed. Knut Schulz (Cologne and Vienna, 1976), pp. 1–32, repr. in Eduard

Hlawitschka, *Stirps regia: Forschungen zu Königtum und Führungsschichten im früheren Mittelalter: ausgewählte Aufsätze: Festgabe zu seinem 60. Geburtstag*, ed. Gertrud Thoma and Wolfgang Giese (Frankfurt, 1988), pp. 11–42.

'Weshalb war die Auflösung der Ehe Friedrich Barbarossas und Adelas von Vohburg möglich?', *Deutsches Archiv für Erforschung des Mittelalters*, 61 (2005), pp. 509–36.

Hoffmann, Hartmut, 'Langobarden, Normannen, Päpste. Zum Legitimitätsproblem in Unteritalien', *Quellen und Forschungen aus italienischen Archiven und Bibliotheken*, 58 (1978), pp. 137–80.

Holladay, Joan A., *Genealogy and the Politics of Representation in the High and Late Middle Ages* (Cambridge, 2019).

'Kings, Notaries, and Merchants: Audience and Image in the Grand'Salle of the Palace at Paris', in *Ritual, Images, and Daily Life: The Medieval Perspective*, ed. Gerhard Jaritz (Geschichte: Forschung und Wissenschaft, 39, Berlin, 2012), pp. 75–93.

Hollingsworth, T. H., 'A Demographic Study of the British Ducal Families', in *Population in History*, ed. D. V. Glass and D. E. C. Eversley (London, 1965), pp. 354–78.

Holt, J. C., 'The *Casus Regis* Reconsidered', *Haskins Society Journal*, 10 (2001), pp. 163–82.

'The *Casus Regis*: The Law and Politics of Succession in the Plantagenet Dominions, 1185–1247', in *Law in Mediaeval Life and Thought*, ed. Edward B. King and Susan J. Ridyard (Sewanee, 1990), pp. 21–42, repr. in J. C. Holt, *Colonial England, 1066–1215* (London, 1997), pp. 307–26.

'Feudal Society and the Family in Early Medieval England: IV. The Heiress and the Alien', *Transactions of the Royal Historical Society*, series 5, 35 (1985), pp. 1–28.

Hudson, John, *The Oxford History of the Laws of England II: 871–1216* (Oxford, 2012).

Huneycutt, Lois L., 'Female Succession and the Language of Power in the Writings of Twelfth Century Churchmen', in *Medieval Queenship*, ed. John Carmi-Parsons (New York, 1993), pp. 189–202.

Hunger, Herbert, 'Die Schönheitskonkurrenz in "Belthandros und Chrysantza" und die Brautschau am byzantinischen Kaiserhof', *Byzantion*, 35 (1965), pp. 150–8.

Hunter, Joseph, 'On the Death of Eleanor of Castile, Consort of King Edward the First, and the Honours Paid to her Memory', *Archaeologia*, 29 (1842), pp. 167–91.

Huth, Volkhard, 'Erzbischof Arnulf von Reims und der Kampf um das Königtum im Westfrankenreich', *Francia*, 21 (1994), pp. 85–124.

Hyam, Jane, 'Ermentrude and Richildis', in *Charles the Bald: Court and Kingdom*, ed. Margaret Gibson and Janet Nelson (2nd edn., London, 1990), pp. 154–68.

Jackman, Donald C., *Studia Luxembourgensia* (Archive for Medieval Prosopography 13, State College, Penn., 2012), pp. 15–20.

Jardin, Jean-Pierre, 'Les prophéties dans la chronique de Pierre Ier de López de Ayala: respect et manipulation du temps', in *La concordance des temps: Moyen Âge et Époque modern*, ed. Gilles Luquet (Paris, 2010), pp. 189–204.

Jarnut, Jörg, 'Chlodwig und Chlothar. Anmerkungen zu den Namen zweier Söhne Karls des Grossen', *Francia*, 12 (1984), pp. 645–51, repr. in Jörg Jarnut, *Herrschaft und Ethnogenese im Frühmittelalter. Gesammelte Aufsätze. Festgabe zum 60. Geburtstag* (Münster, 2002), pp. 247–53.

Jarry, Eugène, 'Instructions secrètes pour l'adoption de Louis Ier d'Anjou par Jeanne de Naples (Janvier 1380)', *Bibliothèque de l'Ecole des Chartes*, 67 (1906), pp. 234–54.

Jaski, Bart, *Early Irish Kingship and Succession* (Dublin, 2000).

Jochens, Jenny, 'The Politics of Reproduction: Medieval Norwegian Kingship', *American Historical Review*, 92 (1987), pp. 327–49.

Johnson, Mark, 'The Porphyry Alveus of Santes Creus and the Mausoleum at Centcelles', *Madrider Mitteilungen* (2008), pp. 388–94.

Jones, William H., *Blanche de Bourbon* (2nd edn., London, 1855).

Jordan, William C., *A Tale of Two Monasteries: Westminster and Saint-Denis in the Thirteenth Century* (Princeton, 2009).

'"*Quando fuit natus*": Interpreting the Birth of Philip Augustus', in *The Work of Jacques Le Goff and the Challenges of Medieval History*, ed. Miri Rubin (Woodbridge, 1997), pp. 171–88.

Jussen, Bernhard, 'Adoptiones franques et logique de la pratique. Remarques sur l'échec d'une importation juridique et les nouveaux contextes d'un terme romain', in *Adoption et fosterage*, ed. Mireille Corbier (Paris, 1999), pp. 101–21.

Spiritual Kinship as Social Practice: Godparenthood and Adoption in the Early Middle Ages (Eng. tr., Newark, 2000).

Juste, David, *Les manuscrits astrologiques latins conservés à la Bibliothèque nationale de France à Paris* (Paris, 2015).

Kaeppeli, Thomas, *Scriptores ordinis praedicatorum medii aevi* (4 vols., Rome, 1970–93).

Kantorowicz, Ernst, *The King's Two Bodies* (Princeton, 1957).

Kasten, Brigitte, 'Chancen und Schicksale "unehelicher" Karolinger im 9. Jahrhundert', in *Kaiser Arnolf: Das ostfränkische Reich am Ende des 9. Jahrhunderts*, ed. Franz Fuchs and Peter Schmid (Munich, 2002), pp. 17–52.

Königssöhne und Königsherrschaft: Untersuchungen zur Teilhabe am Reich in der Merowinger- und Karolingerzeit (MGH, Schriften, 44, Hanover, 1997).

'Noverca venefica. Zum bösen Ruf der Stiefmütter in der gallischen und fränkischen Gesellschaft', *Frühmittelalterliche Studien*, 35 (2001), pp. 145–81.

'Stepmothers in Frankish Legal Life', in *Law, Laity, and Solidarities: Essays in Honour of Susan Reynolds*, ed. Pauline Stafford et al. (Manchester, 2001), pp. 47–67.

Kazhdan, Alexander, 'The Formation of Byzantine Family Names in the Ninth and Tenth Centuries', *Byzantinoslavica*, 58 (1997), pp. 90–109.

Kazhdan, A., and L. F. Sherry, 'The Tale of a Happy Fool: The *Vita* of St. Philaretos the Merciful (BHG 1511z–1512b)', *Byzantion*, 66 (1996), pp. 351–62.

Kelly, Fergus, *A Guide to Early Irish Law* (Dublin, 1988).

Kittredge, George L., *Witchcraft in Old and New England* (New York, 1929).

Klaniczay, Gábor, *Holy Rulers and Blessed Princesses: Dynastic Cults in Medieval Central Europe* (tr. Éva Pálmai, Cambridge, 2002).

Klapisch-Zuber, Christiane, *L'ombre des ancêtres: essai sur l'imaginaire médiéval de la parenté* (Paris, 2000).

Klein, Bruno, 'Comment parler des arts au XIVe siècle? La genèse du panthéon aragonais-catalan à Poblet à l'époque du roi Pierre le Cérémonieux', in *Visualisierung und kultureller Transfer*, ed. Kirsten Kramer and Jens Baumgarten (Würzburg, 2009), pp. 83–99.

Koble, Nathalie, *Les Prophéties de Merlin en prose. Le roman arthurien en éclats* (Paris, 2009).

Koch, Arnim, *Kaiserin Judith: eine politische Biographie* (Husum, 2005).

Kölzer, Theo, 'Das Königtum Minderjähriger im fränkisch-deutschen Mittelater: Eine Skizze', *Historische Zeitschrift*, 251 (1990), pp. 291–323.

Konecny, Silvia, *Die Frauen des karolingischen Königshauses. Die politische Bedeutung der Ehe und die Stellung der Frau in der fränkischen Herrscherfamilie vom 7. bis zum 10. Jahrhundert* (Vienna, 1976).

'Eherecht und Ehepolitik unter Ludwig dem Frommen', *Mitteilungen des Instituts für Österreichische Geschichtsforschung*, 85 (1977), pp. 1–21.

Köpke, Rudolf and Ernst Dümmler, *Kaiser Otto der Grosse* (Jahrbücher der deutschen Geschichte, Leipzig, 1876).

Kotsis, Kriszta, 'Defining Female Authority in Eighth-Century Byzantium: The Numismatic Images of the Empress Irene (797–802)', *Journal of Late Antiquity*, 5, no. 1 (2012), pp. 185–215.

'Mothers of the Empire: Empresses Zoe and Theodora on a Byzantine Medallion Cycle', *Medieval Feminist Forum*, 48 (2012), pp. 5–96.

Krüger, Karl Heinrich, 'Herrschaftsnachfolge als Vater-Sohn-Konflikt', *Frühmittelalterliche Studien*, 36 (2002), pp. 225–40.

Kuehn, Thomas, 'L'adoption à Florence à la fin du Moyen Âge', in *Médiévales*, 35: *L'adoption. Droits et pratiques*, ed. Didier Lett and Christopher Lucken (1998), pp. 69–81.

Kunisch, Johannes, ed., *Der dynastische Fürstenstaat: Zur Bedeutung von Sukzessionsordnungen für die Entstehung des frühmodernen Staates* (Historische Forschungen 21, Berlin, 1982).

Labande-Mailfert, Yvonne, 'Le mariage d'Anne de Bretagne avec Charles VIII vu par Erasme Brasca', *Mémoires de la Société d'histoire et d'archéologie de Bretagne*, 5 (1978), pp. 17–42.

Laborderie, Olivier de, 'A New Pattern for Engish History: The First Genealogical Rolls of the Kings of England', in *Broken Lines. Genealogical Literature in Late-Medieval Britain and France*, ed. Raluca Luria Radulescu and Edward Donald Kennedy (Turnhout, 2008), pp. 45–61.

Histoire, mémoire et pouvoir. Les généalogies en rouleau des rois d'Angleterre (1250–1422) (Paris, 2013).

'La mémoire des origines normandes des rois d'Angleterre dans les généalogies en rouleau des XIIIe et XIVe siècles', in *La Normandie et l'Angleterre au moyen âge*, ed. Pierre Bouet and Véronique Gazeau (Caen, 2003), pp. 211–31.

'Les généalogies des rois d'Angleterre sur rouleaux manuscrits (milieu XIIIe siècle–début XVe siècle): Conception, diffusion et fonctions', in *La généalogie entre science et passion*, ed. Tiphaine Barthelemy and Marie-Claude Pingaud (Paris, 1997), pp. 181–99.

'The First King of England? Egbert and the Foundations of Royal Legitimacy in Thirteenth-Century Historiography', in *The Image and Perception of Monarchy in Medieval and Early Modern Europe*, ed. Sean McGlynn and Elena Woodacre (Newcastle-upon-Tyne, 2014), pp. 70–83.

'The First Manuals of English History: Two Late Thirteenth-Century Genealogical Rolls of the Kings of England in the Royal Collection', *The Electronic British Library Journal* (2014), article 4.

Lachaud, Frédérique, and Michael Penman, eds., *Making and Breaking the Rules: Succession in Medieval Europe, c. 1000–c. 1600/Établir et abolir les normes: la succession dans l'Europe médiévale, vers 1000-vers 1600* (Turnhout, 2008).

Laiou, Angeliki E., 'Imperial Marriages and Their Critics in the Eleventh Century: The Case of Skylitzes', *Dumbarton Oaks Papers*, 46, *Homo Byzantinus: Papers in Honor of Alexander Kazhdan* (1992), pp. 165–76.

Lamarrigue, Anne-Marie, *Bernard Gui, 1261–1331: un historien et sa méthode* (Paris, 2000).

'La rédaction d'un catalogue des rois de France. Guillaume de Nangis et Bernard Gui', in *Saint-Denis et la royauté. Études offertes à Bernard Guenée* (Paris, 1999), pp. 481–92.

Lammers, Walther, 'Ein karolingisches Bildprogramm in der Aula Regia von Ingelheim', in *Festschrift für Hermann Heimpel* (3 vols., Göttingen, 1971–2), 3, pp. 226–89.

Le Jan, Régine, *Famille et pouvoir dans le monde franc (VIIe–Xe siècle): essai d'anthropologie sociale* (Paris, 1995).

Lecuppre, Gilles, *L'imposture politique au Moyen Âge: La seconde vie des rois* (Paris, 2005).

Lecuppre-Desjardin, Élodie, *Le royaume inachevé des ducs de Bourgogne: XIVe–XVe siècles* (Paris, 2016).

Lefebvre-Teillard, Anne, *Autour de l'enfant: du droit canonique et romain médiéval au code civil de 1804* (Leiden, 2008).

Lehmann, Paul, 'Mittelalterliche Beinamen und Ehrentitel', in *Erforschung des Mittelalters: Ausgewählte Abhandlungen und Aufsätze* (Stuttgart, 1949, repr. as vol. 1 of 5, 1959, 1973), pp. 129–54.

Lehugeur, Paul, *Histoire de Philippe le Long, roi de France 1316–1322. 1. Le règne* (Geneva, 1897).

Léonard, Émile-G., *La Jeunesse de la reine Jeanne* (Histoire de Jeanne 1e Reine de Naples 1, Monaco and Paris, 1932).

Lerner, Robert, 'Frederick II, Alive, Aloft and Allayed, in Franciscan-Joachite Eschatology', in *The Use and Abuse of Eschatology in the Middle Ages*, ed. Werner Verbeke et al. (Louvain, 1988), pp. 359–84.

Levick, Barbara, *Augustus: Image and Substance* (Harlow and New York, 2010).

Levison, Wilhelm, 'Die Politik in Jenseitsvisionen des frühen Mittelalters', in *Aus Rheinischer und frankischer Frühzeit* (Düsseldorf, 1948), pp. 229–46.

Lévy, Michel-André, *Louis I, II, III . . . XIV . . . : L'étonnante histoire de la numérotation des rois de France* (Brussels and Paris, 2014).

Lewis, Andrew W., 'Anticipatory Association of the Heir in Early Capetian France', *The American Historical Review*, 83 (1978), pp. 906–27.

'Dynastic Structures and Capetian Throne-Right: The Views of Giles of Paris', *Traditio*, 33 (1977), pp. 225–52.

Royal Succession in Capetian France: Studies on Familial Order and the State (Cambridge, Mass., 1981).

Lewis, Peter, 'War Propaganda and Historiography in Fifteenth-Century France and England', *Transactions of the Royal Historical Society*, 5th series, 15 (1965), pp. 1–21.

Lexikon des Mittelalters (9 vols., Munich, 1977–99).

Lilie, Ralph-Johannes, 'Der Kaiser in der Statistik. Subversive Gedanken zur angeblichen Allmacht der byzantinischen Kaiser', in *Hypermachos: Studien zur Byzantinistik, Armenologie und Georgistik. Festschrift für Werner Seibt zum 65. Geburtstag*, ed. Chrestos Staurakos (Wiesbaden, 2008), pp. 211–34.

Lot, Ferdinand, *La naissance de la France* (5th edn., Paris, 1948).

'Origine et signification du mot "Carolingien"', *Revue historique*, 46 (1891), pp. 68–73.

Loud, Graham A. *The Age of Robert Guiscard: Southern Italy and the Norman Conquest* (Harlow, 2000).

Loudon, Irvine, *Death in Childbirth: An International Study of Maternal Care and Maternal Mortality 1800–1950* (Oxford, 1992).

The Tragedy of Childbed Fever (Oxford, 2000).

Lourie, Elena, 'The Will of Alfonso "El Batallador", King of Aragon and Navarre: A Reassessment', *Speculum*, 50 (1975), pp. 635–51.

'The Will of Alfonso I of Aragon and Navarre: A Reply to Dr Forey', *Durham University Journal*, 77 (n.s. 46) (1984–5), pp. 165–72.

Lydon, James, 'A Land of War', in *A New History of Ireland, 2: Medieval Ireland, 1169–1534*, ed. Art Cosgrove (Oxford, 1987), pp. 240–74.

Lyon, Jonathan R., *Princely Brothers and Sisters: The Sibling Bond in German Politics, 1100–1250* (Ithaca, N.Y., 2013).

MacLean, Simon, *Kingship and Politics in the Late Ninth Century: Charles the Fat and the End of the Carolingian Empire* (Cambridge, 2003).

'Making a Difference in Tenth-Century Politics: King Athelstan's Sisters and Frankish Queenship', in *Frankland: The Franks and the World of Early Middle Ages*, ed. Paul Fouracre (Manchester, 2008), pp. 167–90.

Ottonian Queenship (Oxford, 2017).

Macrides, Ruth, 'Dynastic Marriages', in *Byzantine Diplomacy*, ed. Jonathan Shepard and Simon Franklin (Aldershot, 1992), pp. 263–80, repr. with same pagination in Ruth Macrides, *Kinship and Justice in Byzantium, 11th–15th Centuries* (Aldershot, 1999), item IV.

'Kinship by Arrangement: The Case of Adoption', *Dumbarton Oaks Papers*, 44 (1990), pp. 109–18, repr. with same pagination in Ruth Macrides, *Kinship and Justice in Byzantium, 11th–15th Centuries* (Aldershot, 1999), item II.

'Substitute Parents and their Children', in *Adoption et fosterage*, ed. Mireille Corbier (Paris, 1999), pp. 307–19, repr. with same pagination in Ruth Macrides, *Kinship and Justice in Byzantium, 11th–15th Centuries* (Aldershot, 1999), item III.

Magdalino, Paul, 'Astrology', in *The Cambridge Intellectual History of Byzantium*, ed. Anthony Kaldellis and Niketas Siniossoglou (Cambridge, 2017), pp. 198–214.

L'orthodoxie des astrologues: la science entre le dogme et la divination à Byzance, VIIe–XIVe siècle (Paris, 2006).

Maillard-Luypaert, Monique, 'Jean de Bourgogne, bâtard de Jean Sans Peur, évêque de Cambrai de 1439 à 1480', in *La Bâtardise et l'exercice du pouvoir en Europe du XIIIe au début du XVIe siècle*, ed. Éric Bousmar et al. (*Revue du Nord*, Hors série. Collection Histoire no. 31, 2015), pp. 11–51.

Marafioti, Nicole, *The King's Body: Burial and Succession in Late Anglo-Saxon England* (Toronto, 2014).

Marchandisse, Alain, 'Corneille, Bâtard de Bourgogne (ca 1426–1452)', in *La Bâtardise et l'exercice du pouvoir en Europe du XIIIe au début du XVIe siècle*, ed. Éric Bousmar et al. (*Revue du Nord*, Hors série. Collection Histoire no. 31, 2015), pp. 53–89.

Margue, Michel, 'Bamberger Tafel', in *Kaiser Heinrich II. 1002–1024*, ed. Josef Kirmeier et al. (Stuttgart, 2002), pp. 216–18.

Martin, Russell, *A Bride for the Tsar: Bride-Shows and Marriage Politics in Early Modern Russia* (DeKalb, IL, 2012).

Martin, Therese, *Queen as King: Politics and Architectural Propaganda in Twelfth-Century Spain* (Leiden, 2006).

Mas Latrie, Louis de, *Histoire de l'isle de Chypre sous le règne des princes de la maison de Lusignan* (4 vols., Paris, 1852–82).

Mathieu, Marguerite, 'Les faux Diogènes', *Byzantion*, 22 (1952), pp. 133–48.

Maurel, Christian, 'Un artifice contre l'extinction des familles? La substitution de nom et d'armes à Marseille (fin XIVe–fin XVe siècle)', *Médiévales*, 19 (1990), pp. 29–35.

Maurer, Helen E., *Margaret of Anjou: Queenship and Power in Late Medieval England* (Woodbridge, 2003).

Maurice, Philippe, 'Actes de la pratique, II – L'adoption dans le Gévaudan (XVe siècle)', in *Médiévales*, 35: *L'adoption. Droits et pratiques*, ed. Didier Lett and Christopher Lucken (1998), pp. 101–4.

Mayer, Hans Eberhard, 'Studies in the History of Queen Melisende of Jerusalem', *Dumbarton Oaks Papers*, 26 (1972), pp. 93–182.

'The Succession to Baldwin II of Jerusalem: English Impact on the East', *Dumbarton Oaks Papers*, 39 (1985), pp. 139–47.

'Two Crusaders Out of Luck', *Crusades*, 11 (2012), pp. 159–71.

McCluskey, Stephen C., 'Gregory of Tours, Monastic Timekeeping, and Early Christian Attitudes to Astronomy', *Isis*, 81 (1990), pp. 8–22.

McCracken, Peggy, *The Romance of Adultery: Queenship and Sexual Transgression in Old French Literature* (Philadelphia, 1998).

McDougall, Sara, *Royal Bastards: The Birth of Illegitimacy, 800–1230* (Oxford, 2017).

McNiven, P., 'Rebellion, Sedition and the Legend of Richard II's Survival in the Reigns of Henry IV and Henry V', *Bulletin of the John Rylands University Library of Manchester*, 76 (1994), pp. 93–117.

Médiévales, 35: *L'adoption. Droits et pratiques*, ed. Didier Lett and Christopher Lucken (1998).

Meier, Thomas, *Die Archäologie des mittelalterlichen Königsgrabes im christlichen Europa* (Stuttgart, 2002).

Meller, Harald, et al., eds., *Königin Editha und ihre Grablegen in Magdeburg* (Archäologie in Sachsen-Anhalt, Sonderband 18, Halle, 2012).

Melville, Gert, 'Geschichte in graphischer Gestalt. Untersuchungen zu einem spätmittelalterlichen Darstellungsprinzip', in *Geschichtsschreibung und Geschichtsbewusstsein im späten Mittelalter*, ed. Hans Patze (Vorträge und Forschungen 31, Sigmaringen, 1987), pp. 57–154.

'Vorfahren und Vorgänger. Spätmittelalterliche Genealogien als dynastische Legitimation zur Herrschaft', in *Die Familie als sozialer und historischer Verband*, ed. Peter-Johannes Schuler (Sigmaringen, 1987), pp. 203–309.

Mentgen, Gerd, *Astrologie und Öffentlichkeit im Mittelalter* (Stuttgart, 2005).

Menzel, Gerhard, *Falsche Könige zwischen Thron und Galgen: Politische Hochstapelei von der Antike zur Moderne* (Frankfurt, 2012).

Mérindol, Christian de, 'L'héraldique des princes angevins', in *Les princes angevins du XIIIe au XV siècle: un destin européen*, ed. Noël-Yves Tonnerre and Elisabeth Verry (Rennes, 2003), pp. 277–310.

Michael, Michael, '"The Little Land of England is Preferred before the Great Kingdom of France": The Quartering of the Royal Arms by Edward III', in *Studies in Medieval Art and Architecture Presented to Peter Lasko*, ed. David Buckton and T. A. Heslop (Stroud, 1994), pp. 114–26.

Middle English Dictionary, ed. Hans Kurath and Sherman M. Kuhn (13 vols., Ann Arbor, Michigan, 1952–2001).

Mikat, Paul, *Dotierte Ehe, rechte Ehe: zur Entwicklung des Eheschliessungsrechts in fränkischer Zeit* (Rheinisch-Westfälische Akademie der Wissenschaften, Vorträge G 227, Opladen, 1978).

Moeglin, Jean-Marie, 'Les dynasties princières allemandes et la notion de maison à la fin du Moyen-Age', in *Les Princes et le pouvoir au Moyen Age: 23e Congrès de la Société des Historiens médiévistes de l'enseignement supérieur, Brest, 1992* (Paris, 1993), pp. 137–54.

Möhring, Hannes, *Der Weltkaiser der Endzeit: Entstehung, Wandel und Wirkung einer tausendjährigen Weissagung* (Stuttgart, 2000).

Molina, Luis, 'Las campanãs de Almanzor a la luz de un nuevo texto', *Al-Qantara*, 2 (1981), pp. 209–63.

Monteiro, João Gouveia, 'The Battle of Aljubarrota (1385): A Reassessment', *Journal of Medieval Military History*, 7 (2009), pp. 75–103.

Monter, William, *The Rise of Female Kings in Europe, 1300–1800* (New Haven and London, 2012).

Montesquiou-Fezensac, Blaise de, 'Le tombeau de Charles le Chauve à Saint-Denis', *Bulletin de la Société Nationale des Antiquaires de France* (1965), pp. 84–8.

Morby, John E., 'The Sobriquets of Medieval European Princes', *Canadian Journal of History*, 13. 1 (1978), pp. 1–16.

Morey, Adrian, and C.N.L. Brooke, *Gilbert Foliot and his Letters* (Cambridge, 1965).

Morganstern, Anne McGee, *Gothic Tombs of Kinship in France, the Low Countries, and England* (University Park, Penn., 2000).

Mottahedeh, Roy, *Loyalty and Leadership in an Early Islamic Society* (rev. edn., London and New York, 2001).

Narbona Cárceles, María, 'Les bâtards royaux et la nouvelle noblesse de sang en Navarre (fin XIV siècle–début XVe siècle', in *La Bâtardise et l'exercice du pouvoir en Europe du XIIIe au début du XVIe siècle*, ed. Éric Bousmar et al. (*Revue du Nord*, Hors série. Collection Histoire no. 31, 2015), pp. 421–38.

Nelson, Janet, 'A propos des femmes royales dans les rapports entre le monde wisigothique et le monde franc à l'époque de Reccared', in *Rulers and Ruling Families in Early Medieval Europe: Alfred, Charles the Bald, and Others* (Aldershot, 1999), pp. 469–74 (item XI).

'A Tale of Two Princes: Politics, Text and Ideology in a Carolingian Annal', *Studies in Medieval and Renaissance History*, n.s. 10 (1988), pp. 105–41, repr. with same pagination in Janet Nelson, *Rulers and Ruling Families in Early Medieval Europe: Alfred, Charles the Bald, and Others* (Aldershot, 1999), item XVI.

Charles the Bald (London, 1992).

'Queens as Jezebels: The Careers of Brunhild and Balthild in Merovingian History', in *Politics and Ritual in Early Medieval Europe* (London, 1986), pp. 1–48, originally published in *Medieval Women. Dedicated and Presented to Professor Rosalind M. T. Hill on the Occasion of her Seventieth Birthday*, ed. Derek Baker (Studies in Church History, Subsidia, 1, 1978), pp. 31–77.

Nicholas, Karen S., 'Countesses as Rulers in Flanders', in *Aristocratic Women in Medieval France*, ed. Theodore Evergates (Philadelphia, 1991), pp. 111–37.

Nickson, Tom, 'The Royal Tombs of Santes Creus. Negotiating the Royal Image in Medieval Iberia', *Zeitschrift für Kunstgeschichte*, 72 (2009), pp. 1–14.

Nicol, Donald M., *Byzantium and Venice* (Cambridge, 1988).

'Mixed Marriages in Byzantium in the Thirteenth Century', *Studies in Church History*, 1 (1964), pp. 160–72, repr. with same pagination in Donald M. Nicol, *Byzantium: Its Ecclesiastical History and Relations with the Western World* (London, 1972), item IV.

The Last Centuries of Byzantium 1261–1453 (London, 1972).

The Reluctant Emperor: A Biography of John Cantacuzene, Byzantine Emperor and Monk, c. 1295–1383 (Cambridge, 1996).

Nolan, Kathleen, ed., *Capetian Women* (New York, 2003).

Nonn, Ulrich, 'Karl Martell: Name und Beiname', in *Nomen et Fraternitas – Festschrift für Dieter Geuenich zum 65. Geburtstag*, ed. Uwe Ludwig and Thomas Schilp (Berlin, 2008), pp. 575–85.

Norbye, Marigold Anne, '*Arbor genealogiae*. Manifestations of the Tree in French Royal Genealogies', in *The Tree: Symbol, Allegory, and Mnemonic Device in Medieval Art and Thought*, ed. Pippa Salonius and Andrea Worm (Turnhout, 2014), pp. 69–94.

'Genealogies in Medieval France', in *Broken Lines. Genealogical Literature in Late-Medieval Britain and France*, ed. Raluca Luria Radulescu and Edward Donald Kennedy (Turnhout, 2008), pp. 79–102.

'"Iste non ponitur in recta linea arboris genealogie." Graphische Darstellung und Legitimität in französischen Königsgenealogien', in *Idoneität – Genealogie – Legitimation: Begründung und Akzeptanz von dynastischer Herrschaft im Mittelalter*, ed. Cristina Andenna and Gert Melville (Cologne, 2015), pp. 329–50.

North, J. D., 'Scholars and Power: Astrologers at the Courts of Medieval Europe', in *Actes de la VI Trobada d'Història de la Ciència i de la Tècnica* (Barcelona, 2002), pp. 13–28.

Norton, A. N., 'The Heraldry of the Illegitimate Children of the Nobility', in *Académie Internationale d'Héraldique. VIII Colloquium. Canterbury 29th August–4th September 1993. Proceedings* (Canterbury, 1995), pp. 75–80.

Ó Corráin, Donnchadh, 'Creating the Past: The Early Irish Genealogical Tradition', *Peritia*, 12 (1998), pp. 177–208.

Ó Muraílele, Nollaig, 'The Irish Genealogies: An Overview and Some Desiderata', *Celtica*, 26 (2010), pp. 128–45.

Oexle, Otto Gerhard, 'Die Karolinger und die Stadt des heiligen Arnulf', *Frühmittelalterliche Studien*, 1 (1967), pp. 250–364.

Offergeld, Thilo, *Reges pueri. Das Königtum Minderjähriger im frühen Mittelalter* (MGH, Schriften, 50, 2001).

Onclin, W., 'L'Age requis pour le mariage dans la doctrine canonique médiévale', in *Proceedings of the (Second) International Congress of Medieval Canon Law*, ed. S. Kuttner and J. J. Ryan (Vatican City, 1965), pp. 237–47.

Opll, Ferdinand, *Stadt und Reich im 12. Jahrhundert* (Forschungen zur Kaiser- und Papstgeschichte des Mittelalters 6, Beihefte zu J. F. Böhmer, Regesta imperii, Vienna, 1986).

Oram, Richard, *The Lordship of Galloway* (Edinburgh, 2000).

Ormrod, W. Mark, *Edward III* (New Haven and London, 2011).

Ostrogorsky, Georg, 'Das Mitkaisertum im Mittelalterlichen Byzanz', in Ernst Kornemann, *Doppelprinzipiat und Reichsteilung im Imperium Romanum* (Leipzig and Berlin, 1930), pp. 166–78.

Geschichte des byzantinischen Staates (3rd edn., Munich, 1963).

Oxford English Dictionary, ed. J. A. Simpson and E. S. C. Weiner (20 vols., Oxford, 1989).

Panayotova, Stella, 'Peter of Poitiers' *Compendium in genealogia Christi*: The Early English Copies', in *Belief and Culture in the Middle Ages: Studies Presented to Henry Mayr-Harting*, ed. Richard Gameson and Henrietta Leyser (Oxford, 2001), pp. 327–41, with plates 20–4.

Pangerl, Daniel Carlo, 'Sterndeutung als naturwissenschaftliche Methode der Politikberatung. Astronomie und Astrologie am Hof Kaiser Friedrichs III. (1440–1493)', *Archiv für Kulturgeschichte*, 92 (2010), pp. 309–27.

Pangerl, Mathias, 'Zawisch von Falkenstein', *Mittheilungen des Vereines für Geschichte der Deutschen in Böhmen*, 10 (1872–3), pp. 145–86.

Paravicini, Werner, 'Theatre of Death. The Transfer of the Remnants of Philip the Good and Isabel of Portugal to Dijon, November 1473–February 1474', in *Death at Court*, ed. Karl-Heinz Spiess and Immo Warntjes (Wiesbaden, 2012), pp. 33–115.

Parisse, Michel, 'Sigefroid, abbé de Gorze, et le mariage du roi Henri III', *Revue du Nord*, 86 (2004), pp. 543–66.

Parsons, John Carmi, *Eleanor of Castile: Queen and Society in Thirteenth-Century England* (Basingstoke, 1994).

ed., *Medieval Queenship* (Stroud, 1994).

'Mothers, Daughters, Marriage, Power: Some Plantagenet Evidence, 1150–1500', in *Medieval Queenship*, ed. Parsons (Stroud, 1994), pp. 63–78.

Patlagean, Evelyne, 'Les débuts d'une aristocratie byzantine et le témoinage de l'historiographie: système des noms et liens de parenté aux IXe–Xe siècles', in *The Byzantine aristocracy IX to XIII centuries*, ed. Michael Angold (British Archaeological Reports, International Series 221, 1984), pp. 23–43.

Paulsson, Göte, 'Studier i "Strängnäsmartyrologiet"', in *Historia och samhälle. Studier tillägnade Jerker Rosén* (Malmö, 1975), pp. 22–37.

Penman, Michael, *David II, 1329–71* (East Linton, 2014).

'Diffinicione successionis ad regnum Scottorum: Royal Succession in Scotland in the Later Middle Ages', in *Making and Breaking the Rules: Succession in Medieval Europe, c. 1000–c. 1600/Établir et abolir les normes: la succession dans l'Europe médiévale, vers 1000–vers 1600*, ed. Frédérique Lachaud and Michael Penman (Turnhout, 2008), pp. 43–60.

Périn, Patrick, 'The Undiscovered Grave of King Clovis I (+511)', in *The Age of Sutton Hoo: The Seventh Century in North-Western Europe*, ed. Martin Carver (Woodbridge, 1992), pp. 255–64.

Perrie, Maureen, *Pretenders and Popular Monarchism in Early Modern Russia: The False Tsars of the Time of Troubles* (Cambridge, 1995).

Petit-Dutaillis, Charles, *Étude sur la vie et le règne de Louis VIII (1187–1226)* (Paris, 1894).

Phillips, Seymour, *Edward II* (New Haven and London, 2010).

Pingree, David, 'The Astrological School of John Abramius', *Dumbarton Oaks Papers*, 25 (1971), pp. 189–215.

'The Horoscope of Constantine VII Porphyrogenitus', *Dumbarton Oaks Papers*, 27 (1973), pp. 217–31.

Piskorski, Wladimir, *Las Cortes de Castilla* (Barcelona, 1930).

Pitsakis, Constantin, 'L'adoption dans le droit byzantin', in *Médiévales, 35: L'adoption. Droits et pratiques*, ed. Didier Lett and Christopher Lucken (1998), pp. 19–32.

Platelle, Henri, 'Erreur sur la personne. Contribution à l'histoire de l'imposture au Moyen Âge', *Mélanges de Science Religieuse*, 34 (1977), pp. 117–45.

Pohl, Walter, 'Why Not to Marry a Foreign Woman: Stephen III's Letter to Charlemagne', in *Rome and Religion in the Medieval World: Studies in Honor of Thomas F. X. Noble*, ed. Valerie L. Garver and Owen M. Phelan (Farnham, 2014), pp. 47–64.

Pollock, Frederick, and Frederic William Maitland, *The History of English Law before the Time of Edward I* (2nd edn., 2 vols., Cambridge, 1898, reissued 1968).

Poulle, Emmanuel, 'La date de la naissance de Louis VIII', *Bibliothèque de l'École des Chartes*, 145 (1987), pp. 427–30.

Poupardin, René, 'Généalogies Angevines du XIe siècle', *Mélanges d'archéologie et d'histoire (de l'École française de Rome)*, 20 (1900), pp. 199–208.

Prestwich, Michael, 'Mary [Mary of Woodstock] (1278–c. 1332)', in *ODNB*, 36 (2004), pp. 66–7.

Rabikauskas, Paulius, 'Papstname und Ordnungszahl. Über die Anfänge des Brauches, gleichnamige Päpste durch eine Ordnungszahl zu unterscheiden', *Römische Quartalschrift für christliche Altertumskunde und Kirchengeschichte*, 51 (1956), pp. 1–15.

Raccagni, Gianluca, *The Lombard League 1167–1225* (Oxford, 2010).

Radulescu, Raluca L. and Edward Donald Kennedy, eds., *Broken Lines: Genealogical Literature in Late-Medieval Britain and France* (Turnhout, 2008).

Ramos y Loscertales, José Maria, 'La sucesion del Rey Alfonso VI', *Anuario de la Historia del Derecho Español*, 13 (1936–41), pp. 36–99.

Rapp, Claudia, 'Death at the Byzantine Court: The Emperor and his Family', in *Death at Court*, ed. Karl-Heinz Spiess and Immo Warntjes (Wiesbaden, 2012), pp. 267–86.

Reilly, Bernard F., *The Kingdom of León-Castilla under King Alfonso VI, 1065–1109* (Princeton, 1988).

The Kingdom of León-Castilla under King Alfonso VII, 1126–1157 (Philadelphia, 1998).

The Kingdom of León-Castilla under Queen Urraca, 1109–1126 (Princeton, 1982).

Reimitz, Helmut, 'Anleitung zur Interpretation: Schrift und Genealogie in der Karolingerzeit', in *Von Nutzen des Schreibens. Soziales Gedächtnis, Herrschaft und Besitz im Mittelalter*, ed. Walter Pohl and Paul Herold (Vienna, 2002), pp. 167–81.

Reisinger, Christoph, *Tankred von Lecce. Normannischer König von Sizilien 1190–1194* (Cologne, 1992).

Resende de Oliveira, António, 'Beatriz Afonso, 1244–1300', in *As primeiras rainhas: Mafalda de Mouriana, Dulce de Barcelona e Aragão, Urraca de Castela, Mecia Lopes de Haro, Beatriz Afonso*, ed. Maria Alegria Fernandes Marques et al. (Lisbon, 2012), pp. 383–468.

Reynolds, Susan, *Kingdoms and Communities in Western Europe, 900–1300* (Oxford, 1984).

Richard, Alfred, *Histoire des comtes de Poitou, 778–1204* (2 vols., Paris, 1903).

Riquer, Martin de, 'La littérature provençale à la cour d'Alphonse II d'Aragon', *Cahiers de civilisation médiévale*, 2 (1959), pp. 177–201.

Robbins, Rossell Hope, and John L. Cutler, eds., *Supplement to the Index of Middle English Verse* (Lexington, Kentucky, 1965).

Robinson, Ian S., *The Papacy 1073–1198: Continuity and Innovation* (Cambridge, 1990).

Rodríguez, Bretton, 'Pero López de Ayala and the Politics of Rewriting the Past', *Journal of Medieval Iberian Studies*, 7 (2015), pp. 266–82.

Ross, Charles, *Edward IV* (London, 1974).

Roumy, Franck, *L'adoption dans le droit savant du XIIe au XVIe siècle* (Paris, 1998).

Rouse, Richard H. and Mary A. Rouse, 'Statim invenire: Schools, Preachers, and New Attitudes to the Page', in *Renaissance and Renewal in the Twelfth Century*, ed. Robert Louis Benson and Giles Constable (Oxford and Cambridge, Mass., 1982), pp. 201–25, repr. in Richard H. Rouse and Mary A. Rouse, *Authentic Witnesses: Approaches to Medieval Texts and Manuscripts* (Notre Dame, 1992), pp. 191–220.

Rüdiger, Jan, *Der König und seine Frauen: Polygynie und politische Kultur in Europa (9.–13. Jahrhundert)* (Berlin, 2015).

Ruess, Karl-Heinz, ed., *Frauen der Staufer* (Göppingen, 2006).

Russell, Peter Edward, 'Una alianza frustrada. Las bodas de Pedro I de Castilla y Juana Plantagenet', *Anuarios de estudios medievales*, 2 (1965), pp. 301–32.

Rydén, Lennart, 'The Bride-Shows at the Byzantine Court – History or Fiction?', *Eranos*, 83 (1985), pp. 175–191.

Ryder, Alan, *Alfonso the Magnanimous: King of Aragon, Naples, and Sicily 1396–1458* (Oxford, 1990).

Sághy, Marianne, 'Aspects of Female Rulership in Late Medieval Literature: The Queens' Reign in Angevin Hungary', *East Central Europe/L'Europe du Centre Est*, 20–23/1 (1993–6), pp. 69–86.

Salicrú i Lluch, Roser, 'La coronació de Ferran d'Antequera: l'organització i els preparatius de la festa', *Anuario de Estudios Medievales*, 25 (1995), pp. 699–759.

Salonius, Pippa and Andrea Worm, eds., *The Tree: Symbol, Allegory, and Mnemonic Device in Medieval Art and Thought* (Turnhout, 2014).

Salvador Martínez, H., *Alfonso X, the Learned: A Biography* (Eng. tr., Leiden, 2010).

Santinelli, Emmanuelle, 'Continuité ou rupture? L'adoption dans le droit mérovingien', in *Médiévales*, 35: *L'adoption. Droits et pratiques*, ed. Didier Lett and Christopher Lucken (1998), pp. 9–18.

Il sarcofago dell'imperatore. Studi, ricerche e indagini sulla tomba di Federico II nella Cattedrale di Palermo 1994–1999 (Palermo, 2002).

Saul, Nigel, *Richard II* (New Haven and London, 1997).

Schadt, Hermann, *Die Darstellungen der Arbores consanguinitatis und der Arbores affinitatis: Bildschemata in juristischen Handschriften* (Tübingen, 1982).

Schieffer, Rudolf, 'Karolingische Töchter', in *Herrschaft, Kirche, Kultur. Beiträge zur Geschichte des Mittelalters. Festschrift für Friedrich Prinz zu seinem 65. Geburtstag*, ed. Georg Jenal (Stuttgart, 1993), pp. 125–39.

'Ludwig "der Fromme". Zur Entstehung eines karolingischen Herrscherbeinamens', *Frühmittelalterliche Studien*, 16 (1982), pp. 58–73.

'Väter und Söhne im Karolingerhause', in *Beiträge zur Geschichte des Regnum Francorum*, ed. Schieffer (Beihefte der Francia 22, 1990), pp. 149–64.

Schmid, Karl, 'Ein verlorenes *Stemma Regum Franciae*. Zugleich ein Beitrag zur Entstehung und Funktion karolingischer (Bild)Genealogien in salisch-staufischer Zeit', *Frühmittelalterliche Studien*, 28 (1994), pp. 196–225.

'"De regia stirpe Waiblingensium". Bemerkungen zum Selbstverständnis der Staufer', *Zeitschrift für die Geschichte des Oberrheins*, 124 (NF 85) (1976), pp. 63–73, repr. in Karl Schmid, *Gebetsgedenken und adliges Selbstverständnis im Mittelalter: ausgewählte Beiträge* (Sigmaringen, 1983), pp. 454–66.

'Welfisches Selbstverständnis', in Karl Schmid, *Gebetsgedenken und adliges Selbstverständnis im Mittelalter: ausgewählte Beiträge* (Sigmaringen, 1983), pp. 424–53.

'Zur Problematik von Familie, Sippe und Geschlecht, Haus und Dynastie beim mittelalterlichen Adel', *Zeitschrift für die Geschichte des Oberrheins*, 105 (NF 66) (1957), pp. 1–62, repr. in Karl Schmid, *Gebetsgedenken und adliges Selbstverständnis im Mittelalter: ausgewählte Beiträge* (Sigmaringen, 1983), pp. 183–244.

Schmidt, Heinrich, 'Eine Friesische Fehde: Die "Menalda-Fehde" von 1295', in *Tota Frisia in Teilansichten: Hajo van Lengen zum 65. Geburtstag*, ed. Schmidt et al. (Aurich, 2005), pp. 143–72.

Schmidt, Ulrich, *Königswahl und Thronfolge im 12. Jahrhundert* (Cologne and Vienna, 1987).

Schneider, Reinhard, 'Karolus, qui et Wenceslaus', in *Festschrift für Helmut Beumann zum 65. Geburtstag*, ed. Kurt-Ulrich Jäschke (Sigmaringen, 1977), pp. 365–87.

Schneidmüller, Bernd, 'Constructing the Past by Means of the Present: Historiographical Foundation of Medieval Institutions, Dynasties, Peoples, and Communities', in *Medieval Concepts of the Past. Ritual, Memory, Historiography*, ed. Gerd Althoff et al. (Washington, DC, 2002), pp. 167–92.

'Herrscher über Land oder Leute? Der kapetingische Herrschertitel in der Zeit Philipps II. August und seiner Nachfolger (1180–1270)', in *Lateinische Herrschertitel und Herrschertitulaturen vom 7. bis zum 13. Jahrhundert*, ed. Herwig Wolfram and Anton Scharrer (*Intitulatio* 3: Mitteilungen des Instituts für Österreichische Geschichtsforschung, Ergänzungsband 29, Vienna, 1988), pp. 131–62, plus page of plates.

Schofield, Roger, 'Did the Mothers Really Die? Three Centuries of Maternal Mortality in "The World We have Lost"', in *The World We have Gained: Histories of Population and Social Structure*, ed. L. Bonfield et al. (Oxford, 1986), pp. 231–60.

Schramm, Percy Ernst, and Florentine Mütherich, *Denkmale der deutschen Könige und Kaiser. I: Ein Beitrag zur Herrschergeschichte von Karl dem Grossen bis Friedrich II., 768–1250* (2nd edn., Munich, 1981).

Schreiner, Peter, 'Die kaiserliche Familie: Ideologie und Praxis im Rahmen der internationalen Beziehungen in Byzanz', in *Le relazioni internazionali nell'alto medioevo* (Settimane di studio del Centro italiano di studi sull'alto medioevo 58, 2011), pp. 735–74.

Schultze, Johannes, *Die Mark Brandenburg 1: Entstehung und Entwicklung unter den askanischen Markgrafen (bis 1319)* (Berlin, 1961).

Die Mark Brandenburg 2: Die Mark unter Herrschaft der Wittelsbacher und Luxemburger (1319–1415) (Berlin, 1961).

Schwinges, Rainer Christoph, 'Verfassung und kollektives Verhalten. Zur Mentalität des Erfolges falscher Herrscher im Reich des 13. und 14. Jahrhunderts', in *Mentalitäten im Mittelalter: methodische und inhaltliche Probleme*, ed. František Graus (Vorträge und Forschungen 35, Sigmaringen, 1987), pp. 177–202.

Sesma Muñoz, José Ángel, *El Interregno (1410–1412): concordia y compromiso político en la Corona de Aragón* (Zaragoza, 2011).

Shadis, Miriam, *Berenguela of Castile (1180–1246) and Political Women in the High Middle Ages* (Basingstoke, 2009).

Shukurov, Rustam, 'AIMA: The Blood of the Grand Komnenoi', *Byzantine and Modern Greek Studies*, 19 (1995), pp. 161–81.

Sickel, Wilhelm, 'Das Thronfolgerecht der unehelichen Karolinger', *Zeitschrift der Savigny-Stiftung für Rechtsgeschichte: Germanistische Abteilung*, 24 (1903), pp. 110–47, repr. in Eduard Hlawitschka (ed.), *Königswahl und Thronfolge in fränkisch-karolingischer Zeit* (Darmstadt, 1975), pp. 106–43.

Simms, Katharine, *From Kings to Warlords: The Changing Political Structure of Gaelic Ireland in the Later Middle Ages* (Woodbridge, 1987).

Simonsfeld, Henry, *Jahrbücher des Deutschen Reiches unter Friedrich I., 1: (1152–8)* (Leipzig, 1908).

Sisam, Kenneth, 'Anglo-Saxon Royal Genealogies', *Proceedings of the British Academy*, 39 (1953), pp. 287–348.

Sitges, Juan Bautista, *Las mujeres del rey don Pedro de Castilla* (Madrid, 1910).

Skovgaard-Petersen, Inge, 'Queenship in Medieval Denmark', in *Medieval Queenship*, ed. John Carmi Parsons (Stroud, 1994), pp. 25–42.

Smith, J. Beverley, 'Dynastic Succession in Medieval Wales', *Bulletin of the Board of Celtic Studies*, 33 (1986), pp. 199–232.

Smoller, Laura Ackerman, *History, Prophecy, and the Stars: The Christian Astrology of Pierre d'Ailly, 1350–1420* (Princeton, 1994).

Sonnleitner, Käthe, 'Der Konflikt zwischen Otto I. und seinem Sohn Liudolf als Problem der zeitgenössischen Geschichtsschreibung', in *Festschrift Gerhard Pferschy zum 70. Geburtstag* (Graz, 2000), pp. 615–25.

Spiegel, Gabrielle M., 'The *Reditus regni ad stirpem Karoli Magni*: A New Look', *French Historical Studies*, 7 (1971), pp. 145–74.

Spiess, Karl-Heinz, 'Europa heiratet. Kommunikation und Kulturtransfer im Kontext europäischer Königsheiraten des Spätmittelalters', in *Europa im späten Mittelalter: Politik, Gesellschaft, Kultur*, ed. Rainer C. Schwinges et al. (Historische Zeitschrift, Beihefte, Neue Folge, 40, Munich, 2006), pp. 435–64.

'Lordship, Kinship, and Inheritance among the German High Nobility in the Middle Ages and Early Modern Period', in *Kinship in Europe: Approaches to Long-Term Developments (1300–1900)*, ed. David Warren Sabean et al. (New York, 2007), pp. 57–75.

'Unterwegs zu einem fremden Ehemann: Brautfahrt und Ehe in europäischen Fürstenhäusern des Spätmittelalters', in *Fremdheit und Reisen im Mittelalter*, ed. Irene Erfen and Karl-Heinz Spiess (Stuttgart, 1997), pp. 17–36.

Staaten, Wappen, Dynastien. XVIII. Internationaler Kongress für Genealogie und Heraldik in Innsbruck vom 5. bis 9 September 1988 (Veröffentlichungen des Innsbrucker Stadtarchivs, N. F. 18, 1988).

Stafford, Pauline, 'Charles the Bald, Judith and England', in *Charles the Bald: Court and Kingdom*, ed. Margaret Gibson and Janet Nelson (2nd edn., London, 1990), pp. 139–53.

Queen Emma and Queen Edith: Queenship and Women's Power in Eleventh-Century England (Oxford, 1997).

Queens, Concubines and Dowagers: The King's Wife in the Early Middle Ages (London, 1983).

Stein, Henri, 'Un diplomate bourguignon de XVe siècle, Antoine Haneron', *Bibliothèque de l'École des Chartes*, 98 (1937), pp. 283–348.

Stephenson, Paul, 'A Development in Nomenclature on the Seals of the Byzantine Provincial Aristocracy in the Late Tenth Century', *Revue des études byzantines*, 52 (1994), pp. 187–211.

Strickland, Matthew, *Henry the Young King, 1155–1183* (New Haven and London, 2016).

Stringer, Keith J., *The Reign of Stephen: Kingship, Warfare, and Government in Twelfth-Century England* (London, 1993).

Strück, Wolf Heino, 'Märkische Urkunden aus der Zeit des falschen Woldemar im Anhaltischen Staatsarchiv Zerbst', *Forschungen zur brandenburgischen und preussischen Geschichte*, 55 (1943), pp. 32–82.

Struve, Tilman, 'Die falschen Friedriche und die Friedenssehnsucht im Mittelalter', in *Fälschungen im Mittelalter* (MGH, Schriften, 33, 6 vols., 1988), 1, pp. 317–37.

Stürner, Wolfgang, *Friedrich II.* (2 vols., Darmstadt, 1992–2000).

Sumption, Jonathan, *Trial by Battle (The Hundred Years War I)* (London, 1990).

Taylor, Craig, 'The Salic Law and the Valois Succession to the French Crown', *French History*, 15 (2001), pp. 358–77.

'The Salic Law, French Queenship and the Defence of Women in the Late Middle Ages', *French Historical Studies*, 29 (2006), pp. 543–64.

Tenbrock, Robert Hermann, *Eherecht und Ehepolitik bei Innocenz III.* (Dortmund-Hörde, 1933).

Tessier, Georges, *Diplomatique royale française* (Paris, 1962).

Thacker, Alan, 'The Cult of King Harold at Chester', in *The Middle Ages in the North-West*, ed. T. Scott and P. Starkey (Oxford, 1996), pp. 155–76.

Thoma, Gertrud, *Namensänderungen in Herrscherfamilien des mittelalterlichen Europa* (Munich, 1985).

Thompson, Colin, and Lorne Campbell, *Hugo van der Goes and the Trinity Panels in Edinburgh* (Edinburgh, 1974).

Thompson, Kathleen, 'Affairs of State: The Illegitimate Children of Henry I', *Journal of Medieval History*, 29 (2012), pp. 129–51.

Todt, Klaus-Peter, 'Die Frau als Selbstherrscher: Kaiserin Theodora, die letzte Angehörige der makedonischen Dynastie', *Jahrbuch der Österreichischen Byzantinistik*, 50 (2000), pp. 139–71.

Tolley, Thomas, 'Eleanor of Castile and the "Spanish" Style', in *England in the Thirteenth Century: Proceedings of the 1989 Harlaxton Symposium*, ed. W. M. Ormrod (Stamford, 1991), pp. 167–92.

Tompkins, Laura, 'The Uncrowned Queen: Alice Perrers, Edward III and Political Crisis in Fourteenth-Century England, 1360–1377' (University of St Andrews, PhD thesis, 2013).

Tougher, Shaun, *The Reign of Leo VI (886–912): Politics and People* (Leiden, 1997).

Treadgold, Warren, 'The Bride-Shows of the Byzantine Emperors', *Byzantion*, 49 (1979), pp. 395–413.

'The Historicity of Byzantine Bride-Shows', *Jahrbuch der Österreichischen Byzantinistik*, 54 (2004), pp. 39–52.

Le Trésor de la langue française (16 vols., Paris, 1971–94).

Tschirch, Otto, 'Der falsche Woldemar und die märkischen Städte', *Forschungen zur brandenburgischen und preussischen Geschichte*, 43 (1930), pp. 227–44.

Tuck, Anthony, 'Vere, Robert de, Ninth Earl of Oxford, Marquess of Dublin, and Duke of Ireland (1362–1392), Courtier', in *ODNB*, 56 (2004), pp. 312–15.

Ubl, Karl, 'Der kinderlose König. Ein Testfall für die Ausdifferenzierung des Politischen im 11. Jahrhundert', *Historische Zeitschrift*, 292 (2011), pp. 323–63.

Inzestverbot und Gesetzgebung: die Konstruktion eines Verbrechens (300–1100) (Berlin, 2008).

Vale, Malcolm, *Charles VII* (London, 1974).

Van Houts, Elisabeth, 'Countess Gunnor of Normandy', *Collegium Medievale*, 12 (1999), pp. 7–24.

Married Life in the Middle Ages, 900–1300 (Oxford, 2019).

'The Flemish Contribution to Biographical Writing in England in the Eleventh Century', in *Writing Medieval Biography, 750–1250: Essays in Honour of Professor Frank Barlow*, ed. David Bates et al. (Woodbridge, 2006), pp. 111–27.

Van Winter, J. M., 'Uxorem de militari ordine sibi imparem', in *Miscellanea Mediaevalia in memoriam Jan Frederik Niermeyer* (Groningen, 1967), pp. 113–24.

Vasconcelos Vilar, Hermínia, 'Lineage and Territory: Royal Burial Sites in the Early Portuguese Kingdom', in *Death at Court*, ed. Karl-Heinz Spiess and Immo Warntjes (Wiesbaden, 2012), pp. 159–70.

Vauchez, André, *Sainthood in the Late Middle Ages* (Eng. tr., Cambridge, 1997).

Vaughan, Richard, *Charles the Bold* (London, 1973).

John the Fearless (London, 1966).

Vinson, Martha, 'The Life of Theodora and the Rhetoric of the Byzantine Bride-Show', *Jahrbuch der Österreichischen Byzantinistik*, 49 (1999), pp. 31–60.

Viollet-le-Duc, Eugène, *Dictionnaire raisonné de l'architecture française du XIe au XVIe siècle* (10 vols., Paris, 1854–68).

Vogtherr, Thomas, '"Weh dir, Land, dessen König ein Kind ist". Minderjährige Könige um 1200 im europäischen Vergleich', *Frühmittelalterliche Studien*, 37 (2003), pp. 291–314.

Walker, Simon, 'Rumour, Sedition and Popular Protest in the Reign of Henry IV', *Past and Present*, 166 (2000), pp. 31–65.

Wallace-Hadrill, J. M., *The Long-Haired Kings* (London, 1962).

Ward, Emily Joan, 'Child Kingship in England, Scotland, France and Germany, c.1050–c.1250' (Cambridge University, PhD thesis, 2017)

Warntjes, Immo, 'Programmatic Double Burial (Body and Heart) of the European High Nobility, c. 1200–1400. Its Origins, Geography, and Functions', in *Death at Court*, ed. Karl-Heinz Spiess and Immo Warntjes (Wiesbaden, 2012), pp. 197–259.

'Regnal Succession in Early Medieval Ireland', *Journal of Medieval History*, 30 (2004), pp. 377–410.

Warren, W. L., *King John* (London, 1961, 2nd edn. 1978).

Wartburg, Walther von, *Französisches Etymologisches Wörterbuch* (25 vols., Bonn and Basel, 1922–2002).

Weiler, Björn, 'Kings and Sons: Princely Rebellions and the Structures of Revolt in Western Europe, c. 1170–c. 1280', *Historical Research*, 82 (2009), pp. 17–40.

Kingship, Rebellion and Political Culture: England and Germany, c.1215–c.1250 (Basingstoke, 2007).

Weller, Tobias, *Die Heiratspolitik des deutschen Hochadels im 12. Jahrhundert* (Cologne, etc., 2004).

Werner, Karl Ferdinand, 'Die Legitimität der Kapetinger und die Entstehung des "Reditus regni Francorum ad stirpem Karoli"', *Die Welt als Geschichte*, 12 (1952), pp. 203–25, repr. with same pagination in Karl Ferdinand Werner, *Structures politiques du monde Franc (VIe–XIIe siècles). Etudes sur les origines de la France et de l'Allemagne* (London, 1979), item VIII.

'Die Nachkommen Karls des Grossen', in *Karl der Grosse: Das Nachleben*, ed. Wolfgang Braunfels and Percy Ernst Schramm (*Karl der Grosse* 4, Düsseldorf, 1965), pp. 403–82.

West, M. L., *The East Face of Helicon: West Asiatic Elements in Greek Poetry and Myth* (Oxford, 1997).

Whittow, Mark, 'Motherhood and Power in Early Medieval Europe, West and East: The Strange Case of the Empress Eirene', in *Motherhood, Religion, and Society in Medieval Europe, 400–1400: Essays Presented to Henrietta Leyser*, ed. Conrad Leyser and Lesley Smith (Farnham, 2011), pp. 55–84.

Widdowson, Marc, 'Gundovald, "Ballomer" and the Problems of Identity', *Revue belge de philologie et d'histoire*, 86 (2008), pp. 607–22.

'Merovingian Partitions: A "Genealogical Charter"?', *Early Medieval Europe*, 17 (2009), pp. 1–22.

Wiener, Jürgen, *Das Grabmal des Johann von Brienne: Kaiser von Konstantinopel und König von Jerusalem* (Düsseldorf, 1997).

Williams, John, *The Illustrated Beatus: A Corpus of the Illustrations of the Commentary on the Apocalypse* (5 vols., London, 1994–2003).

Winkelmann, C., 'Zum Leben König Enzio's', *Forschungen zur deutschen Geschichte*, 26 (1886), pp. 308–13.

Wolf, Gunther, 'Königinwitwen als Vormünder ihrer Söhne und Enkel im Abendland zwischen 426 und 1056', in *Kaiserin Theophanu: Prinzessin aus der Fremde*, ed. Gunther Wolf (Cologne, 1991), pp. 39–58.

'Zoe oder Theodora – Die Braut Kaiser Ottos III. 1001/2?', in *Kaiserin Theophanu*, ed. Gunther Wolf (Weimar, 1991), pp. 212–22, repr. in Gunther Wolf, *Satura mediaevalis: Gesammelte Schriften. 2: Ottonenzeit* (Heidelberg, 1995), pp. 457–62.

Wolff, Robert Lee, 'Baldwin of Flanders and Hainault, First Latin Emperor of Constantinople: His Life, Death and Resurrection, 1172–1225', *Speculum*, 27 (1952), pp. 281–322.

Wolffe, Bertram, *Henry VI* (London, 1981).

Woll, Carsten, *Die Königinnen des hochmittelalterlichen Frankreich, 987–1237/38* (Stuttgart, 2002).

Wolverton, Lisa, *Hastening Toward Prague: Power and Society in the Medieval Czech Lands* (Philadelphia, 2001).

Wood, Charles T., *The French Apanages and the Capetian Monarchy 1224–1328* (Cambridge, Mass., 1966).

Wood, Ian, *The Merovingian Kingdoms 450–751* (London, 1993).

Woodacre, Elena, *The Queens Regnant of Navarre: Succession, Politics, and Partnership, 1272–1512* (New York, 2013).

Wright, Georgia Sommers, 'A Royal Tomb Programme', *Art Bulletin*, 56 (1974), pp. 224–43.

Wyss, Robert L., 'Die neun Helden: eine ikonographische Studie', *Zeitschrift für schweizerische Archäologie und Kunstgeschichte*, 17 (1957), pp. 73–106.

Yorke, Barbara, *Nunneries and the Anglo-Saxon Royal Houses* (London, 2003).

'Seaxburh [Sexburga] (d. 674?), Queen of the Gewisse', in *ODNB*, 49 (2004), p. 616.

'The Burial of Kings in Anglo-Saxon England', in *Kingship, Legislation and Power in Anglo-Saxon England*, ed. Gale R. Owen-Crocker and Brian W. Schneider (Woodbridge, 2013), pp. 237–58.

Zacos, G. and A. Veglery, *Byzantine Lead Seals*, 1.1 (Basel, 1972).

Zatschek, Heinz, *Wie das erste Reich der Deutschen entstand* (Prague, 1940).

Zey, Claudia, 'Frauen und Töchter der salischen Herrscher. Zum Wandel salischer Heiratspolitik in der Krise', in *Die Salier, das Reich und der Niederrhein*, ed. Tilman Struve (Cologne, 2008), pp. 47–98.

Zimmermann, Michel, 'La datation des documents catalans du IXe au XIIe siècle: un itinéraire politique', *Annales du Midi*, 93 (1981), pp. 345–75.

Žůrek, Václav, 'Godfrey of Viterbo and His Readers at the Court of Emperor Charles IV', in *Godfrey of Viterbo and his Readers*, ed. Thomas Foerster (London and New York, 2015), pp. 89–104.

Index

People prior to 1400 are alphabetized by first name or, if not, are cross-referenced. Rulers are alphabetized by name of kingdom or people ruled and then by numerical sequence (so Henry I of England precedes Henry I of Germany and Louis VI precedes Louis IX, though the kings of Leon and Castile are listed as a continuous sequence). Roman emperors down to Justinian are termed 'Roman emperor', thereafter 'Byzantine emperor'. Western emperors are termed 'emperor'; rulers elected 'king of the Romans' are termed 'German king'; their dates are always those of their reign as king. For a note on the term 'Holy Roman Emperor', see pp. 437–8. Smaller places in (modern) France are identified by department, smaller places in the British Isles by historic county.

INDEX

Guntram, Merovingian king (d. 592/3), 79, 100, 115, 372, 472

Gustaf III, king of Sweden (1771–92), 247

Guta (d. 1297), wife of Wencelas II, 56, 163

Guy of Burgundy, grandson of Richard II of Normandy, 169

Guy, count of Flanders and margrave of Namur (d. 1305), 101–2

Guy of Lusignan (d. 1194), husband of Sybilla of Jerusalem, 145

Guy-Geoffrey of Poitou, *See* William VIII

Gwynedd, Welsh principality, 221, 443
  princes of, *See* Gruffudd ap Cynan; Owain Gwynedd

Haakon II Sigurdsson, king of Norway (1157–62), 445

Haakon III Sverresson, king of Norway (1202–4), 186

Haakon IV Haakonsson, king of Norway (1217–63), 186, 414

Haakon V Magnusson, king of Norway (1299–1319), 118

Habichtsburg, 'Hawk Castle', 289

Habsburgs, 49, 72, 96, 226, 289, 304, 399, 420, 437, *See also* Albert I; Albert, king of Hungary and Bohemia; Albert, duke of Austria; Frederick III; Frederick (d. 1344); Maximilian; Otto; Rudolf

Hadrian I, pope (772–95), 18

Hadwig (Hedwig) (d. 994), niece of Otto I, 27, 34

Hadwig, countess of Hainault (d. after 1013), daughter of Hugh Capet, 328

Hagarenes (i.e. Muslims), 22

Hagia Sophia, Constantinople, 13, 238

Hainault, 184

Hallfredr Ottarsson, Norse poet (c. 1000), 362

Hamburg, 206

Hamlet (Shakespeare), 374

Hamo de Masci, English landholder (fl. 1199), 166

Hannibal, name, 177

Hanover, Electors of, 402

Harald Hardrada, king of Norway (1046/7–66), 440

Harald Gille, king of Norway (1130–6), 203

Harold Hen, king of Denmark (1074–80), 452

Harold Harefoot, king of England (1035/7–40), 202, 279, 364, 498

Harold Godwinson, king of England (1066), 13, 66, 357, 360, 362, 381, 392

Harthacnut, king of England (1035/40–2), king of Denmark (1035–42), 202, 279

Hartnid, Frankish noble, brother of Nithard, 293

Hastings, battle of (1066), 246, 362

Hathui (d. 1014), niece of Queen Matilda of Germany, 465

Hatto, archbishop of Mainz (891–913), 122, 484

Håtuna, Sweden, 193

Hebrides, 257

Hector, bastard of Bourbon and archbishop of Toulouse (1491–1502), 177

Hector, name, 177

Hedwig (Jadwiga), queen of Poland (1384–99), 146, 441, 446, 447

Hedwig *See also* Hadwig

Heidelberg, 271

Heilsbronn, Franconia, 326

Heimskringla (Snorri Sturluson), 362

Helinand of Froidmont, chronicler (fl. 1197–1229), 86

Helwig (d. 1374), wife of Valdemar IV of Denmark, 452

Hemma (d. 876), wife of Louis the German, 11

Hengist, early Anglo-Saxon leader, 191

'Henries', term for Hohenstaufen, 292

Henry I, king of Castile (1214–17), 125, 219, 257, 445

Henry II of Trastámara, king of Castile (1369–79), 162, 174, 353–4, 413, 439

Henry III, king of Castile (1390–1406), 75, 446, 449

Henry IV, king of Castile (1454–74), 303

Henry I, king of England (1100–35)
  and his brother Robert, 194, 393
  and prophecy, 350–1, 356, 357
  burial of, 252
  daughter of, *See* Matilda (d. 1167)
  illegitimate children of, 165, 166, 178, 330
  marriage of, to Matilda of Scotland, 28, 385, 388
  plans succession of his daughter Matilda, 135–6, 138, 141–2, 170
  plans succession of his son William, 91

INDEX